ONE WEEK LOAN

D1471766

WAR & TERROR

FEMINIST PERSECTIVES

EDITED BY

KAREN ALEXANDER

AND

MARY E. HAWKESWORTH

THE UNIVERSITY OF CHICAGO PRESS

CHICAGO AND LONDON

The essays in this volume originally appeared in various issues of SIGNS: JOURNAL OF WOMEN IN CULTURE AND SOCIETY. Acknowledgment of the original publication data can be found on the first page of each essay.

The University of Chicago Press, Chicago 60637
The University of Chicago Press, Ltd., London
© 2008 by The University of Chicago
All rights reserved. Published 2008
Printed in the United States of America

12 11 10 09 08   5 4 3 2 1

Library of Congress Cataloging-in-Publication Data

War and terror : feminist perspectives / edited by Karen Alexander and Mary Hawkesworth.
    p. cm.
    Includes bibliographical references and index.
    ISBN 978-0-226-01299-5 (alk. paper)
    1. Women and the military. 2. Women and war. I. Alexander, Karen. II. Hawkesworth, Mary, 1952–
UB416.W37 2008
355.0201—dc22   2007044238

The paper used in this publication meets the minimum requirements of American National Standard for Information Sciences—Permanence of Paper for Printed Library Materials, ANSI Z39.48-1984. ⊗

Contents

War as a Mode of Production and Reproduction:
Feminist Analytics

Traditional academic investigations of war seldom link armed conflict to practices of racialization or gendering. Construed as "organized violence between groups of people" (Osterud 2004, 1028), war has been studied in manifold and complex ways—but ways that offer little scope for concerns with race, gender, or sexuality. Historians, political scientists, and international relations scholars have investigated the causes of war in relation to the motives of perpetrators (e.g., wars of conquest, preemption, missionary zeal) and distributions of power within the international system (e.g., bipolarity, multipolarity, hegemonic transition). Within international relations theory, realists have tied the origin of conflict to anarchy in the international system and strategic efforts to secure a balance of power, while liberals highlight domestic roots of war, in particular the role of dictatorships and authoritarian regimes in the instigation of violence. If liberals have been quick to draw the optimistic conclusion that marketization fosters democratization, which will hasten an end to war, Marxian analysts have drawn radically different conclusions, suggesting that war stems from exploitative economic systems, which are a hallmark of capitalism, colonialism, imperialism, and globalization. In recent years, constructivists have resurrected Hegelian notions that depict war as a mode of othering, creating the possibility that war can be interpreted in relation to questions of identity and the production of difference, but the Self/Other dialectic fueling these Hegelian modes of violent assertion has, in their interpretation, far more to do with the production of national identities than with processes of racialization or gendering.

Discussions of women, racial minorities, and indigenous peoples occasionally arise in traditional studies of war in the context of military-civilian relations and the fragility of the civilian/combatant distinction, particularly with the rise of guerrilla war, urban warfare, and terrorism. The focus of these studies, however, is more often asymmetries of warfare, particularly in revolutionary struggles exacerbated by superpower intervention, than concern with issues of race and gender per se. Within the rich literature on nationalisms, war is treated as a mechanism of nation building, but raced-gendered logics and effects are subordinated to concerns about compulsory conscription and the production of nationalist loyalties and sentiments. Racialization surfaces obliquely in studies of the Cold War that document how the balance of terror produced peripheral zones in which proxy wars exacerbated local conflicts. Both the depiction of these so-called peripheral wars and accounts of their causes (boundary disputes, irredentist claims, ethnic and tribal divisions, religious clashes, local warlords, rogue states) depend upon and reinscribe racial hierarchies, although an explicit discussion of such racism is seldom part of mainstream analyses. The extreme violence—expulsion of populations, seizure of land, rape, ethnic cleansing, and genocide—involved in wars in Rwanda, Darfur, and the former Yugoslavia has made some attention to race, ethnicity, and gender inescapable. Situating these horrors in a discourse of failed states, however, has supported justifications of Western military intervention that appeal to ostensibly universal humanitarian concerns, a strategy that simultaneously masks the political causes of these conflicts, appeals to a civilized/barbaric binary that rests upon racist presuppositions, and instrumentalizes the purported concern with issues of race and gender.

In the social sciences and in the popular imagination, race and sex are typically construed as individual attributes or demographic characteristics, but in both cases these are understood as biological or physical traits rather than as political constructs. According to this "primordial view" (Taylor 1996, 885), race and sex are part of the natural or given aspects of human existence and as such are irrelevant to social forces such as war or terrorism. Within this naturalized frame, there is no reason to believe that armed conflict plays any role in shaping individual embodiment or the demographic characteristics of populations. *War and Terror: Feminist Perspectives* differs from all these theorizations by focusing on practices of racialization and gendering in armed conflict, demonstrating how wars and various modes of terrorism produce, naturalize, and maintain racial, ethnic, and gender hierarchies.

Feminist frames

Engaging mainstream studies of war, feminist scholars have challenged constructions of war as gender neutral or as men's business. By asking the question, "where are the women?" Cynthia Enloe (1989) opened new lines of investigation into the multiple roles that women play in war (as mothers, lovers, soldiers, munitions makers, caretakers, sex workers) and the consequences of such gendered divisions of labor for women's citizenship. In the decades since, feminists have documented women's experience of war and the complex dimensions of gender in war. Contrary to stereotypes about war deaths that feature male combatants, women are the majority of casualties in war. Over the past seventy years, the majority of war dead have been civilians, rising from 50 percent of the casualties in World War II to 90 percent of all war casualties in the 1990s—with women and children constituting the vast majority of civilian casualties (Turpin 1998). Women also experience increased levels of domestic violence and sexual violence in wartime. Women's lives and livelihoods are irrevocably affected by displacement and environmental devastation caused by war, even as women assume greater responsibility for subsistence provision during wartime. As military expenditures divert much-needed revenue from domestic programs, including health, education, and social welfare provision, women are often expected to fill the gaps created by cutbacks in state provision. Feminist scholars have also demonstrated that women are directly involved in war making as revolutionaries, militants, soldiers, spies, and participants in the military-industrial complex, just as they are actively engaged in war protesting, peace activism, and war resistance. Moreover, within nationalist symbol systems, particular representations of women circulate as the embodiment of the nation that men seek to protect and defend (Lorentzen and Turpin 1998), while racialized representations of certain groups help constitute both internal and external boundaries of the nation.

Feminist analyses of war have proliferated in the past five years with the escalation of the "war on terror." Working within the growing fields of feminist international relations and feminist political economy, scholars have examined the war on terror as a gendered military intervention, a global population policy, and a new site of "glocalization" (Blanchard 2003; Enloe 2004, 2007). Investigating war as a mechanism of gendered power that perpetuates women's subordination within domestic, national, and international arenas, these studies illuminate how war secures the continuing exclusion of women from decision-making roles despite the passage of UN Security Council Resolution 1325, which requires that women and women's concerns play an integral role in every new security institution and at every decision-making stage in peacekeeping and national reconstruction in the aftermath of armed conflict.

In addition to examining the effects of militarization and securitization on women's lives, some feminist scholars have investigated processes of racialization within the war on terror. Casting an analytic lens on the unsavory racist implications of Samuel Huntington's claims about the "clash of civilizations," for example, Farida Akhter interprets the war on terror as "a population policy" (2002, 298). Within this frame, a war orchestrated by Western powers that targets Islam effectively terminates people who have been constructed as enemies. Inflicting massive harm, this clash of civilizations causes not only the death of combatants and civilians but also the destruction of the civilian infrastructure, the environment, and long-established social relations among disparate groups.

Feminist scholars have also pointed out the mystifying effects of bipolar constructions of the world. Whether cast in terms of Cold War rhetoric pitting the United States against the Soviet Union, the George W. Bush administration's depictions of the forces of freedom versus the axis of evil, or Huntington's clash of Christian versus Muslim civilizations, these polarizing frames mask similar patterns of patriarchy that cut across these juxtaposed worlds (e.g., Christian and Islamic fundamentalism), while also hiding strange and shifting political alliances among putative opponents. Recent depictions of an undifferentiated Islam, organizing across borders to export jihad and create a world in its own image, for example, conjure notions of the clash of civilizations, while eliding half a century of U.S. support for Islamist jihad. From the 1950s to the 1990s, the CIA funneled billions of dollars in aid for weapons, recruitment, and training of thousands of mujahideen from across the Muslim world to fight established governments in Egypt, Iran, Iraq, and Afghanistan (see, e.g., Gallagher 2000/1; Dreyfuss 2005; Russo 2006; Haq in this volume).

Within these complex geopolitical conflicts, the distinctions between local and global break down as local agents are funded by global actors and global causes fuel mobilizations at both local and transnational sites. Both Islamism and neoliberalism circulate globally, uniting supporters across borders, while provoking resistance within particular nations. As transnational forces with roots in specific geopolitical sites, both Islamism and neoliberalism use war and terror to promote gendered and racial orders, as various essays in this collection make clear.

New feminist perspectives on race/gender/war/terror

Drawn primarily from two special issues of *Signs: Journal of Women in Culture and Society*, the essays in this volume build upon and expand feminist analyses of war and terror. Featuring original research by scholars from Australia, Canada, India, Israel, Morocco, Pakistan, Somalia, South Africa, Turkey, the United Kingdom, and the United States, the essays provide innovative analyses of ongoing wars as well as wars long concluded. Several articles examine the war on terror, while others explore armed conflicts ranging from the Partition of India to the antiapartheid struggle in South Africa, civil wars in Sierra Leone and Somalia, and revolutionary anticolonial wars in Algeria, Ethiopia, Guinea-Bissau, Kenya, Mozambique, Namibia, and Zimbabwe. Contributors also investigate diverse modes of terrorism, including Basque separatism in Spain (ETA), terrorist recruitment efforts in Pakistan, antiterrorism campaigns in Morocco, and state terror in Abu Ghraib, in Palestine, and in Turkey's so-called low-intensity war against the Kurds.

By placing race and gender at the center of their analyses, the authors illuminate subjects that have seldom been studied, such as the experiences of girl soldiers in Sierra Leone, women revolutionaries in Africa and the Middle East, female suicide bombers, women terrorists in ETA, and Pakistani mothers who are primed by terrorist organizations to recruit their sons for death missions. Analyzing racial and gender power that operates through new policies concerning securitization, gender integration of the military, the construction of humanitarian facilities at military checkpoints, and demobilization and redomestication, the essays offer new insights into the complex dynamics of violent conflict and terror. Articles investigate changing racial and gender formations within war zones, among combatants, those displaced by war (both internally and in diaspora), and those whose lives remain at some remove from the war front but whose daily routines are profoundly affected by militarization and securitization. Several articles go beyond conflict zones, exploring collateral effects of war on race and gender dynamics and representational practices within a range of contemporary nations such as Australia, Morocco, and the United States.

Illuminating the complex interplay of gender, race, nation, culture, and religion in the context of more than a dozen armed struggles, these essays document the raced-gendered logics, practices, and effects of war. Highlighting women's agency even under conditions of dire constraint, the articles challenge traditional stereotypes of women as perennial victims, perpetual peacemakers, or embodiments of nation that men seek to protect and defend. Contributors demonstrate how women negotiate their survival, enact resistance to oppressive and supposedly liberating forces, mobilize to protest war and counter its effects, participate in redefining war, and appropriate war discourses to advance their own political agendas. Through their substantive breadth, methodological innovation, and theoretical sophistication, these analyses offer new ways of understanding war, shifting the analytic frame from a focus on war as an instrument of statecraft and a means of destruction to war as a mode of production and reproduction. Nations are produced, contested, reproduced, and transformed through war in ways that involve racialization and gendering.

Indeed, practices of racing and gendering are integral both to statecraft and to insurrection.

War as a mode of production and reproduction

Tallying some "two thousand sustained armed conflicts on the face of the earth at the beginning of the new millennium," Hardt and Negri (2004, 31) suggest that, far from being an aberration, war has become the general condition of the world in the twenty-first century. They argue, as did Thomas Hobbes in *Leviathan*, that lethal violence is present as a "constant potentiality"; thus, war "becomes the general matrix for all relations of power and techniques of domination, whether or not bloodshed is involved. War has become a regime of biopower, that is, a form of rule aimed not only at controlling the population but producing and reproducing all aspects of social life. This war brings death but also, paradoxically, must produce life" (Hardt and Negri 2004, 13), and it does so in specific forms.

Exploring the possibility that the strategic deployment of lethal force is also a mode of production and reproduction, the essays in this collection investigate the discursive and material regimes that are being created, nurtured, and sustained, as well as those that are being expunged by military operations. To suggest that war creates as well as destroys is not to claim that it creates ex nihilo. On the contrary, production and reproduction begin with the materials at hand, crafting new forms from contending possibilities, shoring up certain discursive formations and modes of life, while undercutting others. In exploring the intricacies of particular wars, the contributors to this collection demonstrate that war is refiguring old ways of being and doing by creating new subjects (e.g., predatory girl soldiers in Sierra Leone, women who renounce political power yet publicly endorse suicide missions for the sake of the militarized Muslim *ummah* [community]), new practices and policies (e.g., demobilization, redomestication, securitization, feminization, UN Security Council Resolution 1325, gender integration and "overgendering" within the military, politically approved modes of racial profiling, legally sanctioned torture), and new cultural formations and modes of power (e.g., low-intensity war, disfiguration, modes of dress and deportment, racial grammars and visual regimes, gendered nationalisms, and gendered diasporas).

Articles in the collection also call attention to hitherto unnoted continuities between what is considered the "extraordinary violence" of war and the "ordinary violence" to which women are subjected in peacetime. They suggest that it is possible to construe identities negotiated under coercive conditions, mandatory subordination of women's interests to the interests of men, violent modes of domestication, and involuntary displacement either as nodes of gendered normalcy produced in the midst of war or as stark continuities between women's daily experiences in wartime and in peacetime. Thus these detailed analyses show how racial and gender violence produce modes of subordination, challenging claims about natural proclivities and roles and challenging notions of socialization as a noncoercive internalization of norms.

In "Negotiating (In)Security: Agency, Resistance, and Resourcefulness among Girls Formerly Associated with Sierra Leone's Revolutionary United Front," for example, Myriam Denov and Christine Gervais provide a vivid portrayal of the violent production of girl soldiers in Sierra Leone's decade-long civil war. Abducted by warring factions (mainly rebel forces), young girls were forced to assume the roles of combatants, commanders, wives, and slave laborers—often in combination. Girls were assigned an array of domestic and supportive tasks including cooking, washing, taking care of young children, and carrying heavy loads of ammunition, supplies, and arms and were subjected to dire forms of punishment including brutal physical assaults, starvation, and even death for failing to carry out their duties. They were also subjected to severe physical abuse at the hands of those who commanded them, including sexual violence, forced marriages, and coerced childbearing and child rearing. They witnessed brutal forms of violence against men, women, and children—combatants and civilians.

This extreme violence was designed to ensure compliance with a fairly traditional gendered division of labor, but it also produced girl soldiers who perpetrated severe acts of violence as a means of negotiating their survival. Denov and Gervais point out that girls made conscious attempts to protect themselves by developing skill in the use of small arms. Within the ranks of the Revolutionary United Front (RUF), girls became increasingly aware that carrying guns afforded them a measure of protection and decreased their chances of victimization. Seeing armament as a way to increase their safety and security, girls became eager to possess their own weapons. In the words of one former girl soldier, "The gun became my bodyguard and protector. The gun was power, and that's why I was anxious to have one" (45).

The girls also realized that the more aggressive they were seen to be and the more they destroyed and looted, the more valuable they were within the ranks of the RUF. The more violent they were, the safer they became within the armed group. Engaging in extreme forms of violence brought privileges within the RUF, such as better access to food and looted goods, and in some cases led to promotion within the ranks.

Refusing the false opposition of victim/perpetrator, Denov and Gervais trace power dynamics within the RUF that produced girl soldiers who moved from an inability to articulate nonconsent to their sustained sexual exploitation to a strategic mode of consenting deemed essential to their long-term survival. The girls manifested their agency by cultivating their capacity to kill. Far from being the natural disposition of all mankind described by Hobbes in *Leviathan*, the equal capacity to kill emerges as one effect of the brutal militarization of girls within war.

The civil war in Sierra Leone produced the girl soldier who is incorporated into a fighting force unwillingly but who becomes an adept killer to secure her safety. International organizations, however, have not yet found a way to accommodate the gun-wielding girl within recently developed policies concerning disarmament, demobilization, and rehabilitation. As Vanessa Farr points out in her essay in this volume, international law does not accord refugee status to displaced people if they possess arms and are proven to have been members of armed groups or forces. Regardless of their violent abduction, according to international law, girl soldiers of the RUF should be disarmed and interned as prisoners of war. In situations where coercion coexists with complex modes of volition, it becomes extremely difficult for international agencies to classify women and girls associated with armed groups. As a consequence, many are living in appalling conditions in camps for the internally displaced. Often afflicted with HIV/AIDS, former girl soldiers live without support from the wider community because they and their children are perceived as outsiders or indeed as enemies. New racial grammars set them apart from nation-building efforts in the aftermath of conflict. Many who cross borders become invisible, beyond the reach of repatriation, disarmament, demobilization, and reintegration efforts.

Gendered soldiers, gendered citizenship, gendered nations

Racialization and gendering are not simply unintended consequences of war or acts of terror. They are part of nation building and the daily operations of state power, deployed as means for particular states to realize their vision of a national order. Nationalism is intricately tied to armed conflict. Efforts to create and preserve the nation-state inspire, structure, and legitimize violence in revolutionary wars, in civil wars, in terrorist campaigns, and in exercises of state terror. These nationalist ambitions are thoroughly raced and gendered.

Drawing evidence from nationalist struggles in various regions of the world over the past two centuries, feminist scholars have demonstrated that nationalism is a profoundly gendered phenomenon (McClintock 1995; Yuval Davis 1997). Although women have been actively involved in long and dangerous struggles for national independence, organizing against oppressive regimes, mobilizing as citizens, demanding the transformation of the political system, standing publicly against colonial and imperial rule, and participating in revolutionary violence, they hold a very different place in nationalist imaginaries than their male counterparts. Rather than celebrating women's contributions to nationalist struggles, nationalist discourses tend to restrict women to a symbolic role as mother of the nation or as the wives, daughters, sisters, and mothers whom men valiantly struggle to protect and defend. Indeed, feminist scholars have shown that nationalism produces gendered patterns of skilling and de-skilling, gendered differences in political rights and economic opportunities, and gender-specific political visibility and invisibility, while subtly and unsubtly regendering the identities of citizens.[1]

Armed conflict plays a central role in forging nationalism, mobilizing support for a vision of the nation worth dying to defend, developing ties among men who struggle to create, protect, and defend the nation, and creating rights of citizens tied to military service. Carol Pateman has demonstrated how particular states have used mandatory male military service, conscription, and militia duty as means to construct heterosexual men as "bearers of arms," while "unilaterally disarming women" (1998, 248), barring them from military service and from combat duty. Similarly, Shane Phelan (2001) and Gary Lehring (2003) have traced the exclusion of gays and lesbians from military service as a means to privilege particular modes of patriarchal citizenship. By assigning heterosexual men responsibility for the protection of women and children and deploying them in armed combat, states produce the military and citizenship as heteromasculine institutions.

As Orna Sasson-Levy and Sarit Amram-Katz point out in their essay in this volume, militaries are perceived as masculine institutions not only because they are populated mostly with men but also because they constitute a major arena for the construction of masculine identities, which are then given privileged access to social benefits and leadership opportunities afforded by the state. In "Gender Integration in Israeli Officer Training: Degendering and Regendering the Military," they investigate

---

[1] Jaquette 1989; Alvarez 1990; Miller 1991; Parker et al. 1992; Funk and Mueller 1993; Radcliffe and Westwood 1993; Nelson and Chowdhury 1994; Saint Germain 1994; McClintock 1995; Yuval Davis 1997; Jaquette and Wolchik 1998; Nechemias and Kuehnast 2004.

an attempt by the state to alter the gender composition of the military officer corps and in so doing, transcend masculine privilege in the military and in Israeli citizenship. In attempting to disrupt masculine hegemony, Israel heeded the arguments of liberal feminist egalitarian militarists who argue that because the military is a sine qua non of citizenship, women have a right to serve at all levels in the armed forces. Indeed, proponents of this version of egalitarianism insist that women's exclusion from combat duty is discriminatory; it treats women as an inferior category of citizens, limits jobs available to them, and denies them access to educational benefits and routes to power and political leadership. Despite the state's intention to degender the officer training program, however, Sasson-Levy and Amram-Katz demonstrate the enormous difficulty of changing the national gender order.

Through their examination of gender-integration efforts, Sasson-Levy and Amram-Katz show that objective measures of ability are insufficient to trump gender stereotypes. Paradoxically, placing men and women in the same leadership training program created the conditions for greater gendering than had existed when trainees were gender segregated, as gender stereotypes were resurrected and circulated to recreate advantages for men. Contrary to the hopes of feminist egalitarian militarists, gender integration did not generate gender equality. Nor did the presence of women generate gender-neutral modes of military operation: "it did not raise new criteria for leadership evaluation, it did not create new standards for evaluating women's physical performance, and particularly it did not offer a new professional model for the noncombatant staff officer" (355).On the contrary, gender integration reproduced and strengthened the combat model as a universal military norm, entrenching male gender power within the military and within Israeli social and political life.

If transformation of existing racial and gender orders within nations proves difficult, does revolutionary transformation offer better prospects? Several articles in the collection explore the possibility for gender transformation through national independence struggles as men and women fight to build new kinds of nations. One of the most astute critics of colonialism, Frantz Fanon, argued that people's wars—revolutionary struggles to overthrow colonial domination—were essential to reverse the racial inferiority complex created by colonization. Fanon claimed that, by asserting their humanity through a violent confrontation with their oppressors, the colonized could achieve not only national independence but also recognition of their humanity, which had been denied by their colonizers. Fanon broke new ground in suggesting that revolutionary violence held transformative potential for women as well as for men. He claimed that Algerian women's participation in the armed struggle altered their "feminine" colonized identities and family relationships in positive ways that challenged feudal, patriarchal traditions (1967, 99–120).

In "All the Men are Fighting for Freedom, All the Women are Mourning Their Men, but Some of Us Carried Guns," Aaronette White investigates whether anticolonial violence has the psychological effects predicted by Fanon, whether the debilitating effects of colonized identity are transformed through revolutionary violence, and whether participation in revolutionary violence has the same effects for men and women. White suggests that there are many reasons that participation in revolution may fall short of Fanon's emancipatory hopes for men and women: Patriarchal mentalities may be shored up by military systems of command. The authoritarianism deemed essential to military organization may foster hierarchies and systems of command that are inimical to democratic practices. Soldiers trained to obey unquestioningly may lose the autonomy requisite to equal recognition and equal citizenship. Notions of combat as the ultimate test of manliness may generate modes of masculinity in newly independent states that are incompatible with sexual equality.

White argues that gendered dimensions of revolutionary violence produce differing effects for men and women militants. Through an examination of the experiences of women revolutionaries in several African nations, White suggests that gendering in the context of revolutionary war constructs modes of femininity and masculinity that empower men while disempowering women revolutionaries. The sexual division of labor within revolutionary struggles, for example, typically assigns secondary roles—as clerks, couriers, porters, nurses, laundry workers, cooks, child-care providers—to women combatants. Although revolutionary rhetoric suggests that every role in the revolution is valued, every role is not valued equally. Nor is every person, particularly if she is a woman, equally recognized for the role she plays.

In addition to sexual divisions of labor that structure gender inequities, revolutionary cadres captured during armed conflict are often subjected to torture. Some torture techniques—sleep deprivation, physical beatings, and electric shocks to genitals—were used against men and women. Other torture techniques specifically targeted women's sexuality. White notes that most women combatants are ashamed to speak about these incidents, so first-person accounts are few; however, confidential psychological reports suggest that these forms of violence traumatize rather than affirm women cadres, leaving enduring emotional scars that national independence does not erase.

This is especially the case since testimonies by women revolutionaries indicate that sexual torture and abuse were not confined to the activities of enemy forces. Revolutionary armies too engaged in horrific human rights abuses including rape, torture, and brutal abductions. Among their own comrades, women combatants were subjected to sexual duty and sexual politics that could require marriage to a commanding officer to rise through the ranks. Regardless of their training and status as fighters, women were expected to care for, serve, comfort, and sexually satisfy men. Women cadres who resisted these impositions could be judged disloyal to the cause, a fate with dire consequences of imprisonment or death. Speaking about the horrific treatment they endured at the hands of their comrades was also viewed as a form of disloyalty, and the women themselves often chose to remain silent rather than to be accused of betraying their brothers in arms and the cause for which they fought. Their silence often coexists with their erasure as nationalist myth making celebrates the founding fathers of the new nation.

Several articles in this collection demonstrate that demobilization in the aftermath of armed conflict is also gendered. In newly independent states, women combatants may not be celebrated as revolutionary heroes but rather asked to put down their weapons, abjure their active military service, maintain silence about abuses suffered at the hands of their comrades, and return to the domestic sphere. Male nostalgia for "the normal" may mandate wifehood and motherhood for women revolutionaries. Those who resist this mandate may not fare well.

Rather than restoring their dignity through war, participation in violence may subject women combatants to shaming practices that challenge their integrity. Participation in armed struggle may restore male combatants' dignity precisely because it reinscribes dominant conceptions of masculinity. By contrast, the valor of women combatants may violate traditional gender norms (real or imagined), generating public condemnation for loss of femininity and respectability, while posing serious challenges to the dignity and psychological well-being of women combatants. Lying about their war experiences and becoming respectable wives and mothers may be required of demobilized women combatants as an alternative to being ostracized permanently (Lyons 2004). With few exceptions, women revolutionary creators of history, White notes, borrowing Fanon's terms, have been pressured to disappear from history.

If women militants face powerful social pressures to erase their revolutionary valor and conform to fantasies of domesticity, how then can their contributions to nation building be preserved? How can the gendered costs of revolutionary struggle be memorialized? In her contribution to this collection, Meg Samuelson suggests that fiction may afford insights to such questions. Through an analysis of Zoë Wicomb's novel *David's Story* (2000), Samuelson captures the paradoxical position of a female African National Congress (ANC) guerrilla commander during the post-apartheid period of demilitarization and redomestication. Using the novel as well as testimony given at the South African Truth and Reconciliation Commission (TRC) hearings, Samuelson demonstrates how the body of the militant black woman is routinely disfigured within nationalist semiotic systems—both those of the apartheid regime and those of the ANC struggling to overturn it. She also offers an alternative explanation of the silence of women militants who refuse to testify about their wartime experiences, suggesting that a woman's concealment of a painful history of sexual exploitation or indeed sexual torture during her military service may be a "repudiation of a certain kind of femininity" (105), a refusal to be reduced to a victim, a resistance against sexualization, and a rejection of pressures to abandon her revolutionary subject position. Yet, Samuelson points out that even such a tactical deployment of silence was insufficient to avoid sexualization in postapartheid South Africa. "As the TRC became increasingly anxious about its failure to capture both the story of women and the story of sexual violence, it began to conflate the two: a 'woman's' story was reduced to one of sexual violence, and sexual violence was identified as a defining female experience. . . . While only 40 percent of the TRC's cases of sexual abuse, where the victim's sex was specified, concerned women, 'Sexual Abuse' is a central category in the chapter dedicated to the Special Hearings on Women in the *Final Report*" (101). Wicomb's novel disrupts the attempt to reduce women to the sexually violated by developing a far more complicated account of the subjectivity of an ANC woman commander both during and following revolutionary struggle. The insights captured in this fictional account, however, circulate far less widely than the official documents of the TRC. Within the postapartheid national imaginary, black woman qua sexual being is subtly reinscribed.

The discursive sexualization of women discussed by Samuelson is being materially instantiated in contemporary South Africa. Sexual violence against women has increased since the war against apartheid ended, suggesting gendered continuities between conflict and postconflict situations that are masked by constructions of peace as the absence of war. If women experience neither peace nor liberation in the aftermath of revolutionary violence, what exactly does demilitarization mean for women? If the ideology of domesticity is coupled with sexual violence to redomesticate women combatants, then one potent lesson of national independence struggles is that, contrary to the hopes of feminist egalitarian militarists, fighting side-by-side with men is no sure route to gender equality in the nation-state.

Constructing nation, creating tradition, living diaspora

Armed conflict gives birth not only to nations but also to diasporas—the dispersion and resettlement of a people following traumatic deterritorial-ization, a process that often encompasses the obliteration of their home-land or its incorporation within another state. The lives of those living in diaspora are typically marked by the tragedy of displacement, coupled with an intense nostalgia for their lost home and a profound longing to return. Violent displacement also contributes to idealized recollections of the lost homeland, racialized reconstructions of the national community, and the reinvention of traditions at great remove from the daily routines that preceded displacement. Several articles in this collection explore these complex dynamics.

Since the collapse of the Mohamed Siad Barre regime in Somalia in 1991, for example, millions of Somalis have been displaced to Ethiopia, Kenya, Yemen, Europe, and North America. More than half a million sought refuge in camps in Kenya, where their precarious struggle for existence was exacerbated by sexual assault by roving bandits and by hu-manitarian aid workers. In "Convergence of Civil War and the Religious Right: Reimagining Somali Women," Cawo Mohamed Abdi examines how pervasive physical insecurity and the opportunistic interventions of certain Islamist organizations collude in the reinvention of "tradition" that imposes new constraints on women.

Abdi notes that women's heightened vulnerability in conflict and post-conflict situations provides a rationale for changing dress codes and be-haviors associated with conservative Islam. Responding to the danger of sexual assault in a world where protective family networks and state police services as well as traditional mores have been destroyed by warfare, women turn to wearing long dresses with veils (*jalaabiib* or *jilbaab*) as a response to their vulnerability. Indeed, women in Somalia and in adjacent refugee camps in Kenya report that they began wearing trousers for pro-tection—as defense from violence. Although neither trousers nor *jilbaab* were traditional modes of dress in Somalia, women adopted this attire for complex reasons. Some believed that extra layers of clothing might create a barrier to rape by delaying the assault and providing time for someone to come to their aid. Some suggested that the veil lowered their visibility and heightened their respectability, which enabled them to be in public spaces and thereby facilitated their economic efforts to sustain their families. Others adopted conservative forms of dress as an expression of religion, which helped them cope with the hardships and dangers created by war.

Abdi points out that the dress choices available to women were also affected by fundamentalist versions of Islam that Saudi Arabia and Sudan began exporting to war-torn Somalia during the 1990s. These patriarchal Islamists actively politicized gender, interpreting the war as divine punishment for women's deviation from the "authentic" rules of Islam. Women were told that they must repent, and the adoption of the veil was one visible mark of repentance. Although this mode of dress differed markedly from that traditionally worn by Muslim women in Somalia, those who refused to conform were subjected to street harassment including physical assaults such as stoning.

The reinvention of tradition encompassed new modes of education as well as attire. The new Islamist society also introduced gender segregation in schools (madrassas) funded by Saudi Arabia and Sudan. Abdi notes that girls are increasingly excluded from educational opportunities in Somali refugee camps, amounting to only 10 percent of high school students. Far from being a return to traditional practice, new modes of dress and new gendered divisions of labor and knowledge are effects of war, enforced through a potent combination of charity and violence as mechanisms of social control. Somali women operate under new constraints and are subjected to new sanctions as they attempt to preserve their precarious existence within the invented traditions cultivated by foreign nationals engaged in a fundamentalist project to recreate an imagined Islamic society untarnished by colonial influence or Western ideas.

Although nation and diaspora can emerge simultaneously, nationalist and diasporic discourses operate on distinct, albeit related temporal registers. Nationalism resonates with Aristotelian teleology: the nation is first and final cause, that for the sake of which violence is undertaken, both point of origin and final destiny of a people. Diaspora, paradoxically, presupposes and produces nationalism. The process of expulsion from home fuels constructions of nation as space, place, blood, and destiny. Cihan Ahmetbeyzade illuminates the complex relations between nationalism and diaspora in her essay in this collection, "Negotiating Silences in the So-Called Low-Intensity War: The Making of the Kurdish Diaspora in İstanbul." Examining the coerced deterritorialization of the Kurds in Turkey, she demonstrates the complex role of memory, intergenerational narrative, and continuing oppression in the creation of nationalist claims. She traces how blood shed is translated into metaphors of blood ties that combine with claims concerning loss of ancestral lands to ground the nationalist ambitions of the Kurds as a race-nation. Through ethnographic research, she shows how longing for homeland—for "Mother Soil"—operates as a tool of empowerment. Kurdish identity is produced through narratives of the past and narratives of loss circulating among displaced people who understand themselves as a minority nation in exile. Relocated by force and intimidation from the northern countryside to major metropolitan areas within Turkey, the Kurds construct a discourse of blood inextricably tied to territory and to ongoing nationalist struggles to regain that territory as a homeland. Within this internal diaspora, the symbolics of blood link individuals through networks of belonging, claims of identity, and rules of alliance.

Ahmetbeyzade also investigates this internal diaspora as a site of gendered memories and gendered claims making. Thus, she notes that the narrative production of Kurdistan is also gendered. Narratives created by men foreground the idyllic beauty of the local environment, the fertile soil that afforded them rich opportunities to demonstrate their productive powers, which in turn legitimated a patriarchal order in which fathers provided for their families and orchestrated the marriage of their children to ensure individual and collective well-being. Ahmetbeyzade contrasts this construction of an idyllic past with women's recollections of their homeland. Contesting this patriarchal memory of Kurdistan, the women's narratives emphasize the more recent past riddled with violence, bloodshed, and death. Where the men envision a tranquil land where their rule harmonizes the demands of nature and the needs of their families, the women emphasize the loss of their children to violent death. Refusing to acquiesce in the men's idealizations, the women politicize the spilling of blood and the loss of their children as a means to forge a collective identity for women Kurds and to carve out a political role for themselves as "Mothers of the Lost." Although this role ties Kurdish women to the Kurdish nationalist project, it also mobilizes them in alliance with Turkish women who have lost their children to the militarist policies of the Turkish government. Within internal diaspora, the Kurdish women's unrelenting recollection of violence positions them as protesting Turkish citizens even as they dream of future citizenship in Kurdistan.

Women of the Kurdish diaspora find ways around their prescribed role as largely silent supporters by the vivid counterpoint their words offer when they do choose to speak, however quietly. Defying the silence of the Turkish government regarding their treatment of Kurds (and even the existence of the Kurdish nation) and correcting the idealized distortion of Kurdish men's narratives about their homeland, these women speak in terms that demand recognition of the bodily realities of war. Nevertheless, they maintain a respectful silence regarding the social disenfranchisement of their men, of which the men themselves avoid speaking.

In her essay in this volume, Rosemary Marangoly George discusses the comparative merits of nationalist and diasporic frames for understanding the violence associated with the birth of India and Pakistan. Like many struggles for national independence, the 1947 Partition of British India into two nation states, India and Pakistan, was marked by extensive and prolonged violence. Partition provoked the single largest population movement in recent history, with Hindus moving into independent India and Muslims into the newly formed nation of Pakistan. It is estimated that in 1947–48, 10–15 million people crossed the newly created borders in both directions. During the Partition months, the violence against women (in the form of sexual assault, mutilation, murder, and abduction) rose to unprecedented levels. Official estimates suggest that 100,000 or more women were sexually assaulted during this period; an additional 75,000–80,000 women were abducted for the purpose of marriage by men of communities other than their own.

Within the national literatures of both India and Pakistan there is a "general consensus that Partition violence was part of an exceptional moment of insanity in which men went mad" (232). Attending to the gendered dimensions of diaspora, George suggests, challenges this account of the exceptional violence at the moment of nation formation. Indeed, nationalist accounts of Partition elide the disparate experiences of men and women at this moment of political trauma. Men experienced the sense of violation that ensued after Partition as a challenge to the very foundations of their manhood and subjectivity, but "the violence that Partition brought to women is understood to be similar but of a different magnitude than to the usual fare doled out to them in a patriarchal society" (232). Unlike the male experience of diaspora, rooted in national cataclysm, women's diasporic experience is tied to mundane aspects of ordinary life: they marry, leave their natal home, and spend the rest of their lives missing their mother's household, yearning for return, and waiting for their brothers to come and take them for precious visits. Everyday acts of patriarchal control and exchange of women are replicated in the Partition abductions. The life of a Partition abductee both fulfills and parodies this well-worn course of events. More concentrated in their effects, Partition abductions were an intensification of the usual patriarchal discourse about women as property. A daughter is property that is only temporarily attached to her natal home, property whose ultimate destination and destiny lies in the transfer to the marital home.

George suggests that gendered dimensions of diaspora have important implications for our understanding of the nature and frequency of violent conflict. When "read in purely nationalist terms, Partition was a once-in-a-nation's-lifetime event: it was the downside of achieving independence for India and the cost of establishing Pakistan" (237).Located firmly in the past and not subject to repetition, Partition and its communal violence is exceptional, a disordered moment in the shared history of Hindus, Muslims, and Sikhs. Yet when read through a feminist lens that foregrounds women's experiences of diaspora, "partitions and dislocations are routinely replayed from the beginning of settled societies to the present day" (237).Framed within a context of diasporas tied to marriage, trade, indentureship, evictions, forced and economic migrations and dislocations, Partition becomes less of a singular event in a national history and more liable to be repeated in varying form and degree. Indeed, George points out that the horrors of dislocation associated with Partition have been reenacted in the razing of urban slums, the dislocation of rural populations resettled to build dams and power plants, and the destruction of communities in the course of communal riots that swept over entire states such as Gujarat. Within the diasporic frame analyzed by George, Partition demands attention not only because the degree of violence was extraordinary but because this extraordinary violence reveals a great deal about the gendered dynamics of the ordinary.

Gendered nationalism, gendered terrorism

The image of terrorism circulating in the popular press in the aftermath of September 11, 2001, reflects a very recent consensus about the nature and scope of terrorism. The United Nations did not pass a resolution defining terrorism until the 1990s, after the official end of the Cold War. The General Assembly Resolution on Human Rights and Terrorism defines terrorism "wherever and by whomever committed, as activities aimed at the destruction of human rights, fundamental freedoms and democracy, threatening the territorial integrity and security of States, destabilizing legitimate constituted Governments, undermining pluralistic civil society and having adverse consequences on the economic and social development of States" (GA Res 48/122, December 20, 1993).

Situated in a human rights framework that couples democracy with the territorial integrity and security of states, the General Assembly Resolution restricts its definition of terrorism to the acts of those who challenge states' monopoly of the use of violence. Thus, as Ileana Porras notes, "terrorism has come to be the thing against which liberal Western democracies define themselves; . . . terrorism has come to be the repository of everything that cannot be allowed to fit inside the self-image of democracy; and . . . the terrorist has become the 'other' that threatens and desires the annihilation of the democratic 'self' . . . an external force against which democracies therefore must strenuously defend" (Porras 1995, 295). Applied only to nonstate actors, the term *terrorist* in current parlance suggests "a stateless person, an illegitimate combatant who has chosen exile from the law, against whom the state has no obligation to apply laws of war, of civil and international proscriptions on incarceration, deportation, use of torture, or right to legal defense. . . . By placing himself voluntarily outside the law, the terrorist loses his claim to the law" (Porras 1995, 307).

Constructed as illegitimate, evil, and male, the terrorist appears to desire only the destruction of particular nation-states, but this mythic construction masks the fact that terrorism itself is a nationalist project shared by men and women. In "Political Violence and Body Language in Life Stories of Women ETA Activists," Carrie Hamilton investigates the political motives that inspire women to participate in terrorist campaigns organized by Basque separatists in Spain. Noting that armed conflict tends to reinforce male dominance and target women in specifically gendered ways, Hamilton nonetheless suggests that women, who comprise 10–15 percent of ETA membership, find creative ways to articulate their nationalist commitments in a gendered rhetoric that accords women a critical role. Women ETA activists rhetorically move armed struggle to the traditional terrain of women. Deploying metaphors of house/home, they simultaneously feminize armed struggle and claim the ETA military organization as a place for women as well as men. Resisting the dominant tendency to erase women, ETA activists devise metaphors of violence peculiarly related to the female body and to traditional women's roles. Thus Hamilton notes that some women activists use metaphors of birth, casting violent struggle as integral to the emergence of life itself. Refusing to accept the state's depiction of itself as the defender of individual rights and democratic freedoms, women in ETA emphasize the brutality and oppressiveness of the Spanish government's interventions that seek to negate the existence of the Basques: "Brutality is a negation. . . . Identity cards and roadblocks are brutal and negating" (146). By comparison, participating in "violence, with all the harshness and cruelty that it can also entail . . . [is] an act of affirmation. . . . Violence . . . will lead to freedom" (146). Inspired by Fanon's account of the potential of anticolonial violence, women ETA activists continue to embrace liberatory possibilities called into question by the experiences of African women revolutionaries.

If the nationalist ambitions that fuel terrorism are seldom aired in the Western press, the visions of a less patriarchal nationalism cherished by women terrorists are seldom aired in any press. In "Brides of Palestine, Angels of Death: Media, Gender, and Performance in the Case of the Palestinian Female Suicide Bombers," Dorit Naaman examines the elision of the political motives of women who engage in the ultimate act of political violence, sacrificing their lives to politicize the egregious dispossession of their people. If heroic death through ultimate self-sacrifice helps produce a myth that the nation is worth dying for when men commit suicide bombing, why are women suicide bombers interpellated so differently? Naaman points out that the Western media and the Arab media alike distort the motives of women suicide bombers, erasing the women's explicit visions of a nationalism that encompasses gender justice. While Western accounts construct these political agents as deluded, manipulated, disgraced, or depressed, the Arab media and politicians "frame the actions of women suicide bombers in ways that minimize and subvert the overt confrontation of gender politics present in the women's own narratives and actions" (131). The lives of women terrorists are recuperated in ways that perpetuate the gender status quo by their enemies and friends alike. While their enemies insist that they are incapable of principled political action, their friends co-opt their acts to serve patriarchal nationalist projects, rendering their critique of hierarchical gender relations invisible.

Farhat Haq also investigates contemporary terrorist mobilizations with nationalist aims, exploring tensions between creating a civic state that extends equal citizenship to women and imagining a nation that gives women a central cultural mission (raising sons to be martyrs). In "Militarism and Motherhood: The Women of Lashkar-i-Tayyabia in Pakistan," Haq is particularly concerned with religiopolitical movements that mobilize women for the public sphere in order to retraditionalize women's role. Lashkar-i-Tayyabia (LT) is the military wing of Markaz Da'wat wa'l Irshad, an organization founded in 1986 that seeks to create an Islamist polity modeled on a supposedly authentic version of early Islam. Haq argues that it is a mistake to believe that women are proscribed from political roles in the Islamist project. The imagined *ummah* affords women a vital role in forming a Muslim polity: women are to remove themselves willingly from the public arena to reassert and validate the difference between a Muslim and a non-Muslim polity. Covering the female body is inherently political, embodying the culture and value system constitutive of the ideal Islamist political community. To validate the wisdom and superiority of these values, women must voluntarily opt for the veil and purdah. Donning the black burka is not a revival of a local tradition in Pakistan, Haq points out. As in the case of Somalia, it is part of the invention of a tradition to signify the emergence of the jihadi Islamist *ummah.* Adopting the black burka as a uniform, the ideal Islamist woman is expected to shun the language of liberation and employment as detrimental to the Muslim family. Associated with sexual harassment, divorce, and single motherhood, liberation qua employment outside the home is associated with nothing but unhappiness. Within the ideal Islamist *ummah*, the good life for a woman is to be the mother, sister, or daughter of a mujahid. To be effective soldiers for their community, women must choose to stay true to Islamist ideals.

Lashkar-i-Tayyabia uses free education as a recruitment mechanism for poor young men who have no access to formal education. Successful recruitment of suicide bombers, however, requires more than free education. The LT mobilizes women and deploys familial sentiments, particularly the grief of mothers of martyrs, to provide emotional suasion for its recruitment efforts. According to Haq, grieving unspeakable loss is the emotional lifeblood of the movement, for it provides a means to recuperate death in a manner conducive to victory. Within the ideal Islamist *ummah*, nothing is more precious than a son, but mothers in LT profess their willingness to sacrifice their sons because the cause is just. Toward this end, LT has created an active women's wing, which affords women opportunities to participate in political and religious processes, albeit on separate and unequal terms. Although LT attracts thousands of women to its festivals, Haq suggests that there is little evidence that mothers in Pakistan are flocking to the LT mission. On the contrary, her research suggests that impoverished women use the LT festivals for their own purposes, taking advantage of free transportation to participate in an extended religious holiday and to take a break from the arduous work of their everyday existence. Thus Haq cautions against mistaking women's presence at Islamist programs for whole-hearted endorsement of the patriarchal nationalist project.

Racing-gendering in the war on terror

In response to the September 11, 2001, bombing of the World Trade Towers and the Pentagon, the George W. Bush administration launched the "war against terrorism" on October 7, 2001. By executive order, the president mobilized a "coalition of the willing" to invade Afghanistan, remove the Taliban regime, and defeat the Al Qaeda network, a nonstate actor that operates clandestinely within and across national boundaries of some sixty states. One month later, the Bush administration issued a Military Order on the Detention, Treatment and Trial of Certain Non-Citizens in the War Against Terrorism (66 Fed. Reg. 57,833, November 13,

2001), which suspended basic constitutional protections, authorizing the establishment of military tribunals; indefinite detention of enemy combatants and noncitizens associated with newly designated terrorist networks; and denial of detainees' habeas corpus and basic constitutional rights, including a presumption of innocence, the right to be informed of charges against them, and the right to legal representation. The Bush administration also declared that the Geneva Conventions protecting prisoners of war did not apply to terrorists.

Assessing the raced-gendered effects of the ongoing war on terror requires close attention to context, for the effects vary markedly within nations participating in the coalition of the willing, nations drawn into alliance with this antiterror coalition, and nations on whose soil the war is being actively waged. Several articles in this collection explore diverse domestic effects of the war on terror, ranging from women's appropriation of securitization discourses to advance their own political agendas in Morocco to the diversion of funds from domestic violence programs to national security expenditures in Australia to heightened racialization in the United States that legitimates racial profiling, suspension of rights, unlawful detention, and dehumanization of detainees.

Zakia Salime examines effects of the war on terror in a nation whose government has been pressured to join the antiterrorism alliance in "The War on Terrorism: Appropriation and Subversion by Moroccan Women." Salime suggests that the war on terror be understood as a political opportunity structure that creates options for some while heightening constraints on others. In the Moroccan context, the war on terror surfaces on multiple fronts as the state manipulates discourses appealing to modernity and security while succumbing to U.S. pressure to implement neoliberal economic policies, normalize relations with Israel through trade and diplomatic relations, and mitigate its support for the Palestinian cause. The Moroccan monarchy adopts a style of democracy that weds free trade with antiterrorism. While depicting itself as both neoliberal and moderate, the Moroccan government develops securitization measures, including forms of racial profiling that mobilize internal divisions, to produce a docile civil society that does not question the administration.

Within this political opportunity structure, Salime notes that women's groups appropriate the discourse of war for their own political objectives. To counteract the marginalization of women's issues following a terrorist bombing in Casablanca, women's groups utilized the government's war-on-terror framework, adopting the rhetoric of democracy, modernity, and moderation to create space for particular women's voices. Harnessing the language of moderation, liberal feminists constructed themselves as the barrier against religious extremism and pressed for more state intervention to protect secular institutions and civil liberties. Casting themselves as strong allies of the state in its crusade against extreme Islam, liberal feminists created the Modernity/Democracy Network and the Observatory for Women's Rights to monitor and publicize human rights violations by Islamists, such as using street harassment to compel women to wear the *hijab*.

Islamist women also appropriated the language of moderation to enhance their power within religious movements. Defining motherhood and womanhood as the embodiment of moderation, they claimed the right to preach in public. By addressing their appeal to the state rather than to Islamist men, the women secured impressive results. Appealing to the security of the Moroccan people as his justification, the king of Morocco created a new training program for women religious leaders, who were assigned the task of changing the masculine culture of the mosques, providing a feminine alternative to the radical tone of some imams. Coining the term *morshidate* (spiritual guides) to characterize their new role, the king appointed thirty women to councils of *ulama* (religious scholars) in an unprecedented move.

As both liberal and Islamist women cast themselves as the state's ally in fighting terrorism, various women's groups secured some advantages, but Salime points out that they did so at a cost. As the state monitors women's discourse and casts itself as a neutral mediator between liberal feminist and Islamist women's demands, independent organizing by women is diminished. The policies emerging from this state-mediated feminism are a peculiar amalgam of liberalism and Islam unlikely to please either group. The family code introduced in 2003 reflects this tension. Although the new code grew out of more than two decades of liberal feminist activism and incorporates some language pertaining to women's rights and gender equality, in promulgating it the king assured the Islamist community that it was inspired by and consistent with Islamic sharia (personal law adjudicated by the imams).

The bombings of the World Trade Towers and the Pentagon on September 11, 2001, stripped the United States of its sense of invulnerability. As its borders were penetrated by foreign terrorists, the United States joined the ranks of the violated, and gendered images and narratives migrated from embodied subjects to discursive constructions of the nation. The security forces were mobilized and the military put on alert to prevent the further feminization of the United States. Intensive securitization measures at home and deployment of troops abroad were twin tactics adopted by the Bush administration to manifest American military might and performatively restore American virility.

Iris Marion Young (2003) has suggested that the gendered logic of the national security state feminizes the American citizenry. Recycling the patriarchal rationale first vindicated by Thomas Hobbes, which posits threat and fear as endemic and the need for protection as dire, the national security state promises protection of the homeland. Within this discursive frame, the home is lifted from the private sphere and given new geographic purchase; the home qua women's domain is refigured as a "homeland" with borders in need of policing. The private becomes public but not in the democratic sense envisioned by feminist campaigns for the personal as political. At one level of public (mis)appropriations of the private, thousands of vigilantes converge on ranches spanning the Mexican border, pledging their guns and their lives to protect the United States from what they see as security threats lurking south of the border. At a second level, the state withdraws constitutional protections of the private sphere. The USA PATRIOT Act authorizes securitization measures that suspend the right of habeas corpus, as well as Fourth Amendment guarantees against unwarranted searches and seizures. According to the logic of the national security state, the provision of protection necessitates critical trade-offs: civil liberties are eroded; racial and ethnic profiling are legitimated; surveillance is heightened; detention absent due process of law is routinized; foreign nationals passing through American airports are rendered to Egypt, Poland, Romania, or Syria for torture and confinement; and the citizenry is reduced to a subordinate position of dependence and obedience. Rather than enacting their democratic rights through protests against such constitutional violations, citizens of the national security state are expected to be grateful for the protection provided.

In "The Politics of Pain and the Uses of Torture," Liz Philipose examines how racism is deployed to produce the docile feminized citizenry that acquiesces to the violations of homeland security. Drawing attention to parallels between lynching photographs and the photos from Abu Ghraib, both of which circulated widely in different eras, she excavates spectacles of power that consolidate a racial order through a visual regime of domination. Defining a regime of visuality as a system of categorization that organizes differences in predetermined ways, Philipose suggests that images of the abuses at Abu Ghraib play a critical role in producing a popular understanding of the Muslim terrorist as a violent, hyperpatriarchal religious fanatic, an antimodern threat who deserves the brutal treatment enacted on his body. As the lynching photographs so powerfully depict, racialized bodies are marked not only by skin color or physical features but also by their representation as abject, sexualized, decerebrated. Images of the lynched black man and the sexually debauched detainees depict violence in contexts that exonerate the perpetrators of violence by suggesting the culpability of the violated.

Within this racial grammar, the physical traits of the tortured body are taken as cues to interior moral turpitude. Racial profiling becomes a visual technology of power through which the acts of particular terrorists are generalized to lineage, kinship, and heredity as swarthy Middle Easterner and treacherous South Asian morph into the threatening brown man. Torture techniques designed to destroy personality, individuality, and agency produce detainees as subhuman—pathological individuals who can be displayed to the public as deservingly abject. Philipose suggests that the Abu Ghraib photographs demonstrate more than the power of the torturer to turn subjects into objects. They document how the extrajudicial infliction of violence can affirm whiteness and abjectify blackness. Shoring up the privilege of the white hypermasculine racial order in the United States, the Abu Ghraib photos produce new racialized objects on a new world stage, unleashing the power of visuality to justify violence on the tortured body. Constructed as terrorists, Muslim men in detention lose all purchase on innocence, legal rights, and due process guaranteed by the U.S. Constitution and multiple international covenants.

In "Preemptive Fridge Magnets and Other Weapons of Masculinist Destruction: The Rhetoric and Reality of 'Safeguarding Australia,'" Bronwyn Winter explores the gendered and raced operations of the national security state in Australia, a partner in the war on terror's coalition of the willing. Militarization in Australia is a complex phenomenon that combines neoliberal rhetoric, forms of privatization and outsourcing that direct large sums to conservative Christian organizations, diversion of funds originally allocated to address the problem of domestic violence to cover the costs of securitization, and antiterrorism legislation that undermines human rights and civil liberties. Tracing the consequences of these various initiatives for Australian and indigenous women, Winter argues that detrimental effects on women's rights and access to services are not just collateral damages of securitization. Security measures both construct and target women in ways that promote subordination because women must be subdued in order to need protection. Because the politics of fear that sustains securitization turns on control of women, Winter suggests that gendering lies at the heart of a national security agenda, which fails to enhance national security. Thus, she concludes that the "war on terror is largely a fiction endorsed and embellished by the masculinist Australian state to keep the population fearful and submissive. . . . For the macho muscularity of Leviathan Down Under to flourish, the population over which it rules must become, and remain, feminized" (382).

Feminist activism: Toward a new transnational gender order

If racialization and gendering are integral to war and terror, producing
and legitimizing new hierarchies of difference within nations and nationalist imaginaries, then it should not be surprising that feminist activists
have mobilized nationally, transnationally, and in the international arena
to address the direct and indirect effects of war. They have crafted tools
such as gender mainstreaming and worked arduously to deploy those tools
in international conventions. In language developed by the UN Economic
and Social Council following the Beijing Platform for Action, gender
mainstreaming is "the process of assessing the implications for women
and men of any planned action, including legislation, policies or programmes, in all areas and at all levels. It is a strategy for making women's
as well as men's concerns and experiences an integral dimension of the
design, implementation, monitoring and evaluation of policies and programmes in all political, economic and societal spheres so that women
and men benefit equally and inequality is not perpetuated. The ultimate
goal is to achieve gender equality" (UN Economic and Social Council
1997).

Several articles in this collection demonstrate creative approaches to
gender mainstreaming in the context of war. Pam Spees traces the re-
markably successful work of the Women's Caucus for Gender Justice in
the International Criminal Court (ICC). A transnational network of feminist activists concerned that mechanisms be created to hold individuals,
partisan groups, and governments to account for egregious crimes against
women committed in war, the Women's Caucus helped to shape the
Statute of Rome, which created the world's first permanent international
criminal tribunal to try individuals for genocide, war crimes, and crimes
against humanity. Working with diplomats from various regions, the
Women's Caucus succeeded in having sexual violence in war codified as
a crime against humanity, while also expanding the definition of sexual
violence to include rape, sexual slavery, enforced prostitution, forced pregnancy, and enforced sterilization. Through the intervention of the
Women's Caucus, the Rome Statute also identifies trafficking and gender-
based persecution, including crimes based on sexual orientation, as crimes
against humanity. In addition, the intensive lobbying by the Women's
Caucus for increased representation of women on the ICC yielded another
impressive victory: seven of the eighteen judges elected to the ICC in
February 2003 are women. By comparison, only one woman has ever
served on the fifteen-member International Court of Justice.

United Nations Security Council Resolution 1325, a product of the
arduous work of many feminists within the United Nations and in inter-

national nongovernmental organizations, calls for the involvement of women in decision making, peacekeeping, and national reconstruction in the aftermath of armed conflict. In their essay in this volume, Felicity Hill, Mikele Aboitiz, and Sara Poehlman-Doumbouya provide an overview of feminist activism contributing to the passage and implementation of this innovative effort to protect women and girls during armed conflict, heighten gender sensitivity in all UN peacekeeping missions, and incorporate women as equal participants in all postconflict negotiations. The creation of the International Criminal Court and the passage of UN Resolution 1325 laid the groundwork for an international infrastructure for gender equality, but realizing the promise of these international mechanisms remains an enormous challenge. As the articles on postconflict situations in this collection make clear, women and girls face huge hurdles in the processes of disarmament, demobilization, and reintegration. Equal citizenship may be encoded in law, but a great deal remains to be done to realize equal citizenship in practice.

"(En)Gendering Checkpoints: Checkpoint Watch and the Repercussions of Intervention" helps explain why equal citizenship remains so elusive. Through an extended investigation of the intended and unintended consequences of citizen action to hold their government to account for its abusive military practices, Hagar Kotef and Merav Amir demonstrate how gender confounds equal citizenship. Studying and working with Checkpoint Watch (CPW), a women's peace organization created to monitor and to document human rights abuses at Israeli checkpoints inside the Palestinian territories, Kotef and Amir illuminate the gender paradoxes that both enable and impair this intervention. The efficacy of CPW is rooted in gender: traditional assumptions about women's benign and nonthreatening nature underlie women's access to these militarized zones. Checkpoint Watch also trades on what is considered appropriate gendered behavior for its operations, assuming that women will avoid identifying with soldiers or aggressing against them in tense situations. Although CPW activists defy certain gender expectations when they travel to these zones of confrontation and attempt to intervene in army matters, their forms of intervention conform to markedly gendered roles and relations. Confronting the manifold daily humiliations, incidences of violence, and arbitrary impositions of hardship, CPW activists revert to iconic feminine roles to try to mitigate the harms they are witnessing. By mothering the young soldiers and flirting with senior officers, CPW activists use their influence to try to produce more humane treatment of the Palestinians. Kotef and Amir point out, however, that such humanitarian intervention is double edged. Asserting their citizenship rights to be present and to air their concerns at the checkpoints, the CPW activists enact Israeli superiority in the occupied territories, enfeebling the voice of the local population, collaborating with oppressive Israeli authorities, and further entrenching the checkpoints by supporting the creation of humanitarian stations there. Although particular instances of mothering and flirtation may indeed improve the immediate situation for specific Palestinians, the performance of rituals of feminine care and sexuality reinforces norms of gendered citizenship, while simultaneously provoking suspicion. In exercising their feminine wiles for humanitarian purposes, CPW activists make Palestinians the target of their care and thus are seen by some Israelis as betraying the nationalist cause. Political equality in citizen activism is readily confounded as the logics of unfaithful mother, mistress, or whore gain ascendancy.

Conclusion

For more than three decades, feminist scholars have argued that intersectional analysis does far more than add race and gender to existing analytic frameworks; it reframes research questions and alters ways of understanding the world. *War and Terror: Feminist Perspectives* is an example of such transformative scholarship. Essays in this collection demonstrate that racialization and gendering are not simply the unintended consequences of war or acts of terror. They are part of nation building and the daily operations of state power just as they are part of the political arsenal of insurgent groups, deployed as means to realize particular visions of political order.

Contrary to the claims of sociobiology, neither race nor gender is given in nature. As products of culture and society, both shift and change over time. War, armed conflict, and terrorism play crucial roles in disrupting old racial and gender orders, while establishing and maintaining new racial and gender regimes. War alters existing sexual divisions of labor but not necessarily in degendering ways. Organized violence may produce militant women, but it may also feminize nations by increasing their sense of vulnerability and defenselessness or feminize particular men by subjecting them to gendered practices of subordination through sexual assault or torture. Armed conflict may also contribute to significant regendering, as masculinist models are validated through manifestations of physical brutality or as men's longing for a return to "normal life" contributes to the redomestication of women, a pattern of postconflict restructuring sorely in need of further investigation.

Within contemporary social science, racism and sexism are typically understood as attitudes that operate at the level of the individual psyche, whether intentionally or unintentionally. Essays in this volume suggest that a different level of analysis is needed if processes of racialization and feminization in war are to be understood adequately. Racing and gendering are social practices consciously used as instruments of power by states, warring factions, and individuals. Although raced and gendered effects are often unintended consequences of war and terror, this does not preclude the intentional deployment of racial and gender power in particular circumstances. Sexual violence, coerced divisions of labor, formal and informal policing of modes of dress and deportment, and regimes of visibility and invisibility are constitutive of racialization and gendering in war and in peace.

Scholarly attention to race and gender elucidates intricate systems of power far too long omitted from mainstream social science research. As essays in this volume make clear, narrative and analytic frameworks such as nationalism and diaspora are neither neutral nor value free. Within studies of war, nationalist and diasporic frames offer markedly different accounts of the nature and frequency of organized violence. Where nationalist frames vindicate war as a legitimate tool, attention to gendered diaspora challenges legitimations of violence linked to the birth of nations, while also revealing continuities in gender violence in times of war and peace. In attending to race and gender, feminist analysis raises new questions concerning the criteria of demarcation between war and peace.

The essays in the collection illuminate operations of racial and gender power in the context of traditions that are never stagnant. They demonstrate that traditions are volatile cultural formations constantly subject to contestation and challenge and continually recreated through the actions and recollections of individuals as well as the customary practices and laws of nations. While war may accelerate changes in racial and gender hierarchies, it may also shore up old relations of domination or entrench new ones.

Attention to race and gender in the context of armed conflict challenges many received views about war and terror. In contrast to notions that race and gender are irrelevant to international relations, these articles demonstrate that practices of racing and gendering are embedded in nationalism and the production of diasporas and are integral both to statecraft and to insurrection. They also suggest that hard-and-fast distinctions between authoritarian regimes and democratic polities break down when race and gender are placed at the center of analysis. Evidence drawn from more than a dozen armed conflicts over the past half century suggests that suspension of civil liberties, callous disregard for individual rights, racial profiling and racist policies, and gender hierarchies that privilege men and disadvantage women are familiar to both kinds of polity. Although such practices are typically legitimized by appeals to the exceptional circumstances of war, feminist analysis suggests that they are routine practices of liberal democratic, neoliberal, and Islamic orders. By calling attention to the pervasiveness of processes of racialization and gendering in war and terror, the essays in this volume also demonstrate why feminist analysis and feminist activism are needed now more than ever.

Women's and Gender Studies Department
Rutgers University

References

Akhter, Farida. 2002. "Huntington's 'Clash of Civilizations' Thesis and Population Control." In *September 11, 2001: Global Feminist Perspectives*, ed. Susan Hawthorne and Bronwyn Winter, 297–301. Melbourne: Spinifex.

Alvarez, Sonia. 1990. *Engendering Democracy in Brazil: Women's Movements in Transition Politics.* Princeton, NJ: Princeton University Press.

Blanchard, Eric M. 2003. "Gender, International Relations, and the Development of Feminist Security Theory." *Signs: Journal of Women in Culture and Society* 28(4):1289–1312.

Dreyfuss, Robert. 2005. *Devil's Game: How the United States Helped Unleash Fundamentalist Islam.* New York: Metropolitan Books.

Enloe, Cynthia. 1989. *Bananas, Beaches, and Bases: Making Feminist Sense of International Politics.* Berkeley: University of California Press.

———. 2004. *The Curious Feminist: Searching for Women in a New Age of Empire.* Berkeley: University of California Press.

———. 2007. *Globalization and Militarism: Feminists Make the Link.* Lanham, MD: Rowman & Littlefield.

Fanon, Frantz. 1967. *A Dying Colonialism.* Trans. Haakon Chevalier. New York: Grove.

Funk, Nanette, and Magda Mueller. 1993. *Gender Politics and Post-Communism.* New York: Routledge.

Gallagher, Nancy. 2000/1. "The International Campaign against Gender Apartheid in Afghanistan." *UCLA Journal of International Law and Foreign Affairs* 5(2):367–402.

Hardt, Michael, and Antonio Negri. 2004. *Multitude: War and Democracy in the Age of Empire.* New York: Penguin.

Jaquette, Jane, ed. 1989. *The Women's Movement in Latin America: Feminism and the Transition to Democracy.* Boston: Unwin Hyman.

Jaquette, Jane, and Sharon Wolchik. 1998. *Women and Democracy: Latin America and Central and Eastern Europe.* Baltimore: Johns Hopkins University Press.

Lehring, Gary. 2003. *Officially Gay*. Philadelphia: Temple University Press.

Lorentzen, Lois Ann, and Jennifer Turpin. 1998. *The Women and War Reader*. New York: New York University Press.

Lyons, Tanya. 2004. *Guns and Guerilla Girls: Women in the Zimbabwean Liberation Struggle*. Trenton, NJ: Africa World Press.

McClintock, Anne. 1995. *Imperial Leather: Race, Gender, and Sexuality in Colonial Context*. New York: Routledge.

Miller, Francesca. 1991. *Latin American Women and the Search for Social Justice*. Hanover, NH: University Press of New England.

Nechemias, Carol, and Kathleen Kuehnast. 2004. *Post-Soviet Women Encountering Transition: Nation Building, Economic Survival, and Civic Activism*. Washington, DC: Woodrow Wilson Center/Johns Hopkins University Press.

Nelson, Barbara, and Najma Chowdhury, eds. 1994. *Women and Politics Worldwide*. New Haven, CT: Yale University Press.

Osterud, Oyvind. 2004. "War." In *Encyclopedia of Government and Politics*, ed. Mary Hawkesworth and Maurice Kogan, 1039–48. London: Routledge.

Parker, Andrew, Mary Russo, Doris Sommer, and Patricia Yaeger. 1992. *Nationalisms and Sexualities*. New York: Routledge.

Pateman, Carole. 1998. "The Patriarchal Welfare State." In *Feminism, the Public and the Private*, ed. Joan Landes, 241–74. New York: Oxford University Press.

Phelan, Shane. 2001. *Sexual Strangers: Gays, Lesbians, and Dilemmas of Citizenship*. Philadelphia: Temple University Press.

Porras, Ileana. 1995. "On Terrorism: Reflections on Violence and the Outlaw." In *After Identity: A Reader in Law and Culture*, ed. Dan Danielson and Karen Engle, 294–313. New York: Routledge.

Radcliffe, Sara, and Sallie Westwood, eds. 1993. *Viva: Woman and Popular Protest in Latin America*. New York: Routledge.

Russo, Ann. 2006. "The Feminist Majority Foundation's Campaign to Stop Gender Apartheid." *International Feminist Journal of Politics* 8(4):557–80.

Saint Germain, Michelle. 1994. "Women, Democratization, and Public Policy." *Policy Sciences* 27(2–3):269–76.

Taylor, Rupert. 1996. "Political Science Encounters 'Race' and 'Ethnicity.'" *Racial and Ethnic Studies* 19 (October): 884–95.

Turpin, Jennifer. 1998. "Many Faces: Women Confronting War." In *The Women and War Reader*, ed. Lois Ann Lorentzen and Jennifer Turpin, 3–18. New York: New York University Press.

UN Economic and Social Council. 1997. *Agreed Conclusions 1997/2*. General Assembly Official Records; Fifty-second Session, Supplement no. 3. New York: United Nations.

Wicomb, Zoë. 2000. *David's Story*. Capetown: Kwela.

Young, Iris Marion. 2003. "The Logic of Masculinist Protection: Reflections on the Current Security State." *Signs* 29(1):1–25.

Yuval Davis, Nira. 1997. *Gender and Nation*. London: Sage.

Part I. Participation in Violent Conflict

Myriam Denov
Christine Gervais

Negotiating (In)Security: Agency, Resistance, and Resourcefulness among Girls Formerly Associated with Sierra Leone's Revolutionary United Front

When I started looking for girls in numerous war situations, I found silences and empty spaces, punctuated only by a handful of researchers focusing on children in general and girls in particular. Their stories account
only for the smallest percentage of scholarly and popular work on social
and political violence and systems of injustice. . . . Too often the girls are
considered only as silent victims of (sexual) assault—devoid of agency,
moral conscience, economic potential or political awareness. . . . We
need to ask girls to tell their own stories of war . . . rather than assuming the right to speak for them.
—Carolyn Nordstrom 1997, 5, 36

War has traditionally been regarded as a masculine phenomenon and
tends to be inherently linked to male aggression, violence, and brutality. In direct contrast, and perpetuating a misleading binary, depictions and representations of women and girls during war have tended
to focus on their passivity as victims, peacemakers, wives, and mothers,
or as appendages to males who are regarded as the true participants in
war. Moreover, as the above quotation clearly illustrates, although men
have been perceived as the primary agents in war, women have been
rendered largely as silent and invisible victims. Although there is little
question that girls and women endure profound violence during armed
conflict, their roles within the context of armed conflict are increasingly

The first author would like to thank the Children's Rights and Protection Unit at the
Canadian International Development Agency for its generous support of the study upon
which this article is based. Deepest thanks, admiration, and gratitude go to the girls whose
stories are highlighted in this article. The research team was consistently moved and humbled
by their strength, candor, and insights. This article is dedicated to them.

[*Signs: Journal of Women in Culture and Society* 2007, vol. 32, no. 4]

fluid and diverse.[1] In fact, women and girls are involved, often simultaneously, in myriad aspects of armed conflict as perpetrators, actors, porters, commanders, domestic servants, spies, bodyguards, human shields, and sex slaves. Their roles are multidimensional and often contradictory and require that women and girls negotiate and renegotiate their security and well-being in a context that is anything but stable (Moser and Clark 2001). In the case of girls, the chronic quest for safety and security, regardless of the nature of their roles, may be even more challenging because of their vulnerability, which is exacerbated by their gender, age, and relative physical disadvantage (Fox 2004; Denov 2006).

Gender is a significant and unique dimension of security-related experiences and shapes the ways in which security is envisioned, ensured, and experienced (Caprioli 2004; Fox 2004). Moreover, the detrimental impact of sexism and patriarchy on experiences of insecurity reinforces the contention that security is not a gender-neutral concept (Crawley 2000). As Lene Hansen and Louise Olsson claim, "security is gendered through the political mobilization of masculine and feminine identities that are linked to practices of militarism and citizenship" (Hansen and Olsson 2004, 406). Women's and particularly girls' experiences of violence and insecurity differ considerably from those of men and boys, especially because of their sexual and physical vulnerability (Cockburn 2001; Giles and Hyndman 2004; Denov 2006). Caroline Moser and Cathy McIlwaine (2001, 178) echo this contention and add that females and males have different perceptions of the violence that affects them. Gendered perceptions of violence are important considerations in analyses of females' quests for security because perceptions shape individuals' interpretations of and approaches to both dangers and solutions. Acknowledging gender as a noteworthy component of security not only allows for nonstate and more individualized conceptions of security, but such recognition of gendered and personalized dimensions of security may also foster more authentic articulations of security that shed light on relations, experiences, needs, dynamics, variances, and negotiations of security and insecurity (El-Bushra 2000; Macklin 2004).

Although the emerging literature on gender and conflict has begun to highlight the vast insecurities that girls may face in the context of war

[1] These forms of violence include rape, forced impregnation, mutilation, torture, displacement, enslavement, sexual exploitation, trafficking, and death (Meertens 2001; Turshen 2001; Handrahan 2004). The associated conditions of impoverishment, starvation, injury, and disease, as well as the loss of family, employment, residence, and nationality, are equally devastating (Fox 2004).

(see McKay 1998; McKay and Mazurana 2004), given the frequent focus on the wartime victimization of girls, relatively few studies have attempted to articulate or understand the ways in which war-affected girls actively seek to ensure their own security within the highly insecure context of armed conflict, as well as their roles as active agents.[2] A few exceptions to this have been the contributions of Carolyn Nordstrom (1997), Paul Richards (1998), Mats Utas (2003, 2005), and Alcinda Honwana (2006), who have all emphasized the importance of recognizing agency among war-affected children and, in particular, the realities of girls and women. To contribute to and expand upon this growing literature, this article explores the ways in which a sample of girls formerly associated with Sierra Leone's rebel Revolutionary United Front (RUF) experienced and subsequently attempted to avoid, minimize, or resist wartime abuses and insecurities.

We first provide a brief history of the conflict in Sierra Leone and, in particular, its effect on girls. After outlining the methodological approach to the study of girls formerly associated with the RUF, we explore girls' experiences of insecurity and victimization within the context of the decade-long civil war. We then trace the diverse ways in which this sample of girls actively negotiated their insecurity through the use of agency, resourcefulness, and modes of resistance. Finally, we highlight the implications of girls' responses to insecurity for larger debates concerning gender, war, and security.

Sierra Leone's civil war and its effect on girls

Like much of sub-Saharan Africa, Sierra Leone was integrated into the world system in a way that marginalized its traditional social systems and left its economy colonized by international enterprises and a kleptocratic governing elite. Over time, with poor governance and a weak economy, educational and occupational opportunities for young people were consistently undermined (Richards 1998). Moreover, within the context of widespread government corruption, mismanagement, and institutional collapse, and with more than half the population of Sierra Leone under the age of eighteen, disillusionment and anger among young people was

---

[2] The issue of agency and the search for security are clearly applicable to the wartime realities of both boys and girls. However, given their relative invisibility in scholarly literature, this article focuses on the circumstances of girls. For further discussions of agency with a sample of boy soldiers in Sierra Leone, see Maclure and Denov (2006) and Denov and Maclure (forthcoming b).

infectious and volatile. Capitalizing upon the growing mass disillusionment, former Sierra Leonean Army corporal Foday Sankoh (who was backed by Liberian warlord Charles Taylor) formed the rebel Revolutionary United Front of Sierra Leone. Relying on the emancipatory rhetoric of "freedom, justice and democracy to all Sierra Leoneans" (Revolutionary United Front/Sierra Leone 1995), Sankoh systematically recruited largely uneducated, unemployed, and unemployable male youth who were linked to the informal underground economy to join a movement against the government (Abdullah 1998). In circumstances of mounting insurgence, traditional institutions were gradually replaced by militarized structures that were sustained by an ethos of extraordinary violence. When Sankoh's message of political revolution failed to attract popular support, the RUF's aim of broad social emancipation was sidelined by the goals of wealth, power, and control of the country's diamond mines. Marked as one of the most unrestrained fighting forces in recent history, the RUF invaded Sierra Leone from Liberia in 1991 and embarked on a decade-long campaign of terror characterized by indiscriminate violence and brutality against civilians.

Sierra Leone's decade-long conflict had a particularly ferocious effect on girls and women. Although girls and women have been historically relegated to positions of dependency within traditional systems of patriarchy, the political and economic decline and corresponding erosion of civic structures in the 1980s exacerbated female vulnerability. Following the outbreak of hostilities in the early 1990s, the already bleak situation of girls rapidly deteriorated into a nightmare of abuse and horror. Throughout much of the conflict, young females were systematically abducted by warring factions (mainly rebel forces) and forced to assume the roles of combatants, commanders, wives, or slave laborers—often a combination of these roles (Denov and Maclure 2006). In fact, nearly 30 percent of children associated with the RUF were girls (McKay and Mazurana 2004). Alongside the boys, girls became both victims of and participants in brutal forms of violence and terror.[3] Before providing an account of the ways in which a sample of these girls negotiated their safety and security within the militarized context of life with the RUF, we describe our study's methodology.

---

[3] Undoubtedly, child soldiers are simultaneously perpetrators and victims of violence. Their plight is complex: as they actually perpetrate violence, child soldiers remain victims of coercion, terror, and deception.

Methodology

Our examination draws on fieldwork conducted by Myriam Denov and Canadian and Sierra Leonean research partners in 2003 and 2004, which included in-depth qualitative interviews with forty girls formerly associated with the RUF living in the Eastern, Southern, and Northern Provinces and the Western Area of Sierra Leone.[4] At the time of the research field-work, all the girl participants were between fourteen and twenty-one years old. The girl respondents had been under the age of eighteen years before the end of the conflict and had been under the control of the RUF for a period ranging from a few months to seven years. To be included in the study, participants were required to have been associated with an armed group in Sierra Leone (either voluntarily or through coercion) while under the age of eighteen.[5] No stipulations were made regarding the length of time that girls were attached to an armed group or their assigned role within the group. A significant effort was made to gain a "thick descrip-tion" (Geertz 1973) of the mental and experiential world of girls formerly associated with the RUF and the transitions into and out of violent conflict that have been inherent to this world.

The research team also consisted of six female adolescent researchers who had been part of the RUF fighting forces during the conflict. These six girls were involved in several aspects of the project, including the creation of research instruments, the recruitment of research participants, data collection, and dissemination of the research findings at a local com-munity conference in Sierra Leone.[6] Involving the girls in a purposeful activity proved to be educational and empowering for them. Moreover,

---

[4] This research was part of a larger study funded by the Canadian International Devel-opment Agency. The research was conducted by Myriam Denov (the project's principal investigator and this article's primary author), in conjunction with Richard Maclure of the University of Ottawa; Abdul Manaff Kemokai of Defence for Children International, Sierra Leone (DCI-SL); and a Sierra Leonean research team from Defence for Children Interna-tional, Sierra Leone.

[5] In this study, the definition of a child coincides with the definition set out in the UN Convention on the Rights of the Child. According to the convention, a child is defined as "every human being below eighteen years" (article 1). For the text of the convention, see the United Nations Office of the High Commissioner for Human Rights, http://www.unhchr.ch/html/menu3/b/k2crc.htm.

[6] Denov conducted in-depth research training workshops with the adolescent researchers. Training focused on the goals of the research, on interview techniques with children, on gender and cultural aspects of interviewing, on ethical issues, and on the potential challenges they were likely to face in the field. As part of the training, young female researchers undertook mock interviewing and mock focus-group discussions as a way to hone their new skills.

such an inclusive approach reinforced and grounded research on, by, and for girls.

A grounded theory approach to both data collection and analysis, which uses inductive forms of analysis to gain an understanding of the patterns that exist in the social world under study (Glaser and Strauss 1967), was essential to ensuring that the voices and perspectives of participants became the central component of the analysis and facilitated an authentic presentation of girls' experiences (Stasiulis 1993; Lyons 2004, 282).[7] This grounded theory approach also coincides with a human security approach that seeks to move beyond conventional definitions of security, which tend to be state-oriented and as a result tend to exclude relevant human dimensions (Higate and Henry 2004). Our particular interest is to acknowledge and integrate individualized and experiential accounts of both security and insecurity, especially "from the bottom up" (Hoogensen and Rottem 2004, 161); incorporating these accounts through a human dimension into security studies identifies people, and not the state, as security studies' unit of analysis and as their priority of intervention (UN Development Programme 1994, 23).

The human security framework also acknowledges that while security is a political issue, it is also a very personal experience, often associated with fear and agony under threats of violence (Macklin 2004, 82). Such a contention is reinforced in Alexander Wendt's claim that "security is to a large extent what actors make of it" (Wendt 1992, 404). As such, the human security approach legitimizes individualized experiences of security and insecurity (Hansen and Olsson 2004). By placing the security of the person at the forefront of analysis and intervention, the approach extends beyond mere reflection of individual needs and actually enables security to be considered and determined at the individual level (Giles and Hyndman 2004, 12). As a result, security becomes definable both by and for individuals themselves and thereby becomes more authentically understood (Stasiulis 1993). This grounded and "trickle up" approach allows for more personalized and experiential accounts of security and insecurity to ultimately be voiced (Hoogensen and Rottem 2004, 163) and for those

---

[7] We share Tanya Lyons's (2004, 282) concerns about the inappropriateness of using marginalized females' voices to produce a Western academic text. However, we are also cognizant of the openness advocated by Daiva Stasiulis's (1993) antiessentialist position on authentic voice. In light of these considerations, we have attempted to create a space where the marginalized voices of the girls formerly associated with Sierra Leone's RUF can be communicated while being mindful of both dignity and diversity.

most marginalized, particularly women and children, to be prioritized in security concerns (Fox 2004, 475).

The mutually enhancing relation between a grounded theory approach and a human security approach is a useful methodological and conceptual base for our emphasis on the narratives of girls formerly associated with Sierra Leone's RUF. As Gunhild Hoogensen and Svein Rottem (2004) and Mary-Jane Fox (2004) advocate, such a grounded and human-oriented approach opens up spaces for articulations of security, particularly by females. It is within this light that we explore the real-life insecurity experiences of girls from the RUF as they are articulated by the girls themselves.

Life in the RUF: Girls' experiences of insecurity and victimization

Given the war-torn situation in Sierra Leone and the insecurity of people throughout the country, girls inevitably reported feelings of insecurity and victimization prior to their abduction by the rebels. However, it was clear that their sense of insecurity was heightened—to the extreme—when they were coercively and violently separated from their families and communities and forced to join the rebels. All forty girls interviewed reported being abducted by the RUF under circumstances of extreme brutality and fear. In most cases, rebels invaded their villages and communities, and, under the threat of a gun, the girls were ordered to join the movement. As one girl explained: "During one of their numerous attacks, the rebels succeeded in driving the progovernment forces from our community. We hid ourselves in our house. The firing was so intense. Most people were running helter-skelter. After the fighting and firing subsided, rebels entered our house and forcefully picked me among my brothers and sisters. . . . Who would dare refuse? Not even if you were mad. . . . So they took me away. . . . I did not know what we were heading for and what they wanted to do with me. I was in total fear."[8] Following their abduction,

---

[8] All interviews were conducted by Myriam Denov of McGill University, Abdul Manaff Kemokai of DCI-SL, and a number of talented research assistants from DCI-SL. Interviews were conducted in the participant's maternal language (either Krio, Mende, Temne, or Limba), translated into English by the Sierra Leonean research assistants at DCI-SL, and later transcribed. All interview transcripts are in the possession of Myriam Denov, and all quotations in this text emerge from data collected from these interviews. Given that participants were interviewed several times over the course of the two-year research project, often in different locations and regions of the country, information on the date and location of each interview has not been included. To ensure confidentiality and anonymity, all names of participants have been omitted from the text.

and in the context of ongoing fear, girls were assigned an array of domestic and supportive tasks including cooking, washing, taking care of young children, and carrying heavy loads of ammunition, supplies, and arms. Failing to carry out their duties often meant enduring extreme forms of punishment, including brutal physical assaults, starvation, and even death: "If you refused or failed to do what you were told, they would put you in a guardroom or tie you up or one of the commanders might pass a command saying 'kill that person for not taking orders.' If you were obedient, you would be fine. But if you attempted escape and you were caught in the act, you would be killed without delay."

Girls quickly learned of the RUF's culture of violence and constant terror that surrounded them. The violence within the RUF appears to have been an integral feature of daily interaction and ranged along a continuum from verbal abuse to outrageous acts of cruelty. The girls suffered severe physical abuse at the hands of those who commanded them, particularly in the early stages of their recruitment. They were also witnesses to brutal forms of violence against men, women, and children who were both RUF combatants and civilians, acts that were clearly in-tended as public displays of horror. Violence and the threat of violence were used not only as a means to ensure total compliance and obedience but also as a form of indoctrination into and desensitization to the RUF's campaign of terror (Maclure and Denov 2006). Moreover, children were intimidated with terrifying warnings that any attempts to escape their captors would be met with death: "Some children tried to escape and they were caught. They shot some of them and the rest were thrown down a well and drowned. We witnessed this and decided that we should not try to escape."

While a constant aura of menace and terror seems to have been the basis of social structure, cohesion, and authority within the RUF, the patriarchal power structure and institutionalized gender differentiation also rendered almost all girls culturally and physically subservient to their male counterparts. The reality of repeated sexual violence, one of the key sources of insecurity for girls in the RUF, was the embodiment of such patriarchal power relations. Sexual violence, whether gang rape, individual rape, rape with objects, or all three, was a daily occurrence for most girls.[9] In fact, all but two girls interviewed for this study reported being victims of repeated sexual assault by numerous male RUF fighters. These nar-ratives reveal the brutality of these acts: "One afternoon, two rebels raped

---

[9] Sexual violence was reportedly perpetrated predominately by boys and men. However, girls also reported a few instances of sexual abuse by adult female commanders.

me. It was very painful. I cried right through the act. But even when I cried for mercy, they wouldn't listen to me. They tied my hands. . . . After the first man raped me, I was helpless. By the time the second guy was on top of me I didn't even know what was happening. When they had finished, I had blood between my legs and I couldn't walk because of the pain. . . . I felt very awful. I was ashamed of sitting among other people, I really felt like just dying." Similarly, this girl explained: "Rape was just normal with the group. . . . When I was newly captured, I was raped. . . . I was too small to be raped. . . . I cried and pleaded with the man to let go of me. He didn't. He went right on and did exactly as he wanted. . . . That night I cried and cried. . . . I was bleeding profusely. . . . For a whole week I sat and grieved."

In addition to repeated sexual violence, the majority of girls in the sample were forced to marry rebels, whereby a particular girl was deemed the sexual property of a specific RUF male. In Sierra Leone, this sexual slavery was euphemistically referred to as "bush marriage" or "AK-47 marriage": "I was twelve years old at the time. There was one man, a commander, who took me for his own. But other rebels demanded sex from me too. Whenever the commander was away, the other men would come after me and rape me. Some were in full view of others. Sometimes they would take me into the bush to rape me. They seemed to do it more often when they were taking drugs."

Another source of insecurity for girls was their forced involvement in highly dangerous combat activities and the use of small arms and light weapons. As with other countries that have experienced internal civil wars rather than cross-border conflict between countries, small arms were the weapons of choice for combatants in Sierra Leone. Cheap and efficient firearms, often purchased through illicit diamond sales, were widespread throughout the conflict. Following their abduction, girls reported being introduced to the foreign and dangerous world of small arms, and some were provided with rudimentary training. The transition into this world was not an easy one and brought about extreme fear, anxiety, and bitterness. As these girls explained: "I was not happy about it [having to use guns]. It was scary for me because I feared guns a lot." "I wasn't very good at [using weapons]. They took us to a base to learn how to use the weapons. I didn't learn very well. At one point my gun misfired and I was nearly killed. . . . I really had fear in my heart." This girl explained: "It was not the place for a little girl to hold a gun. I was so bitter. . . . I wanted an education, not to know how to fire a gun."

Although many girls were initially delegated supportive roles in the RUF, as the conflict wore on, for some girls, combat activities and the manipulation of small arms formed the crux of their involvement in the conflict: "Initially, my job was to carry heavy loads, but later I became part of the fighting force, to attack and defend. . . . We attacked convoys of vehicles, including military trucks, we killed people randomly and when we overcame them, we took all of their goods and set fire to their vehicles. . . . They normally told me that I was good at attacking when on the offensive, but I did not appreciate it and I was not convinced. I did it to save my life."

These experiences of combat brought forth extreme fear and insecurity. With little experience in handling weaponry, and with chaos and the madness of violence surrounding them, girls were afraid for their lives: "Each time we were preparing for combat, I was afraid for my life. The government soldiers and the Economic Community of West African States Monitoring Group who we were fighting had much more powerful machine guns than us. We were given drugs to overcome our worries and fright."

These testimonies have uncovered gripping perceptions of human and gendered insecurities. These insecurities were gendered through the transposition of patriarchal power structures onto a militarized terrain whereby traditional female roles were entrenched in the daily practices of the conflict. The gendered vulnerability and subservience of girls were manifested through the sexual violence, forced marriages, childbearing and child rearing, domestic chores, and supportive tasks that girls were subjected to during the militarized conflict. Such predominantly girl-specific tasks were performed and required in addition to their duties as fighters and spies.

For the girls formerly associated with the RUF, the terror and brutality of the war in Sierra Leone created a myriad of insecurities that were inevitably related to the limited entitlement that the girls had to even the most basic survival needs. The sexual, physical, personal, spatial, social, political, and health insecurities experienced by the girls occurred within extreme conditions of coercion, chaos, and deceit and consequently generated fear, humiliation, and bitterness. Although such constraining and vulnerable circumstances may seemingly limit girls' capacity to protect themselves, the girls nevertheless attempted to negotiate these challenges and gendered insecurities with resistance and resourcefulness.

Negotiating (in)security: Girls' agency, resourcefulness, and resistance

Amid chaos and vulnerability, females have engaged in alternative mobilization efforts to ensure as much personal survival and communal security as possible (Cordero 2001). In the context of the violence experienced by war-affected girls, ingenuity and creativity became strategic to individual survival and security. Despite their ongoing anxieties and brutal forms of victimization, the girls made conscious attempts to protect themselves and negotiate their security during their time with the RUF. Their attempts to negotiate their safety involved a variety of means, including using small arms, aligning themselves with a powerful male commander, perpetuating severe acts of violence, and engaging in subtle acts of acquiescence as well as bold acts of resistance. These mechanisms, which carried varying degrees of success, highlight the girls' capacity for negotiation and agency as well as resourcefulness, resistance, and mutual forms of support.

Power and small arms

When first coerced into the ranks of the RUF, the girls perceived the use of small arms as a source of insecurity and fear. However, as the conflict dragged on, and through ongoing observations and relations with their commanders and other child soldiers, the girls became increasingly aware that carrying a gun often increased their protection within the ranks of the RUF and in some cases decreased their chances of victimization. In light of this, the girls came to see small arms as a way to increase their safety and security and, reflecting both their agency and resourcefulness, over time became eager to possess their own weapon: "I was eager to become a soldier and have my own gun so that I would be able to resist threats and harassment from other soldiers." In a similar vein, this girl explained: "The gun became my bodyguard and protector. The gun was power, and that's why I was anxious to have one."

Moreover, in a context of continued victimization and powerlessness, ownership and use of a gun often brought the girls a sense of power, authority, and supremacy, particularly over civilians. As one participant described, "I felt powerful when I had a gun. As long as you are holding a gun, you have power over those who don't. It gave me more status and power." Another girl echoed this sentiment: "The gun made a big difference between us and the civilians. Naturally, you feel powerful when you have a gun in a war situation. One of the ways officers used to punish us was to take our guns from us. Some soldiers were not able to live without a gun."

Girls' feelings of power and confidence in relation to handling weaponry must be seen, however, within the context of gender dependency and subservience. Through the use of small arms, girls appear to have experienced a sense of release from previous relations of victimization and submission. More specifically, some girls were able to reframe and transform their original fear of small arms into instances of supremacy and power that afforded them, albeit minimally, a greater sense of security.

Perpetrating acts of violence

The RUF became notorious for its brutal atrocities committed against civilians and entire communities (Abdullah 1998). Being forced to live within this overarching culture of violence, as time went on, children, through a combination of indoctrination, terror, desensitization, and militaristic training, became active participants in conflict (Maclure and Denov 2006; Denov and Maclure forthcoming b). The more aggressive girls were seen to be, and the more destruction and looting they undertook, the more valuable they were within the ranks of the RUF. Girls became increasingly conscious of the fact that the more violent they were, the safer they became within the armed group. As one of the girls described: "I committed a lot of violence. . . . We were cherished by the senior officers for our wicked deeds." "I would tie people up, kill, and loot people's property. . . . I was not too good at shooting, but I was an expert in burning houses. We would enter the house after the enemy left the area and set fire to it using kerosene or petrol. I had to survive, and some of the ways to do it were to get involved in those violent acts."

Importantly, engaging in extreme forms of violence also brought privileges within the RUF, such as better access to food and looted goods, and in some cases led to promotion within the ranks. Promotion to the rank of commander was deemed to be the peak of success within the RUF: "Very violent and obedient soldiers were given positions as commanders. You needed to show enthusiasm, be very active during combat and terrorize and abduct civilians. . . . I was very active in combat and also captured a lot of people, including children. This contributed to my elevation to the status of a commander."

Although a minority of respondents reported being promoted to a commander, those who did recalled this event with nostalgia and even pride. The promotion elevated their status and allowed them to lead their own units of child combatants and contributed to their protection through their entourage of child bodyguards: "I was a commander not only for children but also for soldiers older than myself. Commanders were generally treated better regardless of their age or sex. I had six bodyguards. . . . They were very loyal and they did everything I ordered without questioning. . . . As commanders we needed bodyguards to boost our morale and to show other people our status. [This was important] because we didn't have badges, uniforms, or crowns to depict our status. . . . I was given a lot more status and protection as a commander." It is entirely possible that some girls came to embrace the power of being a perpetrator and the rewards stemming from their violent actions. However, given that extreme acts of violence appeared to ensure girls' survival, reduce their own victimization, and even assure them higher status in the ranks of the RUF, acts of perpetration can be regarded as strategic attempts at negotiation.

Marriage to a powerful commander

Marriage and sexual relations are often referred to as necessary exchanges for the survival and protection of both female combatants and female captives (Dinan 2002). In what have been called sex-for-soap exchanges, some females negotiate their hygienic and food needs "by using their positions as women (being [sexually] available to men)" (Lyons 2004, 191). Others seek protection from physical and sexual abuse through sex or marriage (Ibañez 2001). Depending on the severity of the power dynamics, marriage and sexual relations may be perceived as either active or passive on the part of the girls; in either case, some level of agency or attempt at negotiation is evident.

As noted earlier, the reality of sexual violence was a devastating feature of everyday life for girls in the RUF. Within a powerful patriarchal structure, the girls in this study became mere property of male RUF members, with their bodies being used as resources to be exploited and even as gifts and rewards (Maclure and Denov 2006). Girls were thus constantly aware of the potential threat and danger of sexual violence by their adult commanders as well as by other men within the armed group. Within this context of profound insecurity, girls realized the importance of actively aligning themselves with a high-ranking male commander through a bush marriage. As Utas has argued within the context of war-torn Liberia, "intelligent and smart young women were seen parading with the most powerful commanders" (Utas 2005, 75). Although these marriages to individual male commanders were often highly repressive, violent, and abusive, they were preferable to the alternative of being ongoing victims of gang and individual rape by countless members of the fighting forces.[10] As one girl explained, "When one of the commanders proposed love to you, sometimes you had to accept even if you really were not willing to cooperate. This was preferable to being gang-raped."

---

[10] Here we acknowledge the relativity of security under such repressive circumstances. While marriage may have rendered a girl more secure, the context in which she benefited from a certain level of protection was still very insecure.

As the following narratives illustrate, marriage to a powerful commander not only protected the girls from daily sexual violence and physical abuse by other males in their group but also elevated their overall status within the RUF: "The girls who were serving as wives were treated better, and according to the rank and status of their husbands. . . . At the beginning, I was raped daily. . . . But later an officer had a special interest in me. He then protected me against others and never allowed others to use me. He continued to have sex with me alone and less frequently. . . . He gave me protection from the other men." Similarly, this participant explained, "Girls who were wives of senior officers were treated according to the status of their husbands, so it was good for any girl to have a senior officer as a lover. They had more power and status."

Given the increased security associated with marriage, perhaps not surprisingly girls reported actively trying to gain the sexual attention of powerful males in the RUF. As one girl stated, "I was married in the bush . . . it was more advisable to have a husband than to be single. Women and girls were seeking [the sexual attention of] men—especially strong ones for protection from sexual harassment."

Reflecting agency and resourcefulness, girls' marriage to a powerful commander can thus be seen as a clever strategy to actively find protection, power, status, and survival. Moreover, such strategic instances, albeit in highly insecure conditions, serve as significant examples of girls' abilities to negotiate and in some cases thwart or limit their own potential victimization through the use of conventional gender roles. Although bush marriages may be perceived as a form of sexual slavery, they have also served as a site at which some girls reframe their victimization and, however minimally, transform it into a more secure space. The complexity of bush marriages illustrates how patriarchal norms and gender expectations can sometimes create both insecurity and (relative) security for girls in times of war (Handrahan 2004).

Modes of acquiescence and resistance

Acquiescence to the RUF's doctrines was a resourceful way for girls to ensure their safety. Moreover, acceding to forms of victimization enabled them to stave off more extreme forms of cruelty. As Kinsey Alden Dinan (2002, 1127) and Miranda Alison (2004, 462) have observed elsewhere, girls strategically exploit gendered obedience and gendered divisions of labor to their advantage. For example, some female combatants were intentionally subservient in and deliberately excelled at domestic chores, such as cooking and cleaning, so that they could be relegated to mundane camp tasks and thus avoid being sent into the bush to shoot and kill. In the following narrative, one girl explained her resourceful tactic to avoid warfare: "I was responsible for cooking, and I always did it well because I did not want to leave the [domestic duties] for jobs like combat that were more deadly." Interestingly, this girl's testimony once again demonstrates how other young females use conventional gender roles (e.g., patriarchy-based domestic duties) to their security advantage (Alison 2004).

Strategies of resistance alongside acquiescence by women in conflict situations have been documented across several continents (Jacobs 2000; Preston and Wong 2004). Examples of such resistance include the refusal to act, refusal to assent to violence, silence, escape, and termination of pregnancy in the cases of rape and ethnic cleansing tactics (Jacobs, Jacobson, and Marchbank 2000; Keitetsi 2004). The risks associated with resistance are often grave and even fatal and are thus a testament to the degree of courage exhibited by these women and girls (Denov and Maclure forthcoming a).

For the girls interviewed for this research, there was little room for defiance or opposition in the RUF environment where obedience to authority and conformity to the values of the RUF were imperative to children's very survival. Nonetheless, despite the potential consequences of injury and even death for noncompliance, many girls engaged in acts of resistance. Forms of resistance varied and included developing strong relationships with other girls and women. By creating a sense of female solidarity and by inherently excluding the males, girls within the RUF were able to attain a degree of solace and comfort and could subtly resist patriarchal authority structures. Although some would argue that the creation of strong female relationships can be considered a common survival strategy used by war-affected females historically, one must consider the unique context in which the girls in this study were living. Within the RUF, any form of socializing or sharing of their current thoughts, feelings, or information about their former civilian lives was strictly forbidden and highly punishable, even by death. As one girl explained: "If we came from the same place and we knew each other, we would share a few jokes or sit together and share thoughts and memories of home. This would go on until perhaps one of commanders came and said, 'What are you sitting here for? What are you doing?' We would then pretend we were doing something else so that they would not learn of what we were actually engaged in. Because at those times, if you were caught in acts like that, you [could be killed]."

Given the dangerous and volatile context and the repercussions of being discovered for socializing, engaging in personal discussions and building a sense of solidarity can be considered more passive forms of resistance. Such communicative structures among girls, whether formal or informal, open or secret, were instrumental to their psychological and emotional well-being during armed conflict. As an example, one girl reflected upon the importance of talking to and sharing with other girls about her experience of rape: "One day a girl was brutally raped and she bled so badly she died. . . . I had heard about it and was so affected by it, but I was afraid to discuss it. . . . Two girls began discussing it, and I overheard them. We all sat down and started sharing our stories [of rape]. . . . I felt much better after this because I thought that I was the only one to have this happen to."

Other girls engaged in more active forms of resistance to ensure their survival. For example, girls reported using violent forms of resistance to retaliate against male perpetrators of sexual assault:

I stabbed one guy to death—he was always harassing me for sex. On that day he wanted to rape me and I told him that if he tried, I would stab him. He underestimated me and he never knew I had a dagger. He met me alone in the bush on my way to town after using the bush toilet. I knew that he and others were observing my movements . . . and I took the dagger along [to protect me from] rapists. As he attempted to rape me, I stabbed him twice . . . I was tired of the sexual harassment. He later died [from the stabbing].

Girls also recounted collective efforts at resistance by attempting to escape the RUF, all the while being fully aware of the consequences of violence or death if they were discovered: "It was impossible to escape because they had tight security and those who attempted and were caught were killed. . . . But at times [the children in our group] came together quietly to discuss ways of escaping from our captors. . . . Part of our job was to fetch water for the rebels. . . . On one particular occasion no guards came with us. My sister told me to drop our buckets, and we ran into the bush. We stayed there for nearly a week, living only on fruits and raw cassava until we finally found our way to our own village." Another girl explained the circumstances surrounding her attempted escape: "I became very tired of always carrying the loads. Myself and a group of about five others decided that we would attempt an escape. We decided to use the opportunity of fetching water to do this. But one girl was not involved in the plan and she overheard us talking about it. She informed the commander about our plan . . . we were [punished] and confined to a small space and starved for several days."

In the above case, when the respondent was asked why she thought her colleague had revealed the group's plan of escape to the commander, she replied, "I think that [the girl who revealed our plan to the commander] had a vested interest in having us all stay with her. If we escaped, she would have no friends or companions and she would be left to do all the chores and work by herself." By deceiving her fellow captives by reporting the plan of escape to the commander, the girl in question is herself actively using a survival strategy and a form of resistance. This demonstrates that while the young women acted in solidarity in some moments, in others they were in conflict and competition in their strategies of survival and resistance. Although most respondents were unsuccessful in their attempts to escape, it was clear that girls demonstrated a capacity to organize and to act both individually and collectively with extraordinary courage.

It is important to note that while there may have been a range of opportunities and choices available to girls in the process of exercising agency, in the context of wartime violence, agency often took on a rather defensive form. That is, for victims of incessant violence, especially sexual abuse, and within the context of oppressive hierarchical structures, the agency afforded to girls in conflict zones was often severely constrained (Alison 2004). Where and when agency was exhibited by the girls in this study, it was often under duress involving threats of torture, rape, and death. Under such repressive conditions, it took a significant amount of awareness, skill, vigilance, courage, and strength to avoid risk and to remain as secure as possible (Hoogensen and Rottem 2004). In this sense, the fluidity of the girls' roles is evident in that they were simultaneously victims and aggressors, as well as captives and combatants, often drifting between these categories (Denov and Maclure forthcoming a).

What the girls all had in common was that following their coercive introduction to the war system, they eventually began to understand the intricacies and internal workings of the system and subsequently created different ways to master it. The ways that these girls attempted to subvert the RUF were invariably shaped by the unique individual (psychological, personality, maturity, physical and mental strength, health), and contextual (structural, spatial, relational, geographic) opportunities and circumstances of each girl. Nonetheless, several factors appeared salient to the negotiation process, including age and length of time with the rebels.

Girls fifteen years of age and older who had more life experience and maturity appeared to be able to evaluate, appraise, calculate, and ultimately negotiate their situations with seemingly greater ease and confidence. There were, however, clear exceptions, as the study revealed several instances of very young girls—as young as age nine—who actively planned and executed a successful escape from the RUF. On the whole, it would appear that younger girls who had less life experience and a limited understanding of the war dynamics and who were suddenly catapulted from the safety of their families and communities relied more heavily on modes of calculated acquiescence rather than bold resistance.

It would also appear that girls who lived among the RUF for longer periods of time and had time to observe, learn, and understand the system were more skilled at creating effective means of ensuring their security. For example, it took time and experience to discover that carrying arms, which was initially experienced as frightening and embittering, could actually be protective.

A final factor that appeared to propel girls to develop strategies of resistance was a result of the continued and unrelenting victimization. Girls who lived among the rebels for long periods of time and grew tired and weary from massive sexual, physical, and psychological insecurity developed bold strategies of resistance for their very survival. For example, the young woman who reported killing the man who attempted to rape her explained that she had grown "tired of the sexual harassment."

While there were marked similarities in the responses of girls associated with the RUF, their agency and ability to negotiate their security was invariably shaped largely according to the varying levels of experience, skill, maturity, courage, and opportunity of each girl. Such individual capacities and contextual circumstances were both formed and constrained by the dynamics of the conflict zone.

The implications of girls' negotiations for wartime security

The gendered abuses perpetrated within the RUF were extreme. The girls' efforts to negotiate their own security were thus born out of desperate and vital necessity. The girls made complex and compelling choices in the face of grave danger, inevitable harm, and unimaginable cruelty. The girls' own oral accounts provide several insights into aspects of females' relations to security, violence, agency, and war. In particular, the girls' narratives have uncovered the fact that, despite the horrors of armed conflict, some females find creative ways to bring about change by themselves and for themselves. The hardships endured in their quest for security shed light on the girls' strengths and struggles with negotiation, agency, resistance, resilience, resourcefulness, risk, courage, and support—concepts that were determined inductively through patterns that emerged from the data. Such concepts shed light on the complexities that shape and reshape girls' quests for survival and safety in the face of dire conditions.

In the narratives presented above, the emphasis on negotiation highlights how girls formerly associated with the RUF overcame obstacles and ordeals through various compromises and strategies. For females associated with armed groups, the insecurities and obstacles are extremely difficult to overcome and often require very cautious maneuvering. In the case of RUF girls, negotiation involved both passive acquiescence and active attempts to manipulate situations.

In addition, the attention drawn to the various ways in which girls envisioned and exhibited agency shed light on the deliberate actions, whether as victims or as perpetrators, that the girls took to accomplish particular goals, including survival, safety, and security. The girls' narratives reveal the ways that they actively engage in efforts to minimize their victimization and avoid combat or use combat as a protective measure. Of particular interest here is the courageous capacity of some girls to defend and protect themselves in the most vulnerable of circumstances, often amid state breakdown and in the absence of legitimate and formal support (Fox 2004). Such findings have reflected Judy El-Bushra's (2000) contention that opportunities and choices are often gendered and thus contingent upon and reflective of females' autonomy and capacity to think and act in the face of often oppressive hierarchical structures. It is important to note, however, that these acts of agency and resistance can be perceived as small victories in light of the circumstances of ongoing victimization and terror within the RUF.

In accentuating resourcefulness, examples of the girls' use of clever and competent problem-solving abilities in surmounting difficult situations have been underscored. In the context of the violence experienced by the war-affected girls in Sierra Leone, ingenuity and creativity became vital to individual survival and security. The use of intelligence techniques and physical force as well as the planning of defensive attacks to thwart violence are examples of the seemingly imperative resourcefulness of females during armed conflict. The creative ways that the girls coped with the chaos associated with the RUF certainly "call into question the stereotypical portrayal of women as mere victims of conflict" (Sharoni 2001, 87). Furthermore, in emphasizing resistance, the girls' narratives reveal the ways in which they opposed and struggled against their abusive captors and in so doing demonstrated their ability to counter, albeit on a limited scale, the damaging effects of extremely oppressive structures of violence and armed conflict.

It is important to recognize that the girls' abilities to negotiate security during armed conflict can in no way be constituted as full female emancipation. As noted elsewhere in this article, the oppressive conditions of the conflict and the preexisting inferior social status of women and girls in Sierra Leone certainly shaped the degree of agency and resistance that the girls exhibited and the extent of security that they experienced. Nevertheless, as Valerie Preston and Madeleine Wong (2004, 169) have noted, whether as potential perpetrators or victims, it is possible for females to create new spaces of gender equality through resistance. Susie Jacobs extends this claim by reinforcing the point that an individual instance of resistance "may not amount to mass insurrection but nevertheless signals change in gender relations in directions which may enhance women's gender status" (Jacobs 2000, 232) and by extension their security. The narratives highlighted in this article certainly reinforce this potential. This potential, however, remains fragile given that girls and women are often irreparably scarred and marginalized by the traumatic effects of war, conflict, and displacement.

As the narratives in this study have shown, instances of negotiation, agency, resistance, and resourcefulness do not necessarily occur in isolation. Rather, they tend to be manifested simultaneously and often in mutually reinforcing ways. Although they do not represent the totality of concepts available for the analysis of women and war, they do constitute a point of departure into which other females' experiences of war and other concepts may be integrated, debated, refined, and expanded.

Both the narratives and the conceptual analyses of this article have been framed through a human security lens that emphasizes individual experiences of security and prioritizes the personal security concerns of women and children. Nevertheless, it is imperative to situate these individualized narratives of both perpetration and victimization within broader structural contexts of patriarchal relations, national violence, global economies, and state and extrastate powers (locally, nationally, and internationally). The microlevel experiences of girls in Sierra Leone's RUF and their capacity to engage in negotiation and to act resourcefully and with resistance were undeniably shaped by broader parameters at gendered, political, economic, institutional, state, and extrastate levels. The constraints that exacerbated the vulnerability of young females include, more specifically, preexisting gender inequalities within Sierra Leonean society, the apparent impotency of the Sierra Leonean government in the face of an unrestrained RUF, the international diamond trade, the internal dynamics and institutional controls of the RUF, and weakened national economies and corrupt political governance.

Despite these broader structural forces, our emphasis on the individual voices and experiences of girls remains a component of a more comprehensive analysis of gender, conflict, and security. Indeed, a combined micro- and macroanalysis that sheds greater light on the precursors, experiences, and consequences of females' lack of security within the conflict zones of the past may enable more effective preventative measures and appropriate protective solutions for girls in the future.[11]

Conclusion

In this article, we have sought to enrich current analyses and debates on females' experiences in armed conflict with a particular emphasis on human security. We aimed to project the voices of the girls so that they could relate their own stories. In so doing, we have demonstrated that the girls' accounts should be considered central and indispensable to understandings of female experiences of violence and not as alternative narratives in studies on lack of security during war. As the data reveal, within contexts of profound insecurity, girls were successful negotiators, decision makers, risk assessors, actors, and strategizers in the history of armed conflict in Sierra Leone. In this light, girls associated with the RUF in Sierra Leone challenge the dominant assumptions of females as merely marginalized and vulnerable populations during armed conflicts. This case therefore enlightens our understandings of the various adaptations to lack of security and reclamations of security and survival in which girls may engage simultaneously during war.

The ways in which girls make choices that manifest their agency under extremely adverse conditions have significant implications for long-standing debates within feminist scholarship on structure and agency, as well as within other scholarships on gender, security, and human rights. This study may thus contribute to comparative understandings of females' use of agency in their pursuit of security and rights within other oppressive structures, including domestic settings, repressive state regimes, educa-

---

[11] Both preventative measures and protective solutions should include, among others, gender mainstreaming in peace-building initiatives and conflict-sensitive development (El-Bushra, Adrian-Paul, and Olson 2005, 29), gender sensitivity training among civilian and state officials, greater control over exploitative paramilitary groups, zero-tolerance policies on violence against females and children, fair-trade economies, greater political stability and accountability, and greater access to education and political power for females. Despite their ideal potential, these measures cannot be viewed as a panacea given that their implementation is most often hindered by contradictory policies and practices, lack of political and social will, and lack of funding.

tion, and employment spheres, as well as in other conflict zones. Since this research offers only an initial examination of the conditions of young females' security and insecurity, further research on the interstices between and among conflict, security, and gender is warranted. Moreover, although the findings of this study have shed light on the diverse ways in which girls negotiated their security during the armed conflict, girls' perceptions of their actions during the conflict, as well as an examination of the long-term consequences of the strategies they adopted, were beyond the scope of the current research. Future research would benefit from exploring girls' impressions of their actions over time.

This article's emphasis on the capacity of girls to pursue their own security also has implications at the policy level. With their experiences of agency, negotiation, resistance, and resourcefulness, many girls formerly associated with Sierra Leone's RUF are undoubtedly equipped with incredible potential to contribute to projects of reconstruction, peace, development, justice, and security in the future.[12] Political, social, health, educational, and legal spaces must therefore be granted to allow them to do so. As Hoogensen and Rottem (2004, 165) insist, the resources needed to ensure females' security will only be properly engaged when girls' and women's own articulations of security are acknowledged and heeded by state and nongovernmental authorities who are entrusted with the responsibility of providing protection, security, and healing for war-affected citizens. Such a human- and gender-oriented approach to young women's security needs must be integrated into local, national, and international programs that involve not only disarmament, demobilization, and reintegration processes in the postconflict phase but also and especially processes that encourage gender equality, peace building, and social, political, and economic stability in the preventative stages so as to inhibit potential conflicts and their devastating consequences, especially for girls and women.

Girls' efficacy in postconflict reconstruction initiatives must be carefully facilitated to meet the unique security needs of war-affected girls. Since females' subordinate status and prewar gender roles are often reinforced during postconflict periods, girls often face ostracism, betrayal, repression,

---

[12] Future studies should explore how young and adult women's experiences of insecurity in war affect the interplay of development, peace, justice, and security, on both personal and political levels, not only in the postconflict and reconstruction phases but also in the preventative stages. The interplay of development, peace, justice, and security is identified here as an essential condition to the postconflict reconstruction phases; the simultaneous and mutual reinforcement of these elements are crucial to success in this regard.

and increased poverty, as well as exclusion from reconstruction programs (Cockburn 2001, 26). Under such considerations, their social, health, educational, political, and economic needs and rights must first be addressed. Girls must also be provided with safe and frequent opportunities for inclusion and equal participation in disarmament, demobilization, and reintegration programs and rights-based approaches so that their compelling voices and girl-specific experiences of agency, resilience, and innovation can be appropriately integrated into reconstruction policies and programs. Their participation must be voluntary and guided by supportive counseling; the forums for participation must also be genuinely receptive to the girls' testimonies. Such inclusive opportunities are imperative to maximizing the worthy and essential contributions of war-affected girls to their own postconflict societies. Clearly, their input conveys females' security needs and an informed gender perspective. It is valuable not only to efforts that work toward the long-term security of war-affected girls but also to local, national, and international policies and programs that strive preventatively for peace and security for all.

School of Social Work
McGill University (Denov)

Department of Criminology
University of Ottawa (Gervais)

References

Abdullah, Ibrahim. 1998. "Bush Path to Destruction: The Origin and Character of the Revolutionary United Front/Sierra Leone." *Journal of Modern African Studies* 36(2):203–35.

Alison, Miranda. 2004. "Women as Agents of Political Violence: Gendering Security." *Security Dialogue* 35(4):447–63.

Caprioli, Mary. 2004. "Democracy and Human Rights versus Women's Security: A Contradiction." *Security Dialogue* 35(4):411–28.

Cockburn, Cynthia. 2001. "The Gendered Dynamics of Armed Conflict and Political Violence." In Moser and Clark 2001, 13–29.

Cordero, Isabel Coral. 2001. "Social Organizations: From Victims to Actors in Peace Building." In Moser and Clark 2001, 151–63.

Crawley, Heaven. 2000. "Engendering the State in Refugee Women's Claims for Asylum." In Jacobs, Jacobson, and Marchbank 2000, 87–104.

Denov, Myriam. 2006. "Wartime Sexual Violence: Assessing a Human Security Response to War-Affected Girls in Sierra Leone." *Security Dialogue* 37(3): 319–42.

Denov, Myriam, and Richard Maclure. 2006. "Engaging the Voices of Girls in the

Aftermath of Sierra Leone's Conflict: Experiences and Perspectives in the Culture of Violence." *Anthropologica* 48(1):73–85.

———. Forthcoming a. "Girls and Small Arms in Sierra Leone: Victimization, Participation and Resistance." In *Gender Perspectives on Small Arms and Light Weapons*, ed. Vanessa Farr and Albrecht Schnabel. Tokyo: United Nations University Press.

———. Forthcoming b. "Turnings and Epiphanies: Militarization, Life Histories and the Making and Unmaking of Two Child Soldiers in Sierra Leone." *Journal of Youth Studies*.

Dinan, Kinsey Alden. 2002. "Migrant Thai Women Subjected to Slavery-Like Abuses in Japan." *Violence against Women* 8(9):1113–39.

El-Bushra, Judy. 2000. "Transforming Conflict: Some Thoughts on a Gendered Understanding of Conflict Processes." In Jacobs, Jacobson, and Marchbank 2000, 66–86.

El-Bushra, Judy, with Ancil Adrian-Paul and Maria Olson. 2005. *Women Building Peace: Sharing Know-How, Assessing Impact, Planning for Miracles*. London: International Alert.

Fox, Mary-Jane. 2004. "Girl Soldiers: Human Security and Gendered Insecurity." *Security Dialogue* 35(4):465–79.

Geertz, Clifford. 1973. "Thick Description: Towards an Interpretive Theory of Culture." In his *The Interpretation of Cultures*, 1–16. New York: Basic.

Giles, Wenona, and Jennifer Hyndman, eds. 2004. *Sites of Violence: Gender and Conflict Zones*. Berkeley: University of California Press.

Glaser, Barney, and Anselm Strauss. 1967. *The Discovery of Grounded Theory*. Chicago: Aldine.

Handrahan, Lori. 2004. "Conflict, Gender, Ethnicity and Post-conflict Reconstruction." *Security Dialogue* 35(4):429–45.

Hansen, Lene, and Louise Olsson. 2004. "Guest Editors' Introduction." *Security Dialogue* 35(4):405–9.

Higate, Paul, and Marsha Henry. 2004. "Engendering (In)security in Peace Support Operations." *Security Dialogue* 35(4):481–98.

Honwana, Alcinda. 2006. *Child Soldiers in Africa*. Philadelphia: University of Pennsylvania Press.

Hoogensen, Gunhild, and Svein Rottem. 2004. "Gender Identity and the Subject of Security." *Security Dialogue* 35(2):155–71.

Ibañez, Ana Cristina. 2001. "El Salvador: War and Untold Stories—Women Guerrillas." In Moser and Clark 2001, 117–30.

Jacobs, Susie. 2000. "Globalisation, States and Women's Agency: Possibilities and Pitfalls." In Jacobs, Jacobson, and Marchbank 2000, 217–37.

Jacobs, Susie, Ruth Jacobson, and Jennifer Marchbank. 2000. *States of Conflict: Gender, Violence and Resistance*. London: Zed.

Keitetsi, China. 2004. *La petite fille à la Kalachnikov: Ma vie d'enfant soldat* [The little Kalashnikov girl: My life as a child soldier]. Brussels: Éditions GRIP.

Lyons, Tanya. 2004. *Guns and Guerilla Girls: Women in the Zimbabwean Liberation Struggle*. Asmara, Eritrea: Africa World Press.

Macklin, Audrey. 2004. "Like Oil and Water, with a Match: Militarized Commerce, Armed Conflict, and Human Security in Sudan." In Giles and Hyndman 2004, 75–107.

Maclure, Richard, and Myriam Denov. 2006. "'I Didn't Want to Die So I Joined Them': Structuration and the Process of Becoming Boy Soldiers in Sierra Leone." *Journal of Terrorism and Political Violence* 18(1):119–35.

McKay, Susan. 1998. "The Effects of Armed Conflict on Girls and Women." *Peace and Conflict* 4(4):381–92.

McKay, Susan, and Dyan Mazurana. 2004. "Where Are the Girls?" In their *Where Are the Girls? Girls in Fighting Forces in Northern Uganda, Sierra Leone and Mozambique: Their Lives During and After War*, 17–20. Montreal: Rights and Democracy.

Meertens, Donny. 2001. "The Nostalgic Future: Terror, Displacement and Gender in Colombia." In Moser and Clark 2001, 133–48.

Moser, Caroline O. N., and Fiona Clark, eds. 2001. *Victims, Perpetrators or Actors? Gender, Armed Conflict and Political Violence*. London: Zed.

Moser, Caroline O. N., and Cathy McIlwaine. 2001. "Gender and Social Capital in Contexts of Political Violence: Community Perceptions from Colombia and Guatemala." In Moser and Clark 2001, 178–200.

Nordstrom, Carolyn. 1997. *Girls and Warzones: Troubling Questions*. Uppsala, Sweden: Life and Peace Institute.

Preston, Valerie, and Madeleine Wong. 2004. "Geographies of Violence: Women and Conflict in Ghana." In Giles and Hyndman 2004, 152–69.

Revolutionary United Front/Sierra Leone. 1995. *Footpaths to Democracy: Toward a New Sierra Leone*. n.p.: Revolutionary United Front of Sierra Leone.

Richards, Paul. 1998. *Fighting for the Rainforest: War, Youth and Resources in Sierra Leone*. Oxford: James Currey.

Sharoni, Simona. 2001. "Rethinking Women's Struggles in Israel-Palestine and in the North of Ireland." In Moser and Clark 2001, 85–98.

Stasiulis, Daiva. 1993. "'Authentic Voice': Anti-racist Politics in Canadian Feminist Publishing and Literary Production." In *Feminism and the Politics of Difference*, ed. Sneja Gnew and Anna Yeatman, 35–60. Sydney: Allen & Unwin.

Turshen, Meredeth. 2001. "The Political Economy of Rape: An Analysis of Systematic Rape and Sexual Abuse of Women during Armed Conflict in Africa." In Moser and Clark 2001, 55–68.

UN Development Programme. 1994. *Human Development Report 1994*. New York: Oxford University Press.

Utas, Mats. 2003. "Sweet Battlefields: Youth and the Liberian Civil War." PhD dissertation, Uppsala University.

———. 2005. "Agency of Victims: Young Women in the Liberian Civil War." In

Makers and Breakers: Children and Youth in Postcolonial Africa, ed. Alcinda Honwana and Filip de Boeck, 53–80. Trenton, NJ: Africa World Press.

Wendt, Alexander. 1992. "Anarchy Is What States Make of It: The Social Construction of Power Politics." *International Organization* 46(2):391–425.

Aaronette M. White

All the Men Are Fighting for Freedom, All the Women Are Mourning Their Men, but Some of Us Carried Guns: A Raced-Gendered Analysis of Fanon's Psychological Perspectives on War

> Revolutionary war, as the Algerian people is waging it, is a total war in which the woman does not merely knit for or mourn the soldier. The Algerian woman is at the heart of the combat. Arrested, tortured, raped, shot down, she testifies to the violence of the occupier and to his inhumanity.
> —Frantz Fanon 1967b, 66

Anticolonial revolutionary theorist Frantz Fanon provided a justification for people's wars, suggesting that they contributed to the reversal of the inferiority complex created by colonization. Indeed, by asserting their humanity through a violent confrontation with their oppressors, Fanon claimed, the colonized could achieve recognition of their humanity, which had been denied by their colonizers. Although there is no question that revolutionary violence has been effective in struggles for national independence, has it also had the psychological effects predicted by Fanon? Can the debilitating effects of colonized identity be transformed through revolutionary violence? This is the question I seek to explore. By drawing upon firsthand accounts of the anticolonial war experiences of

This work is dedicated to my former husband and guerrilla fighter D. France Olivieira. The title of this article alludes to Gloria Hull, Patricia Bell Scott, and Barbara Smith's 1982 book titled *All the Women Are White, All the Blacks Are Men, but Some of Us Are Brave: Black Women's Studies* and was also inspired by Cynthia Enloe's allusion to the title in her article "All the Men Are in the Militias, All the Women Are Victims: The Politics of Masculinity and Femininity in Nationalist Wars" (2004a). I would like to thank Aida Hurtado, Lori Ginsberg, Carol Cohn, Paul Zeleza, and James Stewart for comments on a previous draft and the Boston Consortium on Gender, Security, and Human Rights; Harvard University's Women and Public Policy Program; and the College of Liberal Arts at Penn State University for the partial funding of this research.

[*Signs: Journal of Women in Culture and Society* 2007, vol. 32, no. 4]

African women ex-combatants, archival research of government docu-ments, human rights organizations' reports, and current psychological research on the effects of military combat, I suggest that Fanon was overly optimistic about the psychological potential of revolutionary violence. I also argue that his optimism stemmed from his neglect of particular gen-dered aspects of anticolonial war.

Fanon on the psychological benefits of revolutionary violence

Grandson of a former slave, Fanon was born in 1925 in the former French colony of Martinique.[1] After specializing in psychiatry at the University of Lyon in France, he became clinical director of the largest psychiatric hospital in Algeria in 1953, at a time when the Algerian struggle for national independence from France was gaining mass support. Although many scholars focus on Fanon's social and political thought, he was first and foremost a psychiatrist. His psychological works were published in psychiatric, medical, and political journals, and his books incorporated psychological insights to complement, illustrate, and concretize the co-lonial experience and its revolutionary transformation (Bulhan 1985). Placing Fanon in his professional context can enhance understanding of the questions he asked and the psychological theorizing that runs through his better-known works (Fanon 1967a, 1967b, 1967c, 1968).

Fanon argued that the French used violence to usurp Algerian land, deny Algerians full citizenship, and denigrate or destroy their religious and cultural practices. These forms of colonial violence had profound psychological consequences for the colonized. Lacking the economic and military power to protect their own cultural values and beliefs, many indigenous Algerians came to accept what the French colonizers described as their racial inferiority. Fanon suggested that generations of colonial oppression produced an "epidermalization of inferiority" (1967a, 13), an embodied mode of subjugation characterized by fear and the adoption of a variety of behaviors to avoid direct confrontation with the source of

---

[1] Fanon voluntarily fought against Nazi Germany for the French; however, he experienced racism during his military service and during his student days in France after the war. These experiences led him to become active in left-wing gatherings that challenged unjust French policies (Bulhan 1985). While working at the Algerian psychiatric hospital, Fanon began to work secretly for the Front de Libération Nationale (National Liberation Front, or FLN). He eventually became an FLN spokesperson, editor of its major paper, and a doctor in FLN health centers, despite assassination attempts on his life, ongoing "Arab prejudice against his color," and "African discomfort in the presence of his White [French] wife" (Bulhan 1985, 34).

their fear, the colonizer. Rather than strike out directly against the oppressor, the colonized repressed their violent desires for justice, turning their anger, fear, and frustration inward. The result was a high incidence of alcoholism, depression, stress-induced physical ailments, and intracommunal homicides (Fanon 1968, 54).

In contrast to those who internalized the worldview of their colonizers, Fanon observed, there were Algerians who developed nationalist consciousness, which they channeled into revolutionary activity. By redirecting repressed urges outward toward the appropriate target—the colonizer—Algerian nationalists demystified the colonizer's power and restored their self-confidence, cultivating a strong collective identity. Fanon noted that when the colonized began to fully identify themselves with their "wretchedness"—realizing they had nothing to lose, given the daily erosion of their lives under colonial conditions—revolutionary violence became pivotal in transforming their previously self-destructive identities (1968, 35–106). Liberation wars constituted an important means through which the colonized regained their agency and dignity. Rather than remaining victims of historical conquest, they became creators of history. Learning that dignity and equality were more important than life itself, Algerian revolutionaries were willing to risk their lives to achieve recognition of their humanity. Through violence the colonized transcended fear of the colonizer and reclaimed their humanity. According to Fanon, then, "Violence is a cleansing force. It frees the native from his inferiority complex and from his despair and inaction; it makes him fearless and restores his self-respect" (1968, 94). Because it restored balance in everyone's perceptions—the colonized overcame inferiority complexes, and the colonizers overcame superiority complexes—Fanon described the violence of the colonized as humanistic. Emphasizing the transformative importance of revolutionary violence, Fanon insisted that this balance in recognition could not be granted by the colonizer; it had to be seized by the colonized.

Fanon's claims about the transformative power of violence were not restricted to male combatants. To his credit, Fanon acknowledged the important role women played in the Algerian revolutionary struggle. In *A Dying Colonialism* (Fanon 1967b), he discussed the psychological transformation of some Algerian women during the war and defended their right to exist as autonomous human beings. In marked contrast to French archival records and the official accounts of the war in the Algerian Ministry of Veterans, Fanon resisted the patriarchal tendency to exclude women from history. His writings acknowledged the extensive roles Algerian women played during the national war of independence, including the revolutionary role of the sex worker as a political actor (Fanon 1967b,

60). Some Algerian feminists have criticized Fanon for overstating the relationship between national liberation and women's liberation, overestimating Algerian women's military roles as combatants, and assuming women's military status was equal to men's (Hélie-Lucas 1988; Lazreg 1994). Nonetheless, Fanon broke new ground in suggesting that revolutionary violence held transformative potential for women as well as for men. He claimed that Algerian women's participation in the armed struggle altered their feminine colonized identities and family relationships in positive ways that challenged feudal, patriarchal traditions (Fanon 1967b, 99–120), noting that "in Algerian societies stories were told of women who in ever greater number suffered death and imprisonment in order that an independent Algeria might be born. It was these militant women who constituted the points of reference around which the imagination of Algerian feminine society was to be stirred to the boiling point. The woman-for-marriage progressively disappeared, and gave way to the woman-for-action. The young girl was replaced by the militant. . . . The woman ceased to be a complement for man. She literally forged a new place for herself by her sheer strength" (Fanon 1967b, 108–9).

Some critics have suggested that Fanon used psychological jargon merely to romanticize violence, to glorify it for its own sake (Arendt 1970).[2] A series of clinical cases in the final section of *The Wretched of the Earth* (Fanon 1968), however, casts serious doubt on such unfair and oversimplified interpretations of his work. The subsection titled "Series A" explicates reactive psychosis by examining the experiences of a traumatized Algerian fighter whose wife was tortured and raped by French authorities following the discovery of his guerrilla activities and those of a French police interrogator and torturer who ended up torturing his wife and children (Fanon 1968, 254–70). The next subsection, "Series B," investigates the forensic and clinical implications of children murdering children during the war and examines how children on both sides of the struggle coped with the murder of their parents (Fanon 1968, 270–79). "Series C" describes the psychological reactions of torture victims to various techniques of torture (Fanon 1968, 280–89), and "Series D" documents the psychosomatic disorders experienced by war veterans (Fanon 1968, 289–310).

These cases reveal Fanon's sensitivity to the brutality of violence and

[2] See Bulhan (1985) for an overview of Fanon's major critics. A clinical psychologist and biographer of Fanon, Hussein Abdilahi Bulhan is the only scholar who has provided a thorough analysis of all of Fanon's psychological publications.

its potentially corrosive effects on the colonizer and the colonized (Bulhan 1985). Yet the cases also show the degree to which Fanon believed that politically conscious and goal-directed violent confrontation by the colonized against their colonizers could have profoundly rehabilitative psychological effects, despite the risks of trauma. Thus he insisted that the colonizer's institutionalized violence was so devastating and so impervious to reason that only violence in return could transform the oppressive order. Because the colonizer understands and depends on violence, "violence alone, violence committed by the people, violence organized and educated by its leaders, makes it possible for the masses to understand social truths and gives the key to them" (Fanon 1968, 147).

Since he was an existential phenomenologist, Fanon's account of the potential benefits of revolutionary violence was influenced by G. W. F. Hegel's analysis of the constitutive features of consciousness in *The Phenomenology of Mind* (Hegel 1966). Hegel insisted that man becomes conscious of himself only through recognition by the other.[3] To explicate the role of mutual recognition in the development of self-understanding, Hegel explored the complex dynamics of misperception: "false consciousness," mutual dependence, and "pure self recognition in absolute otherness" in the context of bondage or master-slave relations (1966, 229–40). According to Hegel, the master becomes aware of his actual nature only when he recognizes his dependence on the slave.

In *Black Skin, White Masks*, Fanon challenged Hegel's analysis, suggesting that it failed to take seriously the effects of racism in colonial situations (1967a, 210–22). Focusing on the racial dynamics of the master-slave dialectic, Fanon argued that the superiority complex of the white colonizer produced more than an inferiority complex in the black colonized. The colonizer's conviction of superiority rendered the colonized invisible to such an extent that the colonizer never recognized either dependence upon the colonized or the humanity of the colonized. Existing below the threshold of visibility, the colonized had no possibility of achieving mutual recognition through their labor as Hegel had suggested. Only violent confrontation could force the colonizer to see the colonized as agents capable of world making. For this reason, Fanon insisted, revolutionary violence was key to the restoration of the humanity of the colonized.

Fanon died from leukemia less than a year before Algeria won its independence from France and did not witness the challenges that faced

---

[3] Masculine pronouns are used in both Hegel's and Fanon's original writings.

Algeria after the war.[4] He did not have an opportunity to revise his theories concerning the transformative effects of revolutionary violence in light of the anticolonial struggles that transformed Africa over the next decades. Drawing upon a richer historical record, the following sections reexamine Fanon's claims concerning the psychological benefits of participation in violent revolution.

Prewar realities: The differential worth of the wretched

One major dimension of colonized mentality overlooked by Fanon is the gendered, patriarchal underpinnings of most nationalisms. Nationalism can take a variety of forms and can be a powerful, politically mobilizing, and identity-shaping tool for people whose way of life has been demeaned and controlled by others. Nationalism has often enabled men in parts of Africa colonized by Europeans to reclaim both imaginary and real status held prior to colonization. Indeed, as feminist scholars have noted, nationalism often induces nostalgia for a romanticized past when men "controlled the land and the women" without interference from European men (Maitse 2000, 204).[5]

Numerous scholars have documented how colonists generally sought to subordinate African men under European rule in order to exploit their cheap labor.[6] African men experienced loss of status and material resources as a result of forced resettlement, imposed taxation, and the disruption of traditional territorial lineages linked to land ownership, which led to deep resentments. Despite the colonizers' willingness to allow African men to retain varying degrees of authority in their homes and villages, colonial subordination led African men to express their grievances in newly formed nationalist organizations (Schmidt 1991). Nationalist rhetoric often made the case for independence from European control on dual grounds: to restore the autonomy of Africans and to restore the rights of men.

Colonial subjugation diminished the status of African women in complex ways as new fusions of European and African male authority materialized (Schmidt 1991; Kabira and Nzioki 1993; Tamale 1999). Through militant protests, creative entrepreneurship (e.g., beer brewing), militia activity, and

---

[4] Fanon loathed the racism of the United States; however, he reluctantly sought medical treatment there for leukemia. Shortly after his arrival, he died at the age of thirty-six on December 6, 1961. On July 3, 1962, less than a year after Fanon's death, Algeria was declared an independent country (see Bulhan [1985] for additional details).

[5] Some feminists believe that nationalism and feminism can be reconciled if progressive notions of gender and sexuality are included in the ideological policies (see West 1997).

[6] See Isaacman and Isaacman 1984; Cock 1991; Schmidt 1991; Lazreg 1994.

even religious conversion and commitment to convent life, African women resisted these patriarchal efforts to keep them confined to rural areas and the domestic domain.[7] Women's legal status as minors, combined with their lack of independent access to land, housing, and wage employment, made effective resistance difficult, however. Unlike many African men, African women's opportunities to express and act on their gender-specific grievances were hampered by their exclusion from public spaces and from early meetings of revolutionary organizations. Their absence from the circle of intellectuals drafting position papers, advising organizations on policies, and making decisions concerning leadership was particularly constricting (Lazreg 1994, 139). Thus, raced-gendered sociocultural and political processes during colonization were intricately tied to the construction of nationalisms during the anticolonial period. Although the status of African women under colonial rule was severely diminished, as Fanon pointed out, the Front de Libération Nationale (National Liberation Front, or FLN) in Algeria and many other anticolonial movements, such as the Frente de Libertação de Moçambique (Liberation Front of Mozambique, or FRELIMO) in Mozambique; the Partido Africano pola Independencia da Guiné e Cabo Verde (African Party for the Independence of Guinea and Cape Verde) in Guinea-Bisau and Cape Verde; the Movimento Popular de Libertação de Angola (Movement for the Popular Liberation of Angola, or MPLA) in Angola; the South West Africa People's Organization in Namibia; the Zimbabwe African National Union in Zimbabwe; and the African National Congress (ANC) in South Africa mobilized women to join armed struggles. In so doing, they often equated national liberation with women's liberation.[8]

Radical African feminists have argued that African national liberation and African women's liberation movements are related but not identical (Lazreg 1994; Maitse 2000; Mama 2000). They also suggest that the relationship between gender identity and anticolonial revolution needs to be expanded to encompass both men's and women's changing identities. Masculine identities are central to liberation wars, shaping the degree of commitment to gender equity as well as gender-specific political education during prewar mobilization, the liberation war itself, and postwar gender relations.[9]

Although Fanon did not completely ignore the gendered aspects of nationalism and prewar mobilization, he understated their pervasiveness.

---

[7] See Kanogo 1987; Schmidt 1991; Lazreg 1994; Adugna 2001.

[8] See Urdang 1979; Isaacman and Isaacman 1984; Organisation of Angolan Women 1984; Cock 1991; Lazreg 1994; Becker 1995; Lyons 2004.

[9] See Meena 1992; Mama 2000; Campbell 2003; McFadden 2005.

Fanon attributed any narrowness within nationalism to class issues, placing particular emphasis on the myopia of the national bourgeoisie (1968, 148–205). Concerning their efforts to create new governments, Fanon warned the colonized not to perpetuate "the feudal tradition which holds sacred the superiority of the masculine over the feminine" (1968, 202). Despite this warning, Fanon's failure to address the gendered struggles of African men under colonial subjugation as thoroughly as their race and class struggles contributed to his overly optimistic expectations concerning the transformative power of the Algerian revolution. Patriarchal convictions that preexisted independence struggles were further entrenched by war and militarism. Greater attention to these patriarchal legacies may help explain why participation in violence did not have the positive effects for women that Fanon confidently predicted. Closer examination of patriarchal convictions may also show why the active roles African women played during anticolonial struggles did not culminate in gender parity in newly independent nations.[10]

Militarism versus democracy

As social institutions, military forces are not gender neutral. The ideology of militarism interacts with discrete forms of military organizations to produce gender identities consonant with patriarchal ideology and practices (Cock 1991; de Waal 2002; Enloe 2004b). Militarist and patriarchal ideologies and practices often work against democratic values associated with revolutionary transformation. Thus nationalist parties engaged in

---

[10] Western feminists occasionally opine that African women should have refused to participate in liberation wars, given African men's patriarchal nationalist attitudes and practices, or that African women should have created separate feminist organizations as an alternative to the male-led revolutionary organizations. Algerian feminist Marnia Lazreg's response regarding Algerian women can be generalized to the situation of most African women during independence struggles: "Looking at the past from the vantage point of the present is easier than reexperiencing it as it was lived. It is difficult to imagine a feminist movement, by which is meant a movement focused on the promotion of women's rights exclusively, emerging during the war. Who would have been its leaders? Who would have been its adversaries? French men? French women? Algerian men? All of these? Apart from a history of manipulation of women by colonial authorities that made any feminist activity suspect in the eyes of Algerians, native associations were only tolerated and often subjected to harassment, if not banned. An Algerian feminist association that would have inevitably questioned the active complicity of the colonial order in women's exclusion from high school education, training, health care, housing, jobs and so on would have found it difficult to survive" (Lazreg 1994, 139).

armed struggle often end up "shooting democracy in the foot" (Mama 2000).

The patriarchal nature of war, militarism, and military training combined to perpetuate violent injustices and entrench colonized mentalities that Fanon predicted revolutionary violence would eradicate (Mama 2000; de Waal 2002; Campbell 2003). The patriarchal mentality of many African men nurtured under colonial rule was reinforced during independence struggles as nationalist consciousness became militarized through values imparted by involvement with the armed forces (Cock 1991; de Waal 2002; Enloe 2004b). Authoritarianism and the notion of combat as men's work promoted narrow, hypermasculine views of manhood (e.g., manhood as aggressive, competitive, stoic, and the opposite of anything feminine). Revolutionary war also produced sexual divisions of labor that worked against the equal recognition of women by men in military forces.

As an ideology, militarism construes violence in terms of various masculine ideals—courage, virility, chivalry, and superiority (Mama 2000; de Waal 2002; Enloe 2004b). Authoritarianism, deemed essential to military organization, construes power in terms of absolute authority, hierarchy, and obedience (de Waal 2002). By privileging hierarchy and rule by command, authoritarianism works against democratic values such as free expression, consensus, egalitarianism, and transparency in decision making (de Waal 2002). Authoritarian values are important to military organizations because war is strategic, aimed at gaining and exercising power. Combat is the manifestation of power in its most brutal and uncompromising form (de Waal 2002). Authoritarianism molds a soldier who will obey orders without thinking and will internalize unquestioning loyalty to his superiors in ways that minimize the chance that he will flinch in combat (Grossman 1995; de Waal 2002). However, by fostering blind compliance military values work against the autonomy of soldiers, regardless of gender, complicating any sense of agency that Fanon claimed combat would restore. This blind compliance works against women's sense of agency, in particular, because prewar gender inequalities are exacerbated by a predominantly male military leadership more prone to abuse its power during the war given the subordinate status of most female soldiers combined with the stress of life in the camps.

In addition to the authoritarianism that pervades the military as a social institution, the stereotype of the supermacho combat soldier perpetuates hypermasculine attitudes and values that also work against a male soldier's recognition of a woman soldier (or any woman) as his equal. South African feminist sociologist Jacklyn Cock elaborates: "War does not challenge women to prove that they are women, whereas wars have been historically symbolized as the touchstone of 'manliness.' The concept of war as a proving ground of manliness has centered on the notion of combat, which is understood to be the ultimate test of masculinity, and thus crucial to the ideological structure of patriarchy" (1991, 235–36).

The guerrilla warfare tactics used in most of Africa's revolutionary wars did not rely on hand-to-hand combat. They often relied on ambushing patrols, sabotaging communication and transportation lines, and making hit-and-run attacks against enemy posts—tasks women are fully capable of carrying out (Goldman 1982; Cock 1991; Goldstein 2001). Yet the myth of combat as men's work dies hard; even with today's technologically sophisticated war weaponry, the "presumption that a man is unproven in his manhood until he has engaged in collective, violent, and physical struggle against someone categorized as the enemy" is widespread (Enloe 1983, 13). Indeed, Fanon's arguments concerning the transformative potential of war resonate with such masculinist overtones.

Masculinist notions also serve as powerful tools for making men into soldiers because military forces encourage aggressiveness and competitiveness while censuring emotional expression and denouncing physically weak soldiers as effeminate (Enloe 1983; Cock 1991; Goldstein 2001). Combat readiness, male bonding, and social cohesion are achieved through military training by emphasizing the otherness of both women and the enemy: women represent the weaker sex, home and hearth, and the need to be protected, while the enemy represents the weaker force to be dominated and conquered (Enloe 1983; Cock 1991; Goldstein 2001). Given the interactive relationship among militarism, military forces as social institutions, and combat as the test of a man's masculinity, it is not surprising that women have been excluded from most combat, whether in conventional or guerrilla armies (Goldman 1982; Cock 1991; Goldstein 2001).[11]

Gendering African anticolonial wars

Despite the multiple factors working against women's involvement in war,

---

[11] "Women's physical strength, while less than men's on average, has been adequate to many combat situations—from piloting to sniping to firing machine guns. One argument of those opposed to women in combat—that the women would be unable to drag wounded comrades from the battlefield under fire—is refuted by the record of women nurses' doing so. Women's supposedly lower levels of aggressiveness, and their nurturing nature, have been, historically, no obstacle to many women's participation in combat" (Goldstein 2001, 127).

many contemporary African women served in African liberation armies struggling for political independence from European colonial rule.[12] Their war stories are rarely read or heard, however, because of prevalent assumptions that women, African and otherwise, are simply victims of war, not active agents in war. Scholars have now documented women's critical contributions to the economy of armed forces, troop morale, and troop survival (Enloe 1983; Goldstein 2001; Moser and Clark 2001). Recent research also reveals that African women who possessed a strong sense of political agency entered anticolonial fighting forces to demonstrate their support for revolutionary ideology, gain protection for themselves and their families from local or state violence, avoid domestic violence, earn money, improve educational opportunities, and improve career options.[13]

Women have also provided anticolonial wars with unofficial and thus unacknowledged military support as domestic servants, porters, messengers, intelligence officers, disseminators of propaganda, combat trainers, sex workers, and recruiters of other women and children military personnel.[14] Moreover, the number of girls and women in fighting forces is routinely underestimated given the emphasis on their roles as sexual slaves, wives of commanders, prostitutes, and camp followers. These terms, particularly the term *camp follower*, obscure the multiple roles women play during war; furthermore, when sex workers are involved in revolutionary struggles their additional roles and political commitments as spies, assassins, decoys, and, in some instances, combat fighters are understated while their sexual roles are overstated.[15]

African women have been some of the most courageous and fierce fighters in anticolonial armed struggles. It is important not to romanticize their lives, however. Like the posters depicting images of a liberated African woman with her baby in one hand and her rifle in the other, romanticized conceptions of women revolutionaries fail to grapple with the power structure in military organizations. The words of Thandi Modise, ANC member of parliament and former guerrilla commander of the ANC's military wing, help dispel romanticized notions, highlighting frequently overlooked gendered factors that complicated the lives of South African women combatants:

Women face far more difficulties in going underground. . . . They

---

[12] See Urdang 1979; Musialela 1983; Kanogo 1987; Hélie-Lucas 1988; Cock 1991; Becker 1995; West 2000; Adugna 2001; Lyons 2004.

[13] See Cock 1991; Lazreg 1994; Becker 1995; West 2000; Lyons 2004.

[14] See Goldman 1982; Kanogo 1987; Turshen and Twagiramariya 1998; Adugna 2001.

[15] See Enloe 1983; Kanogo 1987; Kesby 1996; Shikola 1998.

have to contend with the traditionally strict attitudes in the society towards women—that we should stay at home and have children. . . . Even though that sort of thinking is challenged by the liberation army not all comrades have unlearned their previous conditioning. . . . In becoming a guerrilla, there is a strong possibility that you will lose your family, your home, and all security. . . . Men are expected to be away from home earning the money or protecting our nation . . . they know that whatever happens to them, their wives will still look after the children. (Quoted in Curnow 2000, 39–40)

Attention to radical African feminist scholarship that focuses on the experience of women cultural workers and fighters such as Modise who played significant roles in challenging European colonialism helps raise questions about the adequacy of Fanon's conception of the transformative potential of revolutionary violence.[16] By examining power relations between women and men in combat and investigating how femininity and masculinity are constructed and inscribed during revolutionary movements, a very different picture emerges of the gendered effects of participation in anticolonial struggles (Enloe 2004c). Although African men were empowered by their role as combatants, African women revolutionaries were at risk of being disproportionately disempowered by their participation in anticolonial wars. First-hand accounts of anticolonial African women combatants suggest that military life often undermined their sense of agency as a result of increased vulnerability to gender-specific human rights abuses perpetrated by enemy troops as well as by their own comrades. These abuses include rape, torture, brutal abductions, forced pregnancies, forced sex work, and other forms of

---

[16] Not all feminists, whether they describe themselves as Western, third world, or African, share a commitment to radical critiques of society. Like North American feminisms, African feminist thought is heterogeneous (Salo 2001). This article selectively highlights the works of radical African feminists while simultaneously including the works of relevant Western feminist scholars. The term *radical African feminist* is not used here as a biological (essentialist) description, nor is it used to promote divisiveness. Rather, it refers to feminists whose theorizing grew primarily out of their experiences with independent and postcolonial movements in Africa and who dispel myths regarding the inevitability of African women's oppression; consider diversity among African women across various ethnic, national, and sexual locations; and challenge the Western misconception of one, essential African culture (Meena 1992; Thiam 1995; Salo 2001; Lewis 2004). Their perspectives fit squarely within a history of international black radicalism characterized by the Black Radical Congress (1998) as opposition to class exploitation (Wilson 1991), racism (Kabira and Nzioki 1993), patriarchy (Thiam 1995), homophobia (Potgieter 1997; Tamale 2003), anti-immigration prejudice (McFadden 2005), and imperialism (McFadden 2000).

sexual harassment, molestation, and discrimination. To assess the merits of Fanon's theories regarding the therapeutic role of revolutionary violence, then, it is important to consider the experiences of both men and women revolutionaries.

The sexual division of labor: Blurring private and public spheres

Although wars have produced some powerful new identities for women, military forces remain distinctively patriarchal institutions. Within carefully controlled sexual divisions of labor in armed forces, most women occupy subordinate positions resembling stereotypical female employment in the civilian sector (e.g., clerks, nurses, social workers, cooks). By keeping women out of the top levels of policy- and decision-making roles and out of most forms of combat, military forces simply reinscribe and expand traditionally gendered roles rather than fundamentally challenge patriarchy (Enloe 1983; Cock 1991; Goldstein 2001).

Firsthand accounts and military records indicate that most anticolonial armies trained women as combatants out of desperation and necessity, not out of enlightened or feminist consciousness.[17] As the following account by a FRELIMO woman guerrilla soldier who fought for Mozambican independence suggests, women revolutionaries had to grapple with powerful cultural constraints: "There was strong opposition to our participation in combat because that was against our tradition. We started a campaign explaining why we also had to fight. . . . We as women were even more oppressed than men and therefore had the right as well as the will and the strength to fight. We insisted on our military training and being given weapons" (quoted in Isaacman and Isaacman 1984, 158).

Women who assumed masculine military roles, including combat, were seen as exceptions, and their nontraditional activities were often interpreted as temporary and as helping the men (Isaacman and Isaacman 1984; Lazreg 1994; Lyons 2004). Although African women in many revolutionary armies were taught to use weapons, they were often deployed in supportive roles, ordered to fight only when necessary, and assigned secondary roles as cooks, child-care providers, laundry workers, and porters. As Algerian feminist Marie-Aimée Hélie-Lucas notes,

Since "there is no humble task in the revolution" we did not dispute the roles we had. . . . What makes me angry, in retrospect, is not the mere fact of confining women to their place, but the brain-

[17] See Cock 1991; Lazreg 1994; Becker 1995; Lyons 2004.

washing which did not allow us, young women, to even think in terms of questioning the women's place. And what makes me even more angry is to witness the replication of this situation in various places in the world where national liberation struggles are still taking place—to witness women engaged in liberation fronts covering the misbehavings of their fellow men, hiding, in the name of national solidarity and identity, crime which will be perpetuated after the liberation. (Hélie-Lucas 1988, 175–76)

The sexual division of labor and the secondary roles assigned to African women combatants have been documented across various anticolonial wars in Africa, including Algeria (Lazreg 1994), Ethiopia (Adugna 2001), Guinea-Bissau (Urdang 1979), Kenya (Kanogo 1987), Mozambique (Isaacman and Isaacman 1984), Namibia (Becker 1995), Zimbabwe (Lyons 2004), and South Africa (Cock 1991). Although revolutionary rhetoric suggests that every role in the revolution is valued, every role is certainly not equally valued—nor is every person, particularly a woman, equally recognized for the role she plays.

African feminist historian Tabitha Kanogo explains how women who took part in the anticolonial war in Kenya struggled to counter men's stereotypes of them and to create new roles and sources of pride for themselves. Male fighters continued to view them as sexual objects, however, despite their new revolutionary roles and contributions:

Since traditionally women did not participate in warfare, their status and roles were initially "highly ambiguous" and tended to shift as the battle lengthened. At the beginning, they were allocated domestic chores, including fetching firewood, cooking, washing, and cleaning. In certain camps, male leaders were each allowed to choose a woman . . . who as well as seeing to the other needs of the leader was also expected to meet his sexual needs. Women were induced to fulfill such "tasks" for "the good of the cause." As one Mau Mau woman stated, "Generally, I would think of sleeping with a man as an individual concern. Here, it seems to me that the leaders consider this as part of the woman's duty in the [Mau Mau] society. I believe that since I could not do any other better service to my people, I would then willingly accept it as my contribution to society." (Kanogo 1987, 87–88)

Although prewar gender norms of behavior instructed most African women to be demure and to resist men's sexual overtures, life in the military camps created different mores for women as well as men. Heterosexual relationships among comrades often highlighted how gender practices lagged behind revolutionary rhetoric, reinforcing women's unequal status to men regardless of their rank. African women struggled with these dynamics in a number of ways. One FRELIMO woman commander lamented, "While many of the male guerrillas accept the fact that women had the right to fight, within the household our husbands continued to treat us as if they were still 'petty chiefs.' . . . We women were still expected to fetch water, clean house, prepare dinner and take care of the children as well as fight for the nation. . . . In general, they didn't do anything in the home and we did not demand that they do anything" (quoted in Isaacman and Isaacman 1984, 168). For some women, regardless of the incongruence between rhetoric and reality, marriage, especially to a commanding officer, was one way to survive military camp life: "I met the father of my first two children during the war. He was a commander, and I got with him because he was single and so was I, and I thought, I had better get hooked with someone so the other men wouldn't put pressure on me" (quoted in Lyons 2004, 195).

Although some comrades created stable unions, the emphasis on nationalism and newly militarized masculine identities, coupled with revolutionary militancy and an absolute commitment to the struggle, provided many male combatants with a convenient excuse for irresponsibility toward the mothers of their children and the children themselves (Kesby 1996; Shikola 1998; Lyons 2004). Some commanders had as many as fifteen to eighteen children (Shikola 1998, 143).[18] Many African armies did not promote contraception as a matter of policy, however, on the grounds that it was expensive, access was unreliable, it was associated with prostitution, and in some cases it was linked to attempts by colonizers to reduce the number of Africans (Lyons 2004). Pregnant women were often sent to special camps, stigmatized as places for prostitutes (Lyons 2004). Many men denied paternity. When a pregnant woman was sent to a camp, this created "a vacuum for the guy," enabling him to "get involved with some other new recruit," ending up with "maybe three or four babies" in the women's camp (Lyons 2004, 201). The official policy of most African armies not to promote contraception or abortion created additional vulnerabilities for women soldiers regarding sex, contraceptives,

---

[18] Some guerrilla armies prohibited sexual relationships between soldiers (however, officers were usually the exception), while other armies did not enforce disciplinary codes, given the protracted nature of the war and the inevitability of such liaisons. Some armies encouraged or forced soldiers to marry if a pregnancy occurred. Women were usually blamed for their pregnancies and any paternity issues that arose (Lyons 2004).

pregnancy, childbirth, and parenting. These same policies, however, contributed to hypermasculine attitudes and sexual practices in the camps. Mutual recognition is highly improbable under these circumstances.

Torture, rape, and abduction by friends and foes

In addition to a sexual division of labor, military forces engaged in anti-colonial wars reinforced patriarchal values and practices through the use of torture, the abuse of military rank to justify rape, and sometimes the abduction of civilians. Although some torture techniques were used against both men and women, the same technique had different meanings for each. Specific techniques targeted women's sexuality. Male interrogators relied on deep-rooted cultural concepts of women's shame and honor to break women combatants. Most women were raped when taken prisoner by enemy forces. In the words of one South African woman fighter, "I don't know what was the worst in jail, the constant threat of being raped or the actual incident itself! Women were made to stand the whole day with blood [from their menstrual cycles and the rapes] flowing down and drying on their legs. Did they gain strength from looking at [and] asking us to drink our own blood?" (quoted in Krog 2001, 204–5). In addition to making women endure sleep deprivation, physical beatings, and electric shocks to their genitals, male guards have engaged in humiliating body searches and vaginal examinations, inserting foreign objects, including rats, in women's vaginas, repeatedly raping women prisoners, and forcing women to have intercourse with other prisoners for the entertainment of prison personnel (Lazreg 1994; Goldblatt and Meintjes 1998; Krog 2001). Women's fallopian tubes have been flooded with gushing water, often resulting in their inability to bear children (Goldblatt and Meintjes 1998). Most women combatants are ashamed to speak about these incidents, so first-person accounts are few, often kept brief, and confidential. Psychological reports verify how these forms of violence traumatized rather than transformed women, leaving enduring emotional scars on women soldiers that national independence does not erase (Goldblatt and Meintjes 1998; Krog 2001).

Testimonies by women revolutionaries indicate that the sexual torture and abuse were not confined to the activities of enemy forces. Revolutionary armies, too, engaged in horrific human rights abuses, including rape, torture, and brutal abductions (Cock 1991; Lyons 2004). Most abducted girls were kept against their will and raped in order to facilitate their submission (Kanogo 1987; Lyons 2004). Ex-combatant Rufaro, abducted from her school when guerrilla soldiers of the Zimbabwe People Revolutionary Army were seeking recruits, became committed to the armed struggle after being "politically educated" (raped; Lyons 2004, 122). She eventually insisted on being trained for combat: "I went to the Botswana/Zimbabwe border and crossed the river with over two hundred children from the school. The guerrillas took us. . . . When we reached Zambia we were taken to Victory Camp. This camp was used by the MPLA freedom fighters. We found other children from the Manama Mission, who were captured by the same guerrillas who captured us. . . . We used to cry saying, 'Why are you discriminating us from men. Men are training in the camps, you just keep us here in Victory Camp. . . . Please we want to train as soldiers'" (quoted in Lyons 2004, 122).

Among their own comrades, women combatants were subjected to combat duty as well as sexual duty, forced marriage, and sexual politics that required marriage to a commanding officer in order to rise through the ranks (Kanogo 1987; Lyons 2004). These double standards make clear that regardless of their training and status as fighters, women were expected to care for, serve, and comfort men (Cock 1991). From the beginning of her military training and throughout her years as a military commander, Modise knew she had to protect herself from the South African apartheid forces as well as from her own comrades. Modise recalled fights among male soldiers, who were bored and felt sexually frustrated in the isolated military camps, over the sexual use of women soldiers. Instances of sexual molestation and harassment were ignored by the ANC leadership (Curnow 2000). Girl soldiers were particularly at risk of rape; poor, young, and illiterate girls and women fighting on the front lines were most vulnerable to such human rights abuses (Kanogo 1987; Curnow 2000; Lyons 2004). Margo Dongo, former Zimbabwe African National Liberation Army guerrilla soldier and the first woman and independent member of the Zimbabwean Parliament, recalled the difficult conditions in the camps:

> When I got to the camps, I was asked who I was, to surrender what little, whatever I had, and choose a name for myself, a pseudonym. . . . From here, I am cutting the story short. I am not talking about the experience I got in those days. It was very nasty. . . . And then I went to the barracks—shelter—thinking I would have somewhere nice to sleep, only to find someone say, "Well there is your grass . . . so you get this grass to make your mattress . . . and you can make your bed. . . . I had to learn to live with it. Nobody forced me to come. . . . I had to adjust, and I did adjust. . . . We could stay for two weeks without enough food, feeding on water or skimmed milk. (Quoted in Lyons 2004, 115–16)

Dongo also reported being raped by a comrade.

Many women negotiated their survival by acquiescing. As one woman fighter for the Zimbabwe African National Liberation Army noted: "Women were given equal treatment . . . going through military training. We were just being mixed up with the men and if we show that military commander we can command and everybody will be saluting you and everything. . . . But [what] was disappointing was that they would try to fall in love with [you] or to make you love the guys and . . . when you're in the hardships promising you that you can have soap, you can have . . . luxury . . . even sugar . . . where you could go for four days without food . . . so they started kind of buying women" (quoted in Lyons 2004, 191). Although Teckla Shikola, formerly of the People's Liberation Army of Namibia (the military wing of the South West Africa People's Organization), avoided being raped, her testimony highlights how abuses were fostered by training and disciplinary regimens that allowed little room for dissent or insubordination: "Sometimes, when you are coming from home, you are new, and they train you in the army to say 'yes.' Whenever someone in charge calls you, you shouldn't refuse, you don't say no, you have to go. You feel scared of saying no, you cannot talk directly to a commander. Sometimes the chiefs would call out these poor young girls fresh from home. The chiefs made love to them and the women became pregnant without knowing the person who impregnated them, sometimes they didn't even know his name" (Shikola 1998, 143).

Authoritarian command structures, exposure to sustained violence, and loyalties cultivated by a gendered warrior ethos produced heinous consequences for women revolutionaries suspected of disloyalty (Grossman 1995). Rita Mazibuko, military-trained South African cadre of the ANC, was detained by her own people after nine comrades in close proximity to her had been shot. Accused of being a spy, she was tortured and raped: "They pushed a pipe with a condom in and out of my vagina. While they did it, they asked how it felt. . . . Someone called Desmond raped me nine times. . . . Comrade Mashego . . . raped me until I approached the authorities. And then, Tebogo, who was also very young, he raped me and cut my genitals—he cut me from number one to number two. And then he put me in a certain room, he tied my legs apart . . . then poured Dettol [an antiseptic] over my genitals" (quoted in Krog 2001, 207–8).

In contrast to Fanon's claims about revolutionary violence as a cleansing force, war is a dirty business and a gendered business. Rather than serving as a transformative, humanistic force, in many contexts violence functions as a degenerative force. The trauma and humiliation caused by debilitating violent acts left many women soldiers serving in anticolonial forces feeling unworthy of any recognition, much less mutual recognition.

Revolutionary warfare: An oxymoron?

Contrary to Fanon's optimistic predictions, revolutionary warfare may be a contradiction in terms. The values and brutal tactics associated with effective warfare (authoritarianism, elitism, secrecy, tight control of information for fear of spies and leaks, and torture to get information from enemies) contradict the values and practices associated with revolutionary social transformation (egalitarianism, freedom of expression, consensus, dissent, and transparency in government decisions and policies). Progressive ideological goals that inspire revolution are diametrically opposed to the tactics taught to achieve victory in warfare. Despite egalitarian slogans, best intentions, and just causes for going to war, such contradictions may explain why some of the most visionary revolutionary organizations and their leaders have over time come to mimic the authoritarian, elitist, and violent characteristics of the regimes they overthrew (de Waal 2002; Campbell 2003).

Discussion of potentially divisive issues such as gender relations and ethnic rivalry are discouraged during active war under the pretext of safeguarding national unity (Kabira and Nzioki 1993; Lazreg 1994; McFadden 2000). Thus, most revolutionary organizations lack clear policies to promote gender-specific political education and transformation. "Equal rights for women" is often a revolutionary call asserting "women's equal right with men to take up arms against repression" (Cock 1991, 197). This narrow militaristic interpretation of equal rights paves the way for the marginalization of women after war.

Postwar realities: Motherhood, wifehood, otherhood

Radical African feminists have noted that androcentric, militarized men require embodiments of feminine womanhood to complement them. For this reason, women combatants have been expected to make any necessary practical and emotional adjustments and go back to their traditional roles as mothers and wives in newly independent nations (Tamale 1999; Mama 2000; McFadden 2000). Visions of social change and gender equity compete with popular patriarchal yearnings to return to normal. This return to the normal is also gendered. Women combatants have been asked to put down their weapons, return to the domestic sphere, and bear children for the new independent nation (Enloe 2004b; McFadden 2005).

In circumstances where extended family networks have been destroyed through abductions, forced removals, and detentions during the course of the revolutionary wars, the return to family life may be a practical and empowering choice for many women ex-combatants. In many other cases, however, motherhood and wifehood were not presented as options but as mandates for all respectable women (McFadden 2005). Pressures to restore traditional gender hierarchies have been accompanied by historical revisionism. Representations of women combatants as equal contributors to the revolution have been censored. Men return as heroes whose roles as independence fighters fortify their evolving masculine identities, but women's identities as revolutionaries have been suppressed in popular accounts of war (Gaba 1997; Shikola 1998; Curnow 2000).

Indeed, in the aftermath of war African women soldiers have been viewed with contempt by civilians and by their fellow comrades, treated as women with declined status or loose morals, women associated with the spread of AIDS, prostitutes, too feisty and difficult for marriage, old and barren if they do not have children, and bad or unnatural mothers if they left their children with family members in order to fight.[19] Subjected to such public denigration, many women conceal their former roles as combatants (Lyons 2004). Rather than restoring their dignity through war, participation in violence has subjected some women combatants to shaming practices that challenge their integrity. Thus participation in anticolonial warfare may restore male combatants' dignity precisely because it reinscribes dominant conceptions of masculinity. By contrast, the valor of women combatants violates traditional gender norms, producing public condemnations for the perceived loss of femininity and respectability, thereby posing serious challenges to the dignity and psychological well-being of women combatants. Lying about their war experiences and becoming so-called respectable wives and mothers are presented as options to avoid being othered and ostracized permanently (Lyons 2004). With few exceptions, female revolutionary "makers of history," to borrow Fanon's term (1968, 69), have been pressured to disappear from history, according to frequent postwar reports.[20]

Postwar research on the adverse effects of violence

Fanon's predictions concerning the transformative psychological effects of political violence have not been clinically substantiated by psychological research on women or men. In fact, the opposite appears to be the case,

[19] See Cock 1991, 153; Shikola 1998, 142, 147; West 2000, 190; Lyons 2004, 223.
[20] See Gaba 1997; Curnow 2000; West 2000; Lyons 2004.

suggesting that Fanon overgeneralized the results of his clinical obser-vations of the Algerian war (Grossman 1995). Fanon did not live long enough to conduct long-term follow-up investigations of Algerian com-batants (Kebede 2001). Psychological research conducted in the aftermath of African wars of national independence suggests that learning to kill exacts a high psychological toll on soldiers, their families, and society at large (Grossman 1995; Mama 2000).

Historian, soldier, and psychologist Lieutenant Colonel Dave Gross-man has conducted comprehensive psychological studies of the effects of combat, studies that suggest that 98 percent of all soldiers involved in close combat become psychiatric casualties, while the remaining 2 percent who endure sustained combat already had a predisposition toward "ag-gressive psychopathic personalities" (1995, 43–44). Heard at close range, the screams and cries of the enemy add to the trauma experienced by soldiers (Grossman 1995, 116). Soldiers who have been involved in close combat "suffer higher incidences of divorce, marital problems, tranquilizer use, alcoholism and other addictions, joblessness, heart disease, high blood pressure, and ulcers" (Grossman 1995, 283). These findings have been corroborated by some studies of African women revolutionaries. African women ex-combatants vary in age, educational level, social class, rural or urban background, marketable skills, physical ability, and both personal and political aspirations (Cock 1994). Most report hardships endured during the war, including hunger, imprisonment, sexual abuse, ongoing fear of death at the hands of the enemy and some comrades, and physical illnesses such as malaria (Cock 1994; Lazreg 1994; Lyons 2004). Many suffer from posttraumatic stress disorder, while others face permanent physical disabilities. However, Fanon theorized that revolutionary eradi-cation of inferiority could occur despite physical and psychic trauma, es-pecially when political education accompanies the armed struggle. African women combatants' published reports suggest that evidence from only a minority of the cases supports his assumption.

Within this minority, women who achieved leadership positions during anticolonial wars provide most accounts that indicate personal empower-ment through combat experiences (Isaacman and Isaacman 1984; Curnow 2000; Lyons 2004). Many of these women now hold positions in govern-ment. Others have reported feeling personally empowered by performing traditional female support roles that they knew were politically important (Isaacman and Isaacman 1984; Kanogo 1987; Cock 1991). A full account-ing of these transformations is difficult, however, because the stories of many women combatants have been censored. Male comrades who engaged in human rights abuses and those who were aware of such abuses but did not intervene to stop them now hold powerful government positions and have vested interests in preserving silence about such abuses.[21]

Despite variations in existing testimonies and the political difficulties associated with efforts to gather additional evidence, there is another aspect of women's war experiences that must be considered in order to assess Fanon's claims concerning the transformative potential of revolutionary violence. Most testimonies by African women combatants who report empowerment during the revolutionary struggle suggest that violence was not integral to the empowerment they achieved. For example, Paulina Mateos, a former FRELIMO guerrilla commander, notes that her ability to survive the harsh elements of military camp life and participating alongside men in collective struggle contributed to her sense of agency and dignity as a woman soldier: "We suffered hunger and thirst and heat as the men did, and we learned to handle all kinds of arms . . . sometimes we even surpassed the men. . . . So, I no longer feel that differences exist between men and myself since we fought side by side. We marched together, organized ambushes together, we suffered defeats together as well as the joys of victory" (quoted in Isaacman and Isaacman 1984, 161, 164, 165).

Ellen Musialela, who first became involved in Namibia's liberation struggle in 1964, when she was fourteen years old, spent seven years as a nurse in the military wing and later was assigned to administrative work in the political wing of the movement after a debilitating snake bite. Her sense of accomplishment had more to do with resistance to shared oppression that grew as she and other women coped with the difficulties that men and everyday military camp life presented:

> Some women have sacrificed their lives on the battlefield; some are very good at communications, reconnaissance, and in the medical field. Of course, you also find that women in the camps are taking a very active role in our kindergartens, in our medical centres, as nurses, as teachers, and in other productive work. . . . Our women in the battlefield especially, are faced with a lot of problems. . . . I saw with my own eyes when I went to the battlefield in May, how women were forced to use grass during their periods and had to go without panties. . . . We feel proud that despite the traditional barriers between men and women, women have started to understand that we have to fight together to fight the system, because we are oppressed as women, and we are oppressed as blacks. (Musialela 1983, 85–86)

[21] See Shikola 1998; Curnow 2000; Krog 2001; Lyons 2004.

Marnia Lazreg's description of the factors that contributed to Algerian women fighters' transformation captures the experiences of many African women combatants: "First, women forged bonds with one another that transcended the usual episodic solidarity that characterized their relationships during peacetime. Second, they gained a sense of responsibility and purpose as well as another perspective on their lives. Third, confidence in themselves and a sense of partaking in history is evident. Fourth, they were exposed to the similarities between men and women, despite differences" (1994, 140). Confirming the multidimensionality of transformative practices, African feminist Patricia McFadden boldly adds, "African [women] do not want to be pitied; they do not want to be studied and interrogated as victimized subjects whose agency is rarely acknowledged, let alone politically supported, at the global level. What African [women] have wanted for the past half-century since independence is the opportunity to craft their own futures and to define their own destinies. . . . Cleaning up the mess of the past three hundred years of supremacist rule . . . cannot be an easy or pleasant task. . . . [However,] it is an opportunity that women are making the most of, a moment that is changing their lives forever" (2005, 17).

Conclusion

In addition to justifying violence as a means of physical self-defense for the colonized, Fanon attributed a therapeutic, psychological role to revolutionary war. To assess the validity of Fanon's claims, feminist scholarship asks additional questions: therapeutic for whom, and in what way? Fanon could not have known that encouraging colonized men to redirect their counterviolent urges could spin out of control both during and after wars of independence. Although Fanon's critique of the psychological harms caused by colonialism remains powerful, his analysis of the power of revolutionary violence to restore human agency and dignity does not fully capture the experiences of African women or African men in anticolonial struggles. Although he acknowledged the role of African women guerrilla fighters and their right to exist as autonomous human beings, he neglected other raced-gendered psychopolitical factors that worked against their recognition as equal contributors to anticolonial wars.

Fanon emphasized the racializing effects of colonial subjugation, what he called "the epidermalization of inferiority" (1967a, 13). As I have shown, however, he paid too little attention to the gendered psychological effects of colonization and revolutionary violence. Drawing his evidence largely from men, he produced an androcentric account that failed to explore patriarchal aspects of men's colonized mentalities. The complex resentments of colonized men against their colonizers contributed to the formation of revolutionary nationalist organizations that privileged the emancipation of the colonized as Africans and as men. Processes of militarization during the anticolonial wars further entrenched male dominance and male privilege. Authoritarianism in military chains of command and the view that combat is so-called men's work created sexual divisions of labor, hypermasculine attitudes and practices, and a form of blind compliance that worked against the equal recognition of women soldiers. In addition, long-standing practices of sexual exploitation subjected women soldiers to human rights abuses by the enemy and their fellow comrades.

Contrary to Fanon's optimistic predictions, participation in revolutionary violence does not necessarily contribute to the mutual recognition and equality of women in the aftermath of war. Indeed, many aspects of gendered violence work against it. Contradictions between the values of democratic revolution and militarism, postwar pressures on women soldiers to censor reports of nontraditional roles as well as gendered tortures that many experienced, and the pressure to resume traditional female roles leave only a select group of women feeling empowered by the war.

To assess the transformative potential of violence, then, it is imperative to examine the complexities and interrelationships of gender, war, and postwar reconstruction. Participation in military operations does not automatically liberate women or men from racially and sexually exploitive relationships. The equal right to engage in combat does not ensure that women soldiers will be equally valued or recognized as equals by men. Women who choose to join military forces have to combat both the external enemy and the patriarchal attitudes and actions of their fellow soldiers. Even in circumstances where revolutionary violence is justified, the long-term psychological costs of war may be far more damaging for women and men than Fanon suggested.

Departments of Women's Studies and African and African American Studies
Pennsylvania State University

References

Adugna, Minale. 2001. *Women and Warfare in Ethiopia: A Case Study of Their Role during the Campaign of Adwa, 1895/96, and the Italo-Ethiopian War, 1935–1941*. Gender Issues Report Series 13. Addis Ababa: Organization for Social Science Research in Eastern and Southern Africa.

Arendt, Hannah. 1970. *On Violence.* New York: Harcourt, Brace & World.

Becker, Heike. 1995. *Namibian Women's Movement, 1980 to 1992: From Anticolonial Resistance to Reconstruction.* Frankfurt: IKO-Verlag für Interkulterelle Kommunikation.

Black Radical Congress. 1998. "Principles of Unity." http://www.blackradical congress.org/unity.html.

Bulhan, Hussein Abdilahi. 1985. *Frantz Fanon and the Psychology of Oppression.* New York: Plenum.

Campbell, Horace. 2003. *Reclaiming Zimbabwe: The Exhaustion of the Patriarchal Model of Liberation.* Trenton, NJ: Africa World Press.

Cock, Jacklyn. 1991. *Colonels and Cadres: War and Gender in South Africa.* Cape Town: Oxford University Press.

———. 1994. *The Forgotten People: The Need for a Soldiers' Charter.* Cape Town: Institute for Democracy in South Africa.

Curnow, Robyn. 2000. "Thandi Modise, a Woman at War." *Agenda: Empowering Women for Gender Equity,* no. 43, 36–40.

de Waal, Alex. 2002. "The Political Cultures of Militarism." In his *Demilitarizing the Mind: African Agendas for Peace and Security,* 73–92. Trenton, NJ: Africa World Press.

Enloe, Cynthia H. 1983. "The Military Needs Camp Followers." In her *Does Khaki Become You? The Militarisation of Women's Lives,* 1–17. London: Pluto.

———. 2004a. "All the Men Are in the Militias, All the Women Are Victims: The Politics of Masculinity and Femininity in Nationalist Wars." In her *The Curious Feminist: Searching for Women in a New Age of Empire,* 99–118. Berkeley: University of California Press.

———. 2004b. "Demilitarization—or More of the Same? Feminist Questions to Ask in the Postwar Moment." In her *The Curious Feminist: Searching for Women in a New Age of Empire,* 217–32. Berkeley: University of California Press.

———. 2004c. "When Feminists Look at Masculinity and the Men Who Wage War: A Conversation between Cynthia Enloe and Carol Cohn." In her *The Curious Feminist: Searching for Women in a New Age of Empire,* 237–67. Berkeley: University of California Press.

Fanon, Frantz. 1967a. *Black Skin, White Masks.* Trans. Charles Lam Markmann. New York: Grove.

———. 1967b. *A Dying Colonialism.* Trans. Haakon Chevalier. New York: Grove.

———. 1967c. *Toward the African Revolution.* Trans. Haakon Chevalier. New York: Grove.

———. 1968. *The Wretched of the Earth.* Trans. Constance Farrington. New York: Grove.

Gaba, Lewis. 1997. "Give Us Our Piece of the Pie: Women Ex–Freedom Fighters Meet in Africa." *AfricaNews* 13, April. Human Rights Information Network. http://www.hartford-hwp.com/archives/30/151.html.

Goldblatt, Beth, and Sheila Meintjes. 1998. "South African Women Demand the Truth." In Turshen and Twagiramariya 1998, 27–61. London: Zed.

Goldman, Nancy Loring, ed. 1982. *Female Soldiers—Combatants or Noncombatants? Historical and Contemporary Perspectives.* Westport, CT: Greenwood.

Goldstein, Joshua S. 2001. *War and Gender: How Gender Shapes the War System and Vice Versa.* Cambridge: Cambridge University Press.

Grossman, Dave. 1995. *On Killing: The Psychological Cost of Learning to Kill in War and Society.* Boston: Little, Brown.

Hegel, G. W. F. 1966. *The Phenomenology of Mind.* Trans. J. B. Baillie. 2nd ed. London: Allen & Unwin.

Hélie-Lucas, Marie-Aimée. 1988. "The Role of Women during the Algerian Liberation Struggle and After: Nationalism as a Concept and as a Practice towards Both the Power of the Army and the Militarization of the People." In *Women and the Military System,* ed. Eva Isaksson, 171–89. New York: St. Martins.

Hull, Gloria T., Patricia Bell Scott, and Barbara Smith, eds. 1982. *All the Women Are White, All the Blacks Are Men, but Some of Us Are Brave: Black Women's Studies.* Old Westbury, NY: Feminist Press.

Isaacman, Allen, and Barbara Isaacman. 1984. "The Role of Women in the Liberation of Mozambique." *Ufahamu: Journal of the African Activist Association* 13(2):128–85.

Kabira, Wanjiku Mukabi, and Elizabeth Akinyi Nzioki, eds. 1993. *Celebrating Women's Resistance: A Case Study of Women's Groups Movement in Kenya.* Nairobi: African Women's Perspective.

Kanogo, Tabitha. 1987. "Kikuyu Women and the Politics of Protest: Mau Mau." In *Images of Women in Peace and War: Cross-Cultural and Historical Perspectives,* ed. Sharon Macdonald, Pat Holden, and Shirley Ardener, 78–99. Houndmills: Macmillan.

Kebede, Messay. 2001. "The Rehabilitation of Violence and the Violence of Rehabilitation: Fanon and Colonialism." *Journal of Black Studies* 31(5):539–62.

Kesby, Mike. 1996. "Arenas for Control, Terrains of Gender Contestation: Guerrilla Struggle and Counter-insurgency Warfare in Zimbabwe, 1972–1980." *Journal of Southern African Studies* 22(4):561–84.

Krog, Antjie. 2001. "Locked into Loss and Silence: Testimonies of Gender and Violence at the South African Truth Commission." In Moser and Clark 2001, 203–16.

Lazreg, Marnia. 1994. *The Eloquence of Silence: Algerian Women in Question.* New York: Routledge.

Lewis, Desiree. 2004. "African Gender Research and Postcoloniality: Legacies and Challenges." In *African Gender Scholarship: Concepts, Methodologies and Paradigms,* by Signe Arnfred, Bibi Bakare-Yusuf, Edward Waswa Kisiang'ani, Desiree Lewis, Oyeronke Oyewumi, and Filomina Chioma Steady, 27–41. Dakar: CODESRIA.

Lyons, Tanya. 2004. *Guns and Guerilla Girls: Women in the Zimbabwean Liberation Struggle.* Trenton, NJ: Africa World Press.

Maitse, Teboho, with Jen Marchbank. 2000. "Revealing Silence: Voices from South

Africa." In *States of Conflict: Gender, Violence and Resistance*, ed. Susie Jacobs, Ruth Jacobson, and Jennifer Marchbank, 199–214. London: Zed.

Mama, Amina. 2000. "Transformation Thwarted: Gender-Based Violence in Africa's New Democracies." *African Gender Institute Newsletter* 6 (May). http://www.uct.ac.za/org/agi/pubs/newsletters/vol6/transf.htm.

McFadden, Patricia. 2000. "Radically Speaking: The Significance of the Women's Movement for Southern Africa." Women's World: Organization for Rights, Literature, and Development. http://www.wworld.org/programs/regions/africa/patricia_mcfadden3.htm.

———. 2005. "Becoming Postcolonial: African Women Changing the Meaning of Citizenship." *Meridians* 6(1):1–22.

Meena, Ruth. 1992. "Gender Research/Studies in Southern Africa: An Overview." In her *Gender in Southern Africa: Conceptual and Theoretical Issues*, 1–30. Harare, Zimbabwe: SAPES.

Moser, Caroline, and Fiona C. Clark. 2001. *Victims, Perpetrators or Actors? Gender, Armed Conflict and Political Violence*. London: Zed.

Musialela, Ellen. 1983. "Women in Namibia: The Only Way to Free Ourselves." In *Third World, Second Sex: Women's Struggles and National Liberation*, comp. Miranda Davies, 83–89. London: Zed.

Organisation of Angolan Women. 1984. *Angolan Women Building the Future: From National Liberation to Women's Emancipation*. Trans. Maria Holness. London: Zed.

Potgieter, Cheryl. 1997. "From Apartheid to Mandela's Constitution: Black South African Lesbians in the Nineties." In *Ethnic and Cultural Diversity among Lesbians and Gay Men*, ed. Beverly Greene. Psychological Perspectives on Lesbian and Gay Issues 3. Thousand Oaks, CA: Sage.

Salo, Elaine. 2001. "Talking about Feminism in Africa with Amina Mama." *Agenda: Empowering Women for Gender Equity*, no. 50, 58–63.

Schmidt, Elizabeth. 1991. "Patriarchy, Capitalism, and the Colonial State in Zimbabwe." *Signs: Journal of Women in Culture and Society* 16(4):732–56.

Shikola, Teckla. 1998. "We Left Our Shoes Behind." In Turshen and Twagiramariya 1998, 138–49.

Tamale, Sylvia. 1999. *When Hens Begin to Crow: Gender and Parliamentary Politics in Uganda*. Boulder, CO: Westview.

———. 2003. "Out of the Closet: Unveiling Sexuality Discourses in Uganda." *Feminist Africa* 2. http://www.feministafrica.org/fa%202/02-2003/sp-tamale.html.

Thiam, Awa. 1995. "Feminism and Revolution." In her *Black Sisters, Speak Out: Black Women and Oppression in Black Africa*, 113–28. Chicago: Research Associates.

Turshen, Meredeth, and Clotilde Twagiramariya, eds. 1998. *What Women Do in Wartime: Gender and Conflict in Africa*. London: Zed.

Urdang, Stephanie. 1979. *Fighting Two Colonialisms: Women in Guinea-Bissau*. New York: Monthly Review.

West, Harry. 2000. "Girls with Guns: Narrating the Experience of War of FRELIMO's 'Female Detachment.'" *Anthropological Quarterly* 73(4):180–94.

West, Lois, ed. 1997. *Feminist Nationalism*. New York: Routledge.

Wilson, Amrit. 1991. *The Challenge Road: Women and the Eritrean Revolution*. Trenton, NJ: Red Sea.

Meg Samuelson

The Disfigured Body of the Female Guerrilla: (De)Militarization, Sexual Violence, and Redomestication in Zoë Wicomb's *David's Story*

In the war zone, women's bodies are simultaneously saturated with and stripped of meaning; in the process, they are rendered invisible. The raped female body suffers a similar fate: figured as a rhetorical sign, its disfigurements slip from view (see Samuelson 2002; Sielke 2002). Feminist discourses have aimed to render such bodies visible in and of themselves but have been embattled when faced with the figure of the female militant. Two strands of feminist thought diverge in conceptualizations of the woman warrior: one finds in war a potential realm of gendered equality and female liberation; another associates women with nurturing and life-giving qualities, linking them to an ethos of peace and pitting them and their interests against war (see Cock 1991, 189–91; D'Amico 1998, 120). Similarly, feminist understandings of rape have variously constructed women as victims of patriarchy and as potential agents of resistance (see Brownmiller 1976; Marcus 1992).

This article explores the implications for feminism of reading and writing about women in the southern African war zone and its aftermath by focusing on Zoë Wicomb's novel *David's Story* (2000), which grapples with the figure of a female militant and the myriad violations to which she is subject. The narrative is set in the context of demobilization following political settlement in South Africa in the early 1990s. During the preceding decades, the conflict between the apartheid state and antiapartheid activists reached civil war proportions, and "militarized constructions

The production of this article was financially supported by the National Research Foundation (NRF), South Africa. Any opinion expressed herein is mine, and the NRF does not accept any liability in regard thereto. I am grateful also to the University of Stellenbosch for providing additional funding. My reading of *David's Story* owes much to Dorothy Driver's pioneering analysis. Employed as Driver's research assistant during her preparation of the afterword, I grappled with the novel, initially, through the prism of her argument; here I expand upon a number of insights gleaned in the process, while developing alternative and parallel readings that will, I hope, add to her scholarship.

[*Signs: Journal of Women in Culture and Society* 2007, vol. 32, no. 4]

of masculinity and femininity became more pronounced" (Goldblatt and Meintjes 1998, 31). Yet South African women entered and were absorbed into the war effort on both sides of the conflict and in a range of capacities. In both the South African Defence Force (SADF) and the liberation armies (particularly Umkhonto we Sizwe [MK], the armed wing of the African National Congress [ANC]), women took up the apparently divergent roles of warriors and supporters. My attention will fall exclusively on women in MK and in ANC homes as I follow Wicomb's complex and nuanced engagement with women in and at war.[1]

Discourse and dis-figuration: Dancing through the representational minefield

> For what we are asking to be scrutinized are nothing less than shared cultural assumptions so deeply rooted and so long ingrained that, for the most part, our critical colleagues have ceased to recognize them as such.
> —Annette Kolodny 1980, 6

David's Story juxtaposes the historical past and the contemporary transition, revealing what it calls "recursions" in attitudes to, and inscriptions of, women, in order to dramatize the paradoxical position inhabited by a female guerrilla subject to abuse in an era of demilitarization and re-domestication (Wicomb 2000, 184). The novel is set in the transitional moment of 1991, "the edge of a new era" (Wicomb 2000, 184). From this vantage point, David, an MK commander, reflects on the recent past of the antiapartheid struggle, while undertaking a historical investigation into his Griqua ancestry.[2]

Pointing to torture in ANC training and detention camps and to general abuse of women within the liberation movement, the novel reveals the contamination of the antiapartheid struggle by the structures against which it set itself, as, in the milieu of suspicion fostered by apartheid counterintelligence, the liberation movement internally replicates the procedures of the apartheid state while offering women cadres a curtailed

---

[1] For a useful comparison of gendered constructions and positions in the SADF and the liberation armies, respectively, see Jacklyn Cock (1991).

[2] The two interpenetrating time frames of the novel thus cover late nineteenth- and early twentieth-century Griqua nationalism and the twentieth-century antiapartheid struggle. I focus entirely on the novel's representation of the recent, and ongoing, past; Driver and Mike Marais both offer useful discussions of the novel's engagements with Griqua history and its implications in the transitional present (Driver 2000, 219–26; Marais 2005, 21–28).

liberation. At the same time, *David's Story* explores the extent to which the abuses and betrayals of the past have seeped into the "new era"—troubling the temporal break between the old and the "new" South Africa—and highlights the gendered shapes that they have taken (see Samuelson 2003, 72). In this period of "treachery and flux" the lines between peace and war are more blurred than ever (Wicomb 2000, 13).

Amid this uncertain present, David approaches an unnamed woman to act as his amanuensis, to ghostwrite his story of the years of conflict. The amanuensis functions as the novel's narrator; the story she relates both "is and is not David's story" (Wicomb 2000, 1). It is David's story in that he figures as its central character and because the story told is, in part, that which David imparts to her. It is not his story in at least two respects: first, as much as the narrator relates David's story, her focus falls on a metafictional exploration into the very act of writing David's story; second, if David is the central character around whom narrative events cohere, his story is shaped and informed by the stories of women, which in turn disrupt his story, fragmenting the coherence David desires to impart to his past and the liberation movement. The narrator is one of these disruptive female figures; David's wife, Sally, herself an ex-MK cadre, is another. The most unsettling character is the elusive Dulcie, an MK commander and the object of David's unspoken desire, whom David describes as "a scream through [his] story" (Wicomb 2000, 134).

David's Story is infused and shaped by these women as it grapples with the various positions taken up by women during the conflict and its aftermath and dramatizes the ways in which two divergent discourses (espoused by David and the narrator, respectively) encode women in and of war.[3] As such, it is profoundly concerned with gendered figurations of war and peace. Highly self-reflexive, *David's Story* is keenly aware of the powers and dangers of representation and of what is risked in writing about women in the war zone and its aftermath: a representational minefield in which women are cast as idealized warriors, silenced victims, and emblems of the domestic world toward which the male warrior ostensibly directs his efforts. Shuttling between idealized warrior and silenced victim in its portrayal of Dulcie, it reveals both figurations as inadequate to her

---

[3] *Discourse* is here understood in the Foucauldian sense as "a body of anonymous, historical rules, always determined in the time and space that have defined a given period, and for a given social, economic, geographical and linguistic area, the conditions of operation of the enunciative function" (Foucault 1972, 117). In other words, *discourse* is the group of statements that describe and constitute a given realm, regulating what can legitimately be said or enunciated about it.

meaning; grappling with the feminine figure of domesticity, the novel dialectically dramatizes its production across the triangular structure set up among David, Dulcie, and Sally. Finally, the novel negotiates the representational minefield by shifting its focus from the representation of bodies to the body of representation itself, from Dulcie's flesh, "marinaded in pain," to the act of "flesh[ing] out the narrative" (Wicomb 2000, 180, 1).

The novel's methodology of dis-figuration tackles the very gendered imagery of war and peace. As Sharon Macdonald asserts, "images of women . . . are never irrelevant or neutral in the discourses of peace and war. . . . [If] women want to question or disrupt these definitions, they must take on . . . the imagery itself" (Macdonald 1987, 23). Dis-figuration entails such a process of taking on the images—or figures—that prop up discourses of war and peace; it deconstructs the gendered figurations that, in turn, disfigure women in order to shape them into ideal images or vessels in which to carry and convey social meaning. At the same time, it attends to the bodily disfigurements veiled beneath and even constitutive of such discourses.

The very attempt to write Dulcie—to figure her—is shown to impose violence on her body, literally disfiguring her. David's first attempts to write Dulcie produce no more than a "mess of . . . peculiar figures" (Wicomb 2000, 135); later he presents the narrator with a "page without words" that she glosses as follows: "There are the dismembered shapes of a body: an asexual torso, like a dressmaker's dummy; arms bent the wrong way at the elbows; legs; swollen feet; hands like claws. . . . I have no doubt that it is Dulcie who lies mutilated on the page" (Wicomb 2000, 205).

As Mike Marais notes in order to develop a related but different argument, "Dulcie cannot be represented in language, because it is *in* and *through* language that the body of the black woman has been dismembered by being reduced to a vocabulary of signs" (Marais 2005, 28).[4] Dulcie's body, mutilated on David's page, points to the violence of representation that is, in turn, linked to the scene of Dulcie's torture, which is literally written onto her body, "meticulously staked out with blue ballpoint before the insertion of a red-hot poker between the bones" (Wicomb 2000, 19).

---

[4] As I do, Marais explores Wicomb's concern with representation and the ways in which the novel dramatizes "the impossibility of representing the body in the absence of discourse" (Marais 2005, 21). His article addresses the delimiting discourses of race, whereas mine attends to the discursively impossible figure of the woman warrior.

Wicomb has said that Dulcie's story is "about the betrayal, about a faction in the Movement no longer requiring powerful coloured women"; such a story can only be told in an antirepresentational mode: "She is in a sense the necessary silence in the text; she can't be fleshed out precisely because of her shameful treatment which those committed to the Movement would rather not talk about" (quoted in Olver 2002, 190–91). As such, Dulcie is presented as a challenge to the writing of David's story and by extension the story of the South African past. Unknown and unknowable to the narrator yet constitutive of the story she is tasked with constructing, Dulcie requires of David's amanuensis that she invent and fabricate, while David remains insistently mum. Dulcie is in turn described by the narrator as "a protean subject that slithers *hither and thither*, out of reach, repeating, replacing, transforming itself"; as David battles to name the subject of his narrative, the narrator notes how, like the story they construct, she and David "*skirt* about a subject that slithers out of reach, and I am reminded of the new screen saver on my computer that tosses the text *hither and thither*" (Wicomb 2000, 34–35; emphasis added). Dulcie, then, is the discursive black hole around which David's story "skirts," in a telling metaphor that ties the act of representation to performances of gender.

Developing a suggestive observation made by Dorothy Driver, I read the "hither and thither" movement of Dulcie's "protean" form as one between two different discourses set up within the narrative. Wicomb attributes her ability "to speak and write" to both Black Consciousness (BC) and feminism (quoted in Hunter 1993, 88; see Driver 2000, 238–39). The discourses that emerge from these two positions at times support each other and at other times pull apart. Informed by BC, Wicomb's feminism differs from what has come to be known as Western feminism, yet she rejects womanism as a viable alternative (see Wicomb 1990) and thus refuses to restrict women to "their conventional supportive roles . . . in male-centred struggles against white oppression" (Lewis 1994, 162–63), particularly those enacted in domestic space. At the same time, while BC authorizes Wicomb's voice, it has been criticized for its failure to offer a discursive space to women. As Pumla Gqola suggests, the figure of Blackwoman "is marked largely by silence and absence" in its discourse (Gqola 2001, 147).

The exchange set up within the novel between David and the narrator is presented as one between a radical, militaristic discourse that has in part emerged from BC and a liberal humanist discourse associated with certain strands of feminism; oscillating between the two, the novel negotiates the demands of gender and race while avoiding what it perceives as the compromise of womanism. What the exchange dramatizes most keenly, however, is the inability of either discourse to accommodate the woman warrior, with the result being that she is effectively consigned to silence. In this way, the novel bears out and extends Jacklyn Cock's observation: "The role of women in militarization has been largely obscured by two competing perspectives—those of sexism and feminism. Both analyses exclude women from war on the grounds that they are bearers of 'special qualities.' . . . The outcome of both positions is that war is understood as a totally male affair" (Cock 1991, 188–89).

Articulating a (misogynistic) militaristic discourse, David bemoans that the narrator has turned his story into "a story of women," demanding, "Who would want to read a story like that? It's not a proper history at all" (Wicomb 2000, 199). Throughout the narrative, he is fundamentally unable to recognize the gendered experiences of women in the movement. His response to the narrator's questions about "the conditions of female guerrillas" is indicative: "Irrelevant, he barks. In the Movement those kinds of differences are wiped out by our common goal" (Wicomb 2000, 78). The barked response reveals that this inability to conceptualize the difference that gender makes stems precisely from the military discourse spoken by and through him. The narrator, however, is drawn to Dulcie out of a fascination fueled by her inability "to imagine a woman who takes that kind of thing seriously—protocol and hierarchy, the saluting and standing to attention, the barking of orders, the uniform" (Wicomb 2000, 79). Neither approach can enunciate the figure of the female guerrilla.

David insists that Dulcie is "not feminine, not like a woman at all"; the narrator's rebuttal issues her feminist insight: "As with the preservation of all prejudices, he will no doubt go on clocking exceptions rather than question the stereotype and its rule" (Wicomb 2000, 80). But she herself is no more able to accommodate Dulcie within her categories. The inventive fragments through which she tries to inscribe Dulcie linger on her "masculinity" and record regretful longings for an earlier "feminine" grace (Wicomb 2000, 18). Like Sally, the narrator appears to doubt that there may be "women in the world who do both": women able to combine military skill and valor with domestic ability and grace (Wicomb 2000, 32). Moreover, she verbalizes a pacifist horror toward war, leading David to retort angrily that those like her "who believe in keeping [their] hands clean at all costs, who reach for *lace handkerchiefs* at the thought of bloodshed, . . . choose not to notice that that fine thing, freedom, is rudely shoved through by *rough guys in khaki*" (Wicomb 2000, 79; emphasis added); in doing so, he again erases the presence of the female guerrilla as his use of imagery—his figuration of war—reiterates the division of war and peace into masculine and feminine domains.

Figurations of war delineate masculine and feminine positions, both depending on and exaggerating constructions of gender difference: men are presented as warriors and protectors, whereas women, cast in turn as the protected, embody hearth and home and are thus rendered passive and inactive. Not only does the iconography of war present such bifurcated gendered figures, but it also appears to depend on them. Cynthia Enloe, who details the military's reliance on femininity in *Does Khaki Become You?* argues that "expectations of what it means to be 'masculine' and what it means to be 'feminine' are . . . among the pillars holding up . . . military ideals" (Enloe 1989, xxxiv). "Militaries need women," she notes, "but they need women to behave *as the gender 'women'*" (Enloe 1989, 212). Hence the narrator's comment, as she grapples with the incongruous spectacle of the military woman while unwittingly suggesting the ways in which a conventional femininity is at war, "Such a woman does presumably not *rifle* in her handbag for a lipstick" (Wicomb 2000, 79; emphasis added).

Searching for an appropriate mode in which to inscribe Dulcie, the narrator idealizes her while mocking David's attempts to do so: "You wouldn't understand the courage and commitment and inviolability of someone like Dulcie, he says, thus placing her on a pedestal, beyond the realm of the human" (Wicomb 2000, 177). As the narrator realizes, such idealizations mean that "Dulcie, like God, must fend for herself" (Wicomb 2000, 177). However, soon after, she herself refers to Dulcie's "super-natural powers," suggesting that "the rumours about her legendary strength, her agility, her incredible marksmanship, her invincibility . . . have grown into truth" (Wicomb 2000, 180).

Dulcie's figuration as superhuman and the more general presence of women in the war zone, of which she is a synecdoche, disrupts the fig-uration of David as warrior and protector. When he is sent a hit list on which both his and Dulcie's names appear, he experiences a radical in-version of gendered positions: it is written "in a girlish hand" and casts him, shockingly, as "the intended," in an allusion to Joseph Conrad's *Heart of Darkness*, which insists anxiously, "They—the women I mean—are out of it—should be out of it. We must help them to stay in that beautiful world of their own, lest ours gets worse" (Conrad [1899] 1973, 69). *David's Story* reveals what Conrad's Marlow cannot countenance: that women are not out of it and never have been and that even Kurtz's Intended, the waiting woman, is implicated in the imperial project—and, in our context, in the war zone—by being the idealized object toward which it is directed. Thus does the novel point to the gendered patterns of war in which women embody and figure the domestic, familiar world that awaits the return of the male soldiers, presenting them with an image of the social order that they, in turn, defend.

Rather than setting women outside the war zone, such configurations of war position "woman as the *raison d'être* for fighting": "When men fight wars as 'the protectors,' women often take on a particular objectified importance as 'the protected.' Women are the custodians of the social values that the men are fighting for; the 'woman left behind' becomes a repository of these values" (Cock 1991, 119). Such gendered positions are stable only insofar as women can be cast as the protected. It is precisely because Dulcie "would not be in need of his protection" that David finds himself thrust into the feminine position of "the girl to be married, a girl in the haze of innocence" (Wicomb 2000, 114, 116).

Given the gendered confusion that Dulcie produces, the narrator recognizes that her story may be rendered best in the "middle voice" (Wicomb 2000, 197), that is, between active and passive voices. The middle voice permits a play of what Jacques Derrida called *différance* between social dichotomies (Derrida 1973, 130). Writing in the middle voice, says Dominick LaCapra, entails engaging with an "anxiety-ridden area of undecidability and the unavailability or radical ambivalence of clear-cut positions" (LaCapra 2001, 20). It is thus appropriate to Dulcie, who confounds available categories: she is an active subject—a powerful MK commander—who is subject to violence inflicted on her passive form; she is a "masculine" woman, habitually clothed in androgynous khaki fatigues; she flits between past and present, suggesting "a recursion" of past violence in the present (Wicomb 2000, 184). The disorientating space in which *David's Story*, and the story of Dulcie, unfolds shatters conventional distinctions—between male and female, war and peace, torture and rape, consensual intercourse and rape, military and domestic roles—by cracking open the gendered myths and constructions, the figurations, that underpin them.

The challenge that Dulcie issues to the gendered status quo fuels the postwar violence against her, as the return to the normalcy of peace issues the demand on women warriors to retreat into the private sphere, to become again, as it were, "women." The feminist position that finds in war the potential for women to establish equality by fighting side by side with men thus comes under pressure, as does that which associates women with the nurturing virtues of the domestic sphere. The "normalcy" to which women are returned, and which they are called upon to represent, requires women warriors to reclaim the home as their natural domain and to render themselves sexually available to men. Ideologies of domesticity and acts of sexual violence are two means by which this return to "normalcy" may be enforced.

Ideologies of domesticity exert a set of pressures upon women warriors in *David's Story* and the represented world, as I discuss at a later point in this article; relatedly, the threat of sexual violence participates in the recasting of militant women as domestic subjects. Sexual violence has certainly been on the ascent in postconflict South Africa, to the extent that it has recently been described as an "epidemic" on the scale of "an unacknowledged gender civil war" (Moffett 2006, 129). This is not an isolated phenomenon: "Evidence confirms that the gender violence women experience in wartime increases when the fighting dies down" (Meintjes, Pillay, and Turshen 2001, 4). What, then, do militarization and demilitarization mean to women? Where does one draw the line between peace and war, if women's experiences are located centrally in social analysis?

Raising questions such as these, and evoking the indeterminacy of the middle voice, Wicomb adds to existing feminist analyses, such as Judith Herman's study of trauma, which links the posttraumatic stress of the war zone to that experienced by women subjected to gendered violence in civilian life and, most often, in the privacy of the home. Herman observes that "the most common post-traumatic disorders are those not of men in war but of women in civilian life" (Herman 2001, 28). Resonant with *David's Story*, which infuses David's story with the stories of women, Herman employs as an emblematic epigraph a quotation from Salman Rushdie's *Shame*: "The women seem to have taken over; they marched in from the peripheries of the story to demand the inclusion of their own tragedies, histories, and comedies, obliging me . . . to see my 'male' plot refracted, so to speak, through the prisms of its reverse and 'female' side" (quoted in Herman 2001, n.p.). The "male" plot of David's story is refracted as provocatively through female plots; *David's Story*, in turn, refracts civil society through the illuminating prism of the war zone.

"Not rape": Sexual violence, torture, and love in war and peace

Writing is also a means of saying that which you can't utter.
—Wicomb (quoted in Olver 2002, 183)

The war zone dramatizes what is true in civil society: that the boundary between coercive and consensual sexual intercourse is fundamentally blurred (see Turshen 1998, 13). This became strikingly evident during the rape trial of suspended South African Deputy President Jacob Zuma in 2006, which revealed the high levels of sexual abuse and abuse of patriarchal power in both the ANC in exile and postapartheid South Africa. Such reports of the sexual abuse women encountered in the ANC in exile have only now begun to trickle out.[5] Beth Goldblatt and Sheila Meintjes note that while women are reticent about the forms of sexual violence encountered in police custody, they are resolutely silent about that experienced in ANC training camps. One informant, Caesarina Kona Makhoere, "expressed an unwillingness to speak about the camps but intimated that her experience had been terrible: 'At least in prison I knew I was in the enemy camp'" (Goldblatt and Meintjes 1998, 48).

Goldblatt and Meintjes surmise, furthermore, that such women "are afraid that their evidence could be used to equate *individual* human rights violations by ANC cadres with the *systemic* violations of apartheid" (1998, 48). Driver proposes instead that "perhaps the fear was, rather, the manifest equation of individual violations with the systematic violence of an African patriarchy, white or black" (Driver 2005, 221). Such recognition would, in turn, lead to another, namely that, for women, neither peace nor liberation necessarily follows formal demobilization.

Some of *David's Story*'s most terrifying ambiguities concern Dulcie's "night visitors," who are "both friend and foe" and who torture and then doctor her body in the postwar aftermath; seeking to recognize them as "friends, family, comrades . . . brings a moment of pure terror" (Wicomb 2000, 179). The novel thus draws attention to the fragile and all-too-permeable boundary between "friend and foe," lover and torturer, and the depth of horror that lies in contemplating its permeability. This terror is present in the relationship between Dulcie and David, as the novel pushes us to ask whether their unspoken love is yet another "variant" on torture (Wicomb 2000, 184; see also Driver 2000, 240).

If torture remains unarticulated by David, so too does his love for Dulcie: love itself is presented as being as unspeakable as its apparent inverse. Dulcie is imagined as longing for yet resisting the enunciation of love, fearful of finding the word itself, like those of "freedom" and "justice," becoming, in the process, "tarnished" (Wicomb 2000, 179): "Worse than any instrument of torture is the thought of such hard-found words being fingered by [the torturers]—jabbed, clubbed, defaced into a gibberish" (Wicomb 2000, 198).

As Dulcie is increasingly tortured by David's refusal to speak his love,

---

[5] Notable, in this respect, is Mtutuzeli Nyoka's brave novel, *I Speak to the Silent* (2004), in which a farm laborer refuses to allow his activist daughter's story of perpetual rape, and eventual death from a botched abortion, to be silenced by the big men of the party in exile.

while being physically tortured by her night visitors, the novel urges us to ask: In the context of the war zone and its aftermath, what is torture and what is tenderness? What, moreover, is love? And what is rape? In this way, it begins to hone in on the currently contested definition of rape in South Africa as nonconsensual rather than coercive intercourse (see South African Law Commission 2003). The legal discourse of rape as nonconsensual intercourse occludes the practices of power and coercion, thrown into relief in the war zone, which may render nonconsent unspeakable. Whereas current rape law presents women as having the power and freedom to say "no," the understanding of rape reached toward here is one cognizant of the power relations in which men and women operate that may prevent women from articulating nonconsent or may even produce them as consenting subjects. Writing of her experience as a female cadre in the liberation army of neighboring Namibia, Teckla Shikola relates, "I didn't really see rape cases as such, but you know, sometimes, when you are coming from home, you are new, and they train you in the army to say yes" (Shikola 1998, 143). Wicomb's Sally similarly recalls her sexual initiation as a young MK cadre in terms that mark it as manifestly coercive yet consensual. Realizing that the inevitable moment has arrived for her to fulfil the "unspoken part of a girl's training," Sally submits, forcing herself to consent in order to avoid having her trainer "force her, lord it over her" (Wicomb 2000, 123).

The novel pushes its inquiry into the definition of rape and the gendered experiences of conflict further by refusing to distinguish between abuses of power that write themselves onto women's bodies in the form of sexual violence and those that write themselves onto bodies—male and female—in the form of torture. The novel asks us to link the two, and, indeed, we are invited to do so by the historical record: Commissar Andrew Masondo, on whom responsibility for excesses at the ANC detention camp Quatro finally came to rest, stated infamously that "the law of supply and demand . . . created some problems" in the camps, with their ratio of fifty men to one woman (TRC 1998, 4.10 par. 104; see also Mngqibisa 1993, 14–15). The novel, Driver contends, "asks us to think about two current issues, and—if we dare—the relation between them: first, about what happened in the African National Congress (ANC) detention camps; and, second, about the sanctioned treatment of ANC women" (Driver 2000, 217).

Following the unveiling of an apartheid spy within the ANC inner circle in 1981, an atmosphere of paranoia and suspicion pervaded the movement in exile, while a group of MK combatants rebelled against the high command. Mutineers and suspected spies were imprisoned in a detention center established in Angola, which came to be known as Quatro and where conditions matched those of the notorious prison in Johannesburg known as Number Four, in which "beatings, starvation and torture were commonplace" (Ellis and Sechaba 1992, 129).

David, we learn, was imprisoned for supporting the mutineers' demands, earning himself "days of interrogation and so forth by the big men from security" (Wicomb 2000, 195). Dulcie was apparently detained after David's release. Having admitted as much, David attempts to erase it from his story: "All that stuff, the things that happened in another country, has nothing to do with this story," he protests feebly before falling silent and then, to the narrator's horror, charging out of the room, having seen "before [his] very eyes, the screen full-bleed with Dulcie" (Wicomb 2000, 201).

Although David remains resolutely silent about his experience in Quatro, his disfigured body speaks what he as a disciplined cadre cannot and will not utter (see TRC 1998, 2.4 par. 160; Wicomb 2000, 11). His torture at Quatro is further inscribed through his persistent tinnitus, which Driver notes "must partly refer to the practice at Quatro of *ukumpompa*, blows and claps on inflated cheeks which often caused ear damage" (Driver 2000, 237). Through David's torture, the text approaches Dulcie's and vice versa; in one of the scenes of her torture, "silence is blasted at high speed" into Dulcie's ears (Wicomb 2000, 199).

At the same time, narratives of coercive sexual intercourse and of sexual torture are threaded into the plot. In Sally's story, as noted, we encounter the "unspoken part of a girl's training" in the antiapartheid struggle (Wicomb 2000, 123). As with abuses committed in camps such as Quatro, sexual abuse did, indeed, remain largely unspoken within the Truth and Reconciliation Commission's (TRC's) public hearings, which aimed to produce national unity during the political transition (see Amupadhi 1998; TRC 1998, 4.10 par. 44). These silences meet in the figure of Dulcie, who has unspeakable violence perpetrated against her in the 1980s at Quatro and again in the novel's transitional present.

Although the ritualistic act of giving voice has dominated the postwar aftermath—most notably in the TRC—the novel urges us to chart instead the meanings produced in the space between voice and silence. Questions of speech and silence are both pertinent and urgent in relation to sexual violence, which functions as a shaming act that imposes a complicit silence on its victims, hence the value granted to breaking the silence. However, giving voice to or recuperating obscured voices presents its own dangers, as Sabine Sielke points out: "In its attempt to break the silence on sexual violence, the (feminist) deployment of rape has nurtured its own silences that are as meaningful as the silences with which dominant culture has veiled sexual violence" (Sielke 2002, 4).

The national discourse of sexual violence during the aftermath was shaped by the TRC. The fabric of *David's Story* is rent by some of the silences that emerge from the TRC's engagement, or lack thereof, with sexual violence in order to express that which cannot be enunciated in discourse. As the TRC became increasingly anxious about its failure to capture both the story of women and the story of sexual violence, it began to conflate the two: a "woman's" story was reduced to one of sexual violence, and sexual violence was identified as a defining female experience (see Ross 2003, 20–26, 87–93). While only 40 percent of the TRC's cases of sexual abuse, where the victim's sex was specified, concerned women, "Sexual Abuse" is a central category in the chapter dedicated to the Special Hearings on Women in the *Final Report* (see TRC 1998, 4.10 pars. 44–69).

Thus, the concern with sexual violence, while ostensibly laudable, re-sulted in familiar representations of women as passive victims and obscured their activism and militancy in the antiapartheid struggle. Such articula-tions of sexual violence reproduced conventional figurations of gender and of war. In the transitional discourse of nation building and national recovery, sexual violence was produced as an experience peculiar to women; in postapartheid civil society, rape continued to be defined as the nonconsensual penetration of the penis into the vagina (South African Law Commission 2003).[6]

One of the silences nurtured in efforts to give voice to rape is thus the gendering of rape as something that happens only to women, which, in turn, produces women as victims of a special kind. If a failure to articulate rape is a matter of concern, perhaps so too are attempts to speak about the raped body within these discursive constraints, which produce women as vulnerable victims in need of male protection and thus reiterate the gendered figurations of war.

Wicomb steps out of discourse in order to destabilize these categories by ungendering rape and torture. Strikingly, in a text so saturated with undercurrents of (often sexualized) violence, the word *rape* appears only

[6] As I was completing this article, a landmark high court ruling began to amend South African common law by extending the definition of rape to include "non-consensual sexual penetration of the vagina and the anus, regardless of whether the victim was male or female" (Venter 2006, 1). Nonetheless, the judgment remains centered upon female anatomical vulnerability, having been reached in response to the anal penetration of a nine-year-old girl-child and with reference to the "close proximity" of the vaginal and anal orifices (Venter 2006, 1). The sentence is currently under appeal.

once, pointedly prefixed by *not*, when we are invited to witness what happens to Dulcie: "On the very first visit, one of them, the wiry one who seems to be in charge, spoke: Not rape, that will teach her nothing, leave nothing; rape's too good for her kind, waving the electrodes as another took off her nightclothes" (Wicomb 2000, 178). The violator's words—"not rape"—veil the sexualized nature of Dulcie's abuse, evident in the removal of her nightclothes. If referential language fails us here, an allusive system of internal cross-referencing conveys the unspeakable, drawing connections between the raped body and the reduction to flesh of the tortured body.

During her torture, Dulcie "run[s] through the vocabulary of recipe books, that which is done to food, to flesh—tenderize, baste, sear, seal, sizzle, score, chop," as her own flesh is seared with hot pokers (Wicomb 2000, 178). When her torturers encourage her to commit suicide by driving off Chapman's Peak, which is a path David later follows, Dulcie imagines feeling "that macerated flesh grow weightless in the water, dissolve in the white spray that beats against the rock. Atomised at Chapman's Peak" (Wicomb 2000, 180). Her thoughts resonate with the description of Sally after coercive sex with her MK trainer: she "found her body dissolving, changing its solid state in the water through which she then moved effortlessly" (Wicomb 2000, 123). Thus do the elusive but highly allusive properties of textuality provide a means of "saying that which you can't utter," to return to the epigraph. If the damage performed on bodies remains unutterable in available discourse, it is spoken through the fragmented and damaged form of the novel itself, which, in turn, creates such allusive echoes and mimetically presents the disfigured bodies that cannot be represented.[7]

Similarly, while the words *not rape* in the above quotation strike through what is happening to Dulcie, the description of her electrode-waving violator as the "wiry one" redirects our focus to the myriad ways in which bodies are violated and asks how we can distinguish between penetrative rape and the torture technique of attaching electrodes to gen-

---

[7] I am indebted here to Lynn Higgins and Brenda Silver's study of rape and representation in which they foreground the necessity of "restoring rape to the literal" by rematerializing the violence so often masked in rhetorical renderings of the raped body. Such a process, they argue, calls attention to "the recurrent motif of disfiguration . . . both in its rhetorical and physical senses (and the ways in which the first hides the second), as both textual and corporeal deformation or mutilation," and recognizes "the secret ways in which representation is linked to the physical, and damaged stories can represent damaged bodies" (Higgins and Silver 1991, 4, 6).

itals. In this way, Wicomb complicates the concept of rape and draws attention to the unspeakable things that are done to bodies, both male and female, in the name of freedom.

Troubling the temporal boundary delineating the "new era" and separating the war zone from civil society, the novel proposes, moreover, that the violence performed on Dulcie is in large part a postrevolutionary backlash against a powerful female militant. Her story suggests that women who have fought for freedom may not, themselves, experience that freedom. The betrayal and appropriation of her revolutionary labor are pointed to in the only passage that stems from Dulcie herself. Dulcie had told David about an incident during the liberation war when, in the face of shrinking rations, she suggests taking honey from a bees' nest. Her comrades ridicule her, "wondering if she were man enough to do it by herself." Dulcie persists through the stings, "since it was a matter of honour, and manages to fill a basket with dripping honeycombs." Afterward, "she swelled up into a roly-poly, hands like loaves of risen dough, eyes buried beneath layers of swellings, mouth a drunken pout, face an undulating hillock of yellow-brown flesh. For several days she writhed in agony, unable to take anything except water. When she recovered sufficiently to try a honeycomb, she found that the others had eaten every scrap of it, had left her nothing" (Wicomb 2000, 82–83).

Dulcie, who knows that "fucking women was a way of preventing them from rising in the Movement" (Wicomb 2000, 179) and who takes up the challenge of being "man enough" to gather honey, is stung by bees until her figure swells, rising like dough, while her comrades devour her share of the honey. In order to participate in the national liberation struggle, of which this passage presents a neat allegory, Dulcie has to prove herself "man enough" to step out of the figuration of woman as fragile victim in need of male protection—and must eschew the performance of female vulnerability enacted through the script of sexual availability, which, in turn, guarantees such protection—while being left nothing of the freedom for which she has fought.

The narrator reworks this revelation in an inventive fragment "about Bronwyn the Brown Witch who can do anything at all": "She uses her magical powers to get her friends out of scrapes, to feed the poor, to stave off hurricanes and earthquakes, to drive back the enemy, until one day her friends, the sticks in the forest, come clattering together, lay themselves down on top of each other until they are a mighty woodpile. There is no way out. Bronwyn the Witch must die on the stake" (Wicomb 2000, 203). Clearly shaken, David acknowledges the truth his amanuensis has touched upon: "Yes, she's grown too big for her boots and they've had enough of her. She must give up her power, hand over her uniform, make way for the big men" (Wicomb 2000, 204).

The novel alludes here to Joan of Arc, "the image of female heroism," to quote the subtitle of Marina Warner's (1981) study. One of the roles in which Joan has been cast is that of "dangerous witch" (Warner 1981, 8); her burning at the stake remains the classic narrative of the sacrifice and betrayal of women who have fought exemplarily in men's wars. The narrator imagines Dulcie's response to her postwar conundrum as follows: "She has taken her training as a revolutionary seriously—the vows, the beliefs—without, some would say, the necessary pinch of salt. Has her life not been devoted to resisting tyranny? Ah, she knows that she has done it too well for a girl, a woman, but she would, and she clenches her teeth, do it again and again" (Wicomb 2000, 180). Dulcie, then, matches the spectacular defiance of Joan of Arc before the court convened to decide her fate for having "done it too well for a girl": "If she was free, she would do exactly as she had done, all over again," Warner paraphrases the court records (1981, 145).

Whereas Dulcie resolutely refuses to "hand over her uniform," Joan's court records expose how "she would rather die than relinquish these clothes [the masculine attire of a knight]" (quoted in Warner 1981, 145). Thus, once again, Dulcie embodies the gendered confusion that sees the narrator wishing to inscribe her in the middle voice. As Warner observes of Joan of Arc, "Through her transvestism, she abrogated the destiny of womankind. She could thereby transcend her sex. . . . At the same time, by never pretending to be other than a woman and a maid, she was usurping a man's function but shaking off the trammels of his sex altogether to occupy a different, third order, neither male nor female" (Warner 1981, 145–46). Dulcie's figure, which remains uncontained both in and by *David's Story*, furthermore resists recuperation into the figure of the ideal, chaste woman, which became Joan of Arc's posthumous fate. Oozing from her orifices onto the narrator's lawn, Dulcie is presented to us at the end of the novel as the figurative opposite of Joan's virginal, saintly form. The novel avoids accommodating her in the idealized codes through which women have been elevated to the category of the heroic; instead it insists on Dulcie's discursive excess.[8]

---

[8] Gillian Gane has read in this concluding image of Dulcie such a recuperative figuration by arguing that she has been "metamorphosed into [an emblem] of the land" (Gane 2002, 110); I have elsewhere argued that such a reading misreads Dulcie as a naturalistic body by ignoring the ways in which her comparison to the black-eyed Suzie flowers presents her, instead, as a "body of writing" (see Samuelson 2007).

Negotiating concealment: Veiling and visibility, (de)mobilization and domesticity

> Concealment . . . becomes a trope for the woman writer who has to ne-
> gotiate the conflicting loyalties of race and gender.
> —Wicomb 1990, 41

Before the book's final scene, in which Dulcie's body "weep[s] like a gargoyle . . . from every orifice, including the man made ones" (Wicomb 2000, 82), her wounds are carefully hidden beneath her khaki, placed precisely by her torturers where they will not be seen. Dulcie complies, veiling her disfigurement beneath clothing that symbolizes her dedication to the cause of freedom and her belief in the necessity of violent struggle to effect it, as well as her refusal to advance this freedom by playing a woman's part. This act of concealment signals both her repudiation of a certain kind of femininity and her commitment to the national liberation struggle, which also silences David and prevents him from revealing un-speakable horrors.

Dulcie tellingly associates her act of concealment with that of women who hide AK-47s under their garments: "They came in traditional dress, gaudy green shifts under pink crossover pinafores draped over straw bol-sters for buttressing the hips and buttocks into exotic insect shapes. When they left days later with piles of wood balanced on their heads, they filed past her searching gaze, their bodies a mere hint of movement within the sculpted shapes, the AK-47s perfectly concealed" (Wicomb 2000, 19). Here, the novel establishes cross-references between women couriers, who are useful to the war effort precisely because they are seemingly invisible in the war zone, and Dulcie's disfigured body, clothed in khaki in order to visibly insist on her presence as a woman warrior in the context of demobilization, while veiling the disfigurements that give the lie to lib-eration.

This trope of concealment is explored in detail in Frantz Fanon's essay "Algeria Unveiled" (1959). In Fanon's analysis, the veil, as marker of both culture and cultural opacity, functions as a scopic barrier, frustrating the surveillance of the colonial gaze. When women joined the Algerian in-dependence struggle as revolutionaries, they unveiled themselves. Their bare faces, heads, and limbs created the disguise enabling them to pass unnoticed in the French quarters. Once the French became wise to this tactic, the women again veiled themselves, concealing weapons beneath their customary covering, as do Dulcie's female couriers. In Fanon's ac-count, according to Diana Fuss, "the woman's body is the contested ideological battleground, overburdened and saturated with meaning" (Fuss 1995, 150). That Dulcie's body is similarly posed as "saturated" with meaning is evident in the final scene, when it oozes its excess on the narrator's lawn. This scene, in which *goggas* (insects) crawl and buzz over Dulcie's body, is in turn prefigured in the "exotic insect shapes" of the women couriers.

Wicomb encourages us to rethink Fanon's mapping of gender liberation upon the topography of an anticolonial revolution. In Dulcie, Wicomb collapses the second and third stages of revolution he describes. Khaki fatigues rather than traditional garb veil her body. Caught between two systems of surveillance—apartheid and ANC intelligence—Dulcie must assent to the covering of her wounds in order to align herself with one, even as she is violated by both.

Again the narrator's intention to cast Dulcie in the middle voice is revealing, along with the narrator's rueful admission that it is "so un-fashionably linked with the sixties and with French letters" (Wicomb 2000, 197). The allusion, one assumes, is to Roland Barthes: distinguishing between middle and active voices, Barthes refers to "the verb *to sacrifice*": "*to sacrifice* (ritually) is active if the priest sacrifices the victim in my place for me, and it is middle voice if, taking the knife from the priest's hands, I make the sacrifice for myself" (Barthes 1986, 142). Dulcie, as the text shows, makes the sacrifice of and for herself, and it is this sacrifice, along with her relentless confounding of gendered categories and configurations, that renders the novel so ethically complex.

Dulcie cannot be figured within a simplistic gendered binary of victim versus perpetrator. When first introduced, she is shown washing blood from her hands and rubbing balm into her wounds. Women may be victims of war, as their disfigured bodies suggest, yet they, too, have bloodstained hands, which are veiled beneath conventional figurations of war. Through its methodology of dis-figuration the text proposes more complex repre-sentations of both gender and war as it maps out the unenunciable position of the woman warrior.

Dulcie's hand washing distinguishes her from stereotypical represen-tations of women as victims, without obscuring the violence enacted upon her; her sacrifice in the middle voice can be read both as a complicit silence and as a refusal to abandon her revolutionary subject position in exchange for male protection. It could be understood, in other words, as a refusal to assent to the domesticity into which previously militant women, such as David's wife, Sally, have been subsumed during a postwar backlash against women that aims to restore the gendered division of spheres par-tially disrupted by the liberation struggle.

The source of this backlash is suggested in Fanon's own anxious phrasing, when he says of the unveiled Algerian woman that she "penetrates a little further into the flesh of the Revolution" (Fanon 1959, 54). As Anne McClintock notes, this "odd image suggests an unbidden fear of emasculation, a dread that the arming of women might entail a fatal unmanning of Algerian men" (1995, 367). Reveiling themselves in a revolutionary gesture during the anticolonial war, the Algerian women of whom Fanon writes consented to their demilitarization and redomestication after independence, when violence against unveiled women created "a climate of fear that was designed to force women's return to the household" (Hatem 1993, 31). Wicomb's complex engagement with the Fanonian trope of concealment foregrounds the dangers to women that Fanon himself was unable to see, as he extolled the Algerian liberation struggle as an arena for gender liberation.

Notably, then, the redomestication of Sally is described in terms similar to the torture of Dulcie. Once again the allusive properties of textuality provide the modus operandi of the novel's analysis. When David and Sally, who met as comrades-in-arms, marry, Sally is summarily released from underground work and returned to the domestic sphere of community matters, household management, and, of course, reproduction. Redomesticated, Sally becomes "an emaciated scarecrow of a woman with uneven, vegetal tufts of hair and liverish spots on her brown skin" (Wicomb 2000, 14); we are told a few pages later that the torture marks burned into Dulcie's skin leave behind "a liverish red crinkled surface of flesh" (Wicomb 2000, 19). One explanation for Dulcie's silence in the text, then, is that both her rape/torture and the redomestication presented in Sally's story enact forms of violence on a woman's sense of self. Dulcie's dilemma is that prevailing discourses of rape threaten to domesticate her should she speak within them.

The novel pushes its analysis further to consider the ways in which the codes of marriage approximate those of the military, just as it has considered the ways in which torture and rape approximate love. Sally and David's domestic life begins as the cover—or veil—behind which they carry out surveillance operations, "inventing personas that spoke quietly about subjects such as gardening or holiday resorts or even a baby called Tracy" (Wicomb 2000, 13); later, however, it becomes the substance of Sally's existence as she is shifted from the role of cadre and comrade to that of mother and wife. Suspecting David of infidelity but unable to question him, Sally busies herself with mundane tasks, reflecting: "It is a trick she has learnt some time ago, part of her training: to block out all else while she concentrates on physical tasks. . . . So, she thinks, and not without bitterness, it has not all been wasted, even for a wife that training has its uses" (Wicomb 2000, 31). Later she realizes that "it is simply a matter of transferring the codes of the Movement to her marriage, for the two can never be separated," and thus she takes up the "intended's" stance of "waiting," donning bright lipstick, "her red badge of courage," which recalls her identifying marker of a red scarf during her days as an MK cadre and again blurs the boundaries between war and domesticity (Wicomb 2000, 172).

For many women combatants in the MK, military life disappointingly approximated domestic life, since "normalcy" was anxiously produced in the very midst of war. Cock's interviews with ex-combatants reveal that while for some the MK offered a space of gender equality, others recall rape and "sexism" in the form of "protectionism," which one informant interprets as encoding a demand for "women to be docile and subservient" (Cock 1994, 160–61). Following the official suspension of the armed struggle, female guerrillas were even more firmly "pushed back into the roles of the protected and defended" (162). In the period in which *David's Story* is set, hundreds of MK cadres were selected for training abroad in order to prepare them for leadership positions in the new national army; no women were included among their numbers (see Cock 1994, 163–64). To unveil Dulcie's disfigurements in such a milieu and within available discourse may mean for her to figure herself as a womanly victim in need of male protection. In this way, her unveiling may further the cause of new postliberation, but fundamentally unliberating, productions of "woman."

Wicomb offers a complicated response to the figurations and disfigurements of women in the war zone and its aftermath. The veil beneath which Dulcie conceals her wounds—or silences her rape/torture—is the khaki uniform of the MK guerrilla rather than the traditional markers of domesticity or modesty. The latter, according to Deniz Kandiyoti, signify a "patriarchal bargain" by which women indicate to men that they are "worthy of protection" (Kandiyoti 1988, 283). Such a femininity functions to underpin a militarism in which women are then not permitted to participate actively. In the novel, military garb is compared to the traditional coverings that encase the female body and is simultaneously distinguished from them and the performance of vulnerable femininity that they represent. If the latter is apparently set outside the war zone, the novel suggests that feminist discourses need to account for the myriad ways in which women are conscripted into militarism in order to forge a discourse able to enunciate the figure of the woman warrior.

This figure, embodied in Dulcie, cracks open the discourses and figurements of femininity and allows for such inquiries, which in turn throw light on Dulcie's attachment to the khaki that conceals her disfigurements. When women's lives beyond the combat zone are inevitably militarized, as Enloe suggests, khaki may indeed "become you" (Enloe 1989). For Dulcie as an ex-combatant, speaking out and unveiling her disfigurement—revealing the wounds concealed beneath her khaki—might entail that she acquiesce to the demand that she "give up her power, hand over her uniform, give way for the big men" (Wicomb 2000, 204), that she, in other words, be figured as "female." Silenced by a political movement that does not recognize its betrayal of her, and that no longer requires her services, Dulcie's dis-figured body allows us to read the ways in which discourses of war and of sexual violence depend on and reproduce the figure of the vulnerable female body. This figure, in turn, delegitimizes female militancy and, by extension, given the foundational national myth of the heroic antiapartheid guerrilla, deauthorizes female citizenship in the liberated state.

Department of English
University of Stellenbosch

References

Amupadhi, Tangeni. 1998. "TRC Ducks Quatro." *Mail and Guardian Online*, June 26. http://archive.mg.co.za.

Barthes, Roland. 1986. *The Rustle of Language*. Trans. Richard Howard. New York: Hill & Wang.

Brownmiller, Susan. 1976. *Against Our Will: Men, Women, and Rape*. New York: Bantam.

Cock, Jacklyn. 1991. *Colonels and Cadres: War and Gender in South Africa*. Cape Town: Oxford University Press.

———. 1994. "Women and the Military: Implications for Demilitarization in the 1990s in South Africa." *Gender and Society* 8(2):152–69.

Conrad, Joseph. (1899) 1973. *Heart of Darkness*. Harmondsworth, UK: Penguin.

D'Amico, Francine. 1998. "Feminist Perspectives on Women Warriors." In *The Women and War Reader*, ed. Lois Ann Lorentzen and Jennifer Turpin, 119–25. New York: New York University Press.

Derrida, Jacques. 1973. *Speech and Phenomena and Other Essays on Husserl's Theory of Signs*. Trans. David B. Allison. Evanston, IL: Northwestern University Press.

Driver, Dorothy. 2000. "Afterword." In Wicomb 2000, 215–71.

———. 2005. "Truth, Reconciliation, Gender: The South African Truth and Reconciliation Commission and Black Women's Intellectual History." *Australian Feminist Studies* 20(47):219–29.

Ellis, Stephen, and Tsepo Sechaba. 1992. *Comrades against Apartheid: The ANC and the South African Communist Party in Exile.* Bloomington: Indiana University Press.

Enloe, Cynthia. 1989. *Does Khaki Become You? The Militarization of Women's Lives.* 2nd ed. London: Pandora.

Fanon, Frantz. 1959. "Algeria Unveiled." In his *A Dying Colonialism.* Trans. Haakon Chevalier, 35–59. New York: Grove Weidenfeld.

Foucault, Michel. 1972. *The Archaeology of Knowledge.* Trans. A. M. Sheridan Smith. New York: Tavistock.

Fuss, Diana. 1995. *Identification Papers.* New York: Routledge.

Gane, Gillian. 2002. "Unspeakable Injuries in *Disgrace* and *David's Story.*" *Kunapipi* 24(1–2):101–13.

Goldblatt, Beth, and Sheila Meintjes. 1998. "South African Women Demand the Truth." In *What Women Do in Wartime: Gender and Conflict in Africa,* ed. Meredeth Turshen and Clotilde Twagiramariya, 27–61. London: Zed.

Gqola, Pumla Dineo. 2001. "Contradictory Locations: Blackwomen and the Discourse of the Black Consciousness Movement (BCM) in South Africa." *Meridians: feminism, race, transnationalism* 2(1):130–52.

Hatem, Mervat. 1993. "Toward the Development of Post-Islamist and Post-nationalist Feminist Discourses in the Middle East." In *Arab Women: Old Boundaries, New Frontiers,* ed. Judith E. Tucker, 29–48. Bloomington: Indiana University Press.

Herman, Judith Lewis. 2001. *Trauma and Recovery: From Domestic Abuse to Political Terror.* 2nd ed. London: Pandora.

Higgins, Lynn A., and Brenda R. Silver. 1991. "Introduction: Reading Rape." In their *Rape and Representation,* 1–11. New York: Columbia University Press.

Hunter, Eva. 1993. "Zoë Wicomb, Interviewed by Eva Hunter." In *Between the Lines II: Interviews with Nadine Gordimer, Menan du Plessis, Zoë Wicomb, Lauretta Ngcobo,* ed. Eva Hunter and Craig MacKenzie, 79–96. Grahamstown, South Africa: National English Literary Museum.

Kandiyoti, Deniz. 1988. "Bargaining with Patriarchy." *Gender and Society* 2(3): 274–90.

Kolodny, Annette. 1980. "Dancing through the Minefield: Some Observations on the Theory, Practice, and Politics of Feminist Literary Criticism." *Feminist Studies* 6(1):1–25.

LaCapra, Dominick. 2001. *Writing History, Writing Trauma.* Baltimore: Johns Hopkins University Press.

Lewis, Desirée. 1994. "Women and Gender in South Africa." In *South Africa: The Challenge of Change,* ed. Vincent Mapai, 158–72. Harare, Zimbabwe: SAPES.

Macdonald, Sharon. 1987. "Drawing the Lines—Gender, Peace, and War: An Introduction." In *Images of Women in Peace and War: Cross-Cultural and Historical Perspectives,* ed. Sharon Macdonald, Pat Holden, and Shirley Ardener, 1–26. London: Macmillan.

Marais, Mike. 2005. "Bastards and Bodies in Zoë Wicomb's *David's Story.*" *Journal of Commonwealth Literature* 40(3):21–36.

Marcus, Sharon. 1992. "Fighting Bodies, Fighting Words: A Theory and Politics of Rape Prevention." In *Feminists Theorize the Political*, ed. Judith Butler and Joan W. Scott, 385–403. New York: Routledge.

McClintock, Anne. 1995. *Imperial Leather: Race, Gender, and Sexuality in the Colonial Contest.* New York: Routledge.

Meintjes, Sheila, Anu Pillay, and Meredeth Turshen. 2001. "There Is No Aftermath for Women." In their *The Aftermath: Women in Post-conflict Transformation*, 3–18. London: Zed.

Mngqibisa, Olefile Samuel. 1993. "Sexual Abuse of Young Women in the ANC Camps." *Searchlight South Africa* 3(3):11–16.

Moffett, Helen. 2006. "'These Women, They Force Us to Rape Them': Rape as Narrative of Social Control in Post-apartheid South Africa." *Journal of Southern African Studies* 32(1):129–44.

Nyoka, Mtutuzeli. 2004. *I Speak to the Silent.* Pietermartizburg, South Africa: University of KwaZulu-Natal Press.

Olver, Thomas. 2002. "Zoë Wicomb Interviewed on Writing and Nation." *Journal of Literary Studies* 18(1–2):182–98.

Ross, Fiona C. 2003. *Bearing Witness: Women and the Truth and Reconciliation Commission in South Africa.* London: Pluto.

Samuelson, Meg. 2002. "The Rainbow Womb: Rape and Race in South African Fiction of the Transition." *Kunapipi* 24(1–2): 88–100.

———. 2003. "Cracked Vases and Untidy Seams: Narrative Structure and Closure in the Truth and Reconciliation Commission and South African Fiction." *Current Writing* 15(2):63–76.

———. 2007. *Remembering the Nation, Dismembering Women? Stories of the South African Transition.* Pietermartizburg, South Africa: University of KwaZulu-Natal Press.

Shikola, Teckla. 1998. "We Left Our Shoes Behind." In *What Women Do in Wartime: Gender and Conflict in Africa*, ed. Meredeth Turshen and Clotilde Twagiramariya, 138–49. London: Zed.

Sielke, Sabine. 2002. *Reading Rape: The Rhetoric of Sexual Violence in American Literature and Culture, 1790–1990.* Princeton, NJ: Princeton University Press.

South African Law Commission. 2003. "Press Statement: South African Law Commission's Project 107; Sexual Offenses." http://www.doj.gov.za/2004dojsite/m_statements/2003/2003%2001%2021_salc%20107.htm.

TRC (Truth and Reconciliation Commission). 1998. *Truth and Reconciliation Commission of South Africa: Report.* 5 vols. Cape Town: TRC. http://www.polity.org.za/html/govdocs/commissions/index.html.

Turshen, Meredeth. 1998. "Women's War Stories." In *What Women Do in Wartime: Gender and Conflict in Africa*, ed. Meredeth Turshen and Clotilde Twagiramariya, 1–26. London: Zed.

Venter, Zelda. 2006. "Landmark Court Ruling Recognises Men Can Be Raped." *Cape Times*, July 26, 1, 3.

Warner, Marina. 1981. *Joan of Arc: The Image of Female Heroism.* Berkeley: University of California Press.

Wicomb, Zoë. 1990. "To Hear the Variety of Discourses." *Current Writing* 2(1): 35–44.

———. 2000. *David's Story.* Cape Town: Kwela; New York: Feminist Press.

Dorit Naaman

Brides of Palestine/Angels of Death: Media, Gender, and Performance in the Case of the Palestinian Female Suicide Bombers

In January 2002, Wafa Idris, a twenty-seven-year-old Palestinian woman, strapped ten kilograms of explosives to her body and killed herself and two Israelis on a crowded Jerusalem street. Idris was the first Palestinian female suicide bomber, to be followed by nine others and several dozen failed attempts. The female suicide bomber is a social phenomenon that has left Israel and the West shocked, signaling (in both Arab and Western views) an escalation in the conflict. Idris was not the first Palestinian woman to be recruited for the fight for national liberation, as women have taken part in the Palestinian struggle from its onset, with some, including Leila Khaled and Dalal el Moughrabi, having partaken in highly publicized hijacking operations. Idris was not the first female suicide bomber either, with Hezbollah and the Tamil Tigers utilizing female suicide bombers since the 1980s. The reactions to Idris's actions vary widely, as labels such as *martyr*, *hero*, *monster*, and *terrorist* indicate. But reactions in the Arab world, in Israel, and in the West cannot be reduced to simple labels. Instead, the reactions all highlight junctures of ideological crises in the perceived roles of women in armed struggles, religion, and traditional gendered settings. Particularly in the Arab world these actions were not simply hailed but actually debated—pragmatically, morally, and, most notably, religiously. For instance, Sheikh Ahmed Yassin, spiritual leader of Hamas until his assassination by Israel in March 2004, objected to the inclusion of women initially, then altered his principled position, and in 2004 Hamas sent its first female suicide bomber, Reem el Riyashi.[1] The

I would like to thank the many individuals who gave me criticism on previous drafts of this article; thanks also for research and editorial assistance from Paul Hanlon, Lisa Davies, and Pamela Robinson. The core of this article was developed during a generous Ford fellowship at the Five Colleges Women's Studies Research Center at Mt. Holyoke College. Finally, to two anonymous readers, my many thanks for reading the article so carefully and making critical suggestions.

[1] For Yassin's and others' positions on the matter, see MEMRI (2002).

[*Signs: Journal of Women in Culture and Society* 2007, vol. 32, no. 4]

debates in the Arab world around Western-style feminism, religion, and the roles women should take in armed struggles are complex and, I would argue, push the already highly charged gender debate to its logical limits.

In this article I focus on the issue of terrorism—especially its performative aspect—and how media representations deal with the loaded image of the Palestinian female suicide bomber and her message. With regard to Western media, my aim is to show the constructed nature of the label *terrorist*, especially as it stands in stark contrast to the highly coded and constructed label *woman*. My claim is that both terms represent ideological expectations of performance rather than reflect actual actions or natural (maybe even essential) states of being in the world. In the case of the Arab media, the term *shaheeda* (martyr) enables people to bypass the loaded deviation from traditional gendered roles and as such mythicizes actions taken rather than engaging with their gender politics. In contrast to news media, filmic representations from Israel and Palestine provide a much more nuanced and complex view of terrorism and the place of women in it. Those images sometimes challenge media stereotypes and sometimes employ them to diverse political ends.[2]

Gender and war

War generally brings with it images that fall into normative gender categories: men are fighters, women the victims. Images of women and children as widows and orphans fleeing war zones to become refugees, or media focus on rape as a war tactic in Rwanda and the former Yugoslavia, figure women as fragile, vulnerable, and in need of defense by men. Rape and forced pregnancies in particular bring forth issues of ethnic purity and position women as vehicles for the production of the next generation of ethnically pure fighters but as defenseless in and of themselves.[3] Furthermore, one aspect of any occupation (and colonization) is the perceived feminization of the occupied men. Men who were used to being sovereign

---

[2] Although the purpose of this study is to look at news media in general, space limitations guided me to limit the scope of the news sources for this article to print media. My selection focuses on leading English-language newspapers from Israel, the United States, Canada, and Britain, which I generally call Western media (although I am aware that reports in German and French might provide a different picture). This article does not attempt a comprehensive media review but uses the examples chosen to substantiate a theoretical argument.

[3] For an extended discussion, see Coomaraswamy (2003). There are also reports of women joining the Liberation Tamil Tiger Eelam in Sri Lanka as a way to defend themselves against the danger of rape by Indian soldiers of the Indian Peacekeeping Force units. I thank Neloufer De Mel for pointing this out.

agents are now subject to the rules, regulations, and whims of the occupier. As the economic situation in the occupied Palestinian territories deteriorated and as the limitations on freedom of movement increased, men were stripped of their stereotypically masculine qualities—independence, courage, ability to provide economically, and protection of the weak (women and children in particular). A video art piece titled *Chic Point* (2003) addresses this feminization by designing men's clothes for the checkpoints. In a fashion show setup, men model shirts with zippers, fishnet, clear material, or patterned holes, all meant to simplify the crossing of the checkpoints. The models all conform to so-called metrosexual ideals (straight men dressing like gay men), and together the catwalk setup, the flirtatious gaze at the camera, and the clothes themselves intentionally blur the categories of masculine and feminine. The video then cuts into documentary black-and-white still photographs of men stripping for soldiers' inspection in the middle of checkpoints, often in front of their entire families. The piece at once exposes the humiliation inherent in the situation while at the same time calling attention to the negative gendered attributes of associating men's humiliation and lack of sovereignty with femininity and submissiveness.

When women opt to fight alongside men, they challenge the dichotomy of woman as victim/man as defender. Women fighters are physically strong, are active (therefore agents), and, most important, are willing to kill (hence, they are violent). They challenge not only the images of women as victims of war but also the traditional patriarchal binary opposition that postulates women as physically and emotionally weak and incapable of determining and defending the course of their own lives. As a result, women fighters have often been represented—especially in mass media—as deviant from prescribed forms of femininity, forms that emphasize a woman's delicacy and fragility but also her generosity, caring nature, motherliness, and sensitivity to others' needs.[4]

Suicide operations complicate these stereotypical dynamics further—not only does the woman willingly sacrifice herself, but her actions also carry a performative aspect typical of terrorist actions by substate groups. Since these groups do not have large and well-equipped armies, they organize their political violence as spectacles that attract media and public attention. When women partake in such operations, their performance of violence and political agency—so drastically different from that of typical female roles in both news and entertainment media—enhances the sense of perplexity, fear, and aversion to the perpetrators of the acts. For instance,

---

[4] A good feminist analysis of those stereotypes can be found in Heinecken (2003).

in response to Ayat Akhras's suicide operation, Anne Applebaum writes, "Not only was she not male, she was not overtly religious, not estranged from her family, not openly associated with any radical groups. She can hardly be described as a woman without a future. She was young, she was a good student, and she was engaged to be married" (2002).

Relying on the stereotypical gap between traditional feminine qualities (i.e., engaged to be married, good student) and political, violent, and supposedly masculine actions, journalists and analysts alike could not explain the phenomenon. The solution was to search for a personal explanation. For instance, after Idris's suicide attack, Western media focused on the fact that Idris was infertile and had allowed her husband to marry another woman, watching him live nearby as he became a father. It was claimed that she was unhappy and, as she could not bear children, that her life was unworthy to her.[5] This explanation is typical, but in many of the cases that followed, the logic of such explanations is unfounded. Some of the women were happy, engaged to be married (Ayat Akhras), good students (Dareen Abu Aisheh), professionals (Hanadi Jaridat), and mothers (Reem el Riyashi). What this attempt at explanation exposes is how gendered the discussion around the female suicide bombers is. While the dozens of male suicide bombers' identities and life stories are hardly ever delved into, their reasons are assumed to be clear and grounded in both political and religious ideology. In contrast, a woman as a suicide bomber seems so oxymoronic that an individualized psychological explanation for the deviation must be found.

However, this sort of psychological explanation fails time and again. The image of woman as the symbolic nurturer, healer, and spiritual mother of the nation is challenged beyond repair, a rupture that is dealt with in the Arab world quite differently than it is in the West. Idris in particular highlights this symbolic contradiction; in her spare time Idris volunteered as a medic on an ambulance, caring for the wounded of the intifada. How did the "angel of mercy" become an "angel of death," asked one headline (Beaumont 2002a). Indeed, the idea that a woman who heals people could turn around and kill others seemed so improbable that it could indicate

---

[5] Fawzia Sheikh (2006) writes: "In Idris' case, Israeli security forces at the time had noted her husband rejected her for being unable to conceive, and as a result she was alienated by a conservative society in which marriage and children are the norm." Peter Beaumont (2002b) writes: "We rationalised that as a woman whose marriage had broken up in a traditional society that somehow she was an outsider, and vulnerable to the persuasion of those who send the bombers out."

to Western media and society only that something was wrong with this particular individual or else that there is something monstrous about the society that produces such a person.[6] In the Arab press the discourse generally focuses on the harshness of the occupation, which drives women to defend the land and the people. Although suicide bombing is met with ambivalence in the Arab world, it is nevertheless understood as an extreme means derived from an extreme situation.[7]

In his feature films, Palestinian director Elia Suleiman bluntly addresses the ways in which the Palestinian woman has become a kind of political femme fatale. In *Divine Intervention* (2002), Suleiman shows the narrator's girlfriend, as she crosses the checkpoint, refusing to stop for the soldiers' inspection. The woman is wearing a short, tight, pink dress and is not carrying anything, so she clearly is not a risk of being a suicide bomber, yet the soldiers point their guns at her. In an extended slow sequence, the woman walks through the checkpoint seductively and assertively while the soldiers objectify her through their guns' viewfinders, but at the same time they fear her. This sequence is particularly poignant since the woman's appearance, hairstyle, and dress are all Western in style; in this way she mocks the idea that (potential) terrorists are Muslim fundamentalists.[8] But even more important, the woman can easily pass as an Israeli, and therefore the danger that Suleiman's mute female protagonist poses clearly is not in political violence but in her challenge to the concept

[6] For instance, Olivia Ward of the *Toronto Star* writes: "The participation of women and, sometimes, teenage girls in an increasing number of deadly acts has horrified the international public, and a wave of revulsion has rolled through the media at female violence in its most ruthless form. Yet, the extent and causes of women's violence are uncertain and remain unpredictable in a world in which aggression has been the province of men, and violent women considered mentally unbalanced or possessed by unimaginable evil" (2004, A6).

[7] For a good overview of the discourse in Arab media surrounding suicide operations and martyrdom, see Hasso (2005). In the conclusion to the article, Frances S. Hasso writes: "My analysis and understanding of suicide/martyrdom attacks takes for granted that Palestinians in the West Bank and Gaza Strip undertake them to resist settler-colonial domination at a historical point of Zionism's almost complete (ideological, economic, diplomatic and military) 'triumph' over the native population" (2005, 43).

[8] Interestingly, in an interview, Zarema Muzhakhoeva, a Chechen who botched a suicide attack, describes how she first dressed in *hijab* (head scarf) and a black dress for the purposes of recording the suicide video, while later being dressed "like a Muscovite—fashionably. Blue Jeans, cross-shoes, T shirt. . . . Also they gave me beautiful dark glasses and a baseball cap" (Muzhakhoeva 2004). It is clear that Muzhakhoeva is dressed to fit in and not draw suspicion, but it is also interesting to note that she sees herself as in costume; she describes her acts (videotaping and suicide operation) almost like performative acts, not necessarily natural.

of ethnic purity and the risk of miscegenation, an issue Israeli cinema has been obsessed with for years.[9]

Toward the end of the film, the still-nameless female protagonist, dressed in the traditional Palestinian checkered kaffiyeh, is left standing as the target in an Israeli shooting range where a dozen Israeli security men are practicing. In a sequence that combines ninja-style aesthetics with a musical's choreography, the woman eliminates all the men. The surreal scene represents the best of Suleiman's style; its political poignancy and depth are not minimized by the supernatural aesthetics. Although the film's shooting preceded the first Palestinian female suicide operation, the film clearly points to the loaded potential of women partaking in combative roles. In order to fully comprehend the genius of this scene, we need to look very briefly at the discourse about terrorism.

Terrorism or political violence

Terrorism is a term that emerged during the French Revolution, when the Jacobins instigated seventeen hundred civilian deaths, in what is now called the Reign of Terror. It is generally agreed that terrorism includes violence (and fear and intimidation) that is directed at civilians, in hopes of obtaining political goals. Terrorism also needs to be regarded as a communication process whereby the terrorists send a message via the act of violence to a target audience or audiences that are usually not the actual victims of the violence.[10] In this way, terrorism is rhetorical and a media event, and mass media become tools of persuasion and propaganda.[11] Since substate groups have limited access to the public sphere (both media and state institutions), terrorism becomes not only a form of communication but also a form of performance, orchestrated to garner as much media and public attention as possible.

Naturally, most of those called terrorists do not see themselves as such; that is, they believe they have legitimate and unheard grievances against a state, and their attacks are directed at voicing those grievances. War rhetoric acknowledges both the positionality of the speaker vis-à-vis the enemy (if you are my enemy, I understand that I am your enemy) and

[9] For an excellent discussion of sexuality and interethnic romance in Israeli cinema, see Loshitzky (2001).

[10] For a good overview of terrorism as a communication process, see Tuman (2003). Interestingly, Joseph Tuman accounts for diverse audiences (state, media, other nations) but does not discuss the primary duality of addressing at once the enemy and one's own society.

[11] In some cases the media are not just transmission tools but actually determinate political agents (Gupta 2002, 19).

the historical reasons that lead to a particular conflict. In contrast, the discourse on terrorism is generally devoid of historical perspectives ("terrorists are pure evil" is one popular trope) and lacks any positionality because, it is assumed, terrorists simply live outside of morality and social norms. But such ahistorical and essentialist attitudes came to haunt this discourse when a former terrorist, Nelson Mandela, became a Nobel Peace Prize winner, or, more recently, when Osama bin Laden, a former American ally, "turned" terrorist. The discourse on terrorism also does not account for state terrorism, whereby state institutions such as the army or police inflict violence on civilian populations, as was the case in Nicaragua and Chechnya (and by the United States via the Contras and Russian forces, respectively). This last point is particularly missing from the discourse on the Palestinian-Israeli conflict.[12] All attacks on Israelis, whether inside the 1967 border or outside, whether targeting soldiers or civilians, are dubbed terrorist attacks. But dropping a one-ton bomb from an Israeli airplane on a five-story Palestinian house, in which a militant may be present, knowing full well that dozens of civilians will be killed, is hardly ever described in Western media as terrorism. One example can be seen in the case of Ayat Akhras, the third female suicide bomber, who killed herself and two others in a supermarket in Jerusalem. One of her victims was seventeen-year-old Rachel Levy, who was buying fish for Shabbat. The two girls looked alike, and the media repeatedly showed their pictures together, juxtaposed as the victim and the perpetrator, the innocent and the monster (see Wente 2003). But in the media discourse it was never mentioned that Levy was just months away from her mandatory army service, which would have directly or indirectly put her in a position that would have endangered the lives of Palestinian civilians. It is, of course, unlikely that Levy would have been in a position to kill (very few women in the Israeli army are in combat positions), but being a soldier is hardly the same as being an innocent civilian. These configurations also fail to account for asymmetric conflicts, in which one side has an army and can play by the rules of war while the other does not have airplanes, tanks, or the privilege of borders (French 2003, 36). Recent theorizing of suicidal terrorism addresses cycles of violence between states and substate groups, but such a discourse is still largely missing from the press

---

[12] Research about suicide bombings indicates that this tactic is chosen only when other means, both diplomatic and less extreme measures of violence, have failed in providing independence. (All conflicts where suicide operations are used are conflicts over the independence of an ethnically occupied or colonized minority.) See Bloom 2005, chap. 2; Pape 2005, 42–44.

(Kapitan 2004, 182–86; Bloom 2005, 37–41). The discourse on terrorism then effaces the root causes of political violence and prevents a sober discussion that explains (but does not necessarily justify) the historical and political reasons for such violence.

One Israeli film that addresses the mutual nature of political violence in Palestine and Israel is Ra'anan Alexandrowicz's documentary *The Inner Tour* (2001). In the film, Alexandrowicz takes a group of Palestinians on a three-day tour of Israel prior to the beginning of the second intifada. Two women befriend each other and have a conversation:

> "Imagine as if the person who killed your husband was here," says Jihad Salah. "What would you do?"
>
> Siham al Ouq, an impoverished widow whose husband was accidentally shot dead by Israeli Defense Forces at his own doorstep, replies, "If he was here, and no one was paying attention, and I wasn't to be held accountable . . . me and my kids would have eaten him alive."
>
> "My husband took part in a mission in which a soldier was killed," says Jihad. "This soldier has a mother too. Imagine as if his mother was here right now. How would she feel about me if she met me here?"

The film then cuts to shots of the bus traveling at night, which allows time for contemplation. The discourse is progressive in that it draws equivalences between the violence, loss, and pain on both sides of the conflict and does not demean or label either one but rather historicizes the situation. But in the film Alexandrowicz never acknowledges the power imbalance between Israel and Palestine, not only as it manifests itself in the reality of both women but also in the power structure of the film.[13] Still, the film is innovative, since unlike most Israeli and Western media coverage, it does not simply demonize the enemy, and it never slides into the simplistic and problematic language of terrorism but employs the more nuanced and historicized language of political violence.

Suicidal terrorism presents a special case in the destructive (rather than demonstrative) category of terrorism, and to a large extent it alienates the

---

[13] The film acknowledges neither the cinematic device nor the fact that the director is Israeli. This masking is problematic, as it is difficult to imagine a Palestinian filmmaker presenting this sequence without acknowledging the power asymmetry in the conflict. Furthermore, the film is in Arabic, but in large sections music overrides the dialogue, so the audience is forced to read subtitles. This is evidence that the film was made for Israeli and Western audiences and not for Palestinian and Arab audiences.

enemy target audience (as well as neutral communities) completely but serves the purposes of coercing the terrorists' own communities (Pape 2005, 9–10). Robert Pape shows that suicidal terrorism campaigns are neither erratic nor religious but primarily nationalistic and that they operate at strategic social and individual levels that need to be accounted for as a complex set (Pape 2005, 21–22). As will be clear from examples used in this article, both Israeli and Western media (as well as some academic research) often focus on one target audience—that of the enemy—and its alienation by such acts and on the individual reasons for the suicidal terror attack. But since such an approach ignores the internal social structures and lacks in historical narratives as they are perceived by the terrorists' communities, Western media generally fail in providing a comprehensive overview of suicidal terrorism.[14]

Suicide operations in the context of gender and media

The phenomenon of Palestinian female suicide bombers ignited the cultural imagination in Western societies, which have produced a Suicide Bomber Barbie, a recent American independent film about a would-be female suicide bomber, and artworks, to name just a few responses.[15] This response highlights the gender discrepancies in reporting, editing, and exposure in mass media coverage. It is a common practice for Palestinian suicide bombers to leave videotapes of themselves, filmed against the Palestinian flag or the Dome of the Rock, holding a rifle.[16] The text is some-

[14] A comprehensive and concise review of this problem in the Palestinian-Israeli conflict can be found in Kapitan (2004). For a problematic account of the same set of issues, see Bloom (2005). Mia Bloom relies almost entirely on Israeli sources; when she uses Palestinian and Arabic sources, they are always secondary sources cited in the English press. As a result, there are numerous blind spots in historicizing and explaining Palestinian suicidal terror.

[15] For the Suicide Bomber Barbie, see http://www.theculture.net/barbie/index.html. *Day Night Day Night* (2006) describes the last forty-eight hours in the life of a would-be female suicide bomber in New York City. The film never explains her personal motivation, her social background, or even the goals of those who sent her on the mission, and as such is vacuous at best. Dror Felier, an Israeli-born Swedish citizen, created an art installation in which Hanadi Jaradat's picture floats in a pool of blood. The work inspired a diplomatic incident whereby the Israeli ambassador to Sweden tried to destroy it during a gala opening. Tamil Tiger female suicide operations in Sri Lanka have already inspired an Indian film, *The Terrorist* (1999).

[16] There are also posters produced in the local towns and villages that are collages of an image of the person with the Dome of the Rock, the flag, and other nationalist symbols as well as accompanying text. These posters produce a narrative of the act of martyrdom that conforms to a script. For a good discussion of the role of the posters, see Abu Hashhash (2006).

what scripted and incorporates a medley of religious and nationalistic language. In Arab media the tapes are aired repeatedly, and the suicide bomber is culturally classified as a *shaheed*.[17] But in the West we rarely see the videos of the men, and even their names are often not disclosed. The case with the women is quite different, as their names are publicly emphasized and the videos aired; furthermore, they are contrasted with photos of the women from their previous lives, photos that emphasize the fact that they were young women engaged in traditional teenage habits and activities. In particular, pictures of Idris and Akhras in ordinary and secular settings were publicized and compared to pictures taken just before they headed out on their missions. Although the verbal text tries to explain the reasoning in psychological terms (revenge or sense of worthlessness, for example), the contrast of the images creates an unbridgeable gap whereby the Western viewer cannot reconcile the image of the young beautiful woman with her fundamentalist, terrorist dark side.[18] The result is a demonization not only of these particular women but also of the society that could produce such monsters. In the context of mass media (especially but not only television outlets), the need for shows to sell advertisements (and ultimately products) make women a major target audience. However, as Dawn Heinecken points out, "it is crucial to note that television producers are less interested in creating shows that appeal to women than they are in building (or reinforcing) an identity for women that is favorable to what advertisers hope to sell" (2003, 15). The notion of an aggressive, violent, and discontented woman is contrary to advertisers' desire to see a docile female becoming active only in the practice of consumption. In addition, what media are selling are not just physical products but a worldview that carries with it ideological ramifications: "Clearly, the media are the contemporary mediators of hegemony, the question being how, and to whose avail, particular ideological constructs of femininity are produced in media content" (van Zoonen 1994, 24). As a result of such media dynamics, the hegemonic Western position

[17] It is important to note that anyone who dies from Israeli fire is considered a *shaheed*, regardless of whether she or he has been violent or involved in fighting.

[18] The layout of Margaret Wente's (2003) article presents an image of Ayat Akhras's grieving mother on the left; in the middle are two pictures of Akhras, one as a teenager, the other wrapped in the kaffiyeh and holding a rifle; and on the right a picture of one of her victims, Rachel Levy. The caption under Akhras's image reads: "The two faces of Ayat Akhras." See also the cover page for *Newsweek* from April 15, 2002. The title reads "War in the Middle East." The accompanying image places side by side Akhras and Levy, and the caption reads: "A Human Bomb and Her Victim: How Two Teens Lived and Died."

cannot tolerate Palestinian female suicide bombers in the context either of Islamic terrorism or of their deviation from desired feminine behavior.

Furthermore, Western media tend to focus on the mothers of both men and women suicide bombers, showing them ululating and celebrating their children's actions. These images are used as supporting evidence for the ills of Palestinian society at large. But Maha Abu-Dayyeh Shamas claims that "compounding their private pain, women are subjected to extreme social pressure to behave in a certain way in public. Their private pain has to be denied for the sake of the public. Some women who have not been able to meet such societal demands (i.e. suppressing their grief in public) have actually been tranquilized by local doctors" (2003, 9). Mothers, then, are expected to perform the loss of their children in certain cultural codes that deny them their own expression of grief and that are used in Western media to mark them as uncaring mothers. This performance masks their personal pain and robs them of a genuine expression of political position, both gender-wise and via the conflict.

The most common way that Western media grapple with the deviation from traditional womanly roles is by adopting a thesis that female suicide bombers are victims of patriarchy. In a *Guardian* article (with the suggestive title "Death and the Maidens"), Giles Foden writes:

> Are men in fact to blame for women in terrorism? Litvak certainly believes the role of women in Muslim suicide bombing is a function of patriarchal control: "Those who send these women do not really care for women's rights," he says. "They are exploiting the personal frustrations and grievances of these women for their own political goals, while they continue to limit the role of women in other aspects of life." He also thinks that the use of women in terrorism has a simple practical application for their leaders. "They believe that women can evade security checks more easily than men, since they arouse fewer suspicions." (2003)

Journalist Barbara Victor utilizes her entire book, *Army of Roses*, to look at the stories of the first four successful Palestinian female suicide bombers, as well as to present interviews with some women whose suicide-bombing attempts failed. Victor finds personal problems among all of the women, mostly emanating from their status as women in a patriarchal society: Idris was unable to bear children, Andaleeb Taktakeh did not want to get married, and Akhras was protecting family honor (her father was accused of collaborating with Israel). In the introduction Victor employs an outdated Western feminist perspective on the matter and claims,

"This book tells the story of four women who died for reasons that go beyond the liberation of Palestine. If nothing else, let it serve as an example of the exploitation of women taken to a cynical and lethal extreme" (2003, 8). Throughout the book, Victor claims that all these women were manipulated by men who convinced them that a suicide operation was the only way to redeem themselves and their family name (2003, 7).

Academic feminist discourse in the West is equally problematic. Although Victor refuses to see the potential agency of individual women and paints them instead as mindless, naive, and manipulable creatures, Andrea Dworkin goes further, blaming gender oppression entirely for the situation: "It is better, easier, and more logical to blame the Israelis for women's suffering than to blame the men who both sexually abuse and then kill them according to honor society rules" (Dworkin 2002). Dworkin applies a universalist feminist framework whereby gender oppression should be considered primary to other forms of oppression or injustice. And Mia Bloom notes that seventeen organizations around the world currently use suicidal terrorism as a tactic, and about half of them employ women in their missions. Her answer to the question of why women carry out suicide bombings is, "So many of these women have been raped or sexually abused in the previous conflict either by representatives of the state or by the insurgents themselves" (Bloom 2005, 143). Elsewhere in her work Bloom makes similar assertions about the Tamil Tigresses and the Black Widows of Chechnya. But nowhere in the book does she provide sources affirming such claims.

Israeli criminologist Anat Berko interviewed would-be suicide bombers in Israeli prison, and she too concludes that "unlike the men, the women had been pushed to suicide by despair at their problematic family situations, such as not being allowed to decide their future, and/or by family members in order to restore the family honour after an illicit relationship" (2004). But in similar interviews Yoram Schweitzer finds that a more nuanced picture emerges from the conversations, whereby nationalist zeal and personal problems (only some of which are gender based) are considered in tandem as motivational reasons (Schweitzer 2006, 40).

Feminist academics in both Israel and North America choose to see the oppression of women in a patriarchal structure as the chief reason for their decision to volunteer for a suicide mission. But in fact, Palestinian feminists have recognized the need to fight simultaneously for national liberation and gender equality. Zahira Kamal, former minister of women's affairs in the Palestinian National Authority, claims that the first intifada "not only challenged the Israelis for the first time in a way that did not provoke negative world reaction, but it changed the second-class status of women within the

Palestinian community" (in Victor 2003, 10–11). Over the last twenty years Palestinian feminist organizations have flourished, and their research accounts for our understanding of the complex interaction among nationalism, religion, gender, and the occupation. These researchers remind us to look at multiple axes of victimization, agency, activism, and empowerment that exist within Palestinian society (see Abdo 2002; Jamal 2004). That is, as with other third-world feminist issues, a comprehensive approach to the Palestinian female suicide bomber cannot reduce or even prioritize gender oppression over other (national, economic) circumstances but rather needs to be accounted for in the complex web of power and social relations in Palestinian society and in the particular political predicament of that society. But until now, the representation of the issue in both Western media and academe is mostly limited to problematic approaches such as those of Dworkin, Bloom, Berko, and Victor.

Meanwhile, in Arab media, the female suicide bombers take on a special role as the symbolic brides of Palestine. For instance, Hanadi Jaradat, who killed herself and twenty-one others, including some Palestinians, in a restaurant in Haifa, is often called "the bride of Haifa."[19] Similarly, in a few cases, men would come to the mourning house and perform symbolic weddings to the *shaheeda*, the mourning scenes transformed into brideless wedding scenes. Taking this feminine symbolism even further, Mufid Fawzie writes, "She bore in her belly the fetus of a rare heroism, and gave birth by blowing herself up!" (quoted in Bennet 2002, A8).

That is, while female suicide bombers are hailed as heroes and martyrs, they are also elevated to mythic realms that solve the problem of dealing with nontraditional gender behavior in their own society. Since women have always been accepted in national liberation struggles as the symbol of the mother nation, the designation of the title *bride* suggests a comfortable place in the patriarchal nationalist project (Abdo 2002, 592).[20] Interestingly, Frances Hasso shows that the application of the title *bride* (implying also "feminine beauty, female weakness and womanly sacrifice" [Hasso 2005, 42]) is selective and does not apply to all female suicide bombers. Particularly telling is the lack of attention in the Arab media to the second female suicide bomber, Dareen Abu Aisheh. Abu Aisheh was a brilliant student of English at Al Najah University in Nablus, an outspoken feminist, and a devout Muslim. She was also a militant and was

[19] "The military wing of Islamic Jihad . . . termed Hanadi Jaradat the 'bride of Haifa' and declared, 'The wedding in Haifa will teach the Zionists an unforgettable lesson'" (Levy-Barzilai 2003).

[20] For a fuller discussion of the mother nation, see Naaman (2000).

the first to leave a videotape recording indicating her intentions and implicating Arab leaders as weak in their response to the Palestinian situation. Hasso argues that Arab media ignored Abu Aisheh "because she can be constructed in no other way but as a militant *woman* and a devout Muslim. The words, images, and known history of Abu Aisheh were not conducive to deployments of heterosexual romance, desire, frailty, and feminized beauty" (2005, 42).[21] Regardless of the narratives the women tried to communicate in their actions and videos, the dominant narrative in the Arab public sphere (political, media, and local) tied these women into heteronormative narratives as mothers and brides, narratives that affirmed the gender status quo. Whether discussing mythic brides or monsters, the discourse in both the Arab world and the West generally avoids uncomfortable questions of subjectivity, agency, and aggression, all qualities that are not befitting women according to patriarchal norms.

Suicide in the context of the Israeli-Palestinian conflict

So far, I have looked at suicide bombing mostly in relation to the discourse on political violence. But it is also important to examine it in the context of suicides and gender. The majority of Palestinian and Arab writers on the topic try to separate suicide from suicide operations. First, Islam (especially in the hadith, or interpretation of the Qu'ran [Dabbagh 2005, 26]) bans suicide altogether and deems the person who commits suicide as weak, despairing, and selfish. In contrast, suicide bombers are referred to as *shaheeds* and are considered brave and selfless warriors in a holy war (jihad). The word suicide (*al-intihar*) is hardly ever mentioned in Arabic-language discussions about suicide operations (Dabbagh 2005, 83). Some Islamist clerics have provided religious justification for such operations by claiming that it is not the person who chooses to die, that it is God who decides when a person dies; martyrdom then is merely "a Muslim's choice of the manner in which he seeks to die" (Sheikh Naim Qassem, quoted

[21] I would also like to point out that while testimonies from Abu Aisheh's friends and family account for diverse reasons for her action, Victor's own selective narrative concludes that "Darine Abu Aisheh is . . . a woman who killed herself because she couldn't face the prospect of an arranged marriage when her goal in life was to continue her education and work in academia" (Victor 2003, 196). Nowhere in the friends' interviews is it suggested that if Abu Aisheh did marry she would be barred from an academic career. Such a reading is not only reductive, but it also conforms to and reaffirms stereotypes about the gender backwardness of Muslim society. Hasso's own (2005) reading—while critical of the manipulation of women in the patriarchal structure of Palestinian society—accounts for the complexity of the situation.

in Reuter 2004, 64). In addition, secularist and nationalist discourses praise suicide operations as a sign of a strong spirit of resistance, a contradiction to the idea of depression leading to suicide. Ghassan Hage writes, for instance, "In this unequal struggle, the Palestinians are always imagined on the verge of being squashed and with them all the Arab masses' aspirations of a dignified life. The suicide bombers become a sign that Palestinians have not been broken" (2003, 74).

But the reality of suicide operations is more complex, as data shows that since 1996 and the Palestinian realization of the failures of the Oslo Accords, the rates of suicide cases in Palestinian society have increased dramatically (although they are still much lower than those in industrialized societies) (Dabbagh 2005, chap. 4). Most psychological research with Palestinian youth shows deep levels of hopelessness and a sense of defeat. Rita Giacaman, who studies youth suicide in Palestine, claims, "Our students generally have an inability to dream, an inability to visualize a better future than their hopelessly miserable life offers" (in Hage 2003, 79). And Hage adds, "Nothing symbolizes social death like this inability to dream a future" (2003, 79). Furthermore, in a study of nine male suicide bombers from the Gaza Strip, it was found that all of the men experienced personal humiliation and physical violence under occupation and/or watched a relative experience such abuses; thus all exhibited signs of being terrorized, some with clear posttraumatic stress disorder symptoms (Fields, Elbedour, and Hein 2002).

For ideological reasons, neither Arab nor Western narratives of suicidal violence explore or emphasize these psychological issues. But two recent films explore the links between the political and the psychological. Golden Globe winner and Academy Award nominee *Paradise Now* (2005) is a Palestinian fiction film discussing the last twenty-four hours in the lives of two male would-be suicide bombers. Said and Khaled live in Nablus, with little or no employment, no possibility of leaving the city (the Israeli authorities hardly ever give permits to young men), and no future prospects in sight. As the two debate the action they are about to take, we find out that the father of one collaborated with the Israelis and was eventually killed, while the father of the other submitted to the occupier's abuse and humiliations to the point of choosing which of his two legs would be shot by an Israeli soldier. As Salman Elbedour argues, exposure to political violence, humiliation, and economic devastation leads to high levels of psychological distress and low levels of self-esteem (1998, 539).[22]

---

[22] Similar results are found with Tamil youth who volunteer for suicide missions. Neloufer De Mel (2004) writes: "It [willingness to go on a suicide mission] mirrors the sense of

Both characters in *Paradise Now* see absolutely no future for themselves, and in fact, when Said falls in love with Suha, he cannot fathom a life where the two could be together because he cannot sustain himself economically or in any other way and he cannot imagine the situation changing. These Palestinian youth can see no personal future but instead see a respectable, even celebrated, way to die.

The situation for women in a patriarchal society poses additional sets of restrictions leading to further humiliation and victimization based on gender. Abu-Dayyeh Shamas claims:

> At present, [women] are victimised by the political violence, living in perpetual fear for their safety and that of their families, while bearing the additional burdens imposed on them under harrowing conditions, such as the destruction of homes, the razing of agricultural property, the uprooting of trees and rampant unemployment. Additionally, they are victims of heightened violence within the home, but are unable to express any of their suffering or anxiety, as they are forced into silence for fear of being blamed at the public level for being selfish and inconsiderate given the national emergency the whole society is undergoing, and at the private level from being blamed for their own victimisation—a vicious circle. (2003, 2)

Breaking out of this vicious cycle is not a simple feat, and depression is a likely and common outcome of the circumstances, even—maybe especially—when the society rarely acknowledges depression in its midst. While personal depression may not be the primal cause of suicidal terrorism, societal depression certainly takes its toll on individuals. In that respect, suicide in the context of a conflict should be examined as a marker not only of depression but also of martyrdom. The Israeli documentary *Avenge but One of My Two Eyes* (2005) investigates the culture of Israeli martyrdom as it is manifested in two foundational myths: the myth of Massada and the tale of the biblical Samson. Samson was the first suicide operator recorded in history, using his immense physical prowess to pull down the roof on himself and hundreds of Philistines after they blinded him. He has been celebrated in Israel as Samson the hero, and there is a cult around his act and choice. Massada was the last fortress held by Jews in the rebellion against the Romans, which ended in AD 73. On Massada— once surrounded and devoid of all hope—a thousand Jews allegedly committed suicide rather than become slaves to the Romans. The site, on the

---

desperation in Tamil youth lacking an alternative meaningful life with opportunities of education, employment and career advancement outside of the armed struggle" (78).

shores of the Dead Sea, was discovered by an archeologist in the early 1940s and quickly became a symbol for proud Zionists who saw themselves as diametrically opposed to the perceived weakness of the European Jewry during the Holocaust. Avi Mograbi follows dozens of tours of Massada, as well as celebrations of Samson, and he intercuts those sequences with footage from the West Bank: shots of the apartheid wall that Israel is erecting, checkpoints, economic devastation, and daily humiliations. As these images of hopeless Palestinians are contrasted with the story of the hopeless Jews at Massada and with the celebrated decision of Samson to take his own life while hurting as many of his enemies as possible, a complex view of martyrdom and suicide emerges. Both Judaism and Islam forbid suicide and consider anyone who takes his or her life to be weak. But both Israeli and Palestinian societies celebrate forms of self-sacrifice that are considered to be serving the better good of the society, even if it emanates from deep desperation and hopelessness. Mograbi's film also shows that martyrdom is not inherent to one monstrous society but is a product of circumstances—sociopolitical as well as interpersonal.

Narratives of martyrdom

In suicide a subject declares "my life is not worth living." But in suicide bombing the subject declares "my life is not worth living, but in my death I will produce a myth that is worth dying for." That is, the subject turns her or his own body into an instrument, a bomb that will not only define her or his life and death but also contribute to a larger national story of heroism and sacrifice (Bilsky 2004). While this account applies for both male and female suicide bombers, I would argue that it reflects women's predicament in patriarchal society rather well. In psychoanalytic terms, since women have no access to the symbolic realms of power, they are relegated to the imaginary, to the realm of the body, emotions, and the irrational. It is therefore not completely surprising that in a society lacking gender equality few women actually make it into fighting forces but dozens are accepted as potential suicide bombers. As suicide bombers they are disposable, one-time instruments and objects in a project designed and controlled by men.[23] Hasso shows that the videotape narratives of the female suicide bombers often use their gendered position to mount a critique of the Arab leadership

---

[23] Kamila Shamise (2002) calls the Palestinian suicide bombers Charlie's Angels, with Yassir Arafat in Charlie's seat: "Men are considered more suited to training recruits, so it's just more efficient to have women kill themselves. No surprise to find men keeping themselves at the centre of things, relegating women to positions of service rather than strategy."

(Hasso 2005, 29–35). Akhras, for instance, says in her video, "I say to the Arab leaders, stop sleeping. Stop failing to fulfill your duty. Shame on the Arab armies who are sitting and watching the girls of Palestine fighting while they are asleep" (quoted in Hasso 2005, 29).

Hasso shows that Arab women, feminists and others, take great inspiration from the women's messages and acts, while Arab men often minimize the loaded gender critique by focusing on nationalist issues instead. One Arab commentator writes in the Jordanian daily *Al Dustour*, "Wafa Idrees, like the rest of the young women of her generation, never dreamed of owning a BMW or of having a cellular phone. Wafa did not carry makeup in her suitcase, but enough explosives to fill the enemy with horror. Wasn't it the west that kept demanding that eastern woman become equal to the man? Well, this is how we understand equality—this is how the martyr Wafa understood equality" (quoted in Chancellor 2002). Similarly, an editorial in a Palestinian paper suggests that "he who marries a good girl will not be asked for a high bride price—a girl marries a warrior and asks for a rifle in place of a dowry" (quoted in Marcus 2002). Thus many Arab men bypass the gender critique and reinscribe a narrative that fits into a more traditional patriarchal structure.

Female suicide bombers use their bodies as weapons, thus circumventing the patriarchal system and entering the symbolic order as (dead) symbols or as myths. Most feminist critics agree that national movements, particularly in the postcolonial context, have for the most part betrayed women's struggle for gender equality and blocked their participation in the newly established nation-state (see, e.g., Abdo and Lentin 2002; Giles et al. 2003). The phenomenon of female suicide bombers highlights some of the problematic relations of gender to the nationalist project of liberation, but at the same time, female suicide bombers get more attention than women combatants because of their ahistorical (either mythic or terrorist) classification. I believe the reason for this discrepancy is that women fighters challenge the patriarchal army order in more profound ways than suicide bombers, ways that are harder to dismiss or subvert. Khaled, perhaps the best-known Palestinian woman fighter, has commented about the reception of the Palestinian female suicide bombers by religious leaders: "When the religious leaders say that women who make those actions are finally equal to men, I have a problem. Everyone is equal in death—rich, poor, Arab, Jew, Christian, we are all equal. I would rather see women equal to men in life" (quoted in Victor 2003, 63–64). Like Khaled and Kamila Shamise, other feminists call for nuanced attention to the way that gender plays into the already complex medley of politics, nationalism, religion, patriarchy, economy, tradition, honor, and social norms in the Palestinian-Israeli conflict.

Conclusion

I close this article with a short detour. In the Hollywood vehicle *So Proudly We Hail* (1943), a group of American nurses are posted to the Pacific front in the Second World War. One of the nurses is the surly Olivia, played by Veronica Lake. She refuses to mingle, party, or socialize and eventually breaks down and tells the others that her fiancé was killed in Pearl Harbor just days before their wedding. She says passionately, "I know what I am doing. I know why I am here. I know what I am going to do. I'm going to kill Japs, every blood-stained one I can get my hands on." Later in the film she requests to be posted in a hospital ward where wounded Japanese prisoners are kept, but ultimately she cannot kill them, as the nurturing nurse in her wins over the vindictive widow. Eventually the women are trapped behind enemy lines, and Olivia saves her friends by taking off her helmet, loosening her blonde long hair, and attracting the Japanese soldiers closer so that she can detonate a hand grenade (hidden in her breast pocket), killing herself and the soldiers. This suicide bombing, interestingly, takes place in the frame's dark background, and the film does not linger on this climax but instead cuts immediately to the escape of the others, and Olivia is rarely even mentioned thereafter. But in the narrative of the film, and in the logic of the Western viewer, it is impossible to label Olivia a terrorist. Nor do we think of the Christian-American nurse Kitty from *Exodus* (1960), last seen armed and ready to fight for Israel's independence, as anything but a freedom fighter.

Now let us return to Idris, the medic and first Palestinian female suicide bomber. Is she a monster? A terrorist? A freedom fighter? A martyr? A victim? The answer clearly lies not in her action or even in her choice of how to represent herself but in the diverse and often competing narratives of politicians and media alike. The politicians' narratives tend to frame the actions of women suicide bombers in ways that minimize and subvert the overt confrontation of gender politics present in the women's own narratives and actions. Ultimately, this co-optation renders the affront on gender politics ineffective, or effective only insofar as it serves the nationalist and patriarchal project. The media treatment of the phenomenon both in the Arab world and in the West relies on convenient stereotypes and conventional narrative frames. Those representations deny women agency and instead represent them as monsters or brides in a hegemonic framework that enables readers and viewers to maintain both the comfortable gender status quo and their preconceived notions about the Palestinian-Israeli conflict.[24] In this respect, the case of the female suicide bomber is not that different from other news events as they are covered by media. That is, while the phenomenon of female suicide bombers is relatively new, its media coverage is organized as news stories packaged to reassert old beliefs. As such, news coverage of the phenomenon is in the end rather old news insofar as gender, terrorism, and the Palestinian-Israeli conflict go.

Department of Film Studies
Queen's University

References

Abdo, Nahla. 2002. "Women, War and Peace: Reflection from the Intifada." *Women's Studies International Forum* 25(5):585–93.

Abdo, Nahla, and Ronit Lentin, eds. 2002. *Women and the Politics of Military Confrontation: Palestinian and Israeli Gendered Narratives of Dislocation*. New York: Berghahn.

Abu-Dayyeh Shamas, Maha. 2003. "Women in Situations of Organized Violence: A Case of Double Jeopardy." Report, Women's Centre for Legal Aid and Counseling. http://www.wclac.org/reports/violence.pdf.

Abu Hashhash, Mahmoud. 2006. "On the Visual Representation of Martyrdom in Palestine." *Third Text* 20(3/4):391–404.

Allan, Stuart, and Barbie Zelizer, eds. 2004. *Reporting War: Journalism in Wartime*. London: Routledge.

Applebaum, Anne. 2002. "Girl Suicide Bombers." *Slate*, April 2. http://slate.msn.com/?id=2063954.

Avenge but One of My Two Eyes. 2005. Directed by Avi Mograbi. Paris: MograbiFilms.

Beaumont, Peter. 2002a. "From an Angel of Mercy to Angel of Death." *Guardian*, January 31. http://www.guardian.co.uk/Archive/Article/0,4273,4346503,00.html.

———. 2002b. "Suicide Notes." *Observer*, December 22. http://observer.guardian.co.uk/2002review/story/0,,862850,00.html.

Bennet, James. 2002. "Arab Press Glorifies Bomber as Heroine." *New York Times*, February 11, A8.

Berko, Anat. 2004. *In the Path to the Garden of Eden*. Tel Aviv: Miscal. English

[24] For a discussion of news narratives and how they reiterate social and cultural narratives, see Johnson-Cartee (2005). For discussions of the media coverage of war, see Hoskins (2004) and also Allan and Zelizer (2004).

excerpt available at http://web.amnesty.org/library/Index/ENGMDE1501
62005?open&of=ENG-ISR.

Bilsky, Leora. 2004. "Suicidal Terror, Radical Evil, and the Distortion of Politics and Law." *Theoretical Inquiries in Law* 5(1). http://www.bepress.com/til/default/vol5/iss1/art5/.

Bloom, Mia. 2005. *Dying to Kill: The Allure of Suicide Terror.* New York: Columbia University Press.

Chancellor, Alexander. 2002. "The Ultimate Equaliser." *Guardian*, February 23. http://www.guardian.co.uk/Archive/Article/0,4273,4360317,00.html.

Chic Point. 2003. Directed by Sharif Waked. Independently produced.

Coomaraswamy, Radhika. 2003. "A Question of Honour: Women, Ethnicity, and Armed Conflict." In Giles et al. 2003, 91–102.

Dabbagh, Nadia Tyasir. 2005. *Suicide in Palestine: Narratives of Despair.* Northampton, MA: Interlink.

Day Night Day Night. 2006. Directed by Julia Loktev. Brooklyn, NY: FaceFilm.

De Mel, Neloufer. 2004. "Body Politics: (Re)Cognising the Female Suicide Bomber in Sri Lanka." *Indian Journal of Gender Studies* 11(1):75–92.

Divine Intervention. 2002. Directed by Elia Suleiman. New York: Avatar Films.

Dworkin, Andrea. 2002. "The Women Suicide Bombers." *feminista!* 5(1). http://www.feminista.com/archives/v5n1/dworkin.html.

Elbedour, Salman. 1998. "Youth in Crisis: The Well-Being of Middle Eastern Youth and Adolescents during War and Peace." *Journal of Youth and Adolescence* 27(5):539–56.

Exodus. 1960. Directed by Otto Preminger. Culver City, CA: Metro-Goldwyn-Mayer.

Fields, Rona M., Salman Elbedour, and Fadel Abu Hein. 2002. "The Palestinian Suicide Bomber." In *The Psychology of Terrorism*, vol. 2, *Clinical Aspects and Responses*, ed. Chris E. Stout, 193–223. Westport, CT: Praeger.

Foden, Giles. 2003. "Death and the Maidens." *Guardian*, July 18. http://www.guardian.co.uk/women/story/0,,1000647,00.html.

French, Shannon E. 2003. "Murderers, Not Warriors: The Moral Distinction between Terrorists and Legitimate Fighters in Asymmetric Conflicts." In *Terrorism and International Justice*, ed. James P. Sterba, 31–46. Oxford: Oxford University Press.

Giles, Wenona, Malathi de Alwis, Edith Klein, and Nekula Silva, eds. 2003. *Feminists under Fire: Exchanges across War Zones.* Toronto: Between the Lines.

Gupta, Suman. 2002. *The Replication of Violence: Thoughts on International Terrorism after September 11th, 2001.* London: Pluto.

Hage, Ghassan. 2003. "'Comes a Time We Are All Enthusiasm': Understanding Palestinian Suicide Bombers in Times of Exighophobia." *Public Culture* 15(1):65–89.

Hasso, Frances S. 2005. "Discursive and Political Deployments by/of the 2002 Palestinian Women Suicide Bombers/Martyrs." *Feminist Review* 81:23–51.

Heinecken, Dawn. 2003. *The Warrior Women of Television: A Feminist Cultural Analysis of the New Female Body in Popular Media.* New York: Peter Lang.

Hoskins, Andrew. 2004. *Televising War: From Vietnam to Iraq.* London: Continuum.

The Inner Tour. 2001. Directed by Ra'anan Alexandrowicz. Tel Aviv: Belfilms.

Jamal, Amal. 2004. "Feminist Media Discourse in Palestine and the Predicament of Politics." *Feminist Media Studies* 4(2):129–46.

Johnson-Cartee, Karen S. 2005. *News Narratives and News Framing: Constructing Political Reality.* Lanham, MD: Rowman & Littlefield.

Kapitan, Tomis. 2004. "Terrorism in the Arab Israeli Conflict." In *Terrorism: The Philosophical Issues,* ed. Igor Primoratz, 175–91. New York: Palgrave.

Levy-Barzilai, Vered. 2003. "Ticking Bomb." *Ha'aretz,* November 16. http://www.haaretz.com/hasen/pages/ShArt.jhtml?itemNo=350272.

Loshitzky, Yosefa. 2001. *Identity Politics on the Israeli Screen.* Austin: University of Texas Press.

Marcus, Itamar. 2002. "PMW Encouraging Woman Terrorists." *Independent Media Review Analysis,* March 19. http://www.imra.org.il/story.php3?id=10761.

MEMRI (Middle East Media Research Institute). 2002. "The Celebration of the First Palestinian Female Suicide Bomber, Part 1." *Al-Sharq Al-Awsat,* February 12. http://www.imra.org.il/story.php3?id=10155.

Muzhakhoeva, Zarema. 2004. "'I Suspected I Had to Commit a Suicide Attack': A Surviving Suicide Bomber Answers Questions of *Izvestia* from a 'Lefortovo' Cell." *Izvestia* 18(5):1–13.

Naaman, Dorit. 2000. "Woman/Nation: A Postcolonial Look at Female Subjectivity." *Quarterly Review of Film and Video* 17(4):333–42.

Pape, Robert. 2005. *Dying to Win: The Strategic Logic of Suicide Terrorism.* New York: Random House.

Paradise Now. 2005. Directed by Hany Abu Assad. Burbank, CA: Warner Independent Pictures.

Reuter, Christoph. 2004. *My Life Is a Weapon: A Modern History of Suicide Bombing.* Trans. Helena Ragg-Kirkby. Princeton, NJ: Princeton University Press.

Schweitzer, Yoram. 2006. "Palestinian Female Suicide Bombers: Reality vs. Myth." In his *Female Suicide Bombers: Dying for Equality?* 25–41. Tel Aviv: Jaffe Center for Strategic Studies.

Shamise, Kamila. 2002. "Exploding the Myths." *Guardian,* April 27. http://www.guardian.co.uk/Archive/Article/0,4273,4401137,00.html.

Sheikh, Fawzia. 2006. "Mideast: Occupation, Conflict Hold Back Palestinian Women." *Inter Press Service,* March 7, Article no. 42424. http://www.globalinfo.org/eng/reader.asp?ArticleId=42424.

So Proudly We Hail. 1943. Directed by Mark Sandrich. Universal City, CA: Universal Studios.

The Terrorist. 1999. Directed by Santosh Sivan. Port Washington, NY: Fox Lorber.

Tuman, Joseph. 2003. *Communicating Terror: The Rhetorical Dimensions of Terrorism.* Thousand Oaks, CA: Sage.

van Zoonen, Liesbet. 1994. *Feminist Media Studies*. London: Sage.

Victor, Barbara. 2003. *Army of Roses: Inside the World of Palestinian Women Suicide Bombers*. Emmaus, PA: Rodale.

Ward, Olivia. 2004. "The Changing Face of Violence." *Toronto Star*, October 10, A6.

Wente, Margaret. 2003. "How to Make a Martyr." *Globe and Mail*, February 8, F6–F7.

Political Violence and Body Language in Life Stories of Women ETA Activists

ETA violence is absolutely political. It's not about testicles. It's not about ovaries.
—Narrator 1 (b. 1946)[1]

There's something that comes from inside you, that you have to let out. And to let out that feeling, that impulse. . . . I think it's born like that, like it can be born equally in a man, in a male activist.
—Narrator 4 (b. 1961)[2]

his article brings together two themes of central interest to feminist scholars in recent years: violence and the body. As the feminist philosopher Bat-Ami Bar On notes, "violent bodies" have often been the focus of feminist theory and activism, but these bodies have normally been defined as male (Bar On 2002, 152). My work has been inspired by and contributes to the growing number of feminist studies on political violence and warfare. But by focusing on the narratives of women who have participated in and supported political violence, specifically in the radical Basque nationalist organization Euskadi Ta Askatasuna (ETA; Basque Homeland and Freedom), I depart from the trend in much of this broader literature of defining female bodies as vulnerable (D'Cruze and Rao 2005). I am interested instead in female activists' descriptions of their relationship to political violence.

The discussion below is based on interviews I conducted in the mid-1990s with women who had been activists in or supporters of ETA from

---

[1] Narrator 1, interview, January 1997, Bilbao.
[2] Narrator 4, interview, March 1997, Bilbao.

[*Signs: Journal of Women in Culture and Society* 2007, vol. 32, no. 4]

the mid-1960s to the early 1980s.[3] The interviews were one of many sources I gathered while writing a history of women and ETA (Hamilton 2007). Given the lack of documentary evidence on women's participation in this armed, illegal nationalist movement, the interviews provide important information on the patterns of women's recruitment into ETA, as well as on their roles and experiences inside the organization. Equally important, however, the interviews reveal the constructions of gender, ethnic, and class identities, as well as the functions of memory in the formation of these identities.

The original group of narrators comprised some twenty-five women born between 1936 and 1961. In selecting the interviewees, I chose a sample that represented a range of backgrounds (age, region, class, and ethnic group) and experiences of activism, and I made contact with potential narrators through references from four sources: (1) Basque women's organizations; (2) radical nationalist organizations; (3) academics, activists, and other acquaintances in the Basque country; and (4) the narrators themselves. Following recommendations in recent works on oral history (Passerini 1987; Thompson 1988), I approached the interviews as life stories, allowing each narrator to recite her story as far as possible according to her own memories. Each interview was conducted in Castilian Spanish, lasted between one and two-and-a half hours, and was tape-recorded with prior agreement from the narrator.[4] I subsequently transcribed the tapes and analyzed the interviews in detail, highlighting common themes in each interview and across the sample. In order to preserve as much as possible the "orality" of the original interviews (Portelli 1981, 97) I transcribed all of them literally, indicating pauses, gaps, repetitions, partial words, and filler words. Although the analysis was conducted on the original Spanish transcripts, the excerpts examined below are my own translations into English. Because of the controversial nature of the topic (i.e., the defense of political violence) and the excerpts studied

---

[3] Euskadi Ta Askatasuna was founded in 1959. Between the late 1960s and the declaration of a permanent ceasefire in March 2006 the organization was involved in a sustained campaign of violence against the Spanish state and Spanish and Basque citizens, resulting in more than eight hundred deaths and thousands of injuries in addition to the deaths, injuries, and imprisonment of hundreds of its own members and supporters. For accounts in English of ETA's history and actions, see Clark (1984), Sullivan (1988), and Zulaika (1988).

[4] My limited fluency in the Basque language *euskera* eliminated the option of interviews in that language. However, only a minority of the narrators were what could be regarded as native speakers of Basque. All were fluent in Castilian Spanish and spoke *euskera* with varying degrees of fluency.

here I have chosen to keep the narrators cited in this article anonymous, withholding their names and other personal details (date and place of birth, profession, time spent in or supporting ETA, etc.); instead I identify them by number in the text.[5]

When I first worked with the interviews, I noted, like others who have interviewed female activists in armed organizations (MacDonald 1991; Passerini 1992), what seemed to be a resounding silence around one very specific theme: participation in and support of political violence. Initially I attributed this to calculated choice on the part of my narrators, one consistent with wider representations of the Basque conflict. Interviews, reports, and images of the conflict show that willingness to acknowledge the violence committed by one's own community is in inverse proportion to the emphasis placed on the violence committed against that community. But, as I read and reread the interview transcripts, I began to see that in spite of my reluctance in many cases to ask direct questions about ETA violence the interviews did contain references to that violence, even if rarely to actual armed actions. What I first interpreted as silence turned out to be a kind of muted language of violence, one often expressed in the interviews in the form of metaphor.

The most recurrent metaphors of violence occur in relation to the body. To date this language of the body has remained stubbornly on the margins of my writing on women in ETA because it never seemed quite to fit within the wider historical narrative in my work about gender, nationalism, memory, and political violence. I struggled, in other words, to find a language with which to address these interview passages. Yet they have continued to both attract and unsettle me and as such seem to demand further consideration. The bodily metaphors of violence in these interviews with female Basque nationalist activists are different from those I have found in other oral histories of conflict. Unlike Gilda Zwerman's (1994) examples of female activists in U.S. armed organizations, who seem to have distanced themselves from the violence of their organizations, these Basque narrators present violence as integral to struggle and to life itself. As distinct from Gyanendra Pandey's (1999) subjects, who situate violence outside themselves and their community, my interviewees locate the origins of violence within their bodies. And in contrast to Luisa Passerini's (1992, 161) metaphor of the "lacerations in the memory," which also suggests a somatic relationship between the subject and the violence she

---

[5] It is common practice in studies of ETA to safeguard informants' anonymity (Alcedo Moneo 1996).

committed, in my interviews with former members and supporters of ETA violence is associated not with wounds but with health and healing.[6]

The association of violence with the body appears in a series of passages in different interviews in which narrators describe ETA violence as a creative force that gives and sustains life. As I show below, there is a lengthy tradition in Western thought associating politics with the body, on the one hand, and violence with life and in particular with reproduction, on the other hand. While scholars have noted the historical importance of organic metaphors of violence, the gendered dimensions of such metaphors have received less attention. In the main section of this article, then, I focus on metaphors relating to reproductive organs and birth. In particular, the image of birth in one interview with a woman formerly active in ETA introduces a novel perspective on the gender politics of political violence in contexts where such violence is typically defined as masculine. I argue that by dissociating political violence from both male and female reproductive organs, or by reworking the military metaphor of male warriors giving birth, the female narrators cited below challenge the common association of violence with masculinity and male sexuality. In so doing they assert what they see as their sexual difference from their male comrades while simultaneously claiming women's capacity to commit violence.

I recognize the political and ethical risks involved in highlighting the accounts of violence of female ETA activists, and it is important to be clear about what this article does and does not set out to do. I do not claim that these interviews tell us anything definitive about female ETA activists' motivations for joining an insurgence movement and committing violence or their feelings about their actions, let alone about the historical roles of women in armed organizations.[7] I am aware that without this wider historical context there is a danger that these interviews will be seen as proof that women have participated as actively as men in ETA violence and that women may indeed have an additional investment in that violence because of their subordinate gender status.[8] The empirical evidence of

---

[6] "Our first impression was that this memory was lacerated, strewn with silences, riddled with holes, as if the recollections of the women who struck had been stricken in their turn by an internal erosion" (Passerini 1992, 198).

[7] I have written extensively on these matters elsewhere; see Hamilton (2000a, 2000b, 2003, 2007).

[8] In "Women's Time" Julia Kristeva ([1979] 1997, 362) argues that "the large number of women in terrorist groups like the Palestinian commandos, the Baader-Meinhoff Gang, and the Red Brigades" may be explained as a kind of paranoid "counterinvestment" in the violence women have encountered. As compelling as her argument is, it is based on an exaggerated claim about women's participation in left-wing and national liberation

ETA membership and activism from the late 1960s to 2003 shows otherwise: the significant majority of armed ETA activists have been men (as have ETA's victims and the members of the Spanish and Basque security forces). In the period when the narrators discussed here were active (late 1960s to early 1980s), women constituted 10–15 percent of ETA's membership, and the majority of female activists were involved in supportive or collaborative roles rather than direct armed activism (Hamilton 2007). In exploring expressions of violence that challenge its popular association with certain forms of masculinity, therefore, I do not argue that ETA and Spanish state violence have no relationship to dominant forms of masculinity or male power. I have detailed elsewhere the material effects of these gender power relations, including the sexual torture of some women arrested for ETA membership (see Hamilton 2007). While I agree with many contemporary feminist studies that war and conflict tend to reinforce male dominance and target women in specifically gendered ways (e.g., Enloe 1988), I stress here that women's resistances to these structures of dominance are not necessarily congruent with that stream of feminism that privileges women's relationship to peace.

Furthermore, there is the danger that my attention to the language of the perpetrators and supporters of ETA violence will obscure the devastation experienced by the victims of that violence. In advocating an analysis of these interviews in the context of traditions of bodily metaphors of war and conflict, I do not intend to reduce violence to discourse. I argue that language is important precisely because intellectual traditions that glorify violence and associate it with creativity and life have played a role in sustaining participation in and support for ETA and that they can tell us something about the gender politics of political violence. By tracing these traditions in the interviews, I take a different tack from that of many oral history studies where interviews are used to highlight the ways in which individuals and subordinate groups challenge dominant discourses. Instead, I hope to show how certain ideas circulate in and across ideological boundaries and shape the identities of participants in political violence and to suggest how this process is gendered.

The bodily metaphors of violence in these interviews highlight the need to listen carefully for signs of those topics that we as interviewers may at first believe to be taboo. Their very idiosyncrasy indicates that they may

movements in the 1970s. Kristeva remains, however, one of the few feminist theorists to address directly the issue of women's possible attraction to terrorism, and as such her argument deserves further attention from feminist scholars. The majority of references to "Women's Time" focus on its argument about different generations of feminists. For an exception that engages with Kristeva's theory of women and violence, see Rose (1993).

have something to say about the complexity of the relationship between gender and political violence and about the ways in which difficult themes such as violence may be expressed in oral history interviews. The fact that references to violence appear in the form of metaphor, rather than through direct rationalization of ETA's actions, does not make the violence they describe any less real or disturbing. To the contrary, through their use of metaphors of life and creativity the passages suggest an affirmation of violence more challenging to the listener than rational justifications of violence as a form of collective national self-defense.

Violence, creativity, and the state as body

The reproductive metaphors I examine in the second half of this article are part of a wider set of organic metaphors in the interviews. I open the current section with examples of such metaphors from three different interviews. The first is taken from an exchange with a woman, Narrator 1, who had been active in ETA in the 1960s and 1970s and remained a supporter of radical nationalism when I spoke with her in the mid-1990s. This excerpt from Narrator 1 is from the opening of her interview, which began with "I was born . . ." and continued into a lengthy reflection on her own personal and political history and that of ETA:

> My human condition, the condition of this people, the freedom of the human being, and the freedom of peoples. It's an important struggle, a good struggle, that gives you hope, that structures your psychology. Because everyone comes from somewhere, and on top of eating and sleeping you have to have something inside, something that makes you get up, live, dream, love, and that means, unfortunately, unfortunately, shooting. I say unfortunately. I wasn't born to shoot, I don't like it, but while the others are shooting, I'm not going to put my head down. . . . The only one the forces of power use, understand, the *only* one, the only kind of struggle, unfortunately, I say it again, that the forces of power don't assimilate, is the armed struggle. Unfortunately . . . human beings, we weren't born to live so others could get fat. Human beings get sick. . . . Human beings were not born to live for others, were not born to be crushed. No . . . we were born to be free, to love, to do things we like. To live. And while they don't let us live, well girl, I—and the struggle doesn't destroy. The struggle is absolutely creative. What destroys

is being slow, keeping quiet, backing down, that *does* make you sick. Struggling, having ideals, is *healthy*. It feels good.[9]

In the first part of this passage the struggle is presented as an internal force, but through its contrast to sleeping and eating, it is implied as something belonging to the soul or spirit as opposed to the body. Further along, however, struggle is associated with food, sustenance, and movement, as that which keeps one healthy and feeling good, physically as well as psychologically. It is worth comparing this passage to the words near the end of a different interview in which similar themes emerge. This second narrator (Narrator 2) had also been active in radical nationalism since the 1960s, largely as an ETA collaborator and supporter. When I asked her if she was optimistic about the future and attaining the goal of national self-determination she replied: "It's a minimum. . . . It's like oxygen . . . if you don't have it. . . . Obviously, if I don't live, I'm not going to let others live. No, no, no. Self-determination is like bread. It's like bread. And if we don't have that bread. No. It can't be."[10]

The land as body, requiring oxygen and bread to live: this excerpt captures the merging of the body and the body politic, the self and the nation implicit in the radical nationalist demand for self-determination. The original Spanish word, *autodeterminación*, makes the link even clearer—*auto* means self but is also the juridical term for edict or writ (hence the title of one book on Basque nationalism and violence, *Auto de terminación* [which literally means termination edict but is a pun on *autodeterminación*, or self-determination; Aranzadi, Juaristi, and Unzueta 1994]). Envisioning national self-determination as oxygen and bread that allow the body to live represents the collapse of the nation and the people. The declaration, repeated almost word for word in the above two excerpts—"if they don't let us live, we won't let them live"—implies that the enemy, that is, the state, is also conceived as a human body.

This image of the state as body appears again in an interview with a third narrator, still active at the time of the interview (1996) in radical nationalist politics, when I asked her what role the armed struggle played in the movement: "The importance of the armed struggle? Well I have thought about this. The armed struggle is necessary—why? Because in the end they're the only actions that can harm them. Because democracy has so many throats, the same as the dictatorship, well maybe not so many.

---

[9] Narrator 1, interview.
[10] Narrator 2, interview, April 1996, Bilbao.

. . . But now in the period of what they call democracy, it has so many throats, so many opportunities to take over, that in the end the only thing it can't swallow is the armed struggle."[11]

Both of these metaphors—violent struggle as a life force and the state as a body—have lengthy traditions in Western thought. In her critique of the "glorification of violence" in New Left writings of the 1960s, Hannah Arendt traces the "old combination of violence, life, and creativity" in philosophical writing to Karl Marx, Friedrich Nietzsche, and Georges Sorel (Arendt 1969, 171).[12] The metaphor of the body politic, the state imagined as a body with different organs representing different functions and constituencies, goes back to ancient Greece (Sontag 1991; Bordo 1993). In the last excerpts above, the enemy/state is imagined as a human body that "swallows" political resistance and denies the Basque people the bread and water they need to live. This image makes literal the contention, dating from ETA's early days, that at stake is the survival of the Basque people, and thus that violence is an act of physical as well as cultural self-defense.[13] This anthropomorphic vision of the state is the necessary reverse of the identification of the bodies of ETA's victims, metonymically, with the state itself, helping justify their deaths in so-called objective terms, as seen in an excerpt from a fourth interview:[14]

[11] Narrator 3, interview, March 1996, Bilbao.

[12] For Arendt this tradition is particularly clear in what she calls the "irresponsible grandiose statements" (1969, 122) in Frantz Fanon's *The Wretched of the Earth* and especially Jean-Paul Sartre's preface to that book. Although it is not possible to locate the source of the above metaphors of violence in any one intellectual or political tradition, there is evidence from my own interviews and the work of other scholars that ETA activists in the 1960s read works by New Left and especially anticolonial thinkers, including Fanon and Sartre (see Zulaika 1988, 285; Letamendia Belzunce 1994, 293). This is the decade when Francoist censorship laws were relaxed somewhat, making previously forbidden texts, including New Left and anticolonial writings, available to a new generation of anti-Francoist youth. Additionally, from the mid-1960s onward increasing numbers of ETA members lived in exile in the French Basque country, where they had contact with nonnationalist leftist movements, including Trotskyist and Maoist organizations. Some ETA activists and supporters traveled to or lived in Paris, where they were involved in the youth movements associated with May 1968. Even though Spain, still under a dictatorship, did not experience a 1960s workers' and student movement in the same form as in its liberal democratic neighbors, anti-Francoist activists, including ETA members, did engage with some of the same political ideas.

[13] An early expression of this idea can be found in the 1963 book *Vasconia* by Federico Krutwig ([1963] 1973), which was made part of ETA's official strategy in the document "Insurrección en Euskadi" (republished in Editorial Txalaparta [1993], 272–89).

[14] Robert Lumley (1990, 287), drawing on the work of Nando Dalla Chiesa, makes a similar point about the "anthropomorphic vision of capital and the state" in the imagery and rhetoric of the Italian Red Brigades in the late 1970s.

Narrator 4 (N4):   I think armed actions are hard for everyone. I'm personally not glad because there's a lieutenant-colonel who's been assassinated. I'm glad about what it means, the step it means in the struggle. I'm not glad about the death of José Jiménez; rather, I'm glad because that man's a lieutenant-colonel and because he plays a role in the conflict.[15]

Carrie Hamilton (CH):   So that makes a step?

N4:   It means a step, in overcoming the conflict. By overcoming, I mean the tension that we have with the state. I think the *losses* of human life are painful for everyone. But I think we know that more than anyone.[16]

In addition to the equation of the individual victim with his part in the conflict, the language of this excerpt works in other ways to excuse killing for political aims. The metaphor of the struggle as a forward journey in which necessary steps must be taken expresses the idea that the end justifies the means. The claim that ETA and its supporters are more familiar than anyone with the pain of death allows the speaker to shift from the position of perpetrator to victim.

Of the interviews I conducted, the one above (that of Narrator 4) is most expressive both of the justification of ETA violence and of women's participation in that violence. The narrator in question was younger than the others cited in this article, and she joined ETA in the late 1970s, a time when there was a small but significant number of female activists in the organization. I will examine here a passage from her interview that incorporates examples of the violence-is-life metaphors outlined above alongside other metaphors of struggle. The excerpt is worth quoting at length because it contains intriguing reflections on the relationship between gender and political violence:

CH: I think lots of women think that they are more emotional, more sensitive. And the logical question in this context is whether women react to death in a different way.

N4:   I, for example, am very opposed to women in mourning. Or to

---

[15] The narrator is not referring here to an actual ETA victim but an imaginary example. The use of a typically Castilian forename and surname adds to the sense of the victim as a representative of the Spanish enemy rather than an individual and can be compared with xenophobic portrayals of Civil Guards as stupid Andalusians with mustaches, which sometimes appeared in radical nationalist cartoons in the 1970s and 1980s.

[16] Narrator 4, interview.

women for peace. Because it seems to me that's taking women back to the role we've always been given. Because we create life we're more sensitive. Because we can be mothers. And I think that's absurd. If not there wouldn't be women who kill. And we all know that isn't true. And I can tell you what I've told you before. I have male comrades who I've talked to, and who're in prison. For whom there's no fun, nor joy, in going to kill someone. But they kill because they believe in the struggle, for liberation. I think Jean Genet said it very clearly: brutality is one thing, violence is another.

CH: What I understand [from what you're saying] is that the struggle is something that goes beyond the person's personality . . . it's a political thing. Explain to me what you were saying before.

N4:   First things first. It's something integral. Men and women, we're a house. And outside the house is a garden, and it's very easy to keep the house tidy and the garden nice and tidy. But inside the house no one sees you. So for me the struggle is the garden and inside the house. And you can't be fighting theoretically or politically for something and inside be very conservative. . . . I think the struggle is something integral. We're a cupboard with lots of drawers. But the cupboard is made from all the drawers, not just the drawer on the top or the drawer on the bottom. That's one thing. The issue of the difference between brutality and violence; for me, brutality is a negation. Genet, the French writer, made it very clear. He said the architecture on the outskirts of many cities is a brutal act. Torture is a brutal act. Identity cards and roadblocks are brutal and negating. In contrast, violence, with all the harshness and cruelty that it can also entail, I think it's an act of affirmation. And violence can be a volcano starting up, a chick breaking an egg and exploding. The birth of a child is a violent act. Or the bud of wheat when it explodes, too. Life has many facts, many violent acts, but which serve to affirm it. And I think that's the difference between brutality and violence. One is a negation and the other is an affirmation. And I think the struggle we have in this nation, violence is hard. I don't think *anyone* likes it. And I know many activists who have been in prison for *many* years, and I don't think anyone likes living the way they live, nor taking someone's life. But we *understand* this violence as a fact that will lead to freedom, to the freedom of this nation, and the *rest* of the people who are in this nation. That's why we fight. . . . The issue isn't arms yes, arms no. Violence, armed struggle, yes or no. No. That's an instrument. Let's say *why* we act like that, what we want. And in that sense being a woman or a man, I don't think it changes anything. I don't consider myself more sensitive than my male comrade, for example.[17]

Between the first and second references to Genet (to which I return below) the narrator describes the struggle with a pair of domestic metaphors. She compares the activist's commitment to keeping one's house in order, making the interior (house) consistent with the exterior (garden). Later she shifts to the image of a cupboard or chest of drawers. I want to consider these domestic metaphors of house, garden, and cupboard with reference to Doreen Massey's (1994) work on space, place, and gender. Massey advocates a mode of thinking in "space-time" (1994, 2), one that conceives of space as "constructed out of social relations" (2) and resists conceiving of place as static. This tendency to envision places as fixed can be found in the "exclusivist claims to places" (4) associated with nationalism, regionalism, and localism. These movements "have been attempts to fix the meaning of particular spaces, to enclose them, endow them with fixed identities and to claim them for one's own" (Massey 1994, 4). In light of this framework for thinking in terms of space-time, I suggest that the term *house* functions in the above excerpt in different ways, producing seemingly paradoxical political meanings that nevertheless encompass the changing position of the narrator herself, in both space and time and geographically and historically. My understanding of the use of *house* here assumes, following contemporary studies of spatial metaphors, a dialectical relationship between metaphor and materiality (Aiken et al. 1998; Brown 2000).

In nationalist discourse generally, the term *house* is related to the common metaphor of the nation as family. This connection is even clearer in the original Spanish in which the same word—*casa*—is used to denote both house and home. The sentence "men and women, we're a house/home" reflects a sentiment akin to "men and women, we're a family/nation," a statement reminiscent of nationalist tributes to a timeless homeland and identity. Feminist scholars of nationalism have argued that the trope of the family functions in nationalist discourses to naturalize hierarchies of gender, class, and race (McClintock 1995, 357). But the reference above to housework, to keeping the "house tidy and the garden nice and tidy," also historicizes the concept *house/home* by evoking a gender division of labor. Elsewhere I have argued that in ETA's early years the organization was defined in opposition to the family and the home, an ideological division that simultaneously reflected and reinforced the

---

[17] Ibid.

exclusion of women from military activism (Hamilton 2007). The activist above, however, was from a younger generation, one whose political activism was conditioned by wider social and political changes in Basque and Spanish society that saw increasing numbers of women enter the labor force and public political activity. By the time the above narrator joined the organization in the 1970s, 10–15 percent of its membership was female (Hamilton 2007). Members were still represented, however—in visual images, songs, and written documents, for example—as overwhelmingly male. Moreover, women's nationalist activism was associated predominantly with family and home through the iconic figure of the mother of the male ETA member. In the excerpt above the narrator's description of activism collapses this popularly perceived gender binary between male activists and female supporters by merging men and women into a single activist, "we." By rhetorically moving the struggle inside the house/home, the narrator feminizes the armed struggle, claiming the military organization as a place for women as well as men. Because of its multiple rhetorical and historical associations, therefore, the trope *house/home* works to claim a static place (the nation) and timeless national identity while it simultaneously locates the narrator within a history of changing gender relations inside ETA.

Reproducing violence

Following the house/garden metaphor, Narrator 4 quotes almost verbatim an article by the French playwright and novelist Jean Genet titled "Violence and Brutality" ([1977] 2004). The piece was originally written as a preface to a collection of writings by members of the German Red Army Faction and was published in the French newspaper *Le Monde* in September 1977 (see White 1993, 683–89). A few years later a Spanish translation appeared in a special issue on political violence of the leftist Spanish magazine *El Viejo Topo* (Genet n.d.). The article sets up a binary opposition between violence and brutality and a series of related categories: revolution, freedom, life, and the violence of the Red Army Faction versus the system, bureaucracy, technology, and the brutality of the West German government. In the first paragraph of his article, Genet writes: "If we reflect on any vital phenomenon, even in its narrowest, biological sense, we understand that violence and life are virtually synonymous" ([1977] 2004, 171). Following Genet, the above narrator claims that the budding of a seed, the hatching of an egg, and the birth of a child are all acts of violence. As Genet's biographer Edmund White notes, the argument rests on a "pseudo-biological" contrast between brutality and violence (White 1993, 688).[18]

Through her reference to Genet, Narrator 4 introduces the theme of violence and its relation to reproduction, one that also appears in the interview with an older narrator (Narrator 1). The two women are from different generations, but both were active in ETA for a number of years. Their proximity to ETA violence may help explain both the intensity and the contradictions that characterize their discussions of women's relationship to political violence. Although both narrators emphatically deny any personal element to political violence, the language of their interviews is most intimate, most rooted in the body, when they refer to violence. The passages I discuss below come in the context of ongoing discussion throughout each interview, between the narrator and me, about the roles of women and men in the military organization. For example, when I asked the older narrator if ETA activism had different meanings for women and men, she declared:

> *N1*: ETA violence is absolutely political. It has nothing to do with a person's violent character. That's something you have to be clear about. ETA violence is absolutely political. It's not about testicles. It's not about ovaries. It's not aggression. It's a front of struggle. You take up arms not because you're violent, and because you like violence. No. It's a way of fighting because unfortunately there are moments when the enemy doesn't understand any other. . . . Violence has nothing to do, absolutely nothing to do, with the feminine sex, or with the masculine.
> *CH*: And with that in mind . . . why haven't there ever been many women in the organization's military front?
> *N1*: Well of course, because there's machismo so the important things are done by men. And the women . . . it's an ideological issue. It's not maternity.

The final statement—"It's not maternity"—echoes the younger narrator's objection to the assumption that women are peaceful because they can give birth. Yet the very recurrence of references to motherhood in these and other interviews underlines the difficulty for female activists of constructing a political identity without reference to the mother, the ar-

---

[18] According to White, the article was roundly condemned on both sides of the Atlantic, and the controversy surrounding it left Genet so isolated that he published nothing further for two years (1993, 687–88).

chetypal Basque nationalist female figure. In most of the interviews—not only those cited here—narrators' attitudes toward motherhood and toward the traditionally celebrated role of mothers in Basque nationalism are marked by ambivalence. More generally there is a tension in the interviews between the frequent motif of the female rebel, which represents a rejection of traditional and restrictive gender roles, including motherhood (Hamilton 2000a), and claims that women and men are different but complementary. In the two interviews cited below the theme of complementary roles surfaces as a caveat to claims of gender equality within ETA:

> *N4*:   I don't like the thing about saying, "I want to be the same as you." I think equality between women and men, I don't like to contain it in that respect. I think we're two different genders, and we do have the same capacity and above all the same opportunities to contribute. But then each one is as she or he is. And each one contributes. And I think we complement one another.[19]

> *N1*:   When I talk about equality, I'm not talking about—if I become like a man, and I take on men's values, and I screw and I smoke like them, are we equal? I don't want to be a man. I don't want to be a man. . . . Do you know why Thatcher didn't wear a miniskirt? . . . Because you could see her balls with a miniskirt. . . . She was the same as men. Thatcher wasn't an oppressed woman. Because she had become a man. I want to be fundamentally different from men in the ways we're different, and then at a social level, be equal. But I don't want to become a man.
>
> *CH*:   But, what is that difference? Is there an essential, a fundamental difference, do you think, between men and women?
>
> *N1*:   Yes.
>
> *CH*:   What is it?
>
> *N1*:   Well, women, we have another kind of energy. . . . Men have a different type of energy, and they're very good for certain types of things, and we for others. We complement each other.[20]

The joke about Margaret Thatcher conjures the fantasy of the powerful

---

[19] Narrator 4, interview.

[20] Narrator 1, interview.

woman who literally becomes a man.[21] Moreover, it implies, against the narrator's previous emphatic claim, that political activism associated with violence is, on some level, "about testicles." If Thatcher's balls represent the imagined dangers of excessive female power, testicles function more widely (in Basque and Spanish as in English) as a metaphor for bravery. In her interviews with men formerly active in ETA, for example, Miren Alcedo Moneo records one male narrator's reference to the *cojonímetro* (ballometer) that ETA militants supposedly used to measure an activist's commitment and valor (Alcedo Moneo 1996, 217–18). The idea that violence is a naturally virile activity is also evidenced in popular representations of female ETA activists. These representations can be classified in what Karrin Anderson and Kristina Sheeler, following the work of Robert L. Ivie, call "metaphoric clusters" (Anderson and Sheeler 2005, 4). Representations of women in ETA have habitually fallen into the following clusters: the masculinized woman, the girlfriend, and the femme fatale (see Calleja 2001, 269; Antolín 2002, 20).[22] Although these metaphoric clusters have changed historically, with the girlfriend model popular in the 1960s and 1970s giving way to the femme fatale by the 1980s, for example (Hamilton 2007), in all three instances women's participation in political violence has been linked to their sexuality.

In their study of gender and metaphor in relation to female politicians in the United States, Anderson and Sheeler argue that "metaphors function both as constraints and rhetorical resources for political figures" (2005, 2). Although stereotypical media portrayals contain and constrain female politicians, the women themselves use metaphors in the construction of their own political identities. A similar dual process can be traced in the interviews with female ETA members. As an example, Narrator 4, by citing Genet's likening of violence to giving birth, has provided an image of women as the privileged agents of violence. Later in her interview she elaborates on this metaphor. Responding to my question about whether activist life was more difficult for women in light of a traditional gender division of roles she states: "I think we did have to demonstrate that we were activists. But activism is not a fact; it's not a rational fact. I think it's an impulse and later it's rational. So it's a conjunction of both. But at the beginning there's something that comes from inside you, that you have to let out. And to let out that feeling, that impulse, that reason

[21] For an analysis of public fantasies of Thatcher as a symbol of female power and excessive violence, see Rose (1993).

[22] For a more detailed discussion of changes in media representations of female ETA members, including references to Spanish and Basque press sources, see Hamilton (2007).

as well, because it's not something entirely spontaneous. I think it's born like that, like it can be born equally in a man, in a male activist."[23] The passage begins with a reference to the experience of women having to prove themselves as armed activists, a popular refrain both among my narrators and in published interviews with female ETA members (del Valle et al. 1985, 246; Alcedo Moneo 1996, 353–66). But almost immediately, as if to preempt any assumption that women had to prove themselves by becoming like men, the passage changes direction, suggesting that it is men who are feminized through violence and specifically through the image of men giving birth. If we read the passage above backward we can trace an image of the activist releasing (letting out) the irrational impulse that has sprouted (literally being born) inside her or his body. The activist—male or female—gives birth to violence.

As do the female politicians studied by Anderson and Sheeler, this narrator uses metaphor creatively in the construction of her own political identity. But whereas Anderson and Sheeler (2005, 2) interpret their subjects' use of metaphors as deliberate strategies for attaining "pragmatic goals," I do not necessarily read the above narrator's metaphor of male birth as strategic. George Lakoff and Mark Johnson (2003, 272), in their work on metaphor, argue that "metaphorical thought is unavoidable, ubiquitous, and mostly unconscious." In this light, I would suggest that the metaphor of male birth is an unconscious cultural reconfiguration of the identity of the armed activist that nevertheless has an explicitly political meaning: that violence is not the natural domain of men.

For Lakoff and Johnson the metaphors that shape all conceptual thought are "grounded in everyday experience" (2003, 272). One of the experiences they discuss is birth, which they claim provides a common metaphor for processes of change. For Lakoff and Johnson metaphors of change that incorporate the ideas of *into* or *out of* "emerge naturally from as fundamental a human experience as there is, namely, birth. . . . The experience of birth (and also agricultural growth) provides a grounding for the general concept of CREATION, which has at its core the concept of MAKING a physical object but which extends to abstract entities as well" (74).

While this argument is suggestive for the importance of the birth metaphor in Western thinking, I depart from the assessment that birth provides a grounding or natural reference for more abstract concepts. As decades of feminist scholarship have shown, the experiences of birth and motherhood are not natural but are historically contingent and socially

---

[23] Narrator 4, interview.

and culturally constructed. Rather than considering natural or everyday experience as the basis for metaphors of violence and reproduction in the interviews with female ETA activists, I suggest that the context for the consideration of these reproductive metaphors is the wider set of gendered discourses of war and violence.

A number of scholars have noted the common motif in Western and non-Western mythology and literature of men giving birth, especially in relation to war, interpreting this as an example of men's desire to usurp female power by appropriating women's most revered—and feared—function: reproduction (Huston 1986; Cohn 1987; Condren 1995). In a recent article Vaheed Ramazani (2003, 26) argues that "the patriarchal appropriation of birthing metaphors serves to naturalize belligerent national ideologies." Following Ramazani I suggest that birth functions in nationalist military discourses as family does in nationalist discourses more generally. In both cases the metaphor works by replacing a political movement (nationalism or militarism) with a supposedly natural phenomenon (family or birth). This rhetorical move operates simultaneously to justify the political claims of nationalism or militarism as natural—and therefore indisputable in political terms—and to obscure the fundamentally political construction and meanings of family and birth. Both metaphors (nation = family, war = birth) depend, moreover, on a wider conceptual binary: masculine = political, feminine = natural.

The metaphor of male birth in the example of the interview with Narrator 4 also depends on a process of naturalization, in this case of violence. As in the examples in the first half of this article, where violence is associated with life, the metaphor of violence as birth serves to justify a political cause as natural or inevitable. According to Nancy Huston (1986), Mary Condren (1995), and others, the birth metaphor in male war narratives has functioned historically to appropriate female reproductive power. But what, we may ask, happens to the metaphor of male birth in war when the speaker is a woman and a female combatant at that? I argue that the metaphor also works as an act of appropriation, but in this case by a woman, of a form of power—military power—habitually associated with men.

As female activists in a nationalist military organization, the two narrators (Narrator 1 and Narrator 4) discussed here were doubly exceptional. On the one hand, in Basque nationalism, as in other nationalist movements, women have been defined historically as mothers, their political roles specified as the reproduction of Basque culture and language as well as giving birth to and rearing new generations of Basque nationalists. On the other hand, in the context of war and conflict women have historically been associated with what Jean Bethke Elshtain has called "history's Beautiful Soul, a collective being embodying values and virtues at odds with war's destructiveness, representing home and hearth and the humble verities of everyday life" (Elshtain 1987, xiii). These female ETA activists form part of the group of women Elshtain (1987, 163) has named the "ferocious few" in contrast to the "noncombatant many." In the context of Basque nationalism the women studied here were also exceptional: like most women active in ETA from the 1960s to 1980s they were not mothers (Hamilton 2007). Their position as exceptional women reflects a paradox noted by Huston (1986, 129) in many Western traditions: childbirth and war are both analogous and mutually exclusive. In other words, male soldiers symbolically "give birth" even while mothers are excluded from the battlefield.

Historical and contemporary discourses of war and conflict in the Basque country and elsewhere are replete with biological and reproductive metaphors: violence as creativity, the state as body, the political activist's bravery as balls, and war as birth. In the interviews with women formerly active in ETA references to maternity and birth, like those to male reproductive organs, are overdetermined. While the older narrator cited above insists that political violence is "not about testicles . . . not about ovaries" (Narrator 1), the repeated references in her and the younger narrator's interviews to reproductive organs and bodies indicates the impossibility for these female activists of constructing an identity as armed activists outside the language of the body, gender, and sexuality. Nonetheless, the interviews demonstrate the fluidity of language and identity through metaphors that denaturalize the relationship between female and male reproduction and sexuality.

Violent bodies

In a chapter titled "Violent Bodies" feminist philosopher Bar On (2002) analyzes the challenges posed for feminism by the production of female violent bodies through women's self-defense classes that train women to defend themselves against male violence. Drawing on the work of Arendt, Bar On argues that since the growth of second-wave feminism in the 1970s in the United States and elsewhere, women's self-defense classes have been justified in "ethicopolitical terms" as part of the feminist struggle to eradicate rape and violence against women (158–59). But, she stresses, the appeal of such classes to women cannot be understood strictly in terms of physical self-defense: "the production of violent women bodies is only in one respect a production of women bodies that are able to defend themselves. In another, it is a production of bodies that break a taboo and are as a result disobedient and transgressive because as implements of violence, they are skilled and competent in ways that are normally reserved for men" (159). To summarize Bar On's argument, for feminism there is an uncomfortable tension between the transgressive character of women's violent bodies, on one the hand, and the evidence that women are not immune to the attractions of violence, on the other hand (164–65). The female ETA members and supporters cited above also defend violence in terms of self-defense, not against rape or male violence but against what they define as the brutality of the Spanish state. Yet the repeated associations in the interviews of violence with creativity, health, life, birth, and the body point to an identification with violence beyond strictly political justifications.

To paraphrase a question Bar On (2002, 152) asks of her own body as she trains it in women's self-defense classes: Are women's violent bodies different from men's violent bodies? The interviews above reject—as does most contemporary feminist theory—any biological differences between women and men as an explanation for the differing levels of participation in violence. But historically in the Basque country, as elsewhere, women's roles in violence and conflict have differed substantially from those of men. If the female narrators cited in this article use a series of bodily metaphors of violence to describe their own relationship to political violence, it is in part because women's bodies are already constructed in wider discourses in particular ways relating to that violence. The interviews are located in a wider cultural context in which women are associated with being naturally nonviolent and peaceful or being more violent and dangerous than men. As childless activists who took on traditionally male roles in an armed organization, the narrators cited here reject both of these stereotypes, by dissociating violence from the activist's personality (Narrator 1) or by imagining men giving birth to violence (Narrator 4). In both cases there is an emphatic rejection of the association of maternity with peace. At the same time, the repeated references to reproductive organs as well as the use of domestic metaphors underscore the extent to which the narrators' constructions of their own relationship to violence are implicated in wider cultural associations of violence with gender and sexuality.

Feminist activism and scholarship (e.g., Enloe 1988) has provided important challenges to discourses and practices of political violence that target and affect women in particular ways. Although such work has not ignored women's capacity for violence, women nonetheless continue to feature more as victims or vulnerable bodies in feminist scholarship on war and conflict. This imbalance is justified to some extent by the extensive historical evidence of the unequal participation of women and men in political violence. But as Bar On (2002, 164–65) insists, feminists cannot afford to treat as marginal the evidence that "women have acted violently not merely because they are not in control but also because, like men of the same socioculture, they also can find something attractive about violence." Interviews with women active or formerly active in armed movements do not explain this attraction in any straightforward way. But they do offer, within the context of a feminist critique of the gender politics of conflict, evidence of the ways in which political violence is gendered through narratives of the body and reproduction and evidence of the multiple challenges of constructing a radical discourse and practice of nonviolence.

Spanish Programme, School of Arts
Roehampton University

References

Aiken, Susan Hardy, Ann E. Birgham, Sallie A. Marston, and Penny M. Waterstone, eds. 1998. *Making Worlds: Gender, Metaphor, Materiality.* Tucson: University of Arizona Press.

Alcedo Moneo, Miren. 1996. *Militar en ETA: Historias de vida y muerte* [ETA activism: Stories of life and death]. San Sebastián, Spain: Haranburu.

Anderson, Karrin Vasby, and Kristina Horn Sheeler. 2005. *Governing Codes: Gender, Metaphor, and Political Identity.* Lanham, MD: Lexington.

Antolín, Matias. 2002. *Mujeres de ETA: Piel de serpiente* [Women of ETA: Skin of the serpent]. Madrid: Ediciones Temas de Hoy.

Aranzadi, Juan, Jon Juaristi, and Patxo Unzueta. 1994. *Auto de terminación: Raza, nación y violencia en el País Vasco* [Self-determination: Race, nation, and violence in the Basque country]. Madrid: El País/Aguilar.

Arendt, Hannah. 1969. "On Violence." In her *Crises of the Republic,* 103–96. New York: Harcourt Brace Jovanovich.

Bar On, Bat-Ami. 2002. "Violent Bodies." In her *The Subject of Violence: Arendtean Exercises in Understanding,* 149–66. Lanham, MD: Rowman & Littlefield.

Bordo, Susan. 1993. *Unbearable Weight: Feminism, Western Culture, and the Body.* Berkeley: University of California Press.

Brown, Michael P. 2000. *Closet Space: Geographies of Metaphor from the Body to the Globe.* London: Routledge.

Calleja, José María. 2001. *¡Arriba Euskadi! La vida diaria en el País Vasco* [Up with Euskadi! Everyday life in the Basque country]. Madrid: Espasa.

Clark, Robert P. 1984. *The Basque Insurgents: ETA, 1952–1980.* Madison: University of Wisconsin Press.

Cohn, Carol. 1987. "Sex and Death in the Rational World of Defense Intellectuals." *Signs: Journal of Women in Culture and Society* 12(4):687–718.

Condren, Mary. 1995. "Sacrifice and Political Legitimation: The Production of a Gendered Social Order." *Journal of Women's History* 6(4)/7(1):160–89.

D'Cruze, Shani, and Anupama Rao, eds. 2005. *Violence, Vulnerability, and Embodiment: Gender and History.* Oxford: Blackwell.

del Valle, Teresa, Joxemartin Apalategi, Begoña Aretxaga, Begoña Arregui, Isabel Babace, Mari C. Díez, Carmen Larrañaga, Amparo Oiarzabal, Carmen Pérez, and Itziar Zuriarrain. 1985. *Mujer vasca: Imagen y realidad* [Basque women: Image and reality]. Barcelona: Anthropos.

Editorial Txalaparta. 1993. *Euskadi eta Askatasuna/Euskal Herria y la Libertad* [Basque country and freedom]. Tafalla, Spain: Editorial Txalaparta.

Elshtain, Jean Bethke. 1987. *Women and War.* New York: Basic.

Enloe, Cynthia. 1988. *Does Khaki Become You? The Militarisation of Women's Lives.* London: Pandora.

Genet, Jean. (1977) 2004. "Violence and Brutality." In his *The Declared Enemy: Texts and Interviews*, ed. Albert Dichy, trans. Jeff Fort, 171–77. Stanford, CA: Stanford University Press.

———. n.d. "Violencia y brutalidad" [Violence and brutality]. *El Viejo Topo* 3 (Extra): 4–7.

Hamilton, Carrie. 2000a. "Changing Subjects: Gendered Identities in ETA and Radical Basque Nationalism." In *Contemporary Spanish Cultural Studies*, ed. Barry Jordan and Rikki Morgan-Tamosunas, 223–32. London: Arnold.

———. 2000b. "Re-membering the Basque Nationalist Family: Daughters, Fathers and the Reproduction of the Radical Nationalist Community." *Journal of Spanish Cultural Studies* 1(2):153–71.

———. 2003. "Memories of Violence in Interviews with Basque Nationalist Women." In *Contested Pasts: The Politics of Memory*, ed. Katherine Hodgkin and Susannah Radstone, 120–35. London: Routledge.

———. 2007. *Women and ETA: The Gender Politics of Radical Basque Nationalism.* Manchester: Manchester University Press.

Huston, Nancy. 1986. "The Matrix of War: Mothers and Heroes." In *The Female Body in Western Culture: Contemporary Perspectives*, ed. Susan Rubin Suleiman, 119–36. Cambridge, MA: Harvard University Press.

Kristeva, Julia. (1979) 1997. "Women's Time." In *The Portable Kristeva*, ed. Kelly Oliver, 349–68. New York: Columbia University Press.

Krutwig, Federico. (1963) 1973. *Vasconia.* Buenos Aires: Ediciones Norbait.

Lakoff, George, and Mark Johnson. 2003. *Metaphors We Live By.* Chicago: University of Chicago Press.

Letamendia Belzunce, Franciso. 1994. *Historia del nacionalismo vasco y de E.T.A* [History of Basque nationalism and ETA]. San Sebastián, Spain: R & B Ediciones.

Lumley, Robert. 1990. *States of Emergency: Cultures and Revolt in Italy from 1968 to 1978.* London: Verso.

MacDonald, Eileen. 1991. *Shoot the Women First.* London: Arrow.

Massey, Doreen. 1994. *Space, Place, and Gender*. Minneapolis: University of Minnesota Press.

McClintock, Anne. 1995. *Imperial Leather: Race, Gender, and Sexuality in the Colonial Contest*. New York: Routledge.

Pandey, Gyanendra. 1999. *Memory, History and the Question of Violence: Reflections on the Reconstruction of Partition*. Calcutta: K. P. Bagchi.

Passerini, Luisa. 1987. *Fascism in Popular Memory: The Cultural Experience of the Turin Working Class*. Trans. Robert Lumley and Jude Bloomfield. Cambridge: Cambridge University Press.

———. 1992. "Lacerations in the Memory: Women in the Italian Underground Organizations." *International Social Movement Research* 4:161–212.

Portelli, Alessandro. 1981. "The Peculiarities of Oral History." *History Workshop Journal* 12(1):6–107.

Ramazani, Vaheed. 2003. "The Mother of All Things: War, Reason, and the Gendering of Pain." *Cultural Critique* 54 (Spring): 26–66.

Rose, Jacqueline. 1993. "Margaret Thatcher and Ruth Ellis." In her *Why War? Psychoanalysis, Politics, and the Return to Melanie Klein*, 41–86. Oxford: Blackwell.

Sontag, Susan. 1991. *Illness as Metaphor and AIDS and Its Metaphors*. London: Penguin.

Sullivan, John. 1988. *ETA and Basque Nationalism: The Fight for Euskadi, 1890–1986*. London: Routledge.

Thompson, Paul. 1988. *The Voice of the Past: Oral History*. Oxford: Oxford University Press.

White, Edmund. 1993. *Genet: A Biography*. London: Picador.

Zulaika, Joseba. 1988. *Basque Violence: Metaphor and Sacrament*. Reno: University of Nevada Press.

Zwerman, Gilda. 1994. "Mothering on the Lam: Politics, Gender Fantasies and Maternal Thinking in Women Associated with Armed, Clandestine Organizations in the United States." *Feminist Review* 47 (Summer): 33–56.

Part II. Feminist Interventions

Hagar Kotef

Merav Amir

(En)Gendering Checkpoints: Checkpoint Watch and the Repercussions of Intervention

This article is the outcome of three years of experience, between the two of us, of weekly shifts, standing with Checkpoint Watch (CPW) at the checkpoints that are spread throughout the Palestinian Occupied Territories. It is the product of these three years of observations, dilemmas, internal conflicts, and contradictory impulses. All of the critiques that this article suggests are thus ones that we as members of CPW often struggled with ourselves. They are by no means an attempt to undermine CPW and the important work it does. To the contrary, we both think CPW is one of the most significant and effective organizations operating today against the Israeli occupation. This article is dedicated to this organization and, in particular, to the remarkable and rare women with whom we have the privilege to stand, week after week, protesting against the occupation.

Introduction

All of a sudden one of the soldiers cracks. . . . He decides to close down the checkpoint, not letting anyone through. We [the activists] tried to call anyone who might assist . . . to no avail; left messages but got no response. . . . It is a cold and rainy day, and it's getting dark. . . . [Suddenly,] one old lady . . . decides that she has had enough. She bypasses the lines and the checkpoint, and simply starts walking home. The soldiers are after her, shouting. . . . She shouts that she cannot bear it any longer and refuses to go back in line. The soldiers panic in light of this "rebellion," and their reaction is a collective punishment: the line for the

We would like to thank Wendy Brown, Amir Engel, Hanna Freund-Chertok, Keren Sadan, Yves Winter, and Effi Ziv for reading different versions of this article and for providing us with many enlightening comments and Adi Ophir for providing the conceptual framework through which we think.

[*Signs: Journal of Women in Culture and Society* 2007, vol. 32, no. 4]

elderly is closed. Whoever was standing in this line must go back and
stand in one of the other lines. But they refuse. They have been standing
there too long to start all over again. In the meantime, the soldiers let
almost no one through. . . . The lines are getting longer and longer, and
the pressure is intolerable. The women start crying. They have a home,
they say, they want to go home.
—Checkpoint Watch report, Beit Iba, January 31, 2005 (translation
ours)[1]

Beit Iba, the checkpoint depicted in this report, is located at the outskirts
of Nablus, one of the major Palestinian cities in the West Bank. The
Palestinian Occupied Territories are paved with hundreds of such checkpoints; some are manned checkpoints, others are roadblocks, metal gates,
and earth mounds.[2] The checkpoints, which create a dense grid of limitations upon the movement of Palestinians, fragmenting both the space
and its population, have become one of the most predominant technologies of the occupation since the 1993 Oslo Accords. Most of these
checkpoints are not located between "Israel" and "Palestine" but inside
the Palestinian territories: on the entrance roads to villages, preventing
all vehicles from entering or leaving them; enclosing the cities, separating
them from the surrounding towns and villages that depend on them; and
fracturing the few roads on which the Palestinians are allowed to move.
They prevent any real possibility of maintaining normal daily lives (getting
to work, school, the doctor, the market) and of establishing a viable
political existence of an independent Palestinian entity (maintaining a political community and territorial continuity).[3]

Checkpoint Watch (*Machsom* Watch in Hebrew) was founded in 2001
by a small group of women who became aware of the expansion and
growing significance of the checkpoints in the ongoing occupation. It is

[1] See http://www.machsomwatch.org/reports/viewReport.asp?step=3&reportId=7545
&link=viewReport&lang=heb.

[2] In January 2006 there were 471 physical obstacles placed by the Israeli army on roads
throughout the Occupied Territories (UN Office for the Coordination of Humanitarian
Affairs 2006). While the term *checkpoint* often serves as a generic term describing all types
of movement-restricting obstacles, CPW activity focuses on checkpoints that are manned by
army personnel, through which both vehicles and pedestrians must pass. Currently there are
approximately fifty manned checkpoints throughout the West Bank.

[3] For a detailed account of the checkpoints and their history, see Keshet (2006) and
Hass (2006). Said Zeedani (2005) provides a Palestinian perspective on the implications of
the checkpoint on Palestinian life. Updated information can be found at the Checkpoint
Watch Web site (http://www.machsomwatch.org) and at the B'Tselem Web site (http://
www.btselem.org).

an all-women Israeli organization, currently including about four hundred volunteers, who stand in small groups of two to five women, in two shifts, morning and evening, at more than forty checkpoints (the main, manned checkpoints throughout the West Bank). The main goal of Checkpoint Watch is to protest against the occupation and in particular against the checkpoints. In a manner similar to that of other watch organizations, the primary practices chosen for that purpose are the regular presence of the activists at the checkpoints, observation, and documentation. The reports, written after every shift, are published on the organization's Web site and are sometimes sent to Israeli and international media, members of parliament, or high-ranking officers in the Israeli army. Later on, forms of intervention were also adopted by the members. These interventions include a wide variety of practices in accordance with each member's disposition and convictions. They range from serving as a physical buffer between violent soldiers and Palestinians, to persuading soldiers to show more consideration to the Palestinians (such as allowing ill individuals hospital visits even when they do not have all the necessary permits), to advocating for rules and regulation changes. These intervening practices were an outcome of growing frustration and a sense of helplessness, as well as the almost instinctive desire to do something, anything, about the distress the activists encounter.

But what does it mean to "do something" in this context? In what follows we will depict some of the more vexing effects of the doings of CPW. To this end, we will trace the body, and in particular the gendered body, within the reality of the checkpoints. Drawing primarily from the conceptual frameworks of Michel Foucault and Judith Butler, we will show that in the case of CPW efficacy is rooted in gender: the bodily presence of the activists at the checkpoints, which is the foundation of the organization's activity, is highly gendered. Gender first creates a breach through which CPW activists can access the checkpoints (the activists gain access to these military zones because they are female) and then materializes into a corporeal excess in the activists' activity. *Corporeal excess*, we argue, is a function of two factors. The first is the seizing of one corporeal axis over others: if a body is a compound matrix, comprised of multiple axes (such as sexuality, reproduction, skin color, size, vulnerability, and so forth), a corporeal excess is produced when one of these axes gains disproportionate dominance over the others. Second, excess is a function of the context in which this seizing is made: it is produced when a particular bodily axis consolidates and emerges within a temporal and spatial field in forms and density that do not comply with a given norm (a norm that is often constructed particularly to constitute this corporeal presence as excessive). Therefore excessiveness, solidified through these two factors, is a historical and social attribute. It is embedded in the normative grids that are at work in particular situations and in the constructions of group identities. (Hence, for example, a heteronormative society, environment, or particular situation would render any presence of same-sex sexual behavior as dominating any other aspect, and thus as "excessive," while the same practices performed in a heterosexual manner would be perceived as coexisting with other dimensions and thus "balanced.") Checkpoints are spatial zones producing, or at least accompanied by, several types of bodily excess: the excess of the bodies of Israelis, whose precarious lives provide the substrate for the ideology that justifies the checkpoints; that of the soldiers' bodies, both in their eruptive violence (from the Palestinian and leftist perspectives) and their vulnerability to Palestinian violence (from the army's perspective); and that of the two types of bodies that are at the focus of this article—those of the Palestinians and those of CPW activists.[4]

The following section attempts to show how Palestinians' bodies function in Israeli mainstream discourses in ways that enable the establishment and sustainment of the checkpoints and how the bodily distresses induced by these sites trigger the pressing need of CPW activists to be effective.[5] The subsequent section analyzes the gendered corporeal excess of CPW women. As CPW is an all-women organization, and for other reasons that this article explores, the forms of intervention of CPW assume gendered traits. Thereby another front is added to the activity of CPW: it is not only a peace organization, challenging nationalism and militarism, but also a feminist organization, operating against sexism. These gendered aspects not only add another axis of analysis, another factor to the ideological and political fronts in which this organization operates but also create a complex matrix in which considerations and countereffects of these two fronts blend into, contradict, and interfere with each other.[6]

---

[4] We borrow the expression "precarious life" from Butler (2004). Although our arguments here diverge from her analysis, we would still like to preserve her comprehension of the political and ethical significance of such a precariousness.

[5] Because this article is about an Israeli nongovernmental organization (NGO) and Israeli rule in the Occupied Territories, we refer to Palestinians predominantly from an Israeli perspective. Consequently, and almost unavoidably, this article duplicates the problematic objectification of the Palestinians made in these discourses.

[6] As Anne McClintock suggests, "Race, gender and class are not distinct realms of experience, existing in splendid isolation from each other; nor can they be simply yoked together retrospectively like armatures of Lego. Rather, they come into existence *in and through* relations to each other—if in contradictory and conflictual ways" (McClintock 1995, 5).

One should therefore take into account the complexities created by the conjunction of these two fronts and aim to map out the effects, profits, and costs of this superimposition.

Suffering, violence, and rudimentary life: Bodies of Palestinians

> On August 26, 2003, twenty-nine-year-old Rula Astia delivered a baby at the Beit Furik checkpoint, on the eastern outskirts of Nablus. Rula and her husband, Da'ud, live in a village ten minutes drive from Nablus, were it not for the checkpoint. Rula was eight months pregnant when she started getting contractions. She recalls: "We took a taxi and got off a fair distance from the checkpoint, since cars are not allowed to reach the checkpoint itself. From there we walked the rest of the way. I was in pain. There were a few soldiers at the checkpoint; they . . . ignored us. Da'ud went to speak to them, and one of them pointed his gun at him. . . . I was in pain and felt that I was going to deliver the baby there. . . . I laid down on the ground, in the dirt, and crawled behind a concrete block to get some privacy, and there I had the baby, in the dirt, like an animal. I held the baby, she moved a little, but a few minutes later she died in my arms." Da'ud continues: "After she had the baby Rula was crying, and then she screamed that the baby has died. She was crying, I was crying. . . . She held the baby in her arms, covered with blood, the umbilical cord was lying in the dirt, still connected, I had to cut it with a rock; I didn't have anything else I could use. Then I picked Rula up in my arms and carried her across the checkpoint to the ambulance, while she was holding our dead baby."
> —Amnesty International 2005, 7 (translation ours)

The singularity of a story creates a breach. Here, the story of the Astia family allows a segment of the actual experience of Palestinians at the checkpoints to penetrate into this article. Yet here we would like to trace how this singularity is dissolved, becomes a form, a figure, a pattern, and how the form of suffering and more specifically the figures of suffering bodies function.

Bodies of Palestinians are the addressees of a wide spectrum of activities, techniques, and tactics deployed by CPW. These activities, techniques, and tactics consist of different ways of addressing not only the extreme cases, such as the one above, or cases of brute violence, but also the mundane dimensions of human existence in the body—needing shelter from the blazing sun in summer and from the rain in winter and basic facilities for water and toilets. We argue that, on the whole, these acts can be understood as at one and the same time humanitarian actions address-ing human suffering and actions subverting the Israeli discourse of national security. We start with the latter.

Palestinian bodies not only inhabit the checkpoints, they also populate mainstream Israeli discourse regarding the occupation at large and the checkpoints in particular. Two main types of bodies, two main figures, constitute this discourse: the explosive body of the terrorist and the woman giving birth at the checkpoint. While the body of the suicide terrorist is the major inhabitant of the discourse of national security, the laboring woman has become an emblem in leftist Israeli discourse of the injustice of the checkpoints. Despite the daily routine of injustice at the check-points, she has become the symbol of all wrongs inflicted upon the in-nocent Palestinians. This iconization is both an outcome and a technique of the feminization of Palestinian suffering. It goes hand in hand with the mirrored masculinization of the Palestinian body that inflicts suffering (upon the Israelis), which produces the second type of body: the explosive body. The body that explodes in suicide attacks is always masculinized, even when the attack is performed by a woman.[7] This allows mainstream Israeli discourse to create a split in Palestinian existence, a split between victims and perpetrators, between those who arouse compassion and those who generate fear. While this is a reconstruction of the worn-out gender division of labor, in which passive suffering is feminized and active agency producing violence is masculinized, here it carries broader political sig-nificance. This gendered split is one of the factors that enable the pro-duction and sustainment of the schizoid Israeli *mentalité* that gives rise to the notion of "enlightened occupation."[8] It breaks the causal link between suffering and terror, separating and molding them into the seem-ingly clean and well-defined masculine/feminine dichotomy. It is because of this operation that the superimposition of humanitarian discourse onto the reality of occupation is sustainable.

Indeed, at the level of mainstream Israeli discourse, Palestinians have a double corporeal excess that is created in tandem with a gender de-marcation. It is an excess constructed by a combination of the two factors introduced above: first, it is a function of an aberrant dominance of one

[7] This is perhaps why female suicide bombers create such perplexity. See, e.g., Naaman 2007.

[8] The term *enlightened occupation* reflects the belief that the Israeli occupation can be administered legally, humanely, and considerately and that the occupation actually benefits the Palestinians by giving them better life conditions than they would otherwise have had. This notion prevailed in Israel at least until the first intifada (1987), and there are still traces of it in mainstream discourses.

axis of embodiment, in this case the axes of reproduction and volatility. Second, it is marked as excess because of the seemingly inappropriate appearance of this axis—giving birth in a war zone and exploding in civilian surroundings. However, at the checkpoint itself this gendered dichotomy collapses and is replaced by two nongendered superfluities: from the perspective of the army, the gender distinction collapses into the axis of explosiveness; from that of CPW activists it collapses into the axis of vulnerability. We begin with the former.

The logic and the grammar of the checkpoints reduce all Palestinians to perilous corporeality. Accordingly, even when a pregnant woman arrives at the checkpoint, she may be denied passage or taken aside to undergo a thorough body inspection to verify that her abdomen is not in fact an explosive belt. As bodies that can explode at any moment and thereby terminate themselves as they terminate others, Palestinians embody death. Moreover, passing daily in front of loaded rifles whose use is not restrained by any law, theirs is a life whose potential end is acutely present at any moment. This state of in-betweenness, of bodies positioned on the threshold of death, is intensified by an additional factor. Palestinian lives are managed as lives whose actuality has been reduced to the minimal sustainment of existence and as such stripped of what is considered normal and full.[9] This form of existence is interlocked with the occupation itself; it is insuperable from its specific form of rule. Checkpoint Watch aims to counter this construction of the Palestinians at the checkpoints by insisting on the mundane aspects of their existence. By demanding that the young man who is detained by the soldiers, presumably for security reasons, be allowed to sit down, drink, or urinate, the group reconstitutes the Palestinian body within Israeli security-oriented discourse as a live body, in contrast to the mere exploding body that is usually present there.[10] By bringing forth an alternative narrative in which the Palestinian body is fully alive and therefore should be attributed with mundane needs and

[9] Herein we only briefly touch on the question of what can be counted as human (or full) life and how the inclusion and exclusion of some lives from the domain of humanity play a part in a normative—many times oppressive—construction of lives. For a more complete account, see Butler (2004).

[10] It is important for us to emphasize that this constitution is an intra-Israeli matter. By no means do we claim here that Palestinians are dependent upon the Israeli grid of meanings in order to construct their own identities. However, within colonial contexts one cannot fully separate the identity of the colonized from his or her construction in the eye of the colonizer (Fanon 1967). This is especially true since the Israeli construction of the Palestinian as an explosive body is what enables the persistence of the Israeli forms of rule in the Occupied Territories in general and the checkpoint system in particular.

allowed to sustain its dignity, CPW opposes not just the construction of the Palestinian as a body on the threshold of death but also the derivative of this liminal positioning, the very discursive conditions that facilitate the forms of rule over the Palestinians.

Yet CPW strives to counter not only the security-oriented discourse but also the complementary iconized construction of Palestinian suffering in mainstream Israeli discourse and its tendency to focus on exceptional and extreme cases by drawing attention precisely to the ongoing and regular hardships inflicted upon Palestinians at the checkpoints. This attempt to resist the iconization of suffering is not just the intention and rhetoric of CPW; it is also the modus operandi of this type of activism: the somewhat Sisyphean character of the activity; the regular, daily shifts (most CPW activists go out once a week, every week, to the same checkpoints); the regular, daily reports (written every day, for each shift, even when nothing out of the ordinary occurs). These reports often look the same: counting the cars waiting to pass; measuring the time it takes one person to go through the checkpoint; the repetitive, almost cyclic encounter with the checkpoints—the same distress, the same routine violation of basic human rights, the same frustrating responses from the army. These forms of operation mirror the suffering they wish to display: a daily, lasting, ongoing suffering that cannot be iconized. By bringing to light the multiple forms of violence that the checkpoints produce, or more accurately the violence that resides in the mere existence of the checkpoints, they undermine the iconization of the woman in labor as a figure that embodies the *surplus* violence of the checkpoints. When it cannot be constructed as a surplus, this violence can no longer be portrayed as a mere byproduct of the occupation that may therefore be contained.

As suggested above, addressing corporeal suffering can also be understood within the framework of humanitarian intervention. Much has been written about the double edge of humanitarian work, and many of the critiques analyzing the complex implications that this type of work carries are applicable to CPW: the enfeeblement of the voice of the local population, the collaboration with the oppressive authorities, and providing the conditions of possibility for the atrocious situation.[11] Drawing from

---

[11] Most critiques of humanitarianism tie these aspects together. Alex De Waal (1997) and John Prendergast (1996) show how these three aspects are interwoven in the case of humanitarian NGOs in Africa. Ariella Azoulay and Adi Ophir (2004) and Rema Hammami (2000) analyze NGOs operating in the Palestinian Occupied Territories. They provide accounts of the complex relations of these organizations with local authorities (Israeli as well as Palestinian) and their role in the perpetuation of the occupation.

this critique, the following analysis examines the humanitarian aspects of CPW's intervention and suggests that additional processes are at play in this case. This examination also provides the framework that the gender-oriented analysis of the next section echoes.

It might seem that expressions such as "elderly people," "women and children," "crying babies," and "the sick" in reference to Palestinians at the checkpoints have become well-worn figures of speech in the discourse of the critical Left. However, arriving at the checkpoints, CPW activists could not overlook the actual and immediate suffering of the Palestinians there, the pressure and crowdedness in which they stand, exposed to the elements, sometimes for hours, and the long, muddy pathways through which they have to walk in order to cross the checkpoint. Activists saw that the sick and the elderly had nowhere to sit while they waited and that men detained for long hours were humiliated by having to relieve themselves in open fields, in full view of others standing in line, since there were no toilets available for them.

Although the principal aims of CPW activists are to protest the existence of the checkpoints and to document what they see there, the encounters with these conditions produced in most CPW activists an urge to alleviate some of the distress they were witnessing. They started by doing what they could: they carried bottles of water in their backpacks in order to supply water to people detained at the checkpoint for long periods of time. However, since CPW is not a humanitarian organization at its core, it lacks the resources and expertise to provide adequate solutions to the immediate bodily distresses at the checkpoints. Moreover, since it does not wish to aid the Israeli authorities in relinquishing their responsibility for the dire circumstances they have created, CPW started demanding that the army supply the basic necessary facilities. First, the organization demanded that the army supply water to any Palestinian, then it insisted that toilet facilities be installed and that shading be constructed in order to protect the people from the Middle Eastern sun in summer and the cold winter rain.

Reluctantly and slowly, the army complied: shadings were erected and toilets installed. Consequently, the checkpoints became entrenched: what started as a cement cube on a dirt path, behind which the soldiers stood, was expanded, developed, and solidified, evolving from a provisory obstacle into a permanent and elaborate construction. At some of the bigger checkpoints a trailer containing diapering posts and first-aid facilities appeared carrying a sign: "humanitarian post." And so, amid a site where suffering is inflicted as a matter of routine and whose mere existence is a violation of human rights, a post suddenly emerges, a post where, so the sign declares, human needs are attended to and human dignity is maintained, perhaps even restored. It may be obvious that we have never witnessed any mother diapering her baby in this trailer or any Palestinian receiving any medical treatment. The absurdity and emptiness of this post is manifested in the fact that for weeks this trailer stood locked. No soldier, and certainly no Palestinian, knew what it contained or what it was for. Yet the fact that these big trailers, which increase the spatial presence of the checkpoints, are called humanitarian posts shows how, in the process of swelling—partly as a result of ingesting humanitarian demands—the checkpoints also swallowed humanitarian language. And so an emphasis given to a corporeal excess of the Palestinians that materializes through the pivot of suffering induces the pervasiveness of the corporeality of the checkpoint itself: the shadings, trailers, roads, water tanks, and toilet facilities. Obviously, CPW was not the sole contributor to this process; the powers of occupation have their own agenda and internal dynamics. Yet being an organization that is dedicated to annulling the checkpoints, CPW's contribution—minor as it is—is particularly vexing.

Toward the end of 2005, a new form of elaborated checkpoint appeared: "the terminal." Unlike the other checkpoints, terminals are built through and through. Surrounded by concrete walls, roofed, and containing clearly marked designated areas (such as a "waiting area" or gates for people in wheelchairs), they are erected as architectural monstrosities. These constructions are equipped with an array of monitoring and control apparatuses—from electric iron turnstiles to security cameras and biometric identification devices—that enable the soldiers to control the checkpoints from an isolated edifice. Despite their title, most of them are located, like most checkpoints, inside Palestinian territory. They are built like border crossings, reinforcing the illusion that they are normal sites marking the border between two sovereign entities and concealing the fact that Israeli rule applies on both sides of the terminal. With seemingly friendly welcome signs, vast parking lots (in which no one parks—the Palestinians have no access by car to the checkpoint area), benches (on which no one sits), toilets (which are often out of order), the terminals present a facade of legitimacy. In a grotesque way, these checkpoints are everything that CPW women, in their humanitarian cast, could have hoped for. If what the CPW activists saw at the checkpoints was corporeal suffering, corporeal suffering has been attended to by the army—so much so that no words were left to describe the monstrosity of these new checkpoints. Reading reports written by CPW members from these checkpoints, one could see the struggle for words, the failed attempts to find ways to describe the enormity of their frustration. Facing these checkpoints, one cannot formulate any coherent critique (except, obviously, for the significant critique of their mere presence), and one cannot ask, say, or demand anything, since all concrete demands have seemingly been attended to and the horror is still there, and since there is no one to talk to. At the new checkpoints one cannot see the soldiers or talk to them. The soldiers control the terminal from a sealed construct behind bulletproof and soundproof glass. The glass is so impenetrable that even if one tries to get the soldiers' attention in light of a specific problem by knocking on it, one's fists make no sound.

Muteness is perhaps what happens to humanitarian organizations when they are digested by the powers they oppose. However, while all resistance to dominant power structures faces the risk of being absorbed into those structures (Foucault 1980; Brown 1995), there are additional factors that make this absorption even more rapid and deleterious in the case of CPW. The first is sociological in nature. It relates to the makeup and structure of the organization, which should be understood in relation to the two main aspects of the multifaceted structural racism in Israel, operating both on the Jewish-Palestinian axis and inside the Jewish population, between the "white" Ashkenazi Jews (of European descent) and the "black" Mizrachi Jews (of North African or Middle Eastern descent). The majority of the women in CPW are middle- to upper-class Jewish Ashkenazi women who belong to the heart of the Israeli establishment, the dominating political, cultural, and intellectual elite in Israel.[12] Thus, the co-optation of the organization by the ruling powers should not take us by surprise. The fact that most CPW women are part of—and perhaps more significantly, are perceived as belonging to—the elite, increases the accessibility and therefore the likelihood of modes of operation that are based on cooperation. In the name of efficacy, CPW implicitly relies on the privileged social positioning of its members to gain access to high-ranking officers, parliament members, and the media, thereby facilitating co-optation by the dominant powers of the occupation.

This sociological factor has been analyzed at length in relation to anti-occupation movements in Israel (Dahan-Kalev 1997; Helman 1999); we would therefore like to introduce a factor of a different order. It is possible that the easy, almost immediate transition from opposition to power to techniques of power in the case of CPW is rooted in a double symmetry that is formed between CPW and the army. The first symmetry is a derivative of an equivalent relation of the army (and more generally, dom-

---

[12] This makeup is not unique to CPW. Most Israeli peace movements are composed, to a large extent, of middle-class Ashkenazi Jews (Helman 1999).

inant Israeli discourses) and CPW (inasmuch as it is a humanitarian organization) to the Palestinians.[13] Both relate to the Palestinians as possessing some form of excessive corporeality, in which one axis of corporeality overshadows all other axes of existence. Both hold opposite yet structurally identical perspectives in which the Palestinian is reduced to either a suffering or an explosive body. Giorgio Agamben makes a similar argument, claiming that both sovereign power and humanitarian NGOs relate to bare life, "and therefore, despite themselves, [humanitarian organizations] maintain a secret solidarity with the very powers they ought to fight" (Agamben 1998, 133). Yet while for Agamben bare life is life excluded from politics (an exclusion that constitutes this life as bare and delineates the political sphere), the lives that the activists of CPW attend to at the checkpoint are saturated with politics; their existence is almost overdetermined by the political situation of the occupation. It would probably also be imprecise to state that both perspectives objectify Palestinians, since suffering is not an attribute of objects. A more accurate account might suggest that both reduce Palestinian lives to *rudimentary lives*—lives that are uncannily dominated by one single mode of existence.

This symmetry to which the Palestinian body serves as a hinge, bearing the two opposite facets of suffering—both enduring and inducing it—does not exhaust the parallels between the army and CPW. If we shift our gaze to the interplay between the bodies of the Palestinians and those of the other permanent inhabitants of the checkpoints, the soldiers, a second type of symmetry between the standpoints of CPW and the army reveals itself. Both see one type of bodies as intrinsically violent and the other type as innately vulnerable. While the army relates to all Palestinians as (potential) suicide bombers and to the soldiers as their designated victims, CPW sees all soldiers as carriers of uncontrollable violence and all Palestinians as jeopardized by this violence, if not as its actual victims. Since both operate within a matrix characterized by a deleterious friction between two types of excessive bodies, that of the Palestinian and that of the soldier, the perspectives of both CPW and the army resonate and therefore lead, intentionally or not, to a solution that maximizes the isolation of these two bodies—the Palestinian's and the soldier's—and both lead to the entrenchment of the checkpoints.

Between these two pivots of structural parallelism, the ground is set for a disturbing resemblance between the army and CPW, a resemblance

---

[13] In all other aspects of its activity CPW does not relate to the Palestinians in forms that produce this reductive effect; quite the contrary—as suggested above—it even aims to counter any attempts of the security forces and the mainstream Israeli discourses to do so.

that produces another form of corporeal excess: the superfluous materiality of the checkpoints. It is this correspondence that enables the army to be attuned to the demands of CPW, granting it the veneer of sensibility to humanitarian consideration and bestowing upon it a cloak of legitimacy, thereby making the new terminals a troublesome product of a treacherous alliance and locating CPW always on the threshold of an abyss, always on the verge of operating against itself.

Mothers, mistresses, and whores: Bodies of CPW activists

An old man of about eighty, clutching a cane and leaning on his daughter, walked slowly across the checkpoint. The old man . . . got into the car lane and almost reached the other side of the checkpoint when the checkpoint commander appeared in front of him and ordered him to go back . . . [and] stand in the lengthening queue like everyone else. I found it difficult to watch. It was simply mean. The man could hardly move. The commander, who could have used his discretion, checked his ID card and let him through, didn't bother to do it. It's not just that I couldn't watch; I couldn't keep quiet either—I went to the commander . . . and called at him: "Look into my eyes, would you let your grandfather walk such a distance?" However, the commander turned his back and snickered. I didn't let him off: . . . "Would you let your grandfather walk like that?" And he snickered. . . . Why should he worry—after all it's not his grandfather. It's only a Palestinian grandfather!
—CPW report, Huwwara, January 23, 2006 (translation ours)[14]

It seems that the fact that CPW is an all-women organization is but another instance of the recent years' trend toward the feminization of Israeli peace NGOs (Isachar 2003; Powers 2006). This feminization is by no means homogenous: the feminist and women-oriented organizations vary, even confront each other on many levels, especially regarding the specific meanings and implications of gender in their ideology and praxis.[15] However, we would like to argue that despite significant differences between them, there is a single thread of reasoning that might be found in all the Israeli

[14] See http://www.machsomwatch.org/reports/viewReport.asp?step = 3&reportId = 14060&link = viewReport&lang = heb.

[15] Some of these organizations include only women (Bat-Shalom) or are defined as women-oriented organizations (Shuvi). Others, such as New Profile, rely on feminist frameworks. Some, like Four Mothers, rely on traditional gender roles; other organizations, on radical feminist grounds (Women in Black) and even queer theory (Black Laundry).

women's peace movements: the fundamental perspective that assumes that the othering of women is a potential source of alternative politics. Most of these organizations share the view that gender is the key to understanding and approaching political circumstances and point to the nexus between the cultivation of heightened masculinity and the militarism of Israeli society.

Analyzing modes of operation, as well as declarative statements made by leading voices in CPW, reveals a different image. While CPW is all-female in its constitution, it nevertheless diverges radically from the common form of gendered politics of most Israeli NGOs. Gender functions in CPW mainly as a tool. The all-female makeup of the organization is utilized to enable forms of activities that would not be tolerated or even feasible otherwise. According to statements made by Yehudit Keshet, one of the three founding members of CPW, and by the organization's former spokesperson, Adi Dagan, the women of CPW believe that including men might jeopardize the delicate interactions with the soldiers at the checkpoints and thereby endanger the type of activism CPW performs. This viewpoint assumes that women may find it easier to avoid one of the two extreme stances while facing the soldiers: either totally identifying with them or aggressively conflicting with them (Deutsch-Nadir 2005, 48; Keshet 2006, 35).

Reasoning that women are more equipped to maintain this balance may be debatable, and experience has shown that the organization has found itself dealing with women who occupied attitudes on these two extremes of the spectrum.[16] Still, this line of reasoning reveals that the determining factor in the decision to restrict its membership to women only was that this makeup would enable the organization to sustain the form of activity its members consider desirable and effective. Furthermore, this reasoning rests on more fundamental grounds that are not openly acknowledged in statements made by CPW members: the conditions of possibility of CPW rely upon its all-female composition. The mere presence of a highly controversial political organization that is considered pro-Palestinian by the Israeli mainstream on the new front line of the

---

[16] Two cases might elucidate this claim. In the first, one of the activists physically attacked a soldier and in the second an active member volunteered to serve in reserve duty at the checkpoints. These uncharacteristic instances of confrontation and identification aroused fierce debates within the organization as to how it may prevent such cases from reoccurring. The intensity of these debates attests to the importance the members of CPW place on keeping a delicate balance when interacting with the soldiers for the integrity and the survival of the organization.

army-controlled checkpoints is tolerable only because of the sexist presuppositions projected onto the activists.

These sexist presuppositions, which are common to many other societies, especially nationalistic and militaristic ones, place women in an external position vis-à-vis the political domain. Women in Israel are considered to be lesser political beings to men; their status as political actors within the discourse of national security is that of caregivers and family agents. Accordingly, the public ear is attuned to political statements that they make in their capacity as mothers and wives (Yuval-Davis 1989; Berkovitch 1999).[17] The women of CPW utilize these preconceptions in order to position themselves, discursively and physically, at the nucleus of political dispute; it is exactly these biases that allow their access to the checkpoints. Nonetheless, once they are there, the type of activities the activists perform clearly deviates from their predetermined womanly roles. They do not position themselves as the carriers of peace values but instead operate on a different ground and from a different basis of legitimacy.

The activity of CPW amounts to a persistent attempt to undercut the man-war/woman-peace division that prevails not just under patriarchal conceptions but in many feminist analyses as well (Ruddick 1992). The women of CPW go out to the confrontational zones and directly intervene in army matters. Often it seems as though CPW activists almost compete with the army over the management of war at the checkpoints. They claim to know the rules, sometimes even better than the soldiers, gaining their authority from their regular and persistent presence at the checkpoints, which most often exceeds that of the soldiers. It is therefore common for CPW activists to confront soldiers, using statements such as "I have been standing at this checkpoint for over a year, you just arrived a few weeks ago; I can tell you that Red Cross vehicles can pass without needing special permits" or "I can tell you that you cannot detain a person just to teach him a lesson." They have access to high-ranking officers, access that most often the soldiers at the checkpoints do not have, access that gives them the opportunity to question specific commands and local decision-making processes. Thus it is not rare for a woman from CPW to demand the brigade commander's intervention in cases where a checkpoint commander seems to be incompetent, violent, or incapable of restraining vi-

---

[17] This claim might seem odd considering the fact that mandatory military service in Israel applies to women as well as men. However, as the social benefits attained by the military service apply only to men, in the political sphere women are desoldierized (Izraeli 1997).

olent soldiers. As we suggest elsewhere (Kotef and Amir 2007), by positioning themselves on the same ground as the military officers and questioning security forces' assertions of privileged access to knowledge, the women of CPW perform a praxis of delegitimization, undermining the very authority of the Israeli rule at the checkpoints.

Still, gender cannot be tamed and restricted to specific and prescribed functions; gender emerges and reemerges in uncalculated forms and unpredictable domains. In the case of CPW, it materializes as an engendered bodily excess of the activists, a bodily excess consolidated through stereotypical gender positions.[18] The most common among these positions is a motherly position toward the soldiers. For some activists this position may be readily accessible, since many of them are indeed mothers and grandmothers of soldiers and most are of that age. More generally, it is a position that may be assumed as a tactical move aiming to constitute a stance from which their message can be heard. The activist consents to place herself in an acceptable and conformist womanly role, assuming that from it she may express highly controversial views regarding Israeli-Palestinian relations and intervene effectively. The motherly stance is most often prompted by a sense of urgency posed by concrete distresses and includes performing as a family agent, an educator, the one who reduces the levels of tension, or any combination thereof. As the family agent, the activist attempts to remind the soldier of his familial context and juxtapose it with the Palestinians' ("would you tolerate the same behavior toward your own grandfather?"). As educators, the activists conduct conversations with soldiers in which "the mother" tries to explain to the soldier why his conduct is unacceptable and that he should "behave." Attempts to calm the soldiers are usually not performed as direct interventions and are more part of the rationale of the all-female presence at the checkpoints—as mentioned above, the decision to make CPW an exclusively women's organization is rooted in the assumption that such a presence will lower the tension at the checkpoints.

More often than not, it is by these acts through which the mother position is assumed that the intervention of CPW at the checkpoint becomes effective. Consequently, when facing a sense of urgency, a form of activism that aims to undermine gender stereotypes and conservative gender-based political divisions eventually materializes in forms that intensify and reify the same stereotypes and divisions. Still, perhaps this account of the double-edged nature of activism is too clean in its attempt to sustain

---

[18] For an additional analysis of gendered bodies in the Israeli Left movement opposing the occupation, see Sasson-Levy and Rapoport (2003).

a dichotomy between subverting gender roles and reproducing them. As with any performance of any identity, gendered or otherwise (Butler 1999), by performing motherhood at the checkpoint CPW women do not simply reproduce and reinforce a traditional prescribed role. Mothers, as a normative and regulatory ideal, care; they feed, they spoil their children. Checkpoint Watch women do not. It is thus a very common occurrence that the soldiers react angrily to this perceived failure and blame the CPW activists for neglecting to bring cookies or soft drinks for them. The "failure" to perform motherly care is rooted in a more critical failure: the main care and concern is not aimed toward members inside "the family" of Jewish-Israelis, and specifically the soldiers, but rather toward the Palestinians. Indeed, examining the explicitly gendered activities performed by the CPW women in the context of their identities as mothers clearly shows a sharp division in the allocation of the resources that this role possesses. While practices of education, appeasing, and making present the familial context are directed toward the soldiers, care and concern are expressed toward the Palestinians. This split may be read as performing a subversive implementation of this gendered position, making use of a prescribed identity that the CPW activists cannot completely avoid. This is particularly true in the Israeli context, in which reproduction is interwoven into racial divisions and constructed as a barrier whose aim is to foreclose the boundaries of race (Melamed 2004).

However, this analysis assumes that occupying one's identity is fully in one's possession and may be activated according to one's will. As Butler (1999) claims, identities in general and gender identities in particular cannot be inhabited in a stable and foreclosing manner; the inherent instability of gendered positions dictates the need to constantly reoccupy them anew, to reperform them in order to inhabit them. Thus, since these positions are never mere tools that are fully controlled by the individual, the meanings and implications derived from these positions are also available for misreadings and appropriation by others. Indeed, such misreadings of the positions of CPW women as mothers often occur at the checkpoints. These readings project onto the activists the Jewish-Israeli normative role of the mother-of-the-soldier in its coherent form, erasing the split between the addressees of the motherly attention mentioned above. The surprise and resentment expressed by the soldiers when CPW women fail to provide the expected care and concern toward them is one example among many. Similarly, parents of soldiers sometimes address the activists and seek their help in caring for the soldiers at the checkpoints.

This analysis may aid in understanding some of the more complex implications of the presence of the CPW activists at the checkpoints. Is it possible that these calls, which interpellate the CPW women as mothers even in terrains they aim to leave clean of motherly traces, carry implications beyond the realm of gender? Is it possible that in their presence at the checkpoints as mothers CPW women have turned the checkpoints into one of the sites in which the army is exposed to parental supervision, one of the sites in which parental inspection necessitates paying more attention to the "working conditions" of soldiers?[19] And is it possible, then, that this supervision—which is never taken on by CPW women as one of their roles but is nonetheless an outcome of their collapse into motherhood—contributed to the form the new terminals took?[20] Can it be that the role CPW played in the entrenchment of the checkpoints is a function not only of the group's humanitarian interventions but also of the gendered attribute of these interventions? Whatever the answers may be, being a mother at the checkpoint is not a position one can simply jump into and out of as one pleases. And yet, being a mother at the checkpoint—and more generally, assuming gendered positions—is not something CPW women can elude. This is not only because the gender role is projected onto them but also because it facilitates a trade-off in which more conservative gender politics allows a radical form of activism to sustain itself.

This trade-off is even more apparent in another gendered and highly embodied figure through which some CPW women operate at the checkpoints: that of the sexualized body. In this domain there are two main positions: that of the sexual object and that which is banished out of the legitimate domains of (racist-delineated) sexuality to the deviate zones of perversion: "the Arabs' whore." Appropriating the role of a sexual object, much like appropriating that of the mother, is a modus operandi at the checkpoint. Though not commonly used, this position often proves to be the most effective. The CPW woman offers the soldier bits of flirtatious attention, which usually takes place in the form of a bargain: she gives him some affection and lets him see her as a sexual being, and he in return performs as a "better person," giving her more considerate treatment of

---

[19] On parental involvement in the Israeli army and its implications, see Herzog (2004).

[20] Unlike the older checkpoints, the new terminals are designed to provide maximal protection to the soldiers. One may therefore argue that when the terminals were designed, parental considerations regarding the well-being of the soldiers at the checkpoints gave this issue precedence.

the Palestinians.[21] This technique achieves effects that no other technique can. To tell one story among many, one of us stood at the Beit Iba checkpoint in January 2005. The lines were unbearably long: people had been standing in them for hours and hours, squeezed almost to the point of not breathing, while the sound of crying babies filled the air. The horrendous pressure was magnified by the malicious conduct of the soldiers, who worked spitefully slowly and completely stopped letting people through every few minutes. A group of officers stopped by. We tried everything we could to make them use their authority and additional personnel to improve the situation; they kept insisting that this was not their job and was none of their business. One of us then started flirting with one of them. In a short while he entered the checkpoint and started checking and letting Palestinians through. The line of people was dramatically reduced in minutes. On releasing a group of men who had been delayed on their way to Nablus, he approached the CPW member, his right hand on his heart, and bowed. "I released them for you," his body language stated.

It is important to ask what happens in these situations, what is produced and ratified, what is contested, and what effects are achieved. This technique duplicates a traditional man-woman relationship in which she offers him sex and he offers her his assets, material and otherwise. The only difference here is that instead of economic benefits, the woman receives the well-being of the Palestinians. Hence, the sexuality of the woman is objectified in an almost commercial transaction. But are other effects produced along the way? Perhaps the fact that this objectification is not a collapse into an assigned position but is instead utilized in order to gain more control over the situation suggests that there is more agency involved. But is this utilization of sexuality not just another case of the prevalent (hetero)sexual game? Moreover, do we find more agency and more subversiveness here than in many other situations? Is not gender itself constituted from these building blocks (Butler 1999)? And perhaps more important, are these the questions we have to ask when dealing with the checkpoints? It is more important to note that this technique objectifies not just the activist but also the Palestinians. It reproduces not just the reification of the activist, making her sexuality a commodity, perhaps

---

[21] Although at some of the checkpoints there are female soldiers, the checkpoints are overwhelmingly manned by male soldiers, and the checkpoint commander is almost always a male. Therefore the interaction between the soldiers and the CPW women is conducted along the lines of a heterogendered dichotomy.

her most valuable commodity; it also reproduces the dehumanization of the Palestinians: they are the property of the soldier to give. Then again, perhaps the only thing that matters here is the effectiveness, the fact that some—sometimes many—people get to go home, to work, to their families with fewer delays or without having to endure the soldiers' violent outbursts.

This measure of effectiveness, assessed by the degree to which the immediate toll of the checkpoints on the lives of the Palestinians is alleviated, is not shared by all CPW members. One of the stances adopted by some of the activists is rooted in the belief that any form of cooperation with the ruling authorities is necessarily flawed and should be avoided at all cost. These women adopt a confrontational stance toward the soldiers; they argue with them fiercely and try to sabotage their ability to manage and control the checkpoints efficiently. They also refuse to align themselves to the gendered positions described above. However, every so often, these women are reminded that falling into traditional gender roles is never completely avoidable. In the eyes of the soldiers, they become Arabs' whores, a common curse in Jewish-Israeli society that is usually hurled at female-left activists or ideologists. This identity claim underscores the manner in which race and sexuality are interlaced in the Jewish-Israeli nationalistic discourse, to the extent that what is regarded as transgression on the axis of nationalism and race is cast as what is perceived as sexual perversion.

In fact, it would be more accurate to speak here not of different types or groups of women but of different strategies, occasions, and incidences in which different women take on this or that role. It is rare to find CPW women who can successfully maintain the same position or those who intentionally aim to make use of a single, stable, and constant strategy. One occurrence that clearly illustrates this point happened to one of the most radical CPW women. Although she consistently endorsed an adversarial attitude toward the soldiers, she discovered that a high-ranking officer had taken a liking to her. Although she was not willing under any circumstances to change her attitude toward him, he claimed that he was willing to do anything as long as she was willing to talk to him. Gradually, she started turning and asking for his help whenever she encountered severe and violent incidents at the checkpoints, despite her strong convictions opposing any cooperation with the army, and reluctantly occupied the role of the flirtatious woman in essence if not in form.

One can claim that the formation of bodily excess in the case of CPW women not only derives but also deviates from the two types of bodily excess with which we began our article, that of one single axis of cor-

poreality gaining dominance over all others and that of contextual diversion from a given norm. First, since the forms of activity we have just
outlined by no means diminish all other actions of CPW activists, the
bodily axes they produce do not dominate the women's corporeal presence. In other words, CPW women are not present at the checkpoint first
and foremost as mothers, mistresses, or whores, but as political activists.
And yet, because the presence of the activists at the checkpoint is always
in jeopardy, negotiable, and in need of reestablishment, when these corporeal axes appear, they always threaten to become the sole logic of this
presence. Second, these appearances do not transgress the norm (as much
as heteronormativity can be thought of in the singular form): reproduction
and sexuality are clearly part of the normative construction of femaleness.
Nonetheless, at the checkpoint reproduction and sexuality appear out of
place: on the front line rather than at home. Perhaps more important,
they exceed and transgress the organization's imaginary self; they radically
diverge from the manner in which CPW sees itself and its activity. Therefore, at the checkpoint, these appearances constitute a bodily excess. It
may then be stated that the bodies of CPW women participate in an
intricate game of give-and-take in which gender functions on multiple
plateaus. Gender provides access to the checkpoints, facilitates certain
forms of activism, and amplifies the effectiveness of some while undoing
others.

Conclusion

In this article we explored ways in which political activism works in spite
of itself. We aimed to mark a trail through which this self-impediment
might be understood, a trail traversing through gender. This trail began
with the way gender functions in the conditions of the occupation itself.
We showed how the Palestinians' occupied bodies are carved into a gender
binary, wherein one side links suffering and femaleness (in the figure of
the woman giving birth at the checkpoint) and the other fuses masculinity
and violence (in the figure of the suicide bomber). We showed how this
male/female binary, which usually serves to preserve gender orders,
operates to sustain a different type of order—that of the occupation.
Although CPW operates to bring about the termination of the checkpoints, its modus operandi also challenges, on many levels, both the
above-mentioned gender division and the positions assigned to women
in Israeli society.

However, the activities performed by CPW members include elements
that repeatedly disrupt the organization's own objectives on these two

fronts. Facing massive injustice at the checkpoints, an almost uncontrollable urge to act effectively arises. Since the ability to alleviate the suffering at the checkpoints demands the soldiers' cooperation, and since the checkpoints are highly gendered military zones, attempting to be effective sometimes results in the activists finding themselves reassigned to traditional and even stereotypical gender roles. Gender overflow is not the sole cause for the organization's digression from its course; the humanitarian impulse to alleviate suffering contributes to this process as well. As the object of this impulse is many times a body that is reduced to one axis of corporeal existence, it resonates with the army's construction of Palestinians as explosive bodies. And as the perspectives both of CPW and of the army position this object in a dyad wherein there is friction between vulnerable and violent bodies that necessitates separation by walls, this resonance results in the ever-progressing material excessiveness of the checkpoints.

Nonetheless, the implications of CPW extend beyond those explored in this article. Before the activity of the organization gained momentum, the reality of the checkpoints—a major aspect of the Israeli rule in the Occupied Territories that has devastating effects on every facet of Palestinian life—was generally overlooked. Not only were the fragmentation of the West Bank, the constant siege, the routine of daily humiliation, incidences of violence, and arbitrary bureaucratic hardship outside the scope of public debates internationally and in Israel, but the mere existence of the checkpoints was also largely unrecognized. The activity of the organization was, and still is, one of the most significant contributors to the effort of bringing the checkpoints into Israeli and international focus. It also manages to affect the manner in which the checkpoints themselves operate in crucial ways that this article did not cover and to diminish in various aspects some of their harmful implications. Though reality produces incalculable effects that might undermine the goals of the organization, and though conceptual frameworks sometime consolidate into concrete apparatuses that prompt a sense of muteness and paralysis, this article is in no way a call for nonaction or political disengagement. Facing the checkpoints, facing catastrophe in the making, neither acting against the occupation nor analyzing the consequences of such interventions can be relinquished.

School of Philosophy
Tel Aviv University (Kotef)

The Cohn Institute
Tel Aviv University (Amir)

References

Agamben, Giorgio. 1998. *Homo Sacer: Sovereign Power and Bare Life*. Trans. Daniel Heller-Roazen. Stanford, CA: Stanford University Press.

Amnesty International. 2005. "Israel Ve-Hashtachim Ha-Kvushim Conflict, Kibush Ve-Patriarchaliyut: Nashim Nos' ot Ba-Netel" [Conflict, occupation, and patriarchy: Women carry the burden]. Report. AI Index: MDE 15/016/2005 http://amnesty.org.il/israel/women042005.doc (in Hebrew).

Azoulay, Ariella, and Adi Ophir. 2004. "The Ruling Apparatus of Control in the Occupied Territories." Paper presented at the Van Leer Jerusalem Institute— the Politics of Humanitarianism in the Occupied Palestinian Territories, Jerusalem, April 20.

Berkovitch, Nitza. 1999. *From Motherhood to Citizenship: Women's Rights and International Organizations*. Baltimore: Johns Hopkins University Press.

Brown, Wendy. 1995. *States of Injury: Power and Freedom in Late Modernity*. Princeton, NJ: Princeton University Press.

Butler, Judith. 1999. *Gender Trouble: Feminism and the Subversion of Identity*. New York: Routledge.

———. 2004. *Precarious Life: The Powers of Mourning and Violence*. London: Verso.

Dahan-Kalev, Henriette. 1997. "The Oppression of Women by Other Women: Relations and Struggle between Mizrahi and Ashkenazi Women in Israel." *Israel Social Science Research* 12(1):31–44.

Deutsch-Nadir, Sharon. 2005. "Capitalizing on Women's Traditional Roles in Israeli Peace Activism: A Comparison between Women in Black and Checkpoint Watch." Masters thesis, Tufts University.

De Waal, Alex. 1997. *Famine Crimes: Politics and the Disaster Relief Industry in Africa*. Bloomington: Indiana University Press.

Fanon, Frantz. 1967. *Black Skin, White Masks*. Trans. Charles Lam Markmann. New York: Grove.

Foucault, Michel. 1980. "Power and Strategies." In his *Power/Knowledge: Selected Interviews and Other Writings, 1972–1977*, 134–45. New York: Pantheon.

Hammami, Rema. 2000. "Palestinian NGOs since Oslo: From NGO Politics to Social Movements?" *Middle East Report* 214 (Spring): 16–19, 27.

Hass, Amira. 2006. "Israeli Restrictions Create Isolated Enclaves in West Bank." *Ha'aretz*, March 24, 1, 3. Available at http://www.kibush.co.il/show_file.asp ?num = 12852.

Helman, Sara. 1999. "From Soldiering and Motherhood to Citizenship: A Study of Four Israeli Peace Protest Movements." *Social Politics: International Studies in Gender, State and Society* 6(3):292–313.

Herzog, Hanna. 2004. "Family-Military Relations in Israel as a Genderizing Social Mechanism." *Armed Forces and Society* 31(1):5–30.

Isachar, Hedva. 2003. *Achayot Le-Shalom: Kolot Ba-Smol Ha-Feministi* [Sisters in peace: Feminist voices of the left]. Tel Aviv: Resling.

Izraeli, Dafna N. 1997. "Gendering Military Service in the Israeli Defense Forces." *Israel Social Science Research* 12(1):129–66.

Keshet, Yehudit Kirstein. 2006. *Checkpoint Watch: Testimonies from Occupied Palestine*. New York: Zed.

Kotef, Hager, and Merav Amir. 2007. "On Imaginary Lines; Biopolitics, Disciplinary Apparati and Sovereign Violence at the Checkpoints." Paper presented at the annual meeting of the Association of American Geographers, San Francisco, April 17–21.

McClintock, Anne. 1995. *Imperial Leather: Race, Gender, and Sexuality in the Colonial Context*. New York: Routledge.

Melamed, Shoham. 2004. "Motherhood, Fertility, and the Construction of the 'Demographic Threat' in the Marital Age Law." *Theory and Criticism* 25 (Fall): 69–96.

Naaman, Dorit. 2007. "Brides of Palestine/Angels of Death: Media, Gender, and Performance in the Case of the Palestinian Female Suicide Bombers." *Signs: Journal of Women in Culture and Society* 32(4):933–55.

Powers, Janet M. 2006. *Blossoms on the Olive Tree: Israeli and Palestinian Women Working for Peace*. Westport, CT: Praeger.

Prendergast, John. 1996. *Frontline Diplomacy: Humanitarian Aid and Conflict in Africa*. Boulder, CO: Lynne Rienner.

Ruddick, Sara. 1992. "Preservative Love and Military Destruction: Some Reflections on Mothering and Peace." In *Feminisms: A Reader*, ed. Maggie Humm, 298–303. New York: Harvester Wheatsheaf.

Sasson-Levy, Orna, and Tamar Rapoport. 2003. "Body, Gender, and Knowledge in Protest Movements: The Israeli Case." *Gender and Society* 17(3):379–403.

UN Office for the Coordination of Humanitarian Affairs. 2006. *West Bank Closure Count and Analysis, January 2006*. New York: United Nations.

Yuval-Davis, Nira. 1989. "National Reproduction and 'the Demographic Race' in Israel." In *Woman, Nation, State*, ed. Nira Yuval-Davis and Floya Anthias, 92–109. Houndmills, UK: Macmillan.

Zeedani, Said. 2005. "A Palestinian Perspective on the Checkpoints." *Occupation Magazine: Life under Occupation*, September 29. http://www.kibush.co.il/show_file.asp?num=9277.

Women's Advocacy in the Creation of the International Criminal Court: Changing the Landscapes of Justice and Power

O n July 1, 2002, the treaty creating the world's first permanent international criminal tribunal to try individuals—any individuals, regardless of their official status or position—for genocide, war crimes, crimes against humanity, and, eventually, aggression entered into force. Known as the Rome Statute, the treaty forms the basis of the future International Criminal Court (ICC, or the Court), an institution intended to pierce the state-centric veil behind which errant state and nonstate actors have often been able to hide in the traditional human rights framework (Rome Statute 1998; see the app.).[1] It is significant that the ICC will be independent of existing institutions such as the United Nations and, more specifically, the UN Security Council (Rome Statute 1998, Preamble and Articles 2, 12, 13, and 16). This aspect alone has incurred the wrath of the defense and foreign policy establishment of the world's "sole remaining superpower," the United States, which is a telling indicator of the potential of the new institution as an independent mechanism of accountability.

Working together as the Women's Caucus for Gender Justice (Women's Caucus), women from different countries, regions, approaches, and disciplines merged energies and interests to help shape this unprecedented instrument as it was brought into being. Though the Women's Caucus

---

[1] Article 5 of the Rome Statute extends the Court's jurisdiction to genocide, war crimes, crimes against humanity, and, eventually, aggression, once a definition of the crime is adopted and amended into the statute. Article 25 affirms the individual criminal responsibility of persons who commit crimes within the jurisdiction of the Court. Article 27 confirms that immunities will not bar the Court from exercising its jurisdiction over such persons without distinction based on official capacity (Rome Statute 1998). The treaty was adopted by 120 votes with twenty-one abstentions and seven "no" votes (China, Iraq, Israel, Libya, Qatar, the United States, and Yemen). On April 11, 2002, the Rome Statute received the sixty ratifications necessary for its entry into force on July 1, 2002, at which time the Court's jurisdiction became active.

[*Signs: Journal of Women in Culture and Society* 2003, vol. 28, no. 4]

is often lauded for the fact that the Rome Statute explicitly codifies for the first time many crimes of sexual and gender violence as war crimes and crimes against humanity, the caucus's advocacy was broader than the effort to include gender crimes and mechanisms for their effective prosecution; it went straight to the heart of the positioning of this Court in the world—its independence, its fairness, and its associations with peace.

The Court began functioning in the first half of 2003 with the inauguration of judges on March 11 and the selection of the chief prosecutor in April. The world is witnessing the strengthening of a system of international criminal justice at the same time as the rhetoric of terror is fueling a rapid rise in militarism and war making. Thus, the ICC will emerge in a climate where militarism and unilateralism are colliding with a convergence of efforts to mold and render enforceable the rule of a fair and just international criminal law—law long considered a matter of convenience, and entirely avoidable when inconvenient, by some of the world's most powerful forces.

This report will first explore the basic structure and function of the ICC and then will briefly discuss the efforts of the Women's Caucus to mainstream gender in the ICC. The third part of the report will present an overview of the nearly unprecedented level of gender mainstreaming in the Rome Statute and opportunities for using the statute as a standard locally. Finally, the report explores the potential of the ICC for fostering a culture of accountability in the current climate where a "war on terror" is being waged ostensibly in the name of security.

The International Criminal Court

As mentioned above, the ICC is the world's first permanent international criminal tribunal set up to prosecute individuals for genocide, war crimes, crimes against humanity, and, eventually, aggression. The ICC follows the establishment of various ad hoc international tribunals that were set up to address specific situations, such as the International Military Tribunals for the Far East and Nuremberg (IMT 1945; IMTFE 1946; see the app.) after World War II, and the International Criminal Tribunals for the former Yugoslavia and Rwanda in the early 1990s (ICTY 1993; ICTR 1994).[2]

---

[2] There was serious discussion about the need for a permanent court with international criminal jurisdiction as early as the end of World War I, though there was no real progress until after World War II when the International Military Tribunals for Nuremberg and the Far East were established to prosecute war crimes and crimes against humanity committed

A crucial step to ensuring the Court's independence and impartiality was ensuring its independence of the UN Security Council. The United States led early efforts to assert Security Council control over the cases that could come before the Court (Scharf 1999). Had the Court been made dependent on the Security Council for the cases it could adjudicate, the permanent members of the Council wielding veto power would have been able to insulate their nationals from the Court's jurisdiction.[3] Instead, the role of the Security Council was greatly circumscribed in the final text of the Rome Statute. The Security Council is thus limited to referring cases to the Court, but this is not the only way that cases can come before the Court (Rome Statute 1998, Article 13). In addition to referrals by the Security Council, States Parties can refer cases to the Court, and, perhaps more significantly, the prosecutor, acting on her own initiative, can institute proceedings (Rome Statute 1998, Articles 12–15). Furthermore, the Security Council has the ability to defer cases for a period of twelve months by affirmative vote acting under Chapter VII of the UN Charter (Rome Statute 1998, Article 16).[4]

The Court's jurisdiction is complementary to national systems, as it will only be able to take a case when the national system is unwilling or unable to genuinely investigate and/or prosecute (Rome Statute 1998, Preamble and Articles 1 and 17). In addition to this complementarity mechanism, the Court's jurisdiction is also limited by several preconditions. Early in the negotiations, there was hope that the Court would be able to exercise universal jurisdiction, which would have allowed it to

---

by Nazi forces and the Japanese Imperial Army, respectively (Bos 1999, 463). Indeed, there was such momentum toward a permanent court in the postwar scene that Article VI of the Genocide Convention (1948) anticipates a permanent tribunal to which cases could be referred. The subsequent onset of the cold war stalled serious consideration of the establishment of such a tribunal for the next fifty years. The idea of a permanent criminal court was finally brought fully to life again in the wake of the violence in the former Yugoslavia and Rwanda. In both of these cases, the Security Council moved to create ad hoc tribunals to address the brutal atrocities taking place. With the polarization of the cold war no longer an obstacle in the early 1990s, the international community could undertake serious efforts to establish a permanent court. Serious deliberations on the establishment of an international criminal court recommenced in 1995. See Bos 1999 and Lee 1999.

[3] The five permanent members of the UN Security Council are China, France, Russia, the United Kingdom, and the United States. Additionally, ten elected members serve two-year terms (UN Charter 1945, Article 23[1]). The five permanent members must concur on all nonprocedural matters (UN Charter 1945, Article 27[3]).

[4] The deferral is renewable after twelve months by another affirmative vote of the Security Council.

prosecute the crimes no matter where they were committed or by whom.[5] However, as a result of intense opposition led by the United States, the preconditions of territoriality or nationality instead qualify the Court's jurisdiction.[6] The preconditions mean that either the territory where the crimes were committed must have been the territory of a State Party or the state of nationality of the person(s) suspected of committing the crimes must be a State Party (Rome Statute 1998, Article 12).[7] The preconditions, however, do not apply to the situations referred to the Court by the UN Security Council (Rome Statute 1998, Articles 12 and 13).

Women's caucus advocacy

In 1995, nongovernmental organizations rallied around the United Nations' renewed efforts to create a permanent international criminal tribunal and formed an official coalition—the Coalition for an International Criminal Court (CICC; Pace and Thieroff 1999). The coalition consisted of human rights monitoring and advocacy groups, faith-based groups, victim/survivor advocacy groups, and others. In 1997, a substantial presence of women advocates and activists joined this effort and formed the Women's Caucus for Gender Justice in the International Criminal Court.[8] They began the work of mainstreaming gender in the creation

---

[5] The concept of "universal jurisdiction" holds that some crimes are so heinous that they harm the international community as a whole and that all states have a duty to investigate and prosecute them no matter where they are committed or who commits them; see Brownlie 1990, 307–9. The Geneva Conventions of 1949 applied this principle and provided that each state party "shall be under the obligation to search for persons alleged to have committed, or to have ordered to be committed, such grave breaches, and shall bring such persons, regardless of their nationality, before its own courts" (Geneva Convention I, Article 49; Geneva Convention II, Article 50; Geneva Convention III, Article 129; and Geneva Convention IV, Article 146). For discussions and advocacy positions relating to universal jurisdiction in the ICC, see Amnesty International 1997; Human Rights Watch 1998; and Women's Caucus 1998b.

[6] For a discussion of the U.S. opposition to universal jurisdiction, see Benedetti and Washburn 1999.

[7] Under this scheme, nationals of countries that have not ratified the Rome Statute could still be hauled before the Court if they are suspected of having committed crimes on the territory of States Parties—one of the most problematic features of the ICC from the perspective of U.S. policy makers.

[8] After the adoption of the Rome Statute in 1998, the Women's Caucus became known as the Women's Caucus for Gender Justice.

of the new institution.[9] The effort built on women's human rights organizing in other arenas such as the Vienna Convention on Human Rights in 1993 where women came together to infuse the discussions with a gender perspective and advance the recognition of women's rights as human rights.[10]

It is important to note that the Women's Caucus was formed in the ICC negotiations at a critical moment in the history of the international women's human rights movement and was thus able to draw on the movement's momentum, as it had gathered strength through the Fourth World Conference on Women in 1995, and strategic objectives that had been formulated to that point (Nainar and Spees 2000, 6–7). At the same time, feminist advocates and legal experts had been monitoring the work of the Yugoslav and Rwandan tribunals that had been established by the UN Security Council in 1993 and 1994, respectively (Copelon 2000; Nainar and Spees 2000). This advocacy and the practice and jurisprudence of the two tribunals also informed the work of the Women's Caucus in the ICC process. The Women's Caucus for Gender Justice quickly expanded to include a regionally diverse pool of advocates and experts with experience advocating in national systems as well as in international forums. These caucus members attended the ICC negotiations as part of the Women's Caucus delegations and helped develop advocacy positions and strategies (Facio 1998). By the time of the Rome Diplomatic Conference in July 1998, the caucus had also developed an expansive network of organizations and individuals who supported the "core principles" of the Women's Caucus and who helped advocate for Women's Caucus concerns in capitals around the world (Facio 1998).

In the ICC negotiations, the Women's Caucus worked to reveal and

---

[9] "Gender mainstreaming" is a concept used in UN parlance and increasingly in national and regional forums. The United Nations Economic and Social Council has defined gender mainstreaming as "the process of assessing the implications for women and men of any planned action, including legislation, policies or programmes, in all areas and at all levels. It is a strategy for making women's as well as men's concerns and experiences an integral dimension of the design, implementation, monitoring and evaluation of policies and programmes in all political, economic and societal spheres so that women and men benefit equally and inequality is not perpetuated. The ultimate goal is to achieve gender equality" (ECOSOC 1997; see the app.). The term *gender* as used in the ICC context is discussed below.

[10] For a discussion of the objectives and methodology of the Women's Caucus, see Facio 1998 and Women's Caucus 1998a. For a discussion of opposition encountered by the Women's Caucus from the Vatican and other conservative states, see Facio 1998; Bedont and Hall-Martinez 1999; Copelon 2000; Nainar and Spees 2000; Rothschild 2000.

correct the deficiencies in existing humanitarian law with respect to crimes of sexual and gender violence. Furthermore, the Women's Caucus was among the strongest voices calling for a more active role for victims and witnesses in the justice process, a broad reparations scheme, strong mandates for protection of victims and witnesses, and gender experts and women on the court and among staff at all levels (Facio 1998; Women's Caucus 1998b; Nainar and Spees 2000). This was in addition to the work concerning issues of jurisdiction and independence of the Court.

The work to mainstream gender continued after the Rome Statute. The statute called for the development of an Elements of Crimes Annex, further defining the crimes within the Court's jurisdiction, and a set of Rules of Procedure and Evidence, which were to be completed by June 30, 2000 (Resolution F 1998; Rome Statute 1998, Articles 9 and 51). Over the course of five preparatory commission meetings beginning in February 1999, the Women's Caucus worked to ensure that the achievements made in Rome were not undermined in the subsequent negotiations and to ensure progressive definitions of the crimes and rules relating to evidence in cases of sexual violence.

Mapping a gender perspective in the Rome Statute: Crimes of sexual and gender violence

There has been much writing on the pervasiveness of sexual violence in armed conflict, both as a strategy of war and as a by-product of militarized aggression.[11] Feminist scholars and legal experts have pointed out both the deficiencies in international humanitarian law with regard to sexual violence and the lack of enforcement of those provisions that did exist, all of which contributed to the culture of impunity for sexual and gender-based violence.[12]

---

[11] See, e.g., Brownmiller 1975; Khushalani 1982; Copelon 1994; and Dolgopol 1998.

[12] Khushalani 1982; Gardam 1992; Meron 1993; Copelon 1994; Askin 1997; Sellers 2000. The recent judgment of the Women's International War Crimes Tribunal on Japan's Military and Sexual Slavery, rendered in December 2001 in The Hague, illustrates one of the clearest examples of the ways in which the international community has ignored these crimes even in the face of egregious and widespread violence against women in armed conflict. More than fifty years after the end of World War II, prosecutors from nine different countries colonized or occupied by Japan during the war presented evidence of the Japanese Imperial Army's system of sexual enslavement, also known as the "comfort women" system, into which more than two hundred thousand women from throughout Asia were forced. The prosecutors before this "people's tribunal" opted to apply the law as it stood at the time that the post–World War II International Military Tribunals for Nuremberg and the Far East

A brief overview of two provisions related to sexual violence in prior humanitarian law is revealing of this problematic treatment. In the regulations attached to The Hague Convention of 1907, Article 46, which mandated respect for "family honour and rights," was commonly understood to encompass rape.[13] In the Fourth Geneva Convention of 1949, Article 27 states that "women shall be especially protected against any attack on their honour, in particular against rape, enforced prostitution, or any other form of indecent assault" (Geneva Convention [IV] 1949).[14]

While the Geneva Conventions became at least a bit more explicit in the provisions relating to sexual violence, especially as compared to the 1907 Hague Convention, they fell short of confirming rape and other sexual violence as grave breaches. The language of Article 27 merely calls for militaries to protect "women" (not men or children) from rape, enforced prostitution, and other forms of indecent assault but does not mandate punitive sanctions or enforcement mechanisms. Thus, the treatment of these crimes in Article 27 and their absence from the lists of grave breaches meant they would not easily give rise to universal jurisdiction, that is, the duty of all states to investigate and prosecute crimes no matter where they are committed or by whom.[15]

A critical aspect of the advocacy in the ICC negotiations was to ensure that the Rome Statute moved beyond such limited treatment and affirmed the gravity of forms of violence that are committed predominately, though not exclusively, against women. As a result, rape, sexual slavery, enforced prostitution, forced pregnancy, enforced sterilization, and sexual violence are included as war crimes and crimes against humanity (Rome Statute

---

were in operation to underscore the idea that rape and sexual enslavement could have been prosecuted had the will to do so existed at the time (Judgment of the Women's International War Crimes Tribunal 2001).

[13] Hague 1907, Article 46. The Hague Convention essentially erased an explicit reference to rape in the Lieber Code, which served as a starting point for the drafting of The Hague Convention. The Lieber Code governed the conduct of the Union Army during the U.S. Civil War and prohibited rape under penalty of death (Lieber Code 1863, Article 44).

[14] It should be noted here that women's groups were instrumental in the formulation of the language of this provision in the Fourth Geneva Convention. The record of the negotiations around Article 27 reveals that the International Council of Women and the International Abolitionist Federation sought to expand the previous language and make it more explicit. They suggested the language as alternative text through a representative of the International Committee of the Red Cross (Final Record of the Diplomatic Conference of Geneva 1949).

[15] The jurisprudence of the International Criminal Tribunal for the former Yugoslavia (ICTY) and the International Criminal Tribunal for Rwanda (ICTR) has contributed significantly to the understanding of crimes of sexual and gender violence as grave war crimes and crimes against humanity in existing humanitarian law. See Askin 1999.

1998, Articles 8[2][b][xxii], 8[2][e][vi], and 7[1][g]). Additionally, trafficking and gender-based persecution are included as crimes against humanity (Rome Statute 1998, Articles 7[1][c], 7[2][c], and 7[1][h]). It is important that these crimes are now delinked from notions of honor or dignity, which will help to place the victims of such crimes at the center of concern rather than on the periphery of family or community, which carries old connotations of women as property. These crimes have also been affirmed as among the gravest (Rome Statute 1998).[16]

After the adoption of the Rome Statute, negotiations of the elements of the crimes began in order to provide more specificity as to the criminal conduct (Elements of Crimes 2002). In these post-Rome negotiations, the Women's Caucus advocated for progressive definitions of the crimes of sexual and gender violence. In the negotiations on the crime of rape, for example, the efforts were to ensure, first, that the elements maintained a focus on the crimes of the perpetrator, and not the victim; second, that the force element was defined broadly enough to encompass the non-physical coercive circumstances that often play on victims, especially in armed conflict but also to a certain extent in peacetime; third, that the definition would avoid unwieldy and harassing specificity; and finally, that the definitions would be gender neutral.[17] The definition of rape that resulted is as follows:

1.   The perpetrator invaded the body of a person by conduct resulting in penetration, however slight, of any part of the body of the victim or of the perpetrator with a sexual organ, or of the anal or genital opening of the victim with any object or any other part of the body;

2.   The invasion was committed by force, or by threat of force or coercion, such as that caused by fear of violence, duress, detention,

---

[16] Article 8(2)(b)(xxii) of the Rome Statute links the crimes of sexual and gender violence occurring in international armed conflict to "grave breaches of the Geneva Conventions"; Article 8(2)(e)(vi) links them to the serious violations contained in "Article 3 common to the four Geneva Conventions," which apply to internal armed conflict.

[17] The Women's Caucus began by advocating that the ICC negotiators follow the trends of the ad hoc tribunals, specifically the ICTR, which identified rape as "a physical invasion of a sexual nature under circumstances which are coercive" (see Women's Caucus 1999–2000; see also Prosecutor v. Jean-Paul Akayesu, Case No. ICTR-96-4-T at pars. 596–98). The jurisprudence of the ICTY and ICTR has been instrumental in helping to reconceptualize the definition of rape for purposes of international criminal law as well as its conceptualization as a form of torture. See also Prosecutor v. Delalic et al., Case No. IT-96-21-A; Prosecutor v. Furundzija, Case No. IT-95-17/1-T; and Prosecutor v. Kunarac et al., Case No. IT-96-23-T and IT-96-23/1-T.

psychological oppression, or abuse of power, against such person or another person, or by taking advantage of a coercive environment, or the invasion was committed against a person incapable of giving genuine consent (Elements of Crimes 2002, Article 7[1][g]-1).

While the efforts to avoid unwieldy specificity were obviously unsuccessful, the definition does maintain a focus on the acts of the perpetrator and not on the victim; that is, a victim's lack of consent is not part of the elements, but, rather, the perpetrator's violation of a victim's physical and sexual autonomy is emphasized. Furthermore, the force element is defined broadly to encompass a range of coercive circumstances and is not restricted to physical force or threat of death.

Parallel to the negotiations on the definitions of the crimes were the negotiations on the Rules of Procedure and Evidence (RPE; Rules of Procedure and Evidence 2002). These negotiations presented an opportunity to avoid the very real danger that the treaty, its supplemental texts, and future Court might replicate many of the evidentiary problems that women have been working to correct in national-level judicial systems the world over regarding the trial of sexual and gender violence crimes.[18] Ultimately, these negotiations yielded rules of evidence in cases of sexual violence that prohibit a defense of consent and the submission of sexual conduct evidence except in very rare circumstances (RPE 2000, Rules 70 and 71). They require that any effort to submit such evidence be conducted in closed proceedings and be shown to be highly relevant and credible (RPE 2000, Rule 72). Additionally, the Court may not require that a victim's testimony be corroborated (RPE 2000, Rule 63).

---

[18] This tendency was avoided, at least in the formulation of procedural rules, when the ad hoc tribunal for the former Yugoslavia was established as a result of the advocacy of nongovernmental organizations and feminist legal experts. See Green et al. 1994 and Helsinki Watch 1995. The ICTY adopted rules of procedure that precluded traditionally discriminatory evidentiary practices such as inquiries into a victim's prior sexual conduct, requirements of corroboratory evidence, and problematic issues of consent that place the focus of the inquiry on the conduct of the victim and not on the perpetrator. The rule was replicated in the rules of procedure for the International Criminal Tribunal for Rwanda. See ICTY Rules 2002, Rule 96; ICTR Rules 2002, Rule 96. The existence of this rule, however, did not in itself prevent harassment of witnesses and similar abuses during the course of trial. See *Prosecutor v. Delalic*, Decision on the Prosecution's Motion for the Redaction of the Public Record, ICTY Trial Chamber (June 5, 1997), Case No. IT-96-21, pars. 47–50 (International Criminal Tribunal for the Former Yugoslavia); Women's Caucus for Gender Justice 1999.

Victims and witnesses

The Rome Statute contains broad mandates concerning the participation and protection of victims and witnesses. Article 68 is the centerpiece of the statute's mandates and provides that victims and witnesses can participate in the proceedings of the Court at appropriate stages (Rome Statute 1998, Article 68[3]). They may be assisted by a legal representative throughout the proceedings (Rome Statute 1998, Article 68[3]). Additionally, Article 68 requires that the Court take measures to protect the "safety, physical and psychological well-being, dignity and privacy of victims and witnesses" (Rome Statute 1998, Article 68[1]). In the process, the Court must also take into account "all relevant factors" including age, gender, health, and the nature of the crime, "in particular . . . where the crime involves sexual or gender violence or violence against children" (Rome Statute 1998, Article 68[1]). The Court may also conduct portions of proceedings in camera, in particular in cases of sexual violence or when the witness is a child. Additionally, evidence may be given via electronic "or other special means" (Rome Statute 1998, Article 69).

The statute also requires the creation of the Victims and Witnesses Unit, to be housed in the Registry of the Court. This unit will be tasked with providing protective measures, security arrangements, counseling, and other assistance and must include staff with "expertise in trauma, including trauma related to crimes of sexual violence" (Rome Statute 1998, Article 43[6]).

The Court will also have the authority to award reparations. Article 75 mandates that the Court develop principles relating to reparations, which include compensation, restitution, and rehabilitation (Rome Statute 1998, Article 75[1]). In some cases, the Court will be able to make awards of reparations against a convicted person (Rome Statute 1998, Article 75[2]). Article 79 of the Rome Statute also requires that the Assembly of States Parties establish a trust fund for the benefit of victims or their survivors (Rome Statute 1998, Article 79).

Women and gender expertise on the court

The Rome Statute contains explicit mandates intended to ensure a presence of women on the Court as well as gender experts and experts on violence against women. Article 36(8) stipulates that in the nomination and election of judges, States Parties must take into account the need for "a fair representation of female and male judges" and the need for "legal expertise on specific issues, including, but not limited to, violence against women or children" (Rome Statute 1998, Article 36[8][a] and [b]). This provision was put to the test in February 2003 when the election of the Court's eighteen judges took place. In a historic and unprecedented development, the elections resulted in a regionally diverse bench that included seven women (Women's Caucus 2003).[19] The presence of seven women on an eighteen-member panel of judges represents a significant advance in light of the traditionally low number of women serving as judges in international judicial institutions.[20]

The criteria relating to fair representation and expertise are also to be applied in the employment of staff for the Office of the Prosecutor and the Registry (Rome Statute 1998, Article 44[2]). Article 42(9) requires the prosecutor to appoint advisors with legal expertise on "sexual and gender violence" as well as other specific issues (Rome Statute 1998, Article 44[2]).

The gender definition

The Rome Statute contains a definition of *gender*—the first in a legally binding international treaty. It is particularly significant that the term was included and a definition agreed on in a treaty that gives rise to individual criminal responsibility and that includes crimes such as gender-based persecution. This is striking when one considers that delegates at the Fourth World Conference on Women were unable to adopt a definition of *gender* for purposes of the Beijing Platform for Action, a nonbinding, unenforceable document.[21]

---

[19] The female judges are Maureen Harding Clark (Ireland); Fatoumata Diarra (Mali); Akua Kuenyehia (Ghana); Elizabeth Odio Benito (Costa Rica); Navanethem Pillay (South Africa); Sylvia Steiner (Brazil); and Anita Usacka (Latvia). See also Spees 2002.

[20] Only one woman has ever served on the fifteen-member International Court of Justice. One woman is currently serving as a judge on the sixteen-member panel of permanent judges at the ICTY, and three of the sixteen permanent judges at the ICTR are women. Currently, no woman is serving on the International Tribunal for the Law of the Sea (Linehan 2001). For a discussion of the rules adopted by the ICC Assembly of States Parties to govern the election process, see Spees 2002.

[21] See Report of the Fourth World Conference on Women 1995. Annex IV of the report simply affirms that *gender* is to be understood according to its commonly understood and generally accepted usage. In a 1996 report on the implementation of the Fourth World Conference on Women, the UN Secretary-General elaborated on what the commonly understood meaning of the term is: "Gender refers to the socially constructed roles played by women and men that are ascribed to them on the basis of their sex. . . . These roles are usually specific to a given area and time, that is, since gender roles are contingent on the

For the purposes of the Rome Statute, *gender* is defined as "the two sexes, male and female, within the context of society" (Rome Statute 1998, Article 7[3]).[22] This definition resulted from one of the most difficult debates at the Rome Conference. Delegates from Roman Catholic countries aligned with a group of Arab delegations to challenge the use of the term in the draft statute (Steains 1999, 371–75; Copelon 2000; Rothschild 2000). Their stated concern was that the definition would be read to encompass sexual orientation. These delegates sought to restrict the concept to biological sex difference and prohibit recognition of the social construction of gender. At one point, a group of delegates sought to substitute the term *sex* for *gender* as one means of preventing the recognition of social construction.

Fortunately, they were not successful. Delegates in favor of maintaining the term *gender* and a definition "capable of being interpreted to include the socially constructed roles" (Steains 1999, 373) won in the long run by the inclusion of the language "within the context of society" (Steains 1999, 374). The statutory definition thus enables the Court to include persecution based on sexual orientation and gender. Persecution on the basis of sexual orientation or differing gender identities could be viewed as targeting a group or collectivity by virtue of its nonadherence to norms or expectations of gender roles in a given societal context. Perhaps the most extensive known historical example of persecution on the basis of sexual orientation is that which was carried out by the Nazis during the Holocaust (Plant 1987; Grau and Shoppman 1997), but more recent examples exist as well (International Gay and Lesbian Human Rights Commission 1998; Amnesty International 2001; Human Rights Watch 2002). Since the crime of persecution involves the "severe deprivation of fundamental human rights" (Rome Statute 1998, Article 7[2][g]) in connection with any other crime against humanity or war crime listed in the statute by reason of the identity of the group or collectivity, it would be

---

social and economic context, they can vary according to the specific context and can change over time. In terms of the use of language, the word 'sex' is used to refer to physical and biological characteristics of women and men, while gender is used to refer to the explanations for observed differences between women and men based on socially assigned roles" (Report of Secretary-General 1996).

[22] The Women's Caucus advocated for an understanding of gender that would encompass "socially constructed differences between men and women and the unequal power relationships that result" and affirmed that "differences between men and women are not essential or inevitable products of biological sex difference" (Women's Caucus 1998a)

difficult for a court to hold that such an egregious crime is permissible under international law.[23]

Local implementation

The complementarity scheme of the Rome Statute that allows the Court to exercise jurisdiction only when national systems are unable or unwilling to genuinely investigate or prosecute the crimes serves as an impetus for countries to ensure that their domestic legal systems are in conformity with the Rome Statute. Unless domestic criminal laws and procedures that allow for the trial of the types of crimes in the ICC's jurisdiction are in place, states would fail the complementarity test on the grounds of inability to prosecute and could be subject to the ICC's assertion of jurisdiction (Rome Statute 1998, Article 17). In many places, the crimes included in the Rome Statute have not been included in domestic criminal codes. This is especially so for some of the crimes of sexual and gender violence, particularly sexual slavery, forced pregnancy, and gender-based persecution.

Furthermore, the definitions of the crimes of sexual and gender violence in the Elements Annex and Rules of Procedure and Evidence are, in many cases, more progressive than their counterparts at the national level. For example, the definition of rape avoids problematic elements commonly found in national systems such as the lack of gender neutrality; requirements of overt, physical resistance on the part of the victim; and inquiries into the prior sexual conduct of the victim. In addition, many jurisdictions require corroboration of a victim's allegations, such as certification by a medical doctor that a rape took place or eyewitness accounts, before law enforcement officials accept charges.

---

[23] Increasingly, there is recognition at the international level that violence and persecution targeting persons of differing sexual and gender identities is impermissible under international legal standards. See *Toonen v. Australia* 1992; HIV/AIDS Guidelines 1998; letter from OHCHR 2001; see the app. Indeed, one conservative opponent of the Court has already acknowledged—and decried—the potential of the Court to address persecution on the basis of sexual orientation. Law professor Richard Wilkins makes a connection between the subject-matter jurisdiction of the Rome Statute and the International Guidelines on HIV/AIDS issued by the Joint UN Program on HIV/AIDS and the UN Office of the High Commissioner for Human Rights; see the app. The guidelines call for, inter alia, the repeal of laws criminalizing sexual acts between consenting adults and the creation of legal penalties for those who vilify "homosexual behavior." Wilkins states: "It is hardly far-fetched to assume that the broad language of Article 7 of the ICC Statute—which among other things, criminalizes 'severs [*sic*] deprivation' of a group's 'fundamental rights'—could be used to achieve the goals set out by [the High Commissioner for Human Rights]" (2002).

In countries that ratify the Rome Statute, the gender provisions could help strengthen the capacity to address violence against women at the national level via the inclusion of additional crimes of sexual and gender violence, progressive definitions of existing crimes, and more gender-sensitive procedures for the trial of these crimes. Moreover, the existence of the crime of gender-based persecution in national systems could have favorable implications for asylum policies and regulations for women fleeing various types of gender-based violence and those endangered as a result of their sexual orientation or gender identity. With respect to crimes such as trafficking, the existence of an international tribunal with criminal jurisdiction can boost efforts to investigate the networks of traffickers and get at the various actors along the way. Furthermore, it is possible that the statute's concern for the protection of victims and witnesses can be used creatively as a standard for ensuring the noncriminalization of trafficked persons and a broader attention to complicated transnational and cross-border issues that often surround situations of trafficking.

More thinking needs to be done along these lines for women's groups to take full advantage of the Rome Statute at the national level and fold the gender gains into national systems in ways that make sense locally. It is thus imperative that women's groups focusing on issues of law reform and violence against women get engaged and help guide the domestic implementation process of this international treaty.

A building block toward human security?

Contrary to many misconceptions, the International Criminal Court will not be only a war crimes tribunal, though the Rome Statute does codify and expand on traditional prohibitions in humanitarian law. The ICC will also be a court for the trial of violators of a developing international criminal law that encompasses violations of the laws of war in addition to genocide and crimes against humanity, which can be committed in times of war as well as in times of so-called peace.

Many nongovernmental organizations actively monitoring the negotiations expected that the Court would be a mechanism that would aid, indeed help revive, the UN mission to "save succeeding generations from the scourge of war" (UN Charter 1948, Preamble) rather than legitimating war as an institution as long as there is compliance with the rules of the game. The extent to which the ICC will be able to withstand the pressure to become a legitimizing agent for the use of armed force as an instrument of foreign policy remains to be seen. Much of this will depend on how the negotiations toward a definition of the crime of aggression play out.

Because the debates around the crime of aggression were so difficult, the Preparatory Committee for the Establishment of the ICC feared that the debate would seriously prolong the negotiations toward the Rome Statute (Von Hebel and Robinson 1999, 79). As a result, they chose to leave it out of the Court's jurisdiction until a definition could be adopted and amended into the statute at a later date (Von Hebel and Robinson 1999, 81–85). After the adoption of the Rome Statute in 1998, a working group was convened to undertake negotiations toward a definition (Resolution F 1998). Among the most sensitive issues at stake in the aggression negotiations are whether the UN Security Council is the sole arbiter in the international community in determining acts of aggression, what the level of force is that would constitute an act of aggression, and how individual criminal responsibility for the crime of aggression would be fixed (Proceedings of Prepcom 2001). As of this writing, the Working Group has labored over the course of eight sessions of the Preparatory Commission and has yet to reach consensus on any of the issues outlined above.

Accountability woes of a lone superpower

While the ICC will by no means be a cure-all, its existence as an institution independent of traditional power plays should have an enormous bearing on the shape of global politics in the future. Indeed, there is reason to believe that it is already having an impact. The International Criminal Court has become a prominent feature of foreign policy in the world. The U.S. foreign policy on the ICC carries an array of disincentives designed to entice less powerful countries away from the Court, while European Union policy carries various incentives for ICC ratification.

The United States has been by far the Court's most hostile opponent.[24] On May 6, 2002, President George W. Bush effectively removed his predecessor's signature of the Rome Statute when he sent a letter to UN Secretary-General Kofi Annan confirming that the United States would not ratify the treaty and therefore had no obligations arising from signature

---

[24] For a full discussion of the U.S. position and policy regarding the ICC, see International Federation of Human Rights 2002 and Spees 2003.

(Spees 2003, 123).[25] Bush's nearly unprecedented nullification of the treaty cleared the way for all-out U.S. opposition and a string of tactics aimed at undermining the future Court. Also in 2002, the U.S. State and Defense Departments embarked on a formal campaign in capitals around the world insisting on bilateral agreements prohibiting the extradition of U.S. nationals to the future Court (Spees 2003, 123–25). The United States has also sought, and obtained, similar language in Security Council resolutions relating to peacekeeping missions.

Shortly after Bush's official nullification of the signing, he signed into law legislation known as the American Servicemembers Protection Act (ASPA; see app.). The act prohibits all assistance to and cooperation with the future Court, authorizes the use of "any means necessary" to free U.S. nationals or allies held on behalf of the Court, and prohibits peace-keeping and other assistance to countries that support the Court (ASPA 2002). Because the Court will be officially seated in The Hague, the Netherlands, opponents of the law have dubbed it "The Hague Invasion Act," though any country holding a U.S. national or ally for the Court could be targeted by the commander-in-chief under this law. United States Senator Jesse Helms (R.-N.C.), who initiated the legislation, declared shortly after the adoption of the Rome Statute: "The ICC is indeed a monster—and it is our responsibility to slay it before it grows to devour us" (Helms 1998).

Conclusion

The ICC will be a critical component of an international framework of accountability aimed at closing the political, practical, and jurisdictional gaps that have long fostered a culture of impunity. It is to be hoped that the Rome Statute will have the more positive effect of ensuring adherence to international law among civilian and military officials and encouraging the pursuit of justice, rather than war, as a response to future acts of genocide, war crimes, and crimes against humanity.

Had an international criminal court been established after World War II as originally intended, it would be a much different court from the one we will see very soon. It would likely have reflected the postwar world order that led to the Allied Powers' control of the UN Security Council and thus would have been susceptible to becoming a mechanism of se-

---

[25] In treaty law signature indicates an intention to ratify and carries the obligation to refrain from actions that would defeat the object or purpose of the treaty. See Vienna Convention 1969, Article 18.

lective justice rather than an independent and impartial judicial institution that affirms the principles of equality before the law—criticisms that have been leveled at the World War II tribunals and the ad hoc tribunals established in the 1990s. Furthermore, it would not have had the advantage of lessons learned through the often tumultuous process of decolonization and the myriad legal, political, and economic issues that would emerge over the next fifty years of international legal development. And, most certainly, women would not have been able to influence the creation of the Court to the extent possible at the end of the twentieth century by drawing on the wealth of transnational feminist thinking, writing, strategizing, and organizing that has grown almost exponentially in the intervening five decades.

Even so, despite the major role played by women's groups in the ICC negotiations, the predominant voices in the ongoing debates and news items about the Court are men. Occasionally in mainstream circles mention is made of the inclusion of rape and other crimes of sexual and gender violence, but the dominant discourse about the Court paints a picture of a remote, elite institution associated with the laws of war that will try and punish individuals who break the rules of war. As ever, the conjured images of those taking part in this new justice system, as defendants, prosecutors, and judges, are men.

These images, however, stand in stark contrast to the reality of the provisions of the Rome Statute and the underlying advocacy of civil society generally and women in particular. Feminist critiques and theories of justice and power underlay the Women's Caucus's advocacy for broader conceptualizations of justice, a more empowered role for victims, mandates relating to the placement of women and gender experts throughout all organs of the Court, and, not least, the insistence on the independence of the Court from traditional power structures. Still, it has yet to fully dawn on many in the international community that this Court will not be business as usual. Women have been and will continue to be a part of it and, in doing so, have altered its trajectory.

MADRE and Coalition for Women's Human Rights in Conflict Situations

Appendix
Treaties, Cases, Legislation, and International Documents

American Servicemembers Protection Act of 2002, Public Law 107-206, 22 USCA 7421 et seq.

Charter of the International Military Tribunal for the Far East, January 19, 1946

(General Orders No. 1), Tokyo, as amended; General Orders No. 20, April 26, 1946, T.I.A.S. No. 1589.

Charter of the International Military Tribunal for the Trial of the Major War Criminals (IMT), appended to the Agreement for the Prosecution and Punishment of Major War Criminals of the European Axis, August 8, 1945, London, 85 U.N.T.S. 251, 59 Stat/1544, as amended, Protocol to Agreement and Charter, October, 1945.

Charter of the United Nations, June 26, 1945, 59 Stat. 1031, T.S. No. 993, 3 Bevans 1153.

Convention on the Regulation of the Laws and Customs of War on Land, The Hague, October 18, 1907, 35 Stat. 2277, 1 Bevans 631 (The Hague Convention).

Convention on the Prevention and Punishment of the Crime of Genocide, approved and opened for signature, ratification, and accession by the United Nations General Assembly Resolution 260 (III), December 9, 1948. Entered into force January 12, 1951, in accordance with Article 12.

Economic and Social Council, *Agreed Conclusions*, U.N. Doc. E/1997/2 (1997).

Elements of Crimes. *Official Records of the First Session of the Assembly of States Parties of the International Criminal Court*, September 3–10, 2002, Doc. ICC/ASP/1/3 at 108; available on-line at http://www.icc-cpi.int/docs/basicdocs/asp_records(e).pdf.

Fourth World Conference on Women: Declaration and Platform for Action, U.N. Doc. A/CONF.177/20 (September 15, 1995).

Geneva Convention (I) for the Amelioration of the Condition of the Wounded, Sick and Shipwrecked Members of Armed Forces in the Field, September 15, 1949, 75 U.N.T.S. 31.

Geneva Convention (II) for the Amelioration of the Condition of Wounded, Sick and Shipwrecked Members of Armed Forces at Sea, August 12, 1949, 75 U.N.T.S. 85.

Geneva Convention (III) Relative to the Treatment of Prisoners of War, August 12, 1949, 75 U.N.T.S. 135.

Geneva Convention (IV) Relative to the Protection of Civilian Persons in Time of War, August 12, 1949, 75 U.N.T.S. 287.

HIV/AIDS and Human Rights: International Guidelines on HIV/AIDS, 1998, Office of the United Nations High Commissioner for Human Rights and the Joint United Nations Programme on HIV/AIDS, Geneva.

Instructions for the Government of the United States in the Field by Order of the Secretary of War, April 24, 1863 (Lieber Code).

Office of the United Nations High Commissioner for Human Rights (OHCHR), letter, June 2001; available on-line at http://www.iglhrc.org/site/iglhrc/section.php?id=5&detail=161.

Proceedings of the Preparatory Commission at its Eighth Session, September 24–October 5, 2001, U.N. Doc. PCNICC/2001/L.3/Rev.1.Annex 3.

Report of the UN Secretary-General on the Implementation of the Outcome of the Fourth World Conference on Women, September 3, 1996, U.N. Doc. A/ 51/322.

Resolution F of the Rome Conference, adopted July 17, 1992, by the United Nations Diplomatic Conference of Plenipotentiaries on the Establishment of an International Criminal Court.

Rome Statute of the International Criminal Court, U.N. Doc. A/CONF.183/9 (July 17, 1998), with corrections on the Web at http://www.un.org/law/icc/ statute/romefra.htm.

Rules of Procedure and Evidence for the International Criminal Court. *Official Records of the First Session of the Assembly of States Parties of the International Criminal Court,* September 3–10, 2002, Doc. ICC/ASP/1/3 at 10; available at http://www.icc-cpi.int/docs/basicdocs/asp_records(e).pdf.

Rules of Procedure and Evidence for the International Criminal Tribunal for Rwanda, as amended July 5, 2002; on-line at http://www.ictr.org/ wwwroot/ENGLISH/rules/index.htm.

Rules of Procedure and Evidence for the International Criminal Tribunal for the Former Yugoslavia, as amended December 12, 2002; available on-line at http://www.un.org/icty/legaldoc/index.htm.

Statute of the International Criminal Tribunal for Rwanda, U.N. Doc. S/RES/ 955, Annex (1994); available on-line at http://www.ictr.org/wwwroot/ ENGLISH/basicdocs/statute.html.

Statute of the International Criminal Tribunal for the Former Yugoslavia, U.N. Doc. S/RES/827, Annex (1993); available on-line at http://www.un.org/ icty/legaldoc/index.htm.

Toonen v. Australia, Communication No. 488/1992, U.N. Doc CCPR/C/50/ D/488/1992 (1994).

References

Amnesty International. 1997. *The International Criminal Court: Making the Right Choices.* Pt. 1. Available on-line at http://web.amnesty.org/ai.nsf/ index/ior400011997.

———. 2001. *Crimes of Hate, Conspiracy of Silence: Torture and Ill-Treatment Based on Sexual Identity.* Available on-line at http://web.amnesty.org/library/ index/engact400162001.

Askin, Kelly. 1997. *War Crimes against Women: Prosecution in International War Crimes Tribunals.* The Hague: Martinus Nijhoff.

———. 1999. "Sexual Violence in Decisions and Indictments of the Yugoslav and Rwandan Tribunals: Current Status." *American Journal of International Law* 93(1):97–123.

Bedont, Barbara, and Katherine Hall-Martinez. 1999. "Ending Impunity for Gender Crimes under the International Criminal Court." *Brown Journal of World Affairs* 6(1):65–85.

Benedetti, Fanny, and John L. Washburn. 1999. "Drafting the International Criminal Court Treaty: Two Years to Rome and an Afterword on the Rome Diplomatic Conference." *Global Governance: A Review of Multilateralism and International Organizations* 5(1):1–37.

Bos, Adrian. 1999. "The International Criminal Court: A Perspective." In *The International Criminal Court: The Making of the Rome Statute—Issues, Negotiations, Results,* ed. Roy Lee, 463–70. The Hague: Kluwer Law International.

Brownlie, Ian. 1990. *Principles of Public International Law.* 4th ed. Oxford: Oxford University Press.

Brownmiller, Susan. 1975. *Against Our Will: Men, Women and Rape.* London: Secker & Warburg.

Copelon, Rhonda. 1994. "Surfacing Gender: Re-engraving Crimes against Women in Humanitarian Law." *Hastings Women's Law Journal* 5(2):243–66.

———. 2000. "Gender Crimes as War Crimes: Integrating Crimes against Women into International Criminal Law." *McGill Law Journal* 46(1):217–40.

Dolgopol, Ustinia. 1998. "Rape as a War Crime—Mythology and History." In *Common Grounds: Violence against Women in War and Armed Conflict Situations.* Manila: Asian Center for Women's Human Rights.

Facio, Alda. 1998. "Report on Rome Conference." Unpublished manuscript, Women's Caucus for Gender Justice, New York City, October 1998.

Gardam, Judith. 1992. "A Feminist Analysis of Certain Aspects of International Humanitarian Law." *Australian Yearbook of International Law* 12:265–78.

Grau, G., and Claudia Shoppman. 1997. *The Hidden Holocaust: Gay and Lesbian Persecution in Germany, 1933–1945.* New York: Taylor & Francis.

Green, Jennifer, Rhonda Copelon, Patrick Cotter, Beth Stephens, and Kathleen Pratt. 1994. "Affecting the Rules for the Prosecution of Rape and Other Gender-Based Violence before the International Criminal Tribunal for the Former Yugoslavia: A Feminist Proposal and Critique." *Hastings Women's Law Journal* 5(2):171–221.

Helms, Jesse. 1998. Letter. *Financial Times,* July 31, 1998.

Helsinki Watch. 1995. "Proposals of States and Organizations for the Rules of Procedure and Evidence of the International Tribunals." In *An Insider's Guide to the International Criminal Tribunal for the Former Yugoslavia,* ed. Virginia Morris and Michael Scharf, 487–504. New York: Transnational Publishers.

Human Rights Watch. 1998. *Justice in the Balance: Recommendations for an Independent and Effective International Criminal Court.* New York: Human Rights Watch.

———. 2002. "Lesbian, Gay, and Bisexual and Transgender Rights." *Human Rights Watch World Report 2002.* Available on-line at http://www.hrw.org/wr2k2/lgbt.html.

International Federation for Human Rights. 2002. *No to American Exceptionalism: Under Cover of the War against Terrorism, a Destructive U.S. Offensive against the ICC.* No. 345/2, December. Available on-line at http://www.fidh.org/justice/rapport/2002/cpi345n8a.pdf.

International Gay and Lesbian Human Rights Commission. 1998. *Public Scandals: Gays and Lesbians Face State-Condoned Violence and Legalized Abuse in Romania*. New York: International Gay and Lesbian Human Rights Commission.

Khushalani, Yougindra. 1982. *Dignity and Honour of Women as Basic and Fundamental Human Rights*. The Hague: Martinus Nijhoff.

Lee, Roy. 1999. "The Rome Conference and Its Contributions to International Law." In *The International Criminal Court: The Making of the Rome Statute*, ed. Roy Lee, 1–39. New York: Kluwer Law International.

Linehan, Jan. 2001. "Women in Public International Litigation." Occasional paper of the Project on International Courts and Tribunals, New York. Available online at http://www.pict-pcti.org/publications/pict_articles/Women1.pdf.

Meron, Theodor. 1993. "Rape as a Crime under International Humanitarian Law." *American Journal of International Law* 87 (July): 424–28.

Nainar, Vahida, and Pam Spees. 2000. *The International Criminal Court: The Beijing Platform IN Action*. New York: Women's Caucus for Gender Justice.

Pace, William, and Mark Thieroff. 1999. "Participation of Non-governmental Organizations." In *The International Criminal Court: The Making of the Rome Statute*, ed Roy Lee, 391–98. The Hague: Kluwer Law International.

Plant, Richard. 1987. *Pink Triangle: The Nazi War against Homosexuals*. New York: Holt.

Rothschild, Cynthia. 2000. *Written Out: How Sexuality Is Used to Attack Women's Organizing*. New York: International Gay and Lesbian Human Rights Commission.

Scharf, Michael. 1999. "The Politics Behind the U.S. Opposition to the International Criminal Court." *New England International and Comparative Law Annual* 5. Available on-line at http://www.nesl.edu/intljournal/volSindx.cfm. Based on the author's remarks at the American Bar Association Standing Committee on Law and National Security Symposium, "The Rome Treaty: Is the International Criminal Court Viable?" Washington, D.C., November 13, 1998.

Sellers, Patricia V. 2000. "The Context of Sexual Violence: Sexual Violence as Violations of International Humanitarian Law." In *Substantive and Procedural Aspects of International Criminal Law*, vol. 1, ed. G. K. McDonald and O. Smaak-Goldman, 263–90. The Hague: Kluwer Law International.

Spees, Pam. 2002. "ASP Adopts Unprecedented Voting Procedures for Election of Judges." *International Criminal Court Monitor* 22 (September): 8, 13.

———. 2003. "The Rome Statute of the International Criminal Court." In *Rule of Power or Rule of Law? An Assessment of U.S. Policies and Actions regarding Security-Related Treaties*, ed. J. Burroughs, N. Deller, and Arjun Makhijani, 113–28. New York: Apex Press.

Steains, Cate. 1999. "Gender Issues." In *The International Criminal Court: The Making of the Rome Statute*, ed. Roy Lee, 357–90. The Hague: Kluwer Law International.

Von Hebel, Hermann, and Daryl Robinson. 1999. "Crimes within the Jurisdiction of the Court." In *The International Criminal Court: The Making of the Rome Statute*, ed. Roy Lee, 79–126. The Hague: Kluwer Law International.

Wilkins, Richard. 2002. "The Right Thing the Wrong Way: Implications of the New International Criminal Court." *The World and I*. Available on-line at http://www.worldandi.com/specialreport/2002/october/Sa22620.htm.

Women's Caucus for Gender Justice. 1999–2000. "Advocacy Papers Submitted to the Preparatory Commission for the International Criminal Court." New York: Women's Caucus for Gender Justice. Available on-line at http://www.iccwomen.org/icc/pcindex.htm.

———. 1999. "Recommendations and Commentary for the Rules of Procedure and Evidence." Submitted to the Preparatory Commission for the International Criminal Court, November 29–December 17. Available on-line at http://www.iccwomen.org/icc/iccpc/111999pc/rpe.htm.

———. 2003. *Report of ICC Elections*. Available on-line at http://www.iccwomen.org/.

Women's Caucus for Gender Justice in the International Criminal Court. 1998a. "Briefing Paper on Gender." Submitted to the Preparatory Committee for the International Criminal Court, March.

Women's Caucus for Gender Justice in the International Criminal Court. 1998b. "Gender Justice and the ICC." Position papers submitted to the United Nations Diplomatic Conference of Plenipotentiaries on the Establishment of an International Criminal Court, June 15–July 17, Rome.

Felicity Hill
Mikele Aboitiz
Sara Poehlman-Doumbouya

Nongovernmental Organizations' Role in the Buildup and Implementation of Security Council Resolution 1325

On October 23, 2000, women from Sierra Leone, Guatemala, Somalia, Tanzania, and international nongovernmental organizations (NGOs) addressed the United Nations Security Council in what has become known as an Arria Formula meeting, revealing the gender-specific conditions and acts that women experience in war. They also addressed the undervalued, underutilized leadership women demonstrate in conflict prevention, peace building, and rebuilding war-torn societies. The following day, under the presidency of Namibia, the Security Council held an open session, during which more than forty speakers addressed the issues of women, peace, and security. As a result of this debate the Security Council unanimously passed Resolution 1325 on October 31, 2000.

The Arria Formula dates back to 1993, when Diego Arria, Venezuela's ambassador to the United Nations, invited members of the Security Council to gather over coffee to hear the views of a Bosnian priest, creating an informal exchange between Security Council members and NGOs. Since 1999, the Arria Formula has been used more regularly to provide expertise and testimony on thematic issues taken up by the Security Council, in particular on humanitarian issues, the protection of civilians in armed conflict, children and armed conflict, and, more recently, on women, peace, and security.

In the past, the Security Council had condemned atrocities against women and stressed women's plight and suffering in armed conflict, as well as urging all parties to take special measures to protect women and girls from rape and other forms of gender-based violence. However, women's issues had not been integrated consistently in the council's activities; nor did the council officially recognize women's roles as agents of peace. All that changed with Resolution 1325.

As Sanam Naraghi-Anderlini writes, "On the face of it, this is just

[*Signs: Journal of Women in Culture and Society* 2003, vol. 28, no. 4]

another Resolution that may or may not be implemented. But for women's groups involved in peace building in war zones worldwide, it is a historic statement, with significant implications" (2000). Because it provides a tool for women to become equal participants at all negotiating tables, for the protection of women and girls during armed conflict, and for gender sensitivity in all UN missions including peacekeeping, Resolution 1325 has been received, quoted, and used by an enthusiastic constituency of women's and peace groups throughout the world. The resolution appears as an appendix to this report.

The resolution has generated many activities. Meetings have occurred between women's organizations and the Security Council; NGOs have produced documents monitoring the progress of its implementation and have held regional consultations in Africa, South Asia, and Europe, developing new information-sharing networks; and the Inter-Agency Taskforce on Women, Peace, and Security at the United Nations has coordinated a system-wide implementation strategy. The United Nations Development Fund for Women (UNIFEM) appointed two independent experts to prepare a report on the issue, and the UN Secretary-General has also prepared a study and report.

The successful introduction and ratification of Resolution 1325 lies in three aspects of the UN system. First, the ideas and language in the resolution were built on documents and treaties passed through the UN system since its inception in 1945. In other words, the concept did not suddenly occur to the UN system. Second, international and grassroots nongovernmental efforts have historically provided information and analysis to the Security Council. Third, cooperation between the Namibian presidency of the Security Council, the Division for the Advancement of Women (DAW), UNIFEM, and NGOs was possible and was very successful in this instance due to a synergistic relationship that had taken decades to establish. All of these elements helped to identify and bring the experiences and expertise of women into the realm of the Security Council.

The buildup to Security Council Resolution 1325

The discussion around women, peace, and security took center stage in 1998, when the Commission on the Status of Women (CSW) debated the obstacles to implementing the chapter of the Beijing Platform for Action, the document that resulted from the Fourth World Conference on Women, devoted to women and armed conflict. During the CSW, Ambassador Anwarul Chowdhury of Bangladesh presided over the Security Council. His statement on March 8, 2000, provided a shot of enthusiasm and encouragement for the women gathered at the CSW by linking equality, development, peace, and the need for women's urgent involvement in these matters. Seeing his statement as an opportunity to take the issue of women, peace, and security to the Security Council, the Women and Armed Conflict caucus, a group of NGOs working around the issue, organized several events to provide further information to Security Council members. At one such event, Security Council members were invited to participate in a discussion with the caucus on the issue. Security Council delegations from Bangladesh, Canada, China, Macedonia, the Netherlands, Russia, the United Kingdom, and the United States accepted the invitation. Women from conflict zones presented their experiences, tailoring their comments and recommendations to the specific mandate of the Security Council. The issues raised included the conversion of military resources to social endeavors, the inclusion of women in all levels of decision making, the implementation of gender- and age-specific measures in conflict situations and for refugees and displaced persons, the allocation of resources to empower women, and the need for peacekeepers to receive sensitivity training before they are assigned to missions.

At this meeting, Ambassador Chowdhury spoke on behalf of the Security Council and reinforced his support for the role of women in peace efforts. He also informed the women that he was working with other colleagues to devote a session of the Security Council to discussing the roles of women in armed conflict and peace and requested their help in garnering support from the fourteen other Security Council members on the issue. He believed that with combined efforts they could achieve the special session. To follow up, the caucus convened another meeting with Security Council members in June, during the Special Session on Women 2000, which was a review of achievements in the five years since the Beijing Women's Conference.

The Women and Armed Conflict Caucus also made the following recommendations to Security Council members in a briefing paper provided to all delegations:

- Commission a report on the requirements for the protection of women and girls in armed conflict and the means to increase the participation of women of all ages in conflict prevention, peacekeeping, peacemaking, and peace building.
- Issue a resolution regarding the requirements for the protection of women and girls in armed conflict and the means for increasing women's participation in peace and security matters.
- Appoint an advisor on gender issues to the Security Council and ensure

that all Security Council actions in regard to conflict, security, and peace include advisors on gender issues.

- Employ a wider range of nonviolent conflict prevention and intervention mechanisms, including unarmed interposition forces and expert teams in conflict resolution comprised of equal numbers of women and men.
- Encourage all member states that contribute to peacekeeping forces to ensure appropriate training of those forces in gender and cultural sensitivity. Additionally, the United Nations should provide on-site training on human rights with special attention to the human rights of women.
- Establish procedures for drawing on the expertise, experiences, and resources of civil society in regard to all matters of conflict, peace, and security, in particular the experience of women's organizations and initiatives.

After the CSW ended, the Hague Appeal for Peace, International Alert (IA), the International Women's Tribunal Center, the Women's Caucus for Gender Justice, the Women's Commission for Refugee Women and Children, and the Women's International League for Peace and Freedom (WILPF) created the NGO Working Group on Women and International Peace and Security. The NGO Working Group agreed to pursue two recommendations—to encourage women's participation in peace agreements and to push for the convening of a special session of the Security Council on women, peace, and security. The WILPF, which had convened the Women and Armed Conflict Caucus, went on to play a coordinating role in the NGO Working Group by initiating meetings among NGOs with Angela King, assistant secretary general and special adviser on gender issues and advancement of women, and working with UNIFEM to discuss the possibility of Security Council action on women.

The first task was to meet with each Security Council mission. The NGO Working Group collected the best contemporary literature on the subject and presented it to each delegation, with a summary of each document. The group generated a list of experts and NGOs that would speak to those issues if Security Council members wished to access a wider range of opinion. Because Namibia had hosted the meeting that led to the Windhoek Declaration and the Namibia Plan of Action on Mainstreaming a Gender Perspective in Multidimensional Peace Support Operations, the NGO Working Group approached the meeting with Namibian Ambassador Martin Andjaba with a great deal of hope that Namibia would consider holding the open session during its October presidency of the Security Council.[1]

Through the months of July and August, the NGO Working Group continued to hold meetings with other members of the Security Council in the hope of widening the base of support beyond Namibia and Bangladesh. To garner support outside the Security Council and increase advocacy efforts, the NGO Working Group strategized and planned with a broad and diverse group of NGOs and the press, informing them of developments in New York and encouraging groups to develop relationships with relevant departments in the capitals of Security Council member states.

Finally, early in September 2000, Namibia announced that the Security Council, under its presidency, would hold an open session on women, peace, and security. Members of the NGO Working Group celebrated with enthusiasm. At last, women would be walking into the Security Council chambers to give their own accounts of the impact of armed conflict on their lives and societies and to present their own appropriate, effective strategies for conflict prevention, resolution, and peace building.

During the months of September and October, NGO Working Group members continued to meet with members of the Security Council and to provide important background documents to help them prepare for the open session. They also prepared a document with NGO recommendations and a draft resolution for the Security Council's consideration. The NGO Working Group invited women experts to bring their concerns and strategies to the open session. Inonge Mbikusita-Lewanika from the Organization of African Unity African Women's Committee on Peace and Democracy, Isha Dyfan from WILPF-Sierra Leone, Luz Mendez from the National Union of Guatemalan Women, and Somali delegate Faiza Jama Mohamed from the Africa Office of Equality Now in Kenya accepted the invitation and came to New York to address the Security Council in the Arria Formula and to observe the open session. Other participants in the Arria Formula were Eugenia Piza-Lopez from IA, Mary F. Diaz from the Women's Commission for Refugee Women and Children, Anne Burke from Amnesty International, Cora Weiss from the Hague Appeal for Peace,

---

[1] The Windhoek Declaration and the Namibia Plan of Action were generated during a seminar on "Mainstreaming a Gender Perspective in Multidimensional Peace Support Operations," organized by the Lessons Learned Unit of the UN Department of Peacekeeping Operations and hosted by the government of Namibia from May 29 to May 31, 2000. Available at http://www.reliefweb.int/library/GHARkit/Docfiles/WindhoekDecl.doc.

and Betty Reardon from the Peace Education Program at Columbia University Teachers College.[2]

The following day, the public gallery of the Security Council chamber was filled with women. There was a lot of clapping—something unheard of in that particular chamber—and the word *historic* was used repeatedly. At last, women's perspectives on war and peace became visible in the Security Council through more than forty speeches.[3] Some of the recommendations from the NGO Working Group, including some of the language from the group's draft resolution, were put into the text of the resolution adopted on October 31.[4]

The implementation of Resolution 1325

Now that Resolution 1325 exists, the task is to implement and put into operation its recommendations and to ensure that women's groups receive concrete, practical financial and technical support. The UN system in general, and the Security Council in particular, must move from words to action. The NGO Working Group remains a solid coalition to ensure the broadest support and implementation for all the elements of Resolution 1325.

Since the passage of Resolution 1325, reports on UN peacekeeping operations in East Timor, Afghanistan (United Nations 2000), the Democratic Republic of Congo (United Nations 2001b), Western Sahara (United Nations 2001a), and other countries have included gender provisions, but the information provided in reports to the Security Council has been limited. However, the demand for women to be included in decision making and in peace and security negotiations has had some effect. Women have been included in the talks on the reconstruction of Afghanistan and in the Inter-Congolese Dialogue.

Second Arria Formula on women, peace, and security, October 30, 2001

On October 30, 2001, Security Council delegations met with women's

---

[2] Arria Formula meetings are "off the record"; therefore, what was discussed at the meeting cannot be disclosed. However, the speeches of all participants can be found at http://www.peacewomen.org/un/sc/arria/arriaindex.html.

[3] All forty-one statements can be found on-line at http://www.peacewomen.org/un/sc/countrystatements/cstatements.html.

[4] For a more detailed analysis of the resolution, see Naraghi-Anderlini 2000.

NGOs for a second time in an Arria Formula meeting at the UN Head-quarters in New York. Council members heard statements from Elisabeth Rehn, an independent expert on the impact of armed conflict on women and women's role in peace building; Natércia Godinho-Adams of East Timor; Jamila, an activist from Afghanistan (who, like many Afghans, uses only one name); Haxhere Veseli from Kosovo/Federal Republic of Yugoslavia; and Maha Muna of the Women's Commission for Refugee Women and Children. During this discussion, women from the grass roots reminded the Security Council that they had decided to "remain actively seized on the matter" and that women still account for the largest number of victims in situations of armed conflict and the smallest number of decision makers.

The NGO Working Group also gave the Security Council members documentation of the implementation of Resolution 1325 in the year since its unanimous adoption. With this meeting, the NGO Working Group tried to maintain the momentum captured a year before and to keep Security Council members committed to the implementation of Resolution 1325. The meeting proved of particular importance given the U.S. attacks in Afghanistan and the limited role women had been able to play in the region.

As a result of the meeting, the Security Council issued a presidential statement on October 31, 2001. In this statement, read by Brian Cowen, minister for foreign affairs of Ireland, the Security Council reaffirmed its strong support for increasing women's role in decision making with regard to conflict prevention and resolution. It also renewed its call for states to include women in negotiations and the implementation of peace accords, constitutions, and strategies for resettlement and rebuilding. On the issue of empowerment, the Security Council urged member states to redouble their efforts to nominate women candidates as special representatives to the Secretary-General or special envoys to peace missions. The Security Council also reiterated its request to the Secretary-General to include, in his reporting, progress in gender mainstreaming throughout United Nations peacekeeping missions and on other aspects relating to women and girls in matters of peace and security.

Efforts of NGOs in the implementation of Resolution 1325

The NGO Working Group on Women, Peace, and Security continues to develop strategies to implement Resolution 1325. Following are some examples of the efforts of member organizations and partner NGOs around the world.

Women's Caucus for Gender Justice. Nearly a year before the second Arria Formula meeting, the Women's Caucus for Gender Justice held a public hearing on December 11, 2000. This one-day public hearing of testimonies on crimes from ongoing war and conflict situations around the world immediately followed the Tokyo Tribunal on Japanese military sexual slavery. This event demonstrated that the crimes against the former "comfort women" during World War II were not isolated incidents specific to the events around the war. Battles are increasingly fought over women's bodies, and women continue to be used as war weapons. The hearing gathered testimony from twelve conflict zones, including Chiapas, Mexico, Colombia, Guatemala, Algeria, Congo, Liberia, Rwanda, Sierra Leone, Somalia, former Yugoslavia, Afghanistan, Burma, Cambodia, East Timor, and Indonesia. The testimonies showed how the lack of accountability for crimes already committed enables the unabated continuation of such crimes. Innocent civilians, women, and children continue to pay the price for the refusal of world powers to learn lessons from the horrendous experiences of war. The hearing not only presented painful experiences of women who had been victimized by war but also provided a forum to discuss initiatives in each of these places to demand justice, exemplified by the experiences of women who joined resistance movements and organized work for peace and justice. The public hearing encouraged the ongoing work of women for genuine justice, peace, and an end to impunity.

The NGO Working Group on Women, Peace, and Security. The NGO Working Group has undertaken a great deal of communication and outreach work, including the printing and distribution of twenty thousand copies of the resolution. To celebrate the first anniversary of Resolution 1325, the NGO Working Group held a luncheon in New York, inviting key government and UN decision makers, and launched a comprehensive listing of all implementation activities undertaken by governments, the UN system, and NGOs (NGO Working Group on Women and International Peace and Security 2001). The NGO Working Group has provided analysis and guidance to Lakhdar Brahimi, the United Nations' special representative for Afghanistan, organizing interfaces between him and Afghan women. During the 2002 Commission on the Status of Women, working-group members held twelve events to bring attention to Resolution 1325. Two interactive workshops organized by the NGO Working Group trained more than one hundred people on ways to advocate and implement the resolution. The NGO Working Group also organized a well-attended panel for International Women's Day. In addition, member organizations conducted three video screenings and discussions; sponsored panels on gender equality in refugee settings, on gender and peace support operations, on media women's perspectives on international peace and security, and on war widows; and organized less formal lunchtime discussions on various aspects of gender and peace issues.

International Alert. On March 8, 2001, IA's Women Building Peace campaign handed Special Advisor Angela King more than 100,000 signatures from more than 140 countries, from women, women's organizations, and civil society groups working for peace and social justice, in support of women's demands for protection, participation in decision making, and an end to impunity for crimes committed against women. During the same month IA published and disseminated "Raising Women's Voices for Peacebuilding: Vision, Impact and Limitations of Media Technologies" (McKay and Mazurana 2001) to a wide range of policy makers, academics, and the media. The publication provides an accessible means for increasing the knowledge of women's responses to violent conflict and peace building, explores how women have used communication technologies in their peace-building work, and highlights the innovative and effective results they have achieved using extremely limited resources. International Alert developed a monitoring framework for core issues in Resolution 1325 that will be used in case study countries, initially Nigeria, the Southern Caucasus, and Nepal. The framework suggests measurable indicators through which key issues of gender mainstreaming can be monitored. It aims to identify the extent to which Resolution 1325 has been internalized and could potentially be developed and supported, as well as to identify gaps in areas not covered by the resolution.

Women's Commission for Refugee Women and Children, Protection, and Participation Project. The Women's Commission is carrying out an assessment to review policies and practices related to the United Nations High Commission for Refugees (UNHCR) protection responsibilities vis-à-vis women refugees and with regard to gender equality. The assessment considers the measures taken by UNHCR over the past decade in response to the particular needs and risks faced by women covered by the UNHCR mandate. It describes how the principles contained in the Guidelines for the Protection of Refugee Women (United Nations High Commissioner for Women [UNHCR] 1991) relate to ongoing practice and analyzes how structures of organization, channels of communication, lines of reporting and accountability, and resource constraints in UNHCR headquarters and in the field may facilitate or impede progress. In April 2001, the Women's Commission released "You Cannot Dance if You Cannot Stand: A Review of the Rwanda Women's Initiative and the UNHCR's Commitment to Gender Equality in Post-conflict Situations" (Women's Commission for

Refugee Women and Children 2001). The report highlights the strengths and weaknesses of the Rwanda Women's Initiative (RWI), providing lessons learned about the potential role for women in postconflict reconstruction and for future women's initiatives. The report also provides specific recommendations for the future of RWI. From May to July 2001, for the second in a series of four participatory studies with adolescents, the Women's Commission carried out a study in northern Uganda that involved fifty-four adolescent researchers and more than twenty adults from the community to identify key concerns facing adolescents and to propose solutions to their problems as part of an international campaign to increase services and protection for and with adolescents affected by armed conflict.

Women's International League for Peace and Freedom. An important lesson learned from the Security Council process is that women's peace initiatives are scattered and diffuse. Without a cohesive front, words sometimes get lost in the wind. To address these issues, WILPF created the Peace Women project. In July 2001, WILPF organized an international seminar in Geneva on the Israeli-Palestinian crisis, featuring women from every country in the Middle East, with a special focus on Security Council Resolution 1325. On October 31, 2001, the first anniversary of Security Council Resolution 1325, WILPF launched the PeaceWomen.org Web site. The concept of PeaceWomen.org evolved and grew, eventually adopting its current format. Through consultations, group meetings, and a generous grant from the Ford Foundation, the Peace Women team brings together information from women and women's organizations working for peace around the world into a repository Web site where communication is nurtured and accurate information is exchanged and made accessible. Thus it became impossible for the United Nations, and the Security Council in particular, to avoid women's voices. This electronic repository of information collects an enormous amount of information, in five main sections:

- *Resources*: This section includes a comprehensive and annotated bibliography of books, articles, and analyses on women's peace theory and activities, as well as NGO, government, and UN position papers and reports and tools for building and reinforcing women's organizations.

- *Contacts*: This section provides listings of contact information for women's NGOs working on peace and justice issues, as well as listings of governmental and UN programs in the field.

- *United Nations*: This part of the site deciphers the UN system so women at the grassroots level can use it. It routinely tracks references to women and peace made in the different forums and departments of the United Nations. The Web site also provides urgently needed information about peacekeeping operations—contact details for those responsible for writing reports and for feeding information to the Security Council. It also provides a detailed listing of UN personnel in the field, through its Peacekeeping Watch campaign.

- *Campaigns*: This section presents the outreach and campaigning tools and materials produced by organizations the world over. In the aftermath of the events of September 11, 2001, and the subsequent events that occurred in Afghanistan, the Peace Women project started its own campaigns by compiling statements from women involved in peace work from around the world. Due to great need and response, the project team developed campaigns on Afghanistan, the Democratic Republic of Congo, and Israel-Palestine to raise the visibility of efforts to include women in peace processes and consequently to exercise pressure for the inclusion of more women.

- *News*: This section provides the latest news on women and peace. It also provides early warnings by linking to extensive networks of women involved in peace efforts.[5]

Conclusions

The words of Security Council Resolution 1325 must continue to be transferred into action. The international community must ensure that women are included at every level of peace and security, from local community action to international criminal tribunals for countries emerging from conflict. This process will take some time. But as the buildup to this resolution and cooperation between NGOs, UN entities, and member states have shown, we can ensure that it will occur. In 2000, the doors were open just wide enough for women to squeeze into a Security Council debate for the first time. Concerned women and men must now act on the words of Resolution 1325 to assure that the door remains open permanently.

---

[5] This Web site is continuously growing, raising visibility, and reinforcing peace efforts. For any additions or comments, contact www.info@peacewomen.org.

Appendix

Resolution 1325 (2000) Adopted by the Security Council at Its 4,213th Meeting, October 31, 2000

The Security Council,

Recalling its resolutions 1261 (1999) of 25 August 1999, 1265 (1999) of 17 September 1999, 1296 (2000) of 19 April 2000 and 1314 (2000) of 11 August 2000, as well as relevant statements of its President, and *recalling also* the statement of its President to the press on the occasion of the United Nations Day for Women's Rights and International Peace (International Women's Day) of 8 March 2000 (SC/6816),

Recalling also the commitments of the Beijing Declaration and Platform for Action (A/52/231) as well as those contained in the outcome document of the twenty-third Special Session of the United Nations General Assembly entitled "Women 2000: Gender Equality, Development and Peace for the Twenty-First Century" (A/S-23/10/Rev.1), in particular those concerning women and armed conflict,

Bearing in mind the purposes and principles of the Charter of the United Nations and the primary responsibility of the Security Council under the Charter for the maintenance of international peace and security,

Expressing concern that civilians, particularly women and children, account for the vast majority of those adversely affected by armed conflict, including as refugees and internally displaced persons, and increasingly are targeted by combatants and armed elements, and *recognizing* the consequent impact this has on durable peace and reconciliation,

Reaffirming the important role of women in the prevention and resolution of conflicts and in peace-building, and *stressing* the importance of their equal participation and full involvement in all efforts for the maintenance and promotion of peace and security, and the need to increase their role in decision-making with regard to conflict prevention and resolution,

Reaffirming also the need to implement fully international humanitarian and human rights law that protects the rights of women and girls during and after conflicts,

Emphasizing the need for all parties to ensure that mine clearance and mine awareness programmes take into account the special needs of women and girls,

Recognizing the urgent need to mainstream a gender perspective into peacekeeping operations, and in this regard *noting* the Windhoek Declaration and the Namibia Plan of Action on Mainstreaming a Gender Perspective in Multidimensional Peace Support Operations (S/2000/693),

Recognizing also the importance of the recommendation contained in the statement of its President to the press of 8 March 2000 for specialized training for all peacekeeping personnel on the protection, special needs and human rights of women and children in conflict situations,

Recognizing that an understanding of the impact of armed conflict on women and girls, effective institutional arrangements to guarantee their protection and full participation in the peace process can significantly contribute to the maintenance and promotion of international peace and security,

Noting the need to consolidate data on the impact of armed conflict on women and girls,

1. *Urges* Member States to ensure increased representation of women at all decision-making levels in national, regional and international institutions and mechanisms for the prevention, management, and resolution of conflict;

2. *Encourages* the Secretary-General to implement his strategic plan of action (A/49/587) calling for an increase in the participation of women at decision-making levels in conflict resolution and peace processes;

3. *Urges* the Secretary-General to appoint more women as special representatives and envoys to pursue good offices on his behalf, and in this regard *calls on* Member States to provide candidates to the Secretary-General, for inclusion in a regularly updated centralized roster;

4. *Further urges* the Secretary-General to seek to expand the role and contribution of women in United Nations field-based operations, and especially among military observers, civilian police, human rights and humanitarian personnel;

5. *Expresses* its willingness to incorporate a gender perspective into peacekeeping operations, and *urges* the Secretary-General to ensure that, where appropriate, field operations include a gender component;

6. *Requests* the Secretary-General to provide to Member States training guidelines and materials on the protection, rights and the particular needs of women, as well as on the importance of involving women in all peacekeeping and peacebuilding measures, *invites* Member States to incorporate these elements as well as HIV/AIDS awareness training into their national training programmes for military and civilian police personnel in preparation for deployment, and *further requests* the Secretary-General to ensure that civilian personnel of peacekeeping operations receive similar training;

7. *Urges* Member States to increase their voluntary financial, technical and logistical support for gender-sensitive training efforts, including those undertaken by relevant funds and programmes, inter alia, the United Nations Fund for Women and United Nations Children's Fund, and by the Office of the United Nations High Commissioner for Refugees and other relevant bodies;

8. *Calls on* all actors involved, when negotiating and implementing peace agreements, to adopt a gender perspective, including, inter alia:

(a) The special needs of women and girls during repatriation and resettlement

and   for   rehabilitation,   reintegration   and   post-conflict   reconstruction;

(b) Measures that support local women's peace initiatives and indigenous processes for conflict resolution, and that involve women in all of the implementation mechanisms of the peace agreements;

(c) Measures that ensure the protection of and respect for human rights of women and girls, particularly as they relate to the constitution, the electoral system, the police and the judiciary;

9. *Calls upon* all parties to armed conflict to respect fully international law applicable to the rights and protection of women and girls, especially as civilians, in particular the obligations applicable to them under the Geneva Conventions of 1949 and the Additional Protocols thereto of 1977, the Refugee Convention of 1951 and the Protocol thereto of 1967, the Convention on the Elimination of All Forms of Discrimination against Women of 1979 and the Optional Protocol thereto of 1999 and the United Nations Convention on the Rights of the Child of 1989 and the two Optional Protocols thereto of 25 May 2000, and to bear in mind the relevant provisions of the Rome Statute of the International Criminal Court;

10. *Calls on* all parties to armed conflict to take special measures to protect women and girls from gender-based violence, particularly rape and other forms of sexual abuse, and all other forms of violence in situations of armed conflict;

11. *Emphasizes* the responsibility of all States to put an end to impunity and to prosecute those responsible for genocide, crimes against humanity, and war crimes including those relating to sexual and other violence against women and girls, and in this regard *stresses* the need to exclude these crimes, where feasible from amnesty provisions;

12. *Calls upon* all parties to armed conflict to respect the civilian and humanitarian character of refugee camps and settlements, and to take into account the particular needs of women and girls, including in their design, and recalls its resolutions 1208 (1998) of 19 November 1998 and 1296 (2000) of 19 April 2000;

13. *Encourages* all those involved in the planning for disarmament, demobilization and reintegration to consider the different needs of female and male ex-combatants and to take into account the needs of their dependants;

14. *Reaffirms* its readiness, whenever measures are adopted under Article 41 of the Charter of the United Nations, to give consideration to their potential impact on the civilian population, bearing in mind the special needs of women and girls, in order to consider appropriate humanitarian exemptions;

15. *Expresses* its willingness to ensure that Security Council missions take into account gender considerations and the rights of women, including through consultation with local and international women's groups;

16. *Invites* the Secretary-General to carry out a study on the impact of armed conflict on women and girls, the role of women in peace-building and the gender dimensions of peace processes and conflict resolution, and *further invites* him to

submit a report to the Security Council on the results of this study and to make this available to all Member States of the United Nations;

17. *Requests* the Secretary-General, where appropriate, to include in his reporting to the Security Council progress on gender mainstreaming throughout peacekeeping missions and all other aspects relating to women and girls;

18. *Decides* to remain actively seized of the matter.

Women's International League for Peace and Freedom, New York

References

McKay, Susan, and Dyan Mazurana. 2001. "Raising Women's Voices for Peacebuilding: Vision, Impact and Limitations of Media Technologies." Discussion paper, International Alert, New York. Available at http://www.internationalalert.org/women/media.pdf.

Naraghi-Anderlini, Sanam. 2000. "The A–B–C to UN Security Council Resolution 1325 on Women and Peace and Security." Report, Ecumenical Women 2000+, New York. Available at http://www.ew2000plus.org/un_womenpeace_res1325 essay.htm.

NGO Working Group on Women and International Peace and Security. 2001. "Security Council Resolution 1325—One Year On." Report, Women's International League for Peace and Freedom, New York. Available at http://www.peacewomen.org/un/UN1325/since1325.html.

United Nations. 2000. "The Situation in Afghanistan and Its Implications for International Peace and Security: Report of the Secretary-General." United Nations, New York. Available at http://ods-dds-ny.un.org/doc/UNDOC/GEN/N00/754/94/PDF/N0075494.pdf.

United Nations. 2001a. "Report of the Secretary-General on the Situation Concerning Western Sahara." United Nations, New York. Available at http://ods-dds-ny.un.org/doc/UNDOC/GEN/N01/252/60/IMG/N0125260.

United Nations. 2001b. "Sixth Report of the Secretary-General on the United Nations Organization Mission in the Democratic Republic of the Congo." United Nations, New York. Available at http://ods-dds-ny.un.org/doc/UNDOC/GEN/N01/246/14/IMG/N0124614.pdf.

United Nations High Commissioner for Women (UNHCR). 1991. "Guidelines for the Protection of Refugee Women." Office of the United Nations High Commissioner for Women, Geneva. Available at http://www.unhcr.org.

Women's Commission for Refugee Women and Children. 2001. "You Cannot Dance if You Cannot Stand: A Review of the Rwanda Women's Initiative and the United Nations High Commissioner for Refugees' Commitment to Gender Equality in Post-conflict States." Women's Commission for Refugee Women and Children, New York. Available at http://www.womenscommission.org/reports/womenscommission-rwi-assessment.pdf.

Vanessa A. Farr

Notes toward a Gendered Understanding of Mixed-Population Movements and Security Sector Reform after Conflict

Armed conflicts in Africa are increasingly characterized by the movements of mixed populations of combatants and civilians. These movements may take place across international borders but sometimes come about from displacement across internal or state boundaries, including cease-fire zones, into territories held by an opposing force. The status of such mixed populations—as refugees or internally displaced people, as mercenaries or prisoners of war—is often difficult to determine.

Their movement has direct implications for postconflict security measures such as repatriation and disarmament, demobilization, and reintegration (DDR) of combatants, their dependents, and most particularly, women and girls associated with armed groups in noncombatant roles. Not surprisingly, however, given the vagueness of current approaches to cross-border and internal movements by militarized groups and the ongoing indifference to using a gender lens as an analytical tool in understanding insecurity, the fact that the movement of armed groups and fighting forces is highly gendered tends to be invisible to policy makers and program planners. In this article, I present a preliminary and largely speculative set of observations and questions on how militarized cross-border and internal movement is affecting women and girls, especially in areas with large internally displaced and refugee communities, and propose some avenues for further research.

Large population movements during wars fought by highly mobile and often informally armed groups and forces populated by both combatants and supporters (usually women and children) raise difficult questions about how to classify individuals as they move across international borders: are they civilians and therefore eligible to claim refugee status, or are they foreign combatants? According to international law, they should not be classed as refugees if they possess arms and are proven to be members of armed groups and forces but should instead be disarmed and interned as

[*Signs: Journal of Women in Culture and Society* 2007, vol. 32, no. 3]

prisoners of war.[1] However, their categorization as foreign combatants might have particular political implications since people defined as mercenaries are engaged in illicit activities and are not eligible for inclusion in DDR processes.[2] In such cases, what should be done to assist women associates who are not combatants with weapons but who have undertaken other forms of work, possibly under coercion, to sustain the armed group? How best should children, especially married girls and girl-mothers associated with fighting forces, be identified, especially when they are being intimidated or hidden by their captors? How should their care, reinsertion or return, and reunification with family or community members be managed? People may claim refugee status on the grounds of persecution, and a case may be made that forced marriage fits into this category, but an additional challenge is that members of armed groups and forces might refuse repatriation after war because they have committed war crimes or, as is often the case with women, have been involved in relationships with men that were unsanctioned by their families or communities. They may feel unable to make claims of refugee status that could facilitate their return, especially with children born of illicit liaisons.

As this brief overview shows, a number of questions arise when mixed populations move around in and with armed forces and groups during and after war. Yet very little research has been conducted to date to work out what such increased mobility—often accompanied by the free movement of illicit small arms and light weapons—actually means for conflict-afflicted populations that have been directly associated with war making. As a result, little is being done to address the problems created for those who find themselves—accidentally or by design—on the wrong side of an international border, or internally displaced in hostile territory, if and when peace is declared and negotiations and postconflict reconstruction programs begin.

My preliminary research on this question reveals that there are four primary ways in which women and girls are affected by cross-border and

---

[1] The separation of armed civilians from armed combatants is always a complicated task in areas where small arms and light weapons are prolific. Most agencies rely on combatants to self-identify, or they look for telltale signs, including obvious things like military uniforms or more subtle signs such as responses to military language and commands.

[2] International law prohibits the recruitment, use, financing, or training of mercenaries, who are defined as foreign fighters specially recruited to fight for compensation at a higher rate than that paid to national combatants of a similar rank and function. They are motivated essentially by the desire for private, not political gain.

internal movements in complex emergencies.[3] The first form of movement is forcible, such as that between northern Uganda and southern Sudan, where women and girls are regularly abducted by rebels (in this case the infamous Lord's Resistance Army [LRA]). Ugandan abductees sometimes escape on the Sudanese side of the border. Some make their way into towns where they look for help; however, it is alleged that some escapees have been picked up and imprisoned by members of the Sudanese Armed Forces, who may be collaborating with the LRA to destabilize communities in southern Sudan. In interviews, nongovernmental organizations (NGOs) and UN officials argued that women and girls may disappear in towns, as they are prime targets for enslavement in households where they are forced into unpaid work or exploited for sex. Those who are imprisoned seem to have no legal rights, although they should be protected by the Geneva Conventions. To my knowledge, no research has been conducted into either of these problems, however, so there is no specific policy in place to deal with them.[4]

Second, as is the case between eastern DRC and western Uganda, women move, possibly of their own accord, when accompanying men who are being deployed back to their country of origin after an armed incursion across an international border. This happened when the Uganda People's Defense Force was forced to retreat from its illegal incursion into the DRC in June 2003, taking local wives back with them.[5] According to women peace activists in the DRC, these women have been abandoned in Uganda, often when they became ill with AIDS or because their husbands returned to official wives. They do not appear to be on any formal lists for repatriation, possibly because of the high levels of social stigma attached to their having taken up with foreign fighters in the first place, but are at least known to peace networks in the DRC who are attempting to raise funds to get them home.[6]

---

[3] Field research on women's peace building in Democratic Republic of Congo (DRC), Uganda, and Sudan was conducted for the International Crisis Group from February to April 2006 but did not focus specifically on mixed-population movements. See International Crisis Group 2006.

[4] Personal interviews with NGOs and UN officials, Juba, South Sudan, March 13–14, 2006. At present, the LRA problem is beyond the mandate of the UN mission in Sudan. A truce signed in southern Sudan on August 26, 2006, between the LRA and the Uganda People's Defence Force will hopefully bring an end to the protracted conflict.

[5] The legality of the marriages between Ugandan military and Congolese civilians is unclear, but it should be assumed that they were neither officially nor culturally sanctioned.

[6] Personal interviews with DRC peace activists, Addis Ababa, Ethiopia, November 23–26, 2005, and Bukavu, DRC, March 24, 2006.

Third, as has happened in many African conflicts, women move as combatants or as women associated with armed groups and fighting forces in noncombat roles. It is often difficult to determine the extent to which they are willing participants in the armed group or force, but I am hesitant to label all the movements of women and girls accompanying armed groups as abductions. While the majority of their participation may be coerced, it is important not to forget that women in war zones, as in peacetime contexts, have very different reasons for doing what they do and often do manage to exercise their own volition, even in terribly difficult circumstances. The problem is that women who take up arms are often excluded from formal DDR processes, even after years of feminist activism to raise their profile, and their invisibility is even more likely when they are able to disappear into groups of civilian refugees and internally displaced people.[7]

The last category of movement of women associated with armed forces is possibly the most complex to define. It happens when women from one ethnic group become associated with armed forces of another ethnic group within the same country in which there is an internal boundary, which has become a conflict zone, such as between North and South Sudan. In the current process of withdrawing Sudan Armed Forces from the territory now governed by the Government of South Sudan, dealing with women associated with enemy fighting forces is proving to be a significant problem because of questions of stigma, illegitimate children, and the women's economic and social dependency on the withdrawing army rather than on local communities.[8] Although the National DDR Commissions and the United Nations are theoretically committed to providing special programs for women associated with the fighting forces as part of the DDR process, there is still a significant struggle ahead to identify the women properly and to develop sustainable programs for their peaceful reintegration, both of which will be a challenge.[9]

In the sea of questions and speculation I have presented here, what emerges as most important is that women peace activists working on the ground in armed conflict are seeing women and girls affected in specific and often horrific ways by the movements of armed men across porous

[7] For more on this issue, see Douglas et al. (2004) and Farr (2005).

[8] Sudan is currently led by a government of national unity. Under an Interim Constitution for Southern Sudan, the south is led by the Government of South Sudan, formed of the National Democratic Alliance, of which the Sudan People's Liberation Movement/Army is a member.

[9] Personal interviews with members of the UN mission in Sudan DDR unit, Khartoum and Juba, March 2006.

borders. They are lamenting that virtually nothing is being done to identify, understand, or properly assist them.[10] My informants in Uganda, DRC, and Sudan reported that abandoned wives are living in appalling circumstances in internally displaced people's settlements or refugee camps, often with HIV/AIDS and without support from the wider community because they and their children are perceived as outsiders or enemies. They have little or no recourse to DDR processes or forms of restitution or justice in the postconflict moment. The invisibility of these women says a lot about how impenetrable security sector reform processes remain for women, even six years after the passing of UN Security Council Resolution 1325 on Women, Peace, and Security (2000).

With more questions than answers, it is difficult to propose better ways to address these problems than through engaging with local researchers working on refugee issues and internal displacement who could help provide more data on the extent of the problems women face, from which the process of developing policies and programs could derive. While this work is being done, women in the three countries propose that a regional women's peace network, possibly attached to an existing process such as the Amani Forum and definitely under the auspices of the African Union, should be set up specifically to discuss cross-border issues and their effects on women and girls.[11] This proposal seems to provide an excellent starting point, not only to address the questions raised in this article but also to further reinforce women's right to participate in innovative ways in regional peace-building forums from which they still remain largely excluded.

UN Institute for Disarmament Research (UNIDIR)

References

Douglas, Sarah, Vanessa Farr, Felicity Hill, and Wendy Kasuma. 2004. *Getting It Right, Doing It Right: Gender and Disarmament, Demobilization and Reintegration.* New York: UNIFEM.

Farr, Vanessa. 2005. "Disarmament, Demobilization and Reintegration: Where Do Women Stand?" In *Women in an Insecure World: Violence against Women,*

---

[10] This conclusion is derived from field research conducted in Sudan, DRC, and Uganda, in March and April 2006, which offered a unique opportunity to consider the cross-border implications for women of complex emergencies in countries with contiguous borders.

[11] The Amani Forum is a regional forum of parliamentarians in the Great Lakes Region of Africa (see http://www.amaniforum.org/index.htm). Sudan is not a member.

Facts, Figures and Analysis, ed. Marie Vlachová and Lea Biason, 193–98. Geneva: Geneva Center for the Democratic Control of Armed Forces.

International Crisis Group. 2006. "Beyond Victimhood: Women's Peacebuilding in Sudan, Congo and Uganda." Africa Report no. 112, June 28. http://www.crisisgroup.org/home/index.cfm?id=4186&l=1.

UN Security Council. 2000. UN Security Council Resolution 1325 on Women, Peace, and Security (S/Res/1325). New York: United Nations.

Part III. Gendering Diasporas and Inventing Traditions

(Extra)Ordinary Violence: National Literatures, Diasporic Aesthetics, and the Politics of Gender in South Asian Partition Fiction

As with similar struggles around the world, independence from British rule in the Indian subcontinent was inaugurated with violence. The 1947 Partition of British India into two nation-states, India and Pakistan, provoked the single largest population movement in recent history, with Hindus moving into independent India and Muslims into the newly formed nation of Pakistan.[1] It is estimated that between 1947 and 1948, 10–15 million people crossed the newly created borders in both directions. The vast body of South Asian Partition–themed fiction has been read, quite understandably, within the framework of nation building as the quintessential national literature documenting the birth pains of the nation(s). In this essay, I will argue that Partition fiction can just as accurately be read as diasporic narrative, more concerned with the trauma of relocation and homesickness for the place left behind than with celebrations of independence. And yet, reading this fictional genre through a gendered and culturally embedded lens reveals that the idiom of diaspora is appropriate not just because of the movement of populations that ensued after Partition but because of diaspora's resonance as metaphor. In these

Earlier versions of this project were presented at the International Conference on the Literature of the Indian Diaspora, St. Augustine, Trinidad, March 2000; at the Thirtieth Annual South Asian Studies Meeting, Madison, Wisconsin, October 2001; as the Westmore Lecture, Brown University, March 2001; at the Rethinking South Asia Conference, University of California, Santa Cruz, May 2001; and at the Center for Race and Ethnicity, University of California, San Diego, April 2005. I thank the organizers and audiences at each of these venues for the opportunity to present my work and for helpful comments. I gratefully acknowledge the help of Chandan Reddy, Parama Roy, and Aparajita Sagar at various stages in the writing of this essay. I especially thank Muhammad Umar Memon for his generous responses to my queries on issues of translation and transliteration between Urdu, English, and Hindi.

[1] For a political chronology of events and forces leading up to Partition, see Sarkar (1983), Hasan (1994), Bhattacharjea (1997), Saint and Saint (2001), and Ludden (2004).

[*Signs: Journal of Women in Culture and Society* 2007, vol. 33, no. 1]

fictional texts, themes that are habitually identified with diasporic aesthetics—the articulation of loss, homesickness, trauma, travel, the longing
for return—are not large-scale expressions of the angst of a people who
have indeed left their home country en masse in tragic circumstances;
rather, such tropes operate on a metaphoric level to articulate the gendered
trauma of Partition on individual lives.

During the Partition months, violence against women (in the form of
sexual assault, mutilation, murder, and abduction) rose to unprecedented
levels, and this gendered violence has mostly been read as metonymic of
the violation of the land.[2] In this essay, I consider the means by which
some of this fiction, written originally in Urdu and Hindi and since translated into English, makes sense of and provides alternatives to the usual
nationalist narrative about Partition's violation of women and of undivided
India.[3] Furthermore, I suggest that when we look more closely at the
fictional articulations of diasporic longing in these texts, we find that such
desires are articulated in very specific and gendered cultural codes. Against
the general consensus that Partition violence was part of an exceptional
moment of insanity in which men went mad, we have stories that theorize
differently: the violence that Partition brought to women is understood
to be similar but of a different magnitude than the usual fare doled out
to them in a patriarchal society. As for the male protagonists in this fiction,
the sense of violation that ensued after Partition challenged the very foundations of their manhood and subjectivity.

National histories written in the first decades after independence tended
to focus on the realm of high politics and therefore on issues of triangular
(British, Pakistani, Indian) national political interests that were served by
Partition. As many scholars have subsequently noted, these early historical
accounts were for the most part silent about the level of gendered violence;
the official narrative seemed to be that it was a time of extraordinary
violence and shame, for men, women, and the two new nations.[4] Silence

---

[2] Besides the hundred thousand or more women estimated to have been sexually assaulted
during this period (1947–48), official estimates state that about seventy-five to eighty thousand women were abducted by men of communities other than their own. See Butalia 1998
and Menon and Bhasin 1998.

[3] I do not consider Partition fiction from Bengal/East Pakistan/Bangladesh in this essay
because while these texts share much of the gender and social dynamics of the north, the
regional political, linguistic, and cultural particularities are significantly different.

[4] Urushi Butalia, Ritu Menon, and Kamla Bhasin, among others, have written eloquently
of the patriarchal nationalist prescription of appropriate femininity and masculinity. Ayesha
Jalal (1998) makes a very simple and yet important statement about Partition violence against

allowed for a saving of face, on both a national and a familial level.[5] And yet, the fiftieth anniversary of independence from British colonial rule arrived in 1997 with no one willing or able to say that the wounds of this Partition have healed or been forgotten, despite the official policy of silence.

In the last decade of the twentieth century, for a variety of reasons, academic and mainstream discussion of the 1947 Partition has been greatly vitalized and intensified.[6] This is especially the case in the Indian context in comparison to Bangladesh and Pakistan.[7] In recent years, a whole new body of social histories has been added to the numerous political histories of Partition written from 1947 onward. Left-leaning and/or feminist scholars have variously revised the official national readings of this event and process called Partition—in what amounts to a distinct body of work that can be called new Partition studies. Gendered analysis is central to this body of multidisciplinary scholarship, primarily because of the pivotal contributions of feminists to this discussion.

This late twentieth/early twenty-first-century scholarly rethinking of Partition has opened up space for more diverse readings that focus more on the social and psychological effects of the trauma of Partition than allowed for in earlier scholarship. New Partition studies goes beyond the official nationalist rhetoric and offers instead "richer definitions of the nation" (Pandey 1991, 559) through an examination of fragmentary evidence such as government documents, memoirs, newspaper articles, interviews with Partition survivors, ethnography, and so on. Gyanendra Pandey writes: "Part of the importance of the 'fragmentary' point of view lies in this, that it resists the drive for a shallow homogenisation *and struggles for other, potentially richer definitions of the 'nation'* and future political community" (1991, 559; emphasis added). Feminist scholarship by Urvashi Butalia (1998), Ritu Menon and Kamla Bhasin (1998), and

---

women: "All said and done, the commonality of masculinity was stronger than the bond of religion. . . . Alas, Punjab had betrayed its patriarchal bent more decisively than the affective affinities of religious community" (Jalal 1998, 2189–90).

[5] See Nandy (2003) for a nuanced account of this silence on Partition.

[6] The resurgence of communal violence in the 1980s and 1990s led both intellectuals and ordinary folk to make comparisons with Partition violence.

[7] The Partition of 1947 has different resonance in all three locations: in independent India it was experienced as a vivisection, as the much lamented loss of bodily parts of Mother India, while in Pakistan it was read as the necessary birth pangs of a new nation. In Bangladeshi history, 1947–71 is the occluded period in national history, a history that is recorded as really beginning in 1971, when East Pakistan became Bangladesh. The violence that ensued during that struggle for independence overshadowed the 1947 Partition.

others has especially forcefully argued for a gendered understanding of communal violence and of state restorations of order. And yet, the focus of much of the new scholarship on Partition remains solidly grounded in the national.

While this focus on the nation-state as *mai-bap*—"mother/father" or protective parent—that intervenes in everyday life is justified in Partition analysis, it effectively restricts women to the bind of being evaluated only in terms of a framework in which they are, of necessity, positioned as symbols, communal sufferers, familial victims, and second-class citizens. This is especially noted in Menon and Bhasin's and also Butalia's moving and impassioned feminist accounts of the particularly gendered victimization of women during Partition. Menon and Bhasin define their project as

> Country, Community. Religion. Freedom itself: a closer examination of what meaning they have for women has led feminists to ask searching questions about women's asymmetrical relationship to nationality and citizenship; and to appreciate the role assigned to them in any renegotiation of identities, whether ethnic, communal or national. Such an analysis of the experience of abducted women, for instance, sheds light not only on the Indian state and its articulation of its role and responsibilities vis-à-vis its female citizens, but also on its perception of its role vis-à-vis Pakistan, Hindu and Muslim communities, and displaced Hindu families. (Menon and Bhasin 1998, 20–21)

This text and the other equally prominent feminist study by Butalia advocate paying attention to the fragments—fragments that may, as Menon and Bhasin write—"at their most subversive . . . counter the rhetoric of nationalism itself" (1998, 8). But neither of these studies nor other work on Partition is quite able to (nor considers it necessary to) theorize Partition outside the "story of the nation," as Menon and Bhasin phrase it (1998, 17).[8]

While this new scholarship on Partition radically altered the terms and practices of knowledge production in several disciplines, literary texts continued to be utilized in unaltered fashion. Historians and other social

---

[8] In her edited collection *No Woman's Land* (2004), Menon's inclusion of texts by Pakistani, Bangladeshi, and Indian women demonstrates her feminist deconstruction of reading within a singular (usually Indian) national framework. What is ironic, of course, is that national identity in all three states is established primarily through differentiation of each from the other, so that even within this cross-border feminist coalition, nation and nationalism are the currency.

scientists have used Partition literature as a means of supplementing their historical analysis: literature is a treasure trove of realistic, even confessional, chronicles of horrors from which examples of "emotional trauma" can be extracted.[9] Not surprisingly, given the tight links that have been forged in literary criticism between third-world literatures and nationalism, the few essays that are written by literary critics mostly assume that the national is the predominant framework within which such literary texts must be read.[10]

The very coherence of the term *Partition fiction* to describe fiction written in several languages in two countries (three countries by 1971) and over a long stretch of time—from 1947 to the 1970s, if not later—is debatable. This coherence comes largely from the new attention that Partition received in both mainstream and scholarly venues in the late 1990s. For example, one of the many manifestations of the yearlong celebrations in 1997 of the fiftieth anniversary of the creation of Pakistan and of Indian independence was the release of several English-language anthologies of Pakistani and Indian national literatures. These anthologies, ostensibly showcasing the best literature of the past fifty years, were shaped by issues of translation, length, availability, editorial taste, and so on. However, despite these constraints, the first few entries in most of these collections are what could be classified as Partition literature, fiction that in some shape or form addresses the trauma of the 1947 Partition.[11]

---

[9] Jill Didur has written of the need to critique "the assumed differences between 'literary' versus 'historical' narratives and the assumed 'value' that each 'type' of text comes to represent for the historiographer reconstructing the events of a particular historical moment" (1997; see also Didur 2006).

[10] See Talbot (1995), Bahri (1999), and Kumar (1999). Also see Jason Francisco's (2000) review of some of the anthologies of Partition fiction.

[11] See anthologies edited by Waqas Ahmad Khwaja (1992), Asif Farrukhi (1997a), Ian Jack (1997), Salman Rushdie and Elizabeth West (1997), and Yasmin Hameed and Asif Aslam Farrukhi (1998). For example, Intizar Hussain, in his preface to *Fires in an Autumn Garden: Short Stories from Urdu and the Regional Languages of Pakistan* (1997), writes: "In the host of stories written in those days [around the creation of Pakistan] I am trying to locate that particular point which can be called the starting point of Pakistani fiction. I am fully conscious of the absurdity of such an attempt. . . . However, at times a literary work turns into a milestone and gives the impression of being the starting point of a new trend or movement or tradition. Manto's short story 'Khol do' [Open It] appears to me a work of this kind. What a dramatic starting point provided to Pakistani fiction!" (Hussain 1997, xvi). Farrukhi, a fiction writer who edited this collection, writes in the introduction: "What follows is an attempt to read my country in its stories, to see how Pakistan is narrated in its stories" (Farrukhi 1997b, xxii). Rushdie and West's (1997) anthology includes a translation of Saadat Hasan Manto's "Toba Tek Singh," the only entry of the total thirty-two entries not written originally in English. This editorial decision displays the apparent necessity of a

Additionally, around the late 1990s, several publishing houses commis-
sioned scholars to assemble anthologies on Partition fiction even as a few
literary critical evaluations of this literary genre were published.[12] Today,
ten years after 1997, Partition fiction/film studies has congealed into an
established field of inquiry (a subfield of Partition studies), and the disparate works gathered under this term do come together as a complex
genre.

Unlike other disciplines, literary criticism has no compulsion (except
for convention) to confine itself to the rubric of the nation. Some Partition
fiction, I argue, adopts the vocabulary, tropes, and aesthetics that we now
readily recognize as endemic to the fictionalization of diasporic situations.
Yet gender prescriptions in this fiction do not automatically change when
the cartographic certainties of nationhood give way to the flexible and
mobile spaces of the diasporic. Of course, during and immediately after
Partition there were very few cartographic certainties, since villages and
even cities that seemed destined for Pakistan stayed in India and vice versa.
Clearly, the birth of the two nations in this case cannot be separated from
the birth of the two diasporas, which are wrenched from one home to a
more "fitting" home. As currently practiced, however, critical discourses
on the national and on the diasporic proceed as if the two were diametrically opposite objects of study. I am arguing, instead, that the two are
intimately intertwined and that it would be productive to bring the diasporic privileging of mobility, travel, memory, split affiliations, and so on,
to bear on the hallowed ground of national discourses because it reveals
the scaffolding on which the national is raised.

As Vijay Mishra defines it, diasporas are ethnic groups that, for a variety
of reasons, "live in displacement" (Mishra 1996, 423). As Partition fiction
repeatedly demonstrates, for those who traveled across newly drawn bor-
derlines, old attachments cannot be submerged into or easily grafted onto
the newly born independent nation. This fiction is diasporic in that it pays
lingering attention to the pains of separation, to the sense of inappropriate
attachment to the place left behind, and to the inability to fall in line with

---

Partition story to even this otherwise nonrepresentative (despite the subtitle of the book)
collection.

[12] On anthologies of Partition fiction, see Cowasjee and Duggal (1995), Memon (1998),
and Bhalla (1999b). On critical evaluations of the genre, see Pandey (2001), Saint and Saint
(2001), and Kumar (2004). Also see special issues of *South Asia* (Low 1995) and *Interventions*
(Menon 1999) as well as innumerable essays in popular newsmagazines in South Asia. Several
Partition novels, memoirs, and other nonfictional essays have been reprinted in recent years;
see Nanda ([1948] 2003), Pritam ([1950] 2003), Manto ([1951] 2003), Hyder ([1959]
1998 and [1960] 1999), and Nahal ([1975] 2001).

the new regime/land/object of patriotism. And yet, fifty years later, these stories of lament and looking back to the land left behind are rounded up in anthologies that canonize the national via the literary.

What, then, is national literature? Literary academics are currently quite familiar and comfortable with the category of national literature, especially when the focus is on literature that emerges from decolonizing contexts. However, what the precise criteria for belonging to this category might be is hard to specify. Such literature is of course not to be equated with straightforward patriotic writing that simply follows the official narrative on the birth and fortunes of the nation. Clearly, there are very few literary examples that cleave to the kind of "no-fault" nationalism that Suvir Kaul suggests is the usual textbook account of national history that school-children are subjected to (Kaul 2001, 9). National literature is usually that which critics assess as the best literary response to national crises, triumphs, or both. As a category it includes literary works that are expressly patterned by authors as a response to significant events in national history, works that even in their dissent from official narratives remain invested in the nation. Unlike diasporic fiction, it is usually understood to be committed to a single national space.

But what, one might ask, is gained from reading Partition fiction through the lens of diaspora-plus-nation? Read in purely nationalist terms, Partition was a once-in-a-nation's-lifetime event: it was the downside of achieving independence for India and the cost of establishing Pakistan. Thus, in terms of national history this Partition is firmly in the past and will not be repeated. As Alok Bhalla writes in his introduction to his best-selling collection of stories, Partition and its communal violence constitute "*an exceptional moment of disorder*" in a continuing history of a life lived together [by Hindus, Muslims, and Sikhs] in all its complex variety" (1999a, xxv; emphasis added). If we read them through a diasporic lens, such partitions and dislocations are routinely replayed from the beginning of settled societies to the present day. Framed in this context of trading diasporas, indentureship, evictions, forced/economic migrations, and dis-locations, this Partition becomes less of a singular event in a national history and more liable to be repeated in varying form and degree.[13] Every aspect of the violence associated with Partition then demands our atten-

---

[13] Today the horrors of dislocation that Partition literature testifies to are reenacted in the razing of urban slums, the dislocation of rural populations that are "resettled" in order to build dams and power plants, and the destruction of communities in the course of com-munal riots that have swept over entire cities in the 1980s and 1990s and as recently as 2002 in Gujarat.

tion, not because it was extraordinary but because of what it reveals about the ordinary. The fiction is very clear on this point.[14]

While diasporic tropes articulate the way national affiliations are presented in crises in the very literature that ostensibly gets the postindependence national literary canon going, one needs to look beyond both national and diasporic features of this literature to get at the radical gender critique that some Partition fiction presents. My reading of the fictional texts by Syed Mohammad Ashraf and Jamila Hashmi demonstrates the ways in which Partition fiction partakes of and in turn reproduces the popular gendered vocabulary in circulation in folktales, iconic religious texts, and Indian cinema to simultaneously register, protest, absorb, and interpret the experiences of 1947 and its aftermath. But first I examine what is possibly the most anthologized Partition story, "Khol do" (Open It), written in Urdu in Pakistan in 1948 by the best known, allegedly antinationalist writer on Partition in both India and Pakistan, Saadat Hasan Manto ([1948] 1999).[15]

In "Open It" Manto's plotting of gendered violence follows the nationalist script in that it reproduces the patriarchal/nationalist prescription of woman standing in for the nation as an object to be either violated or enshrined. In the exceptional moment of disorder that Partition violence is said to stem from, this story easily allows for a reduction of men and

---

[14] This is the central argument of Amrita Pritam's acclaimed Punjabi novel *Pinjar* (The skeleton; [1950] 2003), which chronicles the trials and fortitude of Pooro, a Hindu girl who is abducted by a Muslim youth, Rashid, from her own village eleven years before Partition because of an old vendetta between their two families. At the time of partition, Pooro sees her own story repeated in the many abductions of women that she witnesses. Her outrage, however, is not limited to Partition violence against women. Rather, the plotline for the novel is driven by Pooro's encounters with girls and women who are oppressed in their own families, by their in-laws, or by society at large. Predictably, in the film *Pinjar* (2003) based on this novel the time frame is compressed so that Pooro's abduction seems to take place just prior to Partition, and several of the other plotlines that highlight everyday oppressions that women face are deleted or merely hinted at. In this very arresting film, then, unlike in Pritam's novel, Partition's gendered violence is presented as exceptional.

[15] Manto was born in 1912 into a middle-class Kashmiri Muslim family in Punjab in British India and spent most of his adult life in Bombay, where he worked as a journalist and a screenwriter. It is documented that he moved very reluctantly to Pakistan in 1948. When he published his Partition fiction in the early 1950s, it was negatively received not just by right-wingers in Pakistan and India but also by progressive cultural critics who thought him voyeuristic, pornographic, and irreligious. In recent years, however, Manto's reputation has been resurrected by literary critics. See Mufti (2000) and Gopal (2005) for fuller discussions (in English) of the historical and Urdu literary milieu in which Manto's work was produced and received. For an English translation of some of Manto's critical commentary on his Partition-related writing, see Hasan (1987 and 1991).

women to perfect binaries—rapists and raped, protectors and protected, villains and victims, buyers and bought, sellers and sold. And in making this violence the central event of the tale, some Partition fiction and the literary criticism it engenders further entrench these limited gender categories by allowing no space for either gender outside these binaries. An extreme example of such binary readings is provided by Bhalla, who notes that Manto's stories belong to the category of Partition fiction that is "marked by a sense of rage and hopelessness" (1999a, xxx). Such writers, Bhalla argues, "record with shock as people in an obscene world become either predators or victims, as they either decide to participate gleefully in murder and loot or find themselves unable to do anything but scream with pain as they are stabbed and burnt or raped again and again" (xxxi).

"Open It" is very short and very dramatic in its violence. The story begins innocuously enough: "The special train left Amritsar at two in the afternoon and reached Mughalpura eight hours later" (Manto [1948] 1999, 358). But as Ashis Nandy (2000) has pointed out, to the reader who knows that this distance is about thirty-five miles and can be covered in less than an hour, this is a chilling detail. We know that something awful must have happened en route from Amritsar in India to Mughalpura in Pakistan. Manto forces the reader to participate, to infer from the few details that he does give us the details that he doesn't. In the beginning of this story a refugee family—aged parents and a teenage daughter—is on the run from a rampaging mob. The mother is attacked, and with her dying breath she urges the father to save the daughter. But the father and daughter are soon separated, and while he ends up in a refugee camp, there are no signs of the daughter. We learn that the daughter, Sakina, is rescued by eight young men in a truck—who, because they are associated with the refugee camp where the father is, are, we can assume, of the same community. We are told, "the eight young men were very kind to Sakina" (360). However, a few lines down we read that when the father meets these men, they assure him that they have not found his daughter but that they will keep looking. We are now forced to go back and reread the few lines about the rescue.

A paragraph or so after the father questions these men, we are told that an unconscious Sakina is found abandoned by some railway tracks and is brought to the camp's makeshift hospital. When the male doctor requests that an assistant open a window to let in some reviving air, the semiconscious girl who has been raped so often obeys the male command to "open it" by slowly and painfully unknotting the drawstring to her *salwar* (drawstring pants) and pulling them down. The old father sees her movement as a sign of life and shouts with joy. The story concludes with a single sentence that captures the doctor's mortification: "The doctor broke into a cold sweat" (Manto [1948] 1999, 362).

Most readings of this story have focused on the father's traumatized haplessness and ineffectuality in the face of terror and his inability to protect his daughter from the worst of the violence. In contrast, the refugee camp doctor is assertive and focused, the citizen rebuilding his community. The doctor's shame and mortification at the end of the story becomes a sign of his masculine virtue. Manto is masterful in inducing national/masculine shame. He lets the men of neither community off the hook: clearly both Sakina's Hindu or Sikh (it is not specified) abductors and her Muslim rescuers sexually assault her. As in the final scene in Deepa Mehta's Partition film *Earth* (1998), when the beautiful young heroine is carried aloft by a mob of rapacious men, it is a culmination of all the danger inherent in being female in these locations.[16] In most accounts, these sexual assaults become both symbolic of many other violations and at the same time the embodiment of that violence. Manto's text evokes protective, patriarchal sentiments and a certain helplessness in "decent" male readers and simultaneously makes female readers aware of their gendered vulnerability and their need for protection. It performs a kind of gendering that pulls the reader into the limited gender positions that are available to women (and to men) in this scenario. Such a triangular cast is common in some Partition fiction—the rapacious crowd or individual villain, the helpless innocent male bystander, and the innocent passive female victim—with the shame and details of sexual violation wrapped together.[17]

Very few Partition stories actually produce the forward-looking, patriotic national subject who, one might imagine, is the proper subject of national literature. Hence when I argue that Manto's story performs gen-

---

[16] It is significant that the novel *Ice-Candy Man* by Pakistani writer Bapsi Sidhwa (1988) on which the screenplay for this film was based does not end with this horrific scene. In the novel, Shanta is hardened by this and other violations and refuses to "adjust" (as she is advised to) to her husband, the ice-candy man, who had both raped and pimped her before he married her. The ice-candy man, who is responsible for orchestrating the initial gang rape, is reduced at the end of the novel to a guilt-ridden, tormented, and broken shell of his former self. In Mehta's film, the shock value of this horrific scene makes for a cinematically effective climax scene that unfortunately fixes the feisty, flirtatious Shanta in the final frames as the terrified victim of a horrifying sexual crime.

[17] For another story with this same triangular cast (young female victim, decent but helpless citizen, and a rapacious mob), see "They Are Taking Me Away Father, They Are Taking Me Away!" written by one of Pakistan's most respected women writers, Khajida Mastur ([1984] 1999).

der within the nationalist model, I argue that his terms of critique are specified by notions of nation, of masculine decency (in contrast to masculine madness), and of civic responsibility (evoked in its very abdication).[18] Given the solidly patriarchal social arrangements in the communities affected by Partition, there are very few cultural modes of narrating shame, dislocation, and displacement as experienced by men that do not undermine masculinity as popularly understood. Within the rhetoric of the nation and citizenry, the paucity of words with which normative masculine subjects can express these multiple traumas and still continue to occupy the position of the patriarchal masculine subject/citizen is especially stark. This is an argument that I will explore with the help of another short story, titled "Separated from the Flock," written in the 1970s in Urdu by the Indian writer and civil servant Ashraf (1999).[19]

Ashraf presents a discomfiting masculine narrative of diminished authority in the face of a deep affiliation to the country left behind, an attachment we easily recognize as diasporic. In this first-person narrative, a Pakistani superintendent of police is forced by a series of encounters into a wrenching acknowledgment of his longing for and inability to revisit the Indian state of Uttar Pradesh, or UP, in which he was born and grew up. As a senior Pakistani civil servant based in Lahore, he cannot travel to enemy territory, which is what India has become after the wars of 1965 and 1971. He views this inappropriate homesickness as a weakness that he hopes to keep hidden. In the short story, on his way to a recreational hunting trip, the civil servant is quizzed by his Pakistan-born driver about India and his hometown, which he left thirty years ago at the age of eighteen. At the lakeside where the hunters gather in the early dawn, the

---

[18] For different equations of gender and the national in Manto's work, see Mufti (2000) and Gopal (2005). Aamir R. Mufti focuses on Manto's pre-Partition work to argue that the writer presents the prostitute as protagonist in his short stories as a means of countering the metaphoric use of mother as nation. Mufti writes, "The real point of the debate about Manto's work is the cavalier attitude of his stories not towards sex itself, but rather towards the nation, or more precisely, towards the gendered narratives of national belonging" (2000, 34). Priyamvada Gopal writes, "Manto, one should be clear, has no interest in deconstructing the entire apparatus of masculinity. But the events of Partition would seem to have driven him towards the conclusion that masculinity itself had to be radically reconstituted if there was to be any meaningful societal transformation and, certainly, if the horrors of 1947–8 were not to repeat themselves. This would entail not just a simple reformation of behaviour or attitudes but a more far-reaching transformation wrought from an engagement with contradictions within the self" (2005, 105).

[19] This story was first published in Urdu in the *Aligarh University Journal* (date and citation not given [Bhalla 1999b, 874]). Also see the notes on contributors in Memon (1998, 361).

civil servant meets a childhood friend and reluctantly allows himself to reminisce about the past in a way that he has not done for a while. The third and most discomforting encounter is with his driver's wife who, against her husband's wishes, pleads with the civil servant to get her a travel pass so she can visit her native place in India, which happens to be in the civil servant's own home state. To be able to visit one's natal home, evocatively referred to as one's *maike* (place/home of a married woman's mother), after marriage is culturally understood to be the most poignant wish of all young married women. Men/husbands are understood to be, are supposed to be, at home and not in a position to be pining for a home left behind. After the dislocation forced by Partition, this is no longer such a stable gendered difference and, as the story demonstrates, requires much effort to restabilize. The police superintendent decides to support his driver in this domestic battle and so, when confronted by the tearful wife, feigns his helplessness in expediting such official business.

By the end of the story, however, despite the elaborate arrangements that he and his subordinates made for this duck shoot, the civil servant finds himself unable to shoot the migrating birds. He is himself "separated from the flock." Unable to enjoy the masculine sport of hunting and compelled (most unwillingly) to compare himself both to a woman denied her husband's permission to go to her natal home and to ducks with broken wings, Ashraf's hero is caught in the emasculating discourse of homesickness and displacement. At the end of the story he lies to his friend and subordinates about old cartridges being responsible for his failure to shoot—and he is allowed the ruse. In his introduction to the collection, Bhalla writes that in refusing to shoot the birds, the hunters ensure that "suffering is not forgotten, for it can never be. . . . Their own loss does not have to be repeated" (1999a, xxxix). Interestingly, the understated yet explicit comparison that Ashraf makes between the driver's wife and the protagonist is eclipsed in Bhalla's critical reading. The radical blurring of gender boundaries that is so delicately recorded in this story is covered over by Bhalla's sentimentality.

Ashraf's "Separated from the Flock" does not have the harsh horrific clarity of Manto's "Open It" or of the final abduction scene of Mehta's film *Earth*. The police superintendent's discreet longing for UP leaks the past into the present and disrupts his laboriously disciplined sense of Pakistani citizenship. Written from the perspective of an established male citizen, the diasporic features of the story threaten to unravel the patriarchal certainties of nationalism, but the police superintendent is able (just about) to rein in these disruptions: at the end of the story, self-discipline, proper masculinity, and proper national affiliations continue to hold sway.

I turn to a third and final story, "Banished" (1998), written by the Pakistani woman writer Jamila Hashmi (1929–88), who was a well-known novelist and also a schoolteacher in Lahore.[20] "Banished" was written in Urdu in the 1960s and published under the title "Ban vaas," which has been variously translated as "Banishment" and "Exile."[21] I follow the diasporic trope used in this particular story for the insight it provides into the agency of abducted women who are, as feminist critics have asserted, stripped of the basic rights of citizenship in these new nations.

The original title, "Ban vaas," is taken from the Hindu epic the *Ramayana*—literally translated it would mean "forest dwelling"—a reference to the hero Prince Rama and his wife Sita's banishment from their kingdom and their fourteen years of joint exile in the forest. More poignantly and of specific importance in this story by Hashmi, "Ban vaas" refers to Sita's second exile. When first exiled with her husband Rama, Sita is abducted by Ravana, king of Lanka, and though she is eventually rescued by Rama, her virtue is suspect after the abduction. After the return to his kingdom, Sita is soon banished by her husband to a second round of exile because he is unable to reconcile himself to her abduction. It is not surprising that the *Ramayana* story became a popular metaphor and comforting parallel for the trials faced by Partition refugees (and by other South Asians who are part of the global diaspora). Similarly, some Muslim refugees sought religious solace by comparing their migration in 1947 and the trauma it entailed to the *hijrat* (the flight of Muhammed from Mecca to Medina). The very name given to refugees from India in Pakistan, *Muhajirs*, was a reference to the original *muhajirs* who accompanied the Prophet to Medina. And the Muslims already living in Pakistan were

[20] Two translations of the original story have been consulted: The first, titled "Banished," was translated by Muhammad Umar Memon (see Hashmi 1998, 87–105), and page numbers in the text correspond to this version. The second translation is by Bhalla (1999b, 50–67). For more information on Hashmi, see the notes on contributors in Memon (1998, 363–64). Despite my best efforts, I have been unable to locate the original publication venue and/or date for "Ban vaas" (Banished). None of the English-language anthologies that include translations of this story or critical commentary on it offfer such information about the original. In anthologies published in South Asia around the fiftieth anniversary of Partition in 1997, information about the original publication of each entry is typically not included; rather, the anthologies provide the new, and often only, context for these disparate works.

[21] See Kaul's brief discussion of this story, which he calls "a meditation on human dislocation and loss, but also on resignation, and to a lesser degree, reconciliation" (2001, 27). Also see Bodh Prakash's (2001) discussion of this story as framed by an extremely useful account of the literary representation of women in fiction from this region from the 1900s onward.

seen as *Ansars*, modern equivalents of the people of Medina who, legend has it, had so warmly welcomed the first set of Muslim migrants.[22]

Hashmi's story, "Banished," gives us the first-person narrative of a young upper-class Muslim woman who, at the time of the Partition riots, has been abducted from her home in an unnamed city in India by a Sikh farmer who installs her as his "wife" in his village of Sangraon in Punjab, India. This protagonist, identified only as "Bahu"—the term for daughter-in-law in Hindu and Sikh families—has borne three children to her "husband" and dutifully serves her dominating mother-in-law. From the story: "Whenever anyone calls me Bahu I feel insulted. I have been hearing this word for years, ever since the evening when Gurpal dumped me in this courtyard and cried to Badi Ma, . . . : 'Look ma, I've brought you a bahu. A real beauty! The best of the lot'" (Hashmi 1998, 88).[23] When the army comes to this village in Punjab, several years after Partition, to rescue abducted women like this protagonist, she hides herself in the fields. She will go only if her two brothers come to rescue her. Meanwhile, she compares herself to Sita, and Gurpal, her abductor and now "husband," is her very own Ravana. In the present of the story, about seven or eight years after the abduction, this woman is walking "home" with her "husband" and children from a *Dussehra mela* (a religious country fair). This rare "family" outing is the occasion for her to contemplate her life along the pattern provided by the story of Rama, Sita, and Ravana.[24] Commenting on this story, Kaul sees this "mythic precedent" as "showing up" in Hashmi's story "in a rhetorical reversal," from which he concludes that "Partition stories point out, like no other, the vulnerability of women in times of social turmoil" (2001, 28). A close reading of the story, however, reveals that there are no reversals here—just stark parallels drawn between the experiences of everyday life for women both in patriarchal societies and in times of social turmoil.

In this story Hashmi follows the fine tradition of women and subaltern groups who use the *Ramayana* story to explain and protest their own

[22] See Ansari (1995, 97), Kudaisya (1995, 92), and Talbot (1995, 54) for more on the comforts of religious parallels.

[23] The original Urdu text is much more explicit here: "Aaj jitni larkiyan hamare hath lagin, un mey sab say achchi hai." A more exact translation would be, "Of all the girls we got our hands on today, she was the best." Gurpal, the original Urdu suggests, knows that the woman he chooses to bring home is the best because he has "tried out" the others.

[24] Ironically, Dussehra is a Hindu festival in which the triumph of good against evil is celebrated by the reenactment of the rescue of Sita from the clutches of her abductor Ravana by her husband, Lord Rama.

predicaments.[25] By using the most iconic Hindu story to narrate her own predicament, this Muslim protagonist demonstrates both her integration into the "family" she now belongs to (with all the ownership connotations of *belongs to* intact) and her acknowledgment and incisive critique of the centrality of abduction, sexual dishonoring, doubting of women's virtue—all essential ingredients of the Sita story—in this region. Over the course of this particular short story one is made to appreciate that many of the trials that women suffered as the Partition and exchanges of population proceeded were not new inventions of fanatical menfolk. Against the oft-repeated lament that men went mad during these times, Hashmi makes clear that these *agni parikshas*, or trials by fire, such as the one Sita went through in the *Ramayana*, are scripted into the very texture of everyday life for women in this location. It is noteworthy to add here that in the songs sung by women at traditional Hindu weddings and other related rituals in northern India, Sita's marriage and the trials that follow serve brides as a comforting narrative and as a means of expressing their grief at leaving home as well as their trepidation about the future (Varma 2005, 110, 116, 122, 134, 142, 144).

The protagonist in "Ban vaas" does not draw on the rhetoric of nation in order to articulate her suffering, her compromises, or her process of adjusting to her new life.[26] Rather, she relies on the stories and wisdom that young girls in the Subcontinent are well acquainted with—they marry and leave their natal home, and the rest of their life is spent missing home, waiting for their brothers to come and take them home to their *maike* for precious visits. It is in articulating the ways in which her own life as an abductee both fulfills and parodies this well-worn course of events that this nameless Bahu makes her most trenchant critique of everyday acts of patriarchal control and exchange of women: "And besides, every girl must one day leave her parental home to join her in-laws. Well, maybe Bhaiya and Bhai [a reference to her two brothers] weren't present at my wedding—so what? Hadn't Gurpal rolled out a carpet of corpses for me? Painted the road red with blood? Provided an illumination by burning down city after city? Didn't people celebrate my wedding as they stampeded, screaming and crying? It was a wedding alright. Only the customs were new: celebration by fire, smoke, and blood" (Hashmi 1998, 102).

---

[25] There is a long tradition of variant versions of the *Ramayana* that were produced in Asia over the centuries (see Richman 1991).

[26] *Adjusting* is in fact the favored South Asian English term to describe the degrees of self-negation required and expected of women in difficult or new situations and has consequently been imported into most other Indian languages.

Commenting on this passage, Kaul identifies irony as a central trope in this and other Partition fiction. Irony in his reading is present when "everyday reality is represented via its own inversion" (Kaul 2001, 27). However, one could argue that the irony lies not in inversions but in parallels—in the deftness with which the protagonist presents her own situation through the language of weddings and leave-taking of the natal home. Earlier in the narrative, she notes: "Many such 'brides' were brought to the village of Sangraon, but without the customary fanfare: no festive music, no racy songs to the beat of drums, no comic antics or spins or hip-thrusts of nautch girls. No one oiled my dust-coated hair. No *na'in* was sent for to make me up. I became a bride without a single piece of jewellery, without any sindhur for the parting of my hair. . . . Since that day I too felt like Sita, enduring her exile, incarcerated in Sangraon" (Hashmi 1998, 89). For women, this transfer from natal to "marital" home through abduction as represented in fiction, while severe in its effects, was often presented as an intensification of the usual patriarchal discourse about women as property. A daughter is property that is only temporarily attached (on loan, as it were) to her natal home, property whose ultimate destination and destiny lies in its transfer to the marital home. This cultural understanding of women's inherent transferability, I will argue, is put to work in these accounts of Partition's particular forms of violent dislocation of women and the subsequent attempt to return them to their appropriate place in families. In such texts there is a reliance on cultural vocabulary of women as *paraya dhan* (a stranger's wealth in the temporary safekeeping of a woman's parents), or as guests in their own homes, that was in circulation both prior to and after the trauma of Partition. Such reminders serve as the cultural disciplining that will ease young women's transition from *maike* to *sasural* (the home of a woman's in-laws). Note that colloquially *sasural* is used by men only to refer to a stay in prison; serving a prison sentence, then, is the analogy for men to the transition that women make in marrying. Travel, displacement, the trauma of *bedahi* (the bride's leaving of her natal home, a ritual part of the wedding ceremony, often pronounced and transliterated as *vidai*), and homesickness are all scripted into a commonplace understanding of a woman's normal life cycle and ironically provide a means of narrating and adjusting to Partition's particular forms of violent separation.

The well-documented silence about Partition violence in official historiography is spoken indirectly throughout popular culture. After reading the many accounts (fictional, testimonial) of Partition trauma, one finds the repeated use of available terms for voicing the grief of separation and homesickness that are present everywhere in the culture. Note, for instance, the consistent referencing of grief and longing that is done via parallels to some of the folkloric love stories of this region, especially the Romeo-and-Juliet–like tragic and doomed romances of Heer and Ranjha, Sassi and Punnun, and Soni and Mahiwal. Length constraints and the fact that this trope is not used in the three stories I focus on in this essay prevent me from further examining this rich reference.[27] I would like, however, to speculate on what I see as a subterranean link between Partition trauma and the lost-at-the-*mela* plots of so many North Indian movies that are paralleled in Hashmi's short story. I propose that the very popular filmic plotline of a family that is separated at a country fair or by a traumatic event is obliquely patterned on the many unspoken and unspeakable stories of travel, separation, and sorrow that Partition generated. Note that in most Indian movies that use this formulaic plot, the separation scenes are placed before the opening credits as kind of prelude to the story that will unfold, and the grand finale of the film includes a happy and tearful reunion of lost kin at the end of the three hours. Partition fiction rarely offers such optimistic conclusions. In this short story, the protagonist and her husband Gurpal have a brief argument along the lines of "life is a *mela* in which children may become separated from their parents." Using this trope, Gurpal urges his "wife" to forget the violent separation from kith and kin that he forced on her in the past.

As with the excessive use of the lost-at-the-*mela* trope in Hindi movies, one could note the excessive scripting in postindependence Indian cinema of pathos-laden renditions of *bedahi* scenes in which the new bride leaves her parental home after her wedding for her *sasural*. Many such scenes, presented with and through songs about the sorrows of leaving home, being scattered, torn from the bosom of the family and friends, banished to a foreign land, and so on, can be viewed, I will insist, as Bombay cinema's discreet voicing of the lingering trauma that so many in north India were subjected to around Partition.[28] Many of these filmic *bedahi*

---

[27] For example, the title of Mastur's short story "They Are Taking Me Away Father, They Are Taking Me Away!" does not reference a father-daughter exchange from the story itself but is an easily recognized quotation from the Punjabi epic love poem *Heer Ranjha*, in which Heer protests being taken to a husband she does not love, while Ranjha, her lover, stands by helpless and heartbroken. See Mastur ([1984] 1999) and Naqvi (1999, xix). The popularity of these folkloric romances between beautiful and faithful young women (Soni, Sassi, Heer) and lovelorn young men (Mahiwal, Punnun, Ranjha) is in no way diminished by the fact that each story ends with the tragic death of the young lovers.

[28] See, e.g., Majrooh Sultanpuri's haunting lyrics to the *bedahi* song "Chal re sajni ab kya sochey" (Come [keep walking] dear girl, now what is there to think about) from the 1960 film *Bambai ka Babu* (Gentleman from Bombay), in which a tearful young bride leaves

songs are of course based on traditional Hindu marriage songs from the region and have been sung for generations. A bilingual collection of lyrics for songs that are sung at traditional Hindu marriage rituals and other ceremonies in the states of Uttar Pradesh and Bihar in north India has been recently compiled by Shakuntala Varma (2005). The title for this book, *Kahe Ko Byahi Bidesh*, is taken from a popular wedding song that is particularly able to convey the extra burden that the lyrics may have taken on after Partition.[29] Varma translates this "daughter's lament" as

> Why have you married and sent me so far away
> To an alien land, dear father?
> I am like a bird in your garden
> Here only for the night
> The next morning I fly away, dear father,
> I am like a mute cow tied to a post
> Whichever way you drive me I go, dear father,
> You have given my brother your palatial home
> But you have given me an alien land, dear father.
> (Varma 2005, 104)

The title of the song corresponds to the first two lines of the lyrics with a much clearer sense of being married off to (someone in) an alien land than Varma's English translation can render. The gendering of this banishment to a foreign land via marriage is very clear. Sons, the song wistfully complains, get to stay and inherit the patrimony; daughters are led into exile through marriage arrangements. And yet, after the dislocations of

---

her *maike* while the song in the background laments that the young woman has set off on her journey with no one to call her own. Her father regrets sending "this broken morsel of his heart" out to a foreign land. Her childhood friends are scattered here, there, and who knows where? But none of this bears thinking about, because it is time to leave. The lyricist, Sultanpuri (1919–2000), chose at Partition to remain in India like many other successful and well-entrenched Muslim poets, writers, actors, and others in the Bombay film industry, even as they saw so many of their friends and family leave for Pakistan. The screenplay for this film was written by Rajinder Singh Bedi, author of "Lajwanti," the best-known Partition story about an abducted woman's changed relation with her husband after she is rescued and returned to him.

[29] A version of this traditional song was recorded by singer Jagjit Singh for the film *Umrao Jaan* (1981). A variation on this "daughter's lament," as Pritam calls it, is woven into Pritam's novel *Pinjar* ([1950] 2003, 8). In the film *Pinjar* (2003), based on this novel, the traditional song "Charka Chalati ma" (The mother runs the spinning wheel) is sung by Preeti Uttam, and the lyrics are adapted from the novel.

Partition, sons too found themselves banished to alien lands. As in "Separated from the Flock," this is an emasculating predicament for men.

The presentation of abduction as causing a severe case of homesickness after a woman marries and leaves her natal home continues all through Hashmi's story. For example, the protagonist is envious of other (Hindu, Sikh) village women whose brothers come to take them home: "Every year a father or a brother comes to take one or another woman back home. You should see how Asha, Rekha, Poroo, and Chandra seem to walk on air. They hug everyone before leaving. Their words sound like pure music" (Hashmi 1998, 103). Again, there are countless traditional folk songs (and film songs) from this region that joyfully and hopefully anticipate the next time a married woman's natal family will send a brother to escort his sister home to her *maike* for a visit.[30] In Hashmi's story, the protagonist waits for her brothers to come. And of course they never do. Her abduction has lead to her banishment—there is no return, and yet her thoughts are always on return. In keeping with the general metaphoric bent of this story, it is interesting to note that when the protagonist does talk about her country or her homeland the reference is not so much a geographical one but rather is to be understood in terms of time—past and present. As she states it: "Still, I know well enough now that those dear to me live in a country I cannot possibly hope to reach. Like the pathways leading to Sangraon, all other paths criss-cross each other so often that they make one lose one's way. Besides what is to be gained from searching for *a place which now exists only in stories?*" (Hashmi 1998, 98; emphasis added). The term used in the Urdu original of the story for "country" or "homeland" is, surprisingly, the evocative Hindi term *janam-bhoomi*, which would most closely translate as "birthplace."[31] Like the use of the Sita story, the use of the Hindi term rather than Urdu alternatives such as, say, *watan* by this Pakistani writer deepens the ironic punch of this story. Of course, technically, this woman is still in her *janam-bhoomi*. She is still in India when she is in Sangraon, and yet this is not the "country" she longs to return to. Urdu scholar C. M. Naim (1999) has commented in another context on the "syncretic *ganga-jamni* (Indo-Muslim) culture that was once the primary defining element for much of

---

[30] See Bimal Roy's classic film *Bandini* (Female prisoner; 1963) in which one of these traditional songs is rendered by playback singer Asha Bhosle: "Ab ke baras bhej bhaiya ko babul" (In this coming year, father, send my brother).

[31] I wish to thank Muhammad Umar Memon for this and other details about the original Urdu text of "Ban vaas."

elite society in the towns and cities of the Gangetic plain" (xviii).[32] Naim notes that while Partition destroyed this shared ethos, it often resurfaces in fiction written after 1947. Hashmi's use of Hindu legends and Hindi terms in "Banished" can be understood in this context. What is often dismissed in critical readings as romanticized sentimentalizing of the Other (such as the huge popularity of Hindi films categorized as Muslim socials in postindependence India) could be a nostalgic evocation of the loss of this shared *ganga-jamni* ethos.[33] Thus not only Muslims who leave for Pakistan but also Muslims and Hindus who remain in India are rendered diasporic by time because this pre-1947 place of shared references has been left behind forever. Neither Pakistan nor independent India is adequate to the memory of the past.

In Hashmi's story, then, the language of cartographic displacement—which is how the term *diaspora* is strictly interpreted—is itself simply a deferral of the profound out-of-jointness that this abductee experiences as the Bahu in a rural Sikh family. The Sita story, the diasporic tropes, these are simply metaphoric "paths that criss-cross," allowing her to express her dislocation but ultimately leading her back to the present life in Sangraon. The story ends with the line "How far do I still have to go?" (Hashmi 1998, 105). She is going nowhere, and yet the journey is not done. The narrative repeatedly emphasizes the ordinary drudgery of walking a long distance with a tired child to carry—an ordinary activity that is never sundered from the metaphoric journey: "All the same, I must keep on walking. Exile or not, one is compelled to move on in life's fair [*mela*]" (104).

An abducted woman's suffering in this story is represented as keenly felt homesickness—and yet, while some Partition narratives elevate the horrific events of gendered violence into special stories full of heroism, villainy, and shame, this story consistently represents abduction and banishment as standard events in women's lives. Ashraf's and Hashmi's fiction make diaspora a metaphoric category in itself, one that serves to wrench us from the familiarity of the customary national groves, derails us, and

[32] Literally, the term *ganga-jamni* refers to two rivers (the Ganga and the Yamuna) that flow through this region and that start out from the same source in the Himalayas. Colloquially the term is used to describe two distinct and contrasting strands that are woven into one design.

[33] Muslim socials are films in which north Indian Muslim middle- and upper-class lives are depicted in a manner that stresses a fading but still gracious world of Persianized, Urdu-speaking lead characters stylized to evoke the gentility of the landed classes with their fabled exquisite appreciation of poetry and music.

sometimes allows for a glimpse of a place that, as our protagonist sorrowfully tells us, "now exists only in stories" (Hashmi 1998, 98).

My essay attempts to extend the new scholarship on Partition by bringing literary and diasporic analysis to bear on this discussion, especially where it examines gendered dislocations. I read Partition fiction as a site where the subaltern is voiced through diasporic aesthetics: formative cultural narratives such as the *Ramayana* equip women with a vocabulary for their exile, transferability, banishment, and homesickness. Butalia, Menon, Bhasin, and other feminists in their wake work within the framework of the nation and, in their analysis of Partition's gendered violations, respectfully refrain from forcing into speech the many silences around the issue of rape and abduction. I see my contribution to this discussion as one that points to other routes into an understanding of how gendered expectations and oppressions are voiced and protested in Partition narratives. These routes are made visible and audible within Partition literature, but they are routes that require reading (and listening) outside the official rhetoric of nation and, in the last instance, outside the customary language of diaspora.

Department of Literature
University of California, San Diego

References

Ansari, Sarah. 1995. "Partition, Migration, and Refugees: Responses to the Arrival of *Muhajirs* in Sind during 1947–1948." Special issue, *South Asia: Journal of South Asian Studies* 18(S1):95–108.

Ashraf, Syed Mohammed. 1999. "Separated from the Flock." In Bhalla 1999b, 3–32.

Bahri, Deepika. 1999. "Telling Tales: Women and the Trauma of Partition in Sidhwa's *Cracking India.*" *Interventions: International Journal of Postcolonial Studies* 1(2):217–34.

Bambai ka Babu [Gentleman from Bombay]. 1960. Directed by Raj Khosla. Bombay: Naya Films.

Bandini [Female prisoner]. 1963. Directed by Bimal Roy. Bombay: Bimal Roy Productions.

Bhalla, Alok. 1999a. "Introduction." In Bhalla 1999b, xv–l.

———, ed. 1999b. *Stories about the Partition of India.* New Delhi: HarperCollins.

Bhattacharjea, Ajit. 1997. *Countdown to Partition: The Final Days.* New Delhi: HarperCollins.

Butalia, Urvashi. 1998. *The Other Side of Silence: Voices from the Partition of India.* New Delhi: Penguin.

Cowasjee, Saros, and K. S. Duggal, eds. 1995. *Orphans of the Storm: Stories on the Partition of India*. New Delhi: UBS.

Didur, Jill. 1997. "Fragments of Imagination: Re-thinking the Literary in Historiography through Narratives of India's Partition." *Jouvert: A Journal of Postcolonial Studies* 1(2).

———. 2006. *Unsettling Partition: Literature, Gender, Memory*. Toronto: University of Toronto Press.

Earth. 1998. Directed by Deepa Mehta. New York: Cracking the Earth Films.

Farrukhi, Asif, ed. 1997a. *Fires in an Autumn Garden: Short Stories from Urdu and the Regional Languages of Pakistan*. Karachi: Oxford University Press.

———. 1997b. "Introduction: My Country's Stories." In Farrukhi 1997a, xxi–xxxi.

Francisco, Jason. 2000. "In the Heat of Fratricide: The Literature of India's Partition Burning Freshly (A Review Article)." In *Inventing Boundaries: Gender, Politics, and the Partition of India*, ed. Mushirul Hasan, 371–93. New Delhi: Oxford University Press.

Gopal, Priyamvada. 2005. "Dangerous Bodies: Masculinity, Morality and Social Transformation in Manto." In her *Literary Radicalism in India: Gender, Nation and the Transition to Independence*, 89–122. London: Routledge.

Hameed, Yasmin, and Asif Aslam Farrukhi, eds. 1998. *So That You Can Know Me: An Anthology of Pakistani Women Writers*. New Delhi: HarperCollins.

Hasan, Khalid. 1987. "Introduction." In *Kingdom's End and Other Stories*, by Saadat Hasan Manto, 1–10. New Delhi: Penguin.

———. 1991. "About the Book." In *Partition: Sketches and Stories*, by Saadat Hasan Manto, x–xvi. New Delhi: Viking.

Hasan, Mushirul, ed. 1994. *India's Partition: Process, Strategy and Mobilization*. New Delhi: Oxford University Press.

Hashmi, Jamila. 1998. "Banished." In Memon 1998, 87–105.

Hussain, Intizar. 1997. "Preface." In Farrukhi 1997a, xv–xix.

Hyder, Qurratulain. (1959) 1998. *River of Fire*. Trans. Qurratulain Hyder. New Delhi: Kali for Women.

———. (1960) 1999. *A Season of Betrayals: A Short Story and Two Novellas*. Trans. C. M. Naim. New Delhi: Kali for Women.

Jack, Ian, ed. 1997. "India! The Golden Jubilee." Special issue, *Granta* 57.

Jalal, Ayesha. 1998. "Nation, Reason and Religion: Punjab's Role in the Partition of India." *Economic and Political Weekly* 33 (August 8–14): 2183–90.

Kaul, Suvir, ed. 2001. *The Partitions of Memory: The Afterlife of the Division of India*. New Delhi: Permanent Black.

Khwaja, Waqas Ahmad, ed. 1992. *Pakistani Short Stories*. New Delhi: UBS.

Kudaisya, Gyanesh. 1995. "The Demographic Upheaval of Partition: Refugees and Agricultural Resettlement in India, 1947–1967." Special issue, *South Asia: Journal of South Asian Studies* 18(S1):73–94.

Kumar, Priya. 1999. "Testimonies of Loss and Memory: Partition and the Haunting of a Nation." *Interventions* 1(2):201–15.

Kumar, Sukrita Paul. 2004. *Narrating Partition: Texts, Interpretations, Ideas.* New Delhi: Indialog.

Low, D. A., ed. 1995. "North India: Partition and Independence." Special issue, *South Asia: Journal of South Asian Studies* 18(S1):1–212.

Ludden, David. 2004. *India and South Asia: A Short History.* Oxford: Oneworld.

Manto, Saadat Hasan. (1948) 1999. "Open It." In Bhalla 1999b, 358–62.

———. (1951) 2003. *Black Borders: A Collection of 32 Cameos.* Trans. Rakhshanda Jalil. New Delhi: Rupa.

Mastur, Khadija. (1984) 1999. "They Are Taking Me Away Father, They Are Taking Me Away!" In her *Cool, Sweet Water: Selected Stories,* ed. Muhammad Umar Memon, trans. Tahira Naqvi, 1–6. New Delhi: Kali for Women.

Memon, Muhammad Umar, ed. 1998. *An Epic Unwritten: The Penguin Book of Partition Stories.* New Delhi: Penguin.

Menon, Ritu, ed. 1999. "The Partition of the Indian Sub-continent." Special issue, *Interventions* 1, no. 2, 157–330.

———, ed. 2004. *No Woman's Land: Women from Pakistan, India and Bangladesh Write on the Partition of India.* New Delhi: Women Unlimited.

Menon, Ritu, and Kamla Bhasin. 1998. *Borders and Boundaries: Women in India's Partition.* New Delhi: Kali for Women.

Mishra, Vijay. 1996. "The Diasporic Imaginary: Theorizing the Indian Diaspora." *Textual Practice* 10(3):421–47.

Mufti, Aamir R. 2000. "A Greater Story-Writer than God: Genre, Gender and Minority in Late Colonial India." *Subaltern Studies* 11:1–36.

Nahal, Chaman. (1975) 2001. *Azadi* [Freedom]. New Delhi: Penguin.

Naim, C. M. 1999. "Introduction." In Hyder (1960) 1999, vii–xx.

Nanda B. R. (1948) 2003. *Witness to Partition: A Memoir.* New Delhi: Rupa.

Nandy, Ashis. 2000. "The Invisible Holocaust: Silence and Testimony." Keynote Address, Twenty-ninth Annual Conference on South Asia, October 13, Madison, Wisconsin.

———. 2003. "The Days of the Hyena: A Foreword." In *Mapmaking: Partition Stories from 2 Bengals,* ed. Debjani Sengupta. New Delhi: Shristi.

Naqvi, Tahira. 1999. "Introduction." In *Cool, Sweet Water: Selected Stories,* by Khadija Mastur, ed. Muhammad Umar Memon, trans. Tahira Naqvi, x–xxxvi. New Delhi: Kali for Women.

Pandey, Gyanendra. 1991. "In Defense of the Fragment: Writing about Hindu-Muslim Riots in India Today." *Economic and Political Weekly,* March, 559–72.

———. 2001. *Remembering Partition: Violence, Nationalism and History in India.* New Delhi: Cambridge University Press.

Pinjar [The skeleton]. 2003. Directed by Chandraprakash Dwivedi. Bombay: Lucky Star Entertainment.

Prakash, Bodh. 2001. "The Woman Protagonist in Partition Literature." In Saint and Saint 2001, 194–205.

Pritam, Amrita. (1950) 2003. *Pinjar* [The skeleton]. In her *The Skeleton and Other Writings,* trans. Khushwant Singh, 1–84. New Delhi: Jaico.

Richman, Paula, ed. 1991. *Many Ramayanas: The Diversity of a Narrative Tradition in South Asia.* Berkeley: University of California Press.

Rushdie, Salman, and Elizabeth West, eds. 1997. *The Vintage Book of Indian Writing, 1947–1997.* New York: Vintage.

Saint, Ravikant, and Tarun K. Saint, eds. 2001. *Translating Partition.* New Delhi: Katha.

Sarkar, Sumit. 1983. *Modern India: 1885–1947.* New Delhi: Macmillan.

Sidhwa, Bapsi. 1988. *The Ice-Candy Man.* London: Heinemann.

Talbot, Ian. 1995. "Literature and the Human Drama of the 1947 Partition." Special issue, *South Asia: Journal of South Asian Studies* 18(S1):37–56.

Umrao Jaan. 1981. Directed by Muzaffar Ali. Bombay: Integrated Films.

Varma, Shakuntala. 2005. *Kahe Ko Byahi Bidesh: Songs of the Marriage from the Gangetic Plains.* New Delhi: Roli.

Negotiating Silences in the So-Called Low-Intensity War: The Making of the Kurdish Diaspora in İstanbul

I n Turkey, during the 1990s, while the so-called low-intensity war was deployed against Kurdish armed forces and civilians, many Kurds were violently forced to leave their villages and move to the margins of major cities.[1] Those Kurds not willing to take arms on the side of the state were assumed to be contributors to the Kurdish armed struggle led by the Partiya Karkerên Kurdistan (PKK; Kurdistan worker's party).[2] Their refusal

This article grew out of my dissertation and ethnographic research, which was conducted in a Kurdish exile community in İstanbul, Turkey, between May 1998 and February 2000. Open-ended interviews in both formal and informal settings, e.g., at Kurdish weddings, henna nights, and religious feasts; during afternoon teas and after-dinner visits at Kurdish homes; sitting on sidewalks and knitting, shaping dough, and baking flat bread; and chatting in an empty lot with neighbors, provided most of the collected data. The majority of the data come from twenty-three Kırmançi-speaking families, of which eighteen are three- and four-generation extended families, including women who recently married into these families and children born in exile. Five of the families migrated to this area prior to the 1990s. These economic migrant families are nevertheless politically conscious of the issues concerning many Kurds in the Kurdish Region, and directly or indirectly they have facilitated the relocation of eighteen extended forced-migrant families. There are connecting links among all twenty-three families at various levels: they have all come from border communities of two adjacent cities of the Kurdish region. All twenty-three families have peasant backgrounds, and some continue with peasant activities through various links to the Kurdish region. They are all Shafi'i Muslims. These twenty-three families, while directly or indirectly sharing a violent history and poverty-stricken conditions in exile, also share a political vision. The research data do not indicate that there are class differences or differing class consciousness based on their economic power. I would like to express my gratitude to Karen Alexander, the senior editor of *Signs: Journal of Women in Culture and Society*, for careful reading and providing precious suggestions during the final editing process. I am also grateful to the exiled Kurdish women and their families who enabled me to work among them.

[1] According to a report prepared by the Turkish Parliamentary Commission, 3,428 villages and hamlets were evacuated while the burning of villages and the uprooting of peasants continued (TBMM Araştırma Komisyonu 1997).

[2] In April 2002, three hundred delegates of the PKK voted to change the organization's name to Kongreya Azadî û Demokrasiya Kurdistan (KADEK; Kurdish freedom and democracy congress), and they reelected their imprisoned president, Abdullah Öcalan. The

to take up paramilitary positions was taken as proof that they were terrorists operating against the state, and as a result the state felt justified in
violently intervening. As a means of disciplinary action, security forces
burned the rural villages and hamlets of suspected PKK supporters and
destroyed their means of subsistence—harvests, stables, forests, animals,
and farming implements. These Kurds saw their right to live in their
ancestral homeland violently taken away from them. They were forced
into exile by the military in order to terminate their direct and/or indirect,
real and/or alleged, support of the PKK.

During the low-intensity war, in addition to extrajudicial executions
and disappearances, the waterways of Kurdish villages were diverted, leaving fields, animals, and families without water. Many villages were encircled
by the military. Farmers were banned from their villages and/or not permitted to go to their fields. Identification cards were issued to the male
heads of the families for emergency exits and entrances. A food embargo
was enforced in various cities. Pastoralist tribes were denied pasture rights
in the summer months. These modalities of power resulted in a mass
exodus. Currently millions of Kurds live in the peripheries of the major
cities of Turkey.

Numerous uprooted Kurdish families arrived in Esenyurt, İstanbul,
after 1990, when Esenyurt was a newly established municipality on vast
farming lands. In the following ten years, Esenyurt became one of the
two municipalities of İstanbul that received unprecedented numbers of
Kurdish migrants. Throughout these years, Esenyurt proper developed
more of an industrial center, making room for incoming populations to
settle at its margins, without such basic provisions as water, drainage, or
sewer systems. As sweatshop industries developed, poverty, child labor,
prostitution (including child prostitution), drug problems, infant deaths,
malnutrition, and health problems (including epidemics) also increased in
Esenyurt.

In this article I examine the gender and power relations in a Kurdish
exile community in Esenyurt. Here I employ an analysis of an event/
narrative, a narrative production of history marked by gender differences.
I explore the memories and political forces at play in order to show exiled
Kurdish women's notion of violence as it relates to their memory, silences,
and loss of ancestral land. Memories that women related to me of past
events leading to their deterritorialization led me to realize the critical
role that violent history and memory play in the creation of an internal

---

history, ideology, activities, and complexities surrounding the PKK are beyond the scope of
this article. For details on these issues see, e.g., İmset (1996).

diaspora.[3] Two overlapping processes, the experience of a violent history and continuing oppression in exile, led the women to recognize their conditions as diasporic and Kurdistan as a home to return to.[4] In the following pages I hope to establish a space to conceptualize internal diaspora within the diaspora literature by transgressing the defining theme of transnational border crossings. Then I will situate the diasporic claims of exiled Kurdish women in Esenyurt as claims of social, political, and cultural rights that are different from those claimed by the dominant group in Turkey. These claims delineate the imaginations, memories, and silences of individuals as expressed in their narratives, which were produced through the gendered imageries of Kurdistan.[5]

My examination marks how women who are exiled in Esenyurt challenge the ways in which the diaspora has been conceived while claiming the "real-and-imagined" cultural and historical borders of their Mother Soil (*Ana Toprak*)—a lived space within territorialized geography.[6] These women's narratives of their experiences and their resistance to various forms of power highlight their aims to construct their own histories and

---

[3] My use of the term *internal diaspora* builds on Khachig Tölölyan's (1991) exploration of intrastate diasporas. According to Tölölyan, prior to the Armenian genocide in 1914, about 2.5 million Armenians lived in intrastate diasporas in the Ottoman, Persian, and Russian Empires. However, my reference to the Kurdish internal diaspora differs from Tölölyan's formulation of the Armenian intrastate diaspora. Tölölyan refers to the historical Armenian homeland that is/was divided by and within the contiguous states, whereas my discussion of an internal diaspora considers new Kurdish localities outside of the Kurds' homeland but within Turkey.

[4] Kurdistan or Northern Kurdistan refers to the geographic areas inhabited by Kurds living within the borders of the Turkish nation-state. I use both terms interchangeably, as do the Kurds living in Esenyurt.

[5] My aim is to present a cultural and political vision of a specific group of forced-migrant Kurdish women; therefore, I welcome scholarly efforts to widen the horizon of comparative perspectives and do not suggest that there is a homogenized experience and vision for all Kurdish women living in various other diasporas, both in Turkey and abroad.

[6] I borrowed the concept of "real-and-imagined" from Edward W. Soja, who elaborates the experienced dimension of space mixed with abstracted representations of it (1996, 10–11, 16, 65, 79). A warning about my geographic focus is in order here. It is a fact that there have been different and changing webs of meaning for different Kurdish groups that have settled in areas marginal to various major cities, as well as in İstanbul, both prior to the low-intensity war and after. Members of these groups, with their varied histories, converge in particular regions to support one another. Therefore, the emergence of political and social diversities and related outcomes would be expected in studies of different urban Kurdish settlements with different political visions. Although comparative studies of these groups are most needed, they are not within the scope of this study.

mark their diasporic subjectivity. They also contribute to the reconstruction of gendered differences in the diaspora.

The contested borders of the Turkish nation-state

The establishment of the territorial borders of the Turkish nation-state guaranteed the security and the culture of Turks to the detriment of Kurds. Beginning with its formation, the imagined national community of Turks, as the dominant majority, was armed with specific modalities of power to oppress others who had alternative imaginations in Turkey. The official history texts and documents undermined the differentiated temporal and spatial Kurdish history and homeland. The creation of a hegemonic national master narrative, an ahistorical version that merged Anatolian and Mesopotamian history, appropriated the history of the region by falsely locating Turks within the area for millennia.[7] While in reality Kurds lived in Kurdistan, the name of a geographical region literally meaning "the land of Kurds," the use of the term *Kurdistan* was removed from official and social discourse, and even Turkish encyclopedias have no entries for it.

In line with state domination, oppression, and subjection of Kurds, Kurdish cultural practices and social rituals, such as wedding ceremonies and ethnonational celebrations, as well as the rights to speak Kurdish in public and to teach the Kurdish language, are severely suppressed by the hegemonic state. National ideologies recognized the Turkish language as a marker of homogeneous Turkish culture and the Kurdish language as a marker of the past. The historical names of the Kurdish cities and landmark places were changed to Turkish names in accordance with state policies.[8] The modernizing state projects of the 1930s, deliberately aligning the new state with the West, introduced surnaming practices that through de facto regulations limited the rights of Kurds to choose Kurdish patrinames for themselves.[9] After the 1980s, giving even a Kurdish first

---

[7] In 1935 *Güneş Dil Teorisi* (Sun language theory) and *Milli Tarih Tezi* (National history thesis) were launched by Mustafa Kemal. Academics of the new state devoted their time to claiming that the history of humanity was Turkish history. See Volkan and Itzkowitz (1984, 297–300).

[8] İmset notes that over twenty thousand Kurdish names of the Kurdish provinces, cities, villages, hamlets, mountains, and rivers were changed to Turkish (1996, 49).

[9] See clauses 3, 5, 7, 8, 29, and 33 in Soyadi Kanunu Nizamnamesi, no. 24/12/1934–2/1759 (Regulations of the Last Name Law): http://www.mevzuat.adalet.gov.tr/html/5057.html.

name to a newborn was not permitted by the state, and Kurdish names were changed by court orders.[10]

The creation of master narratives of homogeneous totality, such as Turkishness, Turkish history, and Turkish language, simultaneously gave birth to counterhegemonic Kurdish struggles, signifiers, and narratives.[11] For Kurds, Kurdish languages as institutions became sites for marking Kurdish culture and symbolically representing Kurdistan, the Kurdish homeland. The minority Kurdish nationalism that resulted from modernization, standardization, and state regulations developed as a counterresistance to the impositions of the state. The imposed notion of a Turkish national identity and the prescription of a Turkish self are contested by many Kurds who recognize their own version of history and imagine their own ethnonational identities and communities. Homogenizing the history of the region resulted in Kurdish resistance to the imposed definition and boundaries of space and time and enabled Kurds to nourish their own identities.

In excavating the etymology of the term *diaspora* (Tötölyan 1996) and the history of various diasporas, the corpus of diaspora studies has questioned the notion of ideal or pure diaspora (Safran 1991); problematized the economic and political bases of diasporas; and linked counterhistories and resistance surrounding exile, refugee, and forced migrant communities (Gupta and Ferguson 1999; Ong 1999; Burawoy et al. 2000). Recognizing contemporary diasporas as political constructs shaped by people who were uprooted by (generally violent) forms of coercion, scholars have engaged in fruitful dialogues that have produced studies that differentiate people's claims of multiply positioned diasporic identities; their subjecthood; their collective histories, roots and routes; and their community-building efforts.[12] Many of these works emphasize that the initial formation and definition of contemporary diasporas—unlike the experiences of transnationality—embody the experiences of terror and loss.

---

[10] The U.S. Helsinki Watch Committee confirms and reports that the District Court of Ağri declared that "the first names of Ali Ekrem Kutley's children do not correspond to the record regulations as stated in Article 77. . . . The names Brusk and Bineos are contradictory to good morals, damage the national culture and tradition, and affect the interests of the Turkish Republic. Therefore . . . the names should be amended. . . . The children of the accused . . . will be called Mehmet and Emine. . . . Appeals will not be allowed" (quoted in Gunter 1990, 6).

[11] Brackette Williams (1990) notes that the creation of homogenizing national metanarratives simultaneously highlights the existing distinctions among culturally and ethnically different groups.

[12] Roots and routes is a conceptual tool developed by Paul Gilroy in exploring the meaning of place (1991, 1993).

Systematic crossing of sovereign state borders does not necessarily result in the establishment of diasporas, diaspora cultures, diasporic experiences, or diasporic identities. Khachig Tötölyan, a long-standing editor of *Diaspora*, discussing the elements that constitute diasporas, strategically begins not with the borders of the nation-state but with the boundaries of the homeland: "The paradigmatic diaspora forms due to coercion that leads to the uprooting and resettlement outside the boundaries of homeland of large numbers of people, often entire communities" (1996, 12). For the exiled Kurds who were forced out of their ancestral land, there is a homeland. In their narratives they continually articulate their experiences of displacement and the resulting resettlement outside the conceptual boundaries of their Mother Soil.

Diaspora discourses in Esenyurt highlight roots and routes to create alternative public spheres, collective community consciousness, group solidarity, traditional values, and political mobility among the deterritorialized Kurds to "maintain identifications outside the national time/space in order to live inside, with a difference" (Clifford 1994, 308). Kurds who experienced a violent displacement from their Mother Soil, history, and culture are also forced in diaspora to experience certain practices with implicit and explicit signs that presuppose Turkish homogeneity. In internal diaspora, they experience living in two separate spaces simultaneously; because they are spatially away from their homeland, they bring their old place to the new one. The practices of the diasporic Kurdish community in Esenyurt encapsulate not only the repressive policies of the Turkish nation-state and the community's marginality in Esenyurt but also the chain of Kurdish uprisings during 1923–38 and the PKK resistance of 1984–99.

Kurdish roots and uprooted Kurds in diaspora

The use of the concept of diaspora as a signifier of Kurdish spatial, social, economic, and political deterritorialization and resettlement enables us to critically analyze the underlying reality of uprooted Kurds in articulating and reconstructing their ancestors' now-silenced history of resistance and the ways in which Kurds today challenge the political discourses of the Turkish nation-state. The concept also allows us to understand that the Kurdish political and cultural resistance and struggles, both prior to and after their deterritorialization, are historical experiences that enable this specific group of exiled Kurdish women to explore numerous possibilities in coping with their violent displacement.[13]

In spite of hegemonic processes, continued othering, and economic impositions, the exiled Kurds of this study create links to establish their own localities and communities in Esenyurt. Together with their kin and with other Kurds who share similar experiences, they construct highly heterogenous hybrid communities by combining urban and intercultural elements while persistently highlighting the importance of Kurdish traditions among richly painted sociopolitical, religious, and linguistic differences within the Kurdish population.

The following narrative of an exiled Kurdish woman delineates her new life in Esenyurt, while a collective Kurdish identity marks her attachment to her homeland:

> I don't think we can go back yet. Later. Maybe much later. Our children's blood has not dried yet. . . . Maybe much later . . . when all our children have matured and married. We need security, much more than the signal to go back. The military told our men to be paramilitary. The PKK told us don't be paramilitary. Our men refused the job. We also wanted them to refuse it. They forced us out. We were forced to leave. We lost everything to ashes. Now, we have to wait. A return is very difficult at the present. We are not safe. Did we come here by our own free will? Now, we have built homes here. Our families are here. We have made new friends. Yet, we always think of going back to Kurdistan. Our roots are in Kurdistan. We will go back. We will all go back. The Mother Soil calls us. I don't know when, but I know we will. I am now looking for brides for my sons, not from the city but from our villages, so that I can take our sons and brides back to our land.[14]

A Kurdish sense of diasporic identity makes a strong contribution to the exiles' place-making and community-building activities. Their awareness of demarcated cultural differences and their historical experiences contribute to their survival in Esenyurt, away from their homeland. Kurds' claims of minority nationhood and identity and their persistent preser-

---

[13] See also Anna Secor's (2004) examination of the productions, contestations, and claims of national citizenship, urban citizenship, and cultural citizenship of other women migrants from the Kurdish Region.

[14] All interviews quoted in this article were conducted in Esenyurt and its vicinity between February and September 1999.

vation and reconstruction of Kurdish traditions in the internal diaspora enable them to solidify the relationship with the homeland and with other Kurdish communities in exile. In the meantime, their memories and the lived and retold experiences of state violence cultivate their commitment to Kurdistan, and thus many Kurds consider the return to their ancestral land to be inevitable.

While experiencing continual oppression in Esenyurt, most Kurds in exile speak with an empowered voice about officially distorted constructions, interpretations, and representations of their identities, their history, and their historical homeland. They recognize Kurdistan as a lived space; in doing so, they continually narrate the materiality of Kurdish spatial realities, their historically specific daily activities, struggles, and resistance. This active recognition of their homeland contributes to their understanding of their condition as diasporic. For them Kurdistan is not primordial, permanently fixed; neither is it a passive reflection of their actions. The conception of their homeland as actively defined by their experiences enables uprooted Kurds to participate in the political processes of the homeland. The tradition of linking through kin relations mobilizes blood ties and allows uprooted Kurds to legitimate their rights to their ancestral land.

For exiled Kurds, maintaining their identities rests on the tensions and contradictions that rise from the continual anxiety of violence and loss and from the temporality of setting up living spaces in diaspora here and now while imagining a future in Kurdistan. However, the memory of the homeland, awareness of being both here and not there, and the longing for Mother Soil serve as positive tools of empowerment for crafting exiled Kurdish identities and for empowering the Kurdish community in Esenyurt. This tension of being in both places, home and away from home, enables members of this community to claim and maintain the identity of a minority nation in exile. Home is a conceptual place to which they track back and forth in time and space. Home is a place they were forced to leave and a place to return to. Home is not just one place. Bell hooks reminds us how home is conceived by people struggling and resisting in margins: "One confronts and accepts dispersal and fragmentation as part of the construction of a new world order that reveals more fully where we are, who we can become, an order that does not demand forgetting" (1990, 148).

The violent experiences of diasporic Kurds mark their everyday lives and open up spaces for a new politics of identity that enables them to claim their rights. Their conception of ethnic differences is territorially, historically, and culturally located and counterpoises their understanding of distant and past homes and their present experiences as exiles in an internal diaspora.[15] However, in 2006, seven years after the capture and imprisonment of the PKK's leader, Abdullah Öcalan, which ended the two decades of low-intensity war against so-called Kurdish terrorists, many of the forced-migrant Kurds do not yet feel safe going back to their Mother Soil.[16] The certainty of peace is still questionable in the Kurdish region. This condition does not enforce their attachment to Esenyurt but rather strengthens their commitment to return to their homeland.[17]

Symbolics of blood: Hegemonic discourses, dominance, and the resistance of exiled women

Collective representations of identity in diaspora articulate political voices of oppressed groups and produce a dynamic political mechanism for people to recreate their identities within changing sociopolitical and economic orders. In the case of the exiled Kurds living in Esenyurt, representation and production of Kurdish identities are ingrained in narrative productions of history. The past is reconstructed from individuals' memories of the events. These memories are collectively recognized as empirical claims and are told and retold until they become accepted as the history of the collective subjects. As exiled Kurdish narrators are themselves individual actors of history, their narratives, told facts, and events belong to history. These historical narratives are socially produced discourses, deliberate acts to decide what belongs to the past and to produce knowledge. An analysis of the narrative production of history in an internal diaspora in Esenyurt not only highlights various imposed silences of hopelessness, defeat, and indifference but also brings to the fore the authority of the speakers to narrate a history that has been silenced and thereby to resist a silent history.

In this narrative production, the self-awareness of Kurds as a community in diaspora shows a shift in gender discourses in which Kurdish women rearticulate their identities and redefine the political vision of Kurds within the continually changing details of everyday life. The narratives quoted in this article reflect the speakers' vision in terms of gender differences. These differences, while evoking a Kurdish collective past, also construct

[15] For an elaboration of a diasporic conceptualization of cultural identity in relation to home and far-away places, see, e.g., Hall (1991).

[16] See Aker et al. (2005) for a detailed analysis of the issues that hinder the return of forced migrant Kurds to their homeland.

[17] See, e.g., Tötölyan's similar exploration of the diaspora community's commitment to their homeland (1996, 16–19).

other versions of the events and compose the boundaries between the Kurdish self and other in Turkey. Within these gender discourses, the recollections of exiled Kurdish women about their struggles and resistance experiences leading to their traumatic deterritorialization from their Mother Soil highlight their feelings of loss, horror, and sadness and their desires to return to and reterritorialize their homeland. Often exiled Kurdish women in Esenyurt produce their histories by decentering the patriarchal state's power of writing history and silencing and by simultaneously resisting the silences of Kurdish patriarchy. An analysis of silence and of voices that resist silence allows us to theorize variances in the cultural production of power, hegemony, and identities.[18]

For the exiled Kurds, narrating to preserve Kurdistan in their memories makes imagining their homeland real and makes Kurdish history and culture accessible for the present and the future. For many of the exiled Kurds in Esenyurt, the combination of their experiences in Kurdistan and in exile deepens their commitment to their homeland and simultaneously encourages symbolic politics and political discussions. The active engagement in remembering and recounting tales of their Mother Soil becomes a politically constructive collective process, one that has a genealogical domain emphasizing important blood relations.

Here not only is the discourse of blood linked to territory but also the symbolics of shared blood link individuals and define the rules and norms establishing alliances among Kurdish individuals in diaspora. In the following discussion, women expressed concerns over a lack of running water they had experienced for several days. The women compared the sources of water, the quality of the water, the hardship in fetching water, and the usage of water in Kurdistan and Esenyurt. As in many other cases, this conversation is crystallized in the conditions of guerrilla women.[19] One of the married women thus narrated what happened a decade ago, when she was a young bride; she clearly wanted to register the centrality of the

---

[18] This consideration would be most appropriate with reference to Michel-Rolph Trouillot, who interrogates how histories are made and told. In his reconstructive work, he marks specific kinds of silences that "are silences of resistance, silences thrown against superior silence" (1995, 69).

[19] Exiled Kurds in Esenyurt generally do not use the term *guerrilla*. They refer to the guerrillas as children or youth in the mountains or use the Kurdish term *Peşmerge*, meaning freedom fighters. They are very careful not to mention any identifiable characteristic of any guerrilla they may directly or indirectly know. They use the Turkish term *Korucu* when speaking about paramilitary units or individuals within these units. In the vicinity, there was a retired paramilitary, but as he was regarded as a state agent, and the exile Kurds kept their distance from him.

Kurdish struggle as belonging to all Kurds: "The young women in the mountains were tired, hungry, and dirty. The blood dried on their legs and their hair was full of lice. They had little time to stay. All they wanted from us was some bread to eat, to wash themselves, leaving before the sunrise. We can't send our children back without feeding them. We can't send them back without bathing and without clean underclothes. To host them we always had to be ready." The passage is illustrative of the production of the speaker's overlapping concerns, that is, while she recalls the conditions of the guerrillas to mark the facts, her account also highlights how the symbolics of blood constitute Kurdish belonging. The speaker's usage of the terms *our children*, *us*, and *we* are not simple metaphoric devices. These terms authenticate the ancestral ties, the symbolics of blood as the source of belonging, identity, and inclusion.[20] While this narrative segment highlights my informants' concerns over the debilitated physical state of female guerrillas, it also recenters the importance of blood ties as inextricably linked to Kurdish identity and belonging.

Exiled Kurds' memories of deterritorialization and of creating new Kurdish communities in exile are often embodied in nostalgia for the pastoral beauties of Kurdistan. Kurdistan is depicted as a landscape with snowcapped mountain zeniths in all seasons. Their homeland is in nature with clean air. Their villages are remembered with sown fertile fields, as seen on television programs broadcast from Europe by the Kurdish channel MED/MEDYA-TV. The imagery of the beauty of Kurdistan and the fertile land with clean air is often remembered by exiled men. In Esenyurt, most exiled Kurdish families gather in front of their televisions to watch the Kurdish channel in the evenings. Broadcast images often produce spontaneous memories. While watching such a broadcast, one exiled Kurdish man recalled, "Kesire's marriage was right after the harvest. Fields were as golden as her hair and as tall as she is.[21] Allah's blessings. I only saw such beauty in Kurdistan." Others contribute to remaking Kurdistan from their memories by adding details. Often their nostalgia for Kurdistan and their wish to preserve rural images of the past play a critical role in making Kurdistan a "knowable community" for younger generations (Williams 1973, 165–81).

---

[20] The concept is developed by Michel Foucault and helps us to see how "the blood relation long remained an important element in the mechanisms of power, its manifestation, and its ritual" (1990, 147). The concept is compelling for some scholars precisely because it provides the possibility of analyzing the narratives of diasporic/transnational people through the symbolics of legitimacy and belonging. See, e.g., Clarke 2004.

[21] To protect informants' privacy, all names used in this article are pseudonyms.

In many of the Kurdish narratives, the imagining of Kurdistan coexists with nature. The above statement shows that nature is Kurdistan, the Kurdish people's existence, their daily activities, traditions, rituals, feelings, and sentiments such as the golden color of the harvest that resembles the blond hair of the farmer's daughter. Kurdish peasants' labor, that is, their agricultural and artisanal activities, are also remembered as rejuvenating the Kurdish social existence, enabling Kurdish families to joyously marry their children according to their traditions. In short, nature attaches a powerful meaning to the ways in which it shapes the Kurds' economic activities, culture, and politics, while the symbolic reworking of the meaning of nature is simultaneously shaped by these processes. Nevertheless, the symbolic association often developed by Kurdish men among harvest, women, and marriage is a gendered metaphor: the sexual imagery of Kurdistan, the harvest, the Kurdish landscape, and marriage allows exiled men to highlight the importance of their labor in Kurdish economic and social life.[22]

The symbolic creation of Kurdistan in Esenyurt is constructed by men to highlight the power of familial patriarchy, the power that men once had: a man who owned a piece of land controlled nature and thus had the power of artfully maneuvering Kurdish socioeconomic life and traditions to arrange marriages between young women and men. This patriarchally centered imagery reconstructs the tension between the past and the present and is reflective of life, nature, and reproduction. Distinctively, the patriarchal imagination of Kurdistan is not separate from the Kurdish men's material reality: it highlights the alienation and deterritorialization of men from the land and from their labor in exile. It highlights the fear of losing one's identity as equivalent to losing the land. Kurdish peasant men in exile, aging and with neither the tools of power nor the necessary skills to hold jobs in cities, do recognize their unproductivity. As they yearn for the past, a time when they had the power to control social and economic processes, they recollect Kurdistan as inseparable from their production. This symbolic construction of Kurdistan is inclusive of a specific kind of silence: it is silent about the inability of Kurdish patriarchs to provide for their families, being dependent on the wages their older sons earn in temporary unskilled jobs and the wages their younger sons earn in the sweatshops.

When imagery of Kurdistan is shaped by exiled women in Esenyurt, it

---

[22] It is not a coincidence that the marriage of the farmer's daughter took place after the harvest. Most Kurdish wedding ceremonies take place after the harvest for economic convenience.

highlights a strong resistance to patriarchal constructions. Exiled Kurdish women in Esenyurt contest the patriarchal memory of Kurdistan with historical awareness and produce a counterhegemonic memory in representing the past. Most exiled women's battles over Kurdistan are mediated through their actual memories of violence, death, and blood.[23] Their narratives not only highlight the deliberate destruction of Kurdistan by outsiders, but, more importantly, they reveal how exiled Kurdish women tactically and explicitly situate themselves in the center of political issues in the Esenyurt diaspora as mothers of youth who were killed or were to be killed. Their narratives embody a deeply grounded pain of loss and death. They refuse to disassociate this pain from Kurdistan. This tension informs their oppositional consciousness and, as a result, remembering their Mother Soil is an active oppositional practice: for them the vivid and colorful imageries of Kurdistan are inextricably tainted with the remembering of terror, of the destruction of nature, their homes, their lives, and their loved ones. Their lived experiences in Kurdistan as a whole, in extenso and not in part, are an inalienable substance of their feelings, a part of their commitment to, and the politics of, their Mother Soil. The symbolics of land, nature, and labor are conceived by women as not necessarily constructive for political resistance. For them, blood is more important because it is embedded in their lived experiences.

The politics of place as elaborated by David Harvey allows us to recognize exiled Kurdish women's collective exercise and will in claiming Kurdistan through blood. Harvey points out that "there is, then, a politics to place construction ranging dialectically across material, representational, and symbolic activities which find their hallmark in the way in which individuals invest in places and thereby empower themselves collectively by virtue of that investment. The investment can be blood, sweat, tears and labor" (1996, 323). Kurdish women internalize the symbolics of blood to meaningfully construct a politics of place, Kurdistan as an oppositional response to various forms of domination, and they do so by speaking of the blood of their children who were killed or lost during the low-intensity war. As one exiled mother comments, "The children arrived during the snowstorm. They were fatigued, hungry, and cold. We all opened our doors to them. They were our children. They are our blood."

The historical narratives of women, produced in a variety of contexts, do not share narrative expressions of the men in the Esenyurt diaspora.

---

[23] See, e.g., Lisa Yoneyama's (1994) elaboration of memory and production of contested processes of historical representations. See also Lisa Rofel's argument about memory practice (1999, 128–57).

During family gatherings, where men often talk, Kurdish women, grandmothers, mothers, young daughters, and brides seem to be silently preoccupied with their knitting and lace making. The structure of feeling that allows elder women, grandmothers, and great aunts to have a meaningful relationship with Kurdistan, with their past and memory, is almost silent, a silence that is produced as a response to the conditions of diaspora in Esenyurt.[24] Elderly women, when they were young adults and young married women, experienced the 1923–38 uprisings in Northern Kurdistan. They knew this history as it happened. They experienced the pains of death and rejoiced at the renewal of life. In the end, in diaspora, they have formed a living existence with death and blood. They do not need to be told about the death and suffering. Here, the paternal grandmother of Kesire, whom I addressed as Nene, was resting on a daybed.[25] Hoping that she might express her opinion about the symbolic construction of Kurdistan, I asked for her view. She responded with indifference:

Cihan Ahmetbeyzade (CA): Nene! What do you say for all these talks?
Nene: Nothing!
CA: Do you mean that you agree with both women and men?
Nene: It no longer matters what I think. My time has already passed. I am in "foreign hands." I can't die in my soil.

In diaspora most of the elderly women no longer resist death. Their feelings are in flux because the experience of diaspora produces disorder, fear, and anxiety in their lives.[26] For them time has already stopped, for they can no longer experience Kurdistan. And yet the thought of returning to the land where their ancestors are buried is very important.[27] However, exiled Kurds in Esenyurt do not have the means of such transportation and/or they find such an attempt dangerous. Most elderly women, recognizing their own annihilation in internal diaspora, often prefer to be silent.

In Esenyurt, exiled Kurdish women who have young sons and daughters seem to resist actively the penetrating images of beauty and happy memories of Kurdistan as if they, only they, recognize the danger of yearn-

---

[24] Raymond Williams examines the concept of structure of feeling in relation to space, time, and memory in various works (see, e.g., Williams 1961, 48–71; 1973, 128–41).

[25] *Nene* is a term used for great-grandmothers. It is recognized as a respectful term for referring to a very old woman.

[26] See Doreen Massey on the construction of place and production of fear under certain conditions (1994, 167–72).

[27] This point is highlighted in other cases. See, e.g., Malkki 1999, 56.

ing for tranquil images of Kurdistan. Their feelings as mothers are entangled with the history of death and vitality. Yet they seize hold of the memory of death. Their experiences of state violence, loss, blood, deterritorialization, and the economic difficulties they face in exile without means of subsistence and with their men lacking the suitable skills to make a living are the multiple forces of Kurdish memory in the Esenyurt diaspora. In family gatherings, watching television while the men exchange views, the exiled Kurdish women generally listen quietly. When they speak, they speak as if they are contemplating. They do not need to raise their heads from their work, and they speak very softly. While their voices are tranquil, their words rupture the peaceful imagery that the exiled Kurdish men evoke and invite the listeners to consider the realities of the Kurdish diasporic women. Listening to the bucolic images of Kurdistan being described by the men, Kesire's aunt suddenly began to speak of her missing son: "He was a responsible boy. He helped his father finish the harvest before leaving [i.e., joining the PKK]. He was a good boy. He respected the elders and cared for his juniors. He worked hard. He was my flesh and blood. I knew he was going to leave, leave like the others. Seven years have passed. I am not blaming you. I had given my consent. Kesire was young and she also needed a home. No one wanted to wait. I am waiting. They'll let us know.[28] I am his mother. I can wait." She sighed, and after a brief pause she spoke again: "Where is he? Where are our children? There is only blood. There is blood on the hands of the state. I am not the only one. Other Kurdish mothers are also asking about their children.[29] They are questioning the TC.[30] They have rights. You saw it on the television. And for that, they were beaten? We all know why they left and why our children fight. We all know why we are here. We all know that we will go back to Kurdistan."

Most diasporic Kurdish women, in family and in close-circle gatherings, produce discourses that not only reiterate their power to speak but also empower them to resist their subjugation by the family and the state patriarchy. The consciousness of power here directly arises from their prior

[28] On various occasions my informants told me that the PKK always informed the families upon the death of their family members.

[29] Here she refers to the mothers of missing people who conduct a peaceful sitting demonstration every Saturday in İstanbul under a heavy police cordon backed by machine guns and tanks. More often than not, Kurdish and Turkish mothers and supporting peace activists are raided by the police, beaten, and arrested.

[30] As do other politically conscious Kurds living in the metropolis, the exiled Kurds in Esenyurt refuse to pronounce the name of the political construct Turkish Republic and instead use TC in an act of diminution.

activities and echoes their experiences. Karl Marx advocates that we explore historical processes and recognize that the subjects of history are the product of history; yet they themselves produce history. Kurdish women, too, as subjects of history, produce their own history written "in letters of blood and fire" (Marx [1867] 1987, 669).

Kesire's aunt's intervention articulates the daily realities of exiled women whose children, both male and female, were killed and disappeared during the so-called low-intensity war. My encounters with other Kurdish women revealed that Kesire's aunt's experience and narrative, as personal narrative, does not represent a single event and is not isolated from the experiences of other exiled Kurdish women. Kesire's aunt, resisting the male imageries of Kurdistan, strategically uses motherhood and nurturing as experiences to weave and unify the lost home and blood. Motherhood as a lived experience is uniquely encountered for the exiled Kurdish women in Esenyurt.[31] Motherhood is, in most societies, a socially and economically constructed concept; mothers of most social and economic classes are concerned about the well-being of their children, their children's access and/or lack of access to resources, education, health, and employment possibilities. But, for exiled Kurdish women, there are differing dimensions of motherhood: their lived experiences of motherhood, of annihilation of their children, bring very different experiences from those of most mothers in Turkey. This defining characteristic of motherhood is germane to their experiences of war and the sufferings of their children; it solidifies their commitment to break up various forms of oppression.[32]

This Kurdish mother's narrative, while resisting the male construction of Kurdistan as a spatial image of tranquility, also addresses different issues of gender. In capturing the attention of her audience with minimal gestures and a withdrawn voice, this woman interacts with Kurdish patriarchy; she points out the patriarchal subversion of facts and demands to return to the harsh Kurdish reality. She reminds the Kurdish familial patriarchy that there is a powerful contradiction between the male images of a tranquil rural past and the continuing violence in Kurdistan. She exposes another version of Kurdistan, a gendered version that is oppressed by the violence of power and empowered by notions of motherhood. As an uprooted Kurdish woman speaking in diaspora, she produces oppositional

---

[31] Feminists were quick to point out that motherhood is a lived personal experience. See Rich 1976; Trinh 1991.

[32] See Marjorie DeVault's examination of hegemonic patriarchal discourses that silence women and of the voices of women who challenge patriarchal discourses (1999, 175–91). See also Audre Lorde's (1993) elaboration of the transformation of silence.

images of Kurdistan as painted with blood and physical violence. The bodies of Kurdish youth, flesh and blood, torn apart by the war waged against the Kurds in Turkey, become significant for exiled Kurdish mothers in Esenyurt who are waging a counterhegemonic resistance to state violence. The spatialization of patriarchal state power is elucidated by this diasporic woman who, while resisting familial and state patriarchy, calls for collective and political mobilization of Kurds for their right to live in Kurdistan.[33]

Kurdish men in general have difficulty in speaking about their sorrow and their loss. The events that led to their violent dispersal from their homeland are in general described excluding their personal feelings. Their feelings about their deterritorialization seem to be entangled with their frustration in diaspora. Any question aimed toward understanding how Kurdish men deal with their present conditions at a personal level would only be insulting because the question would be considered as a denunciation of their suffering. Their sorrow is cocooned within their silence. During chats among women, Kurdish women explain that their husbands do not speak with them of their personal feelings about violence and loss in Kurdistan. In diaspora, even while directly criticizing their husbands, women are tactically respectful of the men's silence on this issue. Generally, in the privacy of the family, patriarchal silence is treated with silence.[34]

In the Esenyurt diaspora, silence—including self-imposed silence—is imposed by different forms of power for a variety of reasons. However, diasporic women have developed an ear for hearing what is said and not said. They recognize silence as if it were spoken. As a result, they produce an insurgent voice against the impositions of silence. In the above narrative, the Kurdish mother breaks the silence of the men through her own micropolitical practices.[35] She criticizes and disavows the silence of the

---

[33] See, e.g., Chandra Talpade Mohanty (1987) and Caren Kaplan (1987) on empowerment of displaced women and on spatial identity. Also see bell hooks's (1984) conceptualization of marginality and Gloria Anzaldúa's articulation of "borderland worlds of ethnic communities" (1990, xxvi). Trinh T. Minh-ha (1991) also echoes this sense of empowerment as she challenges the key aspects of identity formation.

[34] Such outcomes are well expressed in Foucault's comments on the imposition of silence: "Silence itself—the things one declines to say, or is forbidden to name, the discretion that is required between different speakers—is less the absolute limit of discourse, the other side from which it is separated by a strict boundary, than an element that functions alongside the things said, with them and in relation to them within over-all strategies" (1990, 27).

[35] See, e.g., Teresa de Lauretis's consideration of the dialectical relationship between the social representation and the subjective construction of gender leading to micropolitical practices at the subjective level (1987, 9–10).

Kurdish patriarchy. There is always an immediate pause after Kurdish women invite everyone not to lose sight of the realities of Kurdistan and to remember the blood that was and is shed by the state in Kurdistan. In these silent moments, my research findings suggest, men do try to reconcile their peaceful representation of Kurdistan with their experiences of the state's oppression, violence, human rights abuses, loss, and their own silenced sorrows.

In response to the men's deflections from their sorrow and pain, Kesire's aunt positions herself as sharing a similar pain with other women, a positioning that is itself a product of history. Her internalization of the death of Kurdish children as a mother allows her to perceive herself as not alone. She has partners in her resistance. Her announcement "I am not the only one" is a step forward to forge a collective identity with others. The presentation of her subjectivity in a diasporic location, here but not in Kurdistan, coalesces other collective identities and expands the boundaries of Kurdish collectivity. Initially, she claims an identity and a group solidarity with people in her patriarchal family and kin, and then she envisions a larger collectivity of Kurds whose children took up arms for the rights of Kurds living in Turkey by asking "Where are our children?" What is also visible in her narrative is that her own self-definition produces an overlapping positionality with other Kurdish women who may be dissimilar in their religious beliefs, spoken languages, and socio-economic locations but who are, nevertheless, mothers concerned with the lives of their children. Her recognition of a possible coalition with other diasporically heterogeneous Kurdish women who share similar experiences enables her to speak as a powerful agent.

The remembering and reviving of the violent past, speaking of blood and forming coalitions with other women, offer Kesire's aunt a communicative tool to create and recreate a collective memory, empowering her to emphasize her differentiated gendered experiences and feelings. The collective group solidarity with other mothers who lost their children as a result of the oppressive policies of the state and the war are constructed not only as her testimonial but also from the television coverage of the Saturday meetings of the Mothers of the Lost, a peaceful public demonstration held every week in İstanbul from May 1995 until March 1999.[36] A hegemonic parody was in play at every Saturday gathering. During the gatherings, the police force was always on duty to control, repress, and

---

[36] The meetings ended because the Mothers of the Lost were raided, beaten, and arrested by police during the last thirty meetings. For more on the Saturday Mothers, see Baydar and İvegen (2006).

practice surveillance. The state-run imitative parody aimed to disrupt the meaning of the silent resistance of women and to show that their claim of missing people was only an illusion. An official minibus, with hotline numbers to report missing people written on both sides, passed every Saturday between solemnly sitting mothers and bystanders. While the silent sittings create a specifically counterhegemonic space, offering a co-alition for a silent voice for both Kurdish and Turkish mothers who lost children who resisted state oppression, Kesire's aunt's reference is strictly concerned with Kurdish mothers who are often sitting in the front row with their traditional Kurdish *pushis* (headdresses). Kesire's aunt's coalition with the Mothers of the Lost is unusual: starting from the excluded cat-egories of women, forced-migrant exiled Kurds, and politically, econom-ically, linguistically, culturally oppressed women in the margins, she moves to form coalitions, to claim solidarity with other Kurdish women, and to return to the issue of silence and silencing.[37] Particularly important here is her marking of different kinds of silences as strategies against oppression. Kurds whose children were killed are forced by the state to be silent. At the same time, Kurdish mothers of the lost respond to the state's silencing with silent sittings.

Kesire's aunt mentions the silent sittings of the Saturday Mothers to criticize the silence of familial patriarchy and the silencing impositions of the state. She is in coalition with other Kurdish mothers because she shares blood with them: the blood of the dead youth. As she identifies herself with a larger community of politically active Kurdish women and with their claims, she demands respectful attention to death and blood. In this context, death and blood are permanently political and are significant in her production of bleeding Kurdistan, Kurdish history, and Kurdish women's present struggles with life in internal diaspora.

The structure of feeling that causes her to recognize the significance of space, being here but not there, also enables her to shape her identity as a deterritorialized Kurdish woman whose right to live in her homeland and to speak is denied by the state that, according to her testimony, already has Kurdish blood on its hands. In Esenyurt, most deterritorialized women's experiences with death give meaning to Kurdish existence in diaspora. Kesire's aunt shares a knowledge with others: "We all know why they left and why our children fight. We all know why we are here." Her explicit claim of epistemic privilege constitutes exiled Kurds as a political collectivity with a differentiated historical experience and voice, a collec-

[37] While working from the margins, feminist critics also highlighted the tension in choos-ing marginality as a strategic space of resistance (Fuss 1991; Trinh 1991).

tivity that has been excluded from majority discourses through various government practices. Through this privilege, she legitimizes the silenced voices and struggles of other Kurds. Although her narrative is directed to the Kurdish patriarchy, her insistence on exploring and exposing the vulnerability of other Kurdish mothers with loss, death, and sorrow allows her to interrogate the state. Positioning herself within multiple subjectivities and balancing her multiple identities, she exposes the state as an agent of destruction: she blames the sovereign power that claims "the right to decide life and death" (Foucault 1990, 135). She concludes: "There is only blood." She holds the state responsible not only for the death of Kurdish youth but also for using gendered techniques of biopower to manipulate, silence, and terrorize women. Her diasporic heterogeneity with her multiple identities as a nontribal Kırmançi speaker, a Shafi'i Muslim, and a Kurdish mother and her plural subjectivities as a wife, a deterritorialized woman, and a minority citizen of Turkey enable and allow her to powerfully claim Kurdistan as Kurdish ancestral land. That is, by "reconfirming a unified subjectivity or 'shared consciousness' through gender" (Alarcón 1990, 364) and through symbolics of the blood of the dead youth, she, as a diasporic Kurd, as a woman, and as a mother legitimizes her right to claim the Mother Soil.

Rethinking diaspora

In September 2002, the Turkish Parliament adopted a reform package as part of its efforts to gain admittance to the European Union. The most disputed amendments of the package abolished the death penalty and proclaimed the rights of Kurds to teach and to learn Kurdish in Turkey. Thus, the Turkish state de facto recognized the heterogeneity of the nation-state, including the existence of the Kurds, their history, cultures, traditions, and the Kurdish languages that marked differences within the state's sovereign borders. And yet this is another uncertain time for Kurds: the legislative performance of the Turkish state in executing the new laws is yet to be finalized. How can the implementation of the laws guaranteeing the rights of the minority Kurdish citizens be actualized after the Kurdish Parties, Halkin Demokrasi Partisi (People's Democracy Party) and Demokratik Halk Partisi (Democratic People's Party), have been closed down? Or are Kurds experiencing a double-voiced word giving two different messages to two different audiences, one to the leaders and citizens of the European Union and one to the citizens of Turkey?

In this article I have explored the forces of history and the historical memory of Kurdish women in relation to their violent deterritorialization and resettlement in Esenyurt in an attempt to further develop a theory of internal diasporas relevant to contemporary Turkey. By examining the narratives of exiled Kurdish women, as well as some of the silences of hopelessness, fear, and resistance, I have focused on the underlying horror resulting from the experiences of the destruction of their homesteads and villages, repression, murders, and their forced migration to show how Kurdish women in internal diaspora in Esenyurt link their past and present. The collective resistance practiced by deterritorialized Kurdish women within the borders of the nation-state forces us to reconsider the creation of diasporas and the differing ways in which diasporas are produced. As I look at the Kurdish communities in internal diaspora, at their specific histories, political oppositions, place-making efforts, reorganization of traditions, and networks, I have come to understand the importance of the notions of homeland and return to homeland in the creation of diasporas. As indices of resistance, violence, loss, death, deterritorialization, and the shared meaning of the construction and representation of their homeland are intertwined with the cultural and political imagining of diaspora communities. In Esenyurt, Kurdish resistance and gendered struggles in the construction and representation of the Mother Soil continue unabated, with the goal of connecting the Kurds' disrupted past and temporality in diaspora to a definite future in which they return to the Mother Soil. The gender-based expressions of internal diaspora and Kurdish women's individual and collective contestations of, and resistance to, the state and familial patriarchal domination create "alternative, resistant spaces occupied by oppositional histories and memories" (Mohanty 1987, 41) and become a tool for empowerment to reproduce Kurdish identities, to invent strategies, and to establish Kurdish communities with articulated Kurdish differences in their struggles in diaspora.

New Jersey

References

Aker, A. Tamer, Betül Çelik, Dilek Kurban, Tugay Ünalan, and Deniz Yükseker. 2005. "The Problem of Internal Displacement in Turkey: Assessment and Policy Proposals." Turkish Economic and Social Studies Foundation (TESEV). http://www.tesev.org.tr/eng/events/TESEV_IDP_Report.pdf.

Alarcón, Norma. 1990. "The Theoretical Subject(s) of *This Bridge Called My Back* and Anglo-American Feminism." In Anzaldúa 1990, 356–69.

Anzaldúa, Gloria, ed. 1990. *Making Face, Making Soul: Haciendo Caras; Creative and Critical Perspectives by Feminists of Color*. San Francisco: Aunt Lute.

Baydar, Gülsüm, and Berfin İvegen. 2006. "Territories, Identities, and Thresholds:

The Saturday Mothers Phenomenon in İstanbul." *Signs: Journal of Women in Culture and Society* 31(3):689–716.

Burawoy, Michael, Joseph A. Blum, Sheba George, Zsuzsa Gille, Teresa Gowan, Lynne Haney, Maren Klawiter, Steven H. Lopez, Seán Ó Riain, and Millie Thayer. 2000. *Global Ethnography: Forces, Connections, and Imagination in a Postmodern World*. Berkeley: University of California Press.

Clarke, Kamari M. 2004. *Mapping Yorùbá Networks: Power and Agency in the Making of Transnational Communities*. Durham, NC: Duke University Press.

Clifford, James. 1994. "Diasporas." *Cultural Anthropology* 9(3):303–38.

de Lauretis, Teresa. 1987. *Technologies of Gender: Essays on Theory, Film, and Fiction*. Bloomington: Indiana University Press.

DeVault, Majorie L. 1999. *Liberating Method: Feminism and Social Research*. Philadelphia: Temple University Press.

Foucault, Michel. 1990. *The History of Sexuality: An Introduction*. Trans. Robert Hurley. New York: Random House.

Fuss, Diana, ed. 1991. *Inside/Out: Lesbian Theories, Gay Theories*. New York: Routledge.

Gilroy, Paul. 1991. *There Ain't No Black in the Union Jack: The Cultural Politics of Race and Nation*. Chicago: University of Chicago Press.

———. 1993. *The Black Atlantic: Modernity and Double Consciousness*. Cambridge, MA: Harvard University Press.

Gunter, Michael. 1990. "The Suppression of the Kurds in Turkey." *Kurdish Times* 3(2):5–16.

Gupta, Akhil, and James Ferguson. 1999. *Culture, Power, Place: Explorations in Critical Anthropology*. Durham, NC: Duke University Press.

Hall, Stuart. 1991. "The Local and the Global: Globalization of Ethnicity." In *Culture, Globalization, and the World-System: Contemporary Conditions for the Representation of Identity*, ed. Anthony D. King, 19–40. Minneapolis: University of Minnesota Press.

Harvey, David. 1996. *Justice, Nature, and the Geography of Difference*. Cambridge, MA: Blackwell.

hooks, bell. 1984. *Feminist Theory: From Margin to Center*. Boston: South End.

———. 1990. *Yearning: Race, Gender, and Cultural Politics*. Boston: South End.

İmset, İsmet. 1996. "The PKK Terrorist or Freedom Fighter." *International Journal of Kurdish Studies* 10(1–2):45–100.

Kaplan, Caren. 1987. "Deterritorialization: Rewriting of Home and Exile in Western Feminist Discourse." *Cultural Critique* 6 (Spring): 187–98.

Lorde, Audre. 1993. "The Transformation of Silence into Language and Action." In her *Zami, Sister Outsider, Undersong*, 40–44. New York: Quality Paperback Book Club.

Malkki, Liisa H. 1999. "National Geographic: The Rooting of Peoples and the Territorialization of National Identity among Scholars and Refugees." In Gupta and Ferguson 1999, 52–74.

Marx, Karl. (1867) 1987. *Capital*. Vol. I. New York: International Publishers.

Massey, Doreen. 1994. *Space, Place, and Gender*. Minneapolis: University of Minnesota Press.

Mohanty, Chandra Talpade. 1987. "Feminist Encounters: Locating the Politics of Experience." *Copyright* 1(1):30–44.

Ong, Aihwa. 1999. *Flexible Citizenship: The Cultural Logics of Transnationality*. Durham, NC: Duke University Press.

Rich, Adrienne. 1976. *Of Woman Born: Motherhood as Experience and Institution*. New York: Norton.

Rofel, Lisa. 1999. *Other Modernities: Gendered Yearnings in China after Socialism*. Berkeley: University of California Press.

Safran, William. 1991. "Diasporas in Modern Societies: Myths of Homeland and Return." *Diaspora: A Journal of Transnational Studies* 1(1):83–99.

Secor, Anna. 2004. "'There Is an Istanbul That Belongs to Me': Citizenship, Space, and Identity in the City." *Annals of the Association of American Geographers* 94(2):352–68.

Soja, Edward W. 1996. *Thirdspace: Journeys to Los Angeles and Other Real-and-Imagined Places*. Cambridge, MA: Blackwell.

TBMM Araştırma Komisyonu (Turkish Grand Assembly Investigation Commission). 1997. Doğu ve Güneydoğu Anadolu'da Boşaltilan Yerleşim Birimleri Nedeniyle Göç Eden Yurttaşlarimizin Sorunlarinin Araştirilarak Alınması Gereken Tedbirlerin Tespit Edilmesi Amaciyla Kurulan Meclis Araştırma Komisyonu (10/25) Raporu" [A report (10/25) of the Grand Assembly Investigation Commission to investigate the problems and to bring solutions for the citizens who used to live in depopulated settlements in Eastern and Southeastern Anatolia]. Ankara: TBMM.

Tölölyan, Khachig. 1991. "Exile Government in Armenian Polity." In *Governments-in-Exile in Contemporary World Politics*, ed. Yossi Shain, 166–87. New York: Routledge.

———. 1996. "Rethinking Diaspora(s): Stateless Power in the Transnational Moment." *Diaspora: A Journal of Transnational Studies* 5(1):3–36.

Trinh T. Minh-ha. 1991. *When the Moon Waxes Red: Representation, Gender, and Cultural Politics*. New York: Routledge.

Trouillot, Michel-Rolph. 1995. *Silencing the Past: Power and the Production of History*. Boston: Beacon.

Volkan, D. Vamik, and Norman Itzkowitz. 1984. *The Immortal Ataturk: A Psychobiography*. Chicago: University of Chicago Press.

Williams, Brackette. 1990. "Nationalism, Traditionalism, and the Problem of Cultural Inauthenticity." In *Nationalist Ideologies and the Production of National Cultures*, ed. Richard G. Fox, 112–29. American Ethnological Society Monograph Series, no. 2. Washington, DC: American Anthropological Association.

Williams, Raymond. 1961. *The Long Revolution*. New York: Columbia University Press.

———. 1973. *The Country and the City.* New York: Oxford University Press.

Yoneyama, Lisa. 1994. "Taming the Memoryscapes: Hiroshima's Urban Renewal." In *Remapping Memory: The Politics of Time Space,* ed. Jonathan Boyarin. Minneapolis: University of Minnesota Press.

Cawo Mohamed Abdi

Convergence of Civil War and the Religious Right: Reimagining Somali Women

T he political crisis that led to the demise of the Somali Democratic Republic in 1991 has had vast, complex effects on Somali women's lives. Somalia remains the only country in the world that has existed without a legitimate central government for the past sixteen years.[1] This lack of government, together with continuing sectarian conflict, has resulted in the forced displacement of millions, affecting Somali women in numerous and drastic ways. The gendered consequences of war go beyond the physical and psychological violence to which women are subjected through rape and terror, extending to insidious practices and invented traditions that further consolidate patriarchy and exacerbate women's social subordination. This article examines the ongoing production and reproduction of gender and sexuality in war-ravaged Somalia and areas to which Somali refugees have fled.[2]

I would like to thank the friends and colleagues who commented on earlier versions of this article. Special thanks to Chris Abuk for her editorial assistance. I am indebted to Mary Hawkesworth and the anonymous reviewers of *Signs* for their critiques and suggestions. Of course, all shortcomings of this article remain my own.

[1] A Somali transitional federal government established in Kenya in 2004 remains weak and barely has any control over any region. This government has thus far failed to establish legitimate functioning institutions to solidify its authority and has very little legitimacy. The Union of Islamic Courts recently emerged in the southern parts of the country as a competing power. These courts applied sharia to bring law and order, and elements of this movement advocated for the establishment of an Islamic state in Somalia. This movement was, however, crushed by invading Ethiopian forces with American air support in December 2006 and January 2007, and Somalia has now returned to its chaotic state, with a very weak federal government trying to establish law and order.

[2] In addition to the general literature on Muslim women, this case study mainly draws from two field research trips to Dadaab refugee camps (Hagadera, Ifo, and Dhagahley) in the Northeastern Province of Kenya in 2001 and 2003. Approximately 130,000 Somalis remain in these camps. I also draw from my doctoral work on continuities and changes in Somali gender relations in the diaspora. I conducted a year of fieldwork with Somali refugee men and women of diverse ages in Minnesota in 2004–5. This ethnographic research included in-depth interviews (sixty-three participants) and eight focus groups (forty participants) with

To explore the intricate dimensions of gender transformation, I investigate the cultural significance of recent dramatic changes in women's modes of dress—the adoption of veiling practices characteristic of conservative Islam but foreign to traditional Somali culture.[3] Through ethnographic fieldwork and in-depth interviews, I explore various reasons that Somali women have for choosing to accept these new modes of dress, ranging from a quest for security from rape and increased piety as a coping mechanism to recover from sexual violation to the adoption of conservative dress so they can move about freely in order to fulfill the survival needs and economic demands of their families. Excavating more subtle means of coercion, I also consider how Somali men, Islamic charities, and the conditions prevailing in refugee camps and conflict zones participate in promoting these new modes of dress.

To deepen understanding of these gender transformations, I draw upon Eric Hobsbawm's (1983) conception of invented tradition to demonstrate that societal and political crises have stimulated the invention of new traditions in Somalia.[4] Under conditions of sustained societal crisis, gender is being reconstructed under the influence of particular religious and ethnic communities. As a consequence of civil war and its devastating effects, people whose lives and livelihoods have been destroyed are turning to versions of religion that were never part of their cultural and traditional repertoire. Despite their recent adoption, these new religious practices are constructed as the natural way of things, neglected out of ignorance for a long time but finally rediscovered and reembraced.

In 1915 Mary Sargent Florence and C. K. Ogden claimed that "in war time, only men matter" (1915, 218–19). One could also argue that it is women who matter more in wartime, because they become the focus of new sanctions in the invented traditions cultivated in conflict and post-conflict situations. When the nation, group, tribe, or clan is in crisis, women's social roles and modes of embodiment become the focal point of male identity constructions (Yuval-Davis 1997). Although myriad other

---

Somali refugees as well as numerous consultations with organizations serving them in the Minneapolis–St. Paul area. Information gathered on recent trips to the northern regions of Somalia also informs the study.

[3] By veil, I refer to the wearing of the *hijab*. Somalis call this dress *jalaabiib* or *jilbaab*, a word related to *galabia*, a flowing gown worn in Arab countries by both men and women.

[4] Hobsbawm defines invented tradition as "a set of practices, normally governed by overtly or tacitly accepted rules, and of a ritual or symbolic nature, which seek to inculcate certain values and norms of behaviour by repetition, which automatically implies continuity with the past" (1983, 1). Whether this past is real or fictitious is irrelevant, as invented traditions "establish their own past by quasi-obligatory repetition" (Hobsbawm 1983, 2).

concerns, such as meeting basic subsistence needs and seeking safe haven, confront a society experiencing conflict, women's roles and practices also receive particular attention as symbols of group identity. Women not only become the first casualties of conflict in terms of the violence inflicted on their bodies and psyches (Niarchos 1995; Lentin 1997; Moser and Clark 2001); they also bear the gendered consequences of war in postwar gender roles and relations within that society.

Marriage of local customs and Islam

The quintessential Muslim woman, often represented by the veil, exists in the imagination of many people in the Western world. In reality, Muslim women in very different regions of the world express their "Muslimness" in hybrid ways, combining local or indigenous customs with the tenets of Islam (El-Solh and Mabro 1994; Bodman and Tohidi 1998; Westerlund and Svanberg 1999). This diversity applies not only to women living in different regions and countries but also to women living within one country (Hasan and Menon 2005). Lived Islam assumes culture-specific characteristics, dependent on the conditions of a particular place and time. That the Islam practiced in these geographically and culturally distinct regions is diverse should not be surprising. Writings on Muslim women, however, often mask this diversity by portraying a monolithic and essentialist view.

It is also an illusion to think that there is a universal monolithic Islam because practiced Islam is often subject to patriarchy. As Deniz Kandiyoti observes, "Different systems of male dominance and their internal variations according to class and ethnicity . . . exercise an influence that inflects and modifies the actual practice of Islam as well as ideological construction of what may be regarded as properly Islamic" (1991b, 24). Although many authors have described these variations, they often concentrate on the central regions of the Middle East, such as Iran, Egypt, and Turkey (Kandiyoti 1991b; Keddie 1991; Ahmed 1992). Muslim women in peripheral regions such as Somalia and Libya, for example, seldom get any mention.

Regardless of the variations of the Islam practiced in geographically distant and culturally distinct societies, one current commonality in many Islamic societies is an ongoing rise in a conservative interpretation of Islam, or what some call the religious right (Imam 2000) or the fundamentalist movement (Moghissi 2000). Though diversity does exist within this movement, characteristics shared by most religious conservatives include a project of reconstructing an imagined Islamic society untarnished by colonial influences and modern ideas (Imam 2000, 127). This reconstruction is based on an imaginary ideal *umma*, or Islamic community, and involves a constant selection and interpretation of what constitutes Islamic society. Among other characteristics identified are intolerance of dissenting views and, most relevant for this article, an obsession with women, women's bodies, and women's sexuality (Mernissi 1996; Moghissi 2000). Scholarly work examining various societies illustrates this obsession and its effect on women.[5] This obsession with the body and focus on women's sexuality as a source of immorality (El-Saadawi 1980; Imam 2000) often has detrimental effects on Muslim women living in these societies.[6] Control and constant scrutiny of women's sexuality can lead to harsh punishments and increased violence against women.[7] This control has been internationalized with the spread of conservative Islam to regions where the dominant religion is Islam but where practiced Islam has previously been generous in its treatment of women and women's sexuality in comparison to many Middle Eastern countries. The imported Islamic interpretation reconfigures preexisting cultural and religious practices, claiming that these communities have mispracticed and thus deviated from true Islam. As this Somali case study will show, such reconfiguration or re-Islamization, which entails the invention of a new Islamic tradition in the Somali context, has been facilitated by the collapse of authority and state apparatus following the civil war of 1991.

Nomadic/agropastoral dress practices: Practical and flexible

Prior to the civil war of the late 1980s, the predominantly nomadic way of life dictated Islamic practices in urban and rural Somalia. Much of the country is semiarid savannah, and nomads' lives entail the search for pasture and water. This search involves extensive physical work by both women and men (Kapteijns 1995; Kapteijns and Ali 1999). Women play a significant role in nomadic life: constructing and dismantling huts, making grass mats used for bedding and for covering the huts, tending livestock, as sole carers for children, and in all other housework-related

[5] See, e.g., Bennoune 1995; Mernissi 1996; El-Saadawi 1997; Bodman and Tohidi 1998; Altinay 2000; Moghissi 2000.

[6] I do not mean to imply that Islam is detrimental to women but rather that interpretations of Islam by specific groups entail detrimental consequences for women. A salient example is the Taliban regime and its treatment of women, which in many respects contradict Islamic prescriptions for societal and gender relations.

[7] See Human Rights Watch 1993; Bennoune 1995; Haeri 1995; Elmadmad 1999.

matters. Like that of women from rural areas around the globe, Somali women's traditional dress was light, reflecting this need for mobility and labor. It consisted of a long piece of cloth, similar to an Indian sari, knotted over one shoulder. The material covers the chest but leaves both arms and shoulders and part of the back bare. These are full-length dresses going down to the ankles. The *guntiino* (also called *guntiimo* or *garays*) was originally made of simple white or red cotton but was later adapted by urban women to include more expensive and elaborate multicolored variations. Somali women in the market wearing the *guntiino* without a shawl while running vegetable stands, selling milk, or even breast-feeding children were a common sight in any town. The *dirac*, a very thin cotton or polyester voile dress worn over a full-length half-slip and a brassiere, was also adapted by women following urbanization. Women also wore the thin *dirac* around their homes and neighborhoods without bras or shawls. Because of this dress norm, breasts were not perceived as sexual.[8] Unlike a veil, which hides everything except the face, the *dirac*, according to one foreign scholar writing about Somalis, was "slightly coquette" (Helander 1999, 48). Yet this dress was never considered deviant, and women were not condemned for showing so much flesh.

Women also wore light scarves over the hair with a knot at the nape, leaving the face, neck, and shoulders uncovered. In the nomadic Somali tradition, scarves worn by married women differentiated them from unmarried women, who did not cover their hair. Girls and young unmarried women braided their hair to indicate their single status and did not wear perfumes or use incense. Urbanization, however, transformed this distinction, with some married women not wearing scarves and, at times, single women wearing them. There were also diverse uses of head scarves among school-age girls, with many never covering their hair while others did.

A small urban minority, often belonging to the middle or upper classes, practiced seclusion of women in Somalia (Kapteijns 1995), whereas the majority remained active in reproduction and production within and outside their households (Abdi 2006a). Veiling, as a practice that is culture/class specific, is consistent with the experience of women in Egypt and other Muslim countries where veiling has been a luxury only befitting women from certain backgrounds. For example, Nikki Keddie

---

[8] By this I mean that breasts were never fetishized as they are in some other parts of the world. This was especially the case for nursing mothers, who could breast-feed anywhere, regardless of whether male strangers were present.

argues that women from the urban middle and upper classes were traditionally the ones veiled and secluded, demonstrating that seclusion was tied to inheritance and to the protection of families' economic interests (1991, 6). In Egypt also, the dress code for women from the lower classes has differed sharply from that of the urban veiled women: "The type of modest female attire meant by veiling among these traditional social strata generally referred to as *milaya laff* (literally enveloping sheet), which 'reveals the graceful bodily curves yet will "cover" what should not be revealed or what is shameful' . . . differed markedly from the veil formerly worn by the more affluent urban Egyptian women in that it did not entail the covering of the face" (El-Solh and Mabro 1994, 10).

There are, however, exceptions to this. Camilla Fawzi El-Solh and Judy Mabro (1994, 10) report that the veil worn by women from the rural "traditional" class in Afghanistan is more conservative, requiring wearing of the burka, which conceals both the face and all the female curves. Despite some exceptions, most research agrees that veiling, at least in earlier times, was culture specific and class based.

Like other Muslim women both in the Middle East and outside it who defy their portrayal as secluded and nonproductive entities in the public sphere (Bovin 1983; Mernissi 1988), Somali women exist first and foremost as economic agents struggling in a precarious economic environment. As Fatima Mernissi (1988) has argued with respect to Moroccan women, the ideal of the Muslim man providing the upkeep, *nafaqa*, of his wife remains just that, an ideal for most Muslim women. Research in other Muslim societies has also found that men's "responsibility for their wives' support, while normative in some instances, is in actual fact relatively low" (Kandiyoti 1988, 277). This also holds true in rural and urban settings in Somalia. For example, nomadic life greatly depends on women, who share equally in household production and perform most household tasks. With urbanization, some women had husbands providing for them and their families at least until the civil war erupted, while they cared for the children and home. But a large proportion of Somali women have continued to work, running cottage industries such as making baskets, selling foodstuffs in the market, operating businesses, or working in more formal settings (Abdi 2006a).

The spread of the Muslim Brethren to Somalia

The Muslim Brethren (*Al-ikhwan al-muslimun*), an organization originally founded in Egypt in 1928 (Ahmed 1992), penetrated Somali urban centers by the late 1970s and early 1980s. For the first time, a small number of Somali women wearing the full chador with face covering (Helander 1999) appeared in the streets of Mogadishu. This was a new phenomenon in Somalia, signifying an internationalization of more conservative interpretations of Islam. This was a period of great discontent with Mohamed Siad Barre's dictatorial regime. Those joining the Muslim Brethren were predominantly young unemployed men who were greatly disenchanted with the bleakness of educational and employment prospects for youth (Ahmed 1999).

A high-ranking female former official in the Ministry of Culture and Higher Education, who requested anonymity, revealed that postsecondary scholarships offered to Somalis by Saudi Arabia during this period were primarily for religious studies, and only men received them. The informant had advocated for diversity in fields of study available to students and also for diversity in the student body. But she reports that she was silenced and even intimidated by the increasing force of the religious right during that period.[9]

Though an increasing number of men and women joined this nascent movement, it did not succeed in changing most Somali women's self-representation and way of life until the late 1980s. Most women, and Somali society in general, perceived the new conservatism as a challenge to their freedom of movement, association, and dress, a challenge to the autonomy that women inherited from their nomadic culture and transplanted to urban centers.

By the very late 1980s, the Somali government turned even more repressive, and rebels against the regime became more active in regions close to the capital, increasing the physical and material insecurity of the whole population. For the first time, most women in Mogadishu began covering their hair with conservative headdress that covered the neck and the shoulders. Those who resisted this new trend received verbal and physical harassment. Whether to veil or not to veil was no longer women's prerogative. The Somali civil war, brewing from the mid-1980s, finally erupted in January 1991, catalyzing a dramatic alteration of Somali women's public self-representation and Islamic identity.[10]

---

[9] Interview in Toronto, May 13, 2003.

[10] The Somali civil war started with the bombardment of the northern cities of Hargaisa and Bur'o in 1988 and the heavy-handed military repression of rebels in this and other regions. The final collapse of the state occurred in early 1991, when Siad Barre fled.

Convergence of civil war and the religious right

> We know that rapid and radical change in the structure and in the norms
> of a given society creates a feeling of insecurity in all its members. The
> result is often a search for well-known values in a more secure past.
> —Inger Rezig 1983, 192

The dictatorship of Siad Barre collapsed in January 1991. More than three hundred thousand Somalis died either from famine or violence (Samatar 1994), and millions were displaced. Of the half million who had sought refuge in Kenya since the early 1990s, there were still about 130,000 in the Dadaab refugee camps in 2001. Refugees' movement is highly curtailed in these camps, which became notorious for sexual violence against women in the early 1990s. About two hundred rape cases were reported in 1993. In the next four years, this dropped to between 70 and 105, but increased to 164 in 1998, dropping back to 71 in 1999, 82 in 2000, 72 in 2001, and 18 in 2002 (UNHCR 2003). The statistics do not convey the terror of rape among camp women, who constantly discuss the insecurity of the camps and their vulnerability to victimization (Abdi 2006b). They report with resignation that any bandit who sets his mind to rape them can do so with impunity because rapes occur on the outskirts of the camps when women gather firewood or at night when camp security is minimal (Abdi 2005, 2006b).

Rape in Somali culture is very stigmatizing. Prior to the war it was rare and severely condemned, making group or clan relations very tense when it occurred. Women's virginity was highly valued, and violating their honor was considered scandalous. With the war and the collapse of law and order, group relations and societal norms were turned upside down. Dispersal of families made women more vulnerable when they were separated from husbands, brothers, or fathers. Furthermore, wider insecurity was already present in the Somali-inhabited northeastern part of Kenya: Somali Kenyans marginalized within the Kenyan state have a hostile relationship with the state, and armed bandits roam freely. The remoteness of the camps, the absence of effective camp security, and the lack of cohesive and tight community among the refugees following the clan-justified war that led to their flight all contribute to the high rates of rapes in these camps.

Not knowing when violence will strike in or outside the camps reinforces women's vulnerability, instilling a permanent fear of disfigurement (Goffman 1961). William I. Thomas and Dorothy Swaine Thomas's famous statement about the importance of the subjective in human life, "If [women] define situations as real, they are real in their consequences"

(1929, 572), illustrates these women's reality (Abdi 2006b). The consequence is even more real for those previously raped during the civil war and the flight from conflict. A practice exemplifying the permanent fear of rape in the camps and also the loss of physical integrity as a result of the civil war is the incorporation of pants (long johns or trousers) in women's dress. Pants were garments that were exclusively worn by men in Somalia. When inquiring about this new addition, I was informed that it started during the civil war era as a result of indiscriminate rapes (Abdi 2006b). As one woman who was in her late teens in the early 1990s put it, "We started wearing these trousers under our clothes during the flight. Women were getting raped. If a woman is wearing a *dirac*, it can just be pulled or torn off in no time; but if she has tight trousers underneath [*naag surweel ku giigsan*], then help may come in time. Women started wearing these trousers for protection and as defense from violence" (Nim'a, a thirty-five-year-old woman).[11]

As the violence that these women fled was replicated in the camps, women continued to wear pants, an additional piece of clothing that has now become a permanent feature of Somali girls' and women's dress. Some women justify this addition in terms of modesty and religious requirement. For example, one woman argued that, "when fleeing, anything can happen: you are climbing a car, you are lifting your leg, and the skirt or whatever you are wearing climbs up and men are standing under you. And religiously, it is preferable. Our prophet, may Allah bless him, praised women who do that, for being modest" (Nim'a again).

In addition to the violence experienced by all refugee women, Muslims often encounter additional stresses related to specific cultural regulations. In her study of Afghan refugees, Sima Wali (1995) reports that Afghan city and tribal women in Pakistani camps who traditionally did not observe purdah are coerced to wear the veil. Moreover she claims that the incidence of rape and forced prostitution inflicted on Afghan women and girls remains very high while simultaneously rigid expectations are enforced for them to maintain so-called Islamic virtues (Wali 1995, 177–79). Similarly, Somali women have reported that Koranic madrassas sprang up everywhere during the flight and that women started taking religious classes. These schools propagated Somali women's changes in dress practices. However, the push for more Islamic practices was also accompanied by

---

[11] Quotations in this article are taken from interviews with Somali women in Dadaab refugee camps from May to August 2001 and with Somali men and women in Minneapolis–St. Paul from May 2004 to March 2005. Interviews were mainly conducted in Somali by the author, who also transcribed and translated them.

the violence intrinsic in civil strife. The Somali civil war reduced all women to representatives of their clans' honor. Violating their integrity and subjecting them to the extreme violence of rape and torture became a key weapon of the war. Islam and all its prescriptions were suspended in the height of the war when law and order had broken down. Refugee camps did not provide any more security than the crisis people had fled in the first place. No woman, whether a child or a grandmother, was safe in these contexts, and women's vulnerability and their search for protection became paramount.

Dadaab refugee camps: Microcosms of social transformation

The Somali political crisis and the permanent insecurity experienced by Somali women resulted in women drastically changing their attire. I contend that these changes differ from a fashion craze or from the adoption of new pieces in a group's everyday wear that occurs within any given society over time. Instead, these changes reflect ideological shifts affecting women's position in society and the norms governing what is permissible. Whether this change was directly imposed on women or indirectly enforced through the violence ensuing from the civil war—rapes, harassment, and so on—is hard to assess. What is unambiguous is that the civil war brought about conditions that heightened women's vulnerability. I was struck by the uniformity of women's dress while doing my first fieldwork in Dadaab. Almost all women are now wearing long, thick, flowing dresses, accompanied by a veil covering the head and shoulders and descending all the way to the knees, covering the dress and leaving only the face showing. Somali women call these *jalaabiib* or *jilbaab*. These are very colorful, in contrast to black chadors with gloves and face coverings worn by a minority of refugee women. One cannot help but be amazed by the dramatic transformations in Somali women's public self-representation in Dadaab compared with their dress habits in prewar times.

Somali women's current conservative dress is directly linked to the vulnerability caused by the civil war and refugeeism. For these women, the veil provides a "response to their vulnerability," pushing them to "retreat into the protective certainties of religious conservatism" (Kandiyoti 1991a, 18). Neither a choice nor direct imposition, this phenomenon exemplifies Mernissi's parallel between the veil and terrorism (Mernissi 1996, xi). Somali women's increased fear of violence translates to the adoption of more conservative attire, which presents them as pious women who attract less attention, and thus less harassment, when outside their homes. Hence, the veil is presently endorsed among Somalis in

Dadaab and in many parts of Somalia and the diaspora as a symbol of respectability without which women may be perceived as publicly available and consequently ostracized (Ahmed 1992, 15). Sadia Ahmed, a Somali activist, has voiced concern about this change, stating "I have seen that the recent increase in veiling has been accompanied, for the first time in Somali history, with extreme forms of censorship of women's behaviour, as extreme versions of Islamic interpretation have found fertile ground" (1999, 71).

With its push for a standardization of religious practices worldwide, conservative Islam carries greater influence in war zones where morale is low and where economic desperation reigns. Since the economic position of refugee women and women caught in war-torn societies remains extremely low, women might embrace the veil for economic reasons. This could be a key factor in women's choice of clothing: the cheaper materials used to make *jalaabiib* are more accessible for poor women, who have been increasing in number for the last two decades because of the economic turmoil in Somalia. Very few women can now afford to pay for the old *dirac* or *guntiino*.

While the majority of women in Dadaab now wear the *jalaabiib*, I found variations in women's garb in the northwestern regions of Somalia. Many wear the new dress, but one still sees some wearing the old *dirac* or *guntiino* in conservative versions. These are no longer made of transparent material, and a thick shawl completely covering the head and shoulders is worn over them. Conversely, when driving through the region where Dadaab camps are located, an area inhabited by Somali pastoral communities, I noted that the garments of the nomadic nonrefugee women herding livestock remain light and are very unlike those of refugee women. Clearly the increased religiosity, or maybe the permanent fear of violence experienced by Somali women in the camps and in urban centers in Somalia, does not extend to rural nomadic women.

Reimagined Somali woman

Somali gender relations were shaken by the civil war, which created unprecedented physical and material insecurity (Abdi 2006a, 2006b). One consequence of this conflict was that women were rendered a depository of culture (Yuval-Davis 1997), leading to a project of inscribing an authentic Islam on their bodies. This interpretation of Islam promotes new prescriptions for women's daily practices within society in terms of dress code. This, I would argue, has resulted in a newly invented tradition for Somali woman's dress habits and a newly imagined Somali woman.

Though Hobsbawm's discussion of invented traditions draws mainly on the European context or on examples from European imperialism in other regions, the characteristics of invented traditions he identifies are applicable to current religious reinterpretations by conservative movements in some parts of the world. For example, Hobsbawm identifies three types of invented traditions: those establishing or symbolizing social cohesion or the membership of groups of real or artificial communities; those establishing or legitimizing institutions, status, or relations of authority; and those whose main purpose is socialization, the inculcation of beliefs, value systems, and conventions of behavior (Hobsbawm 1983, 9). Islamic reinterpretation by the religious right claims to be based on a quest for the common ideology of an Islamic *umma* as the foundation of an imagined Islamic community. More conservative Islamic interpretations often support and legitimize patriarchal gender roles and relations, causing relations of authority within society to become entrenched, especially with regard to gender relations. Finally, the reiteration of these new relations and the enforcement of new prescriptions indoctrinate current and future generations, guaranteeing, to some extent, the reproduction and normalization of these new practices.

To legitimate the new Islamic movement, some Somalis claim that Allah's wrath has descended on Somalia and Somalis because of their digression from authentic Islam. This digression has allegedly caused the complete destruction of the country, the loss of hundreds of thousands of people, and the ongoing absence of law and order. As in other regions where all evil befalling the nation is attributed to women's deviation from the rules (El-Saadawi 1980; Mernissi 1995), a Somali proverb states "*wixii xunba Xaawaa leh*" (All evil originates from Hawa [Eve]). It is accordingly argued that in order to reverse the calamity that has struck the nation, repentance for this deviation must also commence with women. The regulation of women's sexuality and position in society is hence legitimized as a necessary basis on which to salvage the souls of the whole community. In this way the newly invented tradition requiring that all women veil themselves is transformed into a justifiable demand imposed on them.

This case study illustrates the extent to which extreme social transformations affect women's position in society. In times of crisis and civil wars, the first victims are often women. As Valentine Moghadam states, "The politics of gender may be especially strong in patriarchal societies undergoing development and social change; gender becomes politicised during periods of transition and restructuring, when social groups and values clash" (1992, 49). The requirement that Somali women demonstrate their piousness, or Muslimness, by discarding their traditional lingerie-like *dirac* or *guntiino*, which left little to the imagination, for more "respectable" attire becomes compelling in this context. I found that the new project defining behaviors as either Islamic or un-Islamic demonizes earlier Somali women's wear; the only women who are safe from criticism are those appearing to be good Muslims, abiding by the new rules and embracing the new prescriptions.[12] Distinctions are drawn between the new imported discourse of "genuine Islam" and the customs of the people, which are currently equated with *jahilia*, or tainted Somali culture now depicted as un-Islamic. These distinctions are pervasive in discussions with refugee women and men. Those advocating for more authentic Islam offer arguments purporting that the divine law of Islam is contaminated by alien customs (Hjarpe 1983, 12–15). The importation of an imagined Islam, a reinvention of the path to true Islam for Somalia and for Somalis, currently prevails in Dadaab and in much of Somalia and the diaspora.

In a context where law and order have completely collapsed and where violence reigns supreme, women's options to resist such demands are very limited. The minimal version of the new conservative dress is to cover the hair, even if only with a scarf, and to wear the *dirac* or *guntiino* made with heavy fabrics with a large thick shawl. The option not to wear this is no longer open to Somali women in the refugee camps and in Somalia. Those who dare attempt to challenge this prescription become targets of verbal and physical harassment from children, youth, and adult men and women. One Somali researcher from North America who conducted research in Dadaab camps prior to my arrival there was in fact subjected to such treatment, and she was obliged to cover up to pursue her research. Researchers in Gaza and the Palestinian territories have reported similar treatment of women who fail to veil since the intifada (Hammami 1990). Veiling, which until the intifada in the late 1980s was optional and not a required part of daily life for most Palestinian women, became an issue that took center stage. Rema Hammami reports that one informant, discussing the supporters of the veiling campaign, told her that "their main activities in Gaza are to keep demonstrators away from mosques and to make sure women are covering their heads" (1990, 25). Youth and children have subjected women who defied these prescriptions to constant harassment and violence such as stoning. Political and societal crises, both in the Palestinian territories and in war-torn Muslim societies such as

---

[12] This is not always true, as women were still raped at the height of the war and also in the camps despite their conservative dress.

Somalia and Afghanistan, facilitate conservative groups' agenda of pressuring women to conform to certain practices, often reversing the autonomy that these women enjoyed in earlier times.

Somali women living in the diaspora continue to wear the *dirac* and *guntiino* in their old (transparent) form, and fashion in these dresses continues to flourish. Most women, however, wear these dresses only in the contexts of celebrations such as weddings and segregated contexts. I have seen exceptions to this in Somali weddings I have attended in the Minneapolis–St. Paul area, where women dressed in extremely thin *dirac*s, danced, and interacted with men. I even found women who regularly wear the *jalaabiib* but switch to *dirac* when attending celebrations, though these are not always as transparent as they were prior to the Somali conflict. One woman in Minneapolis told me that

> in weddings, we shed it all. There are many women who wear the *jilbaab* every day, but who don't do that during celebrations. It is likely that many women who have been wearing this [*jilbaab*] for a long time might not come as they don't want to remove it. But women who are wearing the *jilbaab*, including those who cover their faces, shed it only at the women's party. I was teasing a woman the other night as the photographer and the video camera person at the party were men. So if you were covering yourself because of men, they are also there at the women's-only party. (Farah, fifty-three-year-old woman)

Women in the diaspora have more leeway about how they and their daughters dress. Young women often wear a head scarf accompanied by a long skirt and shirt. These skirts and shirts are sometimes actually very tight and are similar to what their non-Muslim peers wear. One woman in her early fifties who voiced concerns about the new dress reported:

> Many people ask me, "Why don't you make your daughter wear the *hijab*?" The first time I covered my hair was 1996, at this old age! I grew up in a boarding school; we wore short white dresses. No one ever said anything to me; people were expected to gradually change once they grow up. And there are still many families who are not telling their girls to wear the head scarf [*masar*]. But I still don't allow my daughter to expose her body indecently. I encourage her to wear decent trousers, and a shirt. But the head, I don't care; she can cover it anytime she wants to and I won't enforce. . . . My daughter swims. She plays basketball and football with the boys. Why not? She is growing up. Once she reaches eighteen, we can

talk; I can say you are now a woman, you are grown up. . . . But regarding praying, fasting, etc., I still tell her those things. . . . There are many families like that, modest like me here; my arms are covered, but I am still not wearing the heavy material of the Arabs, and I believe that is culture, that Allah wants me to be modest, but not necessarily to wear the uniforms Arabs wear. (Farah again)

This woman, who was university educated and middle class, criticized the new norms and associated them with an "Arab culture" imposed by a few radical religious leaders. She herself wore ankle-length skirts and long-sleeved shirts, with a head scarf. One thus finds a variety of dress practices in the diaspora, while this diversity is less true for women in Somalia and in Dadaab.

Some women reported that women's changes in dress are closely tied to their discovery of religious education. One interviewee in her forties argued:

There are now many women who are well versed in the Koran. You never saw that in Somalia, except for young girls attending Koranic schools; you did not see adult women pursuing Koranic education. And here there are many madrassas and they are also learning in their homes. We attended a funeral the other day and the verses the woman who was leading the prayer was reading and the way she was reading them were most impressive. She was an older woman who has learned this here. Many beliefs that were taken for truth are now no more. And women pursue Koranic interpretation classes [*tafsiir*]. So women are more religious, and they have changed their dresses due to this. (Sahra, forty-one-year-old woman)

Girls attending Koranic schools in Somalia often stopped in their very early teens without having learned the interpretations of the Arabic verses they memorized. Boys, on the contrary, would pursue this education much further, finishing the whole Koran and sometimes mastering its interpretation. Adult women were therefore mostly uneducated in religious matters and depended greatly on men for Islamic education (Samatar 2000). Women now report that this is no longer the case, and it is particularly so for women in the diaspora, who have more access to new technologies such as the Internet and educational videos and audiotapes as aids with which to learn the Koran. Rima B. McGown, who researched with Somali women in London and Toronto, argues that women's increased religiosity empowers them (1999, 100). Though this is true in part, my research shows that increased religiosity can also be a sign of disempowerment rather than one of empowerment (Abdi 2006a; see also Kandiyoti 1988; Ahmed 1992). McGown's analysis of changing religiosity fails to incorporate women's experiences of violence in Somalia and in transit areas to account for changing Islamic practices in the diaspora.

Because of the limited options in Dadaab, women self-regulate in abiding by the new dress codes, probably drawing on their violent experiences in Somalia, the flight, and the camps. Some young women also circumvent constraints imposed on them by finding small ways of resisting even in an environment where choices seem to be very limited. Many I spoke with in Nairobi and the diaspora reported that young girls and women leave their family homes wearing *jalaabiib* but remove them once they are out of the family neighborhood, using this type of dress to gain freedom that they may not have otherwise. In the camps I also saw that young women wearing the chador come into the nongovernmental organization (NGO) compounds to see the male workers, with whom they engage in relationships in which they are often sexually exploited. One can argue that the latter employ dress with face coverings that prevent recognition to escape family pressure and control. On the other hand, allegations abound of sexual exploitation of refugee women and girls who resort to prostitution because of extreme poverty, and recent scandals of the abuse of power on the part of international organizations' staff, in and outside camp contexts, testifies to refugee children and women's vulnerability to sexual exploitation (WorldNetDaily 2004; Save the Children UK 2006). While these women may use their dress to escape family and societal control, they nevertheless remain victims of other forms of gender abuse in areas where economic insecurity is rife.

How is the new dress code affecting women's participation in the economic sphere? I found that Somali women remain the backbone for the survival of their families in much of Somalia since the collapse of the state. Men were the main perpetrators of the civil unrest, and many either perished in the war or fled outside to escape recruitment by militia, leaving women as the heads and sole providers of families (Abdi 2006a). In the camps, also, women are the ones doing most of the trading, whereas men are often rendered useless; lack of appropriate means of making a living in the camps results in most men spending their days sitting under trees discussing politics, while women sell sugar or tomatoes to gain a few shillings for their children, activities that men perceive as beneath them (Abdi 2006a). Many therefore remain dependent on women and on the rations distributed by the international aid organizations. This fact, however, is never verbally acknowledged, and silence accompanies women's role in family survival (Abdi 2006a). I believe that the conservative push to impose new restrictions on women is closely tied to the scarce livelihood opportunities following the collapse of law and order in Somalia. This insecurity has resulted in a radical protest from men, manifested in the increasing regulation and scrutiny of women's behavior and practices. Despite women's increased role as providers to their families in post–civil war Somalia and in the camps, their real power at home remains constrained by both cultural and social biases (Abdi 2006a). The increase in religiosity and the prominence of particular interpretations of Islam further exacerbate this bias by restricting Somali gender practices, which earlier permitted women great freedom of movement and autonomy.

Women of course remain actors in reinforcing and supporting the new practices. Kandiyoti argues that "women strategize within a set of concrete constraints," and she calls this the "patriarchal bargain" (1988, 275). She asserts that when this patriarchal bargain collapses, for example, in times of crisis, "the response of many women who have to work for wages in this context may be an intensification of traditional modesty markers, such as veiling. Often, through no choice of their own, they are working outside their home and are thus 'exposed'; they must now use every symbolical means at their disposal to signify that they continue to be worthy of protection" (Kandiyoti 1988, 283).

Though Kandiyoti refers above to regions where classical patriarchy prevails, such as the Middle East and Southeast Asia, and although earlier Somali patriarchal relations differed somewhat from the relations prevailing in those areas, the above statement still describes Somali women's support for new practices that rarely existed in their communities prior to the war. One could thus argue that Somali women embrace the new dress code because it at least permits them to remain economic agents in their families, something that has become indispensable since the war. Women strategizing to make the most of difficult circumstances that impose unprecedented control over their autonomy are also reported in other regions, for example, in Iran following the Islamic revolution of 1979. Farah Azari (1983) discusses young women embracing the veil not necessarily out of choice but rather as a survival mechanism. She states, "The restriction imposed on them by an Islamic order was therefore a small price that had to be paid in exchange for the security, stability and presumed respect this order promised them" (Azari 1983, 68). Similarly, the respect and security that women attach to embracing the *jalaabiib* are immeasurable given the chaotic environment of the civil war and refugee camps, where many of them may have been subjected to rape and torture. Arguably, the unarticulated physical and psychological violence many Somali women have experienced since the collapse of the state could be endured only by embracing religion: the attainment of purity in an environment that denied them their basic human and Islamic rights. Female conservatism, directly imposed or chosen in an environment of limited options, is thus one possible outcome in conflict zones, a strategy that permits women to retain some dignity.

Cautionary examples in a changing landscape

Another characteristic attributed to the religious right is the demonization of all that is seen as foreign. Those who dissent from the norms of the religious right are often accused of importing corrupt morals. Several cases from the refugee camps and from Somalia demonstrate new ways of regulating women and their bodies that rely on the rationale that imported morals are corrupting women. Indeed, honor killing, an uncommon practice in prewar Somalia, is surfacing as a means to control women who have been "corrupted."

Female circumcision, which is widely practiced by Somalis, remains a contested topic in Dadaab. Some informants claim that female circumcision is actually on the rise in refugee camps (Imam 2000, 133), whereas educational campaigns are achieving some success in many urban centers in Somalia.[13] On this topic, the religious community is divided. Some condemn it, advocating its eradication, while others endorse it. I heard a preacher during my stay in Dadaab announce over the microphone in a mosque audible by all those in the market "to reject and resist the infidel's message to discontinue female circumcision." He stated that anti–female circumcision campaigns encourage women to deviate from the right path and that Kenyan and expatriate NGO workers are promoting illicit behavior for women. This announcement was a reaction to an anti–female circumcision campaign taking place that day in Hagadera camp. Clearly, the intention of the preacher was to counter and undermine the campaign. Unfortunately, one such sermon can undo the campaigning that a social worker does for the whole year, since whereas the preacher is revered, the NGO workers are distrusted because they are perceived as instruments of foreign and non-Muslim agents.

The above example is not intended to imply that all Somali religious leaders support female circumcision. On the contrary, leaders who denounce female circumcision as un-Islamic and educate the community

---

[13] Personal conversation on April 2, 2003, in Nairobi with Fatima Mohamed, a female circumcision educator with Norwegian Church Aid, which runs projects in southern Somalia.

about its detrimental effects drive most of the progress on this subject. Somalis are generally suspicious of medical discourses on this topic brought by foreign NGOs. The religious community is therefore key to any future progress in the eradication of this un-Islamic custom, since Somalis highly value religion and religious scholars. I present this example to highlight the fear that some religious leaders have of any ideas from outside. Ideas that are beneficial for the community may be vilified as contra-Islam and rejected on the basis of being imported, undermining cultural and religious autonomy.

Another incident that occurred in Somalia relates to women sentenced to death by stoning in the northern region of the country: "Africa Watch has received disturbing reports that in mid-January in the city of Hargeisa six women were accused of prostitution and were stoned and lynched by Islamic fundamentalists. Five of the women subsequently died. The Somaliland authorities have reportedly issued a press release decrying the murders and announcing the arrest of 16 people" (Human Rights Watch 1993, 7). With the lack of any central authority in much of Somalia, it is very probable many more women are persecuted for alleged sexual transgressions and that this does not always get wide publicity.

One last example illustrating the invention of a new tradition in Somalia relates to allegations of the killing of an unmarried pregnant woman by her brother in Dagahaley in 2001. The brother subsequently crossed the border to Somalia to escape the Kenyan justice system. Honor killing was almost unheard of in pre–civil war Somalia. As in many regions, unwed pregnant women fled from their families and settled in other regions, were sent to families in rural areas, or obtained illegal abortions. But nowadays, when the rule of law is nonexistent or very weak in most of Somalia and the religious right is establishing its authority in many regions, there may be many more unreported cases of women falling victims to self-appointed religious leaders and their radical interpretations of Islam.

Petro-Islam: Cultivating conservatism through education

In the Dadaab camps and in Somalia, the promotion of segregation of boys and girls is accompanying the enforcement of women's new dress code. Somali children are presently being indoctrinated into this segregation through formal education. As a result of the scarcity of resources and infrastructure in Somalia, limited educational opportunities are available, which leads to a disproportionate number of girls being excluded from access to learning. As with the scholarships previously proffered to men to pursue religious studies in Saudi Arabia, Islamic charities are now providing educational opportunities mainly to boys in much of Somalia and to a lesser extent in the camps.

A relevant factor in the rise of the religious right is political: the financial aid that oil-rich Middle Eastern countries pour into the less affluent Muslim states (El-Solh and Mabro 1994; Kandiyoti 1995), a practice that Mernissi calls "petro-Islam" (1996). This money in the form of charity often funds religious education in poorer Islamic countries. For example, with the vacuum created by the absence of government, religious leaders have gained new prominence, and Somalia has experienced a proliferation of Islamic charity organizations filling this vacuum (UNDP 2001). Funding from Islamic charity groups has created schools and madrassas all over Somalia, schools that are primarily funded with money from Sudan or Saudi Arabia. Many of these support the Arabic language and Islamic education. For example, some elementary schools in Dadaab camps are run by Al-Haramain, an Islamic NGO operating in Kenya and Somalia.

Women's and girls' exclusion from these educational opportunities is closely tied to the rise in gender conservatism. For example, in Dadaab elementary schools the ratio of boys to girls was 3 : 2, with 11,479 boys compared to 7,222 girls (UNHCR 2003). However, the percentage of girls in schools decreases with each higher grade both in the camps and in Somalia (UNICEF 2002, 8), with only a fraction of girls reaching middle school, and even fewer commencing high school. There were only 69 girls among the 665 high school students in Dadaab in 2003, or 10 percent of all students. This is consistent with girls' high school participation in Somalia (UNDP 2001).

One reason proposed for girls' low attendance in schools relates to economic insecurity, with families requiring girls' labor in the home so that the mother can go out to work. But another reason that cannot be discounted involves the reluctance of parents to send their girls to coed schools, especially as they become teenagers (Ali 2003). Contributing to this reluctance is the heightened violence against women in the form of sexual violence. In the absence of sex-segregated schools, the dropout rate increases as girls get closer to what is considered marriageable age.

It would be wrong to argue that the rise in religiosity is the only factor responsible for the low female participation in education in Somalia and in the camps. As in other Muslim countries (Karmi 1996; Mernissi 1996), there existed a wide gender gap in education even in the prewar era. The situation in Somalia was improving after independence, however, and Somali women made great strides in the educational sphere in the 1970s and 1980s, despite still having one of the lowest school enrollment rates in the world (UNDP 2001). Decreasing numbers of girls in schools, like the changes in dress, illustrate reversals since the war. Increasingly conservative attitudes toward women's education have been exacerbated by the economic insecurity experienced by most Somali families and by the absence of laws enforcing girls' right to education.

The reimagined Somali Muslim woman is also now permanently inscribed in textbooks produced for elementary school children in Somalia. For example, textbooks produced by UNESCO depict Somali girls as young as four or five all wearing the *jalaabiib*, reflecting the current situation. This contrasts with the pre-1990s culture of Somalia, where preteen girls were never expected to cover their hair. One looking at these books would never guess that this is a new tradition dating only to after the civil war. Such reified representations of Somali girls are being reproduced in various images, as well as in patterns of dress, contributing to the reconstruction of gender norms for Somali women and girls. With this new trend we witness a new culture under construction, part of the ongoing project of re-Islamicization of Somali women and girls. Conversations with women in Kenya, Somalia, and the diaspora reveal that there is very little debate about this new dress code or new forms of regulation and normalization, despite their recent invention. The previous dress, the *guntiino*, has already been rendered deviant, at least when worn outside of the home in its old form. An amnesia-like state surrounds this topic, and this amnesia is omnipresent in its naturalness, subversiveness, and subtleness.

Conclusion

The ongoing social transformation experienced by the Somali community everywhere cannot be divorced from the civil war that destroyed the country and left much of its citizenry economically and politically vulnerable. This vulnerability has facilitated and continues to facilitate the rise in prominence of the religious right and its ongoing project of re-Islamizing Somali women. In the vacuum left by the collapse of the state, religious leaders enacting sharia are maintaining peace and order in many regions, providing schooling and other essential social services for marginal communities. And this role increases the conservative groups' legitimacy and power.

The analysis presented in this article does not account for all the challenges currently confronting Somali women in and outside of Somalia. Social, economic, and political setbacks caused by the war and the anarchy that prevailed and still prevails in parts of Somalia have affected women in various ways. This article focuses only on women's circumstances vis-à-vis the rise in the religious right since the late 1980s. My aim is not to blame the religious right for all the ills confronting Somali women. Such an oversimplification of very complex and multifaceted issues would mask the importance of Islam for Somali women. Religion remains the main coping tool available to women, and Islam is an integral part of many women's identities. In the narratives collected from Somali refugee women, Islam remains a salient theme. Women emphasize the importance of Islam in their survival, both during flight and in refugee camps. In prayers women continuously refer to Islam as a source of strength permitting them to keep going despite the myriad obstacles of civil strife.

It is nevertheless important to ask: What does the increasing regulation of Somali women's behavior and body imply for the next decade? Will this newly invented tradition of obligatory veiling persist into future peacetimes? Or will there be a debate over the recent emergence of this conservative phenomenon? Will women be stoned if they choose to return to pre–civil war attire? Will they be accused of non-Islamic behavior? These are interesting but disturbing questions that arise from the analysis in this article.

With no legitimate central government in Somalia, the religious right will surely capitalize on its prominence to promote its conservative agenda for Somali women. After almost two decades of hegemony, it may become difficult to reverse these conservative policies. More research is necessary to document how Somali women are coping with the new and increasing regulation of their bodies and the impact of these regulations on their day-to-day lives. Since my data collection was mainly from refugee camps and the diaspora, more research in different regions of Somalia is required to assess the types of transformations occurring and their impact on women. Moreover, research is required on other aspects of Somali women's lives. For now we can conclude that pervasive insecurity, both physical and material, and the political vacuum existing in Somalia work in favor of legitimizing the religious right's project of regulating women's lives through a combination of charity and violence.

Department of Sociology
University of Minnesota

References

Abdi, Cawo (Awa) Mohamed. 2005. "In Limbo: Dependency, Insecurity, and Identity amongst Somali Refugees in Dadaab Camps." *Refuge: Canada's Periodical on Refugees* 22(2):6–14.

———. 2006a. "Diasporic Lives and Threatened Identities: Gender Struggles of Somalis in America." PhD thesis, Department of Sociology, University of Sussex.

———. 2006b. "Refugees, Gender Based Violence and Resistance: A Case Study of Somali Refugee Women in Kenya." In *Women, Migration and Citizenship: Making Local, National and Transnational Connections*, ed. Evangelia Tastsoglou and Alexandra Dobrowolsky, 231–51. Aldershot: Ashgate.

Ahmed, Leila. 1992. *Women and Gender in Islam: Historical Roots of a Modern Debate*. New Haven, CT: Yale University Press.

Ahmed, Sadia. 1999. "Islam and Development: Opportunities and Constraints for Somali Women." *Gender and Development* 7(1):69–72.

Ali, Mohammud Hassan. 2003. "Status of Girl-Child Education in Dadaab Camps." Kenya Institute of Social Work and Community Development, Nairobi.

Altinay, Ayse Gül. 2000. "Talking and Writing Our Sexuality: Feminist Activism on Virginity and Virginity Tests in Turkey." In *Women and Sexuality in Muslim Societies*, ed. Pınar Ilkkaracan, 403–12. Istanbul: Women for Women's Human Rights.

Azari, Farah. 1983. "Islam's Appeal to Women in Iran: Illusion and Reality." In her *Women of Iran: The Conflict with Fundamentalist Islam*, 1–71. London: Ithaca.

Bennoune, Karima. 1995. "S.O.S. Algeria: Women's Human Rights under Siege." In *Faith and Freedom: Women's Human Rights in the Muslim World*, ed. Mahnaz Afkhami, 184–208. Syracuse, NY: Syracuse University Press.

Bodman, Herbert L., and Nayereh Tohidi, eds. 1998. *Women in Muslim Societies: Diversity within Unity*. London: Rienner.

Bovin, Mette. 1983. "Muslim Women in the Periphery: The West African Sahel." In *Women in Islamic Societies: Social Attitudes and Historical Perspectives*, ed. Bo Utas, 66–103. London: Curzon.

Elmadmad, Khadija. 1999. "The Human Rights of Refugees with Special Reference to Muslim Refugee Women." In *Engendering Forced Migration: Theory and Practice*, ed. Doreen Indra, 261–71. New York: Berghahn.

El-Saadawi, Nawal. 1980. *The Hidden Face of Eve: Women in the Arab World*. Trans. and ed. Sherif Hetata. Boston: Beacon.

———. 1997. *The Nawal El Saadawi Reader*. London: Zed.

El-Solh, Camillia Fawzi, and Judy Mabro. 1994. *Muslim Women's Choices: Religious Belief and Social Reality*. Oxford: Berg.

Florence, Mary Sargent, and C. K. Ogden. 1915. "Women's Prerogative." *Jus Suffragi* 9(4):218–19.

Goffman, Erving. 1961. *Asylums: Essays on the Social Situation of Mental Patients and Other Inmates*. Garden City, NY: Anchor.

Haeri, Shahla. 1995. "The Politics of Dishonor: Rape and Power in Pakistan." In *Faith and Freedom: Women's Human Rights in the Muslim World*, ed. Mahnaz Afkhami, 161–74. Syracuse, NY: Syracuse University Press.

Hammami, Rema. 1990. "Women, the Hijab, and the Intifada." *Middle East Report* 164/165:24–28, 71, 78.

Hasan, Zoya, and Ritu Menon, eds. 2005. *The Diversity of Muslim Women's Lives in India*. New Brunswick, NJ: Rutgers University Press.

Helander, Bernhard. 1999. "Somalia." In Westerlund and Svanberg 1999, 35–55.

Hjarpe, Jan. 1983. "The Attitude of Islamic Fundamentalism towards the Question of Women in Islam." In *Women in Islamic Societies: Social Attitudes and Historical Perspectives*, ed. Bo Utas, 12–25. London: Curzon.

Hobsbawm, Eric. 1983. "Inventing Traditions." In *The Invention of Tradition*, ed. Eric Hobsbawm and Terence Ranger, 1–14. Cambridge: Cambridge University Press.

Human Rights Watch. 1993. " Somalia: Beyond the Warlords; The Need for a Verdict on Human Rights Abuses." *Human Rights Watch* 5, no. 2 (March 7). http://www.hrw.org/reports/1993/somalia/.

Imam, Aisha M. 2000. "The Muslim Religious Right ('Fundamentalists') and Sexuality." In *Women and Sexuality in Muslim Societies*, ed. Pınar Ilkkaracan, 121–39. Istanbul: Women for Women's Human Rights.

Kandiyoti, Deniz. 1988. "Bargaining with Patriarchy." *Gender and Society* 2(3): 274–90.

———. 1991a. "Introduction." In her *Women, Islam, and the State*, 1–21. Basingstoke: Macmillan.

———. 1991b. "Islam and Patriarchy: A Comparative Perspective." In *Women in Middle Eastern History: Shifting Boundaries in Sex and Gender*, ed. Nikki Keddie and Beth Baron, 23–42. New Haven, CT: Yale University Press.

———. 1995. "Reflections on the Politics of Gender in Muslim Societies: From Nairobi to Beijing." In *Faith and Freedom: Women's Human Rights in the Muslim World*, ed. Mahnaz Afkhami, 19–32. Syracuse, NY: Syracuse University Press.

Kapteijns, Lidwien. 1995. "Gender Relations and the Transformation of the Northern Somali Pastoral Tradition." *International Journal of African Historical Studies* 28(2):241–59.

Kapteijns, Lidwien, and Maryan Omar Ali. 1999. *Women's Voices in a Man's World: Women and Pastoral Tradition in Northern Somali Orature, c. 1899–1980*. Portsmouth, NH: Heinemann.

Karmi, Ghada. 1996. "Women, Islam and Patriarchalism." In *Feminism and Islam: Legal and Literary Perspectives*, ed. Mai Yamani, 69–85. New York: New York University Press.

Keddie, Nikki. 1991. "Introduction." In *Women in Middle Eastern History: Shifting Boundaries in Sex and Gender*, ed. Nikki Keddie and Beth Baron, 1–22. New Haven, CT: Yale University Press.

Lentin, Ronit, ed. 1997. *Gender and Catastrophe*. London: Zed.

McGown, Rima Berns. 1999. *Muslims in the Diaspora: The Somali Communities of London and Toronto*. Toronto: University of Toronto Press.

Mernissi, Fatima. 1988. *Doing Daily Battle: Interviews with Moroccan Women*. Trans. Mary Jo Lakeland. London: Women's Press.

———. 1995. "Arab Women's Rights and the Muslim State in the Twentieth

Century: Reflections on Islam as Religion and State." In *Faith and Freedom: Women's Human Rights in the Muslim World*, ed. Mahnaz Afkhami, 33–50. Syracuse, NY: Syracuse University Press.

———. 1996. *Women's Rebellion and Islamic Memory.* London: Zed.

Moghadam, Valentine M. 1992. "Patriarchy and the Politics of Gender in Modernising Societies: Iran, Pakistan and Afghanistan." *International Sociology* 7(1): 35–53.

Moghissi, Haideh. 2000. *Feminism and Islamic Fundamentalism: The Limits of Postmodern Analysis.* London: Zed.

Moser, Caroline O. N., and Fiona Clark, eds. 2001. "Introduction." In their *Victims, Perpetrators or Actors? Gender, Armed Conflict and Political Violence*, 3–12. London: Zed.

Niarchos, Catherine N. 1995. "Women, War, and Rape: Challenges Facing the International Tribunal for the Former Yugoslavia." *Human Rights Quarterly* 17(4):649–90.

Rezig, Inger. 1983. "Women's Roles in Contemporary Algeria: Tradition and Modernism." In *Women in Islamic Societies: Social Attitudes and Historical Perspectives*, ed. Bo Utas, 192–210. London: Curzon.

Samatar, Abdi Ismail. 2000. "Social Transformation and Islamic Reinterpretation in Northern Somalia: The Women's Mosque in Gabilay." *Arab World Geographer* 3(1):22–39.

Samatar, Ahmed I., ed. 1994. *The Somali Challenge: From Catastrophe to Renewal?* Boulder, CO: Rienner.

Thomas, William I., and Dorothy Swaine Thomas. 1929. *The Child in America: Behavior Problems and Programs.* 2nd ed. New York: Knopf.

Save the Children UK. 2006. "From Camp to Community: Liberia Study on Exploitation of Children." Discussion paper. http://www.savethechildren.org.uk/scuk_cache/scuk/cache/cmsattach/4040_libdp.pdf.

UNDP (United Nations Development Program). 2001. "Human Development Report for Somalia: 2001." New York: UNDP.

UNHCR (United Nations High Commissioner for Refugees). 2003. *Camp Brief* 1, no. 1. Dadaab: UNHCR.

UNICEF (United Nations Children's Fund). 2002. *Survey of Primary Schools in Somalia, 2001/2.* Technical Report, vol. 1. UNICEF Somalia Support Center.

Wali, Sima. 1995. "Muslim Refugee, Returnee, and Displaced Women: Challenges and Dilemmas." In *Faith and Freedom: Women's Human Rights in the Muslim World*, ed. Mahnaz Afkhami, 175–183. Syracuse, NY: Syracuse University Press.

Westerlund, David, and Ingvar Svanberg, eds. 1999. *Islam Outside the Arab World.* New York: St. Martin's.

WorldNetDaily. 2004. "The New World Disorder: U.N. 'Peacekeepers' Rape Women, Children." December 24. http://www.worldnetdaily.com/news/article.asp?ARTICLE_ID=42088.

Yuval-Davis, Nira. 1997. *Gender and Nation.* London: Sage.

Part IV. War and Terror: Raced-Gendered Logics and Effects

Militarism and Motherhood: The Women of the Lashkar-i-Tayyabia in Pakistan

> My honorable sisters, you have sacrificed a lot. You have sacrificed your
> sons for the sake of the *deen* [faith], and indeed your sacrifices are the
> most significant for our times. God needs even greater sacrifices. Get
> ready: prepare this generation. I remember the mother I met in a village
> when I went to lead the funeral prayer for her martyred son. After the
> funeral I went to give comfort to the grieving mother, but that elderly
> woman said to me, "My son became a martyr. I have a younger son who
> looks like my martyred son. I want the younger one to follow the same
> path and become a martyr. I am a poor widow; I have done hard labor
> to bring these sons up. Now I have heard the call of jihad. I have no
> money to give, but I have this treasure, these sons. Take my second son,
> and when he is martyred I will have the third one ready." Muslim sisters,
> you have the greater responsibility in the mission of jihad; men give
> money, but you give your sons. Your sacrifice, your hard work, is what
> keeps the jihad going.
> —Hafiz Saeed 2002, 3

These words are part of a longer message by Hafiz Muhammad Saeed
that was played to thousands of men and women at the annual convention of the Lashkar-i-Tayyabia (LT), a Pakistani militant Islamist
group, in November 2002. Saeed himself could not attend the meeting
because he was under house arrest at the time. His message illustrates the
central role assigned to motherhood by this group: its cause must be a
just one if a poor widowed mother who relies on her sons as protectors
and breadwinners is willing to sacrifice these sons for the LT's mission in
the Indian-occupied part of Kashmir. The LT, acting as a proxy for the

I am deeply indebted to Mohsin Masood, Petra Kuppinger, and Ira Smolensky for their
constant encouragement and support. I am grateful as well to Monmouth College for the
faculty development funds to conduct the fieldwork for this article. My colleagues and
students at the Lahore University of Management Sciences provided wonderful hospitality
during my fieldwork. All translations from Urdu in this article are mine.

[*Signs: Journal of Women in Culture and Society* 2007, vol. 32, no. 4]

Pakistani state, carries out insurgency operations in Indian-held Kashmir. The LT recruits mostly poor young men in villages and small towns in Pakistan. Its mobilization of women for the struggle for an Islamic polity that ultimately will severely limit women's rights puts into sharp relief the tensions pointed out by feminist scholars between the imagining of a nation that gives women a central cultural mission, on the one hand, and the creation of a civic state that extends equal citizenship to women, on the other.

By focusing on the LT's mobilization of women, I want to examine the paradoxical relationship between women and contemporary religio-political movements that advocate the retraditionalization of women's role at the same time that they actively mobilize women in the public arena.[1] Since mobilizing mothers' passion and sentiments is a crucial part of the LT's attempt to forge jihadi sensibilities among its target population, I want to illustrate how the group tries to use mothers' grief to address the deficit it faces in winning popular support for its jihadi agenda. The print literature of the LT and published narratives of mothers of martyrs illustrate that the LT has been successful in mobilizing mothers. Yet my research among the LT women's wing in a lower-middle-class neighborhood in Lahore suggests that the majority of the mothers of martyrs are victims of a negligent Pakistani state, not Spartan mothers ready to sacrifice their sons for the mission of the *ummah* (political community; see Elshtain 1991).[2] Before discussing the LT's mobilization of jihadi women, I will provide a brief background of jihadi movements in Pakistan.

Historical background
The United States' support of Islamist movements to fight a jihad against

---

[1] I am using the term *religiopolitical* instead of the more commonly used term *fundamentalist* because the term *fundamentalist* is either used too broadly, including political and nonpolitical movements, or it is used too narrowly to denote extremism. See also Keddie (1999).

[2] During 2002–3 I conducted research in a women's wing of the LT. I attended the Qur'anic study groups, political discussion groups, and other activities such as the graduation ceremony for students of the madrassa (religious school) run out of a mosque controlled by the LT. I also accompanied Sakina, the local women's leader of the LT, as she made recruiting trips to households and attended the annual three-day convention in November 2002. For the last two years I have conducted structured interviews with the young men of Jaish-i-Muhammad, a rival jihadi group, visited households of some of the mothers of martyrs, and interviewed other mothers who resisted the recruitment of their sons into jihadi organizations. All personal names are pseudonyms.

the Soviet Union was one of the more ironic results of the Cold War. With the close cooperation of Inter Services Intelligence (ISI) in Pakistan and the financial and moral support of the Saudi monarchy, the U.S. Central Intelligence Agency channeled billions of dollars in aid for weapons, recruitment, and training of thousands of mujahideen (holy warriors) from across the Muslim world to fight the Soviets in Afghanistan, using Pakistan as a conduit (Rashid 2000; Coll 2004; Mamdani 2004).

The Afghan resistance against the Soviet invasion had a profound impact on neighboring Pakistan, which became the frontline state receiving millions of Afghan refugees, channeling billions of dollars in international aid to fight the Soviets, hosting thousands of foreign fighters, and monitoring dozens of training facilities for the fighters in Afghanistan, who were battling those they saw as godless communists. In Pakistan, Muhammad Zia Ul-Haq's military regime, which had overthrown the democratically elected government of Zulifkar Ali Bhutto in 1977, eagerly supported the mujahideen as a way both to earn Islamic credentials in order to legitimize its military rule and to become a close ally of the United States for the purposes of enhancing Pakistan's military and strategic power in the region.

The Pakistani military viewed the Afghan war as an opportunity to gain strategic depth in its ongoing struggle with India over the contested territory of Kashmir.[3] When the Soviets withdrew from Afghanistan, the ISI increasingly turned its attention toward channeling militant groups to fight in Kashmir. After fighting three wars with India, losing half of the country in 1971 (when East Pakistan became Bangladesh), and facing a stalemate in Kashmir, Pakistan used these groups as important weapons in fighting the Indian army and maintaining a resistance in Kashmir that was loyal to the Pakistani state.

Militant slogans in the form of graffiti, posters, and stickers with images of Kalashnikov rifles touting the fight for Kashmir first appeared in Pakistan in the early 1990s. By the mid-1990s there were several jihadi organizations recruiting volunteers to fight in Kashmir, and there was a growing

---

[3] On the eve of partition of the subcontinent, the Hindu ruler of the predominantly Muslim states of Jammu and Kashmir decided to join India, prompting an immediate challenge from the Pakistani government, which demanded a plebiscite to decide the fate of Kashmir. In 1948 India and Pakistan went to war over Kashmir. By the time a ceasefire was negotiated, India controlled two-thirds of Kashmir, and Pakistan one-third. This line of control (LOC) has held since then. Pakistan calls the area under its control *Azad* (independent) Kashmir and uses the term *Indian-occupied Kashmir* for the rest of the area. Incursions across the LOC by jihadi groups such as the LT have been a constant source of tension between India and Pakistan since the early 1990s.

presence of militant Islamist culture, as manifested in books, pamphlets, posters, and audio and video tapes. The LT became one of the largest groups fighting in India, particularly known for launching spectacular operations, such as the attack on the Indian parliament in New Delhi in December 2001.[4]

The LT is the military wing of the Markaz Da'wat wa'l Irshad, which was founded in 1986 by two professors, Hafiz Muhammad Saeed and Zafar Iqbal. After September 11, 2001, the group's name was changed to Jamaat-i-Dawa as a way to deal with restrictions imposed on militant organizations.[5] The Markaz/Jamaat-i-Dawa headquarters is located in Murdike, a town about thirty miles from Lahore, the second largest city in Pakistan. The group insists on purifying Islam by excising all extraneous influences of popular culture, and it also insists on strictly following the example of the early Muslim community of the prophet Muhammad and his companions (Sikand 2003). In the late 1980s and early 1990s the Markaz opened up hundreds of offices throughout Pakistan. It runs almost two hundred schools, several outpatient medical facilities, and other charity operations in poor urban neighborhoods and villages. It is within these neighborhoods and villages that the group also recruits young men for militant operations. The Markaz publishes newspapers and magazines, issues audio and video tapes, and until recently maintained an active presence on the Internet.

Jihad Inc. and the Lashkar-i-Tayyabia

Jihad, a charged term in Western debates and contexts, evokes an image of angry Muslims with raised fists and theological fury ready to take on the infidels because they are eager to enter paradise.[6] This perception is

---

[4] Steve Coll (2006) points out that the December 13 attack by the LT provoked what he terms the twenty-first century's first nuclear crisis because it led to the Indian government's resolution to retaliate by launching a conventional military operation in Pakistan. This created an unstable situation in which the use of nuclear weapons became a possibility.

[5] Under tremendous pressure from the United States, General Pervez Musharraf's government banned several militant organizations, including Markaz Da'wat wa'l Irshad. The group changed its name to Jamaat-i-Dawa, but everything else remained the same.

[6] The term *Jihad Inc.* was first used by Eqbal Ahmad (1998) to describe how jihad had become a well organized enterprise that offered opportunities for making money and advancing careers. Ahmad used this term in order to desacralize and thus delegitimize the claim of Islamists that they are fighting a holy war. The LT is a good example of Jihad Inc.; within a few years its founders were presiding over a growing industry in schools, hospitals, publishing, and training camps.

based on a false premise of a coherent and historically stable religious framework for fighting jihad. An examination of the genealogy of this concept in Muslim history and theology shows the primacy of politics in shaping what jihad meant in a particular epoch. Roxanne Euben (2002, 368) notes that "many references to jihad in the Qur'an and *Ahl-Hadith* . . . betray a marked ambivalence to violent struggle even in the path of God; jihad . . . appears less a fixed doctrine about warfare than a recurrent and flexible motif with multiple interpretive possibilities."

The LT is an example of a militarist organization attempting to forge jihadi sensibilities among a population that is not directly engaged in an ongoing national liberation struggle. In Chechnya, Palestine, and Iraq the civilian population is directly affected by war, but the conflict in Kashmir is peripheral for most Pakistanis. The LT recruits young men to fight the Indian army in Indian-controlled Kashmir, away from their own homes. The organization also works to produce jihadi culture and sensibilities among women. This is difficult for the LT because much of the population is rather indifferent to the struggle for Kashmir. The LT deploys several strategies to address this indifference. It focuses on charitable activities such as providing free education as a way to recruit poor young men who have no access to formal education, it attempts to create a jihadi culture by adopting various mannerisms of what it deems to be an authentic version of early Islam, and it actively mobilizes women and deploys familial sentiments, particularly the grief of mothers of martyrs, in order to impart emotional depth to its project.[7]

Engendering political Islam

The LT's mobilization of women needs to be viewed within the larger context of Islamist visions of a gendered and hierarchic Islamic polity.[8] Unlike other jihadi organizations, the LT has an active women's wing with its own publications, regular meetings, weekly *dars* (Qur'anic lessons), and girls' madrassas in villages and lower-class and lower-middle-

---

[7] I was able to collect information on about 250 young LT men who died fighting in Kashmir. The general profile that emerges is one of a young man of an average age of seventeen; a middle or youngest son who tended to have difficult relationships with his parents, siblings, and neighbors; someone who did not quite fit in and thus was a source of worry for his parents. With meager means at their disposal, most parents were not able to provide adequate alternatives for their sons, and many felt that by joining the LT their sons might finally find employment and direction in their lives.

[8] The term *Islamists* is used here to indicate followers of political Islam who aim to capture political power in order to establish an Islamic state.

class urban neighborhoods. The importance of an active women's wing becomes clear when one compares the LT with a rival jihadi organization, Jaish-i-Muhammad. All the jihadi groups that emerged in Pakistan in the early 1990s to fight the Indian army in Kashmir competed for government resources, public attention, and leadership of the jihadi movement. Jaish-i-Muhammad launched several military campaigns in Kashmir and was active in the sectarian conflict against the Shia in Pakistan. But as the climate changed for the jihadi groups after September 11, 2001, Jaish-i-Muhammad was eclipsed by the LT, which survived and even thrived because of its better organization. Indeed, the U.S. invasions of Afghanistan and Iraq gave renewed energy to the LT's self-proclaimed mission of fighting Zionists and crusaders.

In addition, the mobilization of women has given the LT advantages over other jihadi groups.[9] Social connections and emotional ties are important factors in its continued strength. Women, particularly mothers and sometimes sisters, have often strongly resisted the recruitment of their sons and brothers into jihadi organizations. During my interviews with young jihadi men belonging to Jaish-i-Muhammad, they often complained that their women did not understand the mission of jihad.[10] The LT's attempt to actively mobilize women is meant to counter this resistance and to create stronger social ties among its members. I know of two instances in which marriages were arranged to strengthen the bonds among the jihadi families. Moreover, as I will discuss below, the frequent evocation of mothers' grief is used to provide emotional depth to the LT's jihadi mission.

Islamists are generally viewed as proscribing political roles for women in an Islamic polity. This is a misreading of the Islamist political project. The Muslim *ummah* imagined by the Islamists gives women a vital role in formulating the Muslim polity precisely because they are to remove themselves willingly from the public arena in order to reassert and validate the difference between a Muslim and non-Muslim polity. The most influential formulation of this gendered Islamic polity was presented by

---

[9] The *New York Times* points out that part of the credit for the surprising victory of Hamas in the 2006 elections in the West Bank and Gaza goes to its mobilization of women: "Hamas used its women to win, sending them door to door with voter lists and to polling places for last-minute campaigning" (Fisher 2006, A1).

[10] I interviewed twenty young men who had connections with Jaish-i-Muhammad; most of them had received training, and five of them had fought in Kashmir. The interviews were conducted in December 2002 and January 2003. Most of the interviews took place in two villages near Sargodha, Pakistan.

Sayyid Abul Ala Maududi (1903–79) and Jamaat-i-Islami, the religio-political movement he founded in South Asia.

The framework for an Islamic polity offered by thinkers such as Maududi is an important precursor to the LT's formulation of a jihadi transnational Islamic community. In his work *Purdah and the Status of Women*, first published in 1938 and in print ever since, with translations in several languages, Maududi ([1938] 2003) notes that there is a fundamental difference in the nature of men and women. Any attempt at creating a just social and political system, he argues, must take these differences into account. He credits the rise of civilization to the proper recognition of natural gender difference and predicts the fall of civilization if gender differences are ignored.[11] He bases his argument on Islamic texts and traditions but also relies heavily on Western sexist biological and psychological literature of the 1920s and 1930s. Quoting such studies, Maududi concludes that women's monthly hormonal and physiological changes and frequent pregnancies put women in a biological and psychological state that does not allow them to consistently perform tasks such as driving, typing, or practicing law or dentistry. Maududi notes that "women will always be inferior to men in performing these tasks. No matter how hard you try you will not be able to create an Aristotle, Avicenna, Kant, Hegel, Shakespeare, Alexander, or a Napoleon among the ranks of women, and no matter how hard they try men can not bear children" ([1938] 2003, 166). Thus one of the main functions of an Islamic polity is to create a just social order by institutionalizing these gender differences. Muslim women are assigned the specific role of forging righteous Muslim male citizens while themselves remaining in the confines of chador and *chardevari* (veil and home).

The biologically deterministic framework enunciated by Maududi in *Purdah and the Status of Women* continues to frame Islamist views about gender. Yet there has also been an important evolution in Islamist practices. Women of Jamaat-i-Islami have become physicians, teachers, politicians, and parliamentarians. Over the years political expediency forced the Islamists to make compromises with regard to women's role in public life for tactical political advantage. The story of *mader-i-millat* (mother of the nation) Fatima Jinnah's candidacy in the 1964 elections in Pakistan illustrates such compromises. Jinnah was the unmarried sister and constant

---

[11] It is important to note here that Maududi's articulation of tradition is itself greatly shaped by Western discourse on gender. The insistence on the absolute sexual division of labor premised on natural or biological differences is a Western concept enthusiastically embraced by thinkers like Maududi.

companion of Muhammad Ali Jinnah, the leader credited with successfully heading a movement to create the separate homeland of Pakistan for Muslims in South Asia. The Combined Opposition Parties (COP) chose Jinnah as their candidate to challenge General Ayub Khan, a secular modernizer. Khan had earlier berated the *ulama* for their regressive attitudes in opposing his women-friendly reforms of Muslim family law. However, confronted with the candidacy of Jinnah, Khan was quick to extract a fatwa from a group of compliant *ulama* declaring that Muslim women were not allowed to run for the top political office and that Jinnah's candidacy was therefore un-Islamic. For Jamaat-i-Islami, as part of the COP, to have a woman such as Jinnah run for the position of head of state was problematic. Jinnah's unveiled body exemplified everything Jamaat-i-Islami found wrong with Westernized Muslim women. Furthermore, the organization had been opposed to giving women the right to vote until 1963.

Supporting Jinnah may have been problematic, but according to Maududi it was a necessary step in order to oust a corrupt general. Herein lies one of the ironies of women and political Islam: the Islamist movements have come to appropriate selective aspects of the democratic process, in this case mobilizing women as a pressure group, to counter what they see as a misguided agenda of Westernized Muslim women and to gain a voting constituency. Political expediency, however, has often led progressive Muslim regimes to backtrack on their attempts at providing greater opportunities and legal protections for women.

The pragmatic need to mobilize women into the public sphere while holding firmly to the ideology that home is the only rightful place for women also shapes the LT's agenda. For the LT the covered female body embodies a culture, a value system, and a politics that constitute the ideal Islamic political community. The group takes Maududi's political framework as foundational and adds to it a militaristic element, thereby making the gun and purdah (literally, a curtain or a screen) two central markers of its Islamic polity. Strict purdah is required of LT women. Their black burkas, gloves, and socks, worn even during the hot summer months, constitute a uniform that marks them as different from others. On the one hand, then, the LT shares Maududi's conviction that women's proper place is in the private realm. But, on the other hand, the LT brings women out of their homes to mobilize other women and to participate in political events, such as the group's annual convention. Although the women are not given military training, many of the women leaders are taken to the training camp to witness the training of young men. The women's magazine *Tayyabiat* often prints letters and short stories by young women who are yearning to take part in active jihad but are told that their jihad is on the home front. At the same time, the LT leaves open the possibility that women may take part in active fighting and suicide missions if that becomes necessary for the survival of the *ummah*.

Given the close association between Muslim women and the veil in the Western imagination, it is important to note that "the vast majority of Muslim women have never veiled or been excluded from appearing in public" (Cole 2003, 774). There was plenty of eye rolling and a number of derogatory comments made by women of the lower-middle-class neighborhood in Lahore about the LT women's radical veiling.[12] Contrary to the LT's claims, it is not reviving an Islamic tradition by making the women wear black burkas, but instead it is inventing a tradition to signify the emergence of a jihadi Islamic *ummah*.

In the weekly training sessions and in the LT literature, Pakistani Muslim women are often scolded for paying too much attention to their mundane chores of housekeeping and not understanding the political peril faced by the Muslim *ummah*. As one of the LT women leaders stated to the weekly gathering of women, "You Muslim women do not have your priorities straight. The Christian women are serving their religion by flying planes in Iraq, the Hindu women are serving their *bagwan* by bombing in Kashmir, and you Muslim women do not even know what is going on outside of your *char-devari* [four walls of the home]."[13] At other points the deficiencies of non-Muslim women are contrasted with the strengths of Muslim women to illustrate that Muslim women are particularly suited to serve their nation. Umm Hammad (2003a, 12) writes that, "according to a news item, American women who are enlisted in the army are experiencing depression and loneliness and are also sexually harassed by men soldiers. Dear readers, you can see what happens to 'liberated' women who work alongside men." She continues to note that starting with Hazarat Kadhija, the wife of the prophet Muhammad, women have played a central role in the growth of the Muslim *ummah*. Her article discusses examples of early Muslim women in battlefields, contrasting them to the role of non-Muslim women who used music and sexual charms to distract the soldiers. She further examines modern politics in which non-Muslim women leaders such as Indira Gandhi and Golda Meir served their nations and reminds her readers that they did this mostly by oppressing Muslims.

---

[12] I heard these comments during my fieldwork in 2002–3.

[13] The following section is based on my observations of weekly meetings of LT women between September 2002 and June 2003 in Lahore, Pakistan, as well as my reading of the LT literature.

Umm Hammad concludes that the Christian West used the misleading language of women's liberation to destroy the Muslim family. She insists that the hope of the Muslim *ummah* rests with a global jihad movement: "The mother of Kashmir, daughter of Palestine, sister of Afghanistan, women of Chechnya and Kosovo have all become one. The color of Muslim blood has become one. Their goal has become one, which is to overthrow those who enslave them. A sixteen-year-old veiled Chechen young woman, an Eve for our times, destroyed the Russian ammunition depot via a martyr operation. A few weeks later a young Palestinian woman, a university student, gave an answer to the barbarism of Jewish soldiers by launching a martyrdom operation against them and thus renewing the memories of pioneer women of early Islam (Umm Hammad 2003a, 14).

The LT aims to produce Muslim women subjects who shun paid employment because it goes against their natural religious duty and because it has only brought divorce, sexual harassment, and single motherhood to the rest of the world's women. This ideal Muslim woman avoids birth control, which is perceived as part of a Western conspiracy to sap the numerical strength of the Muslim *ummah*. She learns to control her jealously and accepts a second or third marriage of her husband because that is the Islamic way and also because the sisters and widows of martyrs need spouses. She urges her husbands, sons, brothers, and fathers to avoid banking or any financial dealings that rely on interest. She does not allow music, television, VCRs, the taking of photographs, or any un-Islamic ritual celebrations. She does not allow Western fast food or soft drinks in her household lest she unwittingly contribute to the profits of the Jewish and Christian capitalists who in turn use this profit to carry on a worldwide crusade against Muslims. She keeps herself informed about political affairs, and she stays ever vigilant against attempts to take away her identity as a Muslim through the seductive traps of fashion, consumerism, or hunger for status. But the central duty of the Muslim woman is to become a daughter, a sister, and most important, a mother of a mujahid, praying for his martyrdom for the cause of the Islamic *ummah*.[14]

The Muslim female subject produced by the LT bears a strong resemblance to female ideals favored by movements of the extremist religious right as disparate as the Rashtriya Swayamsevak Sangh in India or Gush Emumim in Israel (Basu 1998; Keddie 1999). The rest of society may be confused by talk of diversity or tolerance, but women of the religious

---

[14] This information is based on the LT's printed literature and the weekly *dars* meetings for women that I attended.

right—Christian, Muslim, Jewish, or Hindu—understand the enemy and are ready to make any sacrifice necessary to confront the enemy. The women of the extremist religious right also understand that the home front is a crucial battleground. Only by staying true to the traditional ideals of womanhood in their respective traditions can they become effective soldiers for their community. Most important, women of the religious right understand that despite all the chatter about women's liberation, it is their respective traditions that protect and honor them as women.

Women of the religious right present a dilemma to feminist scholars. The patriarchal ideologies of religious movements often demonize feminists as responsible for the many woes of women and thus are understandably anathema to feminist scholars (Basu 1998; Keddie 1999; Moghadam 2001). But it is also clear that religious movements provide opportunities for women to participate in political processes. Islamist movements in particular enable middle- to lower-middle-class women from traditional families to become politically active and even pursue a career since their purdah and affiliation with the Islamists make their lives in public more acceptable to their families. The religious right in Pakistan also illustrates the importance of making distinctions between moderate political movements and more extremist militarist movements when it comes to the kinds of opportunities created for women. Jamaat-i-Islami has had an organized women's wing since its inception in 1941, affording women the chance to participate in the political process, albeit on separate and unequal terms. This includes serving in national and provincial assemblies on seats reserved for women. The LT, however, uses its print literature and a handful of women leaders to expose millions of Pakistani women to its propaganda. Thus women serve more as props or a supporting chorus for the LT's mission rather than as active participants.

Enacting a jihadi counterpublic: The 2002 annual convention at Patoki
The LT's mobilization of women illustrates the shifting and contingent nature of the boundary between private and public and Ruth Lister's point that "the public and private define each other and take meaning from each other" (1997, 42). The LT aims to reshape the private sphere of women to facilitate a new jihadi public. Thus it is women's duty to cleanse the home of all corrupting influences, keep themselves informed of the political struggle between Muslims and the West, actively propagate the jihadi message to other households in their neighborhood, and observe strict purdah so as to become walking billboards for a jihadi mission. As I discuss below, this reshaping also involves reaching into the most intimate

sphere of motherly love: mining private sentiments to produce a jihadi public.

On a hot day in November 2002, I rode a bus with Sakina and other women to Patoki, a town about fifty miles from Lahore, where the annual LT convention took place. For the last several years the LT had been holding its convention at its central headquarters in the suburbs of Lahore. However, in 2000 and 2001 the group was denied permission for the convention until the very last moment, and it was not clear whether it would be able to hold the 2002 convention there. The government issued permission for this convention, but, instead of the Muridke headquarters, the LT was assigned Patoki, a small town further away from Lahore, as a meeting location.

We arrived in Patoki late in the evening; dozens of buses were already parked there. Young men attempted to direct traffic and guide waves of participants toward the dirt path leading to the campsite where the convention was already in full swing. They were holding rifles and wearing uniforms that seemed reminiscent of second-rate Hollywood movies depicting so-called Islamic terrorists: longish camouflage shirts, seemingly inspired by both the Pakistani *kameez* (long overshirts) and the Soviet Red Army coat over short white *shalwars* (baggy cotton pants). Some young men were guarding the low-lying hills as others trotted around on white horses, attempting to convey the ambience of an early Islamic community. As we descended from our bus, several men rushed us to the side of the road where other women and children were waiting. There was pronounced anxiety among the men, who hurried to hail vans that would take us to the campsite instead of us having to walk the mile-and-a-half distance. They were worried that it was getting dark and thought that women should not be walking in the dark even if there were several dozens of us amid so much protection. We finally boarded a van that dropped us in front of a huge tent at the entrance to the women's section. The tent was crowded with women and children of all ages, and more kept coming. There were signs and slogans posted all over, including the following: "The infidels want to conquer Islam by conquering your mind and body, so protect your honor"; "Satan loves a house with TV"; "Every rupee you spend on drinking Coke and Pepsi goes toward war against Islam."

Microphones were blasting the speeches by the all-male LT leadership to the women's camp. There were no microphones in the women's area to address or respond to the men; the women were there only to listen. Young women in green uniforms were performing security duties with obvious pride. Their uniforms were less elaborate than the men's. They were inspired by Pakistani women's *shalwar-kameez* combined with Girl Scouts' shoulder sashes. The uniforms of these young women made them stand out among the thousands of women gathered for the convention. Pointing to the women guards, Sakina noted that "they go through special training." They searched the women and their bags—a search as thorough as any I saw on airports in the aftermath of the September 11, 2001, attacks in the United States. They searched bags, bundles of sleeping gear, and foodstuffs. They performed complete body searches. Some had whispered that Indian government agents might infiltrate the convention. Such rumors helped create an ambience of threat and established symbolic boundaries of the jihadi community.

Lashkar-i-Tayyabia workers had spent days preparing the site, making a camp city out in the wilderness. An important element of these preparations was to provide a separate space for women. It would have been easier for the LT not to bring women and children, since their accommodation required considerable resources. The fact that the LT felt the need to have women present illustrates the central role of women in the enactment of a counterpublic. This construction of the jihadi political community included lines between the public and private and the strict spatial segregation of genders. Yet the segregated female realm remained highly political. Like the men, women LT workers were collecting funds for the families of the martyred, organizing meetings of various regional branches, and performing security duties. The postconvention press coverage by LT publications took great pride in the fact that by providing a safe and segregated space for women the LT had demonstrated its capacity to defend all Muslim women.

However, an examination of the women's section during the three-day convention suggests the limitations of the LT's project to forge jihadi sensibilities among the female participants. As the male leaders made powerful speeches against misguided Muslim rulers, Jews, and so-called crusaders, most of the women in the tents socialized with one another, waited in long lines to get food, attempted to get free medical care for their sick children, and jockeyed to get the attention of the key women leaders to plead for help in the upcoming marriages of their daughters or for jobs for their unemployed sons. For many of the elderly women, this was their opportunity to participate in a religious gathering. One woman explained to me, "we cannot afford to go for pilgrimage to Mecca, so this is our chance to participate in a religious congregation and worship." Many of the nearly fifty thousand women gathered at Patoki had come because of the free transportation. For them this was their only chance to get away for a few days from the daily grind of backbreaking labor. The organizers' pleas to the participants to be respectful and listen to the leaders' speeches were largely ignored. Yet the participants did pay attention to the narratives of the mothers of the martyrs.

Narrating the jihadi *ummah*: Mothers of the martyrs speak

Testimonials by parents of the recently killed are regular features at annual LT conventions and at regional as well as local meetings. Fathers' accounts are played on loudspeakers. The mothers' stories, however, are told in smaller face-to-face meetings, since the LT observes the purdah of the voice, which mandates that women's voices cannot be heard in public. It is mothers' grief and celebration that animates the mission of mobilization and recruitment of young boys by the LT. The mothers' remembrances of their recently martyred sons are given prominent places in all LT magazines. The last will and testament sent by the martyred almost always addresses mothers, requesting that mothers celebrate rather than weep upon hearing the news of the martyrdom.

On the second day of the convention Sakina took me to a tent where mothers of recent martyrs told their stories. About a dozen women sat in a circle, and two mothers were the center of their attention. One narrated the story of her sons' martyrdom by relating the dream she had a few hours before she received the news. It was an elaborate story complete with winged horses, beautiful *houris* (virgins in paradise), and huge red roses. Yet the crowd seemed bored. The story had obviously been told many times. The narrative sounded familiar; indeed it followed too closely the typical official plot of the narratives of martyrs' mothers. The audience, however, was intrigued by the second mother. She shed silent tears and had a hard time speaking despite gentle nudges from those next to her. "This sister lived in London for a long time and worked in a bank; can you believe that?" Sakina noted. It was hard to imagine this woman in her fifties, wrapped in the black burka, as a former London bank employee. "He was a typical teenager growing up in London," the mother finally began the story, after gentle assurances by others that her son was watching her from the heavens. "He liked rock music and new clothes. When he turned seventeen, I started noticing changes in his temperament. He became quieter. He started to grow a beard and to talk about the atrocities against Muslims in Kashmir. He told me, 'Mom, I cannot sleep at night thinking about my Muslim sisters being raped by the Hindu soldiers.' Then he started talking about jihad. He asked for our permission. I told him as a mother I just cannot find it in my heart to let you do this."[15]

She continued that her son eventually disappeared, and after several days of desperate search the family found out that he had gone for training to fight. She talked about her sleepless nights, her journey to Pakistan to convince him to come back, and finally the news of his death. She was struggling to make sense of his death. She had given up her life in London and had come to this convention in hope of finding peace. She now worried about her older son who, after the death of his brother, wanted to fight. "You could be lucky and become the mother of two martyred sons," a younger woman proclaimed enthusiastically. That was too much even for the hardened jihadi women, and they gave her scolding looks. One woman said that she hoped the mother's older son would return a *ghazi* (living warrior), because he was now her only son.

The strength of maternal grief

"How can suffering be made effectively political?" asks Sara Ruddick as she points out that though the figure of *mater dolorosa* (the mother of sorrows) may be the most deeply rooted within war stories, "displays of suffering are notoriously unpredictable in their effects" (Ruddick 1989, 216). Madeleine Vernet, a French feminist socialist, envisioned mothers' grief as mobilizing women to demand peace after the slaughter of the First World War (Siegel 1999). The staggering strength of maternal grief, Vernet argues, "could—indeed, must—be converted into a powerful force for peace" (Siegel 1999, 421). Unfortunately, with a few exceptions the figure of *mater dolorosa* has served to fan the flames of war rather than become a force for peace. All too frequently motherhood is enlisted to carry forward military objectives. The image of motherhood comes to stand for the protection of the nation and the home front.[16]

In a comparative study of the use of maternal imagery in organizations in the United States and Nicaragua, Lorraine Bayard de Volo points out that American mothers were encouraged to send their sons to fight with "a smile on their lips and a prayer in their hearts" and to receive the news of the death of their sons with silent "solemn pride" softened with "cherished memories" (de Volo 1998, 243–44). The Sandinista government

[15] This is a quotation from a martyr's mother who spoke in Patoki during the 2002 annual convention for LT women.

[16] See Elshtain 1991; Cooke and Woollacott 1993; Zeiger 1996; de Volo 1998.

in Nicaragua actively supported the Mothers of Heroes and Martyrs, an organization that represented the mothers of those killed or captured in the revolution or Contra war. The organization urged mothers not to let their selfish love stand in the way of the drafting of their children. Members of the organization were sent to deliver the news of wartime death so that their moral authority could be used to manage the grief of mothers who might blame the government for the deaths of their children. De Volo concludes that "the Mothers of Heroes and Martyrs were an effective conduit through which to construct and disseminate the meaning of death in war in a manner conducive to Sandinista victory" (de Volo 1998, 251).

Similarly, the LT expends great effort to politicize and utilize the suffering of the mothers of those killed in Kashmir. A three-volume collection titled *We Are the Mothers of Lashkar-i-Tayyabia* provides accounts of 184 men killed in action in Kashmir (Umm Hammad 2003b). The title of the collection is somewhat misleading, as not all narratives are first-person accounts by mothers. Umm Hammad, the editor of the volumes, also edits the magazine *Tayyabiat* and is a top LT woman leader. She starts each account by giving the names, places of residence, and family backgrounds of the young men. As editor, Umm Hammad often provides information on what attracted the young man to the jihadi mission of the LT. Often, though, the accounts change from the editor's voice into that of a mother describing the characteristics of her son. The accounts also include stories by other family members, including fathers, brothers, and sisters, who share their memories. There is a pragmatic reason for this focus on mothers. The LT literature frequently repeats, "it is not easy for mothers to sacrifice their sons; therefore the mothers must be educated on the blessings of jihad so that they willingly give permission to their sons" (Saeed 2002, 2). But the LT's focus on mothers goes beyond pragmatics to the requirements of nation making: the mothers speak the language of the global *ummah*. In an editorial warning against negotiating with the Indian government over Kashmir, Saeed writes, "What is more precious to mothers than their sons? But they are willingly sacrificing them for the cause" (3). If these mothers are indeed willingly sacrificing their sons, then the cause of jihad must be just.

The narratives of the mothers of martyrs exemplify the process whereby individual biographies become social texts meant to produce an inspirational narrative for the jihadi community (Das 1998, 128–38). The LT utilizes mothers' grief in order to awaken the *ummah* to the mission of jihad, as the following couplet indicates: "Every mother's heart is wounded, but every mother's lips make this plea / let the tree of my heart be sliced so that the garden of Islam stays green" (Umm Hammad 2003b,

162). For the LT to employ mothers' grief as a political tool, there must be a delicate balance between authentic personal grief and genuine celebration, as the same mothers narrate the Muslim jihadi *ummah*. The mothers must provide the emotional lifeblood for the movement by grieving their unspeakable loss but must also prepare other mothers for such sacrifices by comporting themselves properly. Narratives thus have the pedagogic function of teaching the proper etiquette when one receives the news of a son's martyrdom. The ideal grieving mother is shedding silent tears as she speaks of her son's fine achievements: eternal life for him and the Islamic *ummah*. The official narrative has the mothers assenting to the official plotline: they prayed for the martyrdom of their sons, and upon receiving the news of martyrdom, these mothers fed the bearer of the news, other LT mujahideen, milk and dates, as proper etiquette requires. They bravely asked the question: Where was he hit? And the answer invariably was that he took the bullets in his chest and that he had killed several Hindu infidels before he died.

One of the more effective strategies used by the LT for recruitment is to elaborate on the theme of the imminence of sudden and meaningless death with the promise instead of a meaningful death and eternal afterlife for martyrs. In response to Ruddick's (1989) identification of holding (on, close, dear) as an essential element of maternal thinking, Nancy Scheper-Hughes reminds us that "maternal thinking under conditions of scarcity, political disruption, and violence can instead be guided more by the metaphysical stance of 'letting go'" (1998, 229). She reports that in her research in Brazil the frequent experience of child death in impoverished shantytowns "shapes maternal thinking in a way that extinguishes maternal grief over premature death. Instead it summons another dimension of maternal thinking—one more congenial to military thinking: the notion of inevitable, acceptable, and meaningful death" (229). Mothers remain silent because to show even the slightest doubt is to render the deaths of their sons meaningless.

Sisters, daughters, and mothers: The language of kinship and forging jihadi sensibilities

The alleged rapes of Muslim women in Kashmir and other zones of conflict in the Muslim world (e.g., Gujarat, Palestine, Bosnia, and Kosovo) and the need to exact revenge and protect the honor of sisters and daughters is a persistent theme in LT literature. The language of kinship is invoked to create a sense of solidarity "so that the individual experience of having been violated can be seen as the experience of the whole community"

(Das 1998, 131). Rape has a particular resonance in this context, given the critical role of abduction and sexual violence in the partition of the Indian subcontinent. Young men are urged to sacrifice their lives to protect the honor of their Muslim sisters, making up for the time during the partition and the formation of Pakistan when sufficient protection was not provided to Muslim women. These young men are demonstrating their greater courage and resolve compared with the earlier generation of Muslim men and are sending a signal to the enemy that the violation of Muslim women will not be tolerated.

Veena Das (1998, 56) points out that during the partition of the Indian subcontinent women's bodies "became a sign through which men communicated with each other. The lives of women were framed by the notion that they were to bear permanent witness to the violence of Partition. Thus, the political programme of creating the two nations of India and Pakistan was inscribed upon the bodies of the women." In contemporary jihadi discourse women's bodies are the site of communication with the other in two ways. The veiled body of the Muslim woman is a signal to the rest of the world of the purity of the revitalized Muslim *ummah*. The violated body of the raped Muslim woman turns into a call to action for young Muslim men. This twin theme is illustrated on the February 2003 cover of the Lashkar women's magazine, *Tayyabiat*, which shows a world atlas draped by a chador, with the headline "From Afghanistan to Kashmir, Chechnya, and Europe, Victory of Burka, Congratulations to the Honorable Mothers and Sisters of the Muslim *Ummah*." A sidebar on the cover includes the title of another story, "The Subjugated Sister from Gujarat Cries Out for Your Help." The lead article of this issue chides U.S. President George Bush and British Prime Minister Tony Blair for thinking they were liberating Afghan women from their burkas only to find out that, despite the military occupation and all the talk about the liberation of Afghan women, many of the latter kept their burkas and indeed actively resisted the occupation. The author reports the chagrin of the Western media that Afghan women are still wearing their burkas. She implies that the Taliban might have experienced defeat but the resolve of the Afghani women shows the long-term triumph of the revived Muslim *ummah* (Umm Hammad 2003a, 12). In another article Umm Hammad tells a revealing story about her son, who was fighting in Kashmir. Her son states:

> I was badly injured in one of the military operations and took refuge in a Kashmiri household. I phoned my host family who sent their daughter, my host sister, to bring me back to the safe house. My

sister, who wears a burqa herself, brought one for me to wear. She told me that Hindu soldiers were searching every hundred meters. I was bleeding badly and in a semiconscious state. I lay down in the back seat. She sat in the front seat and instructed me to keep my pistol handy, and if we were stopped by the soldiers I was to shoot her. We were able to make it to the safe house, but I never forgot the sincerity, honor, and faith of that sister. (Umm Hammad 2001, 3)

I want to draw attention to two points in this story. First, wearing the burka for a man is generally considered a grave insult to his masculinity, but in this emergency he could wear the burka as long as he was holding the pistol—although logic would dictate that given his semiconscious state it would have been more effective for his host sister in the front seat to hold the pistol. Like other stories told in jihadi literature, such accounts are less factual reports and more pedagogical narratives meant to reinforce certain key themes. The second point I want to highlight is the sister's instruction that she should be shot if they were stopped. Accepting death rather than being raped is a key theme in the discourse on women's honor in South Asia.[17] Das notes what family narratives about rape and violence during the partition demonstrate: "By choosing violent death for themselves rather than submitting to sexual violence by men of other communities, women are enshrined in these narratives as saviors of family honour" (1998, 63).

Umm Hammad: A Spartan mother

Spartan women shook off expression of sympathy in words that bespeak an unshakable civic identity. Plutarch recounts a woman, as she buried her son, telling a would-be sympathizer that she had had "good luck," not bad: "I bore him that he might die for Sparta, and this is the very thing that has come to pass for me."
—Elshtain 1991, 547

Sakina had invited me for a Friday *dars* to be delivered by a very important person. When I arrived at the girls' madrassa on the second floor of a

[17] In January 2006, on one of the Pakistani television programs broadcast on Geo network, "Ask an Alim" (Islamic expert), a caller asked if a woman who chooses to kill herself rather than be sexually violated would have the status of a martyr because she chose death to protect her honor. It was reassuring for me to see that the Alim was flummoxed by the question, and the host decided to take a commercial break rather than answer the question.

small mosque, the place was overflowing with women from the neighborhood. The event was a graduation ceremony for a dozen young students who had earned their diplomas. The very important person turned out to be Umm Hammad. She was wearing a black head-to-toe burka and dark glasses that she did not remove during the ceremony. She appeared a stern figure, looking straight ahead and not engaging in small talk. When she started speaking, her speech matched her grim persona. She scolded the all-female audience: "So many of you are too busy to attend meetings like this, when Christian and Jewish women are busy serving their religion." She continued with a thorough review of current affairs, reminding the audience that total cooperation with the West had not saved Saddam Hussein's Iraq and nor will it save President Musharraf's Pakistan. She noted that a woman (U.S. Secretary of State Condoleezza Rice) was telling President Bush how to destroy the Muslim world and directly accused the audience: "You Muslim women are so ignorant of what is going on outside of the four walls of your home. In Turkey and France they want to ban the scarf, like the scarf [as opposed to the burka] is anything but a fashion statement. Why do you think they are so worried about our veils? Because these veils are the protection of the Muslim *ummah*. If you do not follow the true sharia and veil, you are giving aid and comfort to the enemies of the Muslims."[18]

In this thirty-minute sermon she directly lectured this crowd of mostly struggling poor women, reprimanding in particular the mothers who dress their girls in Western clothing (there were several children in the crowd who were dressed this way). She thundered: "Don't you know that these young girls are like a blank slate and by dressing them up this way you are writing a script of shamelessness on their bodies?" The crowd listened raptly and was awed by Umm Hammad. "She had two sons martyred," several of them whispered to each other before she started to speak. The women were thoroughly impressed by her knowledge of Islam and world affairs.

Can mothers speak?

Who are these mothers of the martyrs valorized by the LT? Are they like the Spartan mothers willingly sacrificing their sons at the altar of the newly revitalized Muslim *ummah*, or are they victims of a militarized state that cynically deploys jihadi discourse as another form of blood tax, using their sons as cannon fodder? With a few important exceptions, a majority of

[18] Field notes, Lahore, April 28, 2003.

the mothers are victims in the sense that Jean-François Lyotard (1988, 8) identifies: "It is in the nature of a victim not to be able to prove that one has been done a wrong. A plaintiff is someone who has incurred damages and who disposes of the means to prove it. One becomes a victim if one loses these means." The means to show that they are victims or even that they are active agents in the making of the new Muslim *ummah* is lacking for an overwhelming majority of these mothers. Most of them cannot read or write, and thus what is written in the jihadi literature about the mothers is largely not written by the mothers themselves. The ability of jihadi movements to recruit the sons of these mothers with the promise of basic education, medical treatment, a meager stipend, and a glorious afterlife is predicated on the withdrawal of funding for public education by the Pakistani state, leaving the poor to scramble for any means at their disposal to find education for their children. Almost all the young men recruited for jihad face bleak economic circumstances. I illustrate these facts not to argue that economic deprivation is the main dynamic that underwrites jihad but instead to point out that we simply do not have adequate means to adjudicate the question of agency for their mothers. The LT leadership becomes the agent that mines the mothers' private grief to enact a public jihadi community.

"Why does Hafiz Saeed not send his own sons to fight jihad in Kashmir?" asked a mother whom I interviewed and who had successfully rescued her eldest, eighteen-year-old son from the LT's training camp.[19] A widow with several small children, she was worried that he would go back to the training camp and thus was planning a quick wedding for him as a strategy to keep him home. This woman was not alone in resisting the LT's jihadi mission for her son. I encountered several mothers who had used every resource in their power to dissuade their sons from joining LT training camps or similar organizations. The LT mission to create a renewed *ummah* is ultimately a failed project because the overwhelming majority of Pakistani society has not subscribed to its call. It survives because of the patronage of the state and because of its ability to promulgate a culture of jihad that ensnares vulnerable, impoverished youths. The use of the martyrs' mothers' sentiments is an attempt to create a polity that employs selected portions of Muslim history to form a decidedly modern dystopia of a questionable *ummah*. With a few exceptions, notably women such as Sakina or Umm Hammad, there is little evidence that Pakistani mothers are joining the LT's mission.

[19] Interview, Bibi Kurshid, Sargodha, Pakistan, December 20, 2002.

Conclusion: Mother, war, and peace

All too frequently, the staggering strength of mothers' grief is appropriated for making war instead of peace. The few cases where mothers' grief is used effectively to challenge violence offer important insights into the complex relationship between militarism and motherhood. The Madres (mothers) of the Plaza de Mayo in Argentina and the Mothers' Front in Sri Lanka are two examples of politically effective use of mothers' grief to challenge political violence, murder, and mysterious disappearances (Elshtain 1994; de Alwis 1998). In both cases mothers were protesting against their own government's brutality, and in both instances they were protesting disappearances with hopes that their sons or daughters might still be alive. Likewise, both groups employed traditional symbols of motherly grief. In Sri Lanka there were tears, wailing, and even cursing. In Argentina mothers were quietly but persistently marching with the portraits of their disappeared sons and daughters. In both cases the repressive regimes could not ignore or dismiss the mothers. As Jean Bethke Elshtain (1994, 90) notes, "the Mothers remained faithful to the dominant image of the mother of their society. Yet they politicized this tradition against a repressive state, both as a form of protection—the state should fulfill its rhetorical claims to defend motherhood—and as a newfound identity—mothers looking for their children, mothers for human rights." The political space for grieving mothers to challenge the state or to turn their grief into a plea for protection and human rights disappears quickly, however, if the nation is at war. A good example of this is the treatment meted out by the media to U.S. pacifist and grieving mother Cindy Sheehan as she attempted to use the loss of her son in the Iraq war to mobilize for peace (see Rich 2005).

In the current U.S. war against terrorism, President Bush used the liberation of Afghan women as one of the many reasons to overthrow the Taliban. Jihadis in Pakistan and elsewhere chide the Bush administration for believing it can liberate Muslim women from their religion, as they themselves use U.S. foreign policy as a lightning rod to recruit martyrs, sons of impoverished mothers, to continue eternal jihad. In conclusion I want the reader to ponder the following question: are jihadi mothers of the LT and the grieving mothers of Marines from the American heartland really as far apart as we are often led to believe? How do we begin to theorize about gender and militarism in a way that can find commonalities among mothers while avoiding the trap of mistaking our particular cultural contexts and desires for those of the global woman?

Department of Political Science
Monmouth College

References

Ahmad, Eqbal. 1998. "Jihad International, Inc." *Dawn*, February 4, 9–10.

Basu, Amrita. 1998. "Hindu Women's Activism in India and the Questions It Raises." In *Appropriating Gender: Women's Activism and Politicized Religion in South Asia*, ed. Patricia Jeffery and Amrita Basu, 167–84. New York: Routledge.

Cole, Juan. R. I. 2003. "The Taliban, Women, and the Hegelian Private Sphere." *Social Research: An International Quarterly of Social Sciences* 70(3):771–808.

Coll, Steve. 2004. *Ghost Wars: The Secret History of the CIA, Afghanistan, and bin Laden, from the Soviet Invasion to September 10, 2001*. New York: Penguin.

———. 2006. "Atomic Emporium." *New Yorker*, August 7 and 14, 50–63.

Cooke, Miriam, and Angela Woollacott, eds. 1993. *Gendering War Talk*. Princeton, NJ: Princeton University Press

Das, Veena. 1998. *Critical Events: An Anthropological Perspective on Contemporary India*. New Delhi: Oxford University Press.

de Alwis, Malathi. 1998. "Motherhood as a Space of Protest: Women's Political Participation in Contemporary Sri Lanka." In *Appropriating Gender: Women's Activism and Politicized Religion in South Asia*, ed. Patricia Jeffery and Amrita Basu, 185–201. New York: Routledge.

de Volo, Lorraine Bayard. 1998. "Drafting Motherhood: Maternal Imagery and Organizations in the United States and Nicaragua." In *The Women and War Reader*, ed. Lois Ann Lorentzen and Jennifer Turpin, 240–53. New York: New York University Press.

Elshtain, Jean Bethke. 1991. "Sovereignty, Identity, Sacrifice." *Social Research: An International Quarterly of Social Sciences* 58(3):544–64.

———. 1994. "Mothers of the Disappeared." In *Representations of Motherhood*, ed. Donna Bassin, Margaret Honey, and Meryle Mahrer Kaplan, 75–91. New Haven, CT: Yale University Press.

Euben, Roxanne L. 2002. "Jihad and Political Violence." *Current History* 101(638):365–76

Fisher, Ian. 2006. "Women, Secret Hamas Strength, Win Votes at Polls." *New York Times*, February 3, A1.

Keddie, Nikki R. 1999. "The New Religious Politics and Women Worldwide: A Comparative Study." *Journal of Women's History* 10(4):11–34.

Lister, Ruth. 1997. "Citizenship: Towards a Feminist Synthesis." *Feminist Review* 57(1):28–48.

Lyotard, Jean-François. 1988. *The Differend: Phrases in Dispute*. Minneapolis: University of Minnesota Press.

Mamdani, Mahmood. 2004. *Good Muslim, Bad Muslim: America, the Cold War, and the Roots of Terror*. New York: Pantheon.

Maududi, Sayyid Abu Ala. (1938) 2003. *Purdah and the Status of Women*. Lahore: Islamic Publications.

Moghadam, Valentine M. 2001. "Feminism and Islamic Fundamentalism: A Secularist Interpretation." *Journal of Women's History* 13(1):42–45.

Rashid, Ahmed. 2000. *Taliban: Militant Islam, Oil, and Fundamentalism in Central Asia.* New Haven, CT: Yale University Press.

Rich, Frank. 2005. "The Swift Boating of Cindy Sheehan." *New York Times,* August 21, 11.

Ruddick, Sara. 1989. *Maternal Thinking: Toward a Politics of Peace.* Boston: Beacon.

Saeed, Hafiz. 2002. "Negotiation Is a Ploy to Stop Jihad." *Al-Da'wa,* July, 2–5.

Scheper-Hughes, Nancy. 1998. "Maternal Thinking and the Politics of War." In *The Women and War Reader,* ed. Lois Ann Lorentzen and Jennifer Turpin, 227–33. New York: New York University Press.

Siegel, Mona. 1999. "'To the Unknown Mother of the Unknown Soldier': Pacifism, Feminism, and the Politics of Sexual Difference among French *Institutrices* between the Wars." *French Historical Studies* 22(3):421–51.

Sikand, Yoginder. 2003. "Islamic Militancy in Kashmir: The Case of Lashkar-i-Tayyeba." South Asia Citizens Web, http://www.sacw.net/DC/Communalism Collection/ArticlesArchive/sikand20Nov2003.html.

Umm Hammad. 2001. "Yey Tar Tar Dupattay, Ya Azeem Mauen Kay Betu Ka Lahoo Aur Ya Bomb Damaka: Jang Bandi Ka Neehe Jihad Jarie Rakhney Ka Daras Deethay Heen" [These tattered scarves, the blood of the sons of esteemed mothers, and the bomb blasts are teaching the lessons of jihad, not peace]. *Tayyabiat,* February, 2–4.

———. 2003a. "Alami Siyast Aur Askariat Me Muslim Wa Ghair-Muslim Khawateen Kay Kardar Ka Mowaza" [Comparing the role of Muslim and non-Muslim women in military and world politics]. *Tayyabiat,* February, 11–14.

———. 2003b. *Hum Maieen Hay Lashkar-i-Tayyabia Key* [We are the mothers of Lashkar-i-Tayyabia]. Lahore: Dar-al-Andalus.

Zeiger, Susan. 1996. "'She Didn't Raise Her Boy to Be a Slacker': Motherhood, Conscription, and the Culture of the First World War." *Feminist Studies* 22(1): 6–39.

Orna Sasson-Levy

Sarit Amram-Katz

Gender Integration in Israeli Officer Training: Degendering and Regendering the Military

We've already gotten used to the [women's] crying, and we've understood that it's okay, like when men clear their throat. The [female] company commander cried, and the [female] team commanders cried; that's more noticeable, and it bothers the [male] cadets. And everything that goes with it—the hysterics, the outbursts.[1]

This article examines the nature and meaning of gender integration in an officer training course in the Israeli military, in light of the hegemonic status of combat masculinity. The above quote is taken from an interview with Lieutenant Colonel Yoav Golan,[2] a male battalion commander in the newly gender-integrated course. The quote starts by recognizing gender differences as legitimate: women's crying no longer frightens him. However, in the same breath, Yoav recreates the gendered

Earlier drafts of this article were presented at the Annual Conference of the Women's Studies Association (UK and Ireland): Feminism Contesting Globalization, University College Dublin, July 2004; the Hegemonic Masculinities and International Politics Conference, University of Manchester, May 2005; and a conference in honor of Cynthia Enloe: Militarism and Social Inequalities, Bar Ilan University, Israel, December 2005. The research was conducted with the support of the Israel Academy of Sciences and Humanities and in cooperation with the research department of the advisor on women's issues to the chief of staff. We wish to thank the commanding officers and staff of the two bases that enabled this research and cooperated with us. In addition, we want to thank Eyal Ben-Ari, Hadas Ben-Eliyahu, Cynthia Enloe, Henriette Dahan Kalev, Sylvia Fogel-Bijoui, Zeev Lehrer, Judith Lorber, Hanna Nave, and Niza Yanay for their thoughtful comments, Helene Hogri for her invaluable editorial help, and Michal Levy for her intelligent and thorough research assistance.

[1] Quotations in this article are taken from interviews with soldiers and commanders on two bases; see the "Research Strategies and Data" section. All the interviews were conducted by the authors. Interview transcripts are on file with the authors. The interviews were carried out in Hebrew and translated into English by Orna Sasson-Levy.

[2] In order to protect the privacy of our interviewees, all the names are pseudonyms.

[*Signs: Journal of Women in Culture and Society* 2007, vol. 33, no. 1]

hierarchy: the women's crying bothers the male cadets, and "legitimate" tears quickly turn into hysterics. This discursive multiplicity is indicative of the simultaneous degendering and regendering processes that take place in the course. Though the Israeli military has restructured officer training in order to degender its route for promotion, it nonetheless goes on to reconstruct and reify hierarchical gender differences. Since military service is a sine qua non of full citizenship in Israel, the simultaneous processes of degendering and regendering expose the countless barricades that Israeli women have to overcome in order to be considered full citizens.

Israel is the only Western state with compulsory conscription for both men and women. The decision to conscript women was part of the egalitarian ethos of the new Jewish society in Israel. Women, it was said, had proven that they "deserved" the "right to contribute" to the collective and to become soldiers (Berkovitch 1997, 608). Hence, the institution of mandatory conscription for women can be seen as the first wave of degendering, which could signify the construction of a gender-egalitarian citizenship.

However, this bold project of degendering was immediately accompanied by mechanisms of regendering: married women and mothers were exempted from the draft, women served in a Women's Corps, and all female soldiers, including those who had been trained for battle prior to 1948, were transferred to "feminine" jobs, such as social work, nursing, or teaching (Bloom 1982). Thus, from its very beginnings, structural degendering in the Israeli military has been accompanied by structural regendering, and this has remained a male-dominated territory where masculinity is the norm.

The growing awareness that Israeli women are not perceived as equal citizens, partly due to their unequal military service, has raised public criticism of the military's gendered division of labor. This criticism, fortified by Supreme Court rulings, brought about a second wave of degendering in the military in the mid-1990s (Sasson-Levy 2001). As of 1995, women have been integrated into a few select combat roles, the Women's Corps has been dismantled, and some training courses have become gender integrated. The climax of this process was the gender integration of the staff (noncombatant) officer training course, which is the focus of this article.

Our argument is that despite the declared aim of the integrated course to degender the military organization and create an equal-opportunity environment for women, gender integration has actually led to a dual process of degendering and regendering. Degendering, according to Judith Lorber (2005), attacks the structure and process of gender by recognizing that the two genders are not homogeneous groups (as they are intersected by other major social statuses) and by recognizing gender similarities in behavior, thinking, and emotions. Degendering at officer training was the result of deliberate structural changes. In contrast, regendering was a more subtle discursive process that derived from the overbearing centrality of the masculine combat soldier model in the culture of the course. Regendering occurred mostly through the ways in which cultural codes, stereotypical schemas, and hegemonic gender beliefs were enacted and performed in daily interactions. It was thus a more sophisticated and hidden process, harder to expose and change.

To understand the interplay of degendering and regendering, or, in other words, to make some sense of the complexities and paradoxes we encountered in the integrated training course, we apply William H. Sewell's analysis of structures as "constituted by mutually sustaining cultural schemas and sets of resources" (1992, 26). For reasons of clarity, we begin the article with a description of the research. We go on to analyze the links among gender, military service, and citizenship and then discuss the intersection of cultural schemas and resources in order to understand the contradictory dynamics in officer training. The next section explores the processes of degendering and regendering in the integrated course. We conclude with a discussion of the consequences of these dynamics in terms of identity construction, the military organization, and the structure of citizenship.

Research strategies and data

From the establishment of the Israeli military in 1948, staff officer training was carried out in two parallel frameworks: an exclusively women's course on a women's base and an exclusively men's course on a men's base. In May 2003, for the first time, the two courses were gender integrated, organized by designated role and prospective work environment rather than gender. Both courses include a roughly equal number of men and women, who are required to perform the same tasks and participate in all activities equally. This is very different from the typical structure of U.S. military academies; although some (West Point and the U.S. Air Force Academy) began to integrate women as early as 1976, women have never constituted more than 15 percent of the cadets and still feel like outsiders in these "heavily masculinist" institutions (Mitchell 1996, 48). However, it is important to note that only the noncombatant staff officer course is gender integrated in Israel. That is, gender integration is not carried out at the peak of military training but rather seems appropriate only for the secondary course, the one that does not lead to power posts in the military. The more prestigious combat officer training is exclusively masculine.

This study employs a qualitative methodology that stems from a few related paradigms: the phenomenological paradigm, which analyzes social reality from the subjective viewpoint of those living within the society (Taylor 1987); a feminist methodology that emphasizes gender as the main (but not sole) analytic category (Smith 1990); and an organizational perspective that examines the culture and structures of the institution. Specifically, this research is based on participant observation, interviews, and textual and visual content analysis.

The research took place between August and October 2003, during which we interviewed members of the second cohort of the integrated course. During the ten weeks of the course we visited each of the two bases one day a week, participating in many of their activities. In all, we spent thirty-three days and three nights in the two training bases. We observed the entrance exams, physical training classes, theoretical classes, field training (such as range practice and grenade throwing), dismissal committees, and the graduation ceremony. We also participated in a navigation day, two marches, and a day of command-and-control exercises. We ate many meals with cadets, chatted with them while they awaited their turns at shooting ranges, observed their living conditions, and so on. We documented the observations in detailed field reports, describing the daily life of the course, events and interactions, and formal and informal activities.

During our visits, we interviewed seventy male and female cadets, thirty team commanders, eight company commanders, the four battalion commanders, and the two commanding officers (a man and a woman).[3] We also interviewed infirmary staff and base doctors, physical training instructors and officers, and master sergeants. We asked about the personal experience of the course and specifically about attitudes toward gender integration. While the soldiers' narratives teach us about their subjective experience of officer training, the staff interviews shed light on the belief systems of the course. In addition, we analyzed the written texts that saturate the course, such as lesson plans, feedback papers, formal texts

---

[3] The company is the basic administrative and tactical unit. It is located on a command level below the battalion and above the platoon (which is also called a team). A typical battalion has three or four companies, each consisting of three to four platoons (Ben-Ari 1998).

such as "The Rationale of Officer Training," and commanders' position papers.[4]

The qualitative data were accompanied by quantitative data collected from the two bases. This included medical data (visits to the infirmary and medical exemptions from activities), physical training and navigation grades, theoretical test grades, peer evaluations, and percentages of dropouts/dismissals from the course. The quantitative data enabled us to verify or refute certain common assertions, such as women using the medical facilities more than men.

Military, citizenship, and hegemonic masculinity

The military is a critical site for research on gender integration because it is not "just another patriarchal institution" (Enloe 1988, 10); rather, it is the institution most closely identified with the state, its ideologies, and its policies. This is true both in the liberal discourse of citizenship and in the republican discourse. According to the former, military service is perceived as part of the citizen's minimal obligations to the state, in exchange for which the citizen receives equal civic, political, and social rights. Ever since the French and American revolutions, participation in armed conflicts has been an integral aspect of the normative definition of citizenship (Tilly 1995). In the West, military service emerged as a hallmark of citizenship, and citizenship as the hallmark of political democracy (Janowitz 1976).

Whereas the liberal discourse places the rights of the individual front and center, the republican discourse of citizenship highlights the collective and defines citizenship according to the individual's active contribution to the common good (Shafir 1998), which is often articulated in security terms. As serving in the "people's army" is envisioned as the ultimate expression of civic obligation (Pateman 1989), military service is perceived as equivalent to good citizenship and serves to delineate the boundaries of the political collective (Burk 1995).

This close link between military service and citizenship has been modified in the West over the last two decades, following the transition from mandatory service to voluntary professional armies. In Israel, however, military service continues to be associated with good citizenship due to the prolonged Arab-Israeli conflict and the development of civilian mil-

---

[4] The formal texts are occasional messages delivered by the commander that carry an educational value. These texts are formal in that they are distributed and made public within the military but not published.

itarism (Kimmerling 1993). Military service constitutes a central criterion for one's loyalty to the state, and it determines access to differential social, economic, and political resources (Helman 1997).

At the same time, the military has a special role in the ideological construction of patriarchy because of the significance of combat in the construction of masculine identities and in the justification of masculine superiority (Enloe 1988, 2000). Militaries are perceived as masculine institutions not only because they are populated mostly with men but also because they constitute a major arena for the construction of masculine identities (Barrett 1996; Higate 2003). Indeed, despite far-reaching political, social, and technological changes, the warrior seems to maintain his status as a key symbol of masculinity (Morgan 1994, 165).

In Israel, where the military is perceived both as a citizenship-conferring institution and as an initiation rite to masculinity, the Jewish combat soldier has achieved the status of hegemonic masculinity, which in turn is identified with good citizenship.[5] The militarization of citizenship creates a differential and hierarchical gendered structure of belonging to the state (Snyder 1999). Since women are not perceived as men's partners in the ultimate obligation to the state (Pateman 1989, 11), they are not entitled to the same rights and privileges.[6]

Gender integration of officer training can be seen, then, as a step toward equalizing the status of women as soldiers and citizens. This approach is characteristic of "feminist egalitarian militarists" (Feinman 2000, 31; see also Peach 1996, 174–78), who insist that, given that the military is a sine qua non of full citizenship and thus equality, it is the women's right to perform martial service. The exclusion of women from certain military roles, they contend, is discriminatory because it treats all women as if they compose an undifferentiated inferior category and limits the number of jobs for women in the military. Such restrictions extend beyond the military and deny women equal advancement opportunities in the civilian

[5] This hegemony is expressed through a wide range of phenomena, such as economic benefits for combat soldiers, their symbolic social and political power, and even the common use of their image in advertisements, selling everything from cheese to medical insurance.

[6] One of the most blatant examples of women's lower status in Israel is their very low representation in parliament; today, women constitute 15 percent of all Knesset (parliament) members. The military, especially its higher echelons, is a major mobilizing mechanism into Israel's top political positions. Since only (male) combat soldiers can be promoted into higher ranks, this track into politics is virtually closed to women. In addition, women do not enjoy the higher salaries and privileges (such as scholarships) that combat soldiers receive and are not entitled to the prestige that combat commanders hold, which helps them secure better jobs in the labor market.

world after their discharge (Peach 1996; Izraeli 1997). Radical feminists, however, reject military service as a venue for gender equality. The liberal insistence on equal participation in the military, they argue, reifies the armed forces as a citizenship-certifying institution and proposes men as the standard against which women should be measured. They oppose the military for its use of violence and its deeply masculinist culture that depends on the oppression of women (Feinman 2000, 19–31). Whether gender integration will lead to the results hoped for by liberal feminists (i.e., create equality) or bring about the consequences feared by radical feminists (i.e., reaffirm violent masculine institutions) depends largely on the way the organization treats gender.

The military as a gendered organization: Schemas and resources

Feminist analysis has been oscillating between viewing gender as an enduring structure and seeing it as a shifting social construction. Often, the difference can be explained by what one looks at: when considering the division of labor and resource allocation in the public sphere, gender segregation is "an amazingly persistent pattern" (Acker 1990, 145). However, the notion of gender as immutable tends to be deterministic and fails to explain the social and historical variety of gendered identities. Indeed, if we look at the constitution of subjective identities, gender is often seen as a fluid social construction (Connell 1987; Butler 1990). Wendy Brown defines these two "powerful, mutually canceling truths in feminism" as the "radical instability of gender" (2003, 365–66). However, the model that Brown suggests of gender as counterpoint seems to be more metaphoric than sociological.

At first sight, what we found in the integrated course was this radical instability of gender. As the quote at the opening of this article testifies, we heard contradictory statements and witnessed contradictory practices. We observed radical changes and the reproduction of traditional gender concepts at the same time. Sewell's (1992) conceptualization of structure as consisting simultaneously of schemas (which are virtual) and resources (which are actual) can help to bridge this disparity in the understanding of gender. Though this conceptualization has been cited often, it has rarely been applied to the issue of gender (but see Ridgeway and Correll 2004) and even more rarely to the analysis of empirical phenomena such as gender relations in institutions.

The concept, or metaphor, of structure, Sewell explains, is often understood as deterministic, primary, and immutable, and therefore it cannot explain social change. However, we cannot indiscriminately discard this concept, because it teaches about "the tendency of patterns of relations to be reproduced, even when actors engaging in the relations are unaware of the patterns or do not desire their reproduction" (Sewell 1992, 3). In order to build the possibility of change into the notion of structure, Sewell conceptualizes structure as "constituted by mutually sustaining cultural schemas and sets of resources that empower and constrain social action and tend to be reproduced by that action" (26). Cultural schemas are "various conventions, recipes, scenarios, principles of action and habits of speech and gesture" (7), while resources are "anything that can serve as a source of power in social interaction" and can be human (e.g., physical strength, knowledge, dexterity, and emotional commitment) or nonhuman (e.g., land and factories). Resources are always material; even human resources have actual outcomes and operate on the human body itself. This understanding of structure is productive, as it allows room for change, which can occur because societies are based on a multiplicity of intersecting structures, because schemas are transposable, and because resources are polysemic and accumulate unpredictably (18).

Thus, we can understand gender as a structure whose resources (e.g., division of labor) are the effects of schemas (e.g., femininity and masculinity, soldiering, and motherhood), just as schemas are the effects of resources. But this is not a closed circle of reproduction. Rather, gender relations can be dynamic and contradictory. This conceptualization can help us understand both the stability of the gender structure and its ongoing dynamic changes. The question, then, is not whether gender is an immutable structure or a shifting symbol but, rather, what are the dynamics of gender? How do the symbolic and material dimensions of gender interact, and how are they reproduced or challenged in everyday life?

Gender schema and military schema

In order to analyze the dynamics of gender, it is fruitful to analyze the military's cultural schemas and its material resources separately, before exploring their interplay. There are two dominant and intersecting cultural schemas in the officer course: the gender schema and the military schema. The former constructs a binary order based on perceived differences between the sexes and is a primary way of signifying relationships of power. Hegemonic gender beliefs assume that men and women have different traits and skills and that men are more status worthy and competent than women (Ridgeway and Correll 2004, 513). Gender beliefs and social relational contexts help maintain the gender system by modestly, but systematically and repeatedly, biasing men's and women's behaviors and evaluations in ways that reenact and confirm beliefs about men's greater status and competence (521).

Two points that Cecilia Ridgeway and Shelley Correll (2004) make are of special relevance to the study of gender integration in the military. First, when the product of an organization is associated with a domain that is culturally defined as masculine, such as the military, the evaluative bias in favor of men is stronger. Second, gendered biases are more significant when gender is salient in the social setting. This was indeed the case in the second cohort of the integrated course, when gender integration and especially the women's presence in the men's base was a novelty that created much interest and received considerable media attention.

The military schema is based on the gender schema but has a pyramid-like formation that positions the warrior as the hegemonic model for the entire organization. The combat schema—which includes the masculine strong and sturdy body, physical and emotional self-control, and a willingness to risk one's life—is the military's schema in general, and in Israel it has become the schema for achieving and affirming manhood (Ben-Ari 1998, 112). Other military identities are constituted in hierarchical relation to the warrior, and their status is determined by their level of proximity to him. The military schema thus creates hierarchies among men as well: those who do not fit (physically or emotionally) the imperative of warrior masculinity, those who serve in noncombat roles, and those who resist the warrior ethos altogether and refuse to serve in the army are often entitled to fewer privileges and social prestige than the combat soldier (Sasson-Levy 2003b). The intersection of the binary gender schema and the pyramid-like military schema shapes the construction of militarized identities, the military organization's daily practices, the military's social stratification, and the link between military service and citizenship in Israel.

Military resources

Although military service in Israel is mandatory for both men and women, the Israeli army is still a male-dominated territory (Robbins and Ben-Eliezer 2000; Sasson-Levy 2003a). Women, who compose only 32 percent of the regular army, serve a shorter time than men and are easily exempted from service on the grounds of marriage, pregnancy, or religious belief. Structural and organizational differences, together with a male chauvinist culture, have limited the range of roles to which women can be posted and constitute a barrier to women's advancement in the military (Cohen 1997).

Thus far, we see coherence between the military division of resources and the two cultural schemas that operate therein, a coherence that maintains a unified, hierarchical, gendered military structure. However, a process of change in gender relations in the military began in 1995, when the military complied with the intervention of female members of the Knesset and the Supreme Court and integrated women into a few select combat roles, such as pilots, border police, antiaircraft operators, and naval commandos. A battalion of light infantry with 70 percent women, whose main task is to patrol the peaceful border with Jordan, was established in February 2004. Today women in combat roles constitute 2.5 percent of all women in the military. However, women are still barred from "real" infantry, armor, and reconnaissance units, the three specialties that are considered the core of combat and therefore are still excluded from most of the positions that are traditional paths to advancement into top military ranks. This process of change culminated with the dismantling of the Women's Corps and the integration of the staff officer training course (Sasson-Levy 2001).

Gender integration of officer training is of special significance because this course is the sole route for advancement into meaningful military roles in Israel.[7] Data from foreign militaries (such as the Australian Defense Force) indicate that the participation rate of women in the military increases when military academies, as a primary commissioning source for officers, become mixed-gender institutions (Iskra et al. 2002). Moreover, gender integration could signify a shift from a gendered structure to a professionally based structure. Thus, the change in the division of resources could be a step toward degendering the military and bringing about a change in perceptions of femininity and masculinity among those involved in training, as well as throughout the entire military. Why then was our experience in the officers' training so confusing and laden with contradictions?

In the following section we explore how these new relationships between actual resources and virtual schemas affected the experience of the gender-integrated officer training course. We look first at the degendering processes and then at the regendering mechanisms that shaped the course.

Processes of degendering in officer training

On May 13, 2003, with the opening of the newly gender-integrated

---

[7] This is unlike most Western militaries, which offer several paths for military advancement, such as the Reserve Officers Training Corps, military academies, and advancement through the ranks.

course, the commanding officer published his command of the day. Among other things, the text reads (emphasis in original):

> Since the inception of the state women's military training has been separated from men's training. The exclusion of women from the men's training base reflected the policy that differentiates between men and women regarding their utilization and professional development. Without equal opportunities, women's deployment was limited to traditional roles, and blocked from combat roles.
> WE HAVE COME A LONG WAY FROM THERE, AND WE ARE ON THE RIGHT TRACK.
> Integration of men and women in highly responsible roles in the IDF [Israel Defense Forces] is an important strategic move, which carries with it a national message of social renewal that goes beyond the military service.
> The message is clear to the entire nation of Israel, that it is proper and necessary to utilize to the fullest all talents, the best of minds, capabilities, experience and motivation that are embedded in the human resource—men and women alike, in order to assure our security.
> This is an unequivocal declaration (especially for those who have not internalized it yet) that women, like men, have equal rights, value and status, and that all people deserve respect and decency.
> EQUAL AND PARTNERS, NO OTHER RELATION OF OWNERSHIP, PATRONIZING, AUTHORITY, OR PROPRIETARY.

As is clear from this text (which deserves a more thorough analysis than space allows), degendering was the formal declared objective of the new policy, though national security and national renewal are described as the central goals of this move. The aim to degender was expressed through the structure, rules, and formal policies of the integrated courses, which were, on the whole, gender neutral.

The only major exception to this rule was the residential arrangements: male and female cadets resided in the same building, but on different floors, and were not allowed to visit one another's floors. This arrangement appears to be the best compromise between the two other possible arrangements: shared residence or residence in two separate buildings. Shared residence denies the cadets the minimal privacy that most of them want and would deter traditional and religious soldiers from participating in the officer course. Separate residences, however, would split the company into two homogeneous gendered groups, would impair company cohesion and effectiveness, and would reinforce gendered differences. Thus, though the current residence arrangement has its disadvantages, most cadets and commanders found it to be the best solution and were pleased with it.

An important indicator of degendering was the cadets' final grades, which showed only minor gender differences. In the women's base, men graded better on the physical test, while in the men's base, men graded higher on the navigation tests. Women graded higher in the men's base on leadership skills, safety exams, national heritage exams, and the weekly exams, but in all cases these differences were not significant. Peer evaluation tests showed similar scores for men and women on most parameters and slightly higher scores, but again nonsignificant, for women on some parameters.

The data from the infirmaries of the two bases reveal a somewhat different and contradictory picture. In the men's base, where training was more physically intensive, there were no gender differences in infirmary visits, even though women had a more difficult time. This gender similarity is explained by a rumor that spread in the base, which claimed that cadets who were exempted from training for medical reasons for more than five days would be dismissed from the course. This rumor deterred both men and women from taking care of their medical problems. Many women, driven by a very high motivation to survive the training and succeed in it, tended to hide their physical ailments and had more injuries and health problems (see DeFleur, Gillman, and Marshak 1978; Bijur et al. 1997). Curiously enough, female cadets who ignored their medical problems and continued with the training were blamed by the commanding officer for being overmotivated and irresponsible. On the women's base, in contrast, women's visits to the infirmary were double those of men, probably because they were indeed suffering from more problems than the men and because there were no threats involved in taking care of one's body.

Regarding the percentage of dismissals from the course, there was gender similarity in the men's base and a larger percentage of women dropouts in the women's base. On the whole, though, the quantitative data from the two courses indicate that the functioning of men and women was relatively similar and, more important, that differences within each gender group were greater than differences between genders. Differences in age, prior military experience, and education seemed to be more indicative than gender of one's chances of graduating with high grades.

A somewhat unexpected form of degendering concerned the issue of sexual harassment. Unlike the U.S. military academies, where gender integration increased the occurrence of sexual harassment (Firestone and Harris 1994), we did not encounter cases of sexual harassment in the integrated course.[8] It seems that the male cadets were simply afraid of being dismissed from the course due to charges of sexual harassment.[9]

Finally, degendering appeared in a somewhat diluted form in the narratives of both cadets and staff who celebrated gender integration. A male commanding officer said, "Integration did wonders; it had the opposite effect of what we thought it would. In comparison to previous courses, their grades are much higher, their motivation is sky high." Similarly, a female battalion commander said, "I have only had positive experiences with the battalion. I don't understand why it took so long for them to integrate boys and girls. The boys say that it's natural and no big deal; after all, they were at school together. To me, it seems completely natural, the best thing that could possibly have happened."[10]

This affirmative discourse, which is only one among other discourses of gender that we discuss below, seems to testify more to fears and concerns about the new structure than to the degendering of the course itself. Still, these narratives reflect a new perception of gender relations—one that rejects the unique masculine ideology of the military and sees the military as any other organization, similar to school, where gender integration is not often questioned. Thus, in some ways, gender integration did lead to the degendering of officer training and even empowered women by allowing them access to positions that were previously unattainable because they lacked basic military requirements. However, alongside the process of degendering were processes of regendering that restratified the population of the course.

Processes of regendering in officer training
Combat-related physical training
The most visible dynamics of regendering are the combat-related character of the training. Although the integrated course is aimed at noncombatant

---

[8] In U.S. military academies, gender integration increased the occurrence of sexual harassment, even as the percentage of women in the academies grew (Yoder 1991). For example, reports indicated a 12 percent rate of rape and a 70 percent rate of sexual harassment at the Air Force Academy in Colorado Springs (Schemo 2003).

[9] This is not to suggest that there is no sexual harassment in the Israeli military. In research carried out in 2003 by the Advisory on Women's Issues to the Chief of Staff, 20 percent of women soldiers said "yes" to a direct question on sexual harassment during their service, and up to 80 percent said "yes" to specific questions such as "Were you in a situation that contained insulting sexual innuendos or unwanted sexual offers?" (http://www.aka.idf.il/yohalan [Hebrew]). Thus, our impressions are probably reflective only of the specific environment of the officers' course.

[10] In the quotes we use the non–politically correct terms *girls* and *boys*, as this was the language used by both cadets and commanders.

staff officers, combat-related demands were intensified following gender integration. Compared to the previous course, the integrated one included more and longer marches, more navigation exercises (including night navigation), more strenuous fitness tests, and the addition of street warfare exercises and grenade throwing. One of the male senior commanders said bluntly, "I put significant emphasis on toughening, to add more elements of endurance and create a situation of intensive combative challenge. . . . I find it important for them to be able to cope with the stress of combat. Gushing blood, screams, fatigue, sweat, fears, hunger, longing, the whistle of bullets . . . it is very, very difficult to hack it."

The cadets' challenge, then, was more to handle the anxiety and pressure of combat than to develop the leadership skills needed as staff officers. Though the women managed to graduate with the same grades as the men, they had to work harder to achieve them and found some of the course requirements too demanding. While observing the teams performing urban warfare exercises, we could see some of the women enjoying showing off their newly acquired combat abilities. Others, especially those on accelerated courses toward administrative officers' positions, or those assigned to traditional women's roles, expressed feelings of alienation and resentment and did not see the relevance of the overly combat-oriented demands to their prospective jobs. One female cadet complained, "The course ruined my back and my knees. Do I really need this in order to be a good welfare officer?" Another female cadet said, "The idea of shooting a weapon, throwing a hand grenade, shooting a mortar. . . . Emotionally, I had a very hard time dealing with it. There is a difference between boys and girls, and there is no need to be ashamed of it." She seemed to want to maintain the quite popular perception that associates women with ethics of care and peacemaking. As a welfare officer, her military role is a traditional feminine one, wholly unrelated to the combat training required of her in the course.

Why was the level of combat training raised precisely when the decision was made to let women in? None of our respondents provided a satisfactory answer, so we can only speculate. Were the senior commanding officers concerned that gender integration would lower the level of the course? Or were they worried that gender integration would damage the masculine image of the course and therefore of officers in general? Was intensifying the physical training meant to ensure the continued masculine character of the course?

Whatever the case may be, the result was that the entire course was tinged with combat masculinity. Instead of being an instrument for improved soldiering and better general functioning, physical fitness became a goal in itself. This ties in with Robert Connell's (1987) argument that gendered practices create corporeal differences between men and women. Through the soldiering body project, men's bodies become visibly different from those of women. When physical tests are the main rite of passage, they not only reinstate but also naturalize and perpetuate socially constructed distinctions between men and women. These differences are then used to justify and legitimize the original hierarchical social categories. This was clear when looking at the effects of the training program.

The Israeli army has developed a system of comparable training, similar to the one at West Point, based on the premise that the goal is not similar outcomes for men and women but equivalent effort (Cohn 2000). This system, which recognizes physiological differences between men and women and demands that they exert themselves equally, is contrasted with the Virginia Military Institute's (VMI's) single (male) standard for both female and male cadets. Each system has its drawbacks. The VMI's universal training standard can result in more injuries to women or inadequately trained men. Indeed, treating all people identically can produce unequal consequences (Kimmel 2000). However, the comparable training system, which allows different standards, creates resentment among men, undermines the unit's cohesion, and can be used as justification for discrimination against women (Stiehm 1989; Snyder 2003). Moreover, while women are expected to do less than men, the exercises are still modeled according to men's capabilities. The most common fitness test includes push-ups, sit-ups, and a run, which are easier for men. The tests do not include areas in which women tend to excel, such as swimming or flexibility, and thus even the comparable training program works to benefit men (Cohn 2000; Janda 2002). A third and probably better system for physical selection, which is not discriminatory against women, has been developed in the British army. These tests, known as Physical Selection Standards (Recruits), measure job-related criteria, assessing the suitability of individuals for their intended career employment groups. The fitness tests, which are designed to be gender neutral, include a 1.5-mile run, a single lift, carrying, sit-ups, and a loaded march, each with five pass levels (Woodward and Winter 2004). However, even these tests are modeled according to men's capabilities. Moreover, they have not been adopted by the British Navy or the Royal Air Force, which use different test standards for men and women.

In Israel, the system of gender-comparable training was interpreted by male cadets as unequal: the women were accused of doing less than the men, which gave the latter an excuse to debase women or to offer them help in a patronizing way. Male cadets and their commanders claimed that gender integration lowered the level of physical training. A male team commander remarked, "The optimal utilization of men happens when they are separated from women. I see a man navigating with a woman, she holds him back, they don't keep up with the man's pace." The comparable training system was thus another opportunity to create and perform male superiority and contributed to regendering processes. Carol Cohn introduced this dilemma in her essay, wonderfully titled "How Can She Claim Equal Rights When She Doesn't Have to Do as Many Push-Ups as I Do?" (2000). Cohn claims that the men's anger at the physical training issue "is about far more than gender-normed fitness standards: It functions as a socially and institutionally acceptable way of expressing a variety of negative feelings about women in the military—feelings that are no longer as acceptable to state directly" (133). Such feelings of anger and superiority were expressed by both male commanders and male cadets, who said, "Lower physical fitness is an inevitable derivative of gender integration" and "The fitness program is not like it used to be. It's calculated according to the girls' abilities, and this lowered the level" (even though, in actuality, the level of physical fitness was raised). Only one male team commander pointed to the discrepancy between the reality of physical training and hegemonic gender beliefs, saying, "It's all about stigmas. [During the march] all the boys complained and whined that it's too hot, that they're sweaty and stinking, tired and hungry. The girls took it more heroically." This comment reveals, yet again, that physical fitness is not purely physiological; it is socially constructed, perceived through gendered cultural schemas by everyone involved, and therefore works as a regendering mechanism.

"The boys' company"

In addition to its gender complexity, the Israeli military is confronted with religious challenges from Zionist rabbis who object to gender integration, claiming that men who serve alongside women cannot observe modesty laws. In response to these objections an appropriate integration committee was set up, which administered rules for gender integration. The rules for appropriate integration include separate residential arrangements for men and women, a requirement to wear modest clothes at all times (including during physical training), a prohibition on physical contact across gender lines except for purposes of help and support, and allowance for religious men and women to serve in homogeneous companies within the integrated battalion.

Of these rules, the allowance for religious soldiers to serve in homogeneous companies turned out to be a major regendering mechanism.

Not surprisingly, almost no women, but quite a few men, asked to serve in such units. Therefore, there was a men's company on both bases but only one small women's team, within an integrated company, on the women's base. Apparently, the men's request to serve in an all-male company had nothing to do with religiosity, as most were secular. Some of the men asked to serve in the men's company because they were worried that the presence of women would dilute the physical, masculine atmosphere of the course. They wanted to go through this masculinity initiation rite in its "pure" form. "The course is more aggressive in the boys' company," said a male cadet. Other male cadets worried that doing the course with women would be more difficult because they would be expected to help the women and do most of the work. Still others simply figured out that if all their friends asked to serve in the homogeneous unit, they could ensure assignment to the same company.

The presence of a men's company within the integrated battalion created many opportunities for regendering. Complying with patriarchal expectations from men, the cadets of the homogeneous company, and even more so their commanders, strove to prove their superiority over women and to emerge victorious in every formal or informal competition. The "boys' company" was consistently considered the strongest in the battalion, especially in terms of physical capabilities, combat readiness, efficiency, and motivation. A female medic at the women's base said, "The girls' team behaved like they were still in the old women's courses. They were weak in every respect, and the boys' company was the best. They were excellent—they did twice as much as all the other companies. They did individual exercises and team exercises, and even had enough time for a special range practice, while all the others were still doing individual exercises."

This medic's admiration of the men's company was common among other commanders and cadets. Research shows that single-sex education for men often perpetuates feelings of superiority among men and results in arrogance toward women (Kimmel 2000). In the same vein, the men's exclusive companies were a niche where they could develop hypermasculinity and recreate hierarchical gender distinctions.

As the quote above indicates, the women's team was not seen in the same positive way. Female commanders who worked with the team often expressed disappointment. "When it's only girls, they are more spoiled, they're feeble and there's no endurance," said a female commander, exposing her internalization of the military's masculine ideology. However, contrary to the staff's perceptions, the cadets in the women's team talked positively about their experience: "We had the privilege of enjoying both worlds—we were in an integrated course, but we still had our own little female niche in it. The course is very intensive, so you need a place where you can identify with one another. Integration is excellent, but it's important to have a personal niche with the girls."

There was a gap, then, between the positive and empowering experience of the women in the homogenous team and how the team was perceived by the staff. It seems that the evaluation of the different companies' performances correlated with the percentage of men in them. Thus, the existence of an all-male company created a basis for constant gender comparison, which benefited the men and the image of manhood prevalent in the course.

Gendered allocation of duties

A third mechanism of regendering was the method, or, more precisely, the lack of one, for allocating duties. Some of the rotating positions, such as "navigations officer" and "duty officer," were seen as better filled by a cadet with prior combat training. Both men and women had very little combat training prior to the course. Nonetheless, due to the cultural identification of masculinity with combat, the men were perceived as having more combat training and thus as better suited to the more physical, visible, and valued duties. The women were assigned the more educational, "soft" duties, like giving lectures on the heritage of David Ben Gurion or on sexual harassment in the military. This gendered allocation of duties did not result from conscious staff decisions but rather evolved because no formal decision was made on the matter. As one female junior commander said, "It's in the subconscious of the commander—'if I'm looking for assertiveness, I will find it among the boys.' There are more shy women than shy men. A girl who is a 'cannon' has to excel above and beyond; a boy who is a 'cannon' simply knows how to delegate authority." These words make explicit what is usually implicit: that hegemonic gender beliefs create a double standard for judging ability and performance, and that men are likely to be evaluated by themselves and others as having somewhat more ability than the women (Ridgeway and Correll 2004). Since gender is salient in the officer course, it is a persistent source of implicit discrimination in the evaluation of ability and performance and in the distribution of commensurate rewards. The judgment the commander makes contributes to the gendering of the course by biasing decisions through which she steers women or men toward some jobs rather than others. One of the lessons learned from our research and implemented in further courses was to rotate all duties equally among female and male cadets so that each one had an equal chance to meet the challenge and publicly prove his or her capabilities.

Gendered evaluations

The cadets are constantly evaluated by peers and staff. Evaluations are kept on file and provide the basis for the final decision about whether they graduate, which is made by the battalion commander during the last week. Since the course is modeled as a combat course, demands of the battlefield become crucial in the evaluation process. For example, during an evaluation on the men's base, a battalion commander said to a female cadet, "Your academic grades are fine, and socially you're okay, but you didn't participate in most of the physical maneuvers, so I have no way of evaluating your performance." We heard that another cadet "is serious and has a good head on her shoulders, but she has a visibility problem [doesn't carry herself like an officer]." A third female cadet was blamed for "not demonstrating authoritativeness." The evaluation process overrated physical fitness and authoritativeness and underestimated other leadership skills, such as intellectual and academic capabilities, interpersonal communication skills, independent and critical thinking, and taking initiative. A senior commander on the women's base summed this up: "Masculine traits are highly appreciated here. It is always like that in the army, but it became even stronger following the integration with men."

Another measure for evaluating cadets is endurance, understood as the ability to withstand physical and mental difficulties without complaint. This is part of the ethos of the Israeli hegemonic masculinity, which prides itself on physical and emotional self-control as a key element of effective performance in daily situations and especially at times of crisis (Ben-Ari 1998, 45). A male battalion commander explained, "The most important thing is the officer's ability to suffer silently. With girls this doesn't happen. Very few of the girls can carry out a task and suffer it quietly." Endurance, as the ability to withstand pressure, could be measured through other means, such as coping with intellectual challenges, addressing problems, or managing and leading people. When endurance is evaluated only through physical prowess and performance on the (simulated) battlefield, women are often judged as unsuitable. Hence, the evaluation process at the course is a gendered and gendering measure, which creates bias against women.[11]

---

[11] There is a gap between the bias toward men that we witnessed in the evaluation process and the virtually equivalent percentages of dismissals of men and women at the

It is important to note that the evaluation bias not only distinguished between men and women but also created hierarchies of masculinity among men. A week before the end of the course, one of the male cadets was expelled because, as his female commander said, "He's a bit gay, don't you think? He is really like a woman; can he stand in front of his soldiers like that? He has no authority." The gendered distinctions that associate combat with authoritative masculinity were thus applied to a man who seemed not to fit the hegemonic model of masculinity, leading to his expulsion from the core of the military. Thus, even though Israel was one of the first countries to lift the ban on homosexuals in the military—since 1993, gays and lesbians have been able to serve in all military roles (Belkin and Levitt 2001)—the hegemonic cultural schema of combat masculinity is based on stereotypical notions of the effeminate gay man (alongside women) as inferior and unfit for military command. Hence, like the women, the men were also expected to meet the norms of warrior masculinity, and those who deviated from it suffered social and formal sanctions.

Discourses of integration

Finally, the discourses that were prevalent in the course had an important role in regendering. It should be noted that the common military discourse, which objects to gender integration in the name of team cohesion and combat effectiveness (see Woodward and Winter 2004), thereby regendering the armed forces at a macrolevel, was not heard here. The integrated training course under study was for noncombat officers who would be dispersed among different units afterward, and thus this discourse was irrelevant.

Instead, we detected three other main discourses regarding gender integration. The first and most common discourse, which is showcased as the official course discourse, claims that everybody wins from gender integration and that the general level of the course was raised because of it. The female battalion commander said, "In the first [integrated] course, I felt that everyone brought their own relative advantages, and my general impression is that overall their achievements are higher, now that they are together."

According to her and other commanders, the relative advantages brought by the women were criticism, time management, practicality, seriousness, thoroughness, creativity, good learning habits, order, and or-

---

men's base. This interesting gap needs a more thorough explanation. We can only speculate that it might be explained by the higher motivation of the female cadets.

ganization. The men's advantages, it was claimed, were rationality, a sense of proportion, calmness, cleanliness, discipline, learning skills, persistence, and higher willingness to volunteer. We were told that the women learn a lot from the men's experience and that the men's presence contributes to the maturity of the course participants. According to the female battalion commander the men, however, gain from gender integration because "they learn how to work with diverse populations." As is clear by now, these lists of advantages and gains of each gender are contradictory and absurd. Women are said to gain a good deal from gender integration, while the men's benefits are portrayed as insignificant. Similar to the "diversity is good" discourse common in the U.S. and British militaries (Cohn 2000), this discourse sees gender differences as positive and as contributing to the general good. Yet, at the same time, it perceives gender differences as given, which emphasizes and reifies them (Woodward and Winter 2006).

A second widespread discourse argues that the men lose out from gender integration. This, said some, is because a course that includes women is bound to be less combat oriented, so male cadets do not have to push themselves as hard. Others argued that the men lose since they have to work harder to help the women. This line of reasoning was heard mainly from male cadets and staff members, though we heard it from female cadets as well. One female cadet stated, "An integrated course is not good for the boys. It lowers their motivation." Another said, "The boys are not challenged enough in the integrated course." As with the previous discourse, this one is also based on a perception of gender differences, but here they are clearly hierarchical.

A third, rarer, discourse suggests that female cadets lose from gender integration. This discourse is found only among female cadets and female team commanders, mostly those in a position to compare the current course to previous, women-only ones. A few of the female cadets claimed that the course is too physically demanding and out of sync with the requirements of their prospective positions. Female team commanders argued that the women take a less active part in the course because "the boys overshadow them": "The boys gain and the girls lose. Maybe the girls gain something in their training, and the team commanders gain because the level of the course has really gone up, but the girls keep their mouths shut when they're with the boys. You haven't seen a girls-only course—they were really fiery, arguing, talking. Intellectually, they shut up when they're with the boys, they fade away, they're quiet. The boys are dominant, and you've got to be a really, really strong girl to open your mouth when the boys are around."

This commander's analysis is in keeping with research on single-sex education, which found that in coeducational classrooms boys monopolize the linguistic space and the attention of the teacher, in effect silencing the girls. Mixed-gender groups may have the unintended result of "freezing girls out" of the learning process (Salomone 2006, 790). The team commander added more examples to her claim that gender integration restored gendered role divisions: if in the past the girls carried all the heavy loads, such as the generator and field radio, now the men were carrying everything for the women. Gender integration, it seems, reconstructed the men as gallant knights and the women as weak creatures in need of help and protection, thus paradoxically restoring the traditional distinctions between men/women, war/peace, and protector/protected (see Pin-Fat and Stern 2005).

All three discourses emphasize gender differences, be those differences essentialist or cultural, and focus on gender comparison. The discourses differ from one another by the value attributed to gender differences, but none of them allow for images or perceptions of gender sameness. Moreover, the discourses of difference expand well beyond physical differences and are broadened to encompass the description and analysis of multilevel characteristics, such as studying abilities, politeness, and cleanliness.

These three discourses construct the cadets' behavior, the staffs' attitudes toward the cadets, and the relationship between senior and junior staff; in other words, they regender the sphere of relationships and actions, as well the course contents and outcomes. We heard an example of regendering through discourse after the midcourse march, when a male junior officer said to his integrated platoon: "You should all be proud of yourselves, you did the march very well. The girls carried the heavy loads, and even when it was tough you didn't cry and you didn't whine." The commander compliments the women for exceeding his expectations, which are shaped by hegemonic gender beliefs that men suffer quietly while women whine. But, simultaneously, he reconstructs the dominant discourse, which emphasizes gender differences. He compliments them for degendering, but in his words he regenders their experience and their self-perception.

This anecdote is indicative of regendering in the integrated course; it shows that this process is not necessarily planned and orchestrated from above. Rather, it occurs mostly on the cultural level and is performed in daily interactions. Thus, while the restructuring of the course worked to degender it, and surely influenced the awareness of all those involved, hegemonic gender beliefs based on stereotypical schemas were reenacted in everyday practices and relations and reinstituted a gendered (masculine) regime.

Discussion

Since the main thrust of this article is critical of the military attempt at gender integration, we want to begin by giving credit where credit is due. The driving force for gender integration seems to have been a sincere aspiration to elevate the status of women in the army and to degender the organizing principles of military training. This process, which is also taking place in other training frameworks in the Israeli army, not only contributes to the status of women in the military but also enhances the efficiency of the organization by eliminating duplicate frameworks and increases its public legitimacy by creating an image of an egalitarian institution. Hence, the limited success of the degendering processes cannot be attributed to a male conspiracy or bad faith on the part of the military. Rather, degendering should be understood in Sewell's terms, as a discrepancy between the changes that took place on the level of resources and the durability of the virtual gendered schemas that preside in the officer training course.

The analysis of gender integration of officer training highlights the importance of a theory of structure that is dynamic enough to explain both reproduction of and change in institutions. In particular, the case that we studied exemplifies the crucial importance of cultural schemas in the process of change. In recent decades, the cultural schema of gender has undergone a gradual change, from a hierarchical essentialist perception to one that sees gender as socially constructed and calls for equal rights for women. The Israeli military, like most other Western militaries, ultimately could not remain oblivious to these changes and had to find ways to incorporate the new perceptions of gender into the institution through the policy of gender integration. Thus, changes in the cultural schema in civilian society have led to a reallocation of resources within the military in general and in officer training in particular.

Some military resources—such as high-level training, military knowledge and skills, training commands, and especially officer's rank and its accompanying prestige—are no longer allocated strictly along gendered lines. These are, in Sewell's terms, mostly human resources, but their outcome is actual and material: they become "observable characteristics of real people, . . . and it is their actualization in people's minds and bodies that make them resources" (1992, 10). In a militaristic society such as Israel, officer's rank means higher prestige and better life chances not only in the military but also in the civilian labor market. Following gender integration, some women own knowledge they lacked previously, they can serve in roles that used to be closed to them, and they are able to take advantage of the prestige of officer training. Thus, the new division of resources has enabled and even led to a process of degendering.

However, the gradual change in the gender schema in civil society, which led to the policy of integration, has not been internalized in the everyday cultural codes and scripts of the military. Two different, yet connected, cultural schemas continue to operate in the officer course: the binary gender schema and the pyramid-like military schema. At the level of subjective identities, each of the schemas imposes different, almost contradictory, imperatives. The gender schema emphasizes a polarization principle (Bem 1993) demanding that females look and behave like "women" and males look and behave like "men." The military schema, in contrast, positions the masculine body of the warrior as a universal military ideal. This is an androcentric rule demanding that all soldiers, men and women alike, shape their bodies and behavior in accordance with the warrior model, and the closer one gets to the core of the military, the more crucial is his or her resemblance to the combat soldier.

The integration of the officer course purportedly offered women the option to move from their inferior position in the gender schema to a higher position in the military schema. However, since the course is modeled after the combat schema, it positions the warrior, whose identity is based on hypermasculinity, as the only possible and desirable identity for officers. When the warrior is the model for training, masculinity becomes a major organizing principle and regenders the entire course. That is, the military schema is deeply gendered and masculinized in and of itself (Enloe 1988, 2000). This enduring cultural schema affects, in turn, resource allocation. Thus, other resources available to the cadets within the course, such as prestigious duties, the physical fitness program, and social visibility, were distributed unevenly between men and women and thus regendered the course. In other words, though the new structure of the course was meant to degender, its minute practices and cultural schemas perpetuated and emphasized gender differences.

If we understand gender identities as "always doing" (Butler 1990, 25), then gender integration of officer training has led to overgendering of the entire course and especially to the overdoing of masculinity by its participants. This does not mean that all the male cadets took on the image of hegemonic masculinity as their own but that they often mobilized "contesting masculinities," through which they distanced or differentiated themselves from others, by showing rank, status, or simply physical power (see Martin 2001, 603). These behaviors, which conflate the military role with doing masculinity, testify that gender integration posed a threat to the masculinity of the cadets, the masculinity of the course, and, in general, the masculinity of the military and warfare (see Pin-Fat and Stern 2005). Hence, the integrated course became a site of assertion of difference (see Cohn 2000, 138): mixing men and women created the conditions for greater gendering than had existed when trainees were gender segregated, recreating an advantage for men. Moreover, gender integration did not offer new values to the military way of operation: it did not raise new criteria for leadership evaluation, it did not create new standards for evaluating women's physical performance, and particularly it did not offer a new professional model for the noncombatant staff officer.

Hence, the structural change did not alter the cultural model of the army, and, paradoxically, it might have strengthened the combat model as a universal military norm. Thus, while the course we witnessed in summer 2003 was very different from the one that preceded it, it was not different enough to create an equal opportunity environment for women. This supports Christine L. Williams's (1995) argument that a change directed only at altering the sex balance of occupations does little to transform their deeply gendered nature.

Applying Sewell's theory of structure, we have shown how the intersection of resources and schemas shapes both the durability and the changes within a given institution. More important, we have shown how crucial the cultural schemas are in maintaining the gender order despite intentions to modify it. The lesson from this research is that it is not enough to alter the division of resources in order to create a structural change. In order to give gender integration a chance to succeed, a policy of gender integration must take the cultural schemas seriously, at least as seriously as it examines the division of resources. For each organization, we have to ask specifically about its gender schemas. For example, does the organization have a formal public gender ideology, like the military, or is it a latent ideology, like the education system? Are the entrance exams gendered, and if so, how? What is considered achievement or success in the organization—what is its gendered nature? A policy of gender integration that disregards the cultural schemas prevalent in the institution is doomed to fail or at the very least to achieve only a partial success.

Epilogue

In April 2005 the women's base was dismantled, and the two integrated courses are now held on the men's base. In August 2006 we launched a follow-up study on gender integration in officer training. We were surprised to discover that the cadets, men and women alike, were unaware that the course had been gender separated only four years before. They were surprised when we told them gender integration was rather new in the officer course. "Really?" they said, "but why?" The majority did not even know that there used to be a women's base that ran the course. Unlike our interviewees in 2003, now most cadets and commanders saw gender integration as natural and took it for granted. In a sense, this is a sign of the success of gender integration, proving, as Sewell suggests, that resources can accumulate in unpredictable ways. However, the "boys' company" is still considered the best company and still creates a point of gendered comparison, signifying that the military's gendered schemas still work to regender the course in subtle ways.

Department of Sociology and Anthropology and Program in Gender Studies Bar Ilan University (Sasson-Levy)

Department of Behavioral Sciences Israel Defense Forces (Amram-Katz)

References

Acker, Joan. 1990. "Hierarchies, Jobs, Bodies: A Theory of Gendered Organizations." *Gender and Society* 4(2):139–58.

Barrett, Frank. 1996. "The Organizational Construction of Hegemonic Masculinity: The Case of the U.S. Navy." *Gender, Work, and Organization* 3(3): 129–42.

Belkin, Aaron, and Melissa Levitt. 2001. "Homosexuality and the Israel Defense Forces: Did Lifting the Gay Ban Undermine Military Performance?" *Armed Forces and Society* 27(4):541–65.

Bem, Sandra L. 1993. *The Lenses of Gender: Transforming the Debate on Sexual Inequality.* New Haven, CT: Yale University Press.

Ben-Ari, Eyal. 1998. *Mastering Soldiers: Conflicts, Emotions, and the Enemy in an Israeli Military Unit.* New York: Berghahn.

Berkovitch, Nitza. 1997. "Motherhood as a National Mission: The Construction of Womanhood in the Legal Discourse in Israel." *Women's Studies International Forum* 20(5–6):605–19.

Bijur, Polly E., M. Horodyski, W. Egergon, M. Kurzon, S. Lifrak, and S. Friedman. 1997. "Comparison of Injuries during Cadet Basic Training by Gender." *Archives of Pediatrics and Adolescent Medicine* 151(5):456–61.

Bloom, Anne R. 1982. "Israel: The Longest War." In *Female Soldiers—Combatants or Noncombatants? Historical and Contemporary Perspectives*, ed. Nancy L. Goldman, 137–61. London: Greenwood.

Brown, Wendy. 2003. "Gender in Counterpoint." *Feminist Theory* 4(3):365–68.

Burk, James. 1995. "Citizenship Status and Military Service: The Quest for Inclusion by Minorities and Conscientious Objectors." *Armed Forces and Society* 21(4):503–29.

Butler, Judith. 1990. *Gender Trouble: Feminism and the Subversion of Identity.* New York: Routledge.

Cohen, Stuart. 1997. "Towards a New Portrait of the (New) Israeli Soldier." *Israeli Affairs* 3(4):77–117.

Cohn, Carol. 2000. "How Can She Claim Equal Rights When She Doesn't Have to Do as Many Push-Ups as I Do? The Framing of Men's Opposition to Women's Equality in the Military." *Men and Masculinities* 3(2):131–51.

Connell, Robert W. 1987. *Gender and Power: Society, the Person, and Sexual Politics.* Stanford, CA: Stanford University Press.

DeFleur, Lois, David Gillman, and William Marshak. 1978. "Sex Integration of the U.S. Air Force Academy." *Armed Forces and Society* 4(4):607–21.

Enloe, Cynthia. 1988. *Does Khaki Become You? The Militarisation of Women's Lives.* London: Pandora.

———. 2000. *Maneuvers: The International Politics of Militarizing Women's Lives.* Berkeley: University of California Press.

Feinman, Ilene Rose. 2000. *Citizenship Rites: Feminist Soldiers and Feminist Antimilitarists.* New York: New York University Press.

Firestone, Juanita, and Richard Harris. 1994. "Sexual Harassment in the U.S. Military: Individualized and Environmental Contexts." *Armed Forces and Society* 21(1):25–43.

Helman, Sara. 1997. "Militarism and the Construction of Community." *Journal of Political and Military Sociology* 25 (Winter): 305–32.

Higate, Paul R., ed. 2003. *Military Masculinities: Identity and the State.* Westport, CT: Praeger.

Iskra, Darlene, Stephen Trainor, Marcia Leithauser, and Mady Wechsler Segal. 2002. "Women's Participation in Armed Forces Cross-Nationally: Expanding Segal's Model." *Current Sociology* 50(5):771–97.

Izraeli, Dafna. 1997. "Gendering Military Service in the Israeli Defense Forces." *Israel Social Science Research* 12(1):129–66.

Janda, Lance. 2002. *Stronger than Custom: West Point and the Admission of Women.* Westport, CT: Praeger.

Janowitz, Morris. 1976. "Military Institutions and Citizenship in Western Societies." *Armed Forces and Society* 2(2):185–204.

Kimmel, Michael. 2000. "Saving the Males: The Sociological Implications of the Virginia Military Institute and the Citadel." *Gender and Society* 14(4):494–516.

Kimmerling, Baruch. 1993. "Patterns of Militarism in Israel." *European Journal of Sociology* 34(2):196–223.

Lorber, Judith. 2005. *Breaking the Bowls: Degendering and Feminist Change.* New York: Norton.

Martin, Patricia Yancey. 2001. "'Mobilizing Masculinities': Women's Experiences of Men at Work." *Organization* 8(4):587–618.

Mitchell, Billie. 1996. "The Creation of Army Officers and the Gender Lie: Betty Grable or Frankenstein." In *It's Our Military Too! Women and the U.S. Military*, ed. Judith H. Stiehm, 35–60. Philadelphia: Temple University Press.

Morgan, David. 1994. "Theater of War: Combat, the Military, and Masculinities." In *Theorizing Masculinities*, ed. Harry Brod and Michael Kaufman, 165–83. London: Sage.

Pateman, Carole. 1989. *The Disorder of Women: Democracy, Feminism, and Political Theory.* Stanford, CA: Stanford University Press.

Peach, Lucinda Joy. 1996. "Gender Ideology in the Ethics of Women in Combat." In *It's Our Military Too! Women and the U.S. Military*, ed. Judith H. Stiehm, 156–94. Philadelphia: Temple University Press.

Pin-Fat, Véronique, and Maria Stern. 2005. "The Scripting of Private Jessica Lynch: Biopolitics, Gender, and the 'Feminization' of the U.S. Military." *Alternatives: Global, Local, Political* 30(1):25–53.

Ridgeway, Cecilia L., and Shelley J. Correll. 2004. "Unpacking the Gender System: A Theoretical Perspective on Gender Beliefs and Social Relations." *Gender and Society* 18(4):510–31.

Robbins, Joyce, and Uri Ben-Eliezer. 2000. "New Roles or 'New Times'? Gender Inequality and Militarism in Israel's Nation-in-Arms." *Social Politics* 7(3): 309–42.

Salomone, Rosemary C. 2006. "Single-Sex Programs: Resolving the Research Conundrum." *Teachers College Record* 108(4):778–802.

Sasson-Levy, Orna. 2001. "Gender Performance in a Changing Military: Women Soldiers in 'Masculine' Roles." *Israel Studies Forum* 17(1):7–23.

———. 2003a. "Feminism and Military Gender Practices: Israeli Women Soldiers in 'Masculine' Roles." *Sociological Inquiry* 73(3):440–65.

———. 2003b. "Military, Masculinity, and Citizenship: Tensions and Contradictions in the Experience of Blue-Collar Soldiers." *Identities: Global Studies in Culture and Power* 10(3):319–45.

Schemo, Diana. 2003. "Rate of Rape at Air Force Academy 12%." *New York Times*, August 29, A12.

Sewell, William H., Jr. 1992. "A Theory of Structure: Duality, Agency, and Transformation." *American Journal of Sociology* 98(1):1–29.

Shafir, Gershon, ed. 1998. *The Citizenship Debates: A Reader.* Minneapolis: University of Minnesota Press.

Smith, Dorothy E. 1990. *The Conceptual Practices of Power: A Feminist Sociology of Knowledge.* Boston: Northeastern University Press.

Snyder, R. Claire. 1999. *Citizen-Soldiers and Manly Warriors: Military Service and Gender in the Civic Republican Tradition.* Lanham, MD: Rowman & Littlefield.

———. 2003. "The Citizen-Soldier Tradition and Gender Integration of the U.S. Military." *Armed Forces and Society* 29(2):185–204.

Stiehm, Judith H. 1989. *Arms and the Enlisted Woman*. Philadelphia: Temple University Press.

Taylor, Charles. 1987. "Interpretation and the Sciences of Man." In *Interpretive Social Science: A Second Look*, ed. Paul Rabinow and William M. Sullivan, 33–81. Berkeley: University of California Press.

Tilly, Charles. 1995. "The Emergency of Citizenship in France and Elsewhere." *International Review of Social History* 40, suppl. 3: 223–36.

Williams, Christine L. 1995. *Still a Man's World: Men Who Do "Women's Work."* Berkeley: University of California Press.

Woodward, Rachel, and Patricia Winter. 2004. "Discourses of Gender in the Contemporary British Army." *Armed Forces and Society* 30(2):279–301.

———. 2006. "Gender and the Limits to Diversity in the Contemporary British Army." *Gender, Work, and Organization* 13(1):45–67.

Yoder, Janice D. 1991. "Rethinking Tokenism: Looking beyond Numbers." *Gender and Society* 5(2):178–92.

B r o n w y n   W i n t e r

Preemptive Fridge Magnets and Other Weapons of Masculinist Destruction: The Rhetoric and Reality of "Safeguarding Australia"

A **"national security" mind-set** has increasingly informed the policies and practices of the Australian government led by Prime Minister John Howard, who has been in power since 1996. The lead-up to the 2000 Olympic games; the September 11, 2001, attacks in the United States; the bombing of a nightclub in Bali in October 2002, in which Australian tourists were killed; and a hijack attempt on a Qantas jet in May 2003 have all been used as justifications for the Howard government to enhance security measures. In this article I will examine some of the government's agenda of "safeguarding Australia," particularly although not solely as it specifically targets women. In doing so, I will argue that policies and practices of the government that affect women's rights and their access to services are not simply collateral damage as the government shifts its focus from spending on education, health, infrastructure, and welfare to funding the military and boosting corporate capitalism. Diminished spending on public services and welfare and attacks on advocacy groups for the poor and minorities, accompanied by legislation that favors corporate private enterprise, have been a hallmark of neoliberal governments in the West. The current raft of measures both construct and target women in quite particular ways that are directly related to the Howard government's Hobbesian autocratic role as the self-proclaimed safeguarder of Australia. The reality of these measures is more complex than the simple withdrawal of support for services or advocacy groups. In fact, the gov-

Part of the basis for this article was a paper delivered on invitation from the University of Wollongong Legal Intersections Research Centre, at its seminar on "Responses to Terrorism: Comparison of Canadian and Australian Contexts," June 4, 2003. It has been developed and transformed since then with the support of many feminists working in women's services and advocacy groups in Australia, as well as progressive male and female scholars who have taken time to provide me with essential background information. I am indebted to them for their help and dedicate this article to the many women currently under siege as providers and users of feminist women's services in Australia.

[*Signs: Journal of Women in Culture and Society* 2007, vol. 33, no. 1]

ernment has spent considerable money, time, and energy on transforming or assuming control over these services, in scrutinizing and attempting to undermine advocacy groups and human rights watchdogs, and in constructing particular social groups as dangerous and in need of containing (at the same time as they are constructed as needing protection). The government's attacks on women (and on some groups of socioeconomically disadvantaged men, feminized by association) are not a side effect of "Leviathan Down Under's" politics of fear.[1] They are an integral part of it.

The Howard government provides a vivid example of a masculinist state that blurs the boundaries between paternalistic "protector" (Young 2003, 4) and hypermasculine aggressor, boundaries that have figured prominently in several feminist accounts of the state (see Stiehm 1982; Peterson 1992; Young 2003). Iris Marion Young, for example, makes a distinction between "the logic of masculinist protection" (along Hobbesian lines) and "self-consciously dominative" (2003, 4) masculinity. In contrast to the brutal image of the hypermasculine aggressors who "wish to master women sexually for the sake of their own gratification and to have the pleasures of domination," the paternalist protectors appear "more benign," promising to protect their women from the other type, "the selfish, aggressive, othered, hypersexualized predator" (4).

The construction of a demonized, hypersexualized male other (as opposed to good and civilized us) has a long history in the West, surfacing in colonialist, anti-Semitic, racist, and xenophobic literature, philosophy, and statecraft (*barbarian* originally meant *foreigner* in ancient Greece). In recognizing that distinction, I have no argument with Young. I similarly have no argument with her analysis of the protectionist bargain by which only submissive and obedient women (or, by extension, citizens) are good and deserving of protection, as opposed to the bad rebel women (Young 2003, 13–14). I would suggest, however, that the "self-consciously dominative" subjugator of women and the pseudobenign protector are not so easily separated out. Following Robin Morgan (1989), V. Spike Peterson (1992), and Cynthia Enloe (2004), I would suggest that these two representations are simply two sides of the same coin of male domination. The same men and the same institutions embodying masculinist power can present as one or the other depending on the circumstance. The discursive compartmentalization of masculinity into either aggressive or protective only serves to reinforce male domination by preventing one

---

[1] "Down Under" is a nickname for Australia, mostly used ironically or facetiously these days, as I have used it here.

from seeing it in its entirety and complexity. Catharine MacKinnon and Carole Pateman, identified by Young as theorizing only aggressive, "self-consciously dominative" (Young 2003, 4) masculinity, clearly point to the links between the dominative and the more benign protectionist authoritarianism. In her discussion of sex difference and the attribution of sex roles, for example, MacKinnon (1990, 214) states that "'difference' . . . is the velvet glove on the iron fist of dominance," and this is "as true when women are punished for it as it is when they are protected in its name." Pateman thoroughly analyzes the notion of husband (and, by extension, state) as both dominator and benevolent protector, noting in relation to Thomas Hobbes in particular that, "because Hobbes argues that fear and liberty are compatible, 'consent' has the same meaning whether it arises from submission in fear of a conqueror's sword or in fear of exposure by a parent, or whether it is a consequence of the (hypothetical) social contract" (1989, 73). The man who routinely beats and rapes his wife (and perhaps his daughters) may be heroic in protecting those same wife and daughters from a burglar, a fire, or other real or perceived dangers. The state that penalizes women for challenging the male supremacist order or constrains and intimidates them to such an extent that challenge is not a conceivable option may become a champion of women's rights when going off to war, whether it is our women who must be protected or other women who must be rescued (as in the case of the U.S.-led war against Afghanistan; Delphy 2002; Winter 2006).[2]

Subordination of women within the logic of masculinist protectionism is not an effect of protectionism, as Young appears to suggest (2003, 6), but rather a necessary precondition for the relationship of protectionism to exist. The Hobbesian protector is also the "deadly hero" (Morgan 1989, chap. 2), the ironfisted son of the velvet-gloved patriarch, whether sanctioned by the state or acting as subversive revolutionary (or terrorist). The original barbarians, the original threatening and hypersexualized others whom this deadly hero must subdue and appropriate, are women. Once so tamed and controlled, they are transformed into the good submissive women of whom the aggressor can then become protector. Thus they become the justification for further wars. Protecting our women and

---

[2] Young has noted this but curiously lays part of the blame for the masculinist state's appropriation of feminism in the case of the 2001 war against Afghanistan at the door of racism within the feminist movement (2003, 20). I would suggest, without denying that there are issues of oppression and domination among feminists, that, first, the Western state does not need feminism to be paternalistically colonialist and, second, feminists are not responsible for dishonest co-optation of feminism by states.

liberating other women provide a veneer of morality to warmongering. Moreover, the appropriation of "other" women provides a bargaining chip through which control of the enemy can be more effectively secured and through which the enemy can, once subdued, be feminized in turn (Enloe 1990, 34; Winter 1995, 97–146; Young 2003, 19). Throughout the history of modern nation-states and their colonial exploits, and in the rhetoric of their concomitant ideologies, we find the same metaphors of virility—penetrate, subjugate, then jubilate—and the same paternalistic protectionism enacted through punishment, whether this be through direct acts of violence or repression or through more subtle forms of disempowerment.

Nationalists have long understood the centrality of appropriating women into their projects, whether fascist (confining women with and within *Kinder Küche Kirche* [children, kitchen, church]), modern and emancipatory (such as Kemalist Turkey or the early years of the Third Republic in France), colonial and neocolonial, or neo-Hobbesian, as is the case today in the United States and Australia. Protecting our women becomes a way of silencing them, because women's welfare matters only insofar as it serves the cause of the nation (Winter 2002a; Enloe 2004). It is not women's place to say what is good for them; that is the task of the nationalist protector. Recent developments in Australia illuminate this dynamic.

Leviathan Down Under

Deploying discourse and policies to "safeguard Australia," the Howard government has mobilized a politics of fear and demanded submission to a protective authoritarian power.[3] The rhetoric of war on terror, the security of Australia and Australians, and the defense of our values are threaded through the speeches of government ministers in justification of policy, legislation, budget allocations, and mobilization of defense, security, and police forces within and outside the country. "Safeguarding Australia from terrorism, crime, invasive diseases and pests" (ARC 2006, 43) even features as one of four National Research Priorities for academic

[3] Howard is parliamentary leader of Australia's Liberal Party, which is a conservative political party. Governing in coalition with the rural-based National Party, his government has increased its power fairly steadily since its first election in 1996. The September 2001 attacks and the demonization of asylum seekers as part of a security platform have contributed significantly to this success. In its third reelection in 2004, the coalition also gained control of the senate (operative from July 1, 2005), thus removing a substantial barrier to its ability to push through repressive and regressive legislation.

research projects funded by the Australian Research Council (ARC), a public body that is the major funder of nonmedical research in the Australian university system. In outlining this National Research Priority, the ARC Funding Rules state, "The importance of security and safety to Australia has been underscored by recent events. Australia has to be capable of anticipating and tackling critical threats to society, strategic areas of the national economy and the environment. The threats can potentially come from within and outside Australia" (ARC 2006, 43).[4]

Using a strategy similar to George W. Bush's USA PATRIOT Act of 2001, the Howard government exhorted Australian citizens to "Be Alert, But Not Alarmed."[5] This slogan was featured in a twenty-page booklet that arrived on the doorsteps of all Australian households in February 2003 along with a fridge magnet displaying information on the "24-hour National Security Hotline" (Commonwealth Government 2003). The closest a terrorist threat had come to Australia at that point was the bombing of a nightclub in the resort town of Kuta, Bali, on October 12, 2002. Although Australian tourists represented the largest national group of those killed (eighty-nine dead), followed by Indonesians (thirty-eight) and British (twenty-five), it has not been demonstrated that Australians were specifically targeted by the bombers. Nonetheless, the booklet informed Australians that "in a national emergency the Prime Minister will take strategic control" (2003, 6). We were also told that "the public [would] be kept informed with reliable, up-to-date information on the situation at all times" (6).[6]

Despite the ostensibly reassuring message of the fridge magnet campaign, women in particular had cause to be alarmed, all the more when it was revealed how the campaign had been funded. On May 17, 2003, Nicola Roxon, then Australian Labor Party (ALP) shadow minister for children and youth and shadow minister for women, revealed to the Australian media that AU$10.1 million of supposedly "unspent funds relating

[4] Security studies is a burgeoning field in Australian universities, with many political science departments recruiting specialists in this area. This growth in militarization studies is significant in a sector that has suffered massive cuts to its budget over the ten years since the Howard government came to office (an estimated minimum of AU$20 billion is needed to restore higher education to pre-1996 levels of funding).

[5] Uniting and Strengthening America by Providing Appropriate Tools Required to Intercept and Obstruct Terrorism Act (USA PATRIOT Act), Public Law 107-56, 115 Stat. 272 (October 26, 2001).

[6] A few short months later, the Australian public was being given up-to-date and reliable information on the unreliability of the information we had previously been given about Iraqi weapons of mass destruction.

to the Women's programmes" (Commonwealth of Australia 2003b) were diverted in the national budget to the National Security Public Information Campaign (the fridge magnet campaign), which ended up costing AU$18.5 million.[7] The programs in question were Partnerships Against Domestic Violence (PADV; $7.5 million unspent) and the National Initiative to Combat Sexual Assault (NICSA; $2.5 million unspent). Partnerships Against Domestic Violence had received an allocation of over AU$25 million for joint initiatives between commonwealth and state governments concerning violence against women (a separate program from ongoing funding of women's domestic violence services). Women's nongovernmental organizations (NGOs) with many years' experience in working on domestic violence were not consulted about the development of this program or the ways in which the money should be spent. A few days after Roxon's media release, Senator Trish Crossin (ALP) discovered through questions in the Senate Estimates Committee that the budgets for 2003 and 2004 for the Office for the Status of Women, PADV, and NICSA all contained carryovers of unspent funds from the 2002–3 fiscal year. Not only did these funds correspond to the amount spent on the fridge magnet campaign, but it also appeared on paper that they artificially increased government allocations for women's programs in 2003 and 2004. The extra money, however, was not the result of an increased allocation but of a carryover from previous years (Commonwealth of Australia 2003a, 129–77). When told that PADV had "been extended by two years" (because of underspending in 2002–3), Crossin commented that "it has taken an unusually long period of time to spend money in an area that I thought would have been a national priority" (Commonwealth of Australia 2003b, 139). Indeed, in his media release launching PADV, Prime Minister Howard (1997) stated that domestic violence "not only has traumatic personal consequences but also inflicts enormous social and economic costs on the whole community" and that it must be acknowledged that "domestic violence is not a private matter, but a serious issue for our whole society." Yet there had been little constructive activity on this "serious issue" since PADV's inception. Julie Oberin, former National Coordinator and current Victorian Coordinator of the Women's Emergency Services Network (WESNET), a peak (i.e., umbrella) advocacy body that represents and lobbies for some four hundred organizations involved in women's emergency services (e.g., rape crisis services and women's refuges), confirmed that, during the period of underspending, feminist-run women's services were unable to obtain funding crucial to their con-

---

[7] Interview transcript issued by Roxon's parliamentary office, May 17, 2003.

tinuing effective operation. Indeed, Oberin noted that one of the proposals that WESNET submitted for funding did not proceed, although the government gave no particular reason for its failure to fund the proposal. Other women's projects were a year late starting, which saved the government money, and a private consultancy employed as project support for PADV had underspent its budget.[8]

In the state of New South Wales alone in 2001, thirty-nine thousand complaints of domestic violence were made to the courts (Summers 2003a). Yet WESNET has received no government funding since it withdrew in 2001 from a government-imposed amalgamation with homelessness organizations under the umbrella of the Australian Federation of Homelessness Organizations, created specifically for that purpose. This led to specific issues of violence against women being subsumed under a more general homelessness agenda, which was not helpful to the work of WESNET. In 2003, WESNET was so seriously short of funds that it could not pay its national executive officer for more than ten hours' work per week.[9] This is a now familiar scenario affecting peak advocacy bodies in Australia: either they are forced (in order to continue to receive funding) into uncomfortable amalgamations where more radically critical voices are silenced or at the very least diluted, or they are defunded; often they suffer both (Staples 2006).

Compare this to defense spending, which has increased steadily from 1996, although as a percentage of gross domestic product it has remained fairly static. There was a sharp jump in spending in 2001–2 and a planned growth of 3 percent per annum thereafter to meet "emerging strategic priorities" as set out in the 2003–4 budget: border control, Iraq operations, the establishment of a special operations command, and "increased logistics funding" (Commonwealth of Australia 2003b). The May 2006 federal budget provides for spending on defense and "National Security: Preventing Terrorism" (a new subcategory of defense) of roughly AU$20 billion, with further increases planned over coming years. This may appear paltry in comparison to the US$813,500 spent per minute in the United States on national security (US$427.6 billion per annum approved in June 2006 by the U.S. House of Representatives; Allen 2006). Nonetheless, the AU$16 billion budget of 2003 was almost four times the total amount of funding received that year by Australia's thirty-eight public universities (AU$4.31 billion; Commonwealth of Australia 2003b).[10]

---

[8] Julie Oberin, e-mail message to author, June 2, 2003.

[9] Ibid.

[10] The then Federal Education Minister, Brendan Nelson, was subsequently promoted to the defense portfolio, a ministerial hierarchy that is telling in itself.

In his speech introducing the second reading of the 2003–4 budget to the Australian House of Representatives, Treasurer Peter Costello stated that "the security of our people and our nation is the Government's first priority. Today we are faced with the dangers of rising international terrorism and weapons of mass destruction." He went on to say that the government was committed to "confronting these threats to our security and defending our values and way of life" (Costello 2003). In 2006, when introducing the new National Security package, Costello stated: "ongoing review of national security capabilities is critical to meeting the evolving threats to Australia's national security" (Costello 2006). Exactly what these evolving threats are has been left unexplained.

Love me tender . . .

Enloe has observed that "when any policy approach is militarized, one of the first things that happens is that women's voices are silenced. We find that when the United States touts any military institution as the best hope for stability, security, and development, the result is deeply gendered: the politics of masculinity are made to seem 'natural,' the male grasp on political influence is tightened, and most women's access to real political influence shrinks dramatically" (2004, 128). This silencing, however, is neither direct nor complete. As Enloe has also pointed out, some women benefit from militarization and some perceive their interests to lie within it (2000, 294). Moreover, governments have become highly skilled in the art of indirection. In Australia the current silencing of women is happening under the guise of overt government attention to discrimination and violence against women. The government is ostensibly showing its concern for women's safety and even spending a reasonable amount of money to demonstrate this. Yet at the same time it is defunding feminist organizations that advocate on behalf of women and diverting funds from its own women's programs, while adopting other new legislation and policies that in fact make women less safe.

In 2004 the Australian government reconfigured PADV into a National Campaign to Eliminate Violence Against Women (NCEVAW), launched with a glossy twenty-two-page booklet and a television advertising campaign called "Violence Against Women: Australia Says No" (Commonwealth of Australia 2004). On the front page of the booklet, the prime minister smiles from a photograph above the heading: "Good relationships make a great community" (2004, 1). The first paragraph of the letter he addresses to the Australian public under this heading sets the tone: "The Australian Government believes that families are the backbone of a strong and healthy community, and loving supportive relationships are at the heart of happy, well functioning families. Families are the best places for children to learn about love and respect, and how to build and maintain healthy and caring relationships" (2004, 1). The booklet and the television advertising campaign feature case stories, explanations of what constitutes physical and psychological abuse, and information for both women and men on where to go for help. They appear on the face of it to send a positive message, putting government money where feminist mouths have been for many decades, calling for concerted action at a national level.

On closer examination, however, the "Australia Says No" campaign merely puts a gloss on a more sinister reality, including that of the campaign itself. Originally developed as the "No Respect, No Relationship" campaign, it had been intended to air in December 2003 in time for the Christmas holiday period, when the incidence of domestic violence is known to increase. Following protests by groups such as the Men's Rights Agency, the campaign was canceled and relaunched under a new name—and with a new focus on the family—in 2004 (see Bowden 2004; Price 2005).[11] Other disturbing aspects of this reality are the exclusion of feminist-run women's services from national consultations and excessive scrutiny (through, for example, endless reporting requirements) and badgering of organizations that are critical of government policy.[12] Even more disturbing is the fact that women's and other community service provisions were put out to tender, that is, for competitive bidding. Organizations with direct experience in the field, which also play an independent advocacy role for their constituencies, are now competing for funding with private enterprise, conservative, and mostly Christian charities, which provide no sociopolitical analysis of the structural issues contributing to problems of domestic violence, delinquency, homelessness, and so on. Some consultancies have not even had to go through the tendering process but have been awarded directly.

Between 2000 and 2002 consultants awarded PADV funds included international accounting firm KPMG Consulting, concert promoter Brandon Saul, and two businesses run by Tricia Szirom, formerly associated with the Young Women's Christian Association (Summers 2003b, 94–97). The prime minister's report for the 2003–4 financial year shows that some

[11] See the Men's Rights Agency Web site, http://www.mensrights.com.au/index.php ?article_id=255.

[12] Anedoctal evidence from women working in women's, disability, and housing services in New South Wales, the Australian Capital Territory (location of Canberra, the national capital), and Victoria. See also Maddison 2004.

feminist-informed and feminist-run organizations with expertise and experience in working on violence against women, such as the Domestic and Family Violence Clearinghouse at the University of New South Wales, did receive consultancy funding, and government-run departments such as the Australian Bureau of Statistics (ABS) and the Department of Health and Ageing received substantial sums for statistical research.[13] The lion's share, however, went to either Christian charities or public relations and marketing consultancies. Among the largest recipients was Lifeline Australia, an overtly Christian counseling organization, which received almost AU$2 million to run the helpline and referral service for the NCEVAW, while Relationships Australia, a secular but far from feminist organization (founded in 1948 under the name of the Marriage Guidance Council), was awarded AU$275,000 "to trial response strategies and training resources for front-line workers in contact with children living with domestic violence" (Australian Government, Department of the Prime Minister 2004). In fact, only the government's preferred service providers were permitted to tender for the NCEVAW helpline and referral service. Existing women's domestic violence services were barred from doing so.

The many public relations and marketing consultancies awarded included AU$796,455 (more than twice that awarded to the Domestic Violence Clearinghouse) for Haystac Public Affairs Pty Ltd, Melbourne's largest public relations firm, to "provide the public relations services" for the NCEVAW, as well as another AU$197,890 for the same firm to "provide production services for a digital video on women in science" and AU$990,000 for Grey Worldwide Pty Ltd, a communications group that wins a number of government contracts, to "provide the advertising component" of the NCEVAW (Australian Government, Department of the Prime Minister 2004). Overall, four thousand government consultancies in all areas were awarded a total of close to AU$300 million in 2003–4, although this was a lean year compared with the previous one, when more than AU$513 million was spent on consultancies. The total consultancy bill as of February 2005 exceeded AU$2 billion (Seccombe 2005).

State governments have followed the federal model with South Australia, Victoria, Queensland, and New South Wales all now tendering out women's domestic violence services. In South Australia, which led the trend, only one domestic violence consultancy is allowed per region, meaning that women's services are forced to compete with one another for

[13] The Office for the Status of Women was then attached to the prime minister's portfolio. At the start of the 2004–5 financial year it was moved to the Department of Family and Community Services and renamed the Office for Women.

government money—a trend that has spread to other states.[14] Yet a report prepared for the government by WESNET, but buried by the government for fifteen months (and then released only following consistent pressure by WESNET, some state offices for women's policy, and Federal ALP House of Representatives member for Sydney, Tanya Plibersek), showed that women's emergency services were starved of funding, and every second woman fleeing domestic violence had to be turned away by a shelter for lack of space (Weekes and Oberin 2004).

The Australian component of the multicountry *International Violence Against Women Survey* (IVAWS) published in 2004 found that one in ten women had experienced at least one incident of physical and/or sexual violence in the previous twelve months, while 57 percent had experienced such an incident in their lifetime. Incidence was higher among young women and indigenous women, and violence from a former partner was much more likely than violence from a current partner. Among the key recommendations of the report was increased assistance to women escaping conflict situations (Mouzos and Makkai 2004, 4–5). The same year, just prior to the 2004 election, Access Economics published a government-funded study on the costs of domestic violence to the Australian economy. This study was also buried by the government and released only after Michael McKinnon of the *Australian* newspaper filed a freedom of information application. It found that roughly 355,000 women had experienced domestic violence in 2002–3, that 98 percent of the perpetrators were male (which is consistent with findings on domestic violence and sexual assault worldwide, such as those readily available via the United Nations), and that "around 263,800 children were living with victims of domestic violence and 181,200 children witnessed domestic violence" (Access Economics 2004, vi). The total population of Australia at that time was a little under 20 million; half were women, and slightly more than 80 percent were ages 15 and over (67.3 percent ages 15–64, the most probable age group for domestic violence; ABS 2006). This means that in 2002–3 roughly 5 percent of Australian women were known to have suffered domestic violence, that is, 355,000 expressed as a percentage of the female half of 67.3 percent of the overall population ages 15–64. According to the ABS study "Crime and Safety Australia" (ABS 2005), as many as 31 percent of victims of sexual assault did not report the incidents to police, giving as reasons the concern that they would not be

---

[14] Julie Oberin and Betty Green (who work in domestic violence services in Victoria and New South Wales, respectively), contributions to the Feminist Agenda e-mail discussion list, April 18–19, 2006.

taken seriously or an opinion that the issue was a private and not a police matter or that it was a trivial matter. This means that much progress remains to be made concerning another of the IVAWS survey's key recommendations, that violence against women be recognized and responded to as a crime (Mouzos and Makkai 2004, 4–5).

The Access Economics study also found that the annual cost of domestic violence to the Australian economy was AU$8.1 billion, with the largest proportion of the cost being borne by the victims themselves (followed by the general community). While relying too heavily on the argument of cost to the economy of domestic violence is a dangerous path for feminists to tread because it measures women's lives in dollar terms and in terms of the cost to the community rather than to the victims, the figure is nonetheless illuminating, particularly when considered in the light of on what and whom the Australian government is spending women's programs money. The Australian Bureau of Statistics noted in 2004 that there had been a steady increase in reported cases of violence against women over ten years but commented that it was difficult to determine whether the violence had increased or simply that more women were reporting it. It also noted that there was "evidence that most victims of sexual assault do not report the crime to police" (ABS 2004, 14). What is certain, however, is that the national governmental response to what Joy Goodsell, manager of Sutherland Shire Family Services in Sydney's southern suburbs, fittingly termed "terrorism in the home" (Goodsell 2005) is both inappropriate and inadequate.

The government's terror war on women

The government's fanfare about eliminating violence against women trumpets all the more hollowly in the light of its recent changes to the 1975 Family Law Act, which regulates divorce and child custody matters. The stated focus of the 2004 Family Law Rules and the 2006 Family Law (Shared Parental Responsibility) Amendment Act (both of which came into force on July 1, 2006) is the interests of children, but this interest is determined as being achieved through, among other things, mandatory "dispute resolution" (Australian Government 2004, 12) and "shared parenting" arrangements (21). The latter involve "substantially shared parenting time" on a day-to-day basis and a "requirement to consult" concerning things like religious and cultural upbringing and where children reside (14). While fifty-fifty time is the presumption on which Family Court judges should work, it is a rebuttable one in that one or both parties can argue for a different decision. Moreover, the fifty-fifty presumption and the principle of shared parenting are not applicable in cases of violence against women or children. Fathers' rights groups such as the Lone Fathers Association consider that in making fifty-fifty time a recommendation, not a requirement, the government "played into the hands of the people with vested interests: the Family Court, women's groups and the legal profession."[15] The chief justice of the family court, Alastair Nicholson, had long warned against the influence of "discontented litigants" who are "sometimes obviously dysfunctional," saying in 1995 that it was "all too often the experience of this court that its most persistent critics have behaved in a way which cannot stand up to public scrutiny, particularly in relation to issues of violence against women and children. Such persons, who often espouse the rights of fathers, do very little for their cause. . . . The behaviour and attitude of those who espouse so-called fathers' rights leave little opportunity for rational discourse" (Nicholson 1996, 1).

Beginning in 2007, a legal requirement for parents will be cooperative dispute resolution (Australian Government, Attorney-General's Department n.d.) involving mandatory attendance at family dispute resolution sessions before taking a parenting matter to court. Once again, this is not applicable in cases of domestic violence. The new legislation, however, also involves a modification of the definition of family violence that places the onus on individuals fearing violence to demonstrate that they "reasonably fear for . . . their personal wellbeing or safety. The court will consider whether it is reasonable for a person in the shoes of the individual to fear or have an apprehension of violence" (Australian Government, Attorney-General's Department n.d., 1). The import of this is prospective in that it looks to fears for the future while discounting or even ignoring the past existence of violence (Rathus 2005). Yet as Zoe Rathus has pointed out, if the past is not dealt with, neither can the future be; this has been recognized in relation to other matters, such as in the case of the Truth and Reconciliation Commission in South Africa.[16] The dispute resolution process will be mediated through new Family Relationship Centres. As of June 2006 the government had approved AU$90.5 million to establish fifteen Family Relationship Centres, thirty-three early intervention services, and seventeen postseparation services.[17] Most of these are run by Relationships Australia, Centacare Catholic Family Services, and

---

[15] Cited in the *Australian*, December 29, 2003.

[16] Zoe Rathus, e-mail message to the author, June 27, 2006.

[17] See the Department of Family and Community Services Web site, http://www.facs .gov.au/internet/facsinternet.nsf/family/frsp-selection_process.htm.

the Family Life Movement of Australia, an overtly Christian company founded in 1926, trading as Interrelate.

Feminists have expressed significant concerns both about the new Family Law Rules and about the growing influence of fathers' rights groups. A number of studies have demonstrated that women who have suffered domestic violence have initially been supportive of contact between their children and the fathers (contrary to assertions by fathers' rights groups, which routinely accuse women of denying access to fathers). These women have found, however, that in continuing to allow access, they have exposed both themselves and their children to risk of continued or increased violence.[18] As noted in the IVAWS study cited above, women are at greatest risk of violence from former partners. Under the new regime in Australia, where women are forced into dispute resolution brokered by conservative and Christian organizations and the onus of proof is, more than ever before, on them to demonstrate that they have a reasonable fear of violence occurring or recurring, the risks to the security of women and children increase greatly, and it would seem that the major safeguarding is of fathers' rights, as defined by organizations such as the Lone Fathers Association, Men's Rights Agency, and Dads Against Discrimination.

The exact nature and degree of the influence of fathers' rights groups has been difficult to determine with precision, notwithstanding their proliferation, increases in expressions of public support from some politicians, and growing media exposure. This is in part because there is a relative paucity of studies of these movements in Australia to date, but what is certain is that they have had an influence (Kaye and Tolmie 1998; Dunn 2004). Marian Sawer documents the links between "angry white men" (1999) and the rise of the extreme right in Australia, noting that Barry Williams, founder and president of the Lone Fathers Association, was approached to run as a candidate for the extreme-right party One Nation, then headed by Pauline Hanson, and that almost twice as many men as women voted for One Nation. She further notes that "in February 1998 Williams was able to spend an hour with the prime minister to discuss the plight of non-custodial fathers, while Kathleen Swinbourne of the Sole Parents' Union was unable to get even an answer to her letters. She did however receive a message from Dads R Us saying 'We have the Family Court, Child Support Agency embittered self-centered women such as yourself and their effeminite/poofter men supporters, clearly in our sights'" (Sawer 1999, 3).

One of the most popular ideological weapons being used by fathers'

---

[18] See Humphreys 1999; Rendell, Rathus, and Lynch 2000; Brown 2001; Laing 2003.

rights groups at present in their attempts to discredit and intimidate women who speak out about male violence is Parental Alienation Syndrome (PAS), a concept developed in the United States in 1985 by Richard Gardner. Parental Alienation Syndrome is defined by its creator and his supporters as "the systematic vilification by one parent of the other parent and brainwashing of the child, with the intent of alienating the child from the other parent" (Price and Pioske 1994, 9), and, as such, "a form of emotional abuse" that may be "even more detrimental than physically and/or sexually abusing a child" (Gardner 1999, addendum 1). Despite legal and intellectual challenges and official discrediting in some jurisdictions in the United States, PAS has been deployed in recent years by fathers' rights groups in a number of countries, resulting in several custody wins in the United States at least (Childress 2006; see also Wilson 2001). In the United Kingdom the group Families Need Fathers (FNF) produced a lengthy "Guide to the Parental Alienation Syndrome," claiming it is so common that "nearly every FNF member will have some experience of it" (Hayward n.d.).[19] And in France the Association Against Parental Alienation (Association Contre l'Aliénation Parentale, or ACALPA) is organizing a European conference on PAS in Paris, apparently with the support of Xavier Bertrand, Minister for Health with the right-wing government there.[20] In Australia a study conducted over five years in Queensland found that PAS tended to be used by fathers for strategic or tactical reasons in high-conflict custody battles (Berns 2001).

Given that the new Family Law Rules have only just come into effect at the time of this writing, it is difficult to get a sense of their concrete impact in terms of risk of violence to women and children, increased access of abusive or potentially abusive men supported by fathers' rights groups to ex-spouses and children, impact on child support payments, the effect of the involvement of officially sanctioned church organizations, and more generally, of legally enabled intimidation of women within the dispute resolution model. Early indications from women working as researchers and/or practitioners in the field of family law, however, do not augur well for outcomes in terms of safeguarding Australian women.

The Howard government has effectively brought about a paradigm shift in how violence against women, care of children, and women's services are conceptualized. Where before we talked about joint custody, we

---

[19] See the Families Need Fathers Web site, http://www.coeffic.deomn.co.uk/pas.htm.

[20] As announced by its president, Olga Odinetz, during a conference in Lyons, May 2006. Communications posted on June 27 and 28, 2006, to the e-mail discussion list Études Féministes and to me by Léo Thiers-Vidal, who attended the conference.

now talk about shared parenting; where before we talked about women's services, we now talk about family services, counseling, or relationships centers; where before we talked about domestic violence, we now talk about family violence.

"For their own good": Gender, race, and "Australian values"

Indigenous Australian feminists have been outspoken about the obfuscating effect of this shift of focus from women to family. According to Pam Greer, who has been working with indigenous Australian women experiencing domestic violence for twenty years:

> When we hear the definitions of family violence. . . . If the definition is . . . so broad that it's almost like anybody doing violence to anybody else in the community, I think it takes away from what we know domestic violence is. The victims and the survivors know that it's a partner, it's somebody who supposedly loves somebody else who beats them regularly, puts them down and then sometimes murders them. . . . "Family" has become a funny word where people use it in a way that we're all one family . . . while this dreadful thing called domestic violence is going on . . . so it takes away some of the seriousness. (2001, 13–14)

Yet the government does claim to be taking family violence in indigenous communities seriously. In fact, it has used protection of indigenous women and paternalistic care of indigenous Australians more generally as a justification for the removal of indigenous people's rights.

A combination of violence against women and mismanagement of funds by some indigenous leaders was used in 2004 as a pretext for dismantling the elected Aboriginal and Torres Strait Islander Commission (ATSIC) and setting up the government's own appointed body. The same year, then Aboriginal Affairs Minister Amanda Vanstone put out Aboriginal Legal Aid services to competitive tender rather than directly funding a designated service of in-house lawyers familiar with indigenous communities. As human rights lawyer Gwynn MacCarrick pointed out at the time, legal aid cases are low priority for private legal firms, and indigenous Australians would be the big losers in a tendering operation (MacCarrick 2004).

In 2006 Minister for Health and Ageing Tony Abbott, in launching the government's Health Report for that year, even explicitly called for a new paternalism in its approach to indigenous affairs (Abbott 2006). Commenting on poor health and on violence against women and children in indigenous communities, Abbott attributed it not to two centuries of systemic and structural racism and lack of constructive government action in working with indigenous communities (and in particular indigenous women) to resolve demonstrable problems but to poor self-management among semiautonomous rural indigenous communities. This is "why a form of paternalism—paternalism based on competence rather than race" was deemed by the minister to be "really unavoidable if these places are to be well run," as he advocated that the government step in to wrest control from the local indigenous authorities (Abbott 2006).

Less directly, "respect for women" is being mobilized within a governmental push to "defend Australian values," the implied target of which is migrants from Muslim backgrounds. At the time of this writing in late 2006, a national debate is being waged over a government proposal that applicants for Australian citizenship should be given tests not only in English but also in "Australian values" (Shanahan 2006). Those values would include democratic rights, the rule of law, freedom of religion, and nondiscrimination on the grounds of race, religion, or sex: information already communicated in a letter from the government to new migrants. The controversy over Australian values and whether Muslims are able to embrace them was further fueled in October by sexist remarks made by Sheikh Taj al-Din al-Hilaly, Mufti of Australia, to a congregation of five hundred in Sydney at the end of Ramadan. Hilaly called women the "best weapons of Satan" and compared women who go out unveiled in public to "uncovered meat" that has only itself to blame if marauding stray cats eat it (Hilaly 2006). Prime Minister Howard was among the many— including many Muslim women and some Muslim men—who criticized Hilaly for his offensive remarks and urged the Muslim community to remove him from office. Unlike Hilaly's Muslim critics, however, who found his remarks offensive to women, Howard's main concern was Australian values: "I can say without fear of contradiction that what he said is repugnant to Australian values," Howard told the press on October 26 (AAP 2006).

Both indigenous feminists and Muslim-background feminists have criticized white Australia's use of the oppression of women to justify paternalistic attitudes toward racialized groups while concrete and constructive support and solidarity are not forthcoming. Former ATSIC commissioner Alison Anderson characterized professed governmental concern about violence against women in indigenous communities as tokenism and the abolition of ATSIC as a silencing of indigenous voices in an interview on

April 16, 2004, on ABC Radio.[21] Shakira Hussein, writing in the context of a public debate on the empowerment of Australian women versus oppression of women in Muslim countries, noted that white Australian women were not free from discriminations or violence and stressed that Muslim women had no intention of being "silent partners" in debates and actions ostensibly concerning their well-being (Hussein 2006).

"Sacrificing tangible freedoms for a spectral safety"

So wrote Carmen Lawrence in 2006 (5).[22] Many of the freedoms to which she refers have indeed been severely restricted or even curtailed by the twenty-eight pieces of antiterrorism legislation enacted by the Howard government in the five years from September 2001 to September 2006.[23] Among many other things, this legislation empowers the government to prosecute anyone giving funds, directly or indirectly, to any terrorist organization (almost identical legislation was quickly demonstrated to be problematic in Canada; Pue 2003) and extends the definition of sedition to include those who urge violence or assistance to Australia's enemies, which has raised concerns about freedom of speech.[24] In a July 2006 report to the attorney general, the Australian Law Reform Commission made twenty-seven recommendations concerning the sedition law, focusing in particular on the need to distinguish clearly between individual rights to freedom of expression and deliberate incitement to violence. The report also recommends that the term *sedition* no longer be used in any Australian laws and that the unlawful associations provisions be repealed (ALRC 2006). The legislation follows a pattern that has been developing for some time (Head 2000; Ricketts 2002) but has escalated since the September 2001 attacks and the 2002 Bali bombing. Moreover, unlike comparable legislation in the United Kingdom, the Australian antiterrorism laws do not contain adequate provisions for judicial review—some

[21] Anderson's comments appear in Kirk 2004.

[22] This phrase is also an oblique reference to a frequently cited sentence attributed to Benjamin Franklin: "Those who would give up essential liberty to purchase a little temporary safety deserve neither liberty nor safety." Lawrence is an ALP federal member of parliament. She was the only member of the Labor Federal Caucus to publicly oppose her party's support of Australian intervention in Afghanistan and Iraq. She has also been extremely supportive of feminists and has spoken at several activist conferences.

[23] See the Australian Government's National Security Web site, http://www.national security.gov.au.

[24] Anti-Terrorism Act (No. 2) 2005, No. 144 of 2005. Canberra: Commonwealth of Australia.

contain virtually none at all. Even where such review is provided for, "Australian courts cannot examine the compatibility of antiterrorism laws with any human rights instrument" (Michaelsen 2005, 2). Unlike the United States or the United Kingdom, Australia has no bill of rights or specific act of parliament protecting basic rights and freedoms of its citizens and no constitutional watchdogs with legally binding decision-making powers such as the Council of State in France. The Australian Capital Territory and the State of Victoria have, however, addressed this lack within their own jurisdictions.[25] The State of Tasmania is also considering doing so. At the national level Australia does, however, have the Human Rights and Equal Opportunity Commission (HREOC), set up in 1986 by an Act of Federal Parliament, with responsibilities for inquiring into alleged infringements under the Racial Discrimination Act 1975, the Sex Discrimination Act 1984, the Disability Discrimination Act 1992, the Age Discrimination Act 2004, and the Human Rights and Equal Opportunity Commission Act 1986.[26] The Aboriginal and Torres Strait Islander social justice commissioner also has specific functions under the HREOC Act and under the Native Title Act 1993.[27] The Human Rights and Equal Opportunity Commission has played important advocacy, watchdog, and review roles for the protection of human rights in Australia, and the Sex Discrimination Unit and commissioner, often working cooperatively with other units of HREOC, have been highly proactive in the area of women's and, more recently, lesbian and gay rights. The successive sex discrimination commissioners and directors of the unit have maintained strong links with women's and feminist NGOs, with which they have worked constructively and consultatively, including on community research projects—as have the other commissioners with relation to their specific areas.[28] The proactiveness that HREOC has shown in defending rights and engaging with communities that are far from popular with the Howard government (feminists, gay rights organizations) is a key reason why the Howard government attempted to dismantle it via the Australian Human Rights Commission Legislation Bill (2003), which was not the first of

[25] ACT Human Rights Act 2004: A2004–5; Victorian Charter of Human Rights and Responsibilities 2006: No. 43 of 2006. See the New South Wales Council for Civil Liberties Web site, http://www.nswccl.org.au/issues/bill_of_rights/other.php.

[26] Racial Discrimination Act No. 52 of 1975, the Sex Discrimination Act No. 4 of 1984, the Disability Discrimination Act No. 135 of 1992, the Age Discrimination Act No. 68 of 2004, and the Human Rights and Equal Opportunity Commission Act No. 125 of 1986.

[27] Native Title Act No. 130 of 1993.

[28] The last director of the Sex Discrimination Unit, Sally Moyle, now working with overseas aid agency AusAid, is deserving of special mention in this respect.

such attempts (a fairly identical bill to the 2003 one was introduced in 1998). The bill sought not only to replace the specialist commissioners of HREOC, namely Aboriginal and Torres Strait Islander social justice commissioner, disability discrimination commissioner, human rights commissioner, race discrimination commissioner, and sex discrimination commissioner, with three general human rights commissioners, but also to "fetter . . . the power of the Commission to intervene in cases before the courts that involve issues that relate to the jurisprudence of the Commission" by requiring the president of HREOC to seek the attorney general's leave to do so (HREOC 2003).[29] It further sought to remove the power of the commission to seek financial compensation for complainants and of the president to delegate inquiry powers to the human rights commissioner. Among the many submissions opposing the proposed measures was that made by HREOC itself. Its then president, Alice Tay, in a speech delivered on her behalf by William Jonas at the public hearing held in Sydney on April 29, 2003, stressed that "the human rights of Australians will not be better served by limiting the ability of the national human rights body to function independently" (Tay 2003). In its report handed down on May 30, 2003, the Senate Legal and Constitutional Committee set up to inquire into the bill, chaired by Liberal senator Marise Payne, overwhelmingly rejected the provisions of the bill that sought to abolish the specialist commissioners and undermine the independence of the commission in the exercise of its intervention powers and sent it back for a second reading. Other provisions of the bill that undermined the structure of the commission and the president's mandate were rejected by nongovernment members of the committee, who prepared a dissenting report, opposed to a second reading. The bill did not go ahead.

This is not a state that "values our individual rights" or where Australians "respect their obligations to each other" as Prime Minister Howard claimed in his letter to "fellow Australians" sent out in February that same year with the fridge magnet package (Commonwealth Government 2003). This is a state where "mutual obligation" (a term used by the government to describe requirements imposed on recipients of unemployment benefits under the Welfare to Work program) is a unilateral, bottom-up phenomenon. The state has rights over us; we have obligations toward it.[30]

[29] This statement appeared in HREOC 2003 when I conducted my research in late 2006 but has since been removed.

[30] See the Web site of Centrelink, the government welfare benefits agency, http://www .centrelink.gov.au/internet/internet.nsf/payments/newstart_mutual_obligation.htm#ecp.

The demon lover still at large

The rhetoric of safeguarding a supposedly free, just, and open Australian society masks an even deeper fallacy. The costly and rights-abusing measures put in place by the Howard government (and, increasingly, various ALP-led state governments) in the supposed interests of such safeguarding are not even particularly effective in fulfilling their stated aim. This is not, of course, to say that were they effective they would be justified; it is simply to point out that the "protection racket," as Charles Tilly has called it, has failed even on its own terms (quoted in Peterson 1992, 51). To echo Morgan, "political and military leaders . . . address the image but miss the substance. . . . Capturing or killing the leader(s) will no more end terrorism than would Bill Gates' dying of a heart attack end capitalism" (Morgan 2001, xv). In the case of the current "war on terror," even the stated aim of capturing the leaders has not been realized; worse, it is far from sure that this stated aim was the real one (Winter 2002b; Talbot 2003). Morgan wrote the above words just after the September 2001 attacks, in her introduction to the second edition of her 1989 book *The Demon Lover*. In the first edition she had noted the state and media exaggeration of the "threat" of terrorism when many more deaths were due to other causes, both human and natural (Morgan 1989, 30). Similarly, MacKinnon pointed out in the aftermath of September 11, 2001, that, according to FBI statistics, "the number of women who die at the hands of men every year in the United States alone is almost the same as the number of people who died on September 11" (MacKinnon 2002, 426). One might well ask, with MacKinnon, "when is a war?" (2002, 427).

As Morgan, Arundhati Roy (2002), and many others have argued, "when solutions are offered us by the people who originally brought us the problem, we do well to be suspicious" (Morgan 1989, 29). The Howard government offers solutions to a problem that, notwithstanding the demonstrable existence of terrorism (for several decades, in fact), is more fiction than fact—a phantasmagoria reminiscent of the communist scares of Cold War hysteria.[31] These strategies associated with the Hobbesian politics of fear are chillingly familiar to those who lived through the Cold War era, and the comparison has been well argued by many Australian political analysts (see, e.g., Lawrence 2006). Missing from practically all these analyses, however, is recognition of the centrality of the control of women to the construction of such politics. The Howard government is

---

[31] These communist scares were a hallmark of the Menzies administration in Australia during the 1950s and 1960s.

devoting much energy and public money to the production of a paternalist, Christian, family-values security state. At the same time that the government claims to be making Australia into "the most female-friendly environment in the world" (Peter Costello, speech to the National Press Club, March 1, 2006, quoted in Sawer 2006, 2), it is creating laws and policy that do the opposite.

One is tempted to argue that Australia has become a nation of children, infantilized by the politics of fear. But children grow up and in doing so develop the capacity to think for themselves, upon which, argues Lawrence, "the survival of our democracies depends" (2006, 127). Women, however, lack that potential, according to Western masculinist philosophy: Aristotle set the tone by arguing that the faculty of reason, undeveloped in the child, is inoperative in women ([350 BCE] 1962, bk. 1, chap. 13). If the war on terror is largely a fiction endorsed and embellished by the masculinist Australian state to keep the population fearful and submissive, then the protection of women—a class kept insecure, docile, malleable, and both subservient to and grateful to its demon lover, in short, a class kept firmly bound within femininity—is integral to the maintenance of that fiction. For the macho muscularity of Leviathan Down Under to flourish, the population over which it rules must become, and remain, feminized.

Department of French Studies
The University of Sydney

References

AAP (Australian Associated Press). 2006. "Hilaly Comment 'Un-Australian.'" *World News Australia*, SBS TV, October 26. http://www.worldnewsaustralia.com.au/region.php?id = 132243&region = 7.

Abbott, Tony. 2006. "Launch of the Report, Australia's Health 2006." Report presented at the Australian Institute of Health and Welfare's Conference, Canberra, June 21. Department of Health and Ageing, Australian Government. http://www.health.gov.au/internet/ministers/publishing.nsf/Content/health-mediarel-yr2006-ta-abbsp210606.htm?OpenDocument&yr = 2006&mth = 6.

ABS (Australian Bureau of Statistics). 2004. "Sexual Assault in Australia: A Statistical Overview." http://www.ausstats.abs.gov.au/ausstats/subscriber.nsf/0/C41F8B2864D42333CA256F070079CBD4/$File/45230_2004.pdf.

———. 2005. "Crime and Safety Australia 2005." http://www.ausstats.abs.gov.au/ausstats/subscriber.nsf/0/D68F78EDFB7965E4CA25715A001C9192/$File/45090_apr%202005.pdf.

————. 2006. "Population by Age and Sex, Australian States and Territories, June 2006." http://www.abs.gov.au/ausstats/abs@.nsf/0e5fa1cc95cd093c4a256 8110007852b/b52c3903d894336dca2568a9001393c1!OpenDocument.

Access Economics. 2004. "The Cost of Domestic Violence to the Australian Economy." Commonwealth of Australia, Canberra.

Allen, Vicki. 2006. "US House Clears $427.6 Billion for Pentagon." Reuters wire report, June 21. http://political-stuff.blogspot.com/2006/06/us-house-rejects-bid-by-democrats-to.html.

ALRC (Australian Law Reform Commission). 2006. "Fighting Words: A Review of Sedition Laws in Australia (ALRC 104)." http://www.alrc.gov.au/inquiries/title/alrc104/index.html.

ARC (Australian Research Council). 2006. "Discovery Projects: Funding Rules for Funding Commencing in 2007." Australian Government, Canberra. http://www.arc.gov.au/pdf/DP07_FundingRules.pdf.

Aristotle. (350 BCE) 1962. *Politics.* Trans. T. A. Sinclair. Harmondsworth, UK: Penguin.

Australian Government. 2004. "A New Approach to the Family Law System: Implementation of Reforms Discussion Paper." Commonwealth of Australia, Canberra. http://www.ag.gov.au/www/agd/rwpattach.nsf/VAP/(1E76C 1D5D1A37992F0B0C1C4DB87942E)~CleanedA+New+Approach+to+the+ Family+Law+System+zz+-+Discussio.pdf/$file/CleanedA+New+Approach+to +the+Family+Law+System+zz+-+Discussio.pdf.

Australian Government, Attorney General's Department. n.d. "Dealing with Family Violence and Child Abuse." New Family Law System, fact sheet 10. http://www.ag.gov.au/www/agd/rwpattach.nsf/VAP/(22D92C32512757 20C801B3314F7A9BA2)~FactSheet_10.pdf/$file/FactSheet_10.pdf.

Australian Government, Department of the Prime Minister. 2004. "Consultancy Contracts Let during 2003–04 to the Value of $10,000 or more." http://www.pmc.gov.au/annual_reports/2003-04/appendixes/appendix4.htm.

Berns, Sandra. 2001. "Parents Behaving Badly: Parental Alienation Syndrome in the Family Court—Magic Bullet or Poisoned Chalice." *Australian Journal of Family Law* 15:191–214.

Bowden, Tracy. 2004. "No Word on Domestic Violence Campaign." Report from ABC TV's *The 7:30 Report,* March 30. http://www.abc.net.au/7.30/content/ 2004/s1077384.htm.

Brown, Thea. 2001. "Child Abuse in the Context of Parental Separation and Divorce: New Reality and a New Intervention Model." Paper presented at Eighth Australasian Conference on Child Abuse and Neglect, One Child's Reality—Everyone's Responsibility, Melbourne Convention Centre, November 19–22. http://www.ncsmc.org.au/docs/caps.doc.

Childress, Sarah. 2006. "Fighting Over the Kids: Battered Spouses Take Aim at a Controversial Custody Strategy." *Newsweek,* September 25, 35.

Commonwealth of Australia. 2003a. "Senate Finance and Public Administration Legislation Committee Estimates (Budget Estimates), Tuesday, 27 May 2003:

Official Committee Hansard." http://www.aph.gov.au/Senate/committee/ fapa_ctte/estimates/bud_0304/index.htm.

———. 2003b. "2003–4 Commonwealth Budget." http://www.budget.gov.au/ 2003-04/.

———. 2004. *Violence against Women: Australia Says No.* Canberra: Commonwealth of Australia.

Commonwealth Government. 2003. *Let's Look Out for Australia: Protecting Our Way of Life from a Possible Terrorist Threat.* Canberra: Commonwealth of Australia.

Costello, Peter. 2003. "Budget Speech 2003–04." Australian Government. http://www.budget.gov.au/2003-04/speech/html/speech.htm.

———. 2006. "Budget Speech 2006–07." Australian Government. http:// www.budget.gov.au/2006-07/speech/html/speech.htm.

Delphy, Christine. 2002. "A War for Afghan Women?" Trans. Bronwyn Winter. In *September 11, 2001: Feminist Perspectives,* ed. Susan Hawthorne and Bronwyn Winter, 302–15. North Melbourne: Spinifex.

Dunn, M. C. 2004. "The Politics of Fathers' Rights Activists—Do Persistent Critics of the Family Court Behave in a Way Which Stands Up to Scrutiny?" Paper presented to the National Abuse Free Contact Campaign. http://www .xyonline.net/downloads/Politics_of_Father_-WAV.doc.

Enloe, Cynthia. 1990. *Bananas, Beaches, and Bases: Making Feminist Sense of International Politics.* Berkeley: University of California Press.

———. 2000. *Maneuvers: The International Politics of Militarizing Women's Lives.* Berkeley: University of California Press.

———. 2004. *The Curious Feminist: Searching for Women in a New Age of Empire.* Berkeley: University of California Press.

Gardner, Richard A. 1999. *The Parental Alienation Syndrome: A Guide for Mental Health and Legal Professionals.* 2nd ed. Cresskill, NJ: Creative Therapeutics.

Goodsell, Joy. 2005. "Terrorism in the Home on the Rise." *Sydney Morning Herald,* November 25. http://www.smh.com.au/news/opinion/terrorism-in-the-home-on-the-rise/2005/11/24/1132703312579.html?PHPSESSID=ef899 ac86b5d8eb6e78da21cf8883304.

Greer, Pam. 2001. "Pathways to Safety: An Interview about Indigenous Family Violence." Interviewed by Lesley Laing. Australian Domestic and Family Violence Clearinghouse Issues Paper 5. Australian Domestic and Family Violence Clearinghouse, Sydney.

Hayward, Stan. n.d. "A Guide to the Parental Alienation Syndrome." http:// www.coeffic.demon.co.uk/pas.htm.

Head, Michael. 2000. "Olympic Security: Police and Military Plans for the Sydney Olympics; A Cause for Concern." *Alternative Law Journal* 25(3):131–35.

Hilaly, Sheik Taj Din. 2006. "Read Sheik Hilaly's Comments." *World News Australia,* SBS TV, October 28. http://www.worldnewsaustralia.com.au/ region.php?id=132248&region=7.

HREOC (Human Rights and Equal Opportunity Commission). 2003. "Submission of the Human Rights and Equal Opportunity Commission to the Senate Legal and Constitutional Legislation Committee on the Australian Human Rights Commission Legislation Bill 2003." http://www.hreoc.gov.au/ahrc/submission.html.

Humphreys, Catherine. 1999. "Judicial Alienation Syndrome: Failures to Respond to Post-separation Violence." *Family Law* 29 (May): 313–16.

Hussein, Shakira. 2006. "Islam and the West: For a Muslim Feminism." *New Matilda.com: A Different Tune*, August 30. http://www.newmatilda.com/home/articledetail.asp?ArticleID=1779.

Kaye, Miranda, and Julia Tolmie. 1998. "Fathers' Rights Groups in Australia and Their Engagement with Issues in Family Law." *Australian Journal of Family Law* 12(1):19–67.

Kirk, Alexandra. 2004. "ATSIC Abolished to Silence Indigenous Voice: Alison Anderson." *The World Today*, ABC News, April 16. http://www.abc.net.au/worldtoday/content/2004/s1088994.htm.

Laing, Lesley. 2003. "Domestic Violence and Family Law." Topic paper, Australian Domestic and Family Violence Clearinghouse, Sydney. http://www.austdvclearinghouse.unsw.edu.au/topics/topics_pdf_files/family_law.pdf.

Lawrence, Carmen. 2006. *Fear and Politics*. Melbourne: Scribe.

MacCarrick, Gwynn. 2004. "Vanstone Is Dismantling the Right to a Fair Trial for Aboriginal People." *Online Opinion: Australia's E-journal of Social and Political Debate*, May 20. http://www.onlineopinion.com.au/view.asp?article=2223.

MacKinnon, Catharine A. 1990. "Legal Perspectives on Sexual Difference." In *Theoretical Perspectives on Sexual Difference*, ed. Deborah L. Rhode, 213–25. New Haven, CT: Yale University Press.

———. 2002. "State of Emergency." In *September 11, 2001: Feminist Perspectives*, ed. Susan Hawthorne and Bronwyn Winter, 426–31. North Melbourne: Spinifex.

Maddison, Sarah. 2004. "Silencing Dissent." *Australia Institute Newsletter* 39 (June): 1–3.

Michaelsen, Christopher. 2005. "Australia's Antiterrorism Laws Lack Adequate Oversight Mechanisms." Democratic Audit of Australia, November. http://democratic.audit.anu.edu.au/papers/200511_michaelsen_anti_terror.pdf.

Morgan, Robin. 1989. *The Demon Lover: On the Sexuality of Terrorism*. New York: Norton.

———. 2001. *The Demon Lover: The Roots of Terrorism*. Updated ed. London: Piatkus.

Mouzos, Jenny, and Toni Makkai. 2004. *Women's Experiences of Male Violence: Findings from the Australian Component of the International Violence Against Women Survey (IVAWS)*. Research and Policy Series no. 56. Canberra: Australian Institute of Criminology.

Nicholson, Honorable Chief Justice Alistair. 1996. "Welcome." In *Enhancing*

Access to Justice, Family Court of Australia Second National Conference Papers, 20–23 September 1995. Sydney: Family Court of Australia.

Pateman, Carole. 1989. *The Disorder of Women: Democracy, Feminism and Political Theory.* Cambridge: Polity.

Peterson, V. Spike. 1992. "Security and Sovereign States: What Is at Stake in Taking Feminism Seriously?" In her *Gendered States: Feminist (Re)Visions of International Relations Theory,* 31–64. Boulder, CO: Lynne Rienner.

Price, Joseph L., and Kerry S. Pioske. 1994. "Parental Alienation Syndrome: A Developmental Analysis of a Vulnerable Population." *Journal of Psychosocial Nursing and Mental Health Services* 32(11):9–12.

Price, Sue. 2005. "Australian Government Again Demonises Young Men and Boys." Men's Rights Agency, July 26. http://www.mensrights.com.au/index .php?article_id=255.

Prime Minister of Australia. 1997. "Partnerships against Domestic Violence." Media release. Australian Government, Canberra, November 7.

Pue, W. Wesley. 2003. "The War on Terror: Constitutional Governance in a State of Permanent Warfare?" *Osgoode Hall Law Journal* 41(213):267–92.

Rathus, Zoe. 2005. "Submission on Exposure Draft: Family Law Amendment (Shared Parental Responsibility) Bill, 2005." Submission 88. House Standing Committee on Legal and Constitutional Affairs, Canberra. http://www.aph .gov.au/house/committee/laca/familylaw/subs/Sub88.pdf.

Rendell, Kathryn, Zoe Rathus, and Angela Lynch. 2000. *An Unacceptable Risk: A Report on Child Contact Arrangements Where There Is Violence in the Family.* Brisbane: Women's Legal Service.

Ricketts, Aidan. 2002. "Freedom of Association or Guilt by Association: Australia's New Anti-terrorism Laws and the Retreat of Public Liberty." *Southern Cross University Law Review* 6 (October): 133–50.

Roy, Arundhati. 2002. *The Algebra of Infinite Justice.* Rev. ed. London: Flamingo.

Sawer, Marian. 1999. "EMILY's List and Angry White Men: Gender Wars in the Nineties." *Journal of Australian Studies* 62:1–9.

———. 2006. "Paradise Postponed: Women and the House of Representatives." Democratic Audit of Australia Discussion Paper 3/06, March. Australian National University, Canberra.

Seccombe, Mike. 2005. "Governing by Consultants: Now the Bill Hits $2bn." *Sydney Morning Herald,* February 7. http://www.smh.com.au/news/National/ Governing-by-consultants-now-the-bill-hits-2bn/2005/02/06/1107625062 686.html.

Shanahan, Dennis. 2006. "Aussie Value Test for New Migrants." *The Australian,* September 14. http://www.theaustralian.news.com.au/story/0,20867,20408 575-2702,00.html.

Staples, Joan. 2006. "NGOs Out in the Cold: The Howard Government Policy towards NGOs." Democratic Audit of Australia Discussion Paper 19/06, June. Australian National University, Canberra. http://democratic.audit.anu.edu .au/papers/20060615_staples_ngos.pdf.

Stiehm, Judith Hicks. 1982. "The Protected, the Protector, the Defender." *Women's Studies International Forum* 5(3/4):367–76.

Summers, Anne. 2003a. "Callous Treatment for the Victims of Brutal Acts." *Sydney Morning Herald*, May 26. http://www.smh.com.au/articles/2003/05/25/1053801278731.html.

———. 2003b. *The End of Equality: Work, Babies and Women's Choices in 21st Century Australia*. Sydney: Random House Australia.

Talbot, Karen. 2002. "Afghanistan, Central Asia, Georgia: Key to Oil Profits." In *September 11, 2001: Feminist Perspectives*, ed. Susan Hawthorne and Bronwyn Winter, 285–96. North Melbourne: Spinifex.

Tay, Alice. 2003. "Opening Statement." Submission of the Human Rights and Equal Opportunity Commission to the State Legal and Constitutional Legislation Committees on the *Australian Human Rights Commission Legislation Bill 2003*. Legal Information, Australian Human Rights and Equal Opportunity Commission. http://www.hreoc.gov.au/ahrc/opening_statement.html.

Weekes, Wendy, and Julie Oberin, for WESNET. 2004. *Women's Refuges, Shelters, Outreach and Support Services in Australia: From Sydney Squat to Complex Services Challenging Domestic and Family Violence*. Canberra: Australian Government Department of Family and Community Services, Office for Women.

Wilson, Trish. 2001. "Richard Gardner's Parental Alienation Syndrome: Resources for Mothers Who Are Charged with Junk Science." Independent posting, http://members.aol.com/asherah/pas.html.

Winter, Bronwyn. 1995. "Symboles, moteurs et alibis: Critique de l'identification culturelle et nationale des femmes d'origine Maghrébine en France" [Symbols, drivers, and tokens: The national and cultural identification of women of Maghrebian background in France]. PhD dissertation, University of Sydney.

———. 2002a. "If Women Really Mattered . . . " In *September 11, 2001: Feminist Perspectives*, ed. Susan Hawthorne and Bronwyn Winter, 50–80. North Melbourne: Spinifex.

———. 2002b. "Who Will Mourn on October 7?" In *September 11, 2001: Feminist Perspectives*, ed. Susan Hawthorne and Bronwyn Winter, 60–71. North Melbourne: Spinifex.

———. 2006. "Religion, Culture and Women's Human Rights: Some General Political and Theoretical Considerations." *Women's Studies International Forum* 29(4):381–93.

Young, Iris Marion. 2003. "The Logic of Masculinist Protection: Reflections on the Current Security State." *Signs: Journal of Women in Culture and Society* 29(1):1–25.

Liz Philipose

The Politics of Pain and the Uses of Torture

S ince September 11, 2001, the equation of *Muslim* with *terrorist* has
lodged in the popular imagination in the United States. This conflation undermines the ability to distinguish between a few individuals
who have committed or intend to commit acts of extrastate violence (terrorism) and the rest of the Muslim population, a population that consists
of more than 1 billion people worldwide. Although public discussions of
the so-called Muslim terrorist are often accompanied by disclaimers acknowledging that not all Muslims are a problem or that the political abuse
of Islam, rather than Islam itself, is a problem, these caveats fail to dislodge
the increasingly intractable conflation of Muslim with terrorist. This article
examines how the racialized terrorist is produced through various war-
on-terror tactics, including the indefinite detainment and torture of prisoners in U.S. military detention centers and the circulation of torture
photographs.

A long history of Euro-American racialization of Muslim and Arab peoples traverses contemporary discussions.[1] The one-dimensional concept of

I would like to thank the *Signs* editors and the anonymous reviewers for their helpful
comments and assistance in clarifying these arguments. Much of the research and earlier
drafts of this article were completed with the support of the Woodward Professorship in
Women's Studies, Simon Fraser University.

[1] The post- or neocolonial relationships between Euro-Americans and Muslims/Arabs/
Middle Easterners draw upon the historical racialization associated with orientalism (Said
1979). If we consider the orientalist/colonial configuration of modern Western versions of
gender, masculinity is a raced, classed, and sexualized category, encompassing the attributes
of the ideal human as white, Euro-derived, propertied, heterosexual, and male. In this sense,
to be male and called out as raced is also to be feminized as an unfit male, terms that signal
both the abject and the object. Within that dyad is the assumption of deviant sexuality,
impotency, and pollution. To be male and called out as female with the colonial connotations
this predicament entails is to be brought into being as a racialized object, one who is inherently
less than the ideal human, without personality, agency, or individual uniqueness. Heterosexuality, too, in its colonialist connotations, is a commodity of the ideal human that needs
to be continuously proven, protected, and coded as unambiguous. Establishing the masculinity, whiteness, and heterosexuality of U.S. agents demands that they produce themselves
in the image of the ideal human. Orientalism functions as the highly malleable episteme

[*Signs: Journal of Women in Culture and Society* 2007, vol. 32, no. 4]

the Muslim has long circulated as a homogenizing fabrication, having little to do with the diverse beliefs, practices, geographies, histories, or ethnicities of people who identify as Muslim. Yet the new raced-gendered grammar that collapses Muslim into terrorist has certain unique features, peremptorily designating any act, speech, or movement made by a Muslim, or a person perceived to be Muslim, as the act, speech, or movement of a terrorist. Resting on gendered assumptions of men as hyperpatriarchal and misogynistic and women as victimized and ubiquitously burka-clad, the Muslim terrorist becomes the container for gendered attributes that signify the antimodern, religiously fanatical, and sexually deviant terrorist. Like older modes of racialization, this new racial grammar relies on visual cues to signal the deeper, hidden nature of the terrorist. It incorporates faulty biologism, suggesting that physical traits are keys to the interior moral turpitude of the individual terrorist. And it recklessly universalizes terrorist propensities to those marked by the visual cues. Invested in rigid distinctions between masculinity and femininity and in clearly defined parameters of acceptable (hetero)sexuality, this new racial grammar links gender, sexuality, and desire to lineage, heredity, and kinship.

I argue that certain tactics of the war on terror, including the circulation of the Abu Ghraib photos, have contributed to the cultural production of the Muslim terrorist and the solidification of the new racial grammar rooted in a regime of visibility. Racial profiling, a visual technology of power, has played a critical role in the capture and detention of war-on-terror prisoners. People are designated as suspicious based on their ascriptive and surface characteristics—skin color, national origin, and name. Thus, to be arrested and detained in Abu Ghraib, Bagram Air Base, Guantánamo Bay Naval Base (Camp Delta), the Manhattan Detention Center, or in the numerous third-country and secret detention centers across the world is to be racialized as terrorist.[2] But racialization does not rely ex-

---

through which the West continues to come to know itself as the superior agent in contrast to the production of the inferior Oriental (Said 1979).

[2] The U.S. Armed Forces Institute of Pathology autopsy reports, which document the deaths of all detainees throughout the U.S. military prison system, show that there have been homicides of detainees in several different locations, from Abu Ghraib to Camp Sather to Bagram Air Base to Bagram Collection Point. These are available on the American Civil Liberties Union Web site as a result of several Freedom of Information Act challenges, at http://action.aclu.org/torturefoia/released/102405. Ehab Elmaghraby, one of more than one hundred Muslim men detained in the Brooklyn Metropolitan Detention Center in the war on terror successfully sued the U.S. government for his incarceration without trial and for the torture he endured while imprisoned. There have been numerous reports of torture at the Guantánamo Bay Naval Base, and several lawsuits are under way. The Center for

clusively on profiling. The much-publicized treatment of detainees, ranging from the use of torture to forced feeding to indefinite detention, constitutes a racial reduction that turns human subjects into objects. Through techniques designed to destroy personality, individuality, and agency, detainees are brought into being as subhuman. Through sanctioned violence that is at once racialized and racializing, the abject racial object is produced at times under the suspension of law but more recently through the rightful application of law approved by the U.S. Congress.

To enter the public imagination, the racializing technology of the detention centers must be relocated, shifted from clandestine offshore sites to mainstream mechanisms of visuality. Effective racialization requires the development of a new way of seeing the abject. The global circulation of the Abu Ghraib photographs depicting detainees being tortured by U.S. soldiers played a critical role in the cultivation of a new regime of looking. Although the photographs were circulated by the Western media as a manifestation of outrage at the abuses depicted and as a means to provoke official inquiry into prisoner abuse, such benign intentions do not exhaust the uses of images of torture.

Indeed, in the United States the circulation of images of tortured bodies has a peculiar history tied to antiblack racism and vigilante violence in the form of lynchings. The depictions of torture in the Abu Ghraib detention center, particularly those of hooded figures posed with a noose around the neck, mirror the imagery of lynchings. In both instances, violence by whites against men of color produces an abject racialized body. By comparing the regime of looking established by lynching photos with the circulation of Abu Ghraib images, we can learn a great deal about ongoing processes of racialization.[3]

Lynchings disciplined and contained (primarily) black populations after emancipation while quelling white anxieties about social equality. As extrajudicial methods of punishment often against innocent individuals, lynchings entrenched white supremacy and perpetuated an image of black people as property that whites could use as they saw fit. As a mechanism of social

---

Constitutional Rights is one of the leading advocates. Much documentation can be found on the organization's Web site at http://www.ccr-ny.org/v2/home.asp.

[3] The Abu Ghraib photos are not the only archives documenting the use of torture in the war on terror, and Abu Ghraib is not the only site of the use of torture against detainees. There are several reports to draw from, including the multiple autopsy reports from the Armed Forces Institute of Pathology (see n. 2), the Taguba Report (Taguba 2004), and the independent human rights reports made by Amnesty International, the Center for Constitutional Rights (2004), the International Committee of the Red Cross (ICRC 2004), and Human Rights Watch (2004).

control, lynchings contained African Americans, segregating them, fixing them by fear, limiting their mobility and public sphere participation, and constraining their sexuality. The circulation of lynching photos extended a dire warning about the limits of race and place in the United States, well beyond the geographic confines of the lynching locales.

Anxieties in the United States have once again been mobilized. In addition to pervasive concerns about American vulnerability in the aftermath of the September 11, 2001, tragedy, the U.S. National Intelligence Council (2004) has cataloged multiple anxieties about the ways that globalization empowers China, India, political Islam, and terrorists, thus enhancing third world challenges to Euro-American domination and related anxieties about the inability of U.S. military forces to quell the violence in Iraq or Afghanistan. The circulation of images of the torture of detainees in the context of the war on terror can be read as part of a violent and brutal attempt to reestablish and continue Western rule.[4] Regardless of the reasons for their circulation, the visual regime of domination constructed by the global circulation of the torture photographs is deeply imbricated in modes of racialization that affirm the superiority of the torturers by producing the servile, compliant, raced bodies of Muslim men.

To explicate these processes of racialization, I draw upon the insights of Kalpana Sheshadri-Crooks, who develops a theory of race as a "regime of looking" (2000, 2) by creatively extrapolating from Jacques Lacan. To demonstrate how torture and cruel, inhumane, and degrading treatment can produce a racialized visual regime, I will then compare the Abu Ghraib photos with lynching photography from the early twentieth-century United States. This article concludes with a discussion of torture as gendered, raced, and sexualized decerebralization, that is, as part of the process of turning subjects into objects. Drawing on the work of Frantz

---

[4] The Project for the New American Century (1997) clearly states the objective of U.S. domination over global economic and military affairs through the increased use of military means. Just after September 11, Italian Prime Minister Silvio Berlusconi spoke about the obligation of the purveyors of Western civilization to maintain their rule over less civilized peoples (quoted in Said 2001). The Canadian prime minister at the time pledged his commitment to Western domination at a time of crisis and disorder (Chrétien 2001). The British foreign minister wrote a blueprint for British rule titled "Reordering the World," in which he claimed that now, more than even in the nineteenth century, the world needs Western countries to establish authority, rules, laws, and conduct for other countries to follow (quoted in Waugh 2002). The national rhetorics of the United States, Canada, Britain, and Italy do not include all those who live within these states, just those who are considered to be part of the nation.

Fanon, I show how the new racialized subjects and objects produced through torture and the circulation of torture photography take root in our subjectivities as new elements of an emerging racial grammar.

Seeing race

Over the past four decades, critical race theorists in the natural sciences, the social sciences, and the humanities have refuted the mistaken view that race is a biological category.[5] Despite multiple demonstrations that race is a social construct without any concrete foundations in biology or nature, notions of racial embodiment persist. If race is not written on the body in immediately legible ways, how then do we come to see race? Sheshadri-Crooks argues that race is a "practice of visibility" and a "regime of looking" that can neither "be reduced to the look" nor explained as "scientific, anthropological or cultural theory" (2000, 2). She argues that "the regime of visibility secures the investment that we make in 'race' in ways that cannot be easily surrendered" (2). To understand how race works, we need to understand it as a "system of categorization" that, once in place, "organizes differences between humans in predetermined ways" (4). A symbolic rather than natural order of race governs seeing. Operating on the psyche and structuring perception, the symbolic order has palpable effects: "We believe in the factuality of difference in order to see it, because the order of racial difference is an order that promises access to an absolute wholeness of its subjects—white, black, yellow, or brown" (5).

Sheshadri-Crooks suggests that the regime of visibility constructed around race affords fantasies of wholeness akin to those predicated on sexual difference. Following Lacan, Sheshadri-Crooks notes that critical aspects of psychic development are triggered by absence, depend upon lack, and are fueled by incessant misperception. Akin to the elusive wholeness promised by sexual difference and sexual union, "the signifier Whiteness . . . promises a totality, an overcoming of difference itself. For the subject of race, Whiteness represents complete mastery, self-sufficiency and the *jouissance* of humanness" (Sheshadri-Crooks 2000, 56). Unlike sexual difference, however, "race identity can have only one function: it establishes differential relations among the races in order to constitute the logic of domination" (7). Based on exclusivity, exceptionalism, unique-ness, and the pride of being better, race has "no other reason to be but power" (7). Representing the power of being itself, "it is the promise of

---

[5] The literature is extensive and compelling. See, e.g., Gould (1981), Goldberg (1990), Appiah (1992), and Haney-López (1996).

being more human, more full, less lacking. The possibility of this enjoy-ment is at the core of 'race'" (7).

Race is a practice of visibility and a regime of looking, but lodged within the psyche and governing perception, it should not be reduced to mere looking: "Racial visibility . . . is that which secures the much deeper investment we have made in the racial categorization of human beings" (Sheshadri-Crooks 2000, 8). Indeed, racial categorization creates a critical difference between the seer and the seen, between the seeing subject and the object of the gaze: "The subject of the imaginary is constituted as seeing by the signifier, whereas the subject of race is constituted as seen, the subject of the gaze, through a certain logic of the signifier" (38).

Race is related to class and sex but has its own distinct structure and trajectory of power, which operate by positing biological or second-nature attributes. Thus race is accorded far more permanence than class, for example. Although class positions are often intractable, they are relatively mobile when compared with race. If class is cast in terms of biology, blood, or stock, "it lapses into race" (Sheshadri-Crooks 2000, 4), suggesting an inner, hidden quality passed on to all who are born to those who are classed/raced. Family, reproduction, and kinship are integral to the notion of racial differences. Indeed, Sheshadri-Crooks argues that race as the essence and immutable determinant of social worth underlies many surface claims concerning culture, ethnicity, sex, or class. Race "transmutes its historicity, its contingent foundations, into biological necessity" through a process that exploits sexual difference (21).

Race is a regime of looking that moves from surface to depth. As Ann Laura Stoler has pointed out, not only is racism a "visual ideology" but also "Euro-American racial thinking related the visual markers of race to the protean hidden properties of different human kinds" (1997, 205). The surface is where visibility first matters, triggering associations of sur-face features with moral dispositions and character traits. Through this regime of looking we "reproduce the visibility of race as our daily common sense, the means by which we 'tell people apart,' a logic that is best enshrined in the Canadian phrase 'visible minorities'" (Sheshadri-Crooks 2000, 19). Entrenched in the psyche and reproduced in daily interactions, the regime of visibility makes race appear immediate, transparent, and unalterable.

Racializing the terrorist

Operating through a regime of visibility, racialization maps the body with an overlay of discrete meanings. But how are new modes of racialization

concretized in regimes of looking? A comparison of U.S. lynching photography and the Abu Ghraib photographs can shed light on this complex
question. The circulation of both lynching photographs and Abu Ghraib
torture photos contributes to the production of particular regimes of visibility in which racialized bodies are marked not only by skin color or physical
features but also by the representation of bodies as abject, sexualized, and
decerebralized. The images depict racial violence in contexts that exonerate
the perpetrators of violence by suggesting the culpability of the violated.
Just as lynching was taken as evidence of the criminality of the black male,
the torture photos implicate the detainees in practices that produced their
detention.

Within racialized regimes of looking, moral judgment is confounded
as victims are turned into suspects and the perpetrators of violence are
depicted as righteous agents. Despite clear evidence of abuse inflicted by
whites, terror becomes a racial marker reserved for blacks, dissidents, minorities, and Muslims. As bell hooks has noted, "One fantasy of whiteness
is that the threatening Other is always a terrorist. This projection enables
many white people to imagine there is no representation of whiteness as
terror, as terrorizing" (hooks 1992, 174). Although hooks acknowledges
that in certain locations whiteness represents for black people "the terrible,
the terrifying, the terrorizing" (170), it is a terror that cannot be named
within the terms of whiteness. Despite manifold instances of documented
terror by white men, the representation of whiteness as terror is excluded
from public discourse, just as the idea of whiteness as a racial formation
is discounted. In hegemonic discourses, race is attributed only to non-
whites, as a homogenizing and deep biological set of characteristics of
undifferentiated masses. In contrast, white people "are imagined as individuals and as endlessly and ethnically diverse" (Apel 2004, 26).

The terrorist occupies its own discursive field in Western imaginations,
a field that is at once separate from and conjoined with strains of orientalism. In international law, as Ileana Porras has noted, the terrorist is a
distinctly Western invention, a name given to those who challenge states'
monopoly over the use of violence (1995, 294). In her words, "terrorism
has come to be the thing against which liberal Western democracies define
themselves; . . . terrorism has come to be the repository of everything
that cannot be allowed to fit inside the self-image of democracy; and . . .
the terrorist has become the 'other' that threatens and desires the annihilation of the democratic 'self' . . . an external force against which democracies therefore must strenuously defend" (295).

The communist, the religious fanatic, the nomad, the invader, and the
Islamic fundamentalist have all had a place in terrorism studies. Since the

fall of the Soviet system, images of the Arab terrorist have been ubiquitous in U.S. terrorism studies and in media representations, occupying a place in the U.S. discursive imagination once reserved for those of the Soviet Union. Even prior to his conviction for seditious conspiracy in the 1993 World Trade Center bombings, Sheik Omar Abdel Rahman became the face of terrorism in popular media. Porras notes how particular visual cues tied to presumptions about interior states became the defining features of the terrorist:

> It is his turbaned and robed blindness that is immediately familiar. He is more recognizable than the other fourteen accused co-conspirators because he is bedecked with the attributes of his frightening otherness, the cruel Ottoman. The turban and the robe of that other fanatic, nemesis of the west, the Ayatollah Khomeini. Sheik Rahman is frequently described as blind, self-exiled and smiling. These are the further attributes of his fanaticism. The blindness of terrorist violence is visibly conveyed. Sheik Rahman's exile is rendered suspicious. . . . The Sheik's capacity to continue smiling, in the face of the horrors of which he is accused, suggests that he is "crazy" and/or morally degenerate, and therefore, dangerous. (Porras 1995, 303)

Within the Western imaginary the terrorist is an outlaw of a particular sort. Within a framework that restricts terrorism to nonstate actors, the terrorist is constructed as a stateless and illegitimate combatant who has chosen exile from the law. Against such a menace, legitimate states are unconstrained. They have no obligation to adhere to the laws of war or to civil and international covenants concerning incarceration, deportation, the use of torture, or the right to a legal defense: "By placing himself voluntarily outside of the law, the terrorist loses his claim on the law" (Porras 1995, 307).

Consider the ways that U.S. officials characterized the suicides of three men held in Camp Delta, the military prison in Guantánamo Bay. On June 11, 2006, Mani Shaman Turki al-Habardi al-Utaybi, Yasser Talal al-Zahrani, and Ali Abdullah Ahmed hanged themselves with prison-issued bedsheets in their solitary cells. Commenting on the suicides, Colleen Graffy, deputy assistant secretary of state for public diplomacy, attributed cunning to the detainees, saying that "taking their own lives was not necessary, but it certainly is a good PR move" (quoted in Goldenberg and Muir 2006). Navy Rear Admiral Harry Harris suggested that these suicides themselves were acts of terrorism—a devious Al-Qaeda tactic:

"They have no regard for life, neither ours nor their own. I believe this was not an act of desperation, but an act of asymmetrical warfare waged against us" (quoted in Goldenberg and Muir 2006). Avoiding any comment on the unlawful detention of these men over multiple years, Harris instead focused on allegations concerning their terrorist nature: "We hold men who proudly admit membership at the leadership level in al-Qaida and the Taliban, many with direct personal contact and knowledge of the September 11, 2001 attackers. We are keeping terrorist recruiters, facilitators, explosives trainers, bombers and bombmakers, Osama bin Laden bodyguards and financiers" (quoted in Goldenberg and Muir 2006). In contrast to accounts of torture at Guantánamo, Harris described many improvements in prison conditions since 2002, suggesting that prisoners are provided with everything they need—adequate clothing, toothbrushes, soap, shampoo, and safe shelter. "Even so," Harris lamented, "many detainees have taken advantage of this—crafting killing weapons from toothbrushes and garrottes from food wrappers," and he complained that "many detainees persist in mixing a blood-urine-faeces-semen cocktail and throwing this deadly concoction into the faces of the American men and women who guard them, feed them and care for them" (quoted in Goldenberg and Muir 2006).

Suspending the presumption of innocence until proven guilty, the Guantánamo officials assume that the fact of their arrest as suspected terrorists, whether founded on concrete evidence or not, places the detainees outside the law. Graffy and Harris also attribute a tremendous amount of agency to men held in indefinite detention without legal charge or representation. Whether a terrorist is on the loose or imprisoned and stripped of all worldly power, a terrorist remains a dangerous element. Rather than a desperate human being in desperate circumstances, the terrorist is constructed as cunning, violent, and operating in stealth. The terrorist is known by surface appearances, which provide clues to his deeply hidden self. From claims about fashioning weapons from toothbrushes to claims about the terrorist's bodily production of deadly concoctions, Harris moves from surface to interior, from the visible to the biological, from stereotype to racialization, combining "the visuality of the gaze and the invisibility of race's most telling ontological moment" (Stoler 1997, 205).

This racial structure linking surface to interior is reproduced within terrorism studies. As Jasbir Puar and Amit Rai (2002, 121–25) have demonstrated, terrorism studies routinely derive unobservable motivations, belief systems, compulsions, psychopathology, self-destructive urges, disturbed emotions, and problems with authority from observable behavior. These urges are attributed to other unobservables such as inconsistent mothering, family dysfunction, and unconscious feelings of hostility toward parents. By moving from surface to interior, terrorism studies "(1) reduce complex histories of struggle, intervention, and (non)development to Western psychic models rooted in the bourgeois heterosexual family and its dynamics; (2) systematically exclude questions of political economy and the problems of cultural translation; and (3) attempt to master the fear, anxiety, and uncertainty of a form of political dissent by resorting to the banality of a taxonomy" (124).

Michel Foucault (1970) has suggested that movement from surface to interiority is a hallmark of the modern human sciences. Medicojuridical discourses routinely dispense with the complexities of specific histories of struggle that might explain particular instances of violence. Instead they posit hidden truths—violent propensities, dispositions, inclinations lodged deep within the subject—that account for observable behavior. Hidden from the untrained eye but available to expert medical, psychological, criminal justice, and education professionals, the evidence of modern science produces the pathological individual as one whose actions reveal unspoken and invisible character traits (Stoler 1997, 206).

Since September 11, 2001, the production of the pathologized, racialized terrorist has moved beyond the confines of terrorism studies to occupy the public imagination. The mass circulation of the Abu Ghraib photographs played a crucial role in the construction of this new racial regime of visibility. By looking at the tortured bodies of detainees under the gaze of U.S. soldiers, we gain clues to a deep structure of racialized pathology abiding within the so-called Muslim terrorist.

Suffering black bodies

The photographs from Abu Ghraib are reminiscent of the photographs of lynchings distributed during the early part of the twentieth century throughout the United States. Hazel Carby (2004), Susan Sontag (2004), and Dora Apel (2005) note both the similarities between the photographs and the shared effects of publicizing such violence. Although one might be tempted to attribute these similarities to some notion that there are universal but finite ways of humiliating and torturing people, I want to interpret particular features of the Abu Ghraib photos in the historically and culturally specific context of lynchings in the United States. Certain parallels are telling. In both instances, the photographs are staged, and victims are posed in submissive proximity to the agent(s) of violence. In both cases, the photos regularly include onlookers who manifest an air of triumph. And in both episodes, the photographs of tortured bodies have circulated widely, whether deliberately or inadvertently. Indeed, I want to suggest that the deliberately circulated lynching photographs can illuminate the effects of the inadvertently leaked Abu Ghraib photographs. Both serve as spectacles of power within a racial order, visually demonstrating the power of the torturer to turn subjects into objects.

Apel (2004) warns against the easy conflation of all forms of violence with lynchings. She suggests that there is a historically specific context for lynchings that is directly connected to the fears and anxieties of white populations concerning social equality with black people following the abolition of slavery. The form and function of lynchings was ostensibly to punish black men's sexuality, to protect white womanhood, and to prohibit miscegenation. For Apel, extending the metaphor of lynching to any instance of racial violence, racism, or violence collapses the specificities of lynching and erases a history that has yet to be incorporated into U.S. public consciousness. Indeed it is only with the Without Sanctuary exhibit, a collection of lynching postcards and photographs shown first in New York in 2000 and later displayed in several other U.S. venues, that the history of lynching in the United States has been brought back into public consciousness and then only to a limited extent.[6]

Despite the failure of the U.S. public to grapple seriously with the history of lynching, Apel points out that the concept and practice of lynchings have never left the public imagination entirely. A number of contemporary murders have replicated the form and function of lynchings themselves. In 1998 James Byrd was dragged to death from a pickup truck and beheaded in Jasper, Texas; Raynard Johnson was discovered hanging from a tree in front of his home in Kokomo, Mississippi, in July 2002, lynched for dating a white woman; Stanley Forestal, who married a white woman, was hanged in a barn on his Elma, New York, family property in October 2002; Feraris "Ray" Golden was hanged from a tree near his grandmother's home in Belle Glade, Florida, for dating a daughter of a white policeman in 2003; and Leonard Gakinya was hanged from a radio tower in Springfield, Missouri, in 2003, near the site of a 1906 triple lynching (Apel 2004, 16). Besides these cases of actual lynchings, Apel draws attention to "racist pantomimes" in college fraternities and cases of workplace harassment that regularly feature nooses, a potent symbol of race hatred, to threaten black and other minority workers and students (17). In addition, "the echo of lynching memory" (17) reverberated in discussions of what should be done with John Allen Muhammad and Lee

---

[6] See the Web site Without Sanctuary, http://www.withoutsanctuary.org/, for lynching photographs with descriptions. See also Allen 2000.

Boyd Malvo, the Washington, DC, snipers. Clarence Thomas dispensed with sexual harassment allegations by suggesting that he was being subjected to his own "high-tech lynching" (17). There are also instances of violence—sexual, racial, ethnic, and religious—that Apel suggests are increasingly in dialogue with past narratives of lynching and their contemporary use and abuse.

Without flattening out the meaning of lynching, I want to draw attention to particular parallels between the lynching photographs circulated in the early twentieth century and the Abu Ghraib torture photos circulated globally. In each instance, the photographs document the extrajudicial infliction of violence. In each case, a racial regime is constructed through visual records. In each situation, whiteness is affirmed and blackness is abjectified. In each case, masculinity and sexuality are targeted in ways that privilege the white, hypermasculine racial order of the United States.[7]

The iconography of lynching as the violent expression of a racial order is part of U.S. historical consciousness. Each time lynchings are enacted, the history of lynchings and their relationship to the nation are resurrected, and in that resurrection, victims are racialized in ways that have little connection to their actual bodies. The racial regime of visibility consolidated through reenactments of lynching does not erase the history of lynching and antiblack racism. On the contrary, with each enactment the black body is raced again as the new victims are blackened.

Historically, lynchings were regularly staged for an audience. Many photographs in the Without Sanctuary collection show crowds of people, some-

---

[7] While the widely circulated photographs of Abu Ghraib detainees have been of men, there are reports that women are also held in U.S. detentions centers and have been subjected to various forms of torture. The Taguba Report (Taguba 2004) documents the rape of female detainees in Abu Ghraib, and numerous sources report that there are photographs and videotapes attesting to the fact that women are tortured through sexual violence within U.S. military prisons (Rajiva 2004a, 2004b, 2004c). There is nothing surprising about the news that women are also subjects of torture in the context of war. As numerous feminist authors have documented, the targeting of women in war is an integral war tactic, necessary for the destruction of communities, nations, and the masculinity of the enemy (Khushalani 1982; Copelon 1994; Gordon 1995). That the circulation of torture photos has not included photos of women being tortured suggests that the Pentagon withheld these photos for strategic reasons. The U.S. government may have concerns that if the photos circulate they could contribute to a coalescing of public opinion against the war and possibly disrupt the continued occupation of Iraq and the use of military prison and detention centers. It is also possible that if Iraqis were to see such photography, their resistance to the occupation would increase and endanger U.S. soldiers further.

times numbering as many as fifteen thousand, gathered around the black(ened) body, which hangs in the midst of the crowd (Allen 2000, photos 22, 24, 25, and 29). There is rarely a photo of a lynching that does not include a group of onlookers, who typically look directly into the camera (Allen 2000, photos 28, 30, 31, 54, and 79). The onlookers are most often men—members of the lynch mob, although there are several photographs that include women and children among the onlookers (e.g., Allen 2000, photo 57). Most of those who were lynched were men, although some photos of lynched women also circulated (Allen 2000, photos 37 and 38).

The lynching photographs were carefully staged. Not only were on-lookers posed for the camera, but so too were the victims. A few photographs show corpses that have been propped up in chairs, beside trees, or on the ground to face the camera, as though they literally sat for the photograph. There is, for example, a photo of an unidentified corpse propped in a rocking chair, fully clothed, covered in blood, with white and dark paint on his face and head, with an off-camera hand holding a rod propping his head up (Allen and Littlefield 2000–2005, photo 9).

Sometimes lynchings were conducted as live theater, and in certain cases onlookers were invited to participate in the torture of victims before the final act of murder (Allen and Littlefield 2000–2005, photo 70). Lynched bodies were left hanging from utility poles in well-traveled areas. A photo of an unidentified African American man in Oxford, Georgia, in 1908 shows him hanging from a lighted telephone pole near well-used railroad tracks (Allen and Littlefield 2000–2005, photo 12). Corpses were often left in trees in city courtyards, near community billboards, or hanging from bridges to ensure that they would be seen.

Some lynching victims are naked in the photographs, although not as many as might be expected. This might be due to the sensibilities of the viewing audience more than for the protection of the dignity of the victims.[8] A striking example of nudity is in two photographs of Frank Embree, an African American male who in one photo is standing on a buggy, naked and facing the camera, and in another is naked with his back to the camera (Allen 2000, photos 42 and 43). His hands are cuffed and held in front of his genitals, his feet are shackled, and his body is covered with lacer-

---

[8] For instance, the photograph of a naked black man, John (Jack) Holmes, was printed on the front page of the San Jose, California, newspaper the day after he was lynched. The nudity so offended city officials that the entire edition of the newspaper was confiscated (Allen and Littlefield 2000–2005, photo 68, "More information").

ations. This photograph suggests the slave auction in the pose of the man and onlookers who are evaluating and measuring his body.[9]

Several of the photographs indicate that the victims were castrated. Many of the victims of lynching had been accused of raping white women. Although numerous scholars have challenged the validity of such accusations, black men were lynched for their presumed deviant sexuality. Several of the bodies of lynch victims are naked and covered with a blanket around their lower bodies. Streams of blood can be seen running down the legs of some, suggestive of castration (Allen 2000, photos 20, 35, and 44). Apel suggests that lynching involved "indulging a covert form of homoerotic gratification through the subjugated bodies of black men, who would often be humiliated, tortured, and castrated" (Apel 2005, 89–90). Through the lynchings themselves, white women were constructed as paragons of virtue and sexual purity, while black men were constructed as the animalistic, hypersexualized agents whose deviance threatened to destroy white womanhood. Legitimated as a form of punishment for black male infractions of norms of respectable sexuality, lynchings simultaneously exculpated white men who participated in these orgies of homoerotic violence. Acting in defense of white women's purity, white men accorded themselves an unqualified right to defend and protect the desexualized and weak creatures they imagined white women to be.

Traces of lynching iconography appear in the Abu Ghraib photos, which display detainees as the suffering black body, wounded or dead, naked and sexualized. The photos include triumphant poses of the torturers. Thumbs-up signs are enacted by military police who stand proudly next to abused bodies.[10] There is a photo of a grinning military police officer sitting on top of a man who is strapped between two boards on the ground, face down, staged as a trophy photo. There are multiple photos of hooded naked men lying on the cement floor, piled on top of one another or standing beside clothed military police.

The use of dogs by lynch mobs to capture African American men is recalled in the Abu Ghraib photos, where dogs were used to intimidate shackled detainees. There are scenes of lunging dogs with military police surrounding a naked man as he holds his head and crouches in the cellblock. There is a photo of a man kneeling in an orange suit with an unmuzzled dog lunging at his face. A prostrate prisoner held with a dog leash around

---

[9] The third photograph of the same man shows him hanging from a tree with this lower half covered with a blanket. These three photographs were sold in a package, tied together so that they opened like a map (Allen and Littlefield 2000–2005, photo 38).

[10] The Abu Ghraib photos discussed here are posted on Salon.com (see Benjamin 2006).

his neck recalls shackles that dragged black bodies behind horses or vehicles. There is a photo of a naked detainee posed in a manner quite similar to the depiction of nudity in the lynching photos of Embree discussed above. A naked man stands with his hands cuffed in front of his genitals with deep wounds all over his arms, legs, and belly. It is an inspection photo of a sort, a documentation of his body for public appraisal.

Lynching iconography is apparent in the photos of detainees who are metaphorically castrated and emasculated through sexual humiliation. Several of the Abu Ghraib photos depict men who are forced to wear women's underwear on their heads, to touch one another, to simulate fellatio and masturbation, and to be unclothed. Sexualized violence feminizes male detainees by forcing them to enact homosexual sex in scenes of simulated fellatio. Putting women's underwear on their faces suggests a kind of lascivious desire for the intimate apparel of women, evidence of misdirected and immature sexual desire. Forcing detainees to remain naked displays their vulnerability and their lack of decency. Being held on a leash by a white, female soldier dehumanizes the detainee, likening him to a dog, while simultaneously suggesting the image of a dominatrix (Goldstein 2004). As Puar argues,

> The force of feminizing, then, lies not only in the stripping away of masculinity, the "faggotizing" of the male body, or in the robbing of the feminine of its symbolic and reproductive centrality to national-normative sexualities. Rather, it is the fortification of the unenforceable boundaries between masculine and feminine, the rescripting of multiple and fluid gender performatives into petrified sites of masculine and feminine, the regendering of multiple genders into the oppressive binary scripts of masculine and feminine, and the interplay of it all within and through racial, imperial, and economic matrices of power. That is the real force of torture. (Puar 2005, 28)

The Abu Ghraib photos depict a visible regime of sexual desire quite independent of the unknowable desires of specific detainees. This has little connection to the actual bodies at stake; whether they are a priori raced does not necessarily matter, just as it matters little what the actual sexuality of a body is in the process of being "faggotized" (Puar 2005, 28), and just as it matters little whether there is credible evidence to link the majority of the detainees to terrorist activity.[11] Rather, the photos themselves produce

[11] The International Committee of the Red Cross estimates that between 60 percent and 90 percent of the detainees in U.S. detention centers have been mistakenly arrested (ICRC 2004).

the visible difference between those who are appropriately gendered and those who defy gender norms, establishing the clear boundary between masculinity and femininity as marks of the ideal human. That boundary is clarified again by the photos of Lynndie England and Charles Graner having sex with each other and photographs of what look to be young girls in detention, one of whom is exposing her breasts. Among the depictions of homosexualized violence, these photos reassert the heteronormativity that Puar (2005, 13) argues is instrinsic to U.S. patriotism.

In the Abu Ghraib photos, gendered and sexualized violence is used as part of the racializing process that turns someone into an abject racial object. Indeed, the photos are part of a technology that produces the racialized Muslim terrorist. The dynamic process that positions Western viewers as onlookers and witnesses of the torture of Iraqi detainees produces a racial order in which orientalism combines with antiblack racism to give these photos meaning. The photos teach us to see a Muslim terrorist in custody. The photos interpellate the Muslim as an agent of terror through the racialized processes of viewing and being viewed.

Decerebralization as racialization
During the Enlightenment, the official use of torture came to be associated with premodern and barbarous methods of treating suspects or criminals. Arguments cast in terms of the standards of civilization and justice were advanced to minimize the infliction of physical suffering on those held in police custody, and modern states increasingly relied on incarceration to punish criminals. Talal Asad (1997) argues that torture came to be associated with the barbarous and uncivilized in those cases where it was gratuitous, but torture was given a special role tied to drawing subject peoples into modernity. As liberal democracies sought to consolidate their sovereign authority, the use of torture was reserved for noncitizens. Asad demonstrates that the consolidation of these liberal democratic regimes generated new rationales for the legitimate use of torture. Torture was justifiable if it was useful to incorporate subjects into civilization: "Pain endured in the movement toward becoming 'fully human' . . . was seen as necessary because social or moral reasons justified why it must be suffered" (Asad 1997, 295). These uses of torture remained hidden in plain sight (Parry 2005, 521). Awareness of the uses of torture was relegated to the margins of public discourse, shielded both by a moral rationale and by covert practices. Retained as a useful tool for the promotion of civilizing state interests, torture was nonetheless conducted in secrecy (Asad 1997; Parry 2005).

Responding to the images from Abu Ghraib, the George W. Bush administration denied that the practices depicted were widespread, attributing them to a few individuals whose actions were inconsistent with American values.[12] Several soldiers involved, including Graner and England, were charged and tried for prisoner abuse. The commanding officer, Brigadier General Janis Karpinski, was relieved of her position and demoted. Yet at the same time that the practices at Abu Ghraib were being passed off as exceptions, the legitimacy of coercive methods was defended by the U.S. Attorney General's office, which offered a redefinition of torture far removed from that acknowledged in the Geneva Conventions (Levinson 2004, 23–24). Prominent ethics and human rights scholars in the United States advanced various arguments defending the use of torture in the war on terror (Dershowitz 2004; Elshtain 2004; Ignatieff 2004). Preserving both prongs of the Enlightenment ideal, government officials and eminent scholars have argued that torture is necessary to civilize people but that it is best to keep it hidden.

What constitutes torture is a focus of many of these legal and ethical debates, which take detention practices in the war on terror as their point of departure. Several authors make a moral distinction between physical torture and psychological pain, suggesting that psychological tactics necessary for interrogation practices in the war on terror must be differentiated from physical torture (Elshtain 2004; Levinson 2004; Posner 2004). Yet methods of inflicting psychological pain developed by the United States during the Cold War are known to be highly effective coercion techniques. The CIA manual "KUBARK Counter-Intelligence Interrogation" of 1963 suggests that psychological techniques are among the most effective methods of interrogation (CIA 1963). The "Human Resource Exploitation Training Manual," another CIA document, produced in 1983, offers a similar assessment of the merits of psychological techniques, based on case studies gathered from around the world (CIA 1983; McCoy 2004).

Alfred W. McCoy (2004) has argued that "the photos from Iraq's Abu Ghraib prison are snapshots not of simple brutality or a breakdown in

---

[12] Testifying before the Senate and House Armed Services Committee, May 7, 2004, Senator John Warner stated: "This degree of breakdown in military leadership and discipline represents an extremely rare—and I repeat, rare—chapter in the otherwise proud history of the armed forces of the United States. It defies common sense. It contradicts all the values we Americans learned beginning in our homes." Rumsfeld said in his statement to the committee: "So to those Iraqis who were mistreated by members of the U.S. armed forces, I offer my deepest apology. It was inconsistent with the values of our nation. It was inconsistent with the teachings of the military, to the men and women of the armed forces. And it was certainly fundamentally un-American" (Senate Armed Services Committee 2004).

discipline but of CIA torture techniques" developed between 1950 and 1962. Providing vivid depictions of no-touch torture, McCoy notes that these techniques emphasized the value of psychological torture, "the first real revolution in this cruel science since the 17th century" (2004). No-touch torture involves multiple stages. The first stage involves hooding, sleep deprivation, and sexual humiliation. The second stage involves "self-inflicted" (2004) pain, that is, pain and discomfort that come from stress and duress positions. Although the U.S. Agency for International Development (USAID) Office of Public Safety promulgated no-touch torture methods globally to allied militaries and police departments, they were banned in 1975 by an act of the U.S. Congress. Despite this congressional prohibition, no-touch interrogation measures were officially revived as part of the war on terror in early 2002 at Bagram Air Base near Kabul. In a recent report, Physicians for Human Rights (2005) documents the widespread use of psychological torture methods in several U.S.-sponsored detention centers. Contrary to characterization of the treatment of detainees by the Bush administration as light, the methods depicted in the photographs and documented by human rights organizations suggest much more devastating and brutalizing effects on victims of psychological torture.

In debates about the utility of torture, proponents tie torture to interrogation tactics, suggesting that its purpose is to extract crucial strategic information that helps to avert terrorist attacks. In *The Body in Pain* (1985, 28), Elaine Scarry debunks narrow readings that suggest that "torture consists of a primary physical act, the infliction of pain, and a primary verbal act, the interrogation." Although there are few instances of documented torture that do not connect to a question or an investigation, there is more at stake in torture than eliciting information: "While the content of the prisoner's answer is only sometimes important to the regime, the form of the answer, the fact of his answering, is always crucial" (29). The purpose of torture, then, is intricately tied to the wielding of power. Torture demonstrates both the ability and the willingness to inflict great amounts of pain to propagate fear, whether inside or outside the bounds of law. The veracity of the information elicited is far less important than the fact that prisoners surrender to coercion: "What masquerades as the motive for torture is a fiction" (28).

Similarly, Françoise Sironi and Raphaëlle Branche have pointed out that the "real aim of torture is not to make people talk, but to make them keep quiet" (2002, 539). Torture silences and isolates victims through shame, fear, and humiliation. The methods of torture result in psychological destruction and cultural alienation. Concurring with Scarry, Sironi and Branche argue that "intelligence torture" (540) is a euphemism for violence intended to destroy a culture and a nation: "Through the torture victim, the aim is to reach the group to which the victim belongs. . . . It is the collective dimension of the individual that is attacked, the attachment to a group" (539–40).[13]

The process of decerebralization—an integral aspect of torture—entails physical and psychological practices that turn subject into object (Carby 2004). Psychological and mental cruelty, humiliation, shaming, religious and cultural defilement, sexualized violence, and attacks on masculinity and femininity are all elements that further remove the detainee from the terrain of the human. The notion of ghost detainees, which refers to those who are outside of legal protections and public knowledge, exudes a sense of this depersonalized empty presence stripped of self. As John T. Parry (2005, 533) suggests, "when one is a ghost . . . one is already separate from one's body, not to mention from one's family, community, and other support networks. . . . The ghost . . . is by definition hidden, exceptional, and dominated."

The "epidermalization of inferiority" is not the only means through which torture turns subject into object (Fanon 1967, 13). Fanon's astute analysis of the mechanisms of epidermalization or racialization drew upon the French torture of Algerians as well as the effects of colonial occupation on the psyche of the colonized. In *Black Skin, White Masks* (1967), Fanon provides detailed accounts of the phenomenology of racialization, rooted in regimes of visibility entrenched in interpersonal encounters through which the French interpellated the "Negro" as an abject object, altogether other. Yet whether in the context of colonial encounter, lynching, everyday practices of racism, or torture, decerebralization is a primary manifestation of the racialization of people whose human status is displaced by a profound objectification.

The eternal recurrence of racialization

Carby (2004) notes that the publicity of lynchings both secured white power and ensured that black populations remained fearful, segregated, and limited in their mobility and power. Apel suggests that "the lynching photographs served as a means of continuing social control, extended tools of terror which ultimately justified the deeds they represented as protecting whiteness, which was code for America itself" (2005, 90). There are important parallels between the circulation of photos taken at Abu Ghraib and the circulation of lynching photographs. Images that pose victims before mul-

---

[13] For a longer discussion of these authors and related arguments, see Philipose (2007).

tiple, anonymous onlookers while depicting emasculation, castration, and other forms of sexual attack participate in particular forms of decerebralization. Photographing detainees in their abject state and publicizing that abjection racializes the detainee as the suffering, passive, decerebralized object whose terrorist acts have necessitated a powerful response by the U.S. military, charged with the defense of the nation.[14] Circulating images of detainees surrounded by triumphant onlookers resurrect only partially repressed historical consciousness of lynchings. Within this charged racial context, the detainee's punishment appears as deserved as that of the lynched black body. Indeed, the Muslim detainee is blackened in a regime of visibility in which blackness is the marker for the abject or nonhuman. The incorporation of sexual violation into the torture of detainees resurrects modes of emasculation and feminization that resinscribe rigid regimes of white heteronormative sexuality as the property of white Westerners and deviance as the hidden propensity of the orientalized Muslim terrorist.

The circulation of the Abu Ghraib photographs does not merely repeat, reiterate, or reconfigure old racial ideas. By circulating the pain inflicted on Iraqi detainees before a global audience, the Abu Ghraib photographs produce new racialized objects on a new world stage. Invoking the visual authority of the lynching image, the Abu Ghraib photos unleash the power of visuality and justifiable violence onto the tortured body. Constructed as terrorists, Muslim men held in detention lose all purchase on innocence, legal rights, and international covenants. Within the perverse frame constructed by this racialized regime of looking, punishment by white captors proves the criminal propensities harbored within the terrorist body. Documented as threat by free-floating Internet images, the detainees deserve any degree of torture from the defenders of Western liberal democracy. The contradictions manifested in the lynching photos are resurrected in the images from Abu Ghraib. "The relationship of power to helplessness, citizen to outsider, privilege to oppression, subjecthood to objecthood, and community to outcast" (Apel 2004, 7) are played out in these photos in the form of racialized bodies tortured by morally upright white soldiers under the approving gaze of triumphant onlookers.

The complex interpellations proffered by orientalism, terrorism, lynchings, and whiteness mingle in the Abu Ghraib photos to produce a new regime of visibility. The photographs exhibit and simultaneously produce visible racialized difference for the viewer. Whites in military garb pose as

[14] A number of Abu Ghraib detainees' depositions recalled the flash and click of cameras and the knowledge that they were being photographed as elements of the abuse. See the Taguba Report (Taguba 2004).

conquerors. Clothed, armed, and smiling, they stand guard over naked, prostrate, sexualized, wounded, and helpless detainees. Standing powerfully beside, behind, and sometimes on top of prisoners, holding leashes and directing the scene, the men and women in the U.S. military are masculinized. They are the agents of the law defending against those who are outlaws. They are agents of a legitimate state empowered to use the law to serve national interests and military necessity. By contrast, the victims are arrested under conditions of lawlessness—albeit lawlessness created by the U.S. invasion. They are positioned as suspects on the basis of their names, nationality, and religion. Violated while in detention, they have been made abject, and under the racialization's peculiar regime of visibility, they are blamed for their own abuse. Their Muslim religion is interpellated as deviant masculine lawlessness, as threat in need of containment. Circulating globally, the photos of their abjection contain a message "as old as racism itself: this is the material evidence of the wielding of power, of the performance of conquest over an enemy" (Carby 2004). Carby has noted that "in the shadow of the flag, of the Pentagon, and of an imperial democracy, lies the other's tortured body." I would add that the new racial grammar erases any possible empathy for that tortured body. Like the lynched black bodies in the early twentieth century, the tortured Muslim is situated in a regime of visibility that lodges responsibility for the torture beneath the racialized epidermis of the torture victim.

Spectacles of power, such as those embedded in the photographs of Muslim men being humiliated, sexually abused, brutalized, and tortured, may serve domestic purposes. Joseph Hart (2005) has suggested that the visual representation of suffering inflicted through torture is like a "new psychotropic" that quells racial anxiety. These racialized anxieties are national anxieties, and if we take the nation as the embodiment of masculine values of virility and potency as Cynthia Enloe (1990) and Jan Jindy Pettman (1996) have suggested, these are also anxieties about the state of masculinity in the twenty-first-century United States. In an effort to quell white racial anxiety, war and the torture that accompanies it produce new racialized regimes of looking that deploy old racisms for new political ends.

Department of Women's Studies
California State University, Long Beach

References

Allen, James, ed. 2000. *Without Sanctuary: Lynching Photography in America.* Santa Fe, NM: Twin Palms.

Allen, James, and John Littlefield. 2000–2005. *Without Sanctuary: Photographs and Postcards of Lynching in America.* http://www.withoutsanctuary.org.

Apel, Dora. 2004. *Imagery of Lynching: Black Men, White Women, and the Mob.* New Brunswick, NJ: Rutgers University Press.

———. 2005. "Torture Culture: Lynching Photographs and the Images of Abu Ghraib." *Art Journal* 64(2):89–100.

Appiah, Kwame Anthony. 1992. *In My Father's House: Africa in the Philosophy of Culture.* New York: Oxford University Press.

Asad, Talal. 1997. "On Torture, or Cruel, Inhuman, and Degrading Treatment." In *Social Suffering*, ed. Arthur Kleinman, Veena Das, and Margaret Lock, 285–308. Berkeley: University of California Press.

Benjamin, Mark. 2006. "*Salon* Exclusive: The Abu Ghraib Files." Salon.com. http://salon.com/news/feature/2006/02/16/abu_ghraib/.

Carby, Hazel. 2004. "A Strange and Bitter Crop: The Spectacle of Torture." *Open Democracy: Free Thinking for the World,* October 11. http://www.opendemocracy.net/debates/article-8-112-2149.jsp.

Center for Constitutional Rights. 2004. "Composite Statement: Detention in Afghanistan and Guantanamo Bay: Shafiq Rasul, Asif Iqbal, and Rhuhel Ahmed." Report, July 26. http://www.ccr-ny.org/v2/reports/docs/Gitmo-compositestatementFINAL23july04.pdf.

CIA (Central Intelligence Agency). 1963. "KUBARK Counterintelligence Interrogation, July 1963." In the National Security Archive Electronic Briefing Book no. 122. http://www.gwu.edu/~nsarchiv/NSAEBB/NSAEBB122.

———. 1983. "Human Resource Exploitation Training Manual, 1983." In the National Security Archive Electronic Briefing Book no. 122. http://www.gwu.edu/~nsarchiv/NSAEBB/NSAEBB122.

Chrétien, Jean. 2001. "Prime Minister Jean Chrétien: National Day of Mourning 9/11 Memorial Address." American Rhetoric Online Speech Bank. http://www.americanrhetoric.com/speeches/chretian9-14-01.htm.

Copelon, Rhonda. 1994. "Surfacing Gender: Reconceptualizing Crimes against Women in Times of War." In *Mass Rape: The War against Women in Bosnia-Herzegovina*, ed. Alexandra Stiglmayer, 197–218. Lincoln: University of Nebraska Press.

Dershowitz, Alan. 2004. "Tortured Reasoning," In *Torture: A Collection*, ed. Sanford Levinson, 257–80. Oxford: Oxford University Press.

Elshtain, Jean Bethke. 2004. "Reflection on the Problem of 'Dirty Hands.'" In *Torture: A Collection*, ed. Sanford Levinson, 77–89. Oxford: Oxford University Press.

Enloe, Cynthia. 1990. *Bananas, Beaches, and Bases: Making Feminist Sense of International Politics.* Berkeley: University of California Press.

Fanon, Frantz. 1967. *Black Skin, White Masks.* Trans. Charles Lam Markham. New York: Grove.

Foucault, Michel. 1970. *The Order of Things: An Archaeology of the Human Sciences.* London: Tavistock.

Goldberg, David Theo, ed. 1990. *Anatomy of Racism*. Minneapolis: University of Minnesota Press.

Goldenberg, Suzanne, and Hugh Muir. 2006. "Killing Themselves Was Unnecessary. But It Certainly Is a Good PR Move." *Guardian Unlimited*, June 12. http://www.guardian.co.uk/frontpage/story/0,,1795547,00.html.

Goldstein, Richard. 2004. "Bitch Bites Man! Why Lynndie England Is the Face of Torturegate." *Village Voice*, May 10. http://www.villagevoice.com/news/0419,goldstein2,53375,6.html.

Gordon, Melissa. 1995. "Justice on Trial: The Efficacy of the International Criminal Tribunal for Rwanda." *ILSA Journal of International and Comparative Law* 1(1):217–42.

Gould, Stephen J. 1981. *The Mismeasure of Man*. New York: Norton.

Haney-López, Ian F. 1996. *White by Law: The Legal Construction of Race*. New York: New York University Press.

Hart, Joseph. 2005. "War: The New Psychotropic." *Adbusters* 51 (January–February). http://www.adbusters.org/the_magazine/51/War_The_New_Psychotropic.html.

hooks, bell. 1992. "Representations of Whiteness in the Black Imagination." In her *Black Looks: Race and Representation*, 165–78. Cambridge, MA: South End.

Human Rights Watch. 2004. "The Road to Abu Ghraib." Report, June. http://hrw.org/reports/2004/usa0604/.

ICRC (International Committee of the Red Cross). 2004. "Report of the International Committee of the Red Cross on the Treatment by the Coalition Forces of Prisoners of War and Other Protected Persons by the Geneva Conventions in Iraq during Arrest, Internment and Interrogation." In *Torture and Truth: America, Abu Ghraib, and the War on Terror*, ed. Mark Danner, 251–78. New York: New York Review of Books.

Ignatieff, Michael. 2004. "Evil under Interrogation: Is Torture Ever Permissible?" *Financial Times*, May 15. Reprinted at http://www.ksg.harvard.edu/news/opeds/2004/ignatieff_torture_ft_051504.htm.

Khushalani, Yougindra. 1982. *Dignity and Honour of Women as Basic and Fundamental Human Rights*. The Hague: Martinus Nijhoff.

Levinson, Sanford. 2004. "Contemplating Torture: An Introduction." In his *Torture: A Collection*, 23–43. Oxford: Oxford University Press.

McCoy, Alfred W. 2004. "Torture at Abu Ghraib Followed CIA's Manual." *Boston Globe*, May 14. http://www.boston.com/news/globe/editorial_opinion/oped/articles/2004/05/14/torture_at_abu_ghraib_followed_cias_manual/.

Parry, John T. 2005. "The Shape of Modern Torture: Extraordinary Rendition and Ghost Detainees." *Melbourne Journal of International Law* 6(2):516–33.

Pettman, Jan Jindy. 1996. *Worlding Women: A Feminist International Politics*. New York: Routledge.

Philipose, Liz. 2007. "The Politics of Pain and the End of Empire." *International Feminist Journal of Politics* 9(1):60–81.

Physicians for Human Rights. 2005. "Break Them Down: Systematic Use of Psychological Torture by U.S. Forces." *Physicians for Human Rights*, May 1. http://physiciansforhumanrights.org/library/report-2005-may.html.

Porras, Ileana M. 1995. "On Terrorism: Reflections on Violence and the Outlaw." In *After Identity: A Reader in Law and Culture*, ed. Dan Danielsen and Karen Engle, 294–313. New York: Routledge.

Posner, Richard A. 2004. "Torture, Terrorism, and Interrogation." In *Torture: A Collection*, ed. Sanford Levinson, 291–98. Oxford: Oxford University Press.

Project for the New American Century. 1997. "Statement of Principles." Project for the New American Century. http://newamericancentury.org/statementofprinciples.htm.

Puar, Jasbir K. 2005. "On Torture: Abu Ghraib." *Radical History Review* 93 (Fall): 13–38.

Puar, Jasbir K., and Amit S. Rai. 2002. "Monster, Terrorist, Fag: The War on Terrorism and the Production of Docile Patriots." *Social Text* 20(3):117–48.

Rajiva, Lila. 2004a. "Iraqi Women and Torture, Part I: Rapes and Rumors of Rape." *Dissident Voice*, July 27. http://www.dissidentvoice.org/July2004/Rajiva0727.htm.

———. 2004b. "Iraqi Women and Torture, Part II: Theater That Educates, News That Propagandizes." *Dissident Voice*, July 30. http://www.dissidentvoice.org/July2004/Rajiva0730.htm.

———. 2004c. "Iraqi Women and Torture, Part III: Violence and Virtual Violence." *Dissident Voice*, August 4. http://www.dissidentvoice.org/Aug04/Rajiva0804.htm.

Said, Edward W. 1979. *Orientalism*. New York: Vintage.

———. 2001. "The Clash of Ignorance." *Nation*. October 4. http://www.thenation.com/doc/20011022/said.

Scarry, Elaine. 1985. *The Body in Pain: The Making and Unmaking of the World*. Oxford: Oxford University Press.

Senate Armed Services Committee. 2004. "Transcript of the Senate Armed Services Committee Hearing on Iraq Prisoners," May 7. http://wid.ap.org/transcripts/040507iraq.html.

Sheshadri-Crooks, Kalpana. 2000. *Desiring Whiteness: A Lacanian Analysis of Race*. New York: Routledge.

Sironi, Françoise, and Raphaëlle Branche. 2002. "Torture and the Borders of Humanity." *International Social Science Journal* 54(174):539–48.

Sontag, Susan. 2004. "Regarding the Torture of Others." *New York Times*, May 23, sec. 6, 25.

Stoler, Ann Laura. 1997. *Race and the Education of Desire: Foucault's History of Sexuality and the Colonial Order of Things*. Durham, NC: Duke University Press.

Taguba, Antonio, M. 2004. "Article 15-6 Investigation of the 800th Military Police Brigade (The Taguba Report)." In *Torture and Truth: America, Abu*

Ghraib, and the War on Terror, ed. Mark Danner, 279–328. New York: New York Review of Books.

U.S. National Intelligence Council. 2004. *Mapping the Global Future: Report of the National Intelligence Council's 2020 Project*. National Intelligence Council. http://www.dni.gov/nic/NIC_globaltrend2020.html.

Waugh, Paul. 2002. "Blair under Fire over Adviser's Call for 'Imperialism.'" *Independent*, March 28. http://news.independent.co.uk/uk/politics/article194963 .ece.

The War on Terrorism: Appropriation and Subversion by Moroccan Women

I n May 2003, a series of bombing attacks hit the city of Casablanca, killing forty-five people, including the twelve suicide bombers, and hitting five separate targets.[1] The young men involved in the attack were identified as part of the radical group al-Salafiya al-Jihadiya, which up to that point was unknown to the general public. On-the-spot analysts and activists blamed social and economic deprivation for the bombing, after learning that the bombers were from the shantytown of Sidi Moumen and that the majority had very little education and no stable jobs. Links were assumed between this attack and Osama bin Laden's broadcast videotape of February 2003 in which he warned Morocco, along with Jordan, Saudi Arabia, and Sudan, against providing any kind of help to the United States in its war in Iraq.[2]

The war as a package and the war at home

The Casablanca attack brought into sharp relief some of the tensions of the monarchy, which had previously failed to openly ally itself with Washington because of the unpopularity of the U.S. narrative of fighting terrorism. After the Casablanca attack, however, the Moroccan parliament rushed to adopt an antiterrorist law, a Moroccan version of the USA PATRIOT Act. In a continuation of the monarchy's open move to adopt the U.S. agenda for reforming the Middle East, the Moroccan government signed a Free Trade Agreement (FTA) with the United States in April 2004.[3] That same year the government also volunteered to host the first round of the Forum for the Future, a revised version of the Greater Middle East Initiative, which was an all-encompassing vision for the democratization and modernization of the Middle East according to the Bush ad-

---

[1] For details about the attack, see Center for Policing Terrorism (2006).
[2] For excerpts from the videotape, see CNN (2003).
[3] For details about the FTA, see *Arabic News* (2004).

[*Signs: Journal of Women in Culture and Society* 2007, vol. 33, no. 1]

ministration's standards. The Greater Middle East Initiative, presented by the United States to the Group of Eight (G8) members in April of 2004, was adopted by these members during their June summit at Sea Island, Georgia (Wittes 2004).

After the Casablanca attack, the war on terrorism came full circle in Morocco and has become a product for national consumption and control. With the Forum for the Future, the FTA, and the antiterrorist law, the Moroccan state has openly positioned itself against the forces of evil as defined by the Bush administration. As a package the war has been delivered with this prescription: adopt Forum for the Future–style democracy, neoliberal economics, and anti-Islamist moderation. These projects are interconnected. As an economic program neoliberalism needs the war on terrorism because it uses the mass bombing of civilian populations as an excuse for discipline and control through racial profiling and stigma and, as in Iraq, through triggering internal divisions. This mix does not work without tensions, however. While neoliberalism requires a small government and an active civil society, one that can replace the state in the social sectors, the war on terrorism needs a wide-ranging security apparatus and a docile civil society. Yet both the war on terrorism and its underlying neoliberal agenda come packaged in a security narrative that increases the defense apparatus of local governments while reducing the state to its disciplinary dimensions.

As far as Morocco is concerned, the war on terrorism came as a package. The discourse of the war is interwoven with a discourse celebrating neoliberalism and manipulating the themes of modernity and democracy. These themes have been articulated in different versions of the Greater Middle East Initiative and have been presented with a consensual facade in the Forum for the Future.

The Greater Middle East Initiative comprises economic, cultural, and political programs and provides financial aid to help countries implement them. It also requires normalization with the state of Israel through trade exchange and diplomatic relations, which by the same token marginalizes the Palestinian struggle for statehood. All of these projects are couched in a discourse of democratization, modernization, and civil society and are meant to manufacture consent for the controversial U.S. policy in the Middle East and to enhance the poor image of the United States, which has been confirmed by many polls and studies.[4] Morocco is a central piece of this puzzle. The Moroccan government volunteered to host the aforementioned Forum for the Future in December 2004. This meeting was

---

[4] See commentaries about the 2004 Pew Research Center's opinion polls in the Middle East by Abdessalam Maghraoui (2004).

meant to rally civil society, government agents, businesses, and G8 foreign, economic, and other ministers from the Middle East and North Africa in a democratic show.

Morocco also signed the FTA with the United States despite sit-ins and protests against a negotiation process that was handled with secrecy from the time it was launched in January 2003.[5] The country was congratulated by many representatives of the U.S. government for being a good friend and a strong ally of the United States in its war against terrorism. Morocco is also one of the destinations to which the U.S. Central Intelligence Agency has allegedly moved the interrogation of its detainees since the invasion of Afghanistan.

Women in the United States are not exposed to the agenda and effects of the war on terrorism the way women elsewhere are. Even within the vast geographical area known as the Middle East, North Africa, and South and Central Asia, women are located differently vis-à-vis this war and have a different exposure to it. For example, Afghan, Iraqi, Lebanese, and Palestinian women, who live in countries that fall directly within the framework of the U.S. definition of terrorist because they harbor groups considered by the United States to be terrorist groups, are subjected to military operations that require individual as well as collective strategies of survival. But the story of the war does not end there. It continues as a state-generated narrative that has, so far, justified specific policies and more or less discrete forms of policing, control, and discipline, while having severe effects on women's ability to act and to resist acts of war.

Thus, understanding the gender dynamics of the war on terrorism requires examining this entire state of affairs. It entails shifting the lens away from the impact of the war on women and gender policies and focusing instead on women's contributions in reshaping the discourse of the war and using it for political gains. The Moroccan women's movement, represented by two major groups, namely, liberal feminists and prosharia Islamists, provides a good focus for an investigation of the war on terrorism as a culture, an economic rationality, and a technique of government. With Morocco first positioned at the margin of the war on terrorism and then immediately after the Casablanca attack becoming one of its centers, Moroccan women's groups were compelled to strategically position themselves vis-à-vis the war agenda and to respond through specific organizations, programs, and discourses.

---

[5] The secrecy of these negotiations was challenged by sit-ins and demonstrations that were violently suppressed (see Bilaterals.org 2004a, 2004b).

A gender reform

Gender was central to the repositioning of the Moroccan state in this international context. A few months after the Casablanca attack, King Mohamed VI decided to honor two decades of feminist activism by reforming the sharia-based family law, or *moudawana*. Viewed by the international media as a revolution, this reform was in fact the culmination of more than two decades of activism by women's groups, which have managed to work out their demands for gender equality within existing state institutions. By activism, I am referring to the actions of a broad and diverse body of women's groups that have been using the UN conventions about women, notably the Convention on the Elimination of All Forms of Discrimination against Women (CEDAW), and the liberal discourse of equality and individual rights to lobby the state for a reform of the sharia-based family law. These groups have been working mostly on gender mainstreaming, law reforms, and granting women access to the decision-making process. During the parliamentary elections of 2002, these groups increased women's representation in the parliament to 10 percent, managed to open gender units in most ministries and state departments, and saw women represented in the government as ministers and secretaries of state. Some of the women who were appointed to political office were previously active in the feminist movement.

The other part of the story is told by Islamist women who came from within male-dominated Islamist movements and who have attempted to reform women's status in society by rereading the Koran and the sunna (tradition based on the life of the Prophet). By the end of the 1990s these groups had started their own independent women's organizations, having opened up multiple spaces for women's education and interpretations of sharia for more than a decade. More radical in their approach to social change, Islamist women have striven to affect what they call the culture of denigration of women that they found to be widespread in society. They have been engaged in setting up grassroots organizations that have granted them a large and diverse social base of action and support. While feminist groups have been lobbying the state, Islamist women have striven to create a counterdiscourse to the feminist rhetoric of universal rights and gender equality by advancing Islamic alternatives. In contrast to the legalistic approach of law reform as a means to enhance women's status, Islamist women wanted to respond to the culture of denigration of women through communication, mass education, and self-education.

Both the feminist and the Islamist women's movements I refer to in this article now have to organize within the framework of the war in order to prevent worse outcomes. In the case of liberal feminists, the worst is no less than a radicalization of the social body occasioned by the U.S. invasion of Iraq, a marginalization of women's issues, and demands for a reform of family law. To the Islamists the worst would be the secularization of family law, knowing that this code is the only state law that directly derives from the Islamic sharia as interpreted by the Maleki *fikh* (an Islamic school of jurisprudence followed in Morocco). And regardless of their differences, both feminists and Islamist women's groups have had to articulate their demands in an environment where women's issues were not a priority.

Nevertheless, as the Moroccan state strove to position itself as an ally of the United States in its war against terror, a new code of the family that recognized the equality of husband and wife before the law started to make sense to the monarchy. It was, in fact, through the reform of family law that the Moroccan monarchy truly recovered its image as a moderate regime, the Casablanca attack notwithstanding. The new family code was presented by the king in a broadcast speech to the parliament in October 2003. In a gesture to appease the Islamists, who had actively opposed the reform for two decades, the king introduced the new family code as a reform that was inspired by Islamic sharia. The new code is, in fact, closely built on liberal feminist proposals of women's rights and the rhetoric of gender equality. It is worth stating, however, that these reforms in the family code responded to the ways in which feminist and Islamist women's groups have managed to bring gender back to the center stage of the war on terrorism. In what follows, I propose an analysis of these two major groups' appropriations of the war on terrorism as a narrative to pursue their competing agendas about women's rights. This approach will complement feminist studies that have been dominated by cultural and political approaches with a sociological analysis of the way women's groups have used the phenomenon of the war on terrorism to create more space for women's intervention and voices. Nevertheless, by appropriating the war as a valid framework for speaking the language of democracy, modernity, and moderation, these groups have reproduced some of the war's most oppressive aspects. Thus, women are not only resisting the war, they are also contributing to its hegemony while legitimating the policing of the social body and the disciplinary power of local governments.

In order to carry the debate on women's agency beyond the scope of co-optation and resistance, I will ask a new set of questions: How did these two competing women's movements participate in shaping the war's narrative and its agenda? What was the effect of women's voices on domestic gender policy? What are the spaces opened by women through their appropriation and subversion of the war's narrative? My intention is not to imply that the war is good or bad for women. Rather, I would like to shift the gaze from the binary of oppression/resistance to look at the various ways in which women have created new spaces through a selective appropriation of the war's narrative and its main themes: democracy, modernity, and moderation. Since September 11, 2001, these three themes have been recurrent in the U.S. government's plans for remodeling the Middle East. They are also powerful frameworks for the justification of local governments' neoliberal policies and unpopular submission to the might of the U.S. empire.

The war on terrorism: A view from within

In the United States, support for an endless war needs a condition of sustained fear. As Gayatri Chakravorty Spivak puts it, the war on terrorism is "zoomed down to a lawsuit [that of Zacarias Moussaoui] and zoomed up to face an abstraction" (2004, 82). François Debrix calls this state of fear and fascination of the American public with the meanings of terror "abjection," that is, a search for meanings through fascination, acceptance, and rejection (2005, 1158). But if the war on terrorism needs abjection, embracing terror "needs a subtext" (1159). Debrix also explores the work of some U.S. intellectuals in legitimizing the warfare state. "Masters of the abject" or "masters of terror," as he calls them, these "experts" are defined as men of "statecraft" who serve as "relays between public leadership in the media, government, and the military and the [American] public in general" (1159). These intellectuals have constructed the war within the following three paradigms: political realism (Blanchard 2003; Debrix 2005), the clash of civilizations (Huntington 1996), and orientalism (Said 1978).

Feminist writings about the war on terrorism emerged outside of the U.S. academy as an instantaneous reaction to the way the invasion of Afghanistan was marketed as a civilizing mission (Hawthorne and Winter 2003; Sharma 2003; Nnaemeka 2004). Only recently has U.S.-based feminist scholarship seriously identified the centrality of gender as a site for playing out this mission. Feminist studies of the war have been developed within two major paradigms. The first is concerned with the impact of military operations on gender relations and gender norms in the United States, and the second stresses women's responses, agency, and transnational solidarities to resist the war.[6] Both trends converge to identify the

[6] On the impact of military operations on gender relations and gender norms in the United States, see Blanchard (2003), Ruby (2003), Young (2003), Enloe (2004), and Strassberg (2004). On women's responses, agency, and transnational solidarities, see Hawthorne and Winter (2003), Moghissi (2004), and Zerai and Salime (2006).

values of patriarchal domination and protection, as well as masculine fears and desires, as defining principles of the war on terrorism.

Despite this growing feminist interest in international conflict, U.S. scholarship has so far concentrated on the impact of the war on terrorism on women and gender norms domestically. The focus on domestic policy has, however, rendered invisible those women who are directly exposed to the war as a military intervention and as a discursive regime. The narrative of liberation, oppression, and lack of voice attributed to women in the Islamic context, by both U.S. corporate media and U.S. government agents, contributes to victimize Muslim women and deprive them of any form of agency or control over the war's agenda and rhetoric. When women's agency is highlighted, it is considered with regard to direct military intervention, leaving out an important aspect of the war on terrorism, that is, the war as a hegemonic discourse. Studies of women's agency have also reduced agency to women's strategies of survival, modalities of resistance, and solidarity movements to protest the war and counter its effects (Moghissi 2004; Zerai and Salime 2006). In all these cases, women's actual participation in redefining the narrative of the war and shaping its all-encompassing agenda are missing.

The goal of this article is twofold: first, unpacking the war on terrorism by highlighting its economic and geopolitical grounds and, second, identifying the ways women have co-opted these agendas and narratives in order to pursue their long-standing demands for reforming women's status in law, society, and religion. As a regime of truth and a discourse of power, the war on terrorism is not only disruptive, it is also productive. It has created new subjects, policies, and cultural sites of protest, and it has been an agent of manipulation, control, and legitimation. This article identifies some of these sites.

Engendering the war on terrorism: Cultural analyses

Feminist approaches to the war on terrorism are deeply influenced by the two fields of cultural studies and international relations. Cultural studies of the war have articulated poststructuralist analyses of discourse, postmodern definitions of power, and the postcolonial theory of orientalism. In these three conceptual frameworks, discourse is considered in a dialectical relation to power. Discourse is both constituted by and constitutive of structures of power/knowledge (Foucault 1980), identities (Laclau and Mouffe 1985), modes of governmentality (Lemke 2000), and regimes of truth (Foucault 1978). Power, Michel Foucault argues, is productive (Foucault 1980, 119, 1990); it produces subjects and desires,

institutions and techniques of control, and normalization but also subversion (Butler 2003). More important, power does not work through
coercion but rather through consent. Thus, Antonio Gramsci's (1971)
concept of hegemony, which refers to domination through consent, is
also central to these analyses. Hegemony entails adherence to the dominant narratives and ideology at the level of civil society. As Evelina Dagnino (1998) rightly argues, the concept of hegemony brings together
culture, material forces, and politics, which are conceived as interrelated
and embedded into structures of power. Edward Said's (1978) work on
orientalism articulates these definitions. Rather than defining it as a field
of objective knowledge about the Orient, Said defines orientalism as a
discourse of power in which the Oriental or other is constructed through
texts, images, stereotypes, and representations about his or her incom-
mensurable nature. As a hegemonic field of knowledge, orientalism works
at the intersection of cultural (mis)representations and the political and
economic interests of the West. Hegemony is sought through maintaining
a set of binaries—civilized/barbarians, East/West, and modern/archaic—
to nourish and legitimate the colonial enterprise of the West and the
positional superiority of the white male. When the same binaries are appropriated by the agents of what is widely known as al-Qaida, the use of
these binaries is called the clash of civilizations (Huntington 1996).

As a site for theoretical inquiry, the war on terrorism is relevant to
postcolonial feminist analyses. The war has been advertised through powerful institutions such as the corporate media, privately funded think tanks
(Debrix 2005), and evangelical churches, as well as through more general
sources of cultural production that iterate specific images (Nader 1989)
of Western violence as liberation. This regime of truth has enabled the
renewal of post-9/11 traumatized masculine identities and their articulation of essentialized cultural differences. But the symbols and representations released by the terror discourse are gendered. Women's oppression
in Islam is illustrated through selective images of women executed under
the West-sponsored Taliban regime. Similarly, promises to integrate
women into the new Iraqi government and free them from sharia-bound
laws have set the illegal invasion of Iraq in moral terms. The theme of
modernity is also central to these constructions. The main assumption is
that Muslim women will be better off under an invasion represented as
bringing "modernity as a liberation" (Cloud 2004, 285) or, rather, "modernity as media and market" (294). Images of veiled women are deployed
to confirm the need for the white man's protection and establish his
superiority on a renewed civilizing mission, fighting the archaic other to
liberate its women. Thus, if liberating Muslim women has been central

to the legitimation of this war, establishing justice has been central to creating tolerance for the most horrible forms of violence perpetrated against Muslim men. The savagery attributed to these men, themselves feminized through a public humiliation of the kind taking place in Abu Ghraib and Guantánamo Bay, are examples of the ways Muslim men are brought to their knees in this unwinnable war.

But as feminist approaches to international relations have already demonstrated (Enloe 1989, 2004), gender alone does not account for the complexity of national identities in times of war. Rather, it is the interplay of gender, race, nation, and religion that provides a deeper understanding of the issues at stake (Petchesky 2002; Abdo 2003; Akhter 2003). Gender, sexuality, and race contribute to a definition of citizenship and national identities as gendered and racially bound.[7] Similarly, the war on terrorism is gendered, sexualized, and racialized through the ways in which the nations involved are represented. The flag syndrome that contaminated U.S. public space after 9/11 had the double effect of rejecting the notion of a feminized America and its penetration by outside forces and of appealing to the manliest men and women to recover the nation's status as a masculine superpower. The detention camps at Abu Ghraib and Guantánamo work the other way around. They enable those who order the horrors and those who excel in performing them to recover their traumatized masculinities by watching Muslim men on their knees and seeing Muslim men forced into female sexual positions. Though one can resist the thought that Lynndie England, the woman soldier who, with an apparent look of exaltation, posed next to her victims in Abu Ghraib, was animated by the desire to take revenge for millions of oppressed Muslim sisters, as Yasmin Jiwani puts it, as a "discursive regime" (2004, 266), the war on terrorism is founded on "the rescue motif" (271) in which colonization is justified through the motive of saving women. In the United States, the war on terrorism triggers the norms of masculine domination and white male protection, while women are assigned a subordinate position of dependence and obedience (Blanchard 2003, 1294; Young 2003, 2).

In order to understand masculinities at war, Cynthia Enloe (2004, 123) invites us to ask the question, "Are any of the key actors engaging in a violent conflict motivated in part by a desire to appear 'manly' in the eyes of their own principal allies or adversaries?" But while Enloe stresses the logics of masculine domination and masculinist power, Eric M. Blanchard (2003) and Iris Marion Young (2003) suggest instead that the logic of masculine protection functions as a strong anchor for the current U.S.

---

[7] See Enloe 1989, 2004; Blanchard 2003; Ruby 2003; Zerai and Salime 2006.

security state. During the war against the Taliban, it was the masculine United States that had the moral superiority to free "the cowardly and dependent, feminine Afghanistan" (Jiwani 2004, 288). But these images of other men and other women also work as instruments for local consumption and control. Laura Nader asks two fundamental questions: "How can images of women in other societies be prejudicial to women in one's own society?" and "How could images of women in other cultures act as a control to women in one's own culture?" (1989, 324). Thus terror is also gendered, as Jiwani argues, in the "ways in which the Taliban are presented as excessively patriarchal while the same patriarchal impulse and structure that underpins Western society remains unexamined" (2004, 288).

Gender in international relations

The second set of approaches to the war on terror is influenced by feminist scholarship in international relations. Reflecting on the war on terrorism requires opening this field to a gender analysis of this war as a military intervention, a global population policy, and a new site for the repositioning of local actors on the global scene. It also entails exposing the work of gender and power in world politics. Maria Mies (1986) and Enloe (1989) see power as entrenched in the construction of masculinity and femininity and as sustained by the need to maintain women's subordination through a daily exercise of power at all levels—local, national, and international. A gender lens on world politics necessitates taking into account global processes and the way they engage women and gender (Peterson and Runyan 1999).

This means, in Blanchard's terms, the "recovery of women's experiences, the recognition of gender-based exclusion from decision-making roles, and the investigation of women's invisibility in international theory" (2003, 1290). Blanchard argues that feminist studies have, on the one hand, subverted the supposed "irrelevance of women" in international politics and questioned "the extent to which women are secured by state 'protection' in times of war and peace" (1290). On the other hand, feminist international relations studies have contested "discourses wherein women are linked unreflectively with peace" and assumptions that "gendered security practices address only women" (1290). Blanchard also questions the dominance of political realism, considering it "a patriarchal discourse" that is closely tied to a definition of security and politics as the realm of "elite, white, male practitioners" (1292).

But feminist analyses of international conflicts have tended to concentrate on the effects of wars on the militarization of women's lives and the shrinking of social programs and public spaces available to them.[8] Few studies have looked at the war on terrorism as a population policy, and feminist inquiry has yet to uncover the war's effects on increasing internal conflicts and on gender relations in places directly exposed to war and stigmatized by the definition of terrorism, notably, Iraq and Afghanistan or, for a longer period, Palestine. Farida Akhter, referring to Samuel Huntington's worries about the increase in the Muslim population world-wide, defines this war as essentially "a population policy," a "war policy" to terminate the people's considered enemies (Akhter 2003, 328). Put differently, the war on terrorism is based on a Malthusian take on inter-national relations that aims, according to Akhter, to control and dominate the Islamic world. But if one agrees that the war images are predominantly masculine, it is also widely accepted that 90 percent of all war-related casualties are civilians and that the majority of these are women and chil-dren (Nordstrom 1995). As a population policy, the U.S. war in Iraq has caused increased losses of civilian lives, destroyed the civilian infrastruc-ture, and triggered internal divisions that have taken the country to the edge of a long-term civil war.

Once defined as a population policy and a biopower, the war on terrorism finds parallels in other fields such as medicine and bioethics. Barbara Ann Strassberg (2004) looks at the social and cultural construction of the HIV/AIDS epidemic and terrorism in the United States. She links these discourses to processes of transformations in "the interpretation of human sexuality, gender identities, and gender roles within [a] culture of violence" (436). Strassberg calls this transformation "a death spasm of the dominant po-sition of the rugged white Christian heterosexual American male" (436). Both HIV/AIDS and terror are defined, Strassberg argues, within the metaphors of extinction and survival and are mentioned by many sources and with increasing frequency, leading to what she calls an "epidemic of signification" (456). This so-called epidemic is grounded in "metaphors of extinction of the Western world" by "unidentified non-Western agents" (456–57). In both HIV/AIDS and terrorism, the values of the white Christian heterosexual man acquire positional superiority.

Whether the focus is on international relations or global gender issues, feminist studies converge to show that the values of masculine superiority and domination are underlying rationales of both state and nonstate vi-olent conflicts and wars. Enloe paraphrases the U.S. military expansion and "militarized US culture" (2004, 146) in terms of "masculinity as a

---

[8] See Enloe 1989, 2004; Borchorst 2000; Joseph 2000; Moghadam 2000; and Scott 2000.

foreign policy issue" (122) and "macho" policies (126). She argues that the U.S. government has, since the Cold War, strengthened the privileged positions of men in decision making, both in the United States and in the international arena (127). One main idea to retain here is Enloe's claim that the events of 9/11 may be militarizing non-U.S. women's lives, since it was only after 9/11 that the violation of Afghan women's human rights took center stage (147). Jiwani (2004) highlights another dimension of gender in international relations. She claims that the gendering of terror is apparent in the targeting of women as victims of retaliation by means of rape, for example, in the West and the East. She adds that "while patriarchal powers compete for social, cultural, and economic resources, it is women and children who suffer the ensuing of terror" (288).

The challenge for feminist analyses of the war on terrorism relates to its reduction to cultural struggles. The invasions of Iraq and Afghanistan have relied on cultural manipulations, yet they have been motivated at least in part by the urgency to control the natural resources of Central Asia and the Middle East. Both were on the agenda prior to 9/11. The war on terrorism is a technique of power to ensure the hegemony of neoliberal globalization as a promising model for global disparity. James Ferguson (2006) has rightly argued that it is in the shadow zones, in the zones of crises, that the real story of globalization is told. It is in the zones of chaos that capital flourishes, through black market arms trades, part-time jobs, and reconstruction efforts. As I stated earlier, the war on terrorism came as a package. Thus, to look at the war through multiple lenses enables us to enlarge the sphere of feminist inquiry and analysis to the political economy of the war and its geopolitical strategy, notably the marginalization of the Palestinian cause and the supremacy of Israel as the sole military power in the region.

Furthermore, considering how women are articulating these phenomena in their discourses and organizations enables us to tackle differently the question of women's agency in the obviously male-dominated realms of international relations and of political and religious representation in the Middle East. This requires locating the analysis at the interplay among domestic gender struggles, the hegemonic neoliberal agenda, and U.S. imperialist ambition in the region. It also entails deconstructing the binaries assumed between the feminine local and the masculine global (Freeman 2001) by showing how local women are in fact shaping these global processes and discourses. Furthermore, by locating this approach at the interplay of feminism, Islam, and the war on terrorism as a package, my purpose is to show that the local and the global are mutually constitutive.

Restating feminism and the "clash of civilizations"

It was interesting to me to hear Moroccans espousing local versions of Huntington's concept of the clash of civilizations when I talked to leaders of liberal feminist organizations in Morocco. To most of my respondents, the Casablanca attack of May 2003 was the expression of two clashing worldviews, a modernist one represented by liberal feminists and an archaic one promoted by the Islamists. There is, then, a similarity in the way feminist groups perceive the Islamists as a bloc of evil and the way Islamists are represented in the government's discourse, notably through its socialist press. These forces converged to discredit their major political opponents, the Islamists of the party al-Adala w-al-Tanmia (justice and development), who were held responsible for blocking the progress of Morocco through opposing the reform of family law, *moudawana*, and found guilty of disseminating a discourse of hatred of the other. Empowered by the Casablanca attack, liberal feminists started urging the state to adopt with no further delays their project of reform of the *moudawana*. Not only did some leaders of these groups become more assertive about their feminism, but they also managed to define feminism as the fence against religious extremism and the best warrant, if espoused by the state, for blocking the progress of extremist discourse in the mosque and the parliament. Thus, it made sense for these groups to push for a more interventionist state that would protect civil liberties and secular institutions. The Casablanca attack enabled feminist groups to articulate feminism as a new project for transforming Moroccan society along more secular lines. To them, modernity entails the birth of a feminist, anti-Islamist state. As a term, *feminism* is then openly adopted and redefined beyond the scope of a family law reform. The sociologist and president of the Moroccan Association for Women's Rights (Association Marocaine pour les Droits des Femmes; AMDF), Najat Razi, is now open about her feminism. She said, "I used to have a lot of problems with the term feminism and always shied away from calling myself a feminist. I am no longer concerned with the controversy. Yes, I am a feminist, and as a feminist I oppose the injustices based on sexual differences of men and women. To me feminism is an identity and a world vision that enables a progressive political program. Feminism is a modernist, progressive movement that carries a great potential for a true democratic change."[9]

After the Casablanca attack, their opposition to the war on Iraq not-

[9] Personal interview with Razi, a founder of the Association Marocaine pour la Protection des Droits des Femmes and the FAMA Center in Casablanca in June 2003.

withstanding, feminist groups adopted the rhetoric of the war on terrorism but only to redefine its terms and conditions. Najia Zirari, a founder of the network Democratic Association of Moroccan Women (Association Democratique des Femmes du Maroc; ADFM), claimed that "espousing the values of 'democracy' and 'modernity' is the only path for any country to prevent an American military intervention and preserve its territorial sovereignty." More naively, Zirari maintained that "eliminating the motives for an American military intervention definitely depends on the state's handling of 'religious extremism' on the one hand, and its enhancement of women's rights on the other."[10] In a co-optation of the state's discourse of the urgency of democratic reforms, my respondents contended that the state's encouragement of the feminists as democratic players would undermine the advances of religious extremism. Feminism is then both endowed with a normative value and marketed as the strongest ally of the state. The irony is that by defining feminism as an ally of the state, these groups risk becoming feminists of the state. There are also unresolved tensions among feminist activism, discourses of democracy and individual rights, and these activists' call for the eradication of the Islamist component from the political spectrum. And there are tensions between their claim for more political freedoms and their desire to see a more interventionist state that cracks down on those perceived as fundamentalists.

To these activists there is no such a thing as two women's movements in Morocco, one Islamist and one feminist. Zirari, the secretary general of the ADFM in Casablanca, defined the women's movement as "one that prioritizes the cause of women, fights for equality, and recognizes the international norms and conventions about women." She continued that the feminist movement "carries the hopes and aspirations of women for a better world, for fair access to resources, and for equality before the law." Leila Rhiwi, the president of the ADFM section in Rabat, described the feminist movement as "modernist in its approach, democratic in its goals." Another activist, Fatema Maghnawi, a founding member of the Union for Women's Action (Union de l'Action Feminine; UAF), argued that "Islamist women cannot be and are not part of the women's movement." Khadija Rougani from the FAMA Center for the Advocacy of Women's Rights explained to me why Islamist women cannot be considered part of the women's movement. She claimed that "their project is different; because they do not work for the cause of women [*qadiat al-mar'a*] but for the cause of the Islamic state, and women are secondary in this project." In the best-case scenario, the differences between the

---

[10] Personal interview with Zirari, Casablanca, June 2003.

Islamists and the feminists are expressed by Razi, a self-declared secular feminist from AMDF: "We are a civic force; the Islamists are a political force."[11]

To demarcate themselves as a civic force, feminist groups strove to respond to the Casablanca attack through new structures emphasizing their distinguished societal project. The Modernity/Democracy Network is a large concentration of activists and intellectuals united in their struggle against the antidemocratic practices of the Moroccan state as well as against the Islamists' societal project. Feminist groups played a leading role in this network. My own participation in some of the meetings of this large group, in summer 2003, was critical to my understanding of the tensions brought to light by the Casablanca attack. The two-page mission statement published in the network's memorandum captures some of these tensions. The introduction states: "We, the persons signing this memorandum, state our adherence to the values of the enlightenment and modernity. We believe that democracy should be founded on respect of individual freedoms, the right to difference, and the values of solidarity, equality, and tolerance. We believe that this will grant Morocco's full membership in the contemporary human civilization. We are convinced that these universals are a common heritage to humankind. We are also confident that multiple sources of inspiration from our culture have a lot to contribute toward the advancement of these universals."[12]

The Modernity/Democracy Network was formed after many attempts by feminist groups to attract the state's attention to the violations of human rights that were taking place in marginal suburbs, as well as in the streets of big cities, in the name of religion. As women's rights advocates, the feminists were particularly subject to defamation during religious sermons and through audiotapes sold in the streets by unemployed young men. In response, feminist groups have created specific structures to document these violations. For instance, the Observatory for Women's Rights was created by the Ligue Democratique pour les Droits des Femmes (Democratic League for Women's Rights) after the huge Islamist march of 2000 opposing the feminist project for reform of family law. This center has been holding an Islamist Watch in order to document hate speech

---

[11] Quotations in this paragraph are taken from the following personal interviews: Zirari, Casablanca, June 2003; Rhiwi, Rabat, June and July 2003; Maghnaoui, Rabat, July 2003; Rougani, Casablanca, July 2003; Razi, Casablanca, July 2003.

[12] This is a two-page statement that was circulated during the June 2003 meeting of the Modernity/Democracy Network in the offices of the ADFM in Rabat. The network called this statement the Memorandum. This document is available at the ADFM office in Rabat.

and acts of violence committed against persons found guilty of nonobservance of Islamic morals, as defined by some Islamist radicals. It also provides legal assistance to women, helping them bring their cases before the law. It hosts a library and compiles data on violations of individual freedoms of both men and women.

As Bouchra Abdou, an activist in this center, confirmed, various cases of violence were reported by young women assaulted on the street for nonobservance of the *hijab* (wearing of the head scarf). These assaults were more common in poor suburbs where some radical groups were, in the absence of any effective presence of the state, in charge of setting the rules, taxes, and modes of punishments that these radicals dubbed Islamic. In this context, many working-class women were compelled to wear the *hijab* in order to become invisible. That the feminists saw the need for a more interventionist state makes a lot of sense in this context. But it was the Casablanca attack that brought the feminists' frustrations with the state to the fore. It also provided them with the opportunity to rearticulate their demands for a reform of family law that would impede the progress of Islamic radicalism by granting full citizenship and equal rights to women.

Islamism redefined

Islamist women, however, had to carefully articulate their identity politics in a very hostile environment. Leading activists in the movements of Unification and Reform (al-Islah w-al-Tawhid) and Justice and Spirituality (al-Adl w-al-Ihsane), such as Nadia Yassin, Khadija Mufid, and Bassima al-Haqawi, expressed their concern about the disastrous effects of the Casablanca attack on the Islamist movement during our private meeting. In fact, the immediate reaction of the Islamists was to adopt a low profile. Noteworthy also was the way in which women's voices almost disappeared from the Islamist press. The waves of arrests, intimidation of Islamist groups, and systematic calls to close down their organizations from the socialist majority in the government were partly responsible for the fading of Islamist women's voices from the press. There was also a paternalist and protectionist reaction on the part of male Islamist leaders during periods of crisis that is very familiar to the female membership of the Islamist groups. In fact, one can speak of a web of families constituting the Islamist organizations: husbands and wives, brothers and sisters, and the younger generation of children. Thus, the patriarchy, or rather neo-patriarchy (Sharabi 1988), characteristic of these groups is always at work and is more pronounced during periods of crisis. With the exception of a few women such as Yassin from al-Adl w-al-Ihsane, who gave several interviews to the press, or Fouzia Hajbi from the party al-Adala w-al-Tanmia, who maintained her column in the weekly newspaper *al-Asr*, Islamist women did not comment on the attack in the press. The views about the attack that I will outline in the following text are based on personal interviews with the leadership of these two movements.[13]

Both feminist and Islamist women articulated their response to the Casablanca attack by targeting the state and activating a feminist agenda. Both attempted to position themselves as the appropriate agents in this crisis. While feminist groups appropriated the discourse of modernity and democracy to lobby the state and push for a reform of family law, Islamist women directed their efforts to articulate a more radical demand. They wanted to be admitted to positions of religious leadership and to be recognized for their ability to lecture in state-controlled mosques. This also entailed redefining political Islam as it pertains to women and their role as mothers. For example, my respondents defined motherhood according to the Koranic concept of the *wassat*. This term characterizes Muslims as the people of the middle way, which means that they occupy both a median location and a moderate position. The term *wassat* enables Islamist women to steer clear of the politics of radicalism and articulate new identities around an imagined motherhood, this time linked to women's roles as mediators. By claiming the *wassat* as a location, Islamist women appropriated one major discursive theme of the war on terrorism, that of moderation that gave them more space to maneuver.

The narrative of moderation is used by the U.S. government to describe the friendly regimes of the Middle East, such as the Jordanian and the Moroccan monarchies, as moderate states. This term is equally central to the Bush administration's plans for integrating moderate Islamist groups into the political field in the Middle East. After the Casablanca attack, the term *moderation* was manipulated by the Moroccan government to justify reforming the religious field and controlling the discourse of the mosque. Hence, Islamist women's appropriation of this term provided them with negotiating power, first, within their male-dominated movements and, second, in their dealings with the Moroccan state. The discourse of moderation became their entry point to initiate this process of reform, which acquired urgency for the United States after 9/11 and for the Moroccan government after the Casablanca attack. It was then, through defining

[13] These interviews took place in the cities of Casablanca, Rabat, Fez, Meknes, and Tangiers in two consecutive summers. I first met with these activists in the months of June, July, and August of 2003 and conducted additional interviews with some of them, including Mufid and Suad al-Amari, in June of 2004.

motherhood and womanhood as the embodiment of moderation and as sites for enacting a politics of mediation, that Islamist women positioned themselves within the war rhetoric.

Womanhood is defined by this leadership as a set of natural qualities and psychological dispositions that are specific to women, preparing them for their roles as mothers. If womanhood is viewed in essentialized terms, motherhood is defined by Suad al-Amari, an active member in the Unification and Reform movement, as a social location, an "intersecting site," a *wassat*. According to this activist, motherhood is "the point where the social and the individual meet and overlap." As she explained to me during our meeting in June 2003 in Casablanca, motherhood enables women to develop skills and qualities that promote better understanding of interpersonal relations and social connections. "Women carry life, give and maintain life"; this is why they are "predisposed to protect life," contended Ghislane al-Bahraoui, the president of the women's section of al-Adl w-al-Ihsane. Thus women are conflict managers, peacemakers, and moderators. In a more radical stand, Yassin, the spokesperson for al-Adl w-al-Ihsane, claimed that "motherhood does not have to be connected to maternity and procreation." She defined motherhood as "the factor of humanization of the social." It is obvious that these narratives are meant not only to state these activists' distance from Islamist radicalism but also to mark the specific location of women within political Islam and to show the privileged position of women as mediators in times of heightened social crises.

These meanings attributed to motherhood and womanhood are not constructed with reference to a certain feminist theory, at least not consciously, but are rather the outcome of women's interpretations and readings of the Islamic sources of the Koran and sunna as well as the history of Islam. It makes sense then, that Islamist women's call for more space to maneuver would find a large echo in an environment in which the state is looking for these moderate voices to articulate a different message from within Islam. As moderate voices, women and mothers can educate the masses in the true spirit of Islam. Thus, without shying away from their Islamic identities, Islamist women activated their long-standing demand to obtain official recognition from the state as full players on the religious and political scene. It is access to the religious leadership and the podium of *da'wa* (public preaching) to which these activists sought claim. Previously this demand was directed inward, to the male-dominated Islamist movement; it was now directed to the state. Islamist women's discourse of moderation as connected to motherhood is creating its own hegemonic space within the Islamist male-dominated organizations and movements. The Casablanca attack did not change the grounding of this discourse in this emerging culture of gratification of womanhood and celebration of political motherhood. Rather, it provided Islamist women with the opportunity to find an echo to their long-standing demands for access to the mosque and for official recognition of their roles as *dai'yat* (preachers).

The fragmentation and hybridization of the religious field that resulted from the emergence of the Islamist movements through independent preaching and private mosques opened tremendous opportunities for women's entrance into the field. During the 1990s women started opening spaces for discussion and learning in neighborhood mosques, but they were faced with many restrictions because of the state surveillance and co-optation of Islamist discourse and groups. Some of these leaders, such as Naima Benyaich, started taking concrete steps by writing to the Ministry of Islamic Affairs expressing the need for time and space devoted to women's lectures in mosques. In fact, Benyaich, who was one of the first women to pass an exam in Islamic sharia from outside the field of Islamic studies, paved the way for a movement by Islamist women "to take the mosques back," to borrow Yassin's phrasing. In November 2003 Rajaa Naji Mekkaoui, a university professor of law, became the first woman to deliver a religious sermon in the presence of Moroccan royalty. Her sermon opened a series of conferences organized by the palace to commemorate the holy month of Ramadan. Yet Mekkaoui's religious sermon was only the first step toward recognizing women's expertise in religion. A second and more important step was reached when, in an unprecedented move, the king appointed thirty women to the councils of ulema (religious scholars) in May 2004. Among them was Fatouma Kabbaj, who was appointed to the state-controlled supreme council of ulema.

Launched by pioneers like Yassin and Benyaich, this movement by Islamist women to take back Islam found its perfect raison d'être after the Casablanca attack. Not only was this large group of women who were self-educated in the Islamic sciences assigned space and time to preach in mosques but also, in a sign of recognition of women's political impact, the state opened schools to train new groups for the sake of the spiritual security of the Moroccan people. The state also coined the term of *morshidate*, spiritual guides, to define the task of this young generation of women who would carry the burden of moderating the tone of political Islam. A first cohort of fifty women received their degrees in May 2006. As religious leaders, women are now in charge of changing the masculine culture of the mosque and providing a feminine alternative to the radical tone of some imams. Whether we consider this intervention by the state to be a co-optation of women's politics or a smart move in the right direction, the gains made by women were not given by the state but are rather the culmination of two decades of women's readings of the Islamic sources and activism to revise the Islamic sharia and reform the Islamist movements.

The war on terrorism and the gender field

The women's movement has been a major factor in the identification of the centrality of gender in processes of state formation and transformation. Valentine Moghadam (2000) argues that women may become the sign or marker of political goals and of cultural identity not only during processes of revolution and state building but also when power is being contested or reproduced. She states that "representations about women assume political significance, and certain images of women define and demarcate political groups, cultural projects, or ethnic communities" (44). Expanding Moghadam's argument, I see gender as a marker of political shifts at the level of the state and as a site for the positioning of local actors within the context of the war on terrorism. For instance, the reform of family law, resisted by the state for two decades, was implemented only a few months after the Casablanca attack to mark the country's open engagement in this global war and to paint the monarchy as moderate and democratic. Consequently, there was no need to implement radical changes to the structure of political and economic power in which the king remains the central player. Defined within the binaries of modernity/ archaism and progress/stagnation, the agenda of the war has also buttressed the Moroccan state's ability to use gender to position itself as a modern player on the international scene.

Feminist studies stress the fact that some political transformations may increase the political space available to women's organizations while still actively repressing other sectors of civil society (Alvarez 1990, 262; Jelin 1998). Thus, the case of Moroccan women's groups is not merely a success story of how women have subverted the discourse and agenda of the war on terrorism, it is also the story of how they have made this agenda hegemonic. It is true that women's manipulation of the war's narrative has enabled them to carve out new spaces of empowerment and access points (Noonan 1997) to the state. This entailed new definitions of feminism and Islamism as well as a repositioning of women vis-à-vis the neoliberal state agenda for reforms. As I have shown earlier, women on both the feminist and Islamist sides have used the war to support their own politics and affect the opportunities available to their opponents.

Despite their different approaches to social change—a legal reform for liberal feminists and hegemony in civil society for the Islamists—both have responded by adopting the war policy of the state as a valid framework for action. Both have positioned themselves as the appropriate agents for the era of fighting terrorism. Yet, as I argue above, by accepting the framework of the war and speaking its language, both groups, with notable differences, have contributed to making the war hegemonic.

In addition, the state manipulation of the liberal rhetoric of gender equality has decreased the spaces for independent organizing by feminist and Islamist women's groups alike. In addition to co-opting both movements, the state is now able to monitor the discourse and activism of these groups while acting as a neutral mediator. The neoliberal state intervention to facilitate women's access to religious representation and grant them more rights in the family has also enabled the monarchy to regain negotiating power and create local allies among both forms of the women's movement. But since the war is constructed on modernist binaries, the state's intervention to reform family law has definitely increased rather than decreased internal divisions and tensions between the Islamist and feminist movements in Morocco.

Thus, feminists are right to argue for the importance of using a gendered lens when looking at international relations. As far as North Africa and the Middle East are concerned, a promising area of inquiry is yet to emerge in analyses of the war on terrorism, particularly with respect to the state's appropriation of a gendered rhetoric as a means to speak the language of the war, an appropriation that inadvertently triggered local dissent. A feminist analysis of these dynamics will complete the cultural studies of the war on terrorism with a reflection that takes into account gender as a site for the enactment of change.

Department of Sociology
Michigan State University

References

Abdo, Nahla. 2003. "Eurocentrism, Orientalism, and Essentialism: Some Reflections on September 11 and Beyond." In Hawthorne and Winter 2003, 408–29.

Akhter, Farida. 2003. "Huntington's 'Clash of Civilizations' Thesis and Population Control." In Hawthorne and Winter 2003, 328–32.

Alvarez, Sonia E. 1990. *Engendering Democracy in Brazil: Women's Movements in Transition Politics.* Princeton, NJ: Princeton University Press.

Arabic News. 2004. "Morocco Signs Free Trade Agreement with U.S." *ArabicNews .com*, June 17. http://www.arabicnews.com/ansub/Daily/Day/040617/2004061718.html.

Bilaterals.org. 2004a. "Des ONG Marocaines contre l'Accord de Libre-Échange" [Moroccan NGOs against the Free Trade Agreement]. October 24. http://www.bilaterals.org/article.php3?id_article=894.

———. 2004b. "Government Spokesman Deplores False Ideas about Free-Trade Agreement with USA." March 27. http://www.bilaterals.org/article.php3?id_article=746.

Blanchard, Eric M. 2003. "Gender, International Relations, and the Development of Feminist Security Theory." *Signs: Journal of Women in Culture and Society* 28(4):1289–1312.

Borchorst, Anette. 2000. "Feminist Thinking about the Welfare State." In *Revisioning Gender*, ed. Myra Marx Ferree, Judith Lorber, and Beth B. Hess, 99–127. Walnut Creek, CA: AltaMira.

Butler, Judith. 2003. "Performative Acts and Gender Constitutions: An Essay in Phenomenology and Feminist Theory." In *Feminist Theory Reader: Local and Global Perspectives*, ed. Carole R. McCann and Seung-kyung Kim, 415–27. New York: Routledge.

Center for Policing Terrorism. 2006. "Analysis: May 16, 2003, Suicide Bombings in Casablanca, Morocco." Center for Policing Terrorism. Bulletin, January. http://www.cpt-mi.org/pdf_secure.php?pdffilename=Casablancav2.

Cloud, Dana L. 2004. "'To Veil the Threat of Terror': Afghan Women and the <Clash of Civilizations> in the Imagery of the U.S. War on Terrorism." *Quarterly Journal of Speech* 90(3):285–306.

CNN. 2003. "Purported bin Laden Message on War against Infidels." CNN.com. February 12. http://www.cnn.com/2003/WORLD/meast/02//11/binladen.excerpts.

Dagnino, Evelina. 1998. "Culture, Citizenship, and Democracy: Changing Discourses and Practices of the Latin American Left." In *Cultures of Politics, Politics of Cultures: Re-visioning Latin American Social Movements*, ed. Sonia E. Alvarez, Evelina Dagnino, and Arturo Escobar, 33–63. Boulder, CO: Westview.

Debrix, François. 2005. "Discourses of War, Geographies of Abjection: Reading Contemporary American Ideologies of Terror." *Third World Quarterly* 26(7):1157–72.

Enloe, Cynthia. 1989. *Bananas, Beaches, and Bases: Making Feminist Sense of International Politics.* Berkeley: University of California Press.

———. 2004. *The Curious Feminist: Searching for Women in a New Age of Empire.* Berkeley: University of California Press.

Ferguson, James. 2006. *Global Shadows: Africa in the Neoliberal World Order.* Durham, NC: Duke University Press.

Foucault, Michel. 1978. *The History of Sexuality: An Introduction.* Vol. 1. Trans. Robert Hurley. New York: Pantheon.

———. 1980. *Power/Knowledge: Selected Interviews and Other Writings, 1972–1977.* Ed. and trans. Colin Gordon. Brighton: Harvester.

———. 1990. "Sexual Discourse and Power." In *Culture and Society: Contem-*

porary Debates, ed. Jeffrey C. Alexander and Steven Seidman, 199–204. Cambridge: Cambridge University Press.

Freeman, Carla. 2001. "Is Local : Global as Feminine : Masculine? Rethinking the Gender of Globalization." *Signs* 26(4):1007–37.

Gramsci, Antonio. 1971. *Selections from the Prison Notebooks.* Trans. Quintin Hoare and Geoffrey Nowell Smith. New York: International.

Hawthorne, Susan, and Bronwyn Winter, eds. 2003. *After Shock: September 11, 2001; Global Feminist Perspectives.* Vancouver: Raincoast.

Huntington, Samuel P. 1996. *The Clash of Civilizations and the Remaking of World Order.* New York: Simon & Schuster.

Jelin, Elisabeth. 1998. "Toward a Culture of Participation and Citizenship: Challenges for a More Equitable World." In *Cultures of Politics, Politics of Cultures: Re-visioning Latin American Social Movements*, ed. Sonia E. Alvarez, Evelina Dagnino, and Arturo Escobar, 405–14. Boulder, CO: Westview.

Jiwani, Yasmin. 2004. "Gendering Terror: Representations of the Orientalized Body in Quebec's Post–September 11 English-Language Press." *Critique: Critical Middle Eastern Studies* 13(3):265–91.

Joseph, Suad, ed. 2000. *Gender and Citizenship in the Middle East.* Syracuse, NY: Syracuse University Press.

Laclau, Ernesto, and Chantal Mouffe. 1985. *Hegemony and Socialist Strategy: Towards a Radical Democratic Politics.* London: Verso.

Lemke, Thomas. 2000. "Foucault, Governmentality, and Critique." Paper presented at the Rethinking Marxism Conference, University of Massachusetts, Amherst, September 21–24.

Maghraoui, Abdessalam. 2004. "La societe Marocaine se radicalise dans l'indifference" [Indifference to the radicalization of Moroccan society]. *Journal Hebdomadaire* [Weekly Journal], September 5. http://www.lejournal-hebdo.com/article.php3?id_article=714.

Mies, Maria. 1986. *Patriarchy and Accumulation on a World Scale: Women in the International Division of Labor.* London: Zed.

Moghadam, Valentine. 2000. "Gender, National Identity, and Citizenship: Reflections on the Middle East and North Africa." *Hagar: International Social Science Review* 1(1):41–70.

Moghissi, Haideh. 2004. "September 11 and Middle Eastern Women: Shrinking Space for Critical Thinking and Oppositional Politics." *Signs* 29(2):594–97.

Nader, Laura. 1989. "Orientalism, Occidentalism, and the Control of Women." *Cultural Dynamics* 2(3):323–55.

Nnaemeka, Obioma. 2004. "African Voices on September 11: Introduction." *Signs* 29(2):601–3.

Noonan, Rita K. 1997. "Women against the State: Political Opportunities and Collective Action Frames in Chile's Transition to Democracy." In *Social Movements: Readings on Their Emergence, Mobilization, and Dynamics*, ed. Doug McAdam and David A. Snow, 81–111. Los Angeles: Roxbury.

Nordstrom, Carolyn. 1995. "Introduction to Women and War." *Cultural Survival Quarterly* 19(1):1–3.

Petchesky, Rosalind P. 2002. "Phantom Towers: Feminist Reflections on the Battle between Global Capitalism and Fundamentalist Terrorism." In *Nothing Sacred: Women Respond to Fundamentalism and Terror*, ed. Betsy Reed, 357–72. New York: Thunders Mouth/Nation.

Peterson, V. Spike, and Anne Sisson Runyan. 1999. *Global Gender Issues*. 2nd ed. Boulder, CO: Westview.

Ruby, Jennie. 2003. "Is This a Feminist War?" In Hawthorne and Winter 2003, 177–79.

Said, Edward W. 1978. *Orientalism*. New York: Pantheon.

Scott, Joan Wallach. 2000. "Some Reflections on Gender and Politics." In *Revisioning Gender*, ed. Myra Marx Ferree, Judith Lorber, and Beth B. Hess, 70–98. Walnut Creek, CA: AltaMira.

Sharabi, Hisham. 1988. *Neopatriarchy: A Theory of Distorted Change in Arab Society*. New York: Oxford University Press.

Sharma, V. K. 2003. *War against Terrorism*. Jaipur: Book Enclave.

Spivak, Gayatri Chakravorty. 2004. "Terror: A Speech after 9-11." *boundary 2* 31(2):81–111.

Strassberg, Barbara Ann. 2004. "A Pandemic of Terror and Terror of a Pandemic: American Cultural Responses to HIV/AIDS and Bioterrorism." *Zygon: Journal of Religion and Science* 39(2):435–63.

Wittes, Tamara Cofman. 2004. "The New U.S. Proposal for a Greater Middle East Initiative: An Evaluation." Saban Center Middle East Memo no. 2, Brookings Institution, Washington, DC, May 10. http://www.brookings.edu.

Young, Iris Marion. 2003. "The Logic of Masculinist Protection: Reflections on the Current Security State." *Signs* 29(1):1–25.

Zerai, Assata, and Zakia Salime. 2006. "A Black Feminist Analysis of Responses to War, Racism, and Repression." *Critical Sociology* 32(2–3):501–24.

Index